ACTEX ACADEMIC SERIES

Risk Models and Their Estimation

STEPHEN G. KELLISON, FSA, EA, MAAA
UNIVERSITY OF CENTRAL FLORIDA (RETIRED)

RICHARD L. LONDON, FSA
UNIVERSITY OF CONNECTICUT (RETIRED)

ACTEX Publications, Inc.
Winsted, CT

Requests for permission should be addressed to
ACTEX Publications
P.O. Box 974
Winsted, CT 06098

Manufactured in the United States of America

10 9 8 7 6 5 4 3 2 1

Cover design by Christine Phelps and Jeffrey D. Melaragno

Library of Congress Cataloging-in-Publication Data

Kellison, Stephen G.
Risk models and their estimation / Stephen G. Kellison, Richard L. London.
p. cm.
ISBN 978-1-56698-770-7 (pbk. : alk. paper) 1. Risk. 2. Actuarial science. 3. Insurance--Mathematics. I. London, Richard L. II. Title.
HB615.K395 2011
368'.01201--dc23
2011037241

ISBN: 978-1-56698-770-7

PREFACE

The basic subject matter of actuarial science is the analysis and management of financial risk, often within the framework of insurance and other risk-sharing arrangements. To accomplish this, actuaries develop *risk models* to describe and measure the various risks that arise in their work. These models are probabilistic in nature. Increasingly, actuaries are also finding applications for these risk models in a variety of other contexts.

The basic idea is that each risk model is governed by an underlying, operative (but unknown) probability distribution. We attempt to *estimate* this underlying distribution by gathering sample data, and processing the data according to an estimation procedure (possibly involving some simplifying assumptions). We also analyze the quality of the resulting estimate.

There are two major classes of risk models that are of interest to us:

(1) *Survival Models*, which address the number and location in time of failure events. These models are included with the topic commonly referred to as *life contingencies*, and are examined on Exam MLC of the Society of Actuaries (SOA) and Exam 3L of the Casualty Actuarial Society (CAS).

(2) *Loss Models*, subdivided as (a) *frequency models*, which address the number of losses or insurance claims occurring in some interval of time, (b) *severity models*, which address the magnitude of such losses or claims, and (c) *aggregate models*, which combine frequency and severity models to address the total, or aggregate, amount of loss in some interval of time. The study of loss models has traditionally been referred to as *risk theory*. It is examined on SOA Exam C and CAS Exam 4.

In this text we presume a thorough understanding of survival models. For those needing a substantial review of these models, we recommend Chapters 5 and 6 of the textbook *Models for Quantifying Risk* (Fourth Edition), by Cunningham, et al. [7]. A condensed summary of these models is presented in Chapter 3 of this text.

A second area of required background presumed in this text is that of mathematical probability and statistics. We presume that the reader has had (at least) the standard two-semester university course in this topic, covering (at least) discrete and continuous random variables and their distributions, techniques of statistical estimation, and the development of confidence intervals and tests of hypotheses. Again, as a review, we have included here summaries of both probability theory (in Chapter 1), and statistical inference, or estimation (in Chapter 2).

A number of risk models, and some statistical analyses as well, can be conveniently pursued via stochastic simulation. Accordingly, we present, in Chapter 4, the general approach to simulating outcomes from a number of distributions, both discrete and continuous. Applications of simulation techniques to some of the problems discussed in the text are then presented throughout the later chapters.

With an understanding of basic probability theory presumed, the second major class of risk models is then developed in Part II of the text. We follow the logical pattern of developing the frequency models first (in Chapter 5), then the severity models (in Chapter 6), and finally the aggregate models (in Chapter 7). In Chapter 8 we present a common application of aggregate loss models, traditionally known as *ruin theory*. Most of the discrete frequency distributions developed in Chapter 5 and most of the continuous severity distributions developed in Chapter 6 are summarized in Appendices B and A, respectively.

Survival models can be presented in either parametric or tabular (non-parametric) form, with the tabular form predominating in practice. Frequency models are generally parametric, and necessarily discrete. Severity models are mostly parametric and continuous, but can also be tabular. The estimation of tabular models is presented in Part III of the text (Chapters 9 through 12), and estimation of parametric models is presented in Part IV of the text (Chapters 13 through 16). Each part begins with introductory comments describing the contents of that part.

The text includes a number of appendices that summarize some of the text results, provide derivations deemed to be too lengthy for convenient inclusion in the chapters themselves, provide additional background information, or present further topics not considered fundamental to the main subject of the text.

Answers to the textbook exercises are included. A separate solutions manual showing in detail how to solve the exercises is also available from ACTEX Publications. A number of the textbook exercises have been taken from examinations published by the Society of Actuaries and the Casualty Actuarial Society, and we wish to thank the professional societies for making these questions available to us.

A bibliography is included to suggest further reading for those interested in a deeper presentation of certain topics.

This text is appropriate for use in a two-semester university course on the topic of risk theory and the estimation of both classes of risk models.

The aforementioned SOA Exam C and CAS Exam 4 cover three major topics:

(1) Traditional risk theory, as presented in Chapters 5-7 of this text.
(2) Estimation of both survival models and risk models, as presented in Chapters 9-16 of this text.
(3) Basic aspects of *credibility theory*, as presented in Chapters 1-9 of the textbook *Introduction to Credibility Theory* (Fourth Edtion), by T.N. Herzog [15].

The authors would like to thank a number of people for their contributions to the development of this text.

Early drafts of the manuscript were reviewed by Thomas N. Herzog, ASA (National Association of Insurance Commissioners), Samuel A. Broverman, ASA (University of Toronto), Thomas P. Edwalds, FSA (Munich American Reassurance Company), Emiliano Valdez, FSA (University of Connecticut).

Thanks also to the professional staff at ACTEX Publications, particularly Gail A. Hall, FSA, the project editor, Marilyn J. Baleshiski, who did the typesetting and graphic arts, and Christine Phelps and Jeffrey D. Melaragno, who designed the text's cover.

We wish to acknowledge the work of the many authors who have written on these topics before we undertook this project, and whose writings we have researched over the course of our academic careers. We especially wish to thank our mutual instructor, the incomparable Geoffrey Crofts, FSA, to whom we dedicate the publication of this work.

We wish you good luck with your studies and preparation for your professional exams and actuarial careers.

Stephen G. Kellison, FSA
Orlando, Florida

Richard L. London, FSA
Storrs, Connecticut

Winsted, Connecticut
August 2011

TABLE OF CONTENTS

PART I
Review and Background Material

Chapter One
Review of Probability

Chapter Two
Review of Statistical Inference

Chapter Three
Review of Survival Models

Chapter Four
Review of Stochastic Simulation

PART II
Loss Models

Chapter Five
Claim Frequency Models

Chapter Six
Claim Severity Models

Chapter Seven
Models for Aggregate Payments

Chapter Eight
Surplus Process Models (Ruin Theory)

PART III
Estimation of Tabular Models

Chapter Nine
Estimation from Complete Data

Chapter Ten
Estimation from Incomplete Data

Chapter Eleven
Actuarial Survival Model Estimation

Chapter Twelve
Revision of Tabular Models

PART IV
Estimation of Parametric Models

Chapter Thirteen
Parameter Estimation Using Moments or Percentiles

Chapter Fourteen
Parameter Estimation Using Maximum Likelihood

Chapter Fifteen
Bayesian Techniques

Chapter Sixteen
Testing and Selecting Models

PART I

REVIEW AND BACKGROUND MATERIAL

The primary purpose of this text is to present a detailed description of models for insurance losses, including the estimation of those models from sample data. In addition, we also discuss the estimation of survival models from sample data, with the description of such models contained in Cunningham, et al. [7], which could be viewed as a companion text to this one.

The topic of loss models, traditionally referred to as risk theory, relies heavily on general probability theory, and the estimation of models relies on the general theory of mathematical statistics. Accordingly, as background to the major work of this text, we first present a broad review of both probability (in Chapter 1) and statistics (in Chapter 2).

With survival models covered in detail in the Cunningham text, and examined on SOA Exam MLC and CAS Exam 3L, we present a summary review of that topic in Chapter 3 in advance of our discussion of estimating survival models from sample data.

The topic of simulation is treated differently on Exam C/4 than are the other topics reviewed in this part of the text, in that exam questions directly addressing the theory and application of simulation can be expected. In light of this, we have included both examples and end-of-chapter exercises for this topic in Chapter 4.

CHAPTER ONE

REVIEW OF PROBABILITY

In this text we make major use of many results from probability theory. We assume that the reader has completed at least one full semester in calculus-based probability at the university level, so that most of the material contained in this chapter will be somewhat familiar. For several selected topics (see, in particular, Sections 1.5 and 1.6), we are less sure that the reader will have this prior familiarity and we will present those topics in greater detail.

Specialized applications of basic probability concepts to claim frequency models, claim severity models, and sums of random variables models are considered in Chapters 5, 6, and 7, respectively. Extensions of probability theory that are needed for these specialized applications, which would not normally be covered in a basic probability course, will be introduced as needed in the later chapters.

The most basic concepts of probability are not included in this review; the reader should refer to any standard probability textbook if a review of these concepts is needed.[1] Among the basic concepts not reviewed here are the notion of the probability of an event, negation, union, intersection, mutual exclusion, the general addition rule, conditional probability, independence, the general multiplication rule, the law of total probability, and Bayes' Theorem.

1.1 RANDOM VARIABLES AND THEIR DISTRIBUTIONS

The concept of the *random variable* is the foundation for much of the material presented in this text. Levels of risk can be quantitatively represented by random variables, and understanding the properties of these random variables allows us to analyze and manage the risk so represented. In this section of this introductory chapter we review basic aspects of random variables and their properties.

1.1.1 DISCRETE RANDOM VARIABLES

A random variable, denoted X, is said to be *discrete* if it can take on only a finite (or countably infinite) number of different values. Each value it can take on is called an *outcome* of the random variable. The set of all possible outcomes is called the *domain*, or *support*, of the random variable.[2] We let x denote a particular value in the domain.

---

[1] For those needing a good probability text, we recommend Hassett and Stewart's *Probability for Risk Management* [12].

[2] Technically, we should say the domain (or support) of the random variable's probability function, but the shorter phrase "domain of the random variable" is often used.

Associated with each value of x is a probability value for the random variable taking on that particular outcome. The probability value is a function of the value of the outcome, denoted $p(x)$, and is called, appropriately, the *probability function* (PF). That is, $p(x)$ gives the probability of the event $X=x$. (In some textbooks $p(x)$ is called the *probability mass function*.) The set of all probability values constitutes the *distribution* of the random variable. It is necessarily true that

$$\sum_x p(x) \;=\; 1, \tag{1.1}$$

where the summation is taken over all values of x in the domain with non-zero probability.

The *expected value* of the random variable, denoted $E[X]$, is a weighted average of all values in the domain, using the associated probability values as weights. Thus we have

$$E[X] \;=\; \sum_x x \cdot p(x), \tag{1.2}$$

where the summation is again taken over all values of x with non-zero probability. The expected value is also called the *mean of the random variable* or the *mean of the distribution*.

The expected value is a special case of the more general idea of finding the weighted average of a function of the random variable, again using the associated probability values as the weights. If $g(X)$ is any real function of the random variable X, then it can be shown that

$$E[g(X)] \;=\; \sum_x g(x) \cdot p(x) \tag{1.3}$$

gives the expected value of the function of the random variable. Note that the mean of the random variable is simply the special case that results when $g(X)=X$.

An important special case is $g(X)=X^k$, and $E[g(X)]=E[X^k]$ is called the kth *moment* of the random variable. (Note that the mean is therefore the *first moment* of the random variable.) Another special case is $g(X)=(X-E[X])^2$, where the expected value of $g(X)$ is called the *variance* of the random variable and is denoted by $Var(X)$. That is,

$$Var(X) \;=\; E[(X-E[X])^2] \;=\; \sum_x (x-E[X])^2 \cdot p(x). \tag{1.4a}$$

The reader will recall that an equivalent expression for $Var(X)$ is

$$Var(X) \;=\; E[X^2]-(E[X])^2, \tag{1.4b}$$

a form often more convenient for calculating $Var(X)$ than is Equation (1.4a). The positive square root of the variance is called the *standard deviation* of X, and is denoted by $SD(X)$ or sometimes by σ.

The moments of a random variable can be generated from a function called, appropriately, the *moment generating function* (MGF), and denoted by $M_X(t)$. It is defined as

$$\begin{aligned} M_X(t) &= E[e^{tX}] \\ &= \sum_x e^{tx} \cdot p(x). \end{aligned} \tag{1.5}$$

We recognize that this is just another example of finding the expected value of a particular function of the random variable; in this case the function is $g(X) = e^{tX}$. Note that $M_X(t)$ is a function of *t*, with the subscript *X* merely reminding us of what the random variable is for which $M_X(t)$ is the MGF.

The reader will recall that the moments are then obtained from the MGF by differentiating $M_X(t)$ with respect to *t* and evaluating at $t = 0$. The first derivative evaluated at $t = 0$ produces the first moment, the second derivative so evaluated gives the second moment, and so on. In general,

$$E[X^k] = \frac{d^k}{dt^k} M_X(t)\Big|_{t=0} = M_X^{(k)}(0) \tag{1.6}$$

gives the kth moment of the random variable *X*.

Several other characteristics of the random variable are also important.

The *mode* of the distribution is the value of *x* at which the greatest amount of probability is located (i.e., the value of *x* that maximizes $p(x)$). Note that several values of *x* could be tied for the greatest amount, in which case the distribution would have several modes.

The *cumulative distribution function* (CDF) of the random variable, denoted $F(x)$, gives the accumulated amount of probability at all values of the random variable less than or equal to *x*. That is,

$$F(x) = Pr(X \leq x) = \sum_{y \leq x} p(y), \tag{1.7}$$

where the summation is taken over all values of *y* less than or equal to *x*.

The value of *x* for which $F(x) = r$ is called the $100r^{th}$ *percentile* of the distribution. It is the value in the domain of *X* for which the probability of being less than or equal to that value is *r*, and the probability of being greater than that value is therefore $1-r$. In particular, when $r = .50$ we are speaking of the value of *x* for which half the probability lies below (or at) that value and half lies above that value. The value of x in this case is called the *median* of the distribution.[3]

1.1.2 CONTINUOUS RANDOM VARIABLES

A random variable is said to be *continuous* if it can take on any value within a defined interval (or the union of several disjoint intervals) on the real number axis. If this set of possible values, again called the domain or support of the random variable,[4] includes all values between, say, a and b, then we would define the domain as $a < x < b$. If the domain were all non-negative real values of x we would write $x \geq 0$, and if it were all real values of x we would write $-\infty < x < \infty$. Note that the defined values of x could be in several disjoint intervals, so the domain would then be the union of these disjoint intervals. For example, the domain could be all x satisfying $a < x < b$ or $c < x < d$.

Associated with each possible value of x is an amount of *probability density*, given as a function of x by the *probability density function* (PDF), denoted by $f(x)$. Together the PDF and the domain define the distribution of the random variable. It is necessarily true that

$$\int_x f(x)\,dx = 1, \tag{1.8}$$

where the integral is taken over all values of x in the domain.

Analogous with the discrete case, we again consider the weighted average of a function of the random variable, which is the expected value of that function, this time using the density as the weight associated with each value of x. Thus is can be shown that

$$E[g(x)] = \int_x g(x) \cdot f(x)\,dx. \tag{1.9}$$

The same special cases apply here as in the discrete case. For $g(X) = X$ we have

$$E[X] = \int_x x \cdot f(x)\,dx \tag{1.10}$$

as the expected value (or first moment) of the random variable. For $g(X) = X^k$ in general we have

$$E[X^k] = \int_x x^k \cdot f(x)\,dx \tag{1.11}$$

as the kth moment. As before, the variance is given by

---

[3] The median (or any other percentile) in a discrete distribution is not always clear. For example, if $p(0) = \frac{1}{3}$ and $p(1) = \frac{2}{3}$, then what is the median? Clearly there is no unique value of x for which $F(x) = .50$. Either we would say the median does not exist, or we would adopt a definition to resolve the question in each case.

[4] As in the discrete case of Section 1.1.1, the phrase "domain (or support) of the density function of the random variable" is more technically correct, but the briefer phrase "domain of the random variable" is often used.

$$Var(X) = E[(X-E[X])^2] = \int_x (x-E[X])^2 \cdot f(x)\,dx \tag{1.12}$$

and the moment generating function is given by

$$M_X(t) = E[e^{tX}] = \int_x e^{tx} \cdot f(x)\,dx. \tag{1.13}$$

The mode of the distribution is the value of x associated with the greatest amount of probability density, so it can be described as the value of x that maximizes the density function. If several values of x have the same maximum density, then the distribution has more than one mode.

As in the discrete case, the cumulative distribution function (CDF) of the random variable X is defined by $F(x) = Pr(X \leq x)$. It follows that

$$F(x) = \int_{-\infty}^{x} f(y)\,dy, \tag{1.14a}$$

and, conversely,

$$f(x) = \frac{d}{dx}F(x). \tag{1.14b}$$

Just as in the discrete case, the $100r^{th}$ percentile of the distribution is the value of x for which $F(x) = r$, and, in particular, the median of the distribution is the value of x for which $F(x) = .50$.

1.1.3 MIXED RANDOM VARIABLES

On occasion we encounter a random variable that is discrete in one part of its domain and continuous in the rest of the domain. Such random variables are said to have *mixed distributions*. For example, suppose there is a finite probability associated with each of the outcomes $X = a$ and $X = b$, denoted $p(a)$ and $p(b)$, respectively, and a probability density associated with all values of x on the open interval between a and b. Then it would follow that

$$p(a) + \int_a^b f(x)\,dx + p(b) = 1. \tag{1.15}$$

The kth moment of the mixed random variable X would be found as

$$E[X^k] = a^k \cdot p(a) + \int_a^b x^k \cdot f(x)\,dx + b^k \cdot p(b). \tag{1.16}$$

Mixed random variables appear quite often in actuarial models, particularly in connection with insurance coverages involving a deductible, or a policy maximum, or both. We will explore these situations in Chapters 6 and 7.

1.1.4 MORE ON MOMENTS OF RANDOM VARIABLES

Earlier in this section we reviewed the basic idea of the kth moment of a random variable, denoted by $E[X^k]$. This type of moment is called the kth *raw moment of X*, or the kth *moment about the origin.*

By contrast, the quantity $E[(X-\mu)^k]$ is called the kth *central moment of X*, or the kth *moment about the mean*, where $\mu = E[X]$. In particular, the second central moment, denoted by $E[(X-\mu)^2]$, gives the variance of the distribution of X, which is denoted by $Var(X)$ or sometimes by σ^2. Recall that the positive square root of the variance is called the standard deviation, and is denoted by $SD(X)$ or sometimes by σ.

The ratio of the standard deviation to the mean of a random variable is called the *coefficient of variation*, and is denoted by $CV(X)$. Thus we have

$$CV(X) = \frac{\sigma}{\mu}, \tag{1.17}$$

for $\mu \neq 0$. It measures the degree of spread of a random variable relative to its mean.

The *skewness* of a distribution measures its symmetry, or lack thereof. It is defined by

$$\gamma_3 = \frac{E[(X-\mu)^3]}{\sigma^3}, \tag{1.18}$$

the ratio of the third central moment to the cube of the standard deviation. A distribution that is symmetric, such as the normal, will have a skewness measure of zero. A positively skewed distribution will have a right hand tail and a negatively skewed distribution will have a left hand tail.

The extent to which a distribution is peaked or flat is measured by its *kurtosis,* which is defined by

$$\gamma_4 = \frac{E[(X-\mu)^4]}{\sigma^4}, \tag{1.19}$$

the ratio of the fourth central moment to the square of the variance (or the fourth power of the standard deviation). The kurtosis of a normal distribution has a value of 3, so the kurtosis of any other distribution will indicate its degree of peakedness or flatness relative to a normal distribution with equal variance. In addition, kurtosis also relates to the thickness of the tails of the distribution.

It is well known (see Equation (1.4b)) that the second central moment (the variance) is equal to the second raw moment minus the first raw moment (the mean) squared. Similar relationships hold for the higher central moments as well. For example, for the third central moment we have

$$
\begin{aligned}
E[(X-\mu)^3] &= E[X^3 - 3X^2\mu + 3X\mu^2 - \mu^3] \\
&= E[X^3] - 3\cdot E[X^2]\cdot E[X] + 3\cdot E[X]\cdot(E[X])^2 - (E[X])^3 \\
&= E[X^3] - 3\cdot E[X^2]\cdot E[X] + 2(E[X])^3. \qquad (1.20)
\end{aligned}
$$

1.2 SURVEY OF PARTICULAR DISCRETE DISTRIBUTIONS

In this section we will review five standard discrete distributions with which the reader should be familiar. They are included here simply as a convenient reference.

1.2.1 THE DISCRETE UNIFORM DISTRIBUTION

If there are n discrete values in the domain of a random variable X, denoted $x_1, x_2, \cdots, x_n$, for which an equal amount of probability is associated with each value, then X is said to have a *discrete uniform distribution*. Its probability function is therefore

$$p(x_i) = \frac{1}{n}, \qquad (1.21)$$

for all x_i. Its first moment is

$$E[X] = \sum_{i=1}^{n} x_i \cdot p(x_i) = \frac{1}{n}\cdot\sum_{i=1}^{n} x_i, \qquad (1.22a)$$

and its second moment is

$$E[X^2] = \sum_{i=1}^{n} x_i^2 \cdot p(x_i) = \frac{1}{n}\cdot\sum_{i=1}^{n} x_i^2. \qquad (1.22b)$$

In the special case where $x_i = i$, for $i = 1, 2, \cdots, n$, then we have

$$E[X] = \frac{n+1}{2} \qquad (1.23a)$$

and

$$E[X^2] = \frac{(n+1)(2n+1)}{6}, \qquad (1.23b)$$

so that

$$Var(X) = E[X^2] - (E[X])^2 = \frac{n^2-1}{12}. \qquad (1.24)$$

The moment generating function in the special case is

$$M_X(t) = E[e^{tX}] = \frac{e^t(1-e^{nt})}{n(1-e^t)}. \tag{1.25}$$

1.2.2 THE BINOMIAL AND MULTINOMIAL DISTRIBUTIONS

Recall the binomial (or Bernoulli) model, in which we find the concept of repeated independent trials with each trial ending in either success of failure. The probability of success on a single trial, denoted p, is constant over all trials. The random variable X, denoting the number of successes out of n independent trials, is said to have a *binomial distribution*. (The special case of this distribution with $n=1$ is called a *Bernoulli distribution*.) The probability function is

$$p(x) = \binom{n}{x} p^x (1-p)^{n-x}, \tag{1.26a}$$

for $x = 0,1,2,\cdots,n,$ the expected value is

$$E[X] = np, \tag{1.27a}$$

the variance is

$$Var(X) = np(1-p), \tag{1.28a}$$

and the moment generating function is

$$M_X(t) = (q+pe^t)^n, \tag{1.29}$$

where $q = 1-p$.

As the prefix *bi-* implies, there are only two possible outcomes for each of the n trials in the binomial model, which we have called "success" and "failure." Instead of the traditional terminology, we could say that each outcome is either a Type 1 outcome, with probability p_1, or a Type 2 outcome, with probability p_2. If X_1 and X_2 denote the random variables for numbers of Type 1 and Type 2 outcomes, respectively, then X_1 and X_2 have a *joint probability function* given by

$$p(x_1, x_2) = \frac{n!}{x_1!x_2!}(p_1)^{x_1}(p_2)^{x_2}, \tag{1.26b}$$

where $x_1 + x_2 = n$ and $p_1 + p_2 = 1$. It is easy to see that the right sides of Equations (1.26a) and (1.26b) are the same.

Now we generalize the model to one where there are k possible distinct outcomes for each of the n trials. The random variable counting the number of outcomes of Type i is X_i, for

$i=1,2,\cdots,k$, with probability p_i. Then the set of random variables $\{X_1, X_2, \cdots, X_k\}$ has a joint probability function given by

$$p(x_1, x_2, \cdots, x_k) = \frac{n!}{x_1!x_2!\cdots x_k!}(p_1)^{x_1}(p_2)^{x_2}\ldots(p_k)^{x_k}, \tag{1.26c}$$

where $\sum_{i=1}^{k} x_i = n$ and $\sum_{i=1}^{k} p_i = 1$. This is called the *multinomial distribution.*[5]

The expected value of X_i is

$$E[X_i] = n \cdot p_i, \tag{1.27b}$$

its variance is

$$Var(X_i) = n \cdot p_i(1-p_i), \tag{1.28b}$$

and the covariance of any pair of random variables in the set is

$$Cov(X_i, X_j) = -n \cdot p_i \cdot p_j. \tag{1.28c}$$

1.2.3 THE NEGATIVE BINOMIAL DISTRIBUTION

Note that in the binomial distribution the random variable was the number of successes out of a fixed number of trials, n, where n is a fixed parameter of the distribution. In the *negative binomial distribution* the number of successes, denoted r, is a fixed parameter of the distribution and the random variable X represents the number of failures that occur before the rth success is obtained.[6] The probability function is

$$p(x) = \binom{x+r-1}{r-1} p^r (1-p)^x, \tag{1.30a}$$

for $x = 0, 1, 2, \cdots$, the expected value is

$$E[X] = \frac{rq}{p}, \tag{1.31a}$$

the variance is

$$Var(X) = \frac{rq}{p^2}, \tag{1.32a}$$

---

[5] The multinomial distribution is a special case of a multivariate distribution, considered more generally in Section 1.4. We include it here because of its close relationship to the univariate binomial distribution.

[6] Note that if the number of failures, denoted X, is random, then the total number of *trials* needed to obtain r successes, denoted Y, is also random, since we would have $Y = X + r$. Some textbooks (see, for example, Hassett and Stewart [12]), discuss both the "X-meaning" and the "Y-meaning" of the negative binomial distribution.

and the moment generating function is

$$M_X(t) = \left(\frac{p}{1-qe^t}\right)^r, \tag{1.33a}$$

where, in all cases, $q = 1-p$.

Note that the description of the negative binomial distribution given here would require that the parameter r be a nonnegative integer. In Section 5.1.3, where we consider an important use of the negative binomial random variable as a model for the number of insurance claims, we will show that the requirement of an integer value for r can be relaxed.[7]

1.2.4 THE GEOMETRIC DISTRIBUTION

The *geometric distribution* is simply the special case of the negative binomial with $r = 1$. The random variable, X, now denotes the number of failures that occur before the first success is obtained.[8] Its probability function is

$$p(x) = p(1-p)^x, \tag{1.30b}$$

for $x = 0, 1, 2, \cdots$, the expected value is

$$E[X] = \frac{q}{p}, \tag{1.31b}$$

the variance is

$$Var(X) = \frac{q}{p^2}, \tag{1.32b}$$

and the moment generating function is

$$M_X(t) = \frac{p}{1-qe^t}, \tag{1.33b}$$

where $q = 1-p$ in all cases.

1.2.5 THE POISSON DISTRIBUTION

The *Poisson distribution* is a one-parameter discrete distribution with probability function given by

---

[7] Some textbooks use an alternate parameterization for the negative binomial distribution with $p = \frac{1}{1+\beta}$ and $q = \frac{\beta}{1+\beta}$. This is further explored in Exercise 6-38 and summarized in Appendix B.

[8] As with the negative binomial, some textbooks define the geometric random variable to be the number of trials, Y, needed to obtain the first success. In that case the probability function is $p(y) = p(1-p)^{y-1}$, for $y = 1, 2, \cdots$.

$$p(x) = \frac{e^{-\lambda}\lambda^x}{x!}, \tag{1.34}$$

for $x = 0, 1, 2, \cdots$, where $\lambda > 0$. Its expected value is

$$E[X] = \lambda, \tag{1.35}$$

its variance is also

$$Var(X) = \lambda, \tag{1.36}$$

and its moment generating function is

$$M_X(t) = e^{\lambda(e^t - 1)}. \tag{1.37}$$

The Poisson distribution has several delightful properties that make it a convenient one to use in various actuarial and other stochastic applications. These will be reviewed in conjunction with the discussion of the Poisson process and the use of the Poisson distribution as a model for number of insurance losses or insurance claims in Chapter 5.

1.3 SURVEY OF PARTICULAR CONTINUOUS DISTRIBUTIONS

In this section we review four standard continuous probability distributions with which the reader should be familiar from a prior study of probability. Additional continuous distributions are introduced later in the text as claims severity distributions (in Chapter 6).

1.3.1 THE CONTINUOUS UNIFORM DISTRIBUTION

As its name suggests, the *uniform distribution* is characterized by a constant probability density at all points in its domain. If the random variable is defined on the interval $a < X < b$, and if the density function is constant, then it follows that the density function must be

$$f(x) = \frac{1}{b-a}, \tag{1.38}$$

for $a < x < b$. That is, the constant density function is the reciprocal of the length of the interval on which the random variable is defined. The mean of the uniform distribution is

$$E[X] = \frac{a+b}{2}, \tag{1.39}$$

the variance is

$$Var(X) = \frac{(b-a)^2}{12}, \tag{1.40}$$

the moment generating function is

$$M_X(t) = \frac{e^{bt} - e^{at}}{t(b-a)}, \tag{1.41}$$

for $t \neq 0$, and the cumulative distribution function is

$$F(x) = \frac{x-a}{b-a}. \tag{1.42}$$

As a consequence of the constant density function, the median is the same as the mean and the distribution is equimodal, since all points have the same probability density.

1.3.2 THE NORMAL DISTRIBUTION

The *normal distribution* will have use in the models developed later in the text. For now the reader should recall that the density function for this distribution is based on the two parameters μ and σ, where $\sigma > 0$, which are also the mean and standard deviation, respectively, of the distribution. Specifically,

$$f(x) = \frac{1}{\sigma \cdot \sqrt{2\pi}} e^{-\frac{1}{2}\left(\frac{x-\mu}{\sigma}\right)^2}, \tag{1.43a}$$

for $-\infty < x < \infty$, where, as mentioned,

$$E[X] = \mu \tag{1.44}$$

and

$$Var(X) = \sigma^2. \tag{1.45}$$

The moment generating function is

$$M_X(t) = e^{\mu t + \sigma^2 t^2/2}. \tag{1.46}$$

An extremely important property of the normal distribution is that any linear transformation of the random variable will also have a normal distribution. In particular, the random variable Z derived from the normal random variable X by the linear transformation

$$Z = \frac{X-\mu}{\sigma} \tag{1.47}$$

will have a normal distribution with mean

$$E[Z] = \frac{1}{\sigma} \cdot E[X] - \frac{\mu}{\sigma} = 0, \tag{1.48}$$

since $E[X] = \mu$, and variance

$$Var(Z) = \frac{Var(X)}{\sigma^2} = 1, \tag{1.49}$$

since $Var(X)=\sigma^2$ and $Var(\mu/\sigma)=0$. The random variable Z is called the *unit normal random variable* or the *standard normal random variable*. Its probability density function

$$f(z) = \frac{1}{\sqrt{2\pi}} e^{-z^2/2} \tag{1.43b}$$

does not have a closed form antiderivative, so probability values are not found by integrating $f(z)$.[9] Rather, values of the cumulative distribution function $F_Z(z)$ are determined by approximate integration and stored in a table for look-up as needed.[10] Probability values for the normal random variable X are likewise looked up in the table of standard values after making the appropriate linear transformation. A modern alternative to table look-up is that values can be determined by numerical integration using appropriate computer software or even a pocket calculator.

1.3.3 THE EXPONENTIAL DISTRIBUTION

Another standard continuous distribution with some convenient properties is the one-parameter *exponential distribution*. It is defined over all positive values of x by the density function

$$f(x) = \beta \cdot e^{-\beta x}, \tag{1.50a}$$

for $x>0$ and $\beta>0$. The expected value is

$$E[X] = \frac{1}{\beta}, \tag{1.51}$$

the variance is

$$Var(X) = \frac{1}{\beta^2}, \tag{1.52}$$

the moment generating function is

$$M_X(t) = \frac{\beta}{\beta - t}, \tag{1.53}$$

for $t<\beta$, and the cumulative distribution function is

$$F(x) = 1 - e^{-\beta x}. \tag{1.54}$$

[9] The PDF of the unit normal random variable Z is sometimes denoted by $\phi(z)$ instead of $f(z)$.

[10] Similarly, the CDF is sometimes denoted by $\Phi(z)$.

(The reader should note that some textbooks prefer the notation

$$f(x) = \frac{1}{\theta} \cdot e^{-x/\theta}, \tag{1.50b}$$

so that $E[X] = \theta, Var(X) = \theta^2$, and $M_X(t) = (1-\theta t)^{-1}$.)

1.3.4 THE GAMMA DISTRIBUTION

The two-parameter *gamma distribution* is defined by the density function

$$f(x) = \frac{\beta^\alpha}{\Gamma(\alpha)} \cdot x^{\alpha-1} e^{-\beta x}, \tag{1.55}$$

for $x > 0, \alpha > 0$, and $\beta > 0$,[11] where $\Gamma(\alpha)$ is the *gamma function* defined by

$$\Gamma(\alpha) = \int_0^\infty x^{\alpha-1} e^{-x}\, dx. \tag{1.56}$$

By substituting $\alpha = 1$ into the gamma density given by Equation (1.55), and noting that $\Gamma(1) = 1$, we obtain the exponential density given by Equation (1.50a). Thus the exponential is a special case of the gamma with $\alpha = 1$. The mean of the gamma distribution is

$$E[X] = \frac{\alpha}{\beta}, \tag{1.57a}$$

the variance is

$$Var(X) = \frac{\alpha}{\beta^2}, \tag{1.57b}$$

and the moment generating function is

$$M_X(t) = \left(\frac{\beta}{\beta - t}\right)^\alpha, \tag{1.57c}$$

for $t < \beta$. The cumulative distribution function is given by

$$F(x) = \int_0^x f(y)\, dy = \frac{\beta^\alpha}{\Gamma(\alpha)} \int_0^x y^{\alpha-1} e^{-\beta y}\, dy. \tag{1.58a}$$

[11] Some texts prefer to use $\frac{1}{\theta}$ in place of β, as already mentioned for the exponential distribution.

If we let $\beta y = t$, so $y = t/\beta$ and $dy = \frac{1}{\beta} \cdot dt$, then the integral becomes

$$
\begin{aligned}
F(x) &= \frac{1}{\Gamma(\alpha)} \int_0^{\beta x} \beta^{\alpha} \left(\frac{t}{\beta} \right)^{\alpha-1} \cdot e^{-t} \cdot \frac{1}{\beta} \cdot dt \\
&= \frac{1}{\Gamma(\alpha)} \int_0^{\beta x} t^{\alpha-1} e^{-t}\, dt \\
&= \Gamma(\alpha; \beta x),
\end{aligned}
\tag{1.58b}
$$

where $\Gamma(\alpha; \beta x)$ is the *incomplete gamma function* defined by

$$
\Gamma(\alpha; x) = \frac{1}{\Gamma(\alpha)} \int_0^{x} t^{\alpha-1} e^{-t}\, dt. \tag{1.58c}
$$

Further insight into the relationship of the gamma to the exponential distribution will be provided in Section 1.5, and applications of the incomplete gamma function in actuarial models will arise in Chapters 6 and 7. It is further explored in Appendix K, including its evaluation by simulation.

1.4 MULTIVARIATE PROBABILITY

Whenever two or more random variables are involved in the same model we find ourselves dealing with a case of *multivariate probability*. In this section we will review the fundamental aspects of multivariate probability, including the interrelationships among the *joint*, *marginal*, and *conditional distributions*, in both the discrete and continuous cases.

One of the most important aspects of multivariate probability is the process for finding the unconditional mean and variance of a random variable from the associated conditional means and variances. The formulas relating the unconditional and conditional means and variances are given by the *double expectation theorem*. Although this is a result with which the reader might be familiar from prior study, it has so many important applications later in this text that we wish to review it in some detail at this time. We will do this by example, separately for the discrete and continuous cases. An example does not establish the general result, of course; for that purpose the reader is referred to Section 7.4 of Ross [35].

1.4.1 THE DISCRETE CASE

We illustrate the key components of discrete multivariate probability with a numerical example. Suppose the discrete random variable X can assume the values $x = 0,1,2$ and the discrete random variable Y can assume the values $y = 1,2$. Let X and Y have the joint distribution given by the following table, and let $p(x,y)$ denote the joint probability function.

Y \ X	0	1	2
1	.10	.20	.30
2	.10	.10	.20

The marginal distribution of X is given by

$$Pr(X=0) = .10+.10 = .20,$$

$$Pr(X=1) = .20+.10 = .30,$$

and

$$Pr(X=2) = .30+.20 = .50.$$

The moments of X can be calculated directly from the marginal distribution. We have

$$E[X] = (0)(.20)+(1)(.30)+(2)(.50) = 1.30,$$
$$E[X^2] = (0)(.20)+(1)(.30)+(4)(.50) = 2.30,$$

and

$$Var(X) = 2.30-(1.30)^2 = .61.$$

Now we consider an alternative, but longer (at least this time), way to find $E[X]$ and $Var(X)$. First we find the marginal distribution of Y as

$$Pr(Y=1) = .10+.20+.30 = .60$$

and

$$Pr(Y=2) = .10+.10+.20 = .40.$$

Next we find both conditional distributions for X, one given $Y=1$ and the other given $Y=2$. We have

$$Pr(X=0\,|\,Y=1) = \frac{.10}{.60} = \frac{1}{6},$$

$$Pr(X=1\,|\,Y=1) = \frac{.20}{.60} = \frac{2}{6},$$

and

$$Pr(X=2\,|\,Y=1) = \frac{.30}{.60} = \frac{3}{6}.$$

From this conditional distribution we find the conditional moments of X, given $Y=1$. We have

$$E[X\,|\,Y=1] = (0)\left(\frac{1}{6}\right)+(1)\left(\frac{2}{6}\right)+(2)\left(\frac{3}{6}\right) = \frac{8}{6},$$

$$E[X^2\,|\,Y=1] = (0)\left(\frac{1}{6}\right)+(1)\left(\frac{2}{6}\right)+(4)\left(\frac{3}{6}\right) = \frac{14}{6},$$

and

$$Var(X\,|\,Y=1) = \frac{14}{6}-\left(\frac{8}{6}\right)^2 = \frac{20}{36}.$$

Similarly we find the conditional distribution

$$Pr(X=0 \mid Y=2) = \frac{.10}{.40} = \frac{1}{4},$$

$$Pr(X=1 \mid Y=2) = \frac{.10}{.40} = \frac{1}{4},$$

and

$$Pr(X=2 \mid Y=2) = \frac{.20}{.40} = \frac{2}{4},$$

and its associated conditional moments

$$E[X \mid Y=2] = (0)\left(\frac{1}{4}\right)+(1)\left(\frac{1}{4}\right)+(2)\left(\frac{2}{4}\right) = \frac{5}{4},$$

$$E[X^2 \mid Y=2] = (0)\left(\frac{1}{4}\right)+(1)\left(\frac{1}{4}\right)+(4)\left(\frac{2}{4}\right) = \frac{9}{4},$$

and

$$Var(X \mid Y=2) = \frac{9}{4}-\left(\frac{5}{4}\right)^2 = \frac{11}{16}.$$

We now come to the key part of the operation. We recognize that the conditional expected value of X, denoted $E_X[X \mid Y]$, is a random variable because it is a function of the random variable Y. It can take on the two possible values $\frac{8}{6}$ and $\frac{5}{4}$, and does so with probability .60 and .40, respectively, the probabilities associated with the two possible values of Y. We can find the moments of this random variable as

$$E_Y[E_X[X \mid Y]] = \left(\frac{8}{6}\right)(.60)+\left(\frac{5}{4}\right)(.40) = \frac{13}{10},$$

$$E_Y[(E_X[X \mid Y])^2] = \left(\frac{8}{6}\right)^2\cdot(.60)+\left(\frac{5}{4}\right)^2\cdot(.40) = \frac{203}{120},$$

and

$$Var_Y(E_X[X \mid Y]) = \frac{203}{120}-\left(\frac{13}{10}\right)^2 = \frac{1}{600}.$$

Similarly the conditional variance of X given Y, denoted $Var_X(X \mid Y)$, is a random variable because it too is a function of Y. Its two possible values are $\frac{20}{36}$ and $\frac{11}{16}$, so its expected value is

$$E_Y[Var_X(X \mid Y)] = \left(\frac{20}{36}\right)(.60)+\left(\frac{11}{16}\right)(.40) = \frac{73}{120}.$$

Finally we observe that

$$E_Y\left[E_X[X \mid Y]\right] = \frac{13}{10} = E[X],$$

which states that the expected value of the conditional expectation is the unconditional expected value of X. This constitutes the first part of the double expectation theorem. The second part states that

$$E_Y[Var_X(X \mid Y)] + Var_Y(E_X[X \mid Y]) = \frac{73}{120} + \frac{1}{600} = \frac{366}{600} = \frac{61}{100} = Var(X),$$

which says that the expected value of the conditional variance plus the variance of the conditional expectation is the unconditional variance of X.

1.4.2 THE CONTINUOUS CASE

Multivariate probability in the continuous case is handled more compactly than in the discrete case. We cannot list all possible pairs of (x, y) in the continuous joint domain; instead we specify the joint density at the point (x, y) in the form of a joint density function denoted $f(x, y)$. Recall that the marginal density of X is then found by integrating the joint density over all values of Y, and the marginal density of Y is found by integrating the joint density over all values of X. The conditional density of X, given Y, is then found by dividing the joint density by the marginal density of Y, and, similarly, the conditional density of Y, given X, is found by dividing the joint density by the marginal density of X. These basic relationships are illustrated in the following example.

Let the continuous random variable X have a uniform distribution on the interval $0 < x < 12$, and let the continuous random variable Y have a conditional distribution, given $X = x$, that is uniform on the interval $0 < y < x$. We seek the unconditional expected value and variance of Y.

We could, of course, proceed by first finding the marginal distribution of Y and then finding the unconditional expected value and variance of Y directly from this marginal distribution. Since X is uniform we have $f_X(x) = \frac{1}{12}$, and since Y is conditionally uniform we have $f_{Y|X}(y \mid x) = \frac{1}{x}$. Then the joint density is $f(x, y) = \frac{1}{12x}$, and the marginal density of Y is

$$f_Y(y) = \int_y^{12} f(x, y)\, dx = \int_y^{12} \left(\frac{1}{12x}\right) dx = \frac{1}{12}[\ln 12 - \ln y].$$

To then find the first and second moments of Y directly from the marginal density of Y is a bit of a calculus challenge. Instead, we will find the unconditional expected value and variance of Y from its conditional moments by using the double expectation theorem. We have, since Y is conditionally uniform, $E_Y[Y \mid X] = \frac{X}{2}$ and $Var_Y(Y \mid X) = \frac{X^2}{12}$. Then, directly from the double expectation theorem, we have

$$E[Y] = E_X\left[E_Y[Y \mid X]\right] = E_X\left[\frac{X}{2}\right] = \frac{1}{2} \cdot E[X] = 3,$$

since, being uniform on $0<x<12$, we have $E[X]=6$. Similarly,

$$\begin{aligned} Var(Y) &= E_X[Var_Y(Y\,|\,X)] + Var_X(E_Y[Y\,|\,X]) \\ &= E_X\left[\frac{X^2}{12}\right] + Var_X\left(\frac{X}{2}\right) \\ &= \frac{1}{12}\cdot E[X^2] + \frac{1}{4}\cdot Var(X) \\ &= \left(\frac{1}{12}\right)(48) + \left(\frac{1}{4}\right)(12) \;=\; 7, \end{aligned}$$

since $Var(X)=12$ and $E[X^2] \;=\; Var(X)+(E[X])^2 \;=\; 48$.

In the discrete case example, presented in Section 1.4.1, the unconditional mean and variance were found more easily from the marginal distribution than via the double expectation theorem. In this continuous example, however, the opposite is true; the mean and variance of Y are found more easily via the double expectation theorem than from the marginal distribution of Y.

The double expectation theorem will have several applications throughout this text. For future reference we restate it here as

$$E[X] \;=\; E_Y\big[E_X[X\,|\,Y]\big] \tag{1.59a}$$

and

$$Var(X) \;=\; E_Y\big[Var_X(X\,|\,Y)\big] + Var_Y\big(E_X[X\,|\,Y]\big). \tag{1.59b}$$

1.5 SUMS OF INDEPENDENT RANDOM VARIABLES

Consider the random variable S (chosen to stand for "sum"), defined as

$$S \;=\; X_1 + X_2 + \cdots + X_n, \tag{1.60}$$

where the X_i's are all mutually independent. This model arises often in actuarial science, and is referred to there as the *individual risk model*. We will explore this model within the actuarial context more fully in Chapter 7. At this point we wish to review what we already know about the random variable S from a prior study of probability.

1.5.1 THE MOMENTS OF *S*

The expected value of S is simply the sum of the expected values of the X_i's, so we have

$$E[S] \;=\; \sum_{i=1}^{n} E[X_i]. \tag{1.61a}$$

If the X_i's all have the same distribution, so that we may use $E[X]$ to denote the common $E[X_i]$, we then have

$$E[S] = n \cdot E[X]. \tag{1.61b}$$

Because of the assumption of independence, it is also true that

$$Var(S) = \sum_{i=1}^{n} Var(X_i), \tag{1.62a}$$

which, if the X_i's all have the same distribution so they have common $Var(X)$, can be written as

$$Var(S) = n \cdot Var(X). \tag{1.62b}$$

More generally, the moments of S can be found from its moment generating function $M_S(t)$, which is itself found from the MGF's of the X_i's as

$$M_S(t) = M_{X_1}(t) \cdot M_{X_2}(t) \cdot \cdots \cdot M_{X_n}(t). \tag{1.63a}$$

That is, the MGF of the sum of independent random variables is the *product* of the MGF's of the several random variables in the sum. If the X_i's all have the same distribution, and therefore the same MGF, denoted $M_X(t)$, then we have

$$M_S(t) = [M_X(t)]^n. \tag{1.63b}$$

Can we go beyond knowing only the moments of the random variable S and find its actual distribution? The answer is that yes we can, in certain cases; this is pursued in the remaining subsections of this section.

1.5.2 DISTRIBUTIONS CLOSED UNDER CONVOLUTION

If the X_i random variables belong to certain families of distributions, then the random variable S will belong to that same family, albeit with different parameter values. Distributions for which this property holds are said to be *closed under convolution.*

For example, if each X_i is a Poisson random variable with parameter λ_i, then S is a Poisson random variable with parameter $\lambda = \lambda_1 + \lambda_2 + \cdots + \lambda_n$. The result follows from Equation (1.63a). We have

$$\begin{aligned} M_S(t) &= e^{\lambda_1(e^t-1)} \cdot e^{\lambda_2(e^t-1)} \cdot \cdots \cdot e^{\lambda_n(e^t-1)} \\ &= e^{\lambda_1(e^t-1)+\lambda_2(e^t-1)+\cdots+\lambda_n(e^t-1)} \\ &= e^{\lambda(e^t-1)}, \end{aligned}$$

where $\lambda = \lambda_1 + \lambda_2 + \cdots + \lambda_n$, which is the MGF for a Poisson random variable with parameter λ.

Again by using Equation (1.63a) we can show that if each X_i is a binomial random variable, with common value of the parameter p but each with its own parameter value n_i, then S is a binomial random variable with parameters $n = n_1 + n_2 + \cdots + n_n$ and the common value of p.

Similarly we can show that if each X_i is a negative binomial random variable, with common parameter p but each with its own parameter value r_i, then S is a negative binomial random variable with parameters $r = r_1 + r_2 + \cdots + r_n$ and the common value of p.

If each X_i is a geometric random variable with common parameter p, then S is a negative binomial random variable with parameters $r = n$ and the common value of p.

On the continuous side, if each X_i is a normal random variable with parameters μ_i and σ_i, then S is a normal random variable with parameters $\mu = \mu_1 + \mu_2 + \cdots + \mu_n$ and $\sigma^2 = \sigma_1^2 + \sigma_2^2 + \cdots + \sigma_n^2$. (Note that it is *not* true that $\sigma = \sigma_1 + \sigma_2 + \cdots + \sigma_n$.)

If each X_i is an exponential random variable with common parameter β, then S is a gamma random variable with parameters $\alpha = n$ and the common value of β.

Finally if each X_i is a gamma random variable, with common parameter β but each with its own parameter α_i, then S is a gamma random variable with parameters $\alpha = \alpha_1 + \alpha_2 + \cdots + \alpha_n$ and the common value of β.

Note that the uniform random variable is not closed under convolution.

The property of being closed under convolution is a convenient one for the X_i random variables to have. For example, in the continuous case, it is convenient if we are justified in assuming a gamma distribution (including the special case exponential) for the X_i's so that we can then analyze the distribution of S as another gamma random variable. This will be revisited in our further discussion of the individual risk model in Chapter 7.

1.5.3 THE METHOD OF CONVOLUTIONS

Consider the individual risk model in the special case with $n = 2$, so that $S = X_1 + X_2$. Suppose the distributions of X_1 and X_2 are discrete, with only a few points in each distribution. For example, suppose we have the distributions $p_1(1) = .40$ and $p_1(2) = .60$ for X_1, and $p_2(1) = .50$, $p_2(2) = .40$ and $p_2(3) = .10$ for X_2. Then we can simply tabulate the discrete distribution of S. We observe that S can take on the values 2, 3, 4, and 5. We can then easily calculate the probability values associated with each possible value of S:

$$Pr(S{=}2) = Pr(X_1 = 1 \text{ and } X_2 = 1) = (.40)(.50) = .20$$

$$Pr(S{=}3) = Pr(X_1 = 1 \text{ and } X_2 = 2) + Pr(X_1 = 2 \text{ and } X_2 = 1) = (.40)(.40) + (.60)(.50) = .46$$

$$Pr(S{=}4) \;=\; Pr(X_1 = 1 \text{ and } X_2 = 3) + Pr(X_1 = 2 \text{ and } X_2 = 2) \;=\; (.40)(.10) + (.60)(.40) \;=\; .28$$

$$Pr(S{=}5) \;=\; Pr(X_1 = 2 \text{ and } X_2 = 3) \;=\; (.60)(.10) \;=\; .06$$

(Note, as a check on our arithmetic, that the probability values for S sum to unity.) This process for tabulating the distribution of S is called the *method of convolutions*.

If the model has $n = 3$ terms in the sum, we can use the method of convolutions recursively. With $S = X_1 + X_2 + X_3$, we first let $R = X_1 + X_2$ and find the distribution of R by convoluting the distributions of X_1 and X_2, as just discussed, and then we convolute the distributions of R and X_3 to find the distribution of S. This process can then be extended to any number of terms in the sum, noting that we only ever convolute two distributions at one time. Thus if there are n terms in the sum, we would perform $n-1$ sequential convolutions to reach the distribution of S.

The method of convolutions to find the distribution of S in either the individual or collective risk model will be further investigated in Chapter 7 and again in Chapter 8, including the case where each X_i has a continuous distribution.

1.5.4 APPROXIMATING THE DISTRIBUTION OF *S*

If the X_i's do not belong to a family of distributions that is closed under convolution, and if the method of convolutions is too unwieldy (because the domain of each X_i is quite large and/or because we have a large value of n), so that the methods of Sections 1.5.2 and 1.5.3 are either impossible or impractical to use, we can always resort to approximating the distribution of S. If n is "sufficiently large," then we can invoke the Central Limit Theorem to conclude that S has an approximately normal distribution. The mean and variance of S are available by summing the means and variances of the X_i's, and these two values completely define the normal distribution of S. This approach will be utilized at several points throughout the text.

1.6 COMPOUND DISTRIBUTIONS

In this section we consider a variation on the sum of independent random variables model of Section 1.5, in which the number of terms in the sum is itself random. In this case we write

$$S \;=\; X_1 + X_2 + \cdots + X_N, \tag{1.64}$$

where N is used as the subscript of the last term, in contrast to the use of n in Equation (1.60), to remind us that the number of terms in the sum is a random variable. We again assume that the X_i random variables are mutually independent, and that they all have the same distribution. We further assume that each X_i is also independent of the random variable N. In probability theory, S is said to have a *compound distribution*. The distribution of N is called the *primary distribution* and the common distribution of X_i is called the *secondary distribution*.

In the context of actuarial science, the compound distribution is called the *collective risk model*. We will further discuss this model, and contrast it with the simpler individual risk model, in Chapter 7.

1.6.1 THE MOMENTS OF *S*

To find the mean and variance of S when it has the compound distribution defined by Equation (1.64) we make use of the double expectation theorem reviewed in Section 1.4. We consider S to be conditional on the random variable N. Then, conditional on having N terms in the sum, each with expected value $E[X]$ and variance $Var(X)$, we have

$$E[S \mid N] = N \cdot E[X] \tag{1.61c}$$

and

$$Var(S \mid N) = N \cdot Var(X). \tag{1.62c}$$

(We can use the notation $E[X]$ and $Var(X)$, rather than $E[X_i]$ and $Var(X_i)$, because all X_i are assumed to have the same distribution.)

By the first part of the double expectation theorem we then have

$$E[S] = E_N\left[E[S \mid N]\right] = E_N\left[N \cdot E[X]\right] = E[N] \cdot E[X], \tag{1.65}$$

since $E[X]$ is a constant with respect to the random variable N. Similarly, by the second part of the double expectation theorem we have

$$\begin{aligned} Var(S) &= E_N\left[Var(S \mid N)\right] + Var_N\left(E[S \mid N]\right) \\ &= E_N\left[N \cdot Var(X)\right] + Var_N\left(N \cdot E[X]\right) \\ &= E[N] \cdot Var(X) + Var(N) \cdot \left(E[X]\right)^2, \end{aligned} \tag{1.66}$$

since both $E[X]$ and $Var(X)$ are constants with respect to the random variable N.

We can also express the moment generating function of S as a function of the MGF's of N (the primary distribution) and X (the secondary distribution), using the first part of the double expectation theorem, since the MGF of S is just the expected value of e^{tS}. Again conditioning on N we have

$$M_S(t) = E[e^{tS}] = E_N[E[e^{tS} \mid N]].$$

But $E[e^{tS} \mid N]$ is the MGF of S, given that there are N terms in the sum. From Equation (1.63b) we know that this conditional MGF is

$$M_S(t)|N = E[e^{tS}|N] = [M_X(t)]^N,$$

which can also be written as

$$E[e^{tS}|N] = e^{\ln[M_X(t)]^N} = e^{N\cdot\ln M_X(t)}.$$

Let $r = \ln M_X(t)$. Then we have

$$M_S(t) = E_N\left[E[e^{tS}|N]\right] = E_N[e^{rN}] = M_N(r).$$

This tells us that the MGF of S is equal to the MGF of the primary distribution N, evaluated at $r = \ln M_X(t)$. Thus we can conclude that

$$M_S(t) = M_N[\ln M_X(t)]. \tag{1.67}$$

For example, suppose N has a Poisson distribution with MGF given by $M_N(t) = e^{\lambda(e^t-1)}$, as given by Equation (1.37). Then by Equation (1.67) the MGF of S is

$$M_S(t) = M_N[\ln M_X(t)] = e^{\lambda[M_X(t)-1]}, \tag{1.68}$$

in terms of the MGF of the random variable X.

1.6.2 THE COMPOUND POISSON DISTRIBUTION

If N has a Poisson distribution, then S is said to have a *compound Poisson distribution*. In this case the mean of S, by Equation (1.65), can be written as

$$E[S] = \lambda\cdot E[X], \tag{1.69}$$

since $E[N] = \lambda$. Further, since $Var(N) = \lambda$ as well, Equation (1.66) for the variance of S simplifies to

$$\begin{aligned} Var(S) &= \lambda\cdot Var(X) + \lambda\cdot(E[X])^2 \\ &= \lambda[Var(X) + (E[X])^2] \\ &= \lambda\cdot E[X^2], \end{aligned} \tag{1.70}$$

since $Var(X) = E[X^2] - (E[X])^2$. Note that the moments of S can also be obtained from the MGF of S, given by Equation (1.68).

The compound Poisson distribution will be extensively used in our further discussion of the collective risk model in Chapter 7 and the ruin model in Chapter 8.

CHAPTER TWO

REVIEW OF STATISTICAL INFERENCE

2.1 INTRODUCTION

Broadly speaking, *statistical inference* involves the development of techniques for inferring properties of an unknown distribution from data generated by that distribution, a process addressed extensively in this text. In Part III (Chapters 9-12) we consider estimation of *tabular models*. In Part IV (Chapters 13-16) we consider estimation of *parametric models*. In both cases we are dealing with the incorporation of sample data into the models being developed and applied.

We cannot provide a comprehensive review of statistical inference in only one background chapter, and we presume that the reader has previously studied this topic.[1] In this chapter we will review four fundamental issues in statistical inference, namely (1) point estimation, (2) properties of estimators, (3) confidence intervals, and (4) hypothesis testing, with a separate section of the chapter devoted to each.

2.2 POINT ESTIMATION

We first consider the issue of estimating the value of some measure of an unknown population distribution. This value can be any of a wide variety of different measures of the population distribution, such as a moment, percentile, parameter, or probability.

We believe that the true value of this measure in the population exists, but is unknown. The fact that the true value is unknown creates the need for *sampling*, since sampling is the best, and perhaps only, way to learn more about the nature of the underlying population. Even with the most sophisticated and comprehensive sampling, however, we will never know with certainty the true value of the unknown measure.

We quickly discover that different samples will produce different estimates of the measure in question, so a series of estimates from repeated samples will have its own statistical distribution. Despite the fact that there is typically a range of reasonable estimates, there is usually a strong impetus to produce a single value for the estimate. Such a value is called a *point estimate*. This point estimate is often intended to provide a measure of *central tendency* in the underlying population distribution.

---

[1] For those needing a more thorough review of the topic, we recommend any of the following texts: Asimow and Maxwell [2]; Hogg, McKean, and Craig [17]; or Hogg and Tanis [18].

It is important to note that we do not know the accuracy of the point estimate at the time it is made. All we can say at that time is that an appropriate procedure was followed in developing the point estimate. Later, with benefit of hindsight, we may discover how accurate the original estimate actually was. However, even if the original estimate turns out not to have been very accurate, that fact by itself does not necessarily mean that the original estimate was improperly determined.

It might be instructive at this point to define three types of error. The first is *model error*. An example of this type of error would be to use a Poisson distribution, for reasons of simplicity, to model claim frequency, when the more complex negative binomial distribution would have better fit the data. The second is *sampling design error*, in which a sample is used that is not representative of the underlying population. An example would be to use accident experience compiled from a cross-section of all drivers to estimate accident experience for newly-licensed drivers. The third is *statistical error*, and involves the random fluctuations that still occur even when the first two types of error are avoided. We can reduce, or even eliminate, the first two types of error by thorough analysis and comparison of different modeling choices and by carefully designing our sampling techniques. By contrast, the third type of error simply cannot be eliminated, although we can often quantify its possible magnitude.

We also need to clarify certain widely-used terminology that is often misused in connection with point estimation. It is important to distinguish between the two terms *estimate* and *estimator*. The former refers to the value resulting from the estimation process being used. The latter refers to the process itself. An estimator is a random variable, and an estimate is a particular realization of that random variable.

Although our primary focus in this section is the development of point estimates, the dispersion of values around those point estimates is also important. As we discuss three key measures of central tendency in the next three subsections, we will also introduce some commonly-used measures of dispersion that are associated with them for use in later sections.

2.2.1 MEAN

The point estimate most commonly used to provide a measure of central tendency in a statistical distribution is the *mean* or *expected* value. The population mean, which we denote by μ or $E[X]$, is defined as

$$\mu = E[X] = \int x \cdot f(x)\,dx \tag{2.1a}$$

if X is continuous, and

$$\mu = E[X] = \sum x \cdot p(x) \tag{2.1b}$$

if X is discrete.[2] The limits on the integral and the summation in Equations (2.1a) and (2.1b) cover the domain of the random variable X.

[2] In this text we follow the convention of using $f(x)$ for the PDF of a continuous distribution and $p(x)$ for the PF of a discrete distribution. We use $F(x)$ for the CDF, and $S(x)$ for the SDF, where $S(x) = 1 - F(x)$, in both cases.

The *sample mean random variable*, in a sample of size *n* drawn from a population, is defined by

$$\overline{X} = \frac{1}{n}\sum_{i=1}^{n} X_i, \tag{2.2a}$$

where the sample value random variables $X_1, X_2, \ldots, X_n$ have mutually independent outcomes and are identically distributed (generally referred to as i.i.d.). In this text we will assume that sample value random variables are i.i.d. unless stated specifically to the contrary.

It is important to understand that Equation (2.2a) defines the sample mean as a random variable, since it is a function of the underlying random variables $X_1, X_2, \cdots, X_n$. When an actual sample is drawn from the population, and turns out to have realized values $x_1, x_2, \cdots, x_n$, then we can calculate the value of this particular sample mean as

$$\overline{x} = \frac{1}{n}\sum_{i=1}^{n} x_i. \tag{2.2b}$$

In other words, $\overline{X}$ denotes the sample mean random variable and $\overline{x}$ denotes a particular realization of $\overline{X}$. We might then use $\overline{x}$ as our estimate of the true population mean μ, so we would refer to $\overline{X}$ as our estimator random variable for μ.

When using means we are also often interested in variances. The population variance, denoted by σ^2 or $Var(X)$, is defined as

$$\begin{aligned}\sigma^2 = Var(X) &= E\left[(X-\mu)^2\right] \\ &= \int (x-\mu)^2 \cdot f(x)\, dx\end{aligned} \tag{2.3a}$$

if X is continuous, and

$$\begin{aligned}\sigma^2 = Var(X) &= E\left[(X-\mu)^2\right] \\ &= \sum (x-\mu)^2 \cdot p(x)\end{aligned} \tag{2.3b}$$

if X is discrete. The reader might recall that the variance can also be expressed in terms of the second moment about the origin and the mean (the first moment about the origin) as

$$\sigma^2 = Var(X) = E[X^2]-(E[X])^2. \tag{2.4}$$

Equation (2.4) is an attractive formula, since it is often easier to apply than is Equation (2.3a) or (2.3b).

The population *standard deviation* is defined as the positive square root of the population variance. It is denoted by σ or $SD(X)$.

Just as the sample mean is a random variable, so too is the sample variance. A natural way to define the *sample variance random variable* is

$$S_n^2 = \frac{1}{n}\sum_{i=1}^{n}(X_i - \overline{X})^2. \tag{2.5a}$$

However, the reader has likely encountered statistics textbooks and other literature where $n-1$ is used in the denominator rather than n, so that the sample variance random variable is defined as

$$S_{n-1}^2 = \frac{1}{n-1}\sum_{i=1}^{n}(X_i - \overline{X})^2. \tag{2.5b}$$

To avoid ambiguity, we will use a subscript on the sample variance random variable symbol S^2 to indicate which denominator is being used in its definition. The reason why there are two different definitions of the sample variance random variable in widespread use will be discussed in Section 2.3.1. In the remainder of this text we will assume that the sample variance random variable is defined by Equation (2.5a) unless specifically stated to the contrary.

When a particular sample, with values $x_1, x_2, \cdots, x_n$, has been drawn, and the sample mean $\overline{x}$ has been calculated by Equation (2.2b), then the realized value of the sample variance random variable can be determined by

$$s_n^2 = \frac{1}{n}\sum_{i=1}^{n}(x_i - \overline{x})^2 \tag{2.6a}$$

or by

$$s_{n-1}^2 = \frac{1}{n-1}\sum_{i=1}^{n}(x_i - \overline{x})^2. \tag{2.6b}$$

If we use s_n^2 or s_{n-1}^2 as our estimate of the true population variance σ^2, we would refer to S_n^2 or S_{n-1}^2 as the estimator random variable for σ^2.

Since the sample mean is a random variable, which we have denoted by $\overline{X}$, it has its own mean and variance. (We will consider the mean, or expected value, of $\overline{X}$ when we discuss the concept of bias in Section 2.3.1.) Referring to Equation (2.2a), the mutual independence of the X_i's implies that

$$Var(\overline{X}) = \frac{1}{n^2}\sum_{i=1}^{n}Var(X_i). \tag{2.7a}$$

The X_i's are identically distributed, so they have the same variance. Letting $Var(X_i) = \sigma^2$ we can write the variance of the sample mean random variable $\bar{X}$ as

$$Var(\bar{X}) = \frac{n \cdot \sigma^2}{n^2} = \frac{\sigma^2}{n}. \tag{2.7b}$$

Equation (2.7b) is an exact expression for $Var(\bar{X})$ in terms of the (unknown) population variance. To obtain a numerical estimate for the value of $Var(\bar{X})$, we would likely use our estimate of the true population variance σ^2, denoted earlier as either s_n^2 or s_{n-1}^2, in place of σ^2 in Equation (2.7b). The resulting value is then an *estimate of the variance of the sample mean random variable* $\bar{X}$, called the *estimated variance* for short, and is denoted by either

$$Est.Var(\bar{X}) = \frac{s_n^2}{n} \tag{2.8a}$$

or

$$Est.Var(\bar{X}) = \frac{s_{n-1}^2}{n}. \tag{2.8b}$$

When we substitute the expression for s_{n-1}^2 given by Equation (2.6b) into Equation (2.8b), we have

$$Est.Var(\bar{X}) = \frac{\sum_{i=1}^{n}(x_i - \bar{x})^2}{(n)(n-1)}. \tag{2.8c}$$

Although the sample mean is probably the most widely used point estimate when sampling, there are potential problems with it. Perhaps the most significant problem is that extreme values (outliers) can have a disproportionate effect on the sample mean. For example, in sampling personal income, the incomes of people such as top entertainers, sports stars, and business CEOs are so extreme, compared with the rest of the population, that their inclusion in a sample may create a distortion in the sample mean. For example, inclusion of even one such person in a sample of size 25 might well lead to a sample mean for which 24 individual sample values are all smaller than the sample mean. This type of distortion leads some practitioners to prefer using the median (the 50th percentile) instead of the mean as a point estimate in measuring central tendency in certain types of applications. This measure will be explored in the next section.

2.2.2 MEDIAN

Another measure of central tendency in a distribution is the 50th percentile, or the *median*. Values of percentiles in a distribution are directly measured by the cumulative distribution function $F(x)$.

More general notation for percentiles will be introduced in Chapter 13, where we denote the population median by $\pi_{.50}$ and the sample median by $x_{.50}$. Thus we have the general formula

$$F(\pi_{.50}) = .50 \tag{2.9a}$$

or

$$\pi_{.50} = F^{-1}(.50), \tag{2.9b}$$

where F^{-1} is the inverse of the cumulative distribution function.

Finding the median of a continuous distribution is relatively straightforward. If the form of the CDF can be inverted algebraically, then the solution is immediate.[3] If the CDF cannot be inverted algebraically, then other techniques are required. Two common examples of the latter are the normal distribution and the gamma distribution. The CDF for each of these distributions is an integral that does not have a closed form.[4] In the case of the normal distribution, the standard normal tables can be read backwards to produce a value. The gamma distribution will require some type of numerical approach, and can be readily handled with EXCEL or any standard statistical software package.

Challenges arise, however, in evaluating percentiles in discrete distribution. The CDF for a discrete distribution is a stair-step function as illustrated in Figure 2.1, where the values of $F(x)$ appear along the y-axis. Often a given percentile on the y-axis will hit a vertical segment along the x-axis. However, other percentiles will also hit this same vertical segment and generate the same value of x. For example, in Figure 2.1 the 60th, 65th and 70th percentiles are all equal to 3.

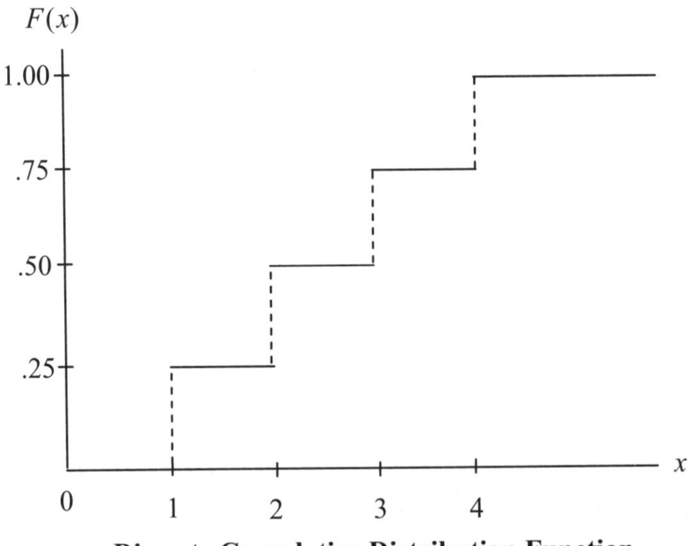

Discrete Cumulative Distribution Function

FIGURE 2.1

On the other hand, in some cases the given percentile on the y-axis will hit a horizontal segment. In these situations, the percentile does not have a unique value and one must be assigned by convention. The authors have seen different conventions used for different appli-

[3] Inverting a CDF is a basic approach used in simulation. (See Chapter 4.)

[4] An exception is the gamma distribution with a positive integer value for the parameter α.

cations. Thus, the reader should be careful when studying various applications by different authors to ascertain the convention being used.

As a simple example, consider the data underlying Figure 2.1, which is contained in Table 2.1. There are four values of the random variable, namely 1, 2, 3, and 4, all of which are equally likely. What is the median?

TABLE 2.1

Values for a Discrete Random Variable		
x	$p(x)$	$F(x)$
0		0
1	.25	.25
2	.25	.50
3	.25	.75
4	.25	1.00

The CDF first hits .50 at $x = 2$. However, the CDF also equals .50 for all values greater than 2 until just to the left of 3. Is the median 2, is it 3, or is it something in between? As a matter of interest, the mean of these four uniformly distributed values is equal to

$$\frac{1+2+3+4}{4} = 2.50.$$

There is no universally accepted answer to this question. A convention must be adopted, and different authors adopt different conventions depending on the application involved.

Another problem arises when working with sample percentiles. Consider a sample of size three in which the three sample values turn out to be $x_1 = 1$, $x_2 = 2$, and $x_3 = 3$. Most people would intuitively think the median should be the middle value, so $x_{.50} = 2$. However, this intuitively comfortable and common-sense answer is not uniquely provided by traditional statistical definitions. In Section 13.4.1 a new measure, called the *smoothed empirical percentile*, is developed that will provide a unique answer of 2 as the sample median.

When the median is being used as the primary measure of central tendency and information about dispersion is desired, the typical approach is to obtain other percentiles. As a simple example, providing the 25th and 75th percentiles along with the median will partition the distribution into four groups each containing 25% of the total probability mass. Many variations along these lines are possible.

2.2.3 MODE

The final measure of central tendency in a distribution that we will discuss is the *mode*. The mode is the *most probable outcome* under a discrete distribution, and the point with greatest density under a continuous distribution. The mode may not be unique, since there may be multiple values of equally great probability or density. A distribution with only one mode is called *unimodal*.

In a continuous distribution, the mode is that value (or those values) of x that maximize the density function $f(x)$. Figure 2.2 below illustrates the mode, denoted by m, in four different situations.

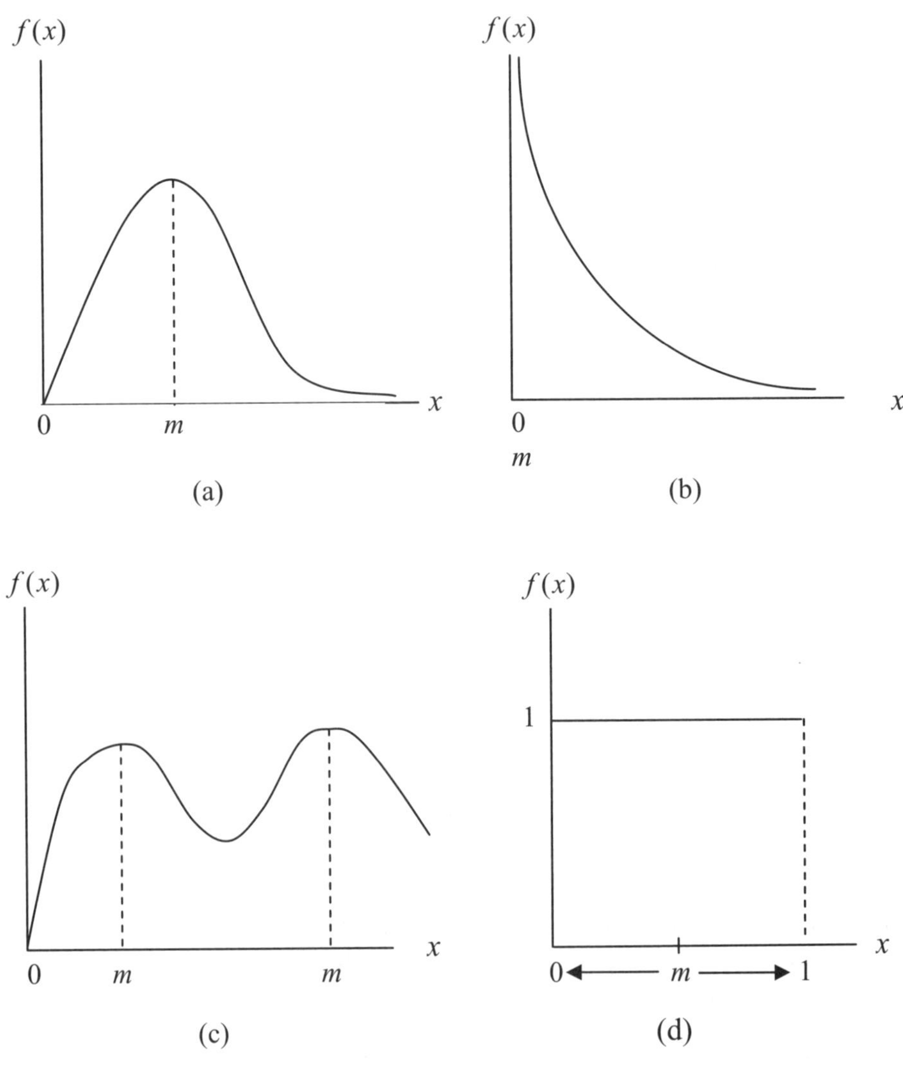

Four Illustrative Modes

FIGURE 2.2

Figure 2.2(a) displays a very common unimodal distribution in which the distribution is heaped in the middle and tails off on each end. Many of the continuous distributions given in Appendix A and discussed in Chapter 1 look like this. Modes of this type may be found by using calculus techniques to find the maximum value of $f(x)$.

Figure 2.2(b) illustrates a monotonically decreasing PDF and shows that the mode may occur at a boundary point. The exponential distribution and the Pareto distribution are two commonly-used distributions having this feature.

Figure 2.2(c) demonstrates a rather unusual bimodal distribution having two distinct modes. Calculus techniques can be used to determine both modes as relative maxima. If the two relative maxima are not of the same height, the taller one might be characterized as the "absolute mode," and the shorter one as a "relative mode." A variation on this type of distribution might be a mixed distribution with a point-mass at $x=0$ and then a shape like Figure 2.2(a) for values of $x>0$.[5]

In Figure 2.2(d) every value of x in the domain of the random variable is a mode! The continuous uniform distribution is a distribution of this type.

The reader should note that the mode has been included in the formulas and properties presented for most of the continuous distributions in Appendix A.

For discrete distributions the concepts are the same, but finding the mode is even simpler. The mode is simply the most probable value of x and typically can be identified by inspection.

Measures of dispersion are generally not applicable when using modes.

2.3 PROPERTIES OF ESTIMATORS

We now turn to a deeper analysis of some important properties of estimators. These various properties provide information on certain key characteristics of estimators and will help us assess their quality. The notation in Section 2.3 will be presented in terms of parameter estimation. This seems appropriate since these properties are widely utilized in connection with parameter estimation, as we will see in more detail in Chapters 13 and 14. However, the properties are somewhat broader than solely for parameter estimation, as we shall also see in this section.

There are three primary properties that we examine in Section 2.3, namely (1) unbiasedness, (2) consistency, and (3) efficiency, with a separate subsection devoted to each.

2.3.1 UNBIASEDNESS

Consider the common situation in which an unknown population parameter θ is being estimated by the estimator $\hat{\theta}$. The estimator $\hat{\theta}$ is said to be *unbiased* if

$$E[\hat{\theta}] = \theta. \tag{2.10}$$

In words, the estimator random variable $\hat{\theta}$ is unbiased if its expected value is equal to the parameter it estimates. If Equation (2.10) does not hold, then the estimator is said to be *biased*, and the bias is defined by

$$Bias(\hat{\theta}) = E[\hat{\theta}]-\theta. \tag{2.11}$$

[5] A picturesque term for a bimodal distribution is a *barbell distribution*.

In some cases, we care about the sign of the bias, and $\hat{\theta}$ is said to be *positively biased* if

$$E[\hat{\theta}] > \theta \tag{2.12a}$$

and *negatively biased* if

$$E[\hat{\theta}] < \theta. \tag{2.12b}$$

In other cases, we do not care about the sign of the bias and just work with its absolute value for convenience.

Some estimators are biased, but the bias is reduced as the sample size increases. For large samples, therefore, the bias becomes insignificant. Such an estimator is called *asymptotically unbiased*. More precisely, a biased estimator is said to be asymptotically unbiased if

$$\lim_{n \to \infty} E[\hat{\theta}_n] = \theta, \tag{2.13}$$

where $\hat{\theta}_n$ is the parameter estimator for a sample of size n.[6]

It is instructive to demonstrate the concept of bias for the sample mean and sample variance random variables, using the notation presented in Section 2.2.1. We first consider using the sample mean random variable $\bar{X}$ as an estimator for the population mean μ, using an i.i.d. sample of size n. From Equation (2.2a) we have

$$\begin{aligned} E[\bar{X}] &= E\left[\frac{1}{n}\sum_{i=1}^{n} X_i\right] \\ &= \frac{1}{n}(n\mu) = \mu, \end{aligned} \tag{2.14}$$

since $E[X_i] = \mu$ for each random variable $X_1, X_2, \ldots, X_n$. Thus, the sample mean random variable is an unbiased estimator for the population mean.

The sample variance random variable is defined by either Equation (2.5a) or (2.5b). To derive expressions for the expected values of these random variables, we first need to find the second moments of the random variables X_i and $\bar{X}$, as well as the expected value of $X_i \cdot \bar{X}$. We are given that $E[X_i] = \mu$ and $Var(X_i) = \sigma^2$, so $E[X_i^2] = \sigma^2 + \mu^2$. Similarly, $E[\bar{X}] = \mu$ (from Equation (2.14)) and $Var(\bar{X}) = \frac{\sigma^2}{n}$ (from Equation (2.7b)), so it follows that $E[\bar{X}^2] = \frac{\sigma^2}{n} + \mu^2$.

---

[6] Notationally we are using $\hat{\theta}$ to denote the estimator random variable used to estimate the unknown population parameter θ. Later we will also use $\hat{\theta}$ to denote a realized value of this estimator random variable. Some texts prefer to use $\hat{\Theta}$ for the estimator random variable and $\hat{\theta}$ for a realization of it. We use $\hat{\theta}$ for both concepts, with the context making clear which meaning of $\hat{\theta}$ is intended.

To find $E[X_1 \cdot \bar{X}]$, for example, we use Equation (2.2a) to write

$$\begin{aligned} E[X_1 \cdot \bar{X}] &= E\left[X_1 \cdot \tfrac{1}{n}\left(X_1+X_2+\cdots+X_n\right)\right] \\ &= \frac{1}{n}\left(E[X_1^2+X_1X_2+\cdots+X_1X_n]\right) \\ &= \frac{1}{n}\left(E[X_1^2]+E[X_1]\cdot E[X_2]+\cdots+E[X_1]\cdot E[X_n]\right), \end{aligned}$$

due to the mutual independence of the X_i's. We already know that $E[X_i]=\mu$ and $E[X_i^2]=\sigma^2+\mu^2$ for all *i*, so it follows that

$$\begin{aligned} E[X_1 \cdot \bar{X}] &= \frac{1}{n}\left(\sigma^2+\mu^2+(n-1)\mu^2\right) \\ &= \frac{\sigma^2}{n}+\mu^2. \end{aligned}$$

By symmetry, it follows that $E[X_i \cdot \bar{X}]=\frac{\sigma^2}{n}+\mu^2$ for all *i*.

Then we can derive the expected value of the sample variance random variable S_n^2, given by Equation (2.5a), as

$$\begin{aligned} E[S_n^2] &= E\left[\frac{1}{n}\sum_{i=1}^{n}(X_i-\bar{X})^2\right] \\ &= \frac{1}{n}\left(E\left[\sum_{i=1}^{n}(X_i^2-2X_i\cdot\bar{X}+\bar{X}^2)\right]\right) \\ &= \frac{1}{n}\left(\sum_{i=1}^{n}E[X_i^2]-2\sum_{i=1}^{n}E[X_i\cdot\bar{X}]+\sum_{i=1}^{n}E[\bar{X}^2]\right) \\ &= \frac{1}{n}\left(n\left(\sigma^2+\mu^2\right)-2n\left(\frac{\sigma^2}{n}+\mu^2\right)+n\left(\frac{\sigma^2}{n}+\mu^2\right)\right), \end{aligned}$$

since each summand is a constant. This easily reduces to

$$\begin{aligned} E[S_n^2] &= \left(\sigma^2+\mu^2\right)-2\left(\frac{\sigma^2}{n}+\mu^2\right)+\left(\frac{\sigma^2}{n}+\mu^2\right) \\ &= \left(\sigma^2+\mu^2\right)-\left(\frac{\sigma^2}{n}+\mu^2\right) \\ &= \frac{n-1}{n}\sigma^2. \end{aligned} \tag{2.15a}$$

Thus we see that S_n^2 is a biased estimator for σ^2, since $E[S_n^2] \neq \sigma^2$. However, if we replace the n in the denominator with $n-1$, we see that

$$E[S_{n-1}^2] = \sigma^2, \tag{2.15b}$$

so that S_{n-1}^2 is an unbiased estimator for σ^2. The motivation for statisticians to use $n-1$ in the denominator, rather than n, in some situations is now clear. However, that is not the entire story. There may be other factors leading statisticians to prefer using n in the denominator anyway even though it produces a biased estimate. The rationale for this possible preference will become clearer in Section 2.3.3.

To illustrate the unbiased sample variance, consider a population with the two equally-likely discrete values 1 and 3, so that $p(1) = p(3) = .50$. The population mean is 2 and the population variance is

$$\sigma^2 = .50\left[(1-2)^2 + (3-2)^2\right] = 1.$$

For a sample of size two, there are four possible equally-likely sample outcomes as displayed in Table 2.2. The expected value of the four unbiased sample variances shown in the final column is equal to $.25(0+2+2+0) = 1$, demonstrating the validity of Equation (2.15b).

TABLE 2.2

Illustration of an Unbiased Sample Variance

X_1	X_2	$\bar{X}$	S_{n-1}^2
1	1	1	$\frac{1}{2-1}\left[(1-1)^2 + (1-1)^2\right] = 0$
1	3	2	$\frac{1}{2-1}\left[(1-2)^2 + (3-2)^2\right] = 2$
3	1	2	$\frac{1}{2-1}\left[(3-2)^2 + (1-2)^2\right] = 2$
3	3	1	$\frac{1}{2-1}\left[(3-3)^2 + (3-3)^2\right] = 0$

One final, and quite important, observation about the biased sample variance random variable S_n^2 is that it is asymptotically unbiased. Whether the denominator in the sample variance is n or $n-1$ essentially becomes irrelevant for large sample sizes.

2.3.2 CONSISTENCY

Instead of looking at the difference between the expected value of an estimator and the true value of the parameter being estimated, as we did in the prior section, let us consider the probability that such a difference is greater than some number ε. The concept of *consistency* is an application of limit theory in calculus, and requires this probability value to become small for large sample sizes. In less precise mathematical language, we want the estimator to be approaching the true value of the parameter as the sample size increases. In mathematical notation, an estimator is said to be *consistent* if, for any $\varepsilon > 0$, we have

$$\lim_{n\to\infty} \Pr\left(\left|\hat{\theta}_n - \theta\right| > \varepsilon\right) = 0. \tag{2.16}$$

The reader might observe that the properties of consistency and asymptotic unbiasedness in a parameter are similar and might possibly be related. It is possible to show that asymptotic unbiasedness is a sufficient (but not necessary) condition for consistency, as long as $Var(\hat{\theta}_n) \to 0$. The proof of this result is beyond the scope of this text.

Readers might assume that the sample mean is a consistent estimator of the population mean. From Equation (2.6) we see that this result follows, as long as the population variance σ^2 is finite.

Consistency is certainly a desirable property for an estimator to possess. However, it is not really that stringent of a property. Most estimators that might be considered as reasonable approaches for estimating a parameter will be consistent. An inconsistent estimator is likely to be easily rejected early in the process of parameter estimation.

2.3.3 EFFICIENCY

The first two properties of estimators have dealt with the point estimate in the estimation process. The third property we discuss is the property of *efficiency*, and it deals with dispersion in the estimation process. Since different samples will produce different point estimates, the estimation process being applied will contain dispersion.

Consider a measure of dispersion defined as the variance of outcomes around a point estimate, which is

$$Var(\hat{\theta}) = E\left[(\hat{\theta} - E[\hat{\theta}])^2\right] \tag{2.17a}$$

$$= E[\hat{\theta}^2] - (E[\hat{\theta}])^2. \tag{2.17b}$$

Equation (2.17a) is the fundamental definition of variance, and Equation (2.17b) expresses the variance as the second moment about the origin minus the mean squared.

Remember that our goal is to estimate the true value of the parameter θ, but θ does not appear in this variance formula. To correct this, another measure of dispersion has been developed to measure the expected squared difference between $\hat{\theta}$ and θ. This measure of dispersion is called *mean square error*, and is defined as

$$MSE(\hat{\theta}) = E\left[(\hat{\theta} - \theta)^2\right]. \tag{2.18}$$

It is possible to derive an alternative expression for $MSE(\hat{\theta})$ that is quite instructive. Starting with Equation (2.18) we have

$$
\begin{aligned}
MSE(\hat{\theta}) &= E\left[(\hat{\theta}-\theta)^2\right] \\
&= E\left[\hat{\theta}^2 - 2\hat{\theta}\theta + \theta^2\right] \\
&= \left(E[\hat{\theta}^2]-(E[\hat{\theta}])^2\right)+\left((E[\hat{\theta}])^2 - 2\theta\cdot E[\hat{\theta}]+\theta^2\right) \\
&= \left(E[\hat{\theta}^2]-(E[\hat{\theta}])^2\right)+\left(E[\hat{\theta}]-\theta\right)^2 \\
&= Var(\hat{\theta})+\left(Bias(\hat{\theta})\right)^2, \qquad (2.19)
\end{aligned}
$$

from Equations (2.17b) and (2.11). Thus, MSE can be conceptualized as a measure of dispersion in the parameter estimator that starts with the variance of the estimator. If the estimator is biased, then additional dispersion arises from the fact that the expected value of the point estimator is not equal to the true value of the parameter being estimated. (We do not worry about the sign of the bias, since it is squared.) If the parameter estimator is unbiased, however, then the MSE equals the variance.

Efficiency is then measured by MSE. Greater efficiency is associated with smaller values of MSE and vice versa. Efficiency is often used in a relative sense to compare two different estimation processes. This leads to a concept called *relative efficiency* that is defined as the ratio of the values of MSE for the two estimation processes.

MSE also sheds light on why unbiased estimators may not always be preferred to biased estimators. It is possible for MSE to actually be lower for a biased estimator than for an unbiased one, if the variance goes in the opposite direction enough to offset the bias. This possibility is actually not that remote, as we shall see in Chapter 14.

Of course, the ideal estimator would be one that is both unbiased and has maximum efficiency (minimum MSE). If such an estimator were also consistent, it would have the best of all three properties. Although they are ideal in terms of our three properties, such estimators may not be that easy to find and apply in practice.

2.4 INTERVAL ESTIMATION

In Sections 2.2 and 2.3 we discussed various aspects of the point estimation of some measure in an unknown population distribution. The technique of point estimation is widely used for many applications, since a single estimated value of the measure is often required. However, it is often useful to also obtain a range of values for the unknown measure being estimated. Typically, the probability that the unknown measure lies in this range of values is also required. This type of estimation process is called *interval estimation*.

2.4.1 CONFIDENCE INTERVALS

The most common type of an interval estimation process used in practice is the determination of a *confidence interval*. Again, we might be estimating a variety of measures from an unknown population distribution, but, as in prior sections, we will state the definition of a confidence interval in terms of estimating an unknown parameter.

The probability that the unknown parameter lies in the confidence interval is called the *confidence level*, and is denoted by $1-\alpha$, so that α is the probability that the parameter value lies outside the confidence interval. For example, if $\alpha = 5\%$, or .05, then the confidence level is equal to 95%, or .95. We will revisit the quantity α in Section 2.5 and discuss it in more depth.

A $100(1-\alpha)\%$ confidence interval is then defined by a pair of values, L and U, computed from the random sample such that

$$\Pr(L \leq \theta \leq U) \geq 1-\alpha, \tag{2.20}$$

for all θ, where L denotes the *lower limit* of the confidence interval and U denotes the *upper limit*.

The $\geq$ sign in Equation (2.20) requires some explanation. In a continuous distribution, this would be an equal sign. The use of the inequality is necessary to accommodate discrete distributions in which probabilities come into the interval is discrete pieces. The goal is to be certain that the interval contains enough probability mass to satisfy the required confidence level.

A confidence interval may be either *two-tailed* or *one-tailed*. A two-tailed confidence interval has some finite amount of the probability α both to the left of L and to the right of U. By contrast, a one-tailed confidence interval has all the probability α either to the left of L or to the right of U.

An important special case of the two-tailed confidence interval for continuous distributions is one in which L and U are chosen so that equal probability of amount $\alpha / 2$ is contained in each tail. This is probably the most common type of two-tailed confidence interval used in practice for continuous distributions.

Confidence intervals require the use of some distribution from which to calculate the associated probabilities and the required values of L and R. The choice of distribution may not be easy to make, since it depends on the measure for which the confidence interval is being constructed and the type of the distribution itself.

We consider two examples. First, consider finding a 90% confidence interval to estimate the value of $Y = \sum_{i=1}^{4} X_i$, where $X_1, \cdots, X_4$ are independent and each has a Poisson distribution with $\lambda = 1$. We know that Y also has a Poisson distribution, but with $\lambda = 4$. The PF and CDF values for this distribution are displayed in Table 2.3 on the following page for values of $x = 0, 1, 2, \cdots, 10$. Although the Poisson distribution is defined on all the non-negative integers, the value of its PF rapidly becomes insignificant past $x = 10$.

Some of the complexities in constructing confidence intervals for discrete distributions are immediately apparent. Confidence intervals of various lengths can be constructed by taking differences of values in the CDF column. There are four approximately 90% confidence intervals of shortest length for their type. These four are displayed in Table 2.4 below.

TABLE 2.3

Poisson Random Variable with $\lambda = 4$		
x	$p(x)$	$F(x)$
0	.01832	.01832
1	.07326	.09158
2	.14653	.23810
3	.19537	.43347
4	.19537	.62884
5	.15629	.78513
6	.10420	.88933
7	.05954	.94887
8	.02977	.97864
9	.01323	.99187
10	.00529	.99716

TABLE 2.4

Confidence Intervals Based on Table 2.3		
Interval $[L,U]$	**Probability Mass**	**Type**
[0,7]	.94887 − 0 = .94887	One-tailed
[1,7]	.94887 − .01832 = .93055	Two-tailed
[2,9]	.99187 − .09158 = .90029	Two-tailed
$[2,\infty]$	1 − .09158 = .90842	One-tailed

The first and fourth confidence intervals are the shortest possible one-tailed confidence intervals that contain at least 90% probability mass. The second and third are two different shortest two-tailed confidence intervals that also contain at least 90% probability mass. Interestingly, each has one end point in common with one of the one-tailed intervals. Moreover, the amount of probability mass in each tail cannot be controlled by the modeler, nor will the two tails have equal amounts of probability mass in general.

The second example involves a two-tailed 90% confidence interval for the mean of a normal distribution based on a random sample of size n. Both the mean and variance of the normal distribution are unknown. A well-known theorem from mathematical statistics specifies use of the t-distribution in this case. Assuming that the two tails are to be equal in size with 5% of the total probability mass in each, the confidence interval is given by

$$L = \overline{X} - t_{.95}^{n-1} \cdot SD(\overline{X}) \tag{2.21a}$$

and

$$R = \bar{X} + t_{.95}^{n-1} \cdot SD(\bar{X}), \tag{2.21b}$$

where $t_{.95}^{n-1}$ is the 95th percentile of a t distribution with $n-1$ degrees of freedom and $SD(\bar{X}) = \sqrt{Var(\bar{X})}$, with $Var(\bar{X})$ given by either Equation (2.7a) or (2.7b).

Clearly the construction of appropriate confidence intervals from first principles varies considerably from situation to situation and can become rather involved and complicated. The above two examples are actually less complicated than many examples that could be given. A simpler approach of widespread utility that works well for large samples will be presented in the next subsection.

2.4.2 CENTRAL LIMIT THEOREM

As we saw in the two examples of Section 2.4.1, determining exact confidence intervals varies from situation to situation and can quickly become complicated in many cases. A popular approach that simplifies this process in the case of large samples is to use the *Central Limit Theorem*, which the reader should recall from a prior study of probability and statistics. This theorem is a bedrock of statistical theory and justifies using the normal distribution in a wide variety of situations involving large sample sizes.

By way of review we will state the basic Central Limit Theorem as it is usually given. Let $X_1, \cdots, X_n$ be a sequence of n i.i.d. random variables each having a finite mean μ and finite variance σ^2. The theorem states that as the sample size n increases, the distribution of the sum of these random variables, $S = X_1 + \cdots + X_n$, approaches the normal distribution with mean $n\mu$ and variance $n\sigma^2$, irrespective of the type of the original distribution.

This version of the Central Limit Theorem is often expressed in terms of the sample mean rather than the sum of the sample values. When this is done, the mean and variance of the sample mean approach μ and $\frac{\sigma^2}{n}$, respectively. The latter result was actually presented earlier in this chapter as Equation (2.7b), without providing any justification at the time.

Many extensions and generalizations of the Central Limit Theorem have been developed to fit a variety of situations that commonly arise in statistical applications. These expansions justify application of the normal approximation to fit a variety of situations involving large samples.

The use of the normal approximation to construct confidence intervals in this fashion is pervasive in statistics. Again, we will express this confidence interval in terms of estimating a parameter, although there are many other types of applications as well.

Let the point estimate for the parameter be denoted by $\hat{\theta}$ and the variance of this estimator be denoted by $Var(\hat{\theta})$. The formulas analogous to Equations (2.21a) and (2.21b) for the 90% confidence interval would then be

$$L = \hat{\theta} - z_{.95} \cdot SD(\hat{\theta}) = \hat{\theta} - 1.645 SD(\hat{\theta}) \tag{2.22a}$$

and

$$R = \hat{\theta} + z_{.95} \cdot SD(\hat{\theta}) = \hat{\theta} + 1.645SD(\hat{\theta}). \tag{2.22b}$$

The percentiles of the standard normal distribution are often expressed in *z-values*, where for a general random variable X we have

$$Z = \frac{X - \mu}{\sigma}. \tag{2.23}$$

In the case of estimating parameters, the reader might question the source of the mean and variance in Equations (2.22a) and (2.22b). This topic will be extensively addressed in Section 14.4.

2.5 HYPOTHESIS TESTING

Hypothesis testing is covered extensively in standard statistics courses and should be familiar to most readers. The purpose of this section is to provide a brief review of the topic as a refresher for readers. Hypothesis testing will be widely used in Chapter 16.

2.5.1 DEFINITIONS AND CONCEPTS

The basic concept in hypothesis testing is to set up two competing hypotheses about some measure of a statistical distribution or process. Ideally, the two hypotheses should be mutually exclusive and exhaustive (sometimes called "either-or") in structure. One of these hypotheses is called the *null hypothesis* and is traditionally labeled H_0. The other is called the *alternative hypothesis* and is traditionally labeled H_1.

Similar to confidence intervals, hypotheses can be one-tailed or two-tailed. A simple example of a one-tailed hypothesis would be

$$H_0: \ \mu \leq 1000$$

or

$$H_1: \ \mu > 1000,$$

where μ denotes the mean of some distribution. By way of contrast, a two-tailed hypothesis in the same situation would be

$$H_0: \ \mu = 1000$$

or

$$H_1: \ \mu \neq 1000.$$

A random sample is obtained, and from this sample a *test statistic* is computed based on the sample values. A subset of the possible values for this test statistic is then defined to be the *critical region*, or the *rejection region* of the test. If the test statistic falls in the critical region, then the null hypothesis H_0 is rejected and the alternative hypothesis H_1 is chosen instead. If the test statistic does not fall in the critical region, then the null hypothesis is chosen. The boundary value(s) between the critical region and the non-critical region is (are) called the *critical value*(*s*).

Continuing the example started above, the test statistic could be the sample mean $\overline{X}$ and the critical region for the one-tailed test might be $\overline{X} \geq 1200$. In this situation, there would be one critical value at 1200. In contrast, the critical region for the two-tailed test might be $\overline{X} \leq 900$ or $\overline{X} \geq 1100$. In this situation there would be two critical values at 900 and 1100.

There are two possible types of errors in hypothesis testing. The first is called *Type I error* and is the event of rejecting H_0 when it is actually the better choice. The probability of making a Type I error is denoted by α and is the probability of obtaining a value of the test statistics in the critical region when H_0 should have been accepted.

The second type of error is called *Type II error* and is the event of accepting H_0 when it should have been rejected. The probability of making a Type II error is denoted by β and is the probability of obtaining a value of the test statistic outside the critical region when H_1 would be the better choice.

The value of α is called the *significance level* of the hypothesis test and is usually established at the outset by the modeler. In other words, the significance level is the amount of Type I error that can be tolerated in the test. The reader is encouraged to go back and reread the beginning of Section 2.4.1 on confidence intervals where the symbol α was used with the same meaning. In the illustration of that section, a two-tailed test was being used in which α was set at 10%, thereby putting 5% in each tail.

Once the significance level of the test is established, then the goal becomes one of trying to minimize β. However, the reader will probably not be surprised to learn that this goal can only be achieved to a limited degree, if it can be achieved at all. In general, when the modeler tries to decrease Type II error, Type I error will increase, and vice versa.

A hypothesis test for which β has been reduced as much as possible for a given level of α is called the *most powerful test*. The word "power" in hypothesis testing generally refers to β, the probability of Type II error. For example, some authors define a *power function* to be equal to $1-\beta$, the probability of not making a Type II error, which is generally a function of the parameters of the underlying distribution.

2.5.2 APPLICATION AND INTERPRETATION

In this final section we discuss some qualitative and interpretative issues involving hypothesis testing. We also discuss the types of applications for which we will use hypothesis testing later in this book.

Asymmetry in the hypotheses

The two hypotheses H_0 and H_1 are not equal in nature, nor is the hypothesis test symmetrical. In other words, switching the roles of H_0 and H_1 may result in a different conclusion than using the two hypotheses in the original order. Thus, a major decision of the modeler, when using hypothesis testing, is the choice of which hypothesis to use as the null hypothesis and which to use as the alternative.

To illustrate this issue of asymmetry, consider again the simple illustration of the hypothetical one-tailed hypothesis test for the mean of a distribution given in Section 2.5.1. Let us assume that the sample mean obtained is $\overline{X} = 1000$, which is exactly equal to the critical value in the hypothesis test. That particular outcome would virtually assure acceptance of the null hypothesis, regardless of which of the two hypotheses were chosen as the null hypothesis!

Meaning of acceptance or rejection of a hypothesis

It is important to characterize what it means to accept or reject a hypothesis. It does *not* mean that either hypothesis is "true" or "false" in any absolute sense. For example, if we run a hypothesis test and accept H_0, it does not mean that H_0 is necessarily "true." It merely means that we did not reject H_0 based on the test statistic actually obtained. Similarly, if we reject H_0 it does not mean that H_1 is necessarily true in any absolute sense. It merely means that we obtained a test statistic sufficiently at variance with H_0 that we are choosing to use H_1 instead of H_0 as the preferable hypothesis.

Readers should avoid using words like "true" or "false" in characterizing the two hypotheses following the hypothesis test. The better way to characterize the result is to say that the sample evidence was, or was not, sufficient to reject the null hypothesis.

Despite the cautionary comments about using descriptive words carefully, there are some usages of the words "true" and "false" that are appropriate. For example, it would be appropriate to say that the size of the critical region α is calculated *assuming* that the null hypothesis is true.

Binary nature of hypothesis testing

Hypothesis testing has a binary nature in the sense that we either accept or reject the null hypothesis. Although this approach is structurally clean and understandable, it is somewhat simplistic. We now present a more sophisticated way of looking at the results of the hypothesis test.

This requires one more definition, which is the *p-value* of a hypothesis test. The letter *p* stands for "percentile" and gives the exact location of the outcome of the test. An example will help to clarify this concept.

Consider a critical region defined as the 5% right-hand tail of the distribution assuming that H_0 is true. An outcome of the test statistic at the 94th percentile will lead to acceptance of H_0, whereas an outcome at the 96th percentile will lead to rejection of H_0. However, these two outcomes are often quite close together numerically.

Disclosure of the p-value of the test conveys much more information than a simple accept/reject criterion. For example, use of the p-value clearly distinguishes between an acceptance at the 20th percentile from one at the 94th percentile, whereas traditional hypothesis testing merely states that both situations lead to an acceptance of H_0. Similarly, use of the p-value clearly distinguishes between a rejection at the 96th percentile from one at the 99.9^{th} percentile, whereas traditional hypothesis testing merely states that both situations lead to a rejection of H_0.

Problems with large samples

It is hard to imagine that there could ever be a downside to having a large sample. However, in hypothesis testing such a counterintuitive problem could happen.

As an example of such, consider a series of hypothesis tests in which the null hypotheses are a series of different, and competing, severity distributions being tested to fit a large volume of claims data. We are trying to identify the distribution that best fits the data. Since the sample consists of real-world data, it is likely that none of the distributions will exactly fit the data. If the volume of sample data is large, this may well result in rejecting the null hypothesis for every distribution being tested! If less sample data were available, it would be more likely that the null hypotheses for one or more of the distributions being considered would not be rejected.

Applications

One of the primary applications of hypothesis testing in Chapter 16 of this text involves performing tests of fit following the process of parameter estimation (covered in Chapters 13, 14, and 15). The purpose of running these tests of fit is to see how well the distribution in question, together with its estimated parameters, fits the sample data. These tests of fit for the parameter estimates will typically involve hypothesis testing.

The situation described immediately above in discussing problems with large samples provides another example. In that discussion we were comparing different (competing) potential distributions in trying to decide which one provides the best fit to the sample data. Hypothesis testing is useful in this process, and this is also discussed in Chapter 16.

CHAPTER THREE

REVIEW OF SURVIVAL MODELS

3.1 INTRODUCTION

As noted earlier, a detailed presentation of survival models is contained in the text by Cunningham, et al. [7], and covered on SOA Exam MLC and CAS Exam 3A. Before proceeding to a discussion of the estimation of such models from sample data, we wish to review the salient features of survival models for the reader's convenience.

Survival models can be either discrete or continuous. When considered in clinical settings, or those of economists and other social scientists, the continuous form is often used. This form is reviewed in Section 3.2. In traditional actuarial settings, generally involving life insurance or pension fund arrangements, survival models are invariably discrete and tabular, and are usually referred to as *life tables* (or, less optimistically, as *mortality tables*). In light of the importance of life table estimation in actuarial work, we review this model extensively in Section 3.3.

The life table model of Section 3.3 is a *single-decrement model*, within which an entity continues to survive until failure occurs. In this model there is only one type (or cause) of failure. In *multiple-decrement models*, on the other hand, survival again continues until failure occurs but this time there can be more than one type, or cause, of failure. We will consider only the *double-decrement model*, and will review it in Section 3.4.

3.2 REVIEW OF PARAMETRIC SURVIVAL MODELS

In a parametric survival model, the random variable X represents the age at failure for an entity known to exist at age 0. Accordingly, the domain of the random variable is restricted to positive values. Like any other continuous random variable, its distribution can be represented by its density function, usually denoted by $f(x)$, or by its cumulative distribution function, usually denoted by $F(x)$. In the special case of a survival model, however, it is customary to define two additional functions.

The first is the *survival distribution function*, denoted by $S(x)$, and defined by

$$S(x) = 1-F(x) = Pr(X \geq x). \tag{3.1}$$

In words we say that $S(x)$ represents the probability of survival from age 0 to age x.

The second special function is the *hazard rate function* (HRF), denoted by $\lambda(x)$, and defined as

$$\lambda(x) = \frac{f(x)}{S(x)}. \tag{3.2}$$

By writing Equation (3.2) as

$$f(x) = S(x) \cdot \lambda(x), \tag{3.3}$$

we can interpret $\lambda(x)$ as the conditional density, or intensity, of failure at age x, conditional on survival up to age x itself. In the context of actuarial science, the hazard rate is generally called the *force of mortality*, and is denoted by μ_x.

In the remainder of this section we review several continuous distribution that might be used to represent parametric survival functions.

3.2.1 THE CONTINUOUS UNIFORM DISTRIBUTION

The mathematically convenient *uniform distribution* has a constant density function over its domain of $a \leq x \leq b$, so the probability density function (PDF) is

$$f(x) = \frac{1}{b-a}. \tag{3.3a}$$

From this it follows that the cumulative distribution function (CDF) is

$$F(x) = \frac{x-a}{b-a}, \tag{3.4a}$$

the survival distribution function (SDF) is

$$S(x) = 1 - F(x) = \frac{b-x}{b-a}, \tag{3.5a}$$

and the hazard rate function is

$$\lambda(x) = \frac{f(x)}{S(x)} = \frac{1}{b-x}. \tag{3.6a}$$

When the uniform distribution is used as a continuous survival distribution, we often have $a = 0$ and use ω in place of b. Then the PDF is

$$f(x) = \frac{1}{\omega}, \tag{3.3b}$$

the CDF is

$$F(x) = \frac{x}{\omega}, \tag{3.4b}$$

the SDF is

$$S(x) = \frac{\omega - x}{\omega}, \tag{3.5b}$$

the HRF is

$$\lambda(x) = \frac{1}{\omega - x}, \tag{3.6b}$$

the expected value is

$$E[X] = \frac{\omega}{2}, \tag{3.7}$$

and the variance is

$$Var(X) = \frac{\omega^2}{12}. \tag{3.8}$$

3.2.2 THE EXPONENTIAL DISTRIBUTION

The popular one-parameter *exponential distribution* has PDF given by

$$f(x) = \beta \cdot e^{-\beta x}, \tag{3.9}$$

for $x > 0$ and $\beta > 0$. From this we find the SDF to be

$$S(x) = e^{-\beta x}, \tag{3.10}$$

and the HRF to be the constant

$$\lambda(x) = \frac{f(x)}{S(x)} = \beta. \tag{3.11}$$

3.2.3 THE GOMPERTZ DISTRIBUTION

This distribution was suggested as a model for human survival by Gompertz [9] in 1825. The distribution is usually defined by its force of mortality as

$$\mu_x = Bc^x, \tag{3.12}$$

for $x > 0$, $B > 0$, and $c > 1$. Then the SDF is given by

$$S(x) = \exp\left[-\int_0^x Bc^y \, dy\right] = \exp\left[\frac{B}{\ln c}(1-c^x)\right]. \tag{3.13}$$

The PDF is given by $\mu_x \cdot S(x)$, and is clearly not a very convenient mathematical form. A closed-form expression for the mean of the distribution, $E[X]$, does not exist, but the mean can be approximated by numerical integration with a large finite upper limit replacing the actual upper limit of infinity.

3.2.4 THE MAKEHAM DISTRIBUTION

In 1860 Makeham [28] modified the Gompertz distribution by taking the force of mortality to be

$$\mu_x = A + Bc^x, \tag{3.14}$$

for $x > 0, B > 0, c > 1,$ and $A > -B.$ Makeham was suggesting that part of the hazard at any age is independent of the age itself, so a constant was added to the Gompertz force of mortality.

The SDF for this distribution is given by

$$S(x) = \exp\left[-\int_0^x (A+Bc^y)\,dy\right] = \exp\left[\frac{B}{\ln c}(1-c^x) - Ax\right]. \tag{3.15}$$

Again it is clear that the PDF for this distribution is not mathematically tractable. As with the Gompertz distribution, there is no closed-form expression for $E[X]$, although it can also be approximated by numerical integration.[1]

3.3 REVIEW OF THE SINGLE-DECREMENT TABULAR SURVIVAL MODEL (THE LIFE TABLE)[2]

In its most basic form, the life table lists values of the survival function $S(x)$ for integral values of x only, with an arbitrary value of x at which the value of $S(x)$ is first presumed to be zero. This value is denoted ω, so $S(\omega-1) > 0$ and $S(x) = 0$ for $x \geq \omega$. Traditionally, each value of $S(x)$ is multiplied by a constant, denoted by ℓ_0, which is called the *radix* of the table. The resulting value is denoted ℓ_x, so we have

$$\ell_x = \ell_0 \cdot S(x), \tag{3.16}$$

for $x = 0, 1, 2, \cdots$.

Converting $S(x)$ values into ℓ_x values does more than just change the scale of values; it also allows for a *deterministic interpretation* of them. If we let ℓ_0 represent the number of entities (persons or otherwise) surviving at age (or time) zero, then ℓ_x denotes the number of them surviving at age (or time) x, in a deterministic view of the model, or the number *expected* to be surviving at age (or time) x in a stochastic view.

Table 3.1 on the following page illustrates an excerpt from a life table with radix 100,000.

---

[1] A generalization of the Makeham distribution is presented in Exercise 5-10 of Cunningham, et al. [7].

[2] For more detail, see Chapter 6 of Cunningham, et al. [7].

TABLE 3.1

Sample Life Table	
x	ℓ_x
0	100,000
1	97,408
2	97,259
3	97,160
4	97,082
⋮	⋮
109	1
110	0

3.3.1 DISCRETE FUNCTIONS DERIVED FROM ℓ_x

From the basic ℓ_x function we can find the conditional probability of survival to age $x+1$, given survival to age x, as

$$p_x = \frac{\ell_{x+1}}{\ell_x}, \tag{3.16a}$$

or, more generally, the conditional probability of survival to age $x+n$, given survival to age x, as

$${}_n p_x = \frac{\ell_{x+n}}{\ell_x}. \tag{3.16b}$$

The conditional probability of failure before age $x+1$, given survival to age x, is

$$q_x = 1-p_x = \frac{\ell_x - \ell_{x+1}}{\ell_x}, \tag{3.17a}$$

or, more generally, the conditional probability of failure before age $x+n$, given survival to age x, is

$${}_n q_x = 1-{}_n p_x = \frac{\ell_x - \ell_{x+n}}{\ell_x}. \tag{3.17b}$$

If we let

$$d_x = \ell_x - \ell_{x+1} \tag{3.18a}$$

denote the number of failures between ages x and $x+1$, given alive at age x, or, more generally,

$${}_n d_x = \ell_x - \ell_{x+n} \tag{3.18b}$$

denote the number of failures between ages x and $x+n$, given alive at age x, then we can write

$$q_x = \frac{d_x}{\ell_x} \tag{3.19a}$$

and

$$_n q_x = \frac{_n d_x}{\ell_x}. \tag{3.19b}$$

Another important function, denoted $_{n|m} q_x$, gives the conditional probability of failure between ages $x+n$ and $x+n+m$, given alive at age x. We have

$$_{n|m} q_x = {_n p_x} - {_{n+m} p_x} = {_n p_x} \cdot {_m q_{x+n}} = \frac{\ell_{x+n} - \ell_{x+n+m}}{\ell_x}. \tag{3.20}$$

The expected future lifetime for an entity alive at age x, counting only *whole years* of future lifetime, is called the *curtate expectation of life* and is given by

$$e_x = \frac{1}{\ell_x} \cdot \sum_{t=1}^{\infty} \ell_{x+t} = p_x + {_2 p_x} + {_3 p_x} + \cdots. \tag{3.21}$$

3.3.2 CONTINUOUS FUNCTIONS DERIVED FROM ℓ_x

Since the underlying survival function $S(x)$ is continuous, then so is ℓ_x, notwithstanding the fact that the life table only shows values of it for integral x. Assuming ℓ_x to be differentiable as well as continuous, we define the *force of failure* (or *force of mortality* in traditional actuarial terminology) at age x to be

$$\mu_x = \frac{-\frac{d}{dx}\ell_x}{\ell_x} = -\frac{d}{dx}\ln \ell_x.^3 \tag{3.22}$$

The *central rate of failure* over the interval $(x, x+1]$, given alive at age x, is the weighted average of the force of failure, using the number surviving, ℓ_y, as the weight for each value of μ_y. That is,

$$m_x = \frac{\int_x^{x+1} \ell_y \mu_y \, dy}{\int_x^{x+1} \ell_y \, dy}. \tag{3.23}$$

From Equation (3.22) we see that $\ell_y \mu_y = -\frac{d}{dy}\ell_y$, so Equation (3.23) becomes

$$m_x = \frac{\int_x^{x+1} -d\,\ell_y}{\int_x^{x+1} \ell_y \, dy} = \frac{\ell_x - \ell_{x+1}}{L_x} = \frac{d_x}{L_x}, \tag{3.24a}$$

[3] The force of failure is the same concept as the hazard rate function defined for continuous models in Section 3.2.

where we use L_x to denote $\int_x^{x+1} \ell_y \, dy$. More generally, the central rate of failure over $(x, x+n]$, given alive at age x, is

$$ {}_n m_x = \frac{\int_x^{x+n} \ell_y \mu_y \, dy}{\int_x^{x+n} \ell_y \, dy} = \frac{{}_n d_x}{{}_n L_x}. \tag{3.24b} $$

Finally, the expected future lifetime for an entity alive at age x, counting *all years* of future lifetime, is called the *complete expectation of life* and is given by

$$ \mathring{e}_x = \frac{1}{\ell_x} \cdot \int_0^\infty \ell_{x+t} \, dt = \int_0^\infty {}_t p_x \, dt. \tag{3.25} $$

Since we do not generally know the continuous functional form for ℓ_x, but only have values of ℓ_x at integral values of x, then we can calculate e_x (but not $\mathring{e}_x$) and intuitively approximate $\mathring{e}_x$ as

$$ \mathring{e}_x \approx e_x + \frac{1}{2}. \tag{3.26} $$

3.3.3 APPROXIMATION OF CONTINUOUS FUNCTIONS

With values of ℓ_x available only at integral values of x, we need to approximate values of ℓ_{x+t}, for $0 < t < 1$, from the known values of ℓ_x and ℓ_{x+1}. The most common approach is to use *linear interpolation*[4] between ℓ_x and ℓ_{x+1}, producing

$$ \ell_{x+t} = t \cdot \ell_{x+1} + (1-t) \cdot \ell_x = \ell_x - t \cdot d_x. \tag{3.27} $$

From this expression for ℓ_{x+t} we easily find, for $0 < t < 1$,

$$ {}_t q_x = t \cdot q_x, \tag{3.28} $$

$$ {}_t p_x = 1 - {}_t q_x = 1 - t \cdot q_x, \tag{3.29} $$

$$ \mu_{x+t} = \frac{q_x}{1 - t \cdot q_x}, \tag{3.30} $$

$$ L_x = \ell_x - \frac{1}{2} \cdot d_x, \tag{3.31} $$

[4] In traditional actuarial terminology, this use of linear interpolation is called the *uniform distribution of decrement* (or *uniform distribution of deaths* in a life insurance context) assumption.

$$m_x = \frac{d_x}{L_x} = \frac{d_x}{\ell_x - \frac{1}{2} \cdot d_x} = \frac{q_x}{1 - \frac{1}{2} \cdot q_x}, \tag{3.32}$$

and

$$\overset{\circ}{e}_x = e_x + \frac{1}{2}, \tag{3.33}$$

which we had already developed intuitively in Section 3.3.2.

An alternative to linear interpolation is to use *exponential interpolation*, producing, for $0 < t < 1$,

$$\ell_{x+t} = (\ell_{x+1})^t \cdot (\ell_x)^{1-t}. \tag{3.34}$$

From this expression for ℓ_{x+t} we can derive the results

$$_t p_x = (p_x)^t, \tag{3.35}$$

$$_t q_x = 1 - (p_x)^t = 1 - (1 - q_x)^t, \tag{3.36}$$

and

$$\mu_{x+t} = -\ln p_x, \tag{3.37}$$

a constant, which we denote by simply μ. Then

$$p_x = e^{-\mu} \tag{3.38a}$$

and

$$_t p_x = (p_x)^t = (e^{-\mu})^t = e^{-t\mu}. \tag{3.38b}$$

It also follows that

$$L_x = \frac{d_x}{\mu} \tag{3.39}$$

so

$$m_x = \frac{d_x}{L_x} = \mu, \tag{3.40}$$

the constant value of μ_{x+t} for $0 < t < 1$. This is not surprising, since we earlier defined m_x as the weighted average value of μ_{x+t}. If μ_{x+t} is constant, then m_x will be that same constant, which is μ.

3.3.4 ESTIMATION OF THE LIFE TABLE MODEL

In this review of the life table model, we began by assuming values of ℓ_x, for integral x, from which we developed all other functions, either exactly or approximately. When we estimate the life table from sample data, which we pursue in Part III of this text, we will proceed to estimate a sequence of the conditional probability function q_x (or the conditional central rate function m_x). We would likely then revise (generally by smoothing) this sequence of estimates (see Chapter 12) before constructing the life table.

We begin this construction by selecting a radix value ℓ_0. Then we would calculate

$$d_0 = \ell_0 \cdot q_0, \tag{3.41a}$$

then

$$\ell_1 = \ell_0 - d_0, \tag{3.42a}$$

then

$$d_1 = \ell_1 \cdot q_1, \tag{3.41b}$$

then

$$\ell_2 = \ell_1 - d_1, \tag{3.42b}$$

and so on. Then all other functions can be determined from ℓ_x as described above.

If the estimation process naturally produces a sequence of m_x, rather than q_x, we then generally interpret m_x as μ, a constant value of μ_{x+t} for $0<t<1$, and estimate q_x as $1-e^{-\mu}$, using Equation (3.38a). The development of the rest of the life table then proceeds as above.

3.4 REVIEW OF THE DOUBLE-DECREMENT TABULAR SURVIVAL MODEL (THE DOUBLE-DECREMENT TABLE)[5]

In the life table of Section 3.3, the initial number of entities (often persons) surviving at time (or age) zero is decremented eventually down to $\ell_\omega = 0$ *by a single cause of decrement.* In the double-decrement model the initial group, which is denoted by $\ell_0^{(\tau)}$, is decremented down to $\ell_\omega^{(\tau)} = 0$ by two causes, denoted (1) and (2). The total decrements in the interval $(x, x+1]$, denoted $d_x^{(\tau)}$, is the sum of those from each cause, so we have

$$d_x^{(\tau)} = d_x^{(1)} + d_x^{(2)}. \tag{3.43a}$$

It also follows that

$$d_x^{(\tau)} = \ell_x^{(\tau)} - \ell_{x+1}^{(\tau)}. \tag{3.44a}$$

Over the interval $(x, x+n]$ the corresponding relationships are

$${}_nd_x^{(\tau)} = {}_nd_x^{(1)} +_n d_x^{(2)} \tag{3.43b}$$

and

$${}_nd_x^{(\tau)} = \ell_x^{(\tau)} - \ell_{x+n}^{(\tau)}. \tag{3.44b}$$

[5] For more detail, see Chapter 13 of Cunningham, et al. [7].

The one-year survival probability is

$$p_x^{(\tau)} = \frac{\ell_{x+1}^{(\tau)}}{\ell_x^{(\tau)}}, \tag{3.45a}$$

and the corresponding n-year survival probability is

$${}_np_x^{(\tau)} = \frac{\ell_{x+n}^{(\tau)}}{\ell_x^{(\tau)}}. \tag{3.45b}$$

The one-year failure probability, for any cause, is

$$q_x^{(\tau)} = 1 - p_x^{(\tau)} = \frac{d_x^{(\tau)}}{\ell_x^{(\tau)}}, \tag{3.46a}$$

and the corresponding n-year failure probability is

$${}_nq_x^{(\tau)} = 1 - {}_np_x^{(\tau)} = \frac{{}_nd_x^{(\tau)}}{\ell_x^{(\tau)}}. \tag{3.46b}$$

We also define

$$q_x^{(1)} = \frac{d_x^{(1)}}{\ell_x^{(\tau)}} \tag{3.47a}$$

and

$$q_x^{(2)} = \frac{d_x^{(2)}}{\ell_x^{(\tau)}} \tag{3.48a}$$

as the one-year failure probabilities due to causes (1) and (2), respectively, and their n-year counterparts as

$${}_nq_x^{(1)} = \frac{{}_nd_x^{(1)}}{\ell_x^{(\tau)}} \tag{3.47b}$$

and

$${}_nq_x^{(2)} = \frac{{}_nd_x^{(2)}}{\ell_x^{(\tau)}}. \tag{3.48b}$$

Then it follows that

$$q_x^{(\tau)} = q_x^{(1)} + q_x^{(2)} \tag{3.49a}$$

and

$${}_nq_x^{(\tau)} = {}_nq_x^{(1)} + {}_nq_x^{(2)}. \tag{3.49b}$$

In the double-decrement model, the probability of failure in $(x, x+1]$ due to cause (j), for $j = 1,2,$ denoted $q_x^{(j)}$, is less than the *absolute rate* at which cause (j) operates due to the possibility of failure due to cause $(\bar{j})$.[6] (This is called the *theory of competing risks.*) We denote the absolute rate[7] of cause (*j*) failures as $q_x'^{(j)}$, so we have

$$q_x'^{(j)} \geq q_x^{(j)} \tag{3.50a}$$

and

$${}_nq_x'^{(j)} \geq {}_nq_x^{(j)}. \tag{3.50b}$$

The absolute rate of avoiding failure by cause (*j*) over $(x, x{+}1]$, given survival to age *x*, is

$$p_x'^{(j)} = 1 - q_x'^{(j)} \tag{3.51a}$$

with the corresponding relationship

$${}_np_x'^{(j)} = 1 - {}_nq_x'^{(j)} \tag{3.51b}$$

for the interval $(x, x{+}n]$. If the causes are independent, then we have

$$p_x^{(\tau)} = p_x'^{(1)} \cdot p_x'^{(2)} \tag{3.52a}$$

and

$${}_np_x^{(\tau)} = {}_np_x'^{(1)} \cdot {}_np_x'^{(2)}. \tag{3.52b}$$

The relationship between $q_x^{(j)}$ and $q_x'^{(j)}$, for $j = 1, 2$, requires an assumption regarding the distribution of decrements (1) and (2) over the interval $(x, x{+}1]$. If the decrements are uniformly distributed within the double-decrement model, then

$$q_x'^{(j)} = 1 - p_x'^{(j)} = 1 - \left(p_x^{(\tau)}\right)^{q_x^{(j)}/q_x^{(\tau)}}, \tag{3.53}$$

for $j = 1, 2$. That is, given a double-decrement model showing values of $q_x^{(\tau)}$, $p_x^{(\tau)}$, and $q_x^{(j)}$, and assuming uniform distribution of decrements in that model, $q_x'^{(j)}$ can be found from Equation (3.53).

Conversely, given single-decrement models for each of causes (1) and (2) showing values of $q_x'^{(1)}$ and $q_x'^{(2)}$, and assuming uniform distribution of each decrement in its own single-decrement model, then $q_x^{(1)}$ and $q_x^{(2)}$ can be found from

$$q_x^{(1)} = q_x'^{(1)} \cdot \left(1 - \frac{1}{2} \cdot q_x'^{(2)}\right) \tag{3.54a}$$

---

[6] Cause $(\bar{j})$ is read as "Cause (not *j*)."

[7] Other texts refer to the absolute rate as the *absolute probability of failure* due to cause (*j*), or the *pure probability of failure* due to cause (*j*).

and

$$q_x^{(2)} = q_x^{\prime(2)} \cdot \left(1 - \frac{1}{2} \cdot q_x^{\prime(1)}\right). \tag{3.54b}$$

(We would not expect the two different assumptions to produce consistent results.)

Finally, it should be noted that the force of total failure at age $x+t$, denoted $\mu_{x+t}^{(\tau)}$, and forces of failure due to causes (1) and (2), denoted $\mu_{x+t}^{(1)}$ and $\mu_{x+t}^{(2)}$, respectively, can be defined and used to establish several additional important relationships. Since they are not used in the estimation work developed later in this text, we have chosen not to include them in this summary.

CHAPTER FOUR

REVIEW OF STOCHASTIC SIMULATION

4.1 INTRODUCTION

In this chapter, we review a number of techniques for using a computer to *imitate*, or *simulate*, a wide range of financial and insurance problems. Such problems, either stochastic or deterministic, typically cannot be solved easily using analytic methods but are readily amenable to stochastic simulation procedures. The term "stochastic" is used to modify simulation in order to emphasize that we are confining our attention to simulation in which values are randomly selected from one or more probability distributions.

The term "Monte Carlo" was coined as a synonym for stochastic simulation during U.S. research work on the development of the hydrogen bomb in the years immediately following World War II. Monte Carlo methods were rarely performed prior to the advent of electronic computers. The nearly universal availability of high-speed electronic computers today makes simulation a cheap and effective method for solving a wide variety of complex, practical problems.

The actuarial applications of this technique include (1) model offices of life insurance and annuities, (2) analysis of investment and asset allocation strategies (e.g., bond call properties), (3) asset/liability management, (4) product design and pricing studies, (5) dynamic solvency testing of insurance company (or pension fund) solidity and resilience, (6) collective risk models in general, and (7) aggregate loss distributions in particular.

Various applications of simulation to the models and analyses considered in this text are scattered throughout the following chapters.

4.1.1 THE SIMULATION PROCEDURE

The crucial steps of a simulation are the following:

(1) The construction of an appropriate model.
(2) The design of the experiment.
(3) The repeated generation of *simulated output values* from one (or more) probability distributions.
(4) The analysis of the results.

The focus of this chapter is on the efficient generation of simulated outputs. The other steps, which are heavily dependent on the specific nature of the problem at hand, are illustrated in the applications scattered throughout the remainder of the text. Since the generation of simulated outputs is crucial to any simulation, this chapter contains a discussion of algorithms for the computer generation of them from a number of frequently-used probability distributions. Such generation procedures were used in the past, and are still being used today, because they produce a large number of simulated outputs in a short period of time and do not require much computer storage space, as would a large table of random numbers permanently stored in the computer's memory.

In this text we use the special term *random number*, denoted by u, where $0 \le u < 1$, to refer specifically to a simulated output value from the continuous uniform distribution over the interval $[0,1)$. For convenience, we use the abbreviation $U[0,1)$ to denote this distribution.

When we wish to generate a simulated output value from a distribution other than $U[0,1)$, we normally first generate a random number u from $U[0,1)$ and use it to then generate our desired simulated output value. This two-step process is described in the sections that follow.

4.1.2 LINEAR CONGRUENTIAL RANDOM NUMBER GENERATORS

A frequently-used type of random number generator is known as a *linear congruential generator*, which was introduced by Lehmer [23]. In order to fully specify an individual linear congruential generator we must select the following four integer-valued parameters:

Parameter Name	Symbol	Restrictions
The modulus	m	$m > 0$
The multiplier	a	$0 \le a < m$
The increment	c	$0 \le c < m$
The starting value	X_0	$0 \le X_0 < m$

The $(n+1)^{st}$ term of the random sequence specified is

$$X_{n+1} \equiv a \cdot X_n + c \quad \text{mod } m. \tag{4.1}$$

In other words, X_{n+1} is the remainder when $(a \cdot X_n + c)$ is divided by m, so the possible values of X_n are $0, 1, \cdots, m-1$. Because such sequences of numbers are in fact deterministic, they are sometimes called *pseudo-random* instead of random.

A *multiplicative congruential generator* is the special case of a linear congruential generator which is obtained when $c = 0$. Because the generation process is a little faster when $c = 0$, and most other desirable features are preserved, many practitioners prefer to use multiplicative congruential generators.

The multiplicative congruential random number generator given by

$$X_{n+1} \equiv 16{,}807 \cdot X_n \ \text{ mod } 2^{31} - 1, \tag{4.2}$$

where $X_0 = 16{,}807 = 7^5$ is known as GGL. It was developed by Lewis, Goodman, and Miller [24] at IBM. GGL has a cycle length of $2^{31} - 2 \approx 2$ billion. This is the maximum possible length because, if X_n is ever zero, then all subsequent terms must be zero. Prior to its implementation, this generator successfully passed a wide range of statistical tests as described in Lewis, Goodman, and Miller. GGL is still the random number generator employed as the "?" operator in IBM's version of the APL computer programming language. This generator works well for many problems as noted on page 189 of Knuth [22].

For the initial step in the generation of simulated output values from distributions other than the uniform distribution over $[0,1)$, we generally employ output values (random numbers) drawn from the uniform distribution over $[0,1)$. This is easily accomplished by dividing X_n by m, the modulus of the multiplicative congruential generator.

Unfortunately, there is no all-purpose random number generator, let alone one that is both easy to program and also has a long cycle length. As a consequence, Knuth [22] recommends (see page 189) that "each Monte Carlo" application should be run "at least twice using quite different sources of random numbers, before taking the answers of the program seriously; this will not only give an indication of the stability of the results, it will also guard against the danger of trusting in a generator with hidden deficiencies." Thus the burden is on the analyst to determine the random number generator(s) which are appropriate for the task at hand. The interested reader should see either Herzog and Lord [16] or Knuth [22] for more details about random number generators.

EXAMPLE 4.1

In Equation (4.1), let $a=3,\ c=2,\ m=7$, and let the starting value be $x_0=5$. Generate the values x_1 through x_7.

SOLUTION

The calculations are shown in the following table:

i	x_i	$3\cdot x_i+4$	x_{i+1}
0	5	17	3
1	3	11	4
2	4	14	0
3	0	2	2
4	2	8	1
5	1	5	5
6	5	17	3
7	3	--	--

The sequence of "random" numbers will now recycle as 5,3,4,0,2,1 forever. ❒

4.2 THE INVERSION METHOD FOR CONTINUOUS DISTRIBUTIONS

In this section, we describe a general method, known as the *inversion method*, for generating simulated random outputs from continuous probability distributions. We illustrate this approach with some examples applying the technique to important distributions. We also include a few clever *ad hoc* techniques that are superior to some of the more general approaches in certain situations.

Let X denote a continuous random variable with cumulative distribution function $F(x) = Pr(X \le x)$. Since $F(x)$ is a nondecreasing function of x, its inverse function, F^{-1}, may be defined for any value z between 0 and 1 as the smallest x satisfying $F(x) \ge z$. We may write this definition mathematically as

$$F^{-1}(z) = inf\{x \mid F(x) \ge z\}, \tag{4.3}$$

for $0 \le z \le 1$, where $F^{-1}(0) = -\infty$ and $F^{-1}(1)$ may be equal to $+\infty$. This definition of F^{-1} is selected because it always exists.

If the random variable U is uniformly distributed over the interval [0,1), then the continuous random variable

$$X = F^{-1}(U) \tag{4.4}$$

has cumulative distribution function F. This may be shown as

$$\begin{aligned} Pr(X \le x) &= Pr\{X \le F^{-1}[F(x)]\} = Pr\{F^{-1}(U) \le F^{-1}[F(x)]\} \\ &= Pr[U \le F(x)] = F(x). \end{aligned}$$

Hence, to generate a simulated value x from the distribution of X, we first draw a random number u from the uniform distribution over [0,1) and then set $x = F^{-1}(u)$. The inversion method is illustrated in Figure 4.1 below and in the examples which follow.

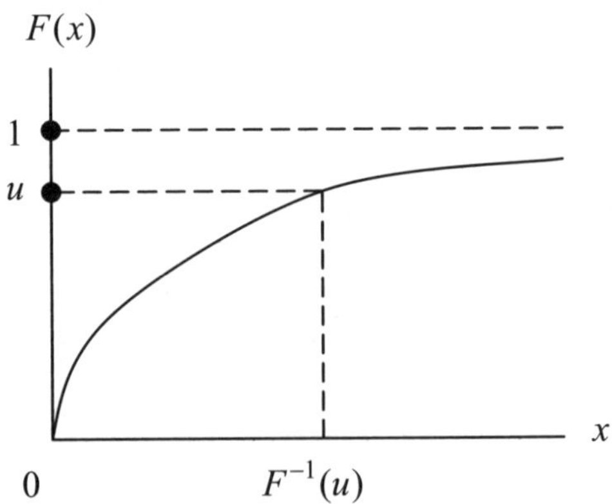

Graphic Representation of the Inversion Method

FIGURE 4.1

If $F^{-1}(u)$ is easily calculated, as illustrated in Sections 4.3.1 and 4.3.2, then this is perhaps the easiest way to generate simulated output values of the random variable X. Most of the other methods are designed for situations where it is not easy (or even possible) to calculate $F^{-1}(u)$ directly.[1]

4.2.1 THE EXPONENTIAL DISTRIBUTION

If we let

$$u = F(x) = 1-e^{-\beta x}, \tag{4.5a}$$

and solve for x, we obtain

$$x = F^{-1}(u) = \frac{-\ln(1-u)}{\beta}. \tag{4.5b}$$

In order to generate a simulated value x from the exponential distribution with multiplicative parameter β, we proceed as follows:

Step 1: Draw a random number u from the $U[0,1)$ distribution.

Step 2: Set $x = F^{-1}(u) = \frac{-\ln(1-u)}{\beta}$.

Note that if U is uniformly distributed over $[0,1)$, then so is $1-U$; a slightly faster generation method is obtained by setting $x = \frac{-\ln u}{\beta}$ in Step 2. On any one simulation, a different answer is obtained if $1-U$ is used instead of U. When a large number of simulations is performed, however, the results should be nearly equivalent whether U or $1-U$ is used.[2]

4.2.2 THE PARETO DISTRIBUTION

Consider the density function

$$f(x) = \frac{\alpha \cdot \theta^{\alpha}}{(x+\theta)^{\alpha+1}}, \tag{4.6a}$$

where $x>0, \theta>0$, and $\alpha>0$. Now we have

$$u = F(x) = 1-\frac{\theta^{\alpha}}{(x+\theta)^{\alpha}}, \tag{4.6b}$$

which implies that

$$x = F^{-1}(u) = \frac{\theta}{(1-u)^{1/\alpha}}-\theta. \tag{4.6c}$$

---

[1] If $x = F^{-1}(u)$ does not exist in closed form, we can still generally solve the equation $u = F(x)$ iteratively for x given the uniform output value u. This would be true even if $F(x)$ does not exist in closed form (as, for example, with the normal distribution), because we can iteratively solve the equation $u = \int_{-\infty}^{x} f(y)\,dy$.

[2] The reader should carefully note, in any application, whether random numbers are going from 0 to 1 (i.e., U is being used) or from 1 to 0 ($1-U$ is being used).

Then we can generate a random number u from the $U[0,1)$ distribution, and use Equation (4.6c) to generate a simulated output value of x from the Pareto distribution.

4.2.3 ADDITIONAL CONTINUOUS DISTRIBUTIONS

Suppose the random variable X has a cumulative distribution function given by

$$F(x) = 1 - \frac{1}{1+\exp\left(\frac{x-1}{2}\right)},$$

for $-\infty < x < \infty$, and suppose the random number $u = .40$ is generated from the $U[0,1)$ distribution. We can then use the inversion method to determine a simulated value of the random variable X.

We first need to solve $u = F(x)$ for $x = F^{-1}(u)$. We have

$$1+\exp\left(\frac{x-1}{2}\right) = \frac{1}{1-u},$$

so

$$\frac{x-1}{2} = \ln\left(\frac{1}{1-u}-1\right) = \ln\left(\frac{u}{1-u}\right),$$

and finally $x = 1+2\cdot\ln\left(\frac{u}{1-u}\right)$. Since the random number is $u = .40$, the simulated value of x will be

$$x = 1+2\cdot\ln\left(\frac{.40}{.60}\right) = .18907.$$

EXAMPLE 4.2

Determine the simulated value of x from an exponential distribution with $\beta = .50$, based on the random number $u = .30$, using (a) u directly or (b) by substituting $1-u$.

SOLUTION

(a) Using Equation (4.5b) directly, we obtain

$$x = \frac{-\ln(1-.30)}{.50} = .71335.$$

(b) Using Equation (4.5b) with $1-u$ replacing u, we obtain

$$x = \frac{-\ln(.30)}{.50} = 2.40795.$$ ❐

4.3 THE TABLE LOOK-UP METHOD FOR DISCRETE DISTRIBUTIONS

The *table look-up method* may be considered to be the discrete analog of the inversion method. However, with the table look-up method we do not need to know the mathematical distributional form.

Let X be a discrete random variable having positive probability at the points $x_1, x_2, \cdots$. The probability function is

$$p(x_i) = Pr(X=x_i),$$

where the probabilities $p(x_i)$ satisfy the condition that $p(x_i) > 0$ for all i, and

$$\sum_{i=1}^{\infty} p(x_i) = 1 .$$

Without loss of generality we can assume that $x_1 < x_2 < \cdots$. The table look-up method proceeds by the following steps. First we select a random number u from the $U[0,1)$ distribution. Then we set

$$x = x_1 \quad \text{if} \quad 0 \le u < p(x_1) \tag{4.7a}$$

or

$$x = x_j \quad \text{if} \quad \sum_{i=1}^{j-1} p(x_i) \le u < \sum_{i=1}^{j} p(x_i) . \tag{4.7b}$$

Going in order through the x_i's is a brute-force approach that suffers from a possibly high expected number of comparisons, as mentioned below. If computational speed is an issue (which, with today's computing power, would occur only for a very large number of x_i's), then the expected number of comparisons could be reduced substantially either by employing a smart search algorithm (*e.g.*, successive bisections) or applying appropriate ad hoc procedures as illustrated later in this section. We note that the average number of comparisons is $\sum_{i=1}^{\infty} i \cdot p(x_i)$. The table look-up method works best if the cumulating sums of probabilities reduce to a simple expression, as in the negative binomial distribution discussed below.

4.3.1 THE DISCRETE UNIFORM DISTRIBUTION

Let $p(x) = \frac{1}{b-a}$, where $x = a, a+1, \cdots, b-1$, and $a < b$. Then if u is a random number from $U[0,1)$, we set

$$x = a + \lfloor (b-a)u \rfloor , \tag{4.8}$$

where $\lfloor y \rfloor$ denotes the largest integer less than or equal to y.

4.3.2 THE BERNOULLI DISTRIBUTION

Let $p(0)=1-p$ and $p(1)=p$. Then if u is a random number from $U[0,1)$, we set

$$x = 0 \quad \text{if} \quad u < 1-p \tag{4.9a}$$

or

$$x = 1 \quad \text{if} \quad u \geq 1-p. \tag{4.9b}$$

4.3.3 THE BINOMIAL DISTRIBUTION

Table Look-Up for the Binomial Distribution

One procedure for simulating output values from a binomial distribution using the table look-up method is as follows. Let the binomial cumulative distribution function be

$$F(k) = \sum_{j=0}^{k} \binom{n}{j} p^j (1-p)^{n-j}, \tag{4.10}$$

for $k=0,1,\ldots,n$, with the obvious extension between integer points. A value, s, may be generated by first generating a random number u from $U[0,1)$, and then setting s equal to zero if $u<F(0)$ or else setting s equal to r, where r satisfies

$$F(r-1) \leq u < F(r). \tag{4.11}$$

Note that this is a brute force type of strategy.

Modified Table Look-Up for the Binomial Distribution

For this distribution, $p(0)=(1-p)^n$ and $\frac{p(k+1)}{p(k)} = \frac{(n-k)p}{(k+1)(1-p)}$ (see Section 5.1.1), so we have the recursion expression

$$Pr(K=k+1) = Pr(K=k)\cdot\frac{(n-k)p}{(k+1)(1-p)}. \tag{4.12}$$

This is an acceleration strategy, as opposed to the brute-force strategy of the table look-up method described above. The algorithm for this process follows the following steps:

Step 1 (Initialization): Define $C=\frac{p}{1-p}$, set the initial value of the counter at $K=0$, set the initial value of $PR=Pr(K{=}0)=(1-p)^n$, and set the initial value of the cumulative sum at $CS=PR$.

Step 2: Generate a value u from $U[0,1)$.

Step 3: If $u<CS$, output K and stop.

Step 4 (Apply recursive formula): Set $PR = PR\cdot C\frac{n-K}{K+1}$.

Step 5: Set $CS = CS{+}PR$ and $K = K{+}1$.

Step 6: Return to Step 3.

We note two other methods for simulating output values from a binomial distribution. Because each binomial random variable may be considered to be a sum of Bernoulli random variables, one approach is to use convolutions as discussed in Section 5.2.1. The second is the normal approximation that we describe next.

Normal Approximation to the Binomial Distribution

The normal approximation to the binomial distribution is generally assumed to apply if either (1) $np > 10$ and $p > .50$, or (2) $n(1{-}p) > 10$ and $p < .50$. In this case, we employ the statistic

$$Z \;=\; \frac{K - np + .50}{\sqrt{np(1{-}p)}}, \tag{4.13}$$

which is asymptotically distributed as a standard normal random variable. Thus we can simulate a standard normal variable, Z, according to the strategy of Section 4.4 and then solve the above equation for K.

4.3.4 THE NEGATIVE BINOMIAL DISTRIBUTION

The regular table look-up method can be used with the negative binomial distribution just as with the binomial. We now present two alternative approaches to use with the negative binomial distribution. A third approach, the *convolution approach*, is described in Section 4.2 of Herzog and Lord [16].

Modified Table Look-Up Approach (with recursion)

For this distribution we have $p(0) = p^r$ and $\frac{p(x+1)}{p(x)} = \frac{(x+r)(1-p)}{x+1}$ (see Section 5.1.3). We can use the recursion relationship

$$Pr(X = x{+}1) \;=\; Pr(X = x)\cdot\frac{(x{+}r)(1{-}p)}{x+1}. \tag{4.14}$$

The algorithm for this is as follows:

Step 1 (Initialization): Set the initial value of the counter at $X = 0$, set the initial value of $PR = Pr(X{=}0) = p^r$, and set the initial value of the cumulative sum $CS = PR$.

Step 2: Generate a value u from $U[0,1)$.

Step 3: If $u \le CS$, output X and stop.

Step 4 (Apply recursive formula): Set $PR \;=\; PR\cdot\frac{(X{+}r)(1{-}p)}{X+1}$.

Step 5: Set $CS = CS{+}PR$ and $X = X{+}1$.

Step 6: Return to Step 3.

The expected number of iterations of Steps 3-6 required to simulate one value from this distribution using this algorithm is $\frac{1+r(1-p)}{p}$.

Tossing a Biased Coin Approach[3]

We use the following algorithm to execute this event simulation approach:

Step 1 (Initialization): Set the initial counter values at $X=0$ and $R=0$.

Step 2: Generate a value u from the uniform distribution over $[0,1)$.

Step 3: If $u \geq 1-p$, go to Step 7.

Step 4: Set $R=R+1$.

Step 5: If $R=r$, output X and stop.

Step 6: Go to Step 2.

Step 7: Set $X=X+1$.

Step 8: Return to Step 2.

This approach is relatively inefficient. We might use it only if it were the only available strategy.

4.3.5 THE POISSON DISTRIBUTION

Again we note that the regular table look-up method can be used with the Poisson distribution, and we again present two alternative approaches. A third approach, the exponential interarrival time approach, is described in Section 3.2 of Herzog and Lord [16].

Modified Table Look-Up

Here we have $p(0)=e^{-\lambda}$ and $\frac{p(k+1)}{p(k)}=\frac{\lambda}{k+1}$ (see Section 2.2.5), leading to the recursion

$$Pr(K=k+1) = Pr(K=k)\cdot\frac{\lambda}{k+1}. \tag{4.15}$$

The algorithm for this is as follows:

Step 1 (Initialization): Set the initial value of the counter at $K=0$, set the initial value of $PR=Pr(K=0)=e^{-\lambda}$, and set the initial value of the cumulative sum $CS=PR$.

Step 2: Generate a value u from $U[0,1)$.

Step 3: If $u<CS$, output K and stop.

---

[3] This procedure should be employed only when r is a positive integer.

Step 4 (Apply recursive formula): Set $PR = PR \cdot \frac{\lambda}{K+1}$.

Step 5: Set $CS = CS + PR$ and $K = K+1$.

Step 6: Return to Step 3.

Normal Approximation to the Poisson Distribution

Another simulation approach is to use a normal approximation. This pertains if the Poisson mean, λ, is large, such as, for example, $\lambda > 10$. In this case we employ the statistic

$$Z = \frac{K - \lambda + .50}{\sqrt{\lambda}}, \tag{4.16}$$

which is asymptotically distributed as a standard normal random variable. We can draw standard normal variates Z according to the strategy of Section 4.4, and then solve the above equation for K.

4.3.6 APPLICATIONS OF THE MATERIAL OF SECTION 4.3

The material discussed in Section 4.3 has a wide range of applications. The binomial, Poisson, and negative binomial are often used to model the frequency of loss among groups of insureds (see Chapter 5). In a case study involving home equity conversion mortgages (see Chapter 11 of Herzog and Lord [16]), the authors assume that the mortality experience of the insureds can be modeled as a Bernoulli trial.

EXAMPLE 4.3

We wish to simulate values from a binomial distribution with parameters $n = 3$ and $p = 60$. The following five random numbers have been generated from the $U[0,1)$ distribution:

.560, .213, .013, .875, .352

Using the standard table look-up method, find the corresponding simulated binomial outcome values.

SOLUTION

We first tabulate the probability function $p(x)$ and the cumulative distribution function $F(x)$ for this distribution. The results are shown in the following "look-up" table:

x	$p(x)$	$F(x)$
0	.064	.064
1	.288	.352
2	.432	.784
3	.216	1.000

Applying Equation (4.11) we find that $u_1 = .560$ generates $x_1 = 2$, $u_2 = .213$ generates $x_2 = 1$, $u_3 = .013$ generates $x_3 = 0$, and $u_4 = .875$ generates $x_4 = 3$. The value $u_5 = .352$ calls for special attention, since .352 is the exact value of $F(1)$. Referring to the rule established by Equation (4.11), we conclude that $x_5 = 2$.

The reason for the rule is that 1000 three-place decimal values can be generated from $U[0,1)$, namely .000 through .999. The first 64 of them, namely .000 through .063, generate $x = 0$; the next 288 of them, namely .064 through .351, generate $x = 1$; the next 432 of them, namely .352 through .783, generate $x = 2$; the last 216 of them, namely .784 through .999, generate $x = 3$.

This example illustrates the challenge in interpreting the CDF of a discrete distribution. (A further discussion of this is found on pages 32-33 of Chapter 2.) ❐

4.4 GENERATING SIMULATED NORMAL DISTRIBUTION VALUES

In this section we present two methods for generating simulated normal distribution values, which are quite useful since the normal distribution CDF does not possess a closed-form expression.

4.4.1 THE POLAR METHOD

Our first method for simulating normal output values is the *polar method*, which produces a pair of output values x_1 and x_2, drawn independently from the standard normal distribution. Here we inscribe a circle (of radius 1, centered at the origin of a two-dimensional Cartesian coordinate system) within a square and accept only those values falling inside the circle.

To perform the polar method, we first generate two random numbers, u_1 and u_2, from $U[0,1)$. Then we compute

$$v_i = 2 \cdot u_i - 1,$$

for $i = 1,2$, and form the ordered pair (v_1, v_2), where v_1 and v_2 represent output values drawn independently from the uniform distribution over $[-1, 1)$.
If (v_1, v_2) is in the interior of the unit circle defined in the first paragraph, we then compute x_1 and x_2 as

$$x_1 = v_1 \cdot \sqrt{(-2 \cdot \ln s)/s} \tag{4.18a}$$

and

$$x_2 = v_2 \cdot \sqrt{(-2 \ln s)/s}, \tag{4.18b}$$

where the square of the radius is $s = v_1^2 + v_2^2$. Then x_1 and x_2 are the desired standard normal output values. If (v_1, v_2) is outside the unit circle, we generate another pair of random numbers and repeat the above procedure.

EXAMPLE 4.4

Using the polar method, calculate the simulated standard normal values x_1 and x_2, given the random numbers $u_1 = .823$ and $u_2 = .317$.

SOLUTION

First we calculate

$$v_1 = 2 \cdot u_1 - 1 = (2)(.823) - 1 = .646,$$

$$v_2 = 2 \cdot u_2 - 1 = (2)(.317) - 1 = -.366,$$

and

$$s = v_1^2 + v_2^2 = (.646)^2 + (-.366)^2 = .551272.$$

Then we apply Equations (4.18a) and (4.18b) to obtain

$$x_1 = .646 \cdot \sqrt{\frac{-2 \cdot \ln(.551272)}{.551272}} = .9495$$

and

$$x_2 = -.366 \cdot \sqrt{\frac{-2 \cdot \ln(.551272)}{.551272}} = -.5380.$$ ❐

4.4.2 THE BOX-MULLER METHOD

A second method for simulating standard normal output values is the *Box-Muller method.*[4] Under this method, we first obtain two random numbers u_1 and u_2 from $U[0,1)$. We then produce a pair of independent simulated values from the standard normal distribution as

$$x_1 = \sqrt{-2 \cdot \ln u_1} \cdot \cos(2\pi u_2) \tag{4.19a}$$

and

$$x_2 = \sqrt{-2 \cdot \ln u_1} \cdot \sin(2\pi u_2). \tag{4.19b}$$

EXAMPLE 4.5

Rework Example 4.4 using the Box-Muller method.

SOLUTION

Using Equations (4.19a) and (4.19b), and a calculator with sin and cos functions, we directly obtain $x_1 = -.2551$ and $x_2 = .5697$. ❐

[4] The original presentation is found in Box and Muller [5]. The technique is also described in Ross [37].

4.5 SAMPLE SIZE

We have thus far presented methods for simulating random outcomes from a wide range of probability distributions. Now we address the question of how many repetitions of the simulation process should be performed in any particular application.

In general, the answer will depend on the distribution being simulated as well as the importance and nature of the quantity being approximated. For example, suppose we wish to estimate the mean of a continuous distribution with PDF given by $f(x)$. If we denote the mean by θ, then the exact value of θ is given by

$$\theta = \int_x x \cdot f(x)\ dx,$$

and our natural estimator of θ would be

$$\hat{\theta}_n = \frac{1}{n} \cdot \sum_{i=1}^{n} x_i, \tag{4.20}$$

where x_i is a simulated outcome of the random variable X_i, and the random variables $X_1, X_2, \cdots, X_n$ are independent and identically distributed with common PDF $f(x)$ and known variance. What should be the value of n?

To answer this question we need to specify a level of precision, d, and a significance level, α. Suppose we want our estimator to satisfy the condition

$$Pr\left[\left| \hat{\theta}_n - \theta \right| \geq d \right] \leq \alpha, \tag{4.21}$$

where $d > 0$ and $0 < \alpha < 1$. Then we seek the smallest value of n satisfying Inequality (4.21). By symmetry, it suffices to find the smallest n satisfying

$$Pr\left[\hat{\theta}_n - \theta \geq d \right] \leq \frac{\alpha}{2}, \tag{4.22}$$

which can be written as

$$Pr\left[\frac{\hat{\theta}_n - \theta}{\sigma / \sqrt{n}} \geq \frac{d}{\sigma / \sqrt{n}} \right] \leq \frac{\alpha}{2}, \tag{4.23}$$

where σ denotes the common standard deviation of X_i. If n is sufficiently large we can invoke the Central Limit Theorem, in which case the statistic $\frac{\hat{\theta}_n - \theta}{\sigma/\sqrt{n}}$ has a standard normal distribution. Thus we seek the smallest integer n satisfying

$$\Phi\left(\frac{d}{\sigma / \sqrt{n}} \right) \geq 1 - \frac{\alpha}{2}, \tag{4.24a}$$

or

$$\frac{d}{\sigma/\sqrt{n}} \geq \Phi^{-1}\left(1-\frac{\alpha}{2}\right), \tag{4.24b}$$

which leads to

$$n \geq \left[\frac{\sigma}{d} \cdot \Phi^{-1}\left(1-\frac{\alpha}{2}\right)\right]^2. \tag{4.25}$$

EXAMPLE 4.6

Suppose $Var(X_i) = 4$, so that $\sigma = 2$, and our condition to be satisfied by $\hat{\theta}_n$ is

$$Pr\left[\left|\,\hat{\theta}_n - \theta\right| \geq .03\right] \leq .01.$$

Find the smallest value of n that will satisfy this condition.

SOLUTION

With $\alpha = .01$, we need the value of $\Phi^{-1}\left(1-\frac{.01}{2}\right) = \Phi^{-1}(.995) = 2.576$. Then from Equation (4.25) we have

$$n \geq \left[\left(\frac{2}{.03}\right)(2.576)\right]^2 = 29{,}492.34,$$

so we conclude that $n = 29{,}493$. ❐

4.6 THE BOOTSTRAP METHOD

As described in Section 2.1, statistical inference is the process of estimating some unknown measure (such as moment, percentile, probability, and so on) of a population by sampling. The *bootstrap method* is a technique that attempts to obtain additional information about the quality of the estimated measure from the sample that has been taken. It is important to note that the original estimate of the measure in question does not change. Indeed, there is no basis for changing the original estimate, since the entire sample has already been used. What the bootstrap method attempts to do is to estimate the *dispersion* that may exist around the original estimate.

The first instinct of the modeler when additional information is sought is often to just do additional sampling. However, additional sampling may be impractical, or even impossible, due to the nature of population data, time, money, or some other constraint. The bootstrap method is an option to consider when additional sampling cannot be conducted.

The bootstrap method starts with some function g calculated from the n sample values. As indicated above, the function g can be any measure of the population. The fact that the bootstrap method is quite flexible and can be applied for any function g is one of its major advantages.

The next step in the bootstrap method is to *resample* from the original sample. There are two basic approaches that can be used for this resampling.

The first approach is the *exact method* and is based on taking all possible samples of size n from the original sample. The number of bootstrap samples possible is equal to n^n, which is the number of permutations of n items taken n at a time with repetition. For example, consider an original sample of size 2 whose sample values are x_1 and x_2. This original sample leads to the following $2^2 = 4$ bootstrap samples:

$$\{x_1, x_1\}; \quad \{x_1, x_2\}; \quad \{x_2, x_1\}; \quad \{x_2, x_2\}$$

Although the exact method is theoretically the ideal technique to use in applying the bootstrap method, it quickly becomes impractical for other than extremely small sample sizes. The function n^n is an explosive number as n increases. For example, consider a small sample of size 10. This one sample can generate 10 billion bootstrap samples using the exact method! Thus, the bootstrap sample is not feasible for other than extremely small samples of, say, 6 or less.

The second approach is the *simulation method* in which the bootstrap samples are obtained through simulation. This is why the bootstrap method appears in a chapter of this book devoted to simulation. Note that no new sample values are used in constructing the bootstrap samples. All the bootstrap samples are obtained by resampling from the original sample. The number of bootstrap samples obtained can be any number and is totally under the control of the modeler.

Once the bootstrap samples are obtained by whatever method is being used, the next step in the process is to compute $\hat{g}(x_i)$ for each of the bootstrap samples. The caret is used on the g function to distinguish it from the g function (without the caret) calculated on the original sample.

The final step in the bootstrap method is to compute the *mean square error* (*MSE*) of the estimate, which is defined as the average value of square deviations of bootstrap estimates around the estimate in the original sample. In mathematical symbols this result can be expressed as

$$MSE = E\left[(\hat{g} - g)^2\right]. \tag{4.26}$$

Thus, the new information provided by the bootstrap method is not any change in the original estimate of the measure in question, but rather the calculation of estimated dispersion around this value, as measured by *MSE* obtained by resampling from the original sample.

EXAMPLE 4.7

A sample of size two contains the values $x_1 = 1$ and $x_2 = 3$. We wish to calculate the MSE of the unbiased estimator of the true population variance using the bootstrap method.

SOLUTION

The sample mean is $\bar{x} = (.50)(x_1 + x_2) = 2$, and the unbiased version of the sample variance is

$$g(x_1, x_2) = s_1^2 = \frac{1}{2-1} \cdot \sum_{i=1}^{2} (x_i - \bar{x})^2 = (1-2)^2 + (3-2)^2 = 2.$$

The exact method can be applied in this case since the sample size is so small. There are $2^2 = 4$ bootstrap samples. The sample mean and the unbiased sample variance for each of these four bootstrap samples are shown in the following table:

Sample	x_1	x_2	$\bar{x}$	$\hat{g}(x_1, x_2) = s_1^2$
1	1	1	1	$(1-1)^2 + (1-1)^2 = 0$
2	1	3	2	$(1-2)^2 + (3-2)^2 = 2$
3	3	1	2	$(3-2)^2 + (1-2)^2 = 2$
4	3	3	3	$(3-3)^2 + (3-3)^2 = 0$

Finally, we take the average of the squared deviations between the g value of the original sample and the $\hat{g}$ value of each bootstrap sample, producing

$$MSE = E\left[(\hat{g} - g)^2\right] = (.25)\left[(0-2)^2 + (2-2)^2 + (2-2)^2 + (0-2)^2\right] = 2.$$ ❐

EXAMPLE 4.8

A sample of size ten is drawn from a distribution with unknown mean and unknown variance. The ten sample values are as follows:

{3, 4, 4, 5, 6, 7, 7, 7, 8, 9}

We wish to estimate $Pr(X < 5)$ for this distribution. Find an estimate for the MSE of this probability using the bootstrap method, if the following five bootstrap samples are generated by simulation:

{3, 3, 4, 4, 4, 6, 7, 7, 8, 8}
{4, 4, 5, 6, 7, 7, 8, 9, 9, 9}
{3, 3, 4, 5, 5, 6, 6, 7, 7, 9}
{3, 3, 4, 4, 6, 7, 7, 7, 8, 8}
{3, 4, 4, 4, 5, 5, 7, 8, 9, 9}

SOLUTION

From the original sample we have $g = Pr(X < 5) = .30$. From the five bootstrap samples we obtain the following estimates of g: $\hat{g}_1 = .50$, $\hat{g}_2 = .20$, $\hat{g}_3 = .30$, $\hat{g}_4 = .40$, and $\hat{g}_5 = .40$. The MSE of this probability is

$$MSE = E\left[(\hat{g}-g)^2\right] = \frac{1}{5}\left[(.50-.30)^2+(.20-.30)^2+(.30-.30)^2+(.40-.30)^2+(.40-.30)^2\right]$$
$$= .014.$$

❑

As an interesting addendum to Example 4.8, the sample mean is

$$\bar{x} = \frac{1}{5}(.50+.20+.30+.40+.40) = .36,$$

and the (biased) sample variance is

$$s_5^2 = \frac{1}{5}\left[(.50-.36)^2+(.20-.36)^2+(.30-.36)^2+(.40-.36)^2+(.40-.36)^2\right] = .0104.$$

By Equation (2.19) in Section 2.3 we know that $MSE = Var + Bias^2$. If we apply this relationship to this example, we have $MSE = .0104+(.36-.30)^2 = .014$, confirming the MSE calculation above. This demonstration indicates the rationale for characterizing the measure of dispersion in the bootstrap method as an MSE.

4.7 APPLICATIONS IN LOSS MODELS AND STATISTICAL ESTIMATION

We will present various applications of simulation in our discussion of various modeling techniques to be discussed in Parts II, III, and IV of this book. Simulation is a very general technique that can be applied to a wide array of situations. Typically, it is most often used when a direct, analytical approach would be quite difficult, or even impossible, to apply. Although there are a wide variety of possible applications, we will briefly discuss two here.

The first example of a potential application of simulation is in connection with the development of loss models to be discussed in detail in Part II. Such models typically involve the *frequency* of losses (or claims) and the *severity* (or amount) of such losses (or claims), either separately or in combination. Although simulation can be applied in virtually any such situation, the most frequent use of simulation in practice involves the combined effect of frequency and severity to produce aggregate loss distributions.

Such aggregate loss distributions often result in compound distributions that require the use of convolutions to obtain analytical solutions. (The reader is referred to Sections 1.5 and 1.6 for a basic introduction to these concepts that will be expanded upon in Chapter 7.) Applying analytical solutions to such compound distributions can become quite complicated, and even impossible, to apply in certain situations. This is particularly true in the presence of coverage limitations, such as deductibles and policy limits. When the level of complexity reaches a certain level, the use of simulation as an alternative becomes an attractive approach.

A related area in which simulation techniques are often applied is in the use of process models discussed in Chapter 8. These models typically involve both frequency and severity and include various risk theory and ruin theory models to be developed in that chapter. Much of the discussion above about aggregate loss distribution models is equally applicable to these risk theory and ruin theory models as well.

The second example of the application of simulation is in connection with hypothesis testing to be discussed in various situations in Chapter 16 in Part IV. In particular, simulation can facilitate the calculation of p-values in hypothesis testing. (The reader is referred to Section 2.5 for a basic review of hypothesis testing, in general, and more specifically to the subsection on the *binary nature of hypothesis testing* in Section 2.5.2 for more background on these concepts.)

The calculation of the p-value involves the determination the percentiles of the process in question. Depending upon the situation, the calculation of such percentiles may be onerous and, again, simulation offers an attractive alternative. An application of this type will be illustrated in Chapter 16.

The applications illustrating the use of simulation for topics discussed in later chapters will appear as numbered Examples including the phrase "Simulation Illustration" alongside the Example number for the convenience of the reader in identifying such illustrative simulation applications.

4.8 EXERCISES

4.1 Introduction

4.2 The Inversion Method for Continuous Distributions

4-1 Use the three random numbers .84507, .05634, and .80282 to simulate the sum of three values of X drawn from a distribution with CDF given by

$$F(x) = 1-\frac{1}{x^2},$$

for $x \geq 1$.

4-2 The random variable Y has a two-point mixture distribution. With probability .30, Y is exponential with mean .50. With probability .70, Y is uniform over $(-3,3)$. Use the uniform random numbers .25 and .69, in that order, to first choose the distribution and then to simulate a value from that distribution. What is the simulated value of Y?

4-3 In searching for sunken treasure, the probability is .80 that no treasure will be found, so the value is zero. The probability is .20 that some treasure will be found, with value uniformly distributed over $(1000, 5000)$. Using the random numbers .75 and .85, calculate the average of the treasure values simulated by these two trials.

4.3 The Table Look-up Method for Discrete Distributions

4-4 We wish to simulate outcomes obtained from throwing a six-sided die by using the discrete uniform distribution defined by $p(n) = \frac{1}{6}$, for $n = 1,2,\cdots,6$. Find the average total obtained by throwing a pair of dice three times, if the first six random numbers are .25, .92, .63, .03, .85, and .68.

4-5 A company insures 100 people age 65, with probability of death $q_{65} = .03$. The lives are independent. We wish to simulate the number of deaths in a year using the random numbers $u_1 = .20$, $u_2 = .03$, and $u_3 = .09$. Calculate the average of the simulated values.

4.4 Generating Simulated Normal Distribution Values

4-6 A theorem in mathematical statistics states that if $X_1, X_2, \cdots, X_n$ are n independent standard normal random variables, then $\sum_{i=1}^{n} X_i^2$ has a chi-square distribution with n degrees of freedom. Suppose losses follow a chi-square distribution with 2 degrees of freedom. The following three pairs of standard normal values were generated by simulation: $(-1.10, -0.80)$, $(0.70, -0.10)$, and $(2.00, 1.20)$. Find the total amount of three simulated losses.

4.5 Sample Size

4-7 We wish to estimate the mean of the random variable X. A total of 16 values of X_i have been simulated with the results $\sum_{i=1}^{16} X_i = 172$ and $\sum_{i=1}^{16} X_i^2 = 1985$. Based on these data, if we want the unbiased standard deviation of the estimator of the mean of X, which is $\frac{s_{n-1}}{\sqrt{n}}$, to be less than .30, how many *additional* simulation runs will be needed?

4-8 We wish to use simulation to estimate the value of $F_X(300)$, where X has an exponential distribution with mean 100. Determine the minimum number of simulations needed such that there is at least a 99% probability that the estimate is within $\pm 1\%$ of the correct value.

4-9 A random variable has a standard deviation that is 20% larger than its mean. We wish to estimate the mean using simulation. Using the Central Limit Theorem, estimate the smallest number of trials needed so that we are at least 95% confident that the simulated mean is within 5% of the true mean.

4.6 The Bootstrap Method

4-10 Three observed values of the random variable X are 1, 1, and 4. We use the estimator

$$g(X_1, X_2, X_3) = \frac{1}{3}\sum_{i=1}^{3}(X_i - \bar{X})^3$$

to estimate the third central moment of X. Determine the bootstrap estimate of the mean squared error of the estimator g.

4-11 A random sample of size five taken from the distribution of X is $\{1, 3, 4, 7, 10\}$. The following six bootstrap samples are then generated by simulation:

Bootstrap 1:	1	1	4	7	7
Bootstrap 2:	3	4	4	7	10
Bootstrap 3:	1	4	4	10	10
Bootstrap 4:	3	3	3	4	10
Bootstrap 5:	4	4	7	7	10
Bootstrap 6:	1	7	7	10	10

The median of X is estimated as the third order statistic of a sample. Find the bootstrap MSE of this estimator for the sample median based on these six bootstrap samples.

4.7 Applications in Loss Models and Statistical Estimation[5]

4-12 A city purchases insurance to cover its snow removal costs over the next four winter months, with a deductible of 10,000 per month. The insurer assumes the monthly costs are independent and normally distributed with mean 15,000 and standard deviation 2,000. The insurer wishes to estimate (using simulation) the total claim amount over the next four months, using the values .5398, .1151, .0013, and .7881 drawn from the $U[0,1)$ distribution.

4-13 A compound claims distribution has the following properties:

(i) The number of claims, N, is binomial with $n = 3$ and mean 1.80.
(ii) Claim amounts, which are independent and independent of N, are uniformly distributed over the values $x = 1, 2, 3, 4, 5$.

We first simulate the value of N, and then the amounts of these N claims (unless the simulated value of N is zero). Using, in order, the sequence of random numbers

$$\{.70, .10, .30, .10, .90, .50, .50, .70, .30, .10\},$$

find the aggregate claim amount associated with the third simulated value of N.

[5] The reader may wish to defer these two exercises until after studying, later in the text, the topics upon which they are based.

PART II

LOSS MODELS

In the Preface to this text we identified two major class of actuarial risk models, namely survival models and loss models.

Survival models are described in detail in Cunningham, et al. [7], reviewed in Chapter 3 of this text, and appear in the sequence of the actuarial examinations in SOA Exam MLC and CAS Exam 3L. How these models are estimated from sample data is addressed in Parts Three and Four of this text.

In this part of the text we describe the development of models for the *aggretate loss*, or *aggregate risk*, arising from a collection (or portfolio) of individual risks. These models are often called "risk theory models" in actuarial tradition, which is somewhat of a misnomer since actuarial models, in general, involve the theory of risk.

Aggregate loss models are normally constructed by considering separately a model for the number (i.e., frequency) of losses (or insurance claims) and a model for the size (i.e., severity) of those losses. These frequency and severity models are then combined in a compound distribution to reach a model for aggregate losses. The three topics of frequency models, severity models, and aggregate (compound) models are presented in Chapters 5, 6, and 7, respectively.

The concept of a *surplus process model*, also called a *ruin model*, is presented in Chapter 8. These models track both positive and negative cash flows of an insurance system model over some defined future time period to assess its financial viability over this period.

Several simulation illustrations are presented throughout these chapters. Generally speaking, simulation is not needed when closed-form solutions are possible. Thus, when distributions are known or assumed, as for claim frequency and severity in Chapters 5 and 6, simulation techniques are not generally used.[1] When models become more complex, as they do for the aggregate and ruin models of Chapters 7 and 8, then simulation approaches become more useful and are illustrated more frequently in those chapters.

[1] An exception to this appears in Section 6.4 on risk measures.

CHAPTER FIVE

CLAIM FREQUENCY MODELS

5.1 INTRODUCTION

It is the presumption in this textbook that the probability material reviewed in Chapter 1 has been previously studied by the reader in a standard university course in mathematical probability. In the next three chapters, we will expand on this core material, and present probability models with special applications within the topic of aggregate loss models.

5.2 SECTION 1.2 (DISCRETE DISTRIBUTIONS) REVISITED

We begin that expansion in this chapter by returning to the several standard discrete (counting) random variables reviewed in Section 1.2, now with a particular view to their suitability as models for the number of insurance losses incurred or number of insurance claims filed. Several additional properties of these distributions are described here because they are relevant to the use of these distributions in the loss frequency (or claim frequency) context.[1]

5.2.1 THE BINOMIAL DISTRIBUTION

It should be clear that the binomial distribution would be well qualified for use as a loss or claim frequency distribution in any circumstance where the assumptions of the Bernoulli model are met. Thus if we have n sufficiently identical risks, such that the probability of a loss or claim from each individual risk might reasonably be presumed to be the same over all risks, and if all risks might be presumed independent, then the binomial distribution for the number of events (losses or claims) is appropriate.[2] For example, the number of losses from a collection of n identical amount life insurance policies on men of the same age and insured class might have a binomial distribution.

A property of the binomial distribution not mentioned in Section 1.2.2 that we wish to develop here relates to the idea of calculating probability values recursively. From the binomial probability function given by Equation (1.26a) we can show that

[1] The presence of insurance coverage modifications, especially deductibles, will have an impact on the distribution of claim frequency. This is explored in Section 6.3.6, after the concept of coverage modification is introduced.

[2] Note that here the event of a loss or claim plays the role of the generic idea of a "success" under the binomial distribution, although the person experiencing the loss might not be as inclined as we have been to refer to it as a "success."

$$\frac{p(x)}{p(x-1)} = \frac{\binom{n}{x} p^x (1-p)^{n-x}}{\binom{n}{x-1} p^{x-1} (1-p)^{n-x+1}} = \frac{n-x+1}{x} \cdot \frac{p}{1-p}. \tag{5.1a}$$

This enables us to calculate binomial probabilities recursively using

$$p(x) = \left(\frac{n-x+1}{x} \cdot \frac{p}{1-p} \right) \cdot p(x-1), \tag{5.1b}$$

for $x = 1, 2, \cdots, n$. To begin the recursion we need the value of $p(0)$, obtained from the probability function as

$$p(0) = (1-p)^n. \tag{5.2}$$

Our reasons for developing this recursive relationship will become clearer in Section 5.3.1 and again in Chapter 7.

5.2.2 THE POISSON DISTRIBUTION

If the value of p is small and the value of n is large in a binomial distribution, then the binomial probabilities can be reasonably approximated as Poisson probabilities with the Poisson parameter λ set equal to np, the mean of the binomial distribution. (This well-known result is discussed in a number of standard probability textbooks.) Therefore it may be reasonable to use a Poisson distribution to model insurance losses or claims in place of a binomial distribution.

The recursive relationship for Poisson probabilities is particularly convenient. From Equation (1.34) we have

$$\frac{p(x)}{p(x-1)} = \frac{\frac{e^{-\lambda}\lambda^x}{x!}}{\frac{e^{-\lambda}\lambda^{x-1}}{(x-1)!}} = \frac{\lambda^x (x-1)!}{\lambda^{x-1} \cdot x!} = \frac{\lambda}{x}, \tag{5.3a}$$

for $x = 1, 2, \cdots$. Poisson probabilities can then be calculated recursively as

$$p(x) = \frac{\lambda}{x} \cdot p(x-1), \tag{5.3b}$$

for $x = 1, 2, \cdots$, starting with the value

$$p(0) = e^{-\lambda}. \tag{5.4}$$

Recall the property noted in Section 1.5.2 that the Poisson distribution is closed under convolution. By that we mean that if $X_1, X_2, \cdots, X_k$ are independent Poisson random variables, with $E[X_i] = \lambda_i$, then the random variable $X = X_1 + X_2 + \cdots + X_k$ will also have a Poisson distribution with expected value $E[X] = \lambda = \lambda_1 + \lambda_2 + \cdots + \lambda_k$. Another useful result, and perhaps a more surprising one, is that the converse is also true.

Suppose the Poisson random variable X, with parameter (mean) λ, counts the number of events, such as insurance claims, that can occur, and suppose the events can be classified as being of one (and only one) out of k distinct types. (For example, each claim could be classified by the size group into which it falls.) Let p_i denote the probability that the event is of Type i, given that an event has occurred, for $i=1,2,\cdots,k$, and let X_i denote the random variable for the number of Type i events. Note that $\sum_{i=1}^{k} p_i = 1$. Then the random variables $X_1, X_2, \cdots, X_k$ are mutually independent and each has a Poisson distribution with parameter (mean) $\lambda_i = \lambda \cdot p_i$, where λ is the parameter of the random variable X. This result is called the *decomposition property* of the Poisson distribution.

To show that this is true, we first note that given the total number of claims to be $X=x$, then the (conditional) joint distribution of the X_i's is multinomial, with parameters $x, p_1, p_2, \cdots, p_k$. The conditional multinomial probability function is

$$Pr(X_1{=}x_1, X_2{=}x_2, \cdots, X_k{=}x_k \mid X{=}x) = \frac{x!}{x_1!x_2!\cdots x_k!} \cdot p_1^{x_1} \cdot p_2^{x_2} \cdot \cdots \cdot p_k^{x_k}, \tag{5.5}$$

where $x_1 + x_2 + \cdots + x_k = x$. The probability that, in fact, $X = x$ (the probability of the conditioning event) is

$$Pr(X = x) = \frac{e^{-\lambda}\lambda^x}{x!}, \tag{5.6}$$

since X has a Poisson distribution. Then the (unconditional) joint distribution of the X_i's is found as the product of Equations (5.5) and (5.6), so

$$Pr(X_1{=}x_1, X_2{=}x_2, \cdots, X_k{=}x_k) = \frac{x!}{x_1!x_2!\cdots x_k!} \cdot p_1^{x_1} \cdot p_2^{x_2} \cdot \cdots \cdot p_k^{x_k} \cdot \frac{e^{-\lambda}\lambda^x}{x!}. \tag{5.7}$$

We cancel the two $x!$ terms and note that $x = x_1 + x_2 + \cdots + x_k$ and $1 = p_1 + p_2 + \cdots + p_k$. Then Equation (5.7) becomes

$$\begin{aligned} Pr(X_1{=}x_1, X_2{=}x_2, \cdots, X_k{=}x_k) &= \frac{p_1^{x_1} \cdot p_2^{x_2} \cdot \cdots \cdot p_k^{x_k} \cdot e^{-\lambda(p_1+p_2+\cdots+p_k)} \lambda^{x_1+x_2+\cdots+x_k}}{x_1!x_2!\cdots x_k!} \\ &= \frac{(\lambda p_1)^{x_1} \cdot (\lambda p_2)^{x_2} \cdot \cdots \cdot (\lambda p_k)^{x_k} \cdot e^{-\lambda p_1} \cdot e^{-\lambda p_2} \cdot \cdots \cdot e^{-\lambda p_k}}{x_1!x_2!\cdots x_k!} \\ &= \prod_{i=1}^{k} \frac{e^{-\lambda p_i} \cdot (\lambda p_i)^{x_i}}{x_i!}, \end{aligned} \tag{5.8}$$

showing that the joint distribution of the X_i's is the product of k Poisson probability functions.

Parallel to the above analysis of the joint distribution of the X_i's, we note that given $X=x$, then the (conditional) marginal distribution of each X_i is binomial with parameters x and p_i. That is,

$$Pr(X_i=x_i \mid X=x) = \binom{x}{x_i} p_i^{x_i}(1-p_i)^{x-x_i}, \tag{5.9}$$

where $x_i = 0,1,2,\cdots,x$. Again the probability of the conditioning event is Poisson with probability function given by Equation (5.6). Then by the law of total probability the (unconditional) marginal distribution of X_i is

$$Pr(X_i=x_i) = \sum_{x=x_i}^{\infty} Pr(X_i=x_i \mid X=x)\cdot Pr(X=x), \tag{5.10}$$

where the summation is taken over all values of x greater than or equal to x_i. Thus we have

$$Pr(X_i=x_i) = \sum_{x=x_i}^{\infty} \frac{x!}{x_i!(x-x_i)!} p_i^{x_i}(1-p_i)^{x-x_i}\cdot\frac{e^{-\lambda}\lambda^x}{x!}. \tag{5.11}$$

Again we cancel the two $x!$ terms, we write the λ^x term as $\lambda^{x_i+(x-x_i)}$, and we take outside the summation all terms not involving x. We then have

$$Pr(X_i=x_i) = \frac{p_i^{x_i}\cdot e^{-\lambda}\lambda^{x_i}}{x_i!}\sum_{x=x_i}^{\infty}\frac{(1-p_i)^{x-x_i}\cdot\lambda^{x-x_i}}{(x-x_i)!}. \tag{5.12}$$

Making the change of variable $y=x-x_i$, the summation term becomes $\sum_{y=0}^{\infty}\frac{[\lambda(1-p_i)]^y}{y!}$, which is the series expansion of $e^{\lambda(1-p_i)}$. Thus we have

$$Pr(X_i=x_i) = \frac{p_i^{x_i}\cdot e^{-\lambda}\lambda^{x_i}}{x_i!}\cdot e^{\lambda(1-p_i)} = \frac{e^{-\lambda p_i}(\lambda p_i)^{x_i}}{x_i!}, \tag{5.13}$$

showing that each X_i has a Poisson distribution with parameter (mean) λp_i, as asserted. Furthermore, since the joint probability function of all the X_i's, given by Equation (5.8), is the product of the marginal probability functions for each separately, given by Equation (5.13), the assertion of mutual independence is established. This important result will be cited in some of the application areas that follow.

EXAMPLE 5.1

The number of accidents incurred in a year by a family of drivers has a Poisson distribution with $\lambda=3$. An accident is considered major if the resulting damage exceeds the family's auto insurance deductible, and minor otherwise. One-third of the accidents that occur are major. Find the probability of there being no major accidents in a year.

SOLUTION

Since the total number of accidents is Poisson, then the number of major accidents is also Poisson with parameter $\lambda' = \frac{\lambda}{3} = 1$. The probability of no major accidents in a year is then $e^{-\lambda'} = e^{-1} = .36787$. ❐

Another property of the Poisson distribution that makes it a useful one for modeling insurance claims is that if the number of homogeneous risks in a portfolio is changed, then the number of claims from the modified portfolio will still have a Poisson distribution with a proportionally adjusted parameter.[3] This is illustrated in the following example.

Example 5.2

A portfolio is made up of m independent and homogeneous risks, and the total number of claims from the portfolio has a Poisson distribution with parameter λ. If the number of homogeneous risks in the portfolio is changed to m', show that the total number of claims now has a Poisson distribution with parameter $\lambda' = \lambda\left(\frac{m'}{m}\right)$.

SOLUTION

Let N denote the random variable for total number of claims in the original portfolio of m risks. Then we have

$$N = X_1 + X_2 + \cdots + X_m,$$

where X_i denotes the number of claims from the ith risk. If the risks are homogeneous, then the X_i's are identically distributed and the MGF of N is

$$M_N(t) = [M_X(t)]^m$$

from Equation (1.63b). Similarly, if N' denotes the random variable for total claims in the modified portfolio of m' risks, then we have

$$M_{N'}(t) = [M_X(t)]^{m'} = [M_N(t)]^{m'/m}.$$

But if N has a Poisson distribution, with MGF $M_N(t) = e^{\lambda(e^t-1)}$, then the MGF of N' is

$$M_{N'}(t) = \left[e^{\lambda(e^t-1)}\right]^{m'/m} = e^{\lambda(m'/m)(e^t-1)},$$

which identifies N' as a Poisson random variable with parameter $\lambda' = \lambda\left(\frac{m'}{m}\right)$. ❐

---

[3] Distributions possessing this property are said to be *infinitely divisible*.

5.2.3 THE NEGATIVE BINOMIAL DISTRIBUTION

The negative binomial distribution, defined in Chapter 1 by its probability function (see Equation (1.30a)), is a two-parameter counting distribution. The presence of two parameters can give it more flexibility to fit various circumstances than might be true of the one-parameter Poisson distribution. Furthermore, we want to point out here that the parameter r need not be restricted to the positive integers, as it seemed must be the case when the distribution was first defined in Section 1.2.3.

Consider the binomial coefficient $\binom{x+r-1}{r-1}$ of Equation (1.30a). The customary way to evaluate this coefficient is to use factorials, producing

$$\binom{x+r-1}{r-1} = \frac{(x+r-1)!}{(r-1)!\,x!}. \tag{5.14}$$

The factorials are only defined if $r \geq 1$ is an integer. However, since x *must* be an integer, then it follows that

$$\begin{aligned}\frac{(x+r-1)!}{(r-1)!\,x!} &= \frac{(x+r-1)(x+r-2)\cdots(x+r-x)(x+r-x-1)(x+r-x-2)\cdots}{x!\,(r-1)(r-2)\cdots} \\ &= \frac{(x+r-1)(x+r-2)\cdots(r)(r-1)(r-2)\cdots}{x!\,(r-1)(r-2)\cdots} = \frac{(x+r-1)(x+r-2)\cdots(r)}{x!}.\end{aligned} \tag{5.15}$$

Next recall the gamma function, defined in Section 1.3.4 in conjunction with the gamma distribution. In particular, recall that

$$\Gamma(\alpha) = (\alpha-1)\cdot\Gamma(\alpha-1) = (\alpha-1)(\alpha-2)\cdot\Gamma(\alpha-2), \tag{5.16}$$

and so on, so that $\Gamma(\alpha) = (\alpha-1)!$ if α is a positive integer. However, even if α is not a positive integer, we can still represent a series of factors reducing by 1 each time as a ratio of two gamma functions. In particular, it is now easy to see that

$$\frac{\Gamma(x+r)}{\Gamma(r)} = \frac{(x+r-1)(x+r-2)\cdots(r)(r-1)(r-2)\cdots}{(r-1)(r-2)\cdots} = (x+r-1)(x+r-2)\cdots(r). \tag{5.17}$$

Finally, since $x! = \Gamma(x+1)$, because x is a positive integer, then we can see from Equations (5.14), (5.15), and (5.17) together that the negative binomial coefficient $\binom{x+r-1}{r-1}$ can be evaluated as

$$\binom{x+r-1}{r-1} = \frac{\Gamma(x+r)}{\Gamma(r)\cdot\Gamma(x+1)}. \tag{5.18}$$

Applications of the negative binomial distribution might require values of the gamma function with non-integral r. Such values are easily obtained using the widely-available mathematical software of modern computers.

The recursive relationship for the negative binomial distribution is similar in form to that for the binomial distribution. Starting with Equation (1.30) we have

$$\frac{p(x)}{p(x-1)} = \frac{\binom{x+r-1}{r-1}p^r(1-p)^x}{\binom{x+r-2}{r-1}p^r(1-p)^{x-1}} = \frac{\frac{\Gamma(x+r)}{\Gamma(r)\cdot\Gamma(x+1)}p^r(1-p)^x}{\frac{\Gamma(x+r-1)}{\Gamma(r)\cdot\Gamma(x)}p^r(1-p)^{x-1}} = \frac{x+r-1}{x}(1-p), \tag{5.19a}$$

so we can calculate negative binomial probabilities recursively as

$$p(x) = \left(\frac{x+r-1}{x}(1-p)\right)\cdot p(x-1), \tag{5.19b}$$

for $x=1,2,\cdots$. To begin the recursion we need the value of $p(0)$, obtained from the probability function as

$$p(0) = p^r. \tag{5.20}$$

EXAMPLE 5.3

Suppose N has a negative binomial distribution with $E[N]=20$ and $Var(N)=24$. Find the values of the parameters r and p.

SOLUTION

From Section 1.2.3 we have

$$E[N] = \frac{rq}{p} = 20$$

and

$$Var(N) = \frac{rq}{p^2} = 24.$$

Then we have

$$\frac{E[N]}{Var(N)} = \frac{rq}{p}\cdot\frac{p^2}{rq} = p = \frac{20}{24} = \frac{5}{6}$$

and

$$r = \frac{20p}{q} = \frac{(20)\left(\frac{5}{6}\right)}{\frac{1}{6}} = 100.$$

❐

EXAMPLE 5.4

Repeat Example 5.2 assuming that N has a negative binomial distribution.

SOLUTION

This time we have

$$M_N(t) = \left(\frac{p}{1-qe^t}\right)^r$$

(see Equation (1.33)), so

$$M_{N'}(t) = [M_N(t)]^{m'/m} = \left(\frac{p}{1-qe^t}\right)^{r(m'/m)},$$

which identifies N' as a negative binomial random variable with parameter $r' = r\left(\frac{m'}{m}\right)$. ❐

5.2.4 THE GEOMETRIC DISTRIBUTION

Recall that this is simply the special case of the negative binomial with $r=1$. The probability function then reduces to $p(x) = p(1-p)^x$, as already discussed in Section 1.2.4. The negative binomial recursive relationship simplifies to

$$p(x) = (1-p)\cdot p(x-1), \tag{5.21}$$

for $x = 1,2,\cdots$, with initial value $p(0) = p$.

5.2.5 SUMMARY OF THE RECURSIVE RELATIONSHIPS

All four of the recursive relationships, as given by Equations (5.1b) for the binomial, (5.3b) for the Poisson, (5.19b) for the negative binomial, and (5.21) for the geometric, can be arranged in the general form

$$p(x) = \left(\alpha + \frac{\beta}{x}\right)\cdot p(x-1), \tag{5.22}$$

where the values of α and β in each of the four cases are given in the following table. The derivation of α and β in all four cases is left as an exercise.

TABLE 5.1

Values for the Recursive Relationships			
Distribution	α	β	$p(0)$
Binomial	$-\frac{p}{1-p}$	$\frac{(n+1)p}{1-p}$	$(1-p)^n$
Poisson	0	λ	$e^{-\lambda}$
Negative Binomial	$1-p$	$(r-1)(1-p)$	p^r
Geometric	$1-p$	0	p

In some textbooks, these four distributions are said to constitute the $(\alpha, \beta, 0)$ class of distributions, and are the only distributions contained in that class.

EXAMPLE 5.5

Suppose X is a counting random variable of the $(\alpha, \beta, 0)$ class, with probability function $p(x)$ satisfying

$$\frac{p(x)}{p(x-1)} = -\frac{1}{3}+\frac{4}{x},$$

for $x=1,2,\cdots$. Identify the distribution of X.

SOLUTION

From Equation (5.22) we know that

$$\frac{p(x)}{p(x-1)} = \alpha+\frac{\beta}{x},$$

so here we have $\alpha=-\frac{1}{3}$ and $\beta=4$. Table 5.1 shows us that only the binomial distribution has $\alpha<0$, so we have $\frac{p}{1-p}=\frac{1}{3}$ which solves for $p=.25$. Then

$$\beta = (n+1)\left(\frac{p}{1-p}\right) = (n+1)\left(\frac{.25}{.75}\right) = 4,$$

which solves for $n=11$, so the distribution is binomial with $n=11$ and $p=.25$. ❐

5.2.6 PROBABILITY GENERATING FUNCTIONS

Just as each discrete distribution presented in this section has a moment generating function to generate the moments of that distribution (see also pages 5 and 7 and Section 1.2), it also has a *probability generating function* (PGF) to generate the respective probability values. Of course, we do not really need a PGF to do this, since we already have the probability function for that purpose. But just as the MGF can be used for purposes other than the actual generation of moments, similarly the PGF can be used to establish results other than the actual generation of probabilities.

Recall that the MGF is defined as $M_X(t)=E[e^{tX}]$, and the kth moment of X is obtained from the MGF as $E[X^k]=M_X^{(k)}(0)$. The PGF is defined as

$$P_X(s) = E[s^X], \tag{5.23}$$

for all s for which the expectation exists, which is just another example of finding the expected value of a function of the random variable where the function is $g(X)=s^X$. From the definition it follows that

$$\begin{aligned} P_X(s) &= \sum_{k=0}^{\infty} s^k \cdot p(k) \\ &= p(0) + s \cdot p(1) + s^2 \cdot p(2) + \cdots. \end{aligned} \tag{5.24}$$

Thus if the PGF is expanded in a series, the probability values appear as the coefficients of the various powers of s in that expansion. Furthermore, Equation (5.24) shows us that

$$P_X(0) = p(0), \tag{5.25a}$$

$$P'_X(0) = 1 \cdot p(1), \tag{5.25b}$$

$$P''_X(0) = 2 \cdot 1 \cdot p(2), \tag{5.25c}$$

$$P'''_X(0) = 3 \cdot 2 \cdot 1 \cdot p(3), \tag{5.25d}$$

and, in general,

$$P_X^{(k)}(0) = k! \cdot p(k), \tag{5.25e}$$

for $k = 0, 1, 2, \cdots$, where $P_X^{(k)}(0)$ stands for $\frac{d^k}{ds^k} P_X(s)\big|_{s=0}$. Then the probability value $p(k)$ is found as

$$p(k) = \frac{P_X^{(k)}(0)}{k!}. \tag{5.25f}$$

For example, the PGF of the Poisson distribution is $P_X(s) = e^{\lambda(s-1)}$. We can write

$$\begin{aligned} P_X(s) &= e^{\lambda(s-1)} \\ &= e^{-\lambda} \cdot e^{\lambda s} \\ &= e^{-\lambda}\left[1 + \lambda s + \frac{\lambda^2 s^2}{2!} + \frac{\lambda^3 s^3}{3!} + \cdots\right] \\ &= e^{-\lambda} + s(e^{-\lambda} \cdot \lambda) + s^2\left(\frac{e^{-\lambda} \cdot \lambda^2}{2!}\right) + s^3\left(\frac{e^{-\lambda} \cdot \lambda^3}{3!}\right) + \cdots. \end{aligned}$$

Clearly the first term (actually the coefficient of s^0) is $p(0)$, the coefficient of s^1 is $p(1)$, the coefficient of s^2 is $p(2)$, and so on.

There is a convenient relationship between the PGF and the MGF of a discrete random variable, as shown in the following example.

EXAMPLE 5.6

Show that the PGF of a random variable is the MGF evaluated at $t = \ln s$, and the MGF is the PGF evaluated at $s = e^t$.

SOLUTION

$$\begin{aligned} M_X(t)\big|_{t=\ln s} &= E[e^{tX}]\big|_{t=\ln s} \\ &= E[e^{X \cdot \ln s}] \\ &= E[e^{\ln s^X}] \\ &= E[s^X] = P_X(s) \end{aligned}$$

Conversely,

$$\begin{aligned} P_X(s)\big|_{s=e^t} &= E[s^X]\big|_{s=e^t} \\ &= E[e^{tX}] \\ &= M_X(t). \end{aligned}$$

□

5.3 CREATING ADDITIONAL COUNTING DISTRIBUTIONS

The four standard counting distributions discussed in Section 5.1 can be very useful as models for the frequency of insurance losses or insurance claims, and have been used extensively in this way. They might not be suitable in all circumstances, however, so we might ask how we can develop additional distributions for this application. In this section we will consider three methods for doing this, which are the method of *compounding*, the method of *mixing*, and the method of *truncation or modification at zero*.

5.3.1 COMPOUND FREQUENCY MODELS

We return to the notion of the compound distribution, defined in Section 1.6, now with a view to developing compound counting distributions to be used as models for claim frequency. Recall that the general form of a compound distribution is

$$S = X_1 + X_2 + \cdots + X_N, \tag{5.26}$$

where the X_i's are mutually independent and have the same distribution, and where each X_i is also independent of N. Recall that the distribution of N is called the primary distribution and the common distribution of the X_i's is called the secondary distribution. It is clear that S will be a counting distribution, taking on only the integer values $s = 0,1,\cdots$, if and only if both N and X_i have counting distributions. The mean and variance of S are given by Equations (1.65) and (1.66), respectively, and the moment generating function of S is obtained from the MGF's of N and X by Equation (1.67).

But how do we find the complete distribution of the random variable S?

One way is to use the law of total probability to state that

$$\begin{aligned} Pr(S=s) &= \sum_{n=0}^{\infty} Pr(S=s \mid N=n) \cdot Pr(N=n) \\ &= \sum_{n=0}^{\infty} Pr(X_1+X_2+\cdots+X_n=s) \cdot Pr(N=n), \end{aligned} \quad (5.27)$$

and then to use convolutions to evaluate $Pr(X_1+X_2+\cdots+X_n=s)$ for each value of n. (See Section 1.5.3.) This approach could entail a considerable amount of calculation.

In the special case where the primary distribution N is one of the four standard distributions reviewed in Section 5.2, there is a recursion formula that will tabulate the counting distribution of S much more easily. If we let $p_S(k)$ denote $Pr(S=k)$ and $p_X(k)$ denote $Pr(X=k)$, then the probability function of S can be calculated as

$$\begin{aligned} p_S(s) &= \frac{\sum_{k=1}^{s} \left(\alpha+\frac{\beta k}{s}\right) \cdot Pr(X=k) \cdot Pr(S=s-k)}{1-\alpha \cdot Pr(X=0)} \\ &= \frac{\sum_{k=1}^{s} \left(\alpha+\frac{\beta k}{s}\right) \cdot p_X(k) \cdot p_S(s-k)}{1-\alpha \cdot p_X(0)}, \end{aligned} \quad (5.28)$$

for $s=1,2,3,\ldots,$ where the values of α and β are determined from the parameters of the distribution of N as shown in Table 5.1. (For a derivation of Equation (5.28), see Section 12.4 of Bowers et al. [4].) Note that the value of $p_S(0)$ is needed to initialize the recursion.

A numerical example will demonstrate the steps involved in using Equation (5.28).

EXAMPLE 5.7

Let the primary distribution N be binomial with parameters $n=2$ and $p=.50$, and let the distribution of X be $p_X(0)=.50$, $p_X(1)=.30$, and $p_X(2)=.20$. Use Equation (5.28) to tabulate the counting distribution of S.

SOLUTION

First we note that the possible values of S will be $0,1,2,3,4$. Next we note that the distribution of N is $p_N(0)=.25$, $p_N(1)=.50$, and $p_N(2)=.25$. Finally, from Table 5.1 we find $\alpha=-\frac{p}{1-p}=-1$ and $\beta=(n+1)\frac{p}{1-p}=3$. Then Equation (5.28) simplifies to

$$p_S(s) = \frac{\sum_{k=1}^{s}\left(\frac{3k}{s}-1\right)\cdot p_X(k)\cdot p_S(s-k)}{1-(-1)(.50)}$$

$$= \frac{2}{3}\sum_{k=1}^{s}\left(\frac{3k}{s}-1\right)\cdot p_X(k)\cdot p_S(s-k),$$

for $s=1,2,3,4$. The starting value $p_S(0)$ can be found from Equation (5.27) as

$$p_S(0) = Pr(S{=}0) = \sum_{n=0}^{2} Pr(S{=}0\,|\,N{=}n)\cdot Pr(N{=}n)$$

$$= \frac{1}{4}\cdot Pr(S{=}0\,|\,N{=}0)+\frac{1}{2}\cdot Pr(S{=}0\,|\,N{=}1)+\frac{1}{4}\cdot Pr(S{=}0\,|\,N{=}2)$$

$$= \frac{1}{4}(1)+\frac{1}{2}(.50)+\frac{1}{4}(.50)^2 = .5625.$$

Then, recursively, we have for $s=1$

$$p_S(1) = \frac{2}{3}\sum_{k=1}^{1}\left(\frac{3k}{1}-1\right)\cdot p_X(k)\cdot p_S(1-k)$$

$$= \frac{2}{3}[(3-1)\cdot p_X(1)\cdot p_S(0)]$$

$$= \frac{2}{3}[(2)(.30)(.5625)] = .2250.$$

For $s=2$ we have

$$p_S(2) = \frac{2}{3}\sum_{k=1}^{2}\left(\frac{3k}{2}-1\right)\cdot p_X(k)\cdot p_S(2-k)$$

$$= \frac{2}{3}\left[\left(\frac{3}{2}-1\right)\cdot p_X(1)\cdot p_S(1)+\left(\frac{6}{2}-1\right)\cdot p_X(2)\cdot p_S(0)\right]$$

$$= \frac{2}{3}[(.50)(.30)(.2250)+(2)(.20)(.5625)] = .1725.$$

For $s=3$ we have

$$\begin{aligned} p_S(3) &= \frac{2}{3}\sum_{k=1}^{3}\left(\frac{3k}{3}-1\right)\cdot p_X(k)\cdot p_S(3-k) \\ &= \frac{2}{3}\big[(1-1)\cdot p_X(1)\cdot p_S(2)+(2-1)\cdot p_X(2)\cdot p_S(1)+(3-1)\cdot p_X(3)\cdot p_S(0)\big] \\ &= \frac{2}{3}[(0)(.30)(.1725)+(1)(.20)(.2250)+(2)(0)(.5625)] \\ &= .0300. \end{aligned}$$

For $s=4$ we have

$$\begin{aligned} p_S(4) &= \frac{2}{3}\sum_{k=1}^{4}\left(\frac{3k}{4}-1\right)\cdot p_X(k)\cdot p_S(4-k) \\ &= \frac{2}{3}\Bigg[\left(\frac{3}{4}-1\right)\cdot p_X(1)\cdot p_S(3)+\left(\frac{6}{4}-1\right)\cdot p_X(2)\cdot p_S(2) \\ &\qquad +\left(\frac{9}{4}-1\right)\cdot p_X(3)\cdot p_S(1)+\left(\frac{12}{4}-1\right)\cdot p_X(4)\cdot p_S(0)\Bigg] \\ &= \frac{2}{3}[(-.25)(.30)(.0300)+(.50)(.20)(.1725)] \\ &= .0100, \end{aligned}$$

since $p_X(3)=p_X(4)=0$. As a check on our calculations, we note that

$$\sum_{s=0}^{4} p_S(s) = .5625+.2250+.1725+.0300+.0100 = 1.0000,$$

as required. ❐

Note that Equation (5.28) is valid as long as the primary distribution N is one of the four standard distributions (Poisson, binomial, negative binomial, or geometric), but the secondary distribution X is *not* required to be of these families, as Example 5.7 shows.

Finally, there is another way to calculate the starting value $p_S(0)$ than the method shown in the solution to Example 5.7, namely

$$p_S(0) = M_N[\ln p_X(0)], \tag{5.29}$$

the MGF of the primary variable N evaluated at the natural log of $p_X(0)$. This result is derived as follows:

$$\begin{aligned} p_S(0) &= \sum_{n=0}^{\infty} Pr(S=0 \mid N=n) \cdot Pr(N=n) \\ &= \sum_{n=0}^{\infty} [p_X(0)]^n \cdot Pr(N=n) \\ &= \sum_{n=0}^{\infty} [e^{\ln[p_X(0)]^n}] \cdot Pr(N=n) \\ &= \sum_{n=0}^{\infty} \left[e^{n \cdot \ln p_X(0)}\right] \cdot Pr(N=n) \\ &= M_N\left[\ln p_X(0)\right]. \end{aligned}$$

In Example 5.7, where N is binomial with $n=2$ and $p=.50$, its MGF is

$$M_N(t) = (q+pe^t)^n = (.50+.50e^t)^2.$$

Then

$$\begin{aligned} M_N[\ln p_X(0)] &= (.50+.50e^{\ln p_X(0)})^2 \\ &= \left(.50+.50p_X(0)\right)^2 \\ &= \left[.50+(.50)(.50)\right]^2 = .5625, \end{aligned}$$

as already known.

Further practice with compound counting distributions is provided in the exercises at the end of the chapter.

5.3.2 MIXTURE FREQUENCY MODELS

Another technique for creating additional counting (frequency) distributions is the method of mixing. Here we view one or more of the parameters of a specified frequency model as a random variable, with a known or presumed distribution.[4]

Consider a Poisson frequency model with parameter λ, but where λ is itself a realization of a random variable Λ. For example, consider a collection of accident insurance risks that can be classified into three distinct classes according to risk of accident, say, low, medium, and high. Then the precise PF for the number of accidents will depend on which risk class is under consideration, and the unconditional PF for the number of accidents would be

[4] A *mixture* distribution is not to be confused with a *mixed* distribution, as defined in Section 1.1.3.

$$\begin{aligned} p_N(n) &= Pr(N{=}n) \\ &= \frac{e^{-\lambda_1}\lambda_1^n}{n!}\cdot p_\Lambda(\lambda_1)+\frac{e^{-\lambda_2}\lambda_2^n}{n!}\cdot p_\Lambda(\lambda_2)+\frac{e^{-\lambda_3}\lambda_3^n}{n!}\cdot p_\Lambda(\lambda_3), \end{aligned} \tag{5.30a}$$

where $\lambda_1, \lambda_2, \lambda_3$ are the expected numbers of claims for the three different risk classes, and $p_\Lambda(\lambda_i)$ denotes the probability of selecting the ith class.

Here the distribution of Λ is called the *mixing distribution,* which is a discrete distribution in this example. When the mixing distribution is discrete, the overall (unconditional) distribution of N is called a *discrete mixture distribution.*

Suppose Λ, the random variable generating the parameter value λ, has a continuous distribution with PDF denoted by $f_\Lambda(\lambda)$. In this case the distribution of N is called a *continuous mixture distribution*, notwithstanding the fact that the distribution of N is still discrete. The PF of N is given by

$$\begin{aligned} p_N(n) &= Pr(N{=}n) \\ &= \int_\Lambda Pr(N{=}n \mid \Lambda=\lambda)\cdot f_\Lambda(\lambda)\,d\lambda \\ &= \int_\Lambda \frac{e^{-\lambda}\lambda^n}{n!}\cdot f_\Lambda(\lambda)\,d\lambda, \end{aligned} \tag{5.30b}$$

where the integral is taken over all values in the continuous domain of Λ.

Some interesting results can occur when new distributions are created by mixing. For example, it turns out that if a Poisson distribution is based on a parameter λ that is generated by a gamma distribution (see Section 1.3.4), then the resulting mixture distribution (called a Poisson-gamma continuous mixture) is the negative binomial distribution, so that no new type of distribution is created.

To verify this result, recall from Equation (1.55) that the PDF of Λ is

$$f_\Lambda(\lambda) = \frac{\beta^\alpha}{\Gamma(\alpha)}\cdot\lambda^{\alpha-1}e^{-\beta\lambda},$$

for $\lambda>0, \alpha>0$, and $\beta>0$. Then from Equation (5.30b) we have

$$\begin{aligned} p_N(n) &= \int_0^\infty \frac{e^{-\lambda}\lambda^n}{n!}\cdot\frac{\beta^\alpha}{\Gamma(\alpha)}\cdot\lambda^{\alpha-1}e^{-\beta\lambda}\,d\lambda \\ &= \frac{\beta^\alpha}{n!\cdot\Gamma(\alpha)}\int_0^\infty e^{-\lambda(1+\beta)}\lambda^{n+\alpha-1}\,d\lambda. \end{aligned}$$

Now make the variable change $x = \lambda(1+\beta)$, so that $\lambda = \frac{x}{1+\beta}$ and $d\lambda = \frac{dx}{1+\beta}$. This gives us

$$\begin{aligned} p_N(n) &= \frac{\beta^\alpha}{n!\cdot\Gamma(\alpha)}\int_0^\infty e^{-x}\left(\frac{x}{1+\beta}\right)^{(n+\alpha)-1}\cdot\frac{dx}{1+\beta} \\ &= \frac{\beta^\alpha}{n!\cdot\Gamma(\alpha)}\left(\frac{1}{1+\beta}\right)^{n+\alpha}\int_0^\infty e^{-x}x^{(n+\alpha)-1}\,dx \\ &= \frac{\beta^\alpha}{n!\cdot\Gamma(\alpha)}\left(\frac{1}{1+\beta}\right)^{n}\left(\frac{1}{1+\beta}\right)^{\alpha}\cdot\Gamma(n+\alpha), \end{aligned}$$

by the definition of the gamma function. This can then be written as

$$p_N(n) = \frac{\Gamma(n+\alpha)}{\Gamma(\alpha)\cdot\Gamma(n+1)}\left(\frac{\beta}{1+\beta}\right)^{\alpha}\left(\frac{1}{1+\beta}\right)^{n},$$

since, with n being an integer, $\Gamma(n+1) = n!$. Finally, if we let $p = \frac{\beta}{1+\beta}$, so that $1-p = \frac{1}{1+\beta}$, and recall from Equation (5.18) that

$$\binom{n+\alpha-1}{\alpha-1} = \frac{\Gamma(n+\alpha)}{\Gamma(\alpha)\cdot\Gamma(n+1)},$$

then we finally have

$$p_N(n) = \binom{n+\alpha-1}{\alpha-1}p^\alpha(1-p)^n,$$

which is the negative binomial PF given by Equation (1.30), with α replacing r and n replacing x.

EXAMPLE 5.8

A claim count random variable N has a Poisson distribution with mean Λ, where Λ has a gamma distribution with mean 1 and variance 2. Evaluate $Pr(N=1)$.

SOLUTION

For the gamma distribution (see Section 1.3.4), we have $E[\Lambda] = \frac{\alpha}{\beta} = 1$ and $Var(\Lambda) = \frac{\alpha}{\beta^2} = 2$, which implies $\alpha = \beta = .50$. Since N is a Poisson-gamma mixture, it has a negative binomial distribution with $r = \alpha = .50$ and $p = \frac{\beta}{1+\beta} = \frac{1}{3}$. (Recall that r is not required to be an integer.) Recall that

$$Pr(N=n) = \frac{\Gamma(n+r)}{\Gamma(r)\cdot\Gamma(n+1)}\cdot p^r(1-p)^n$$

so

$$\begin{aligned} Pr(N=1) &= \frac{\Gamma(1.50)}{\Gamma(.50)\cdot\Gamma(2)}\left(\frac{1}{3}\right)^{1/2}\left(\frac{2}{3}\right)^1 \\ &= \frac{(.50)\cdot\Gamma(.50)}{\Gamma(.50)\cdot\Gamma(2)}\left(\frac{1}{3}\right)^{1/2}\left(\frac{2}{3}\right) \\ &= (.50)\left(\frac{1}{3}\right)^{1/2}\left(\frac{2}{3}\right) \\ &= .19245, \end{aligned}$$

since $\Gamma(\alpha)=(\alpha-1)\cdot\Gamma(\alpha-1)$ and $\Gamma(2)=1$. ❒

5.3.3 TRUNCATION OR MODIFICATION AT ZERO

The four standard counting distributions presented in Section 5.1 all have the property of $x=0$ as a possible event. That is, $p(0)>0$. Cases might arise where we seek to model the distribution of the number of events in a circumstance where at least one event is known to have occurred, so that $p(0)=0$ and the domain of the counting random variable is $x=1,2,\cdots$.

We can create such a counting distribution simply by modifying an existing distribution to eliminate $x=0$ as a possible event. The remaining probability values, which would otherwise sum to $1-p(0)$, are each divided by $1-p(0)$ to create a proper distribution. Since the outcome of $x=0$ has been truncated from the distribution, we refer to the resulting distribution as a *zero-truncated distribution.*

On the other hand, many cases arise in actuarial models where the probability of the event $x=0$ is much larger than the value given by the standard distributions discussed earlier in this chapter. For many insurance applications, for example, the probability of no claim occurring could be very large. To address this we might modify an existing distribution by first assigning a new value to $p(0)$ and then modifying the other values of $p(x)$ to create a proper distribution. The new distribution is referred to as a *zero-modified distribution*.

Note that the zero-truncated distribution mentioned earlier is a special case of a zero-modified distribution with the new value of $p(0)$ set at $p(0)=0$. We will therefore develop the zero-modified case in general, and then the special zero-truncated case.

We consider only the four standard counting distributions presented in Section 5.2, and recall that they are said to constitute the $(\alpha,\beta,0)$ class of distributions. We continue to let $p(x)$ denote the probability function of the standard distribution from which the modified distribution is created.

Let $p_{ZM}(x)$ denote the probability function for the zero-modified distribution, so that $p_{ZM}(0)$ denotes the reassigned value of $Pr(X=0)$. The values of $p_{ZM}(x)$ are given by the general relationship

$$p_{ZM}(x) = \left(\frac{1-p_{ZM}(0)}{1-p(0)}\right)\cdot p(x), \tag{5.31a}$$

for $x=1,2,\cdots$. In the special case of the zero-truncated distribution, where $p_{ZM}(0)=0$, we denote the probability function by $p_{ZT}(x)$, so we have

$$p_{ZT}(x) = \frac{p(x)}{1-p(0)}, \tag{5.31b}$$

for $x=1,2,\cdots$.

EXAMPLE 5.9

Show that the probability functions given by Equations (5.31a) and (5.31b) define proper distributions.

SOLUTION

We need to show that $\sum_{x=0}^{\infty} p_{ZM}(x)=1$. Using Equation (5.31a) we have

$$\begin{aligned}
\sum_{x=0}^{\infty} p_{ZM}(x) &= p_{ZM}(0)+\sum_{x=1}^{\infty} p_{ZM}(x) \\
&= p_{ZM}(0)+\left(\frac{1-p_{ZM}(0)}{1-p(0)}\right)\cdot\sum_{x=1}^{\infty} p(x) \\
&= p_{ZM}(0)+\left(\frac{1-p_{ZM}(0)}{1-p(0)}\right)\cdot(1-p(0)) = 1.
\end{aligned}$$

Similarly, using Equation (5.31b) we have

$$\begin{aligned}
\sum_{x=0}^{\infty} p_{ZT}(x) &= p_{ZT}(0)+\sum_{x=1}^{\infty} p_{ZT}(x) \\
&= p_{ZT}(0)+\left(\frac{1}{1-p(0)}\right)\cdot\sum_{x=1}^{\infty} p(x) \\
&= p_{ZT}(0)+\frac{1-p(0)}{1-p(0)} = 1,
\end{aligned}$$

since $p_{ZT}(0) = 0$. ❒

Since $p_{ZM}(x) = c \cdot p(x)$, where $c = \frac{1-p_{ZM}(0)}{1-p(0)}$ is a constant, then it follows that the shape of the zero-modified distribution from $x=1$ onward is the same as the basic $(\alpha, \beta, 0)$ distribution represented by $p(x)$. Furthermore, the ratio

$$\frac{p_{ZM}(x)}{p_{ZM}(x-1)} = \frac{c \cdot p(x)}{c \cdot p(x-1)} = \frac{p(x)}{p(x-1)}, \tag{5.32}$$

so it follows that the general recursive relationship given by Equation (5.22) for the basic distribution holds for the zero-modified distribution as well, except that it begins at $x=2$ instead of $x=1$, since $p_{ZM}(0)$ has an assigned non-zero value that does not fit the recursive pattern.

The MGF and the PGF for a zero-modified distribution can be obtained from the corresponding generating functions of the associated basic distribution. For the MGF we have

$$\begin{aligned}
M_X^{ZM}(t) &= E[e^{tX}] \\
&= \sum_{x=0}^{\infty} e^{tx} \cdot p_{ZM}(x) \\
&= p_{ZM}(0) + \left(\frac{1-p_{ZM}(0)}{1-p(0)} \right) \cdot \sum_{x=1}^{\infty} e^{tx} \cdot p(x),
\end{aligned}$$

using Equation (5.31a) for $p_{ZM}(x)$ and the fact that $e^{tx} = 1$ at $x=0$. But

$$\sum_{x=1}^{\infty} e^{tx} \cdot p(x) = \sum_{x=0}^{\infty} e^{tx} \cdot p(x) - p(0) = M_X(t) - p(0),$$

again since $e^{tx} = 1$ at $x=0$, so we have

$$\begin{aligned}
M_X^{ZM}(t) &= p_{ZM}(0) + \left(\frac{1-p_{ZM}(0)}{1-p(0)} \right) \left(M_X(t) - p(0) \right) \\
&= p_{ZM}(0) - p(0) \cdot \left(\frac{1-p_{ZM}(0)}{1-p(0)} \right) + \left(\frac{1-p_{ZM}(0)}{1-p(0)} \right) \cdot M_X(t) \\
&= \frac{p_{ZM}(0) - p(0)}{1-p(0)} + \left(\frac{1-p_{ZM}(0)}{1-p(0)} \right) \cdot M_X(t). \qquad (5.33a)
\end{aligned}$$

To find the PGF of the zero-modified distribution we use the general relationship developed in Example 5.6. We have

$$
\begin{aligned}
P_X^{ZM}(s) &= M_X^{ZM}(t)\Big|_{t=\ln s} \\
&= \frac{p_{ZM}(0)-p(0)}{1-p(0)} + \frac{1-p_{ZM}(0)}{1-p(0)} \cdot M_X(t)\Big|_{t=\ln s} \\
&= \frac{p_{ZM}(0)-p(0)}{1-p(0)} + \frac{1-p_{ZM}(0)}{1-p(0)} \cdot P_X(s). \qquad (5.33b)
\end{aligned}
$$

The special cases of $M_X^{ZT}(t)$ and $P_X^{ZT}(s)$ follow from Equations (5.33a) and (5.33b) by substituting $p_{ZM}(0)=0$, resulting in

$$M_X^{ZT}(t) = \frac{M_X(t)-p(0)}{1-p(0)} \qquad (5.34a)$$

and

$$P_X^{ZT}(s) = \frac{P_X(s)-p(0)}{1-p(0)}. \qquad (5.34b)$$

Further practice with zero-modified and zero-truncated distributions is provided in Exercises 5-19 through 5-21.

5.4 COUNTING PROCESSES

Suppose the discrete random variable *N*, with $n=0,1,2,\cdots$, counts the number of events occurring in some interval of time, where the distribution of *N* will naturally vary depending on the length of the underlying time interval. Let us consider *N* to be the counting random variable for the number of events in one unit of time. Then for any fixed value t_0, where $t_0>0$, we let $N(t_0)$ denote the random variable which counts the number of events occurring in the time interval $(0,t_0]$. Note that $N(1)$ would have the same meaning as *N* itself.

Now consider $N(t)$, for $t>0$, where $N(t)$ is viewed as a function of time. For a *specific value* of *t*, $N(t)$ is a counting random variable as described in the previous paragraph. But when viewed as a function of *t*, $N(t)$ is called a *counting process*. Note that $N(0)=0$.

5.4.1 PROPERTIES OF COUNTING PROCESSES

Since the counting process $N(t)$ counts the number of events occurring in the time interval $(0,t]$, several properties of $N(t)$ naturally follow. First, it will necessarily be true that $N(t)\geq 0$ and can take on only integer values. Furthermore $N(t)$ must be a non-decreasing function. That is, if $t_1<t_2$, then necessarily $N(t_1)\leq N(t_2)$, as illustrated in the following diagram.

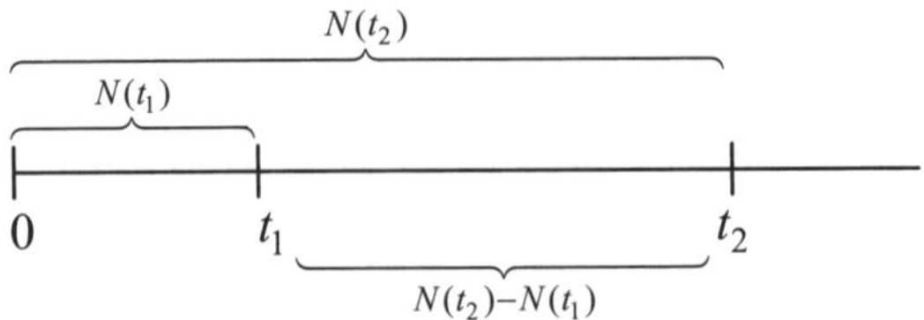

Illustration of $N(t)$

FIGURE 5.1

Note that $N(t_2)$ counts the number of events occurring in $(0,t_2]$, not in $(t_1,t_2]$, so $N(t_2)$ cannot be less than $N(t_1)$. We will use the notation $N(t_2)-N(t_1)$, where $t_1 < t_2$, to denote the number of events occurring in the interval $(t_1,t_2]$.

A counting process is said to possess the property of *independent increments* if the numbers of events occurring in disjoint (i.e., non-overlapping) time intervals are independent random variables. Whether or not a particular counting process possesses the property of independent increments will depend on the nature of the events being counted in each case.

A counting process is said to possess the property of *stationary increments* if the distribution of number of events occurring in any time interval depends only on the *length* of that time interval, and not on its location on the general time axis. For example, Figure 5.2 shows two separate time intervals of length 10, namely (5, 15] and (20, 30].

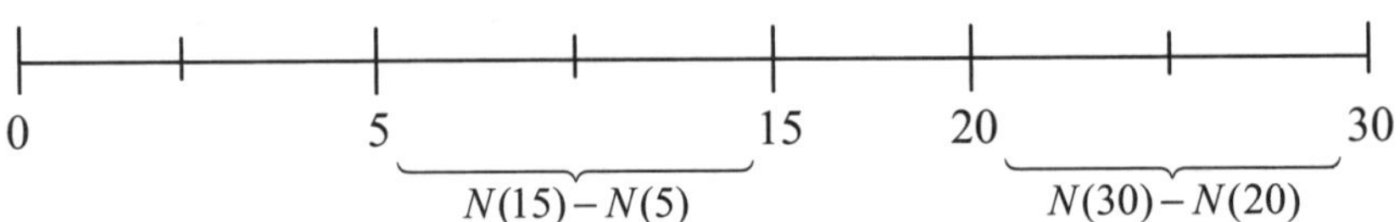

Illustration of Stationary Increments

FIGURE 5.2

If the distribution of the number of events occurring in $(5,15]$, denoted $N(15)-N(5)$, is the same as the distribution of number of events occurring in $(20,30]$, denoted $N(30)-N(20)$, and is the same as the distribution in *any* interval of length 10, then the counting process $N(t)$ possesses the property of stationary increments. The significance of the stationary increments property will become clearer in later sections of the text. The reasonableness of the stationary increments assumption will depend on the nature of each case. (See Section 5.4.5.)

5.4.2 THE POISSON COUNTING PROCESS

Suppose a counting process $N(t)$ satisfies the basic requirement of $N(0)=0$ and possesses the property of independent increments. Suppose the probability function for the number of events occurring in *any* interval of length *t*, regardless of where such interval is located on the general time axis, is given by

$$p_{N(t)}(n) = \frac{e^{-\lambda t}(\lambda t)^n}{n!}, \tag{5.35}$$

for $n = 0,1,2,\cdots$. (Note that this supposition establishes the property of stationary increments.) A counting process meeting these criteria is called a *Poisson counting process*, and the parameter $\lambda > 0$ is called the *rate of the process*.[5] Due to the property of stationary increments, we can use the notation $N(t)$ to denote the random variable counting the number of events occurring in *any* interval of length t, not just the specific interval $(0,t]$. It follows that

$$E[N(t)] = \lambda t \tag{5.36}$$

and

$$Var[N(t)] = \lambda t \tag{5.37}$$

as well.

5.4.3 FURTHER PROPERTIES OF THE POISSON COUNTING PROCESS

Suppose the events being counted by a Poisson counting process occur as indicated by the X's in the following diagram.

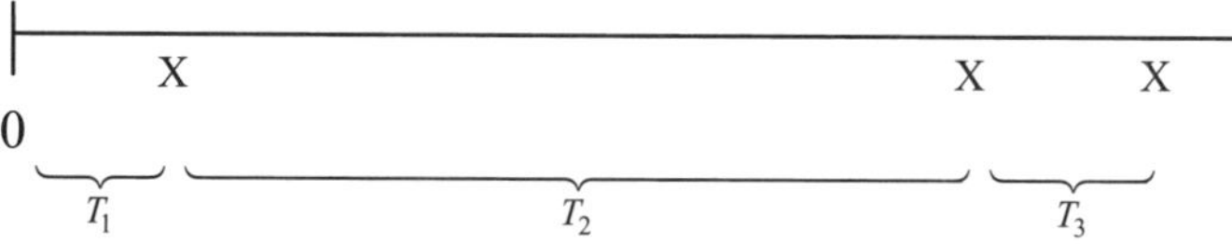

Illustration of Interarrival Times

FIGURE 5.3

In Figure 5.3, T_1 denotes the (random) length of time until the first event occurs, T_2 denotes the length of time after the first event occurs until the second event occurs, and so on. In general, T_i denotes the length of time after the $(i-1)^{st}$ event occurs until the ith event occurs and is called the ith *interarrival time*. (The entire sequence $\{T_i, i = 1,2,\cdots\}$ is called the *sequence of interarrival times*.) What can we say about the distribution of each T_i random variable?

Consider first the random variable T_1. The event $T_1 > t$ means that no events occur in the interval $(0,t]$, since the time until the first event occurs exceeds t. Thus we have

$$Pr(T_1 > t) = Pr[N(t) = 0] = e^{-\lambda t}, \tag{5.38}$$

since $N(t)$ has a Poisson distribution with parameter λt. Equation (5.38) shows that T_1 has an exponential distribution with parameter λ, and therefore with mean $\frac{1}{\lambda}$ (see Section 1.3.3). Fur-

[5] For an alternative, but equivalent, definition of the Poisson counting process, see Section 5.3.2 of Ross [36].

thermore, each subsequent T_i behaves the same as T_1 (i.e., each T_i is exponential with $E[T_i]=\frac{1}{\lambda}$), as a consequence of the independent and stationary increments properties of the Poisson process, and all of the T_i's are mutually independent of each other.

Next we consider the random variable

$$S_n = T_1+T_2+\cdots+T_n, \tag{5.39}$$

which represents the time until the nth event occurs. (S_n is often called the *waiting time* until the nth event.) Since each T_i is an independent and identically distributed exponential random variable, then it follows that S_n has a gamma distribution with parameters λ and n. (See Section 1.5.2.)

Finally, recall the decomposition property of the Poisson distribution discussed in Section 5.2.2. By reasoning totally parallel to that used in Section 5.2.2 for the Poisson random variable itself, we can show that if the events being counted by the Poisson process $N(t)$ can be classified as one out of k distinct types, then the process counting the events of Type i will be a Poisson counting process $N_i(t)$ with rate $\lambda_i = \lambda \cdot p_i$, where p_i is the probability of a Type i event. Furthermore each of the $N_i(t)$ will be mutually independent. (See Exercise 5-26.) Of course it must be true that

$$N(t) = \sum_{i=1}^{k} N_i(t) \tag{5.40a}$$

and

$$\lambda = \sum_{i=1}^{k} \lambda_i, \tag{5.40b}$$

since $\sum_{i=1}^{k} p_i = 1$.

Here we have assumed that the probability of a Type i event, denoted p_i, is constant over time. Conversely, suppose the probability of a Type i event depends on the time the event occurs, with the probability that an event occurring at time s is a Type i event denoted by $p_i(s)$. In this case the process counting the events of Type i will still be a Poisson counting process $N_i(t)$, but with rate $\lambda_i(t)$ that varies with the value of t and is given by

$$\lambda_i(t) = \lambda \int_0^t p_i(s)\, ds. \tag{5.41}$$

In this case, the process counting the number of Type i events is a nonstationary one, as described in Section 5.4.5.

In Chapter 8 we will consider $N(t)$ as a Poisson counting process for the number of insurance losses or claims, and will make use of the decomposition property to create the Poisson counting process $N_i(t)$ for the number of insurance losses or claims of Type i. The converse of the decomposition property is also true. That is, if $N_i(t)$, for $i=1,2,\cdots,k$, are independent Poisson counting processes with respective rates λ_i, then

$$N(t) = \sum_{i=1}^{k} N_i(t) \tag{5.42}$$

will be a Poisson counting process with rate $\lambda = \sum_{i=1}^{k} \lambda_i$.

EXAMPLE 5.10

Claims in insurance Portfolio P occur according to a Poisson counting process with rate $\lambda_P = 3$ and claims in Portfolio Q occur according to an independent Poisson counting process with rate $\lambda_Q = 5$. Find the probability that 3 claims occur from Portfolio P before 3 claims occur from Portfolio Q.

SOLUTION

The total claims from both portfolios together is also a Poisson counting process with rate $\lambda = \lambda_P + \lambda_Q = 8$, and the probability that a claim comes from Portfolio P is $p = \frac{\lambda_P}{\lambda} = \frac{3}{8}$. In order that 3 claims from P occur before 3 from Q, it is necessary that at least 3 claims from P occur within the first 5 claims in total. (Otherwise, if fewer than 3 from P occur within the first 5 then at least 3 from Q will occur before the third one from P.) The number of claims from P out of 5 in total has a binomial distribution with $p = \frac{3}{8}$ and $n = 5$. Then the desired probability is

$$Pr(3 \text{ from P before 3 from Q})$$
$$= \binom{5}{3}\left(\tfrac{3}{8}\right)^3\left(\tfrac{5}{8}\right)^2 + \binom{5}{4}\left(\tfrac{3}{8}\right)^4\left(\tfrac{5}{8}\right)^1 + \left(\tfrac{3}{8}\right)^5 = .20599 + .06180 + .00742 = .27520. \quad \square$$

5.4.4 POISSON MIXTURE PROCESSES

The discussion in Section 5.3.2 on mixture counting distributions (and Poisson mixtures in particular) is easily extended to the notion of *mixture counting processes*. In particular, if a Poisson counting process has rate λ which is itself a realization of a random variable Λ, where Λ has PDF given by $f_\Lambda(\lambda)$, then $N(t)$ is a *Poisson mixture process* where

$$\begin{aligned} p_{N(t)}(n) = Pr[N(t)=n] &= \int_\Lambda Pr[N(t)=n \mid \Lambda=\lambda] \cdot f_\Lambda(\lambda)\, d\lambda \\ &= \int_\Lambda \frac{e^{-\lambda t}(\lambda t)^n}{n!} \cdot f_\Lambda(\lambda)\, d\lambda, \end{aligned} \tag{5.43}$$

where the integral is taken over all values in the continuous domain of Λ.

Conditional on $\Lambda = \lambda$, $N(t)$ is a Poisson process, so it follows that

$$E[N(t) \mid \Lambda] = Var[N(t) \mid \Lambda] = \Lambda t.$$

Then by the double expectation theorem (see Section 1.4) we find

$$E[N(t)] = E_{\Lambda}\big[E[N(t) \mid \Lambda]\big] = t \cdot E[\Lambda] \tag{5.44}$$

and

$$\begin{aligned} Var[N(t)] &= Var_{\Lambda}\big[E[N(t) \mid \Lambda]\big] + E_{\Lambda}\big[Var[N(t) \mid \Lambda]\big] \\ &= Var_{\Lambda}(\Lambda t) + E_{\Lambda}[\Lambda t] \\ &= t^2 \cdot Var(\Lambda) + t \cdot E[\Lambda]. \end{aligned} \tag{5.45}$$

It should be noted that the Poisson mixture process has stationary increments but does not generally have independent increments, so the Poisson mixture process is not itself a Poisson process.

5.4.5 THE NONSTATIONARY POISSON COUNTING PROCESS

The assumption of the stationary increments property for a Poisson counting process is not always a reasonable one. For example, suppose $N(t)$ counts the number of customers arriving at a popular town diner, where $t = 0$ corresponds to 6:00a.m. To suppose that the distribution of the number of arriving customers (i.e., the number of events being counted) is the same over any interval of fixed length, regardless of its location in time, is not reasonable. Surely the number of arrivals between, say, 7:00a.m. and 9:00a.m., denoted $N(3) - N(1)$, has a very different distribution from that of the random variable denoted $N(5) - N(3)$, the number of arrivals between 9:00a.m. and 11:00a.m., although both random variables relate to an interval of two hours in length.

To address such cases, we discard the property of stationary increments. Since the constant parameter λ governs the distribution of $N(t)$ in the stationary case, we will replace the rate λ by a *rate function*, denoted $\lambda(t)$, in the nonstationary case. (The nonstationary Poisson process is also called a *nonhomogeneous Poisson process*.) Note that our nonstationary Poisson process will still possess the property that $N(0) = 0$ and the property of independent increments. The only difference will be that the rate of the process will be a function of time, denoted $\lambda(t)$, rather than a constant λ. In this sense, we can say that the nonhomogeneous process is the general case, and the stationary process is a special case with $\lambda(t) = \lambda$.

For the specific time interval $(0,t]$, again let $N(t)$ denote the random variable counting the number of events occurring in that time interval. If the probability function for $N(t)$ is given by

$$p_{N(t)}(n) = \frac{e^{-m(t)}[m(t)]^n}{n!}, \tag{5.46}$$

for $n = 0,1,2,\cdots$, where

$$m(t) = \int_0^t \lambda(r)\, dr, \tag{5.47}$$

then we say that $N(t)$ is a nonstationary (or nonhomogeneous) Poisson process. Clearly in the special case of $\lambda(t) = \lambda$, a constant, then $m(t) = \lambda t$ and Equation (5.46) simplifies to the familiar Poisson counting process. Furthermore it is clear that

$$E[N(t)] = Var[N(t)] = m(t) \tag{5.48}$$

in the nonstationary case. Since $m(t)$ is the mean of the distribution, it is sometimes called the *mean value function* of the nonstationary process.

For the more general time interval from t_1 to t_2, the random variable $N(t_2) - N(t_1)$ has a Poisson distribution with parameter (mean) equal to

$$m(t_2) - m(t_1) = \int_{t_1}^{t_2} \lambda(r)\, dr, \tag{5.49}$$

so that its probability function is

$$p_{N(t_2)-N(t_1)}(n) = \frac{e^{-[m(t_2)-m(t_1)]}[m(t_2) - m(t_1)]^n}{n!}, \tag{5.50}$$

for $n = 0,1,2,\cdots$.

EXAMPLE 5.11

A nonhomogeneous Poisson process has a rate function given by $\lambda(t) = t$ for $0 \le t \le 10$ and $\lambda(t) = 10$ for $t > 10$. Determine the expected number of events to occur during the interval $(5,15]$.

SOLUTION

The expected number of events is given by the mean value function over the desired interval. We have

$$\begin{aligned} m(15) - m(5) &= \int_5^{10} t\, dt + \int_{10}^{15} 10\, dt \\ &= \tfrac{1}{2}t^2\Big|_5^{10} + 10t\Big|_{10}^{15} \\ &= 50 - 12.50 + 150 - 100 \\ &= 87.50. \end{aligned}$$

❐

Exercise 5-32 shows how to recognize a nonstationary process and how to identify its mean value function.

5.5 SUMMARY

In this chapter we expanded on our brief description of discrete counting distributions found in Section 1.2, to further explore their use as models for claim frequency. Emphasis was given to the binomial, negative binomial, and Poisson distributions, including their recursive relationships and probability generating functions.

We then explored the creation of additional counting distributions via compounding, mixing, and modification at zero.

The important concept of the counting process, especially the Poisson process, was then developed. This concept will have extensive application in Chapters 7 and 8.

5.6 EXERCISES

5.1 Introduction
5.2 Section 1.2 (Discrete Distributions) Revisited

5-1 Derive the α and β values shown in Table 5.1.

5-2 The probability function for a certain discrete random variable obeys the recursive relationship

$$p(k) = \frac{2}{k} \cdot p(k-1),$$

for $k = 1, 2, \cdots$. Find the value of $p(4)$.

5-3 Let X be a discrete random variable whose probability function satisfies Equation (5.22). Given that $Pr(X=0) = Pr(X=1) = .2500$ and $Pr(X=2) = .1875$, find the value of $Pr(X=3)$.

5-4 A discrete distribution has the properties that $p(0) = .50$ and

$$p(x) = c\left(1 + \tfrac{1}{x}\right) \cdot p(x-1),$$

for $x = 1, 2, \cdots$. Find the value of c.

5-5 Suppose the random variable for claim frequency is Poisson, and 50 claims are expected in a one-month period. Claims are categorized by size as small, medium, or large. The probability of a small claim is .50, the probability of a medium claim is .40, and the probability of a large claim is .10. Find the probability that more than three large claims occur in the month.

5-6 Show that

$$p(3) = \frac{P_X'''(0)}{3!}$$

for the Poisson distribution.

5-7 Find the PGF's of (a) the binomial, (b) the negative binomial, and (c) the geometric distributions.

5.3 Creating Additional Counting Distributions

5-8 A compound frequency model has a primary Poisson distribution with parameter λ_1 and a secondary distribution that is also Poisson with parameter λ_2. Find the MGF of the compound random variable S.

5-9 Simplify Equation (5.28) for the special case where the primary distribution N is Poisson with parameter λ.

5-10 Find the starting value $p_S(0)$ for the compound Poisson model of Exercise 5-9.

5-11 Show that the PGF for a compound distribution with primary distribution N and secondary distribution X is given by

$$P_S(s) = P_N[P_X(s)].$$

5-12 Consider a compound frequency model whose primary distribution is negative binomial with $r=2$ and $p=.25$, and whose secondary distribution is Poisson. If $Pr(S{=}0)=.067$, use the result of Exercise 5-11 to find the value of the Poisson parameter λ.

5-13 Find the MGF for each of the following models.

(a) A compound distribution with a negative binomial primary and a Poisson secondary.

(b) A Poisson mixture distribution with a negative binomial mixing distribution.

5-14 A claim frequency distribution is a Poisson mixture with a mean that is uniformly distributed over the interval (0, 5). Find the probability of 2 or more claims.

5-15 The number of claims for an individual insured has a Poisson distribution, whose mean is distributed over the population of insureds according to a gamma distribution. The number of claims for an insured chosen at random from the population has a negative binomial distribution with mean .20 and variance .40. Find the variance of the gamma mixing distribution.

5-16 The number of broken windshield claims per driver per year has a Poisson distribution with parameter λ, where λ follows a gamma distribution with mean 3 and variance 3. Find the probability of no more than 1 broken windshield claim in the next year for a driver selected at random.

5-17 In a game of chance, the player receives a payment of $w=2^n$ if the player has n successes, for $n=0,1,2,\cdots$. The random variable N has a Poisson distribution with mean Λ, where Λ is a random variable uniformly distributed on the interval $(0,4)$. Find the expected payment for this game.

5-18 The beta function is defined as

$$\beta(a,b) \;=\; \int_0^1 t^{a-1}(1-t)^{b-1}\,dt \;=\; \frac{\Gamma(a)\cdot\Gamma(b)}{\Gamma(a+b)},$$

and the (continuous) beta distribution is defined by its PDF as

$$f_T(t) \;=\; \frac{\Gamma(a+b)}{\Gamma(a)\cdot\Gamma(b)}\cdot t^{a-1}(1-t)^{b-1},$$

for $0\le t\le 1$. This would be a natural mixing distribution for the parameter p in a binomial or negative binomial mixture distribution. Find, in terms of gamma functions, the probability function for (a) the binomial - beta mixture, and (b) the negative binomial - beta mixture.

5-19 Show that

$$p_{ZM}(x) \;=\; \big(1-p_{ZM}(0)\big)\cdot p_{ZT}(x),$$

for $x=1,2,\cdots$.

5-20 The probability function for a discrete random variable satisfies the relationship

$$\frac{p(n)}{p(m)} = \frac{m!}{n!},$$

for all $m\ge 0$ and $n\ge 0$. Find the value of $p_{ZM}(1)$, the probability that $x=1$ in the associated zero-modified distribution with $p_{ZM}(0)=.10$.

5-21 From a basic Poisson distribution with parameter λ, find the probability functions for the corresponding (a) zero-truncated distribution and (b) zero-modified distribution with reassigned value $Pr(X=0) = .35$.

5.4 Counting Processes

5-22 Workers Compensation claims occur according to a Poisson process with mean 100 per month. 2% of the claims exceed 30,000. How many full months of data are needed to have at least a 90% chance of observing at least 3 claims that exceed 30,000?

5-23 Losses occur according to a Poisson process with rate 100 per year. Loss amounts are exponentially distributed with mean 500; only losses in excess of 100 produce claims. Find the expected number of claims over a two-year period.

5-24 Events occur according to a Poisson process with rate 2 per hour. What is the probability that the second event occurs after one hour has passed?

5-25 Events occur according to a Poisson process with rate 2 per day.

(a) What is the expected waiting time until the tenth event occurs?

(b) What is the probability that the 11th event will occur more than two days after the 10th event?

5-26 Repeat the reasoning of the Poisson decomposition property in Section 5.1.2, this time applied to the Poisson counting process.

5-27 While taking his daily one-hour walk, a man finds coins on the ground according to a Poisson process at a rate of .50 coins per minute. 60% of the coins are pennies, 20% are nickels, and 20% are dimes.

(a) Given that he collected ten nickels, calculate the expected value (in cents) of the total coins collected.

(b) Calculate the variance of the value of total coins collected.

(c) Calculate the probability of finding at least two dimes in the first ten minutes and at least three dimes in the first twenty minutes.

5-28 Suppose, in Exercise 5-27, the Poisson rate per minute of finding coins on the ground is constant each day, but varies from day to day according to a gamma distribution with mean 2 and variance 4. Calculate the probability of finding exactly one coin during the sixth minute of the walk.

5-29 For the nonhomogeneous Poisson process of Example 5.11, if the 50th event occurs at time 9 find the probability that the 51st event will occur by time 9.10.

5-30 Under a nonhomogeneous Poisson process, the interarrival times are no longer identically exponentially distributed, so the distribution of S_n, the waiting time for the nth event, does not have a gamma distribution. Show that the PDF of S_n in this case is

$$f_{S_n}(t) \;=\; \lambda(t)\cdot e^{-m(t)}\cdot\frac{[m(t)]^{n-1}}{(n-1)!}.$$

5-31 Customers arrive at a store at a Poisson rate that increases linearly from 6 per hour at 1:00pm to 9 per hour at 2:00pm. Calculate the probability that exactly two customers arrive between 1:00pm and 2:00pm.

5-32 During a certain type of epidemic, infections occur in a population at a Poisson rate of 20 per day, but are not immediately identified. The time elapsed from onset of the infection to its identification is an exponential random variable with mean of 7 days. Find the expected number of identified infections over a 10-day period.

CHAPTER SIX

CLAIM SEVERITY MODELS

6.1 INTRODUCTION

In this chapter we continue our expansion of the basic probability material presented in Chapter 1. In Chapter 5 we addressed discrete (counting) distributions and in this chapter we continue our expansion of probability by investigating continuous distributions. In particular, we explore the use of continuous random variables and their distributions specifically as models for the random amount of financial loss or financial payment made under contingent payment arrangements. In this context we refer to the amount of the loss as the *loss severity*, and the probability distribution describing the amount of loss as a *severity distribution*.

We also include a discussion of the use of tabular distributions in place of the more commonly used parametric distributions.

Another specialization of the basic continuous distribution material found in Chapter 1 was addressed in Chapter 5 of Cunningham, et al. [7], in the special context of a *survival distribution*. The reader will discover that severity distributions and survival distributions have much in common, although the two topics are generally presented in slightly different terminology.

Although we discuss here a variety of common distributions and means of creating new distributions from existing ones, we do not yet address the actual fitting of a given distribution to a set of observed data. Both the topic of selecting the best model type and that of estimating the parameters for a given model are deferred to Part IV of the text.

Most of the parametric probability distributions regularly employed by actuaries can be developed through transformations from elementary distributions with which the reader should already be familiar. In this section we identify three such fundamental continuous distributions, from which others may be generated by transformation (see Section 6.2). (Of course these distributions also have applications in their own right.) Two of these fundamental distributions are old friends, and are reviewed in Chapter 1. The third is described in detail in Section 6.1.2.

6.1.1 THE NORMAL AND EXPONENTIAL DISTRIBUTIONS

Along with the continuous uniform distribution, which is not widely used to generate other distributions, the two most basic probability distributions are the *normal distribution* and the *exponential distribution*. The properties of both these distributions were reviewed in Chapter 1. The reader may accept the fundamental nature of the normal distribution as given. We also saw in Chapter 5 that the exponential distribution is closely related to the very important

Poisson counting distribution. Because the exponential distribution arises so naturally in this and other contexts, we treat it as fundamental as well.

6.1.2 THE PARETO DISTRIBUTION

A third fundamental distribution that is useful for modeling severity of loss is the *Pareto distribution*. An important distinguishing feature of the Pareto distribution, compared to the exponential distribution, is that it allows for a higher probability of very high loss amounts. That is, it has a heavier right-hand tail than the exponential distribution.[1] Although the Pareto distribution can itself be produced from the exponential distribution through a series of random variable transformations, we prefer to treat it as one of our three fundamental distributions.

The Pareto distribution is defined over all positive values of x by the density function

$$f_X(x) = \frac{\alpha \cdot \theta^\alpha}{(x+\theta)^{\alpha+1}}, \tag{6.1}$$

where $\alpha > 0$ and $\theta > 0$. The parameter α is called the *shape parameter* because it affects the "shape" of the cumulative distribution function by impacting how much of the probability is concentrated at low values, and θ is called the *scale parameter* of the distribution for reasons that will be made clear later in the chapter. By integrating the PDF given by Equation (6.1) the CDF is found to be

$$F_X(x) = 1 - \left(\frac{\theta}{x+\theta}\right)^\alpha. \tag{6.2}$$

When $\alpha > 1$ the expected value exists and is given by

$$E[X] = \frac{\theta}{\alpha - 1} \tag{6.3a}$$

and for $\alpha > 2$ the second moment exists as well and is given by

$$E[X^2] = \frac{2\theta^2}{(\alpha-1)(\alpha-2)}, \tag{6.3b}$$

so the variance, when it exists, is

$$\begin{aligned} Var(X) &= E[X^2] - (E[X])^2 \\ &= \frac{2\theta^2}{(\alpha-1)(\alpha-2)} - \frac{\theta^2}{(\alpha-1)^2} = \frac{\alpha\theta^2}{(\alpha-1)^2(\alpha-2)}. \end{aligned} \tag{6.4}$$

The moment generating function of the Pareto distribution does not exist, since $E[e^{tX}] = \infty$ for any positive t. The facts that $E[X]$ and $Var(X)$ do not exist for small values of α are

[1] The importance of accurately modeling the probability of high loss amounts cannot be overemphasized, in light of the severe effect of high loss amounts on an insurer's financial results.

symptoms of how heavy the tail is for this type of distribution, especially for small values of α. This is also the reason why the moment generating function does not exist.

Figure 6.1 shows the density functions for (a) an exponential distribution with parameter $\beta = .02$, (b) a Pareto distribution with parameters $\alpha = 2$ and $\theta = 50$, and (c) a Pareto distribution with parameters $\alpha = 6$ and $\theta = 250$. Note that all three distributions have expected value 50.

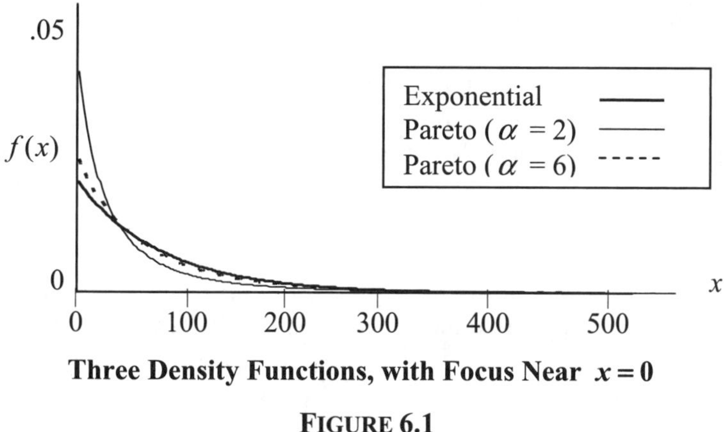

Three Density Functions, with Focus Near $x = 0$

FIGURE 6.1

Figure 6.1 shows the weight of each distribution near $x = 0$, but creates a very misleading impression of the relative sizes of the tails of each distribution. Figure 6.2 is the same graph but with a different scaling.

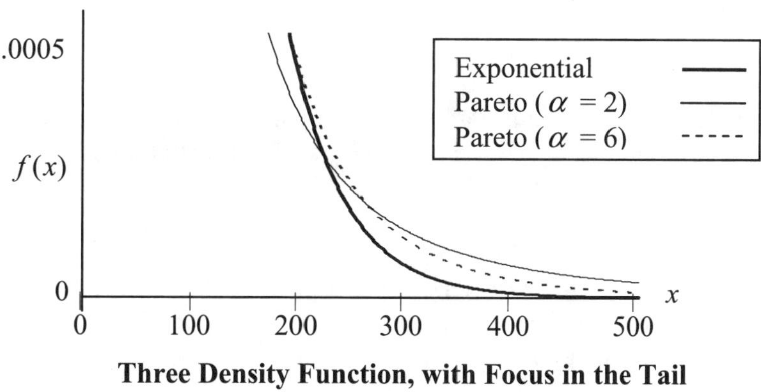

Three Density Function, with Focus in the Tail

FIGURE 6.2

Figure 6.2 makes the tail behavior more apparent. The exponential distribution has almost no probability mass to the right of $x = 500$, and the Pareto distribution with $\alpha = 6$ has very little compared to the Pareto distribution with $\alpha = 2$. For the exponential distribution, in fact, more than 99.9% of the probability is to the left of $x = 500$, whereas the corresponding percentages for the Pareto distribution are approximately 98.2% with $\alpha = 6$ and only 82.6% with $\alpha = 2$. The Pareto distributions have much higher probabilities associated with values of x above 500. This demonstrates their heavier tails relative to the exponential distribution.

6.1.3 ANALYTIC MEASURES OF TAIL WEIGHT

In Section 6.1.2 we informally observed the relative right-hand tail weights of the exponential and Pareto distributions (see Figure 6.2). Because this tail weight is an important property of severity distributions, we should develop more rigorous analytic methods for measuring it and for comparing tail weights of alternative distributions. For now, we will illustrate these analytic measures by applying them only to the exponential and Pareto distributions. After additional distributions are introduced in Section 6.2, we will apply our tail weight measures to them as well. (See Section 6.4.)

One such analytic measure of tail weight is the existence of the moments of the severity distribution. As stated in Section 6.1.2, moments of the Pareto distribution might not exist (depending on the value of the shape parameter α), whereas all moments do exist for the exponential distribution. The existence of moments implies a lighter right-hand tail, and the nonexistence of some (or all) moments implies a heavier tail.

A second measure of the relative tail weights of the distributions of two random variables X and Y is provided by evaluating the limit of the ratio of their density functions, which is given by

$$L = \lim_{x\to\infty} \frac{f_X(x)}{f_Y(x)}. \tag{6.5}$$

If this limit is infinite, we say that X has a heavier tail than has Y, and is thus more appropriate to model loss distributions with relatively large probabilities of very high loss amounts. If the limit is 0, we conclude that Y has the heavier tail. If the limit is positive but finite, we can think of the tails as being proportionate.

EXAMPLE 6.1

Show that, in general, if X is any Pareto random variable and Y is any exponential random variable, the distribution of X has a heavier tail than the distribution of Y.

SOLUTION

The Pareto distribution with parameters $\alpha > 0$ and $\theta > 0$ has PDF given by Equation (6.1), and the exponential distribution with parameter $\beta > 0$ has PDF given by Equation (1.50a). The limit of the ratio of the PDF's is

$$L = \lim_{x\to\infty} \frac{f_X(x)}{f_Y(x)} = \lim_{x\to\infty} \frac{\frac{\alpha\cdot\theta^\alpha}{(x+\theta)^{\alpha+1}}}{\beta\cdot e^{-\beta x}} = \frac{\alpha\cdot\theta^\alpha}{\beta}\cdot \lim_{x\to\infty} \frac{e^{\beta x}}{(x+\theta)^{\alpha+1}} = \infty.$$

The limit can be seen to be infinite either by repeated applications of L'Hospital's rule or by recognizing that $e^{\beta x}$ grows much more quickly than any power of x. Therefore Pareto distributions have heavier tails than exponential distributions, as already known. ❐

An equivalent approach, possessing the same limit, would be to evaluate the limit of the ratio of the survival functions of X and Y. This is left as Exercise 6-4.

A third measure of tail weight is provided by the *hazard rate function*, defined as the ratio of the density function to the survival function. Heavy-tailed distributions have decreasing HRFs, and light-tailed distributions have increasing HRFs. For the Pareto distribution, the HRF is

$$\begin{aligned}\lambda_X(x) = \frac{f_X(x)}{S_X(x)} &= \frac{-S'_X(x)}{S_X(x)} \\ &= -\frac{d}{dx}\ln S_X(x) \\ &= -\frac{d}{dx}\left[\ln \theta^{\alpha}(x+\theta)^{-\alpha}\right] \\ &= -\frac{d}{dx}\left[\ln \theta^{\alpha} - \alpha\cdot\ln(x+\theta)\right] \\ &= \frac{\alpha}{x+\theta},\end{aligned}$$

which is a decreasing function of x. This shows once again that the Pareto distribution has a heavier tail than the exponential distribution, which has a constant hazard rate function.

A fourth measure of tail weight, the mean excess loss function, will be considered (see Section 6.4) after that function is defined in Section 6.3.1.

6.2 GENERATING ADDITIONAL DISTRIBUTIONS

Starting with our set of only three fundamental loss random variables, namely the normal, exponential, and Pareto, we can generate a very wide set of parametric random variables using the various operations described in this section.

6.2.1 SUMMATION

Summation of several identically distributed random variables is of critical importance in modeling aggregate loss amounts, as we have seen in Chapter 1 and will see again in Chapter 7. Here, however, we are concerned only with the generation of a new random variable for use as a model of a single loss amount. For our purposes, the properties of sums of random variables have already been reviewed in Chapter 1 and need not be discussed further here. One useful example of a sum of random variables that may be used as a single severity distribution is the *gamma distribution* with parameters β and α (where α is an integer) that was mentioned in Section 1.5.2. The sum of α identically distributed independent exponential random variables is a gamma random variable.[2] Other properties of the gamma distribution were covered in Section 1.3.4.

[2] Note that α must be an integer only when the gamma distribution is derived from the exponential by summation. (In general, α is constrained to be positive, but not necessarily an integer.) The gamma distribution with integral α is also called the *Erlang distribution*.

6.2.2 SCALAR MULTIPLICATION

In this and the following two sections we will consider the transformation $Y = g(X)$, where X has a known distribution and g is a one-to-one invertible operation used to produce the new random variable Y. In all cases we assume that $Pr(X \geq 0) = 1$. The reader should recall from probability theory that

$$F_Y(y) = Pr(Y \leq y) = Pr[g(X) \leq y] = Pr[X \leq g^{-1}(y)] = F_X[g^{-1}(y)],$$

so, when the transformation is increasing, we have

$$F_Y(y) = F_X\left[g^{-1}(y)\right]. \tag{6.6a}$$

If the transformation is decreasing, then

$$F_Y(y) = 1 - F_X\left[\, g^{-1}(y) \,\right]. \tag{6.6b}$$

Differentiating both sides with respect to y and applying the chain rule produces the corresponding relationship between the PDF's of X and Y as

$$f_Y(y) = f_X\left[g^{-1}(y)\right] \cdot \left| \frac{d}{dy} g^{-1}(y) \right|. \tag{6.7a}$$

Now for *scalar multiplication* of a random variable we have $Y = c \cdot X$, where $c > 0$ is a constant. Then $g^{-1}(y) = \frac{y}{c}$, and Equation (6.7a) for the PDF of Y becomes

$$f_Y(y) = f_X\left(\frac{y}{c}\right) \cdot \frac{1}{c}. \tag{6.7b}$$

Scalar multiplication can be used to show that the entire family of exponential distributions arises from the standard exponential model, with mean 1, defined by $f_X(x) = e^{-x}$. Then if $Y = c \cdot X$, we find

$$f_Y(y) = \frac{1}{c} \cdot e^{-y/c}, \tag{6.8}$$

which is the alternative form of the exponential density function given by Equation (1.50b) with $\theta = c$. Furthermore it can be shown (see Example 6.2) that if X is *any* exponential random variable (not just the standard exponential), then the random variable $Y = c \cdot X$, where $c > 0$, has an exponential distribution as well. Thus the family of exponential distributions is closed under scalar multiplication. A family of distributions that is closed under scalar multiplication is called a *scale family*.

It is left to the reader (see Exercise 6-6) to show that the family of normal distributions also forms a scale family.

A scale family is said to have a *scale parameter* θ if whenever X is a member of the family, then so is $Y = c{\cdot}X$ (where $c > 0$), and the parameters of Y are the same as those of X except that θ is replaced by $c{\cdot}\theta$. In Exercise 6-7 the reader will show that the family of Pareto distributions has a scale parameter. Scale families and scale parameters are particularly useful in dealing with the effects of inflation on loss severity distributions (see Section 6.3.5).

EXAMPLE 6.2

(a) Show that the exponential distribution with PDF given by Equation (1.50a) belongs to a scale family, but the parameter β is *not* a scale parameter.

(b) Show that for the exponential distribution with PDF given by Equation (1.50b), the parameter θ *is* a scale parameter.

SOLUTION

(a) If X has the density function given by Equation (1.50a), and $Y = c{\cdot}X$ so $g^{-1}(y) = \frac{y}{c}$, then the density of Y is

$$f_Y(y) = \beta \cdot e^{-\beta(y/c)} \cdot \frac{1}{c} = \beta' \cdot e^{-\beta' y},$$

where $\beta' = \frac{\beta}{c}$, which is again an exponential density so the exponential belongs to a scale family. But we see that $\beta' = \frac{\beta}{c}$, not $\beta' = c{\cdot}\beta$ as required for a scale parameter.

(b) When X has the density function given by Equation (1.50b), and $Y = c{\cdot}X$ so $g^{-1}(y) = \frac{y}{c}$, then the density of Y is

$$f_Y(y) = \frac{1}{\theta} \cdot e^{-(y/c)/\theta} \cdot \frac{1}{c} = \frac{1}{\theta'} \cdot e^{-y/\theta'},$$

where $\theta' = c{\cdot}\theta$. This shows that the parameter θ is a scale parameter. (This is a major reason why the Equation (1.50b) form of the exponential distribution is used in the context of loss severity models.) ❐

6.2.3 POWER OPERATIONS

As the name implies, the *power operation* involves raising a random variable to a power. We consider both the cases of $Y = X^{1/\tau}$ and $Y = X^{-1/\tau}$, where $\tau > 0$ in both cases. In the first case, where the exponent of X is positive, we say the new random variable Y has a *transformed X distribution*. In the second case, where the exponent of X is negative, we say the new random variable Y has an *inverse transformed X distribution*. In the special case where $Y = X^{-1}$, we say that Y has an *inverse X distribution*.

In the transformed case, where $y = x^{1/\tau}$ so that $x = g^{-1}(y) = y^{\tau}$, the PDF of Y is

$$f_Y(y) = \tau \cdot y^{\tau-1} \cdot f_X(y^{\tau}). \tag{6.9a}$$

In the inverse transformed case, where $y = x^{-1/\tau}$ so that $x = g^{-1}(y) = y^{-\tau}$, the PDF of Y is

$$f_Y(y) = \tau \cdot y^{-\tau-1} \cdot f_X(y^{-\tau}). \tag{6.9b}$$

In the inverse case, where $y = x^{-1}$ so that $x = g^{-1}(y) = y^{-1}$, the PDF of Y is

$$f_Y(y) = y^{-2} \cdot f_X(y^{-1}). \tag{6.9c}$$

(The reader should verify the accuracy of Equations (6.9a), (6.9b), and (6.9c).)

EXAMPLE 6.3

(a) Derive the PDF of the inverse exponential distribution starting with the Equation (1.50a) form of the exponential density. Does this inverse exponential distribution possess a scale parameter?

(b) Repeat part (a) starting with the Equation (1.50b) form of the exponential density.

SOLUTION

(a) For the inverse transformation, $Y = X^{-1}$ so $g^{-1}(y) = y^{-1}$ and $\left|\frac{d}{dy} g^{-1}(y)\right| = y^{-2}$. The density of Y is given by Equation (6.9c). If X has the exponential density given by Equation (1.50a), then the density of Y is

$$f_Y(y) = \beta \cdot e^{-\beta/y} \cdot y^{-2} = \frac{\beta \cdot e^{-\beta/y}}{y^2}. \tag{6.10a}$$

Now let $Z = c \cdot Y$ so $g^{-1}(z) = \frac{z}{c}$. Then the density of Z is

$$f_Z(z) = \frac{\beta \cdot e^{-\beta/(z/c)}}{(z/c)^2} \cdot \frac{1}{c} = \frac{(c^2 \cdot \beta) \cdot e^{-c \cdot \beta/z}}{c \cdot z^2} = \frac{\beta' \cdot e^{-\beta'/z}}{z^2},$$

where $\beta' = c \cdot \beta$. This is again an inverse exponential density with $\beta' = c \cdot \beta$, which shows that this inverse exponential distribution belongs to a scale family and the parameter β is a scale parameter. Equation (6.10a) will be our preferred form of the inverse exponential distribution.

(b) When X has the density given by Equation (1.50b), we find

$$f_Y(y) = \frac{1}{\theta} \cdot e^{-(y^{-1}/\theta)} \cdot y^{-2} = \frac{\frac{1}{\theta} \cdot e^{-1/\theta y}}{y^2}, \tag{6.10b}$$

which is again the inverse exponential density with $\beta = \frac{1}{\theta}$. To test for scale parameter, we again let $Z = c \cdot Y$ so $g^{-1}(z) = \frac{z}{c}$. Then the density of Z is

$$f_Z(z) = \frac{\frac{1}{\theta} \cdot e^{-(1/\theta)(c/z)}}{(z/c)^2} \cdot \frac{1}{c} = \frac{\frac{c^2}{\theta} \cdot e^{-(c/\theta)/z}}{c \cdot z^2} = \frac{\frac{1}{\theta'} \cdot e^{-1/\theta' z}}{z^2},$$

where $\theta' = \frac{\theta}{c}$ rather than $c \cdot \theta$, so θ is not a scale parameter in this form of the inverse exponential distribution. ❐

Since the form of the inverse exponential developed in part (a) of Example 6.3 possesses a scale parameter, it should be considered the preferred form. Only this form is included in the summary of severity distributions in Table 6.1.

EXAMPLE 6.4

Let X be exponentially distributed with parameter β, and let $Y = X^{1/\tau}$. Find the CDF and PDF of the transformed exponential random variable Y.

SOLUTION

We have

$$F_Y(y) = F_X\left[g^{-1}(y)\right] = F_X(y^\tau) = 1 - e^{-\beta \cdot y^\tau}. \tag{6.11a}$$

Then by differentiation we find

$$f_Y(y) = (-e^{-\beta \cdot y^\tau})(-\tau \cdot \beta \cdot y^{\tau-1}) = \tau \cdot \beta \cdot y^{\tau-1} \cdot e^{-\beta \cdot y^\tau}. \tag{6.11b}$$

❐

A special case of the transformed exponential distribution, called the *Weibull distribution*, results when we let $\beta = 1/\theta^\tau$, producing

$$F_Y(y) = 1 - e^{-(y/\theta)^\tau} \tag{6.12a}$$

and, by differentiation,

$$f_Y(y) = -e^{-(y/\theta)^\tau} \cdot -\tau(y/\theta)^{\tau-1} \cdot \frac{1}{\theta} = \frac{\tau(y/\theta)^\tau \cdot e^{-(y/\theta)^\tau}}{y}, \tag{6.12b}$$

where $\tau > 0$ and $\theta > 0$. The family of Weibull distributions is a scale family with a scale parameter (see Exercise 6-9).

6.2.4 EXPONENTIATION AND THE LOGNORMAL DISTRIBUTION

The final type of algebraic transformation we consider is the *exponentiation operation* where $Y = e^X$. In this case we have

$$F_Y(y) = F_X(\ln y) \tag{6.13a}$$

for the CDF of Y and

$$f_Y(y) = f_X(\ln y) \cdot \frac{1}{y} \tag{6.13b}$$

for the PDF of Y. The moments of Y are given by

$$E\left[Y^k\right] = E\left[(e^X)^k\right] = E\left[e^{kX}\right] = M_X(k), \tag{6.14}$$

where $M_X(t)$ is the MGF of the random variable X.

This is the technique used to create the *lognormal distribution* from the normal distribution, as shown in the following example.

EXAMPLE 6.5

Let X be normally distributed with mean μ and variance σ^2. Find the PDF, mean, and variance of the lognormal random variable $Y = e^X$.

SOLUTION

The exponential transformation gives us

$$f_Y(y) = \frac{1}{y} \cdot f_X(\ln y).$$

We know from Equation (1.43a) that

$$f_X(x) = \frac{1}{\sigma\sqrt{2\pi}} \cdot e^{-\frac{1}{2}\left(\frac{x-\mu}{\sigma}\right)^2},$$

so we have

$$f_Y(y) = \frac{1}{y} \cdot \frac{1}{\sigma\sqrt{2\pi}} \cdot e^{-\frac{1}{2}\left(\frac{\ln y-\mu}{\sigma}\right)^2}. \tag{6.15}$$

The mean is given by

$$E[Y] = M_X(1) = e^{\mu+\sigma^2/2} \tag{6.16a}$$

and the second moment is given by

$$E[Y^2] = M_X(2) = e^{2\mu+2\sigma^2}, \tag{6.16b}$$

so the variance is given by

$$Var(Y) = e^{2\mu+2\sigma^2} - (e^{\mu+\sigma^2/2})^2 = e^{2\mu}(e^{2\sigma^2} - e^{\sigma^2}). \tag{6.16c}$$

❒

Probability calculations from a lognormal distribution are made from a table of standard normal values, just as they are for a normal distribution. In general, for any continuous random variable X, we know that

$$Pr(a < X \le b) = Pr(X \le b) - Pr(X \le a) = F_X(b) - F_X(a).$$

The CDF of the lognormal distribution is given by

$$F_X(x) = \Phi\left(\frac{\ln x - \mu}{\sigma}\right), \tag{6.17}$$

where $\Phi(z)$ is the CDF of the standard normal random variable. (The derivation of Equation (6.17) is left as Exercise 6-13.)

EXAMPLE 6.6

Let X have a lognormal distribution with parameters $\mu = 7$ and $\sigma = 1.50$. Find the probability that X exceeds 4000.

SOLUTION

We have

$$\begin{aligned} Pr(X > 4000) &= 1 - Pr(X \le 4000) \\ &= 1 - Pr(\ln X \le \ln 4000) \\ &= 1 - Pr\left(\frac{\ln X - 7}{1.50} \le \frac{\ln 4000 - 7}{1.50}\right) = 1 - \Phi(.863) = .1941. \end{aligned}$$

❒

The lognormal distribution is often used to model loss amounts under various forms of property and casualty insurance. It is also extensively used as a model for stock prices in financial analysis.

6.2.5 SUMMARY OF SEVERITY DISTRIBUTIONS

By this point of the text we have identified nine continuous distributions, all with nonnegative domains, that might be used to model claim severity. The first three (uniform (with $a = 0$), exponential, and gamma) are old friends with which the reader should be familiar from a prior study of probability. (They are also reviewed in Chapter 1.) The fourth distribution, the Pareto, was presented in Section 6.1.2. The final five (inverse exponential, Weibull (a member of the transformed exponential family), inverse Weibull, inverse Pareto, and lognormal) were developed earlier in this section or in its exercises.

Table 6.1 summarizes many of the details of these nine distributions. The second column of the table shows the location in the text where the distribution is derived or reviewed. An additional important detail of a severity distribution, the limited expected value (LEV), is described in Sections 6.3.2 and 6.3.3. Expressions for the LEV for each of the nine distributions in Table 6.1 are given in Table 6.2 at the end of Section 6.3.3. These distributions are also summarized in Appendix A.

TABLE 6.1

Summary of Severity Distributions

Distribution	Reference	PDF	Parameters
Uniform	Section 1.3.1	$\frac{1}{\omega}$	$\omega>0$
Exponential	Section 1.3.3	$\beta\cdot e^{-\beta x}$ or $\frac{1}{\theta}\cdot e^{-x/\theta}$ *	$\beta>0$ or $\theta>0$
Gamma	Section 1.3.4 and Exercise 6-5	$\frac{\beta^{\alpha}}{\Gamma(\alpha)}\cdot x^{\alpha-1}\, e^{-\beta x}$ or $\frac{(x/\theta)^{\alpha}\cdot e^{-x/\theta}}{x\cdot\Gamma(\alpha)}$ *	$\alpha>0, \beta>0$ or $\alpha>0, \theta>0$
Pareto	Section 6.1.2	$\frac{\alpha\cdot\theta^{\alpha}}{(x+\theta)^{\alpha+1}}$	$\alpha>0, \theta>0$
Inverse Exponential	Example 6.3	$\frac{\beta\cdot e^{-\beta/x}}{x^2}$ *	$\beta>0$
Weibull (Transformed Exponential)	Example 6.4	$\frac{\tau(x/\theta)^{\tau}\cdot e^{-(x/\theta)^{\tau}}}{x}$	$\tau>0, \theta>0$
Inverse Weibull	Exercise 6-10	$\frac{\tau(\theta/x)^{\tau}\cdot e^{-(\theta/x)^{\tau}}}{x}$	$\tau>0, \theta>0$
Inverse Pareto	Exercise 6-12	$\frac{\alpha\theta\cdot x^{\alpha-1}}{(x+\theta)^{\alpha+1}}$	$\alpha>0, \theta>0$
Lognormal	Section 6.2.4	$\frac{1}{y}\cdot\frac{1}{\sigma\sqrt{2\pi}}\cdot e^{-\frac{1}{2}\left(\frac{\ln y-\mu}{\sigma}\right)^2}$	$\sigma>0$

* These are the preferred forms for the exponential, gamma, and inverse exponential densities, respectively, since these forms possess a scale parameter.

TABLE 6.1

Summary of Severity Distributions			
CDF	**$E[X]$**	**$E[X^2]$**	**Distribution**
$\frac{x}{\omega}$	$\frac{\omega}{2}$	$\frac{\omega^2}{3}$	Uniform
$1-e^{-\beta x}$ or $1-e^{-x/\theta}$	$\frac{1}{\beta}$ or θ	$\frac{2}{\beta^2}$ or $2\theta^2$	Exponential
$\Gamma(\alpha;\beta x)^*$ or $\Gamma(\alpha;x/\theta)^*$	$\frac{\alpha}{\beta}$ or $\alpha\theta$	$\frac{\alpha(\alpha+1)}{\beta^2}$ or $\alpha(\alpha+1)\theta^2$	Gamma
$1-\left(\frac{\theta}{x+\theta}\right)^\alpha$	$\frac{\theta}{\alpha-1}$ (if $\alpha>1$)	$\frac{2\theta^2}{(\alpha-1)(\alpha-2)}$ (if $\alpha>2$)	Pareto
$e^{-\beta/x}$	Does Not Exist	Does Not Exist	Inverse Exponential
$1-e^{-(x/\theta)^\tau}$	$\theta\cdot\Gamma(1+\frac{1}{\tau})$	$\theta^2\cdot\Gamma(1+\frac{2}{\tau})$	Weibull (Transformed Exponential)
$e^{-(\theta/x)^\tau}$	$\theta\cdot\Gamma(1-\frac{1}{\tau})$ (if $\tau>1$)	$\theta^2\cdot\Gamma(1-\frac{2}{\tau})$ (if $\tau>2$)	Inverse Weibull
$\left(\frac{x}{x+\theta}\right)^\alpha$	Does Not Exist	Does Not Exist	Inverse Pareto
$\Phi\left(\frac{\ln x-\mu}{\sigma}\right)$	$e^{\mu+\sigma^2/2}$	$e^{2\mu+2\sigma^2}$	Lognormal

* The CDF of the gamma distribution is expressed as an incomplete gamma function. See Section 1.3.4 and Appendix K for a review of this function.

6.2.6 MIXTURES OF DISTRIBUTIONS

When we model loss severity in this text, we accept the appropriate severity distribution as given and assume the loss amount is then a random draw from that single distribution. *Mixing of distributions* allows us to make the severity distribution itself a random variable. We consider two types of mixture severity distributions:

(1) *Discrete mixing*: Each of several severity distributions is specified, and each is assigned a probability a_i of being the appropriate distribution for a given severity, where $\sum_i a_i = 1$. The appropriate distribution is then the ith one, with probability a_i.

(2) *Continuous mixing*: A parametric severity distribution is specified, but the parameter is not assumed to be a fixed constant. Instead, the parameter itself is treated as a random variable giving rise to a continuous spectrum of distributions, one for each possible value of the parameter. The result is a new parametric family of distributions.

In Section 5.2.2 we considered the case where the primary distribution was the discrete Poisson distribution, as we developed the idea of mixture frequency models. In this section the primary distribution will be continuous, and the mixing distribution can be either discrete or continuous, as we develop mixture severity models.

We let $f_{X|\Lambda}(x\,|\,\lambda)$ denote the PDF for the continuous random variable X with parameter λ. If λ is viewed as a realization of the random variable Λ with PDF given by $f_\Lambda(\lambda)$, then the joint density of X and Λ is given by

$$f_{X,\Lambda}(x,\lambda) = f_{X|\Lambda}(x\,|\,\lambda)\cdot f_\Lambda(\lambda) \tag{6.15}$$

and the marginal (unconditional) density of X is given by

$$f_X(x) = \int_\Lambda f_{X|\Lambda}(x\,|\,\lambda)\cdot f_\Lambda(\lambda)\,d\lambda \tag{6.16a}$$

if Λ is continuous and

$$f_X(x) = \sum_\Lambda f_{X|\Lambda}(x\,|\,\lambda)\cdot p_\Lambda(\lambda) \tag{6.16b}$$

if Λ is discrete.

When working with mixture distributions, it is useful to keep in mind the double expectation theorem reviewed in Section 1.4. In the notation of our current discussion we have

$$E\left[X^k\right] = E_\Lambda\left[E\left[\,X^k\middle|\Lambda\,\right]\right] \tag{6.17a}$$

which has the important corollary

$$Var(X) = E_\Lambda[Var(X\,|\,\Lambda)] + Var_\Lambda\left(E[X\,|\,\Lambda]\right). \tag{6.17b}$$

Note that when the mixing distribution is discrete, mixing is just the weighted average of two or more probability densities where the weights are positive and sum to 1.

EXAMPLE 6.7

A refrigerator manufacturer provides lifetime guarantees on both its Standard and Deluxe models. Repair costs for the Deluxe model follow an exponential distribution X_1 with parameter $\beta_1 = .01$ and repair costs for the Standard model follow an exponential distribution X_2 with parameter $\beta_2 = .02$. Each required repair has probability .30 of being on a Deluxe model and probability .70 of being on a Standard model.

(a) Find the PDF for the repair cost of a single repair selected at random.

(b) Find the expected cost and the variance in the cost of each repair.

SOLUTION

(a) This is a discrete mixture with $p(.01) = .30$ and $p(.02) = .70$. Then the PDF for a repair cost selected at random is the weighted average of the separate PDF's, producing

$$f_X(x) = (.30)(.01e^{-.01x}) + (.70)(.02e^{-.02x}) = .003e^{-.01x} + .014e^{-.02x}.$$

(b) The expected cost is

$$E[X] = \int_0^\infty x \cdot f_X(x)\, dx = 65,$$

which is equal to $.30E[X_1] + .70E[X_2]$. In the case of a discrete mixing distribution, it is easy to show (see Exercise 6-16) that for any integer k

$$E[X^k] = \sum_{\Lambda} p_\Lambda(\lambda) \cdot E\left[X^k \mid \Lambda = \lambda\right]. \tag{6.18}$$

There are two possible approaches to calculating the variance. The first is to note that $E[X_i^2] = \frac{2}{\beta_i^2}$, and then use Equation (6.18) to find

$$E[X^2] = (.30)\left(\frac{2}{.0001}\right) + (.70)\left(\frac{2}{.0004}\right) = 9500.$$

Then the variance is

$$Var(X) = 9500 - (65)^2 = 5275.$$

The second approach is to use the second part of the double expectation theorem given by Equation (6.17b). We have

$$Var(X) = E_\Lambda\left[Var(X \mid \Lambda = \lambda)\right] + Var_\Lambda\left(E[X \mid \Lambda = \lambda]\right) = E_\Lambda\left[\frac{1}{\lambda^2}\right] + Var_\Lambda\left(\frac{1}{\lambda}\right).$$

Then we calculate

$$E_\Lambda\left[\frac{1}{\lambda^2}\right] = (.30)\left(\frac{1}{.0001}\right)+(.70)\left(\frac{1}{.0004}\right) = 4750$$

and

$$Var_\Lambda\left(\frac{1}{\lambda}\right) = E_\Lambda\left[\frac{1}{\lambda^2}\right]-\left(E_\Lambda\left[\frac{1}{\lambda}\right]\right)^2 = 4750-\left[(.30)\left(\frac{1}{.01}\right)+(.70)\left(\frac{1}{.02}\right)\right]^2 = 525.$$

Finally we have

$$Var(X) = 4750+525 = 5275,$$

as before. ❐

The following example illustrates a severity mixture with a continuous mixing distribution.

EXAMPLE 6.8

Consider an exponential-gamma mixture model, where the gamma mixing distribution has parameters $\alpha=2$ and $\beta=.50$. Find $Pr(X\leq.50)$ in the marginal (unconditional) distribution.

SOLUTION

Let λ denote the exponential parameter. Then we have

$$f_{X|\Lambda}(x\,|\,\lambda) = \lambda\cdot e^{-\lambda x}$$

and

$$f_\Lambda(\lambda) = \frac{(.50)^2}{\Gamma(2)}\cdot\lambda\cdot e^{-.50\lambda} = .25\lambda\cdot e^{-.50\lambda},$$

since $\Gamma(2)=1$. Then the unconditional probability is given by

$$\begin{aligned}Pr(X\leq.50) &= \int_0^\infty(1-e^{-.50\lambda})(.25\lambda\cdot e^{-.50\lambda})\,d\lambda \\ &= .25\left[\int_0^\infty\lambda\cdot e^{-.50\lambda}\,d\lambda-\int_0^\infty\lambda\cdot e^{-\lambda}\,d\lambda\right].\end{aligned}$$

Both integrals are evaluated using integration by parts. The first evaluates to 4 and the second to 1, so we find

$$Pr(X\leq.50) = .25(4-1) = .75.$$

❐

6.2.7 FRAILTY MODELS

An interesting example of a mixture distribution is that of the *frailty model.* This model arises more naturally within the context of a survival model, rather than that of a loss severity model, but we choose to present it at this point of the text since its mathematics is essentially that of a mixture distribution.

Recall that the hazard rate function (HRF), denoted by $\lambda_X(x)$, is the ratio of the density function to the survival function. Rather than define the HRF of X by this function, we introduce a *measure of uncertainty* about the HRF by allowing it to be $\delta \cdot \lambda_X(x)$ instead, where $\delta > 0$. (Note that $\delta > 1$ would enlarge the hazard, whereas $\delta < 1$ would reduce it.)

In turn, the value of δ is a realization of a random variable Δ, which we call the *frailty random variable.* (It is really our confidence in fixing the HRF of X that is "frail" and the use of $\delta \cdot \lambda_X(x)$ is meant to quantify the extent of that frailty.) The distribution of Δ is the *frailty distribution* for the model.

Then given $\Delta = \delta$, the HRF $\delta \cdot \lambda_X(x)$ is a conditional HRF, so we have

$$\lambda_{X|\Delta}(x \mid \delta) = \delta \cdot \lambda_X(x). \tag{6.19a}$$

The conditional survival function of X, given $\Delta = \delta$, is therefore

$$\begin{aligned} S_{X|\Delta}(x \mid \delta) &= \exp\left[-\int_0^x \lambda_{X|\Delta}(y \mid \delta)\, dy\right] \\ &= \exp\left[-\int_0^x \delta \cdot \lambda_X(y)\, dy\right] \\ &= e^{-\delta \cdot S_X(x)}, \end{aligned} \tag{6.19b}$$

where $S_X(x)$ would be the SDF of X if the distribution of X were based on the HRF given by $\lambda_X(x)$ without introducing the uncertainty (or frailty) embodied in the distribution of Δ.

Finally, we can then find the unconditional (marginal) SDF of X in the usual way as

$$S_X^F(x) = \int_0^\infty S_{X|\Delta}(x \mid \delta) \cdot f_\Delta(\delta)\, d\delta, \tag{6.20a}$$

where $f_\Delta(\delta)$ denotes the PDF of the frailty random variable Δ. Note that we must distinguish the marginal SDF of X *in the presence of the frailty concept* from the SDF of X without introducing this concept (i.e., if based on the HRF $\lambda_X(x)$). Since the latter has always been denoted by $S_X(x)$, we use $S_X^F(x)$ to denote the marginal SDF of X in this special circumstance.

Several special cases can be observed. For example, if we let $\lambda_X(x) = \lambda$, a constant, so that $\lambda_{X|\Delta}(x \mid \delta) = \delta \cdot \lambda$ is also a constant, then the conditional distribution of X given $\Delta = \delta$ is exponential and the overall mixture distribution is an exponential-Δ mixture, where Δ identifies the mixing distribution.

The SDF of X with the frailty concept incorporated, which we denote by $S_X^F(x)$, is easily determined from the MGF of the frailty random variable Δ. The integral in Equation (6.20a) expresses the expected value, with respect to Δ, of $S_{X|\Delta}(x\,|\,\delta)$. That is,

$$S_X^F(x) = E_\Delta[S_{X|\Delta}(x\,|\,\delta)]. \tag{6.20b}$$

Substituting for $S_{X|\Delta}(x\,|\,\delta)$ from Equation (6.19b) we have

$$\begin{aligned} S_X^F(x) &= E_\Delta\left[e^{-\delta \cdot S_X(x)}\right] \\ &= M_\Delta[-S_X(x)]. \end{aligned} \tag{6.20c}$$

6.2.8 SPLICED DISTRIBUTIONS

A *spliced distribution* is one for which the form of the distribution is different in different portions of the domain of the random variable. Thus if the distribution is that of loss amounts, we would be using different types of distributions for smaller versus larger losses.

The simplest example is that of a two-component spliced distribution, breaking at the point $x=c$, where the density $f_1(x)$ applies in the interval $0<x<c$ and the density $f_2(x)$ applies in the interval $c<x<\infty$. This is illustrated in the following figure.

$f_1(x)$ $f_2(x)$

0 c

Two-Component Spliced Distribution

FIGURE 6.3

Both $f_1(x)$ and $f_2(x)$ must be legitimate density functions within their respective intervals. Then the density function for the spliced distribution is

$$f_X(x) = \begin{cases} k_1 \cdot f_1(x) & \text{for } 0<x<c \\ k_2 \cdot f_2(x) & \text{for } c<x<\infty \end{cases}, \tag{6.21}$$

where $k_1+k_2=1$. Since $f_1(x)$ and $f_2(x)$ are legitimate density functions within their respective intervals, then

$$\int_0^c f_1(x)\,dx = 1 \tag{6.22a}$$

and

$$\int_c^\infty f_2(x)\,dx \;=\; 1. \tag{6.22b}$$

Then the property $\int_0^\infty f_X(x)\,dx = 1$ will result as long as $k_1 + k_2 = 1$, so we conclude that

$$f_X(x) \;=\; \begin{cases} k \cdot f_1(x) & \text{for } 0 < x < c \\ (1-k)\cdot f_2(x) & \text{for } c < x < \infty \end{cases}, \tag{6.23}$$

where we have substituted k for k_1 and $1-k$ for k_2. Note that we do not require $f_1(c) = f_2(c)$, so the spliced density function $f_X(x)$ is not necessarily continuous at $x = c$. This in turn implies that neither $f_X(x)$ nor the hazard rate function $\lambda_X(x)$ is defined at $x = c$. Note, however, that continuity at $x = c$ could be added as part of the specifications of the spliced model. (See Exercise 6-20.)

EXAMPLE 6.9

Find the density function for a two-component spliced distribution that is uniform on $(0,c)$ and exponential thereafter. Modify the general result by adding the specification that $f_X(x)$ be continuous at $x = c$.

SOLUTION

Here we have $f_1(x) = \frac{1}{c}$ and $f_2(x) = \beta \cdot e^{-\beta(x-c)}$. (Note that both $f_1(x)$ and $f_2(x)$ integrate to 1 over their respective intervals.) Then the general form of the spliced distribution is

$$f_X(x) \;=\; \begin{cases} k/c & \text{for } 0 < x < c \\ \beta(1-k)\cdot e^{-\beta(x-c)} & \text{for } c < x < \infty \end{cases}.$$

(The reader should confirm that

$$\int_0^\infty f_X(x)\,dx \;=\; \int_0^c \frac{k}{c}\,dx + \int_c^\infty \beta(1-k)\cdot e^{-\beta(x-c)}\,dx \;=\; 1$$

for any value of k.) To have continuity at $x = c$, we must have

$$f_X(c) \;=\; \beta(1-k) \;=\; \frac{k}{c},$$

which implies that

$$k \;=\; \frac{\beta c}{1+\beta c}.$$

Then we have

$$f_X(x) = \begin{cases} \frac{\beta}{1+\beta c} & \text{for } 0 < x \leq c \\ \frac{\beta}{1+\beta c} \cdot e^{-\beta(x-c)} & \text{for } c \leq x < \infty \end{cases}. \qquad \square$$

6.2.9 LIMITING DISTRIBUTIONS

For some of our severity distributions, it turns out that the limit of the PDF, as the distribution parameters approach infinity or zero, is the PDF of another distribution. Consequently, the limiting operation does not produce a new distribution, but simply shows how certain distributions are related to others. An illustration of this is provided in the following example.

EXAMPLE 6.10

Show that the limit of the Pareto density, as $\theta \to \infty, \alpha \to \infty$, and $\frac{\theta}{\alpha} \to c$, a constant, is the exponential density.

SOLUTION

To hold the ratio θ / α constant while both θ and α approach infinity, we set $\theta / \alpha = c$, so that $\theta = c\alpha$, substitute $c\alpha$ for θ in the Pareto density, and then take the limit as $\alpha \to \infty$. (Since $\theta = c\alpha$, this forces $\theta \to \infty$ as well.) Thus we have

$$\lim_{\substack{\theta \to \infty \\ \alpha \to \infty \\ \frac{\theta}{\alpha} \to c}} \left(\frac{\alpha \cdot \theta^{\alpha}}{(x+\theta)^{\alpha+1}} \right) = \lim_{\alpha \to \infty} \frac{\alpha (c\alpha)^{\alpha}}{(x+c\alpha)^{\alpha+1}} = \frac{1}{c} \cdot \lim_{\alpha \to \infty} \frac{(c\alpha)^{\alpha+1}}{(x+c\alpha)^{\alpha+1}}.$$

To find the limit we use the standard technique of log transformation. (If $\lim_{\alpha \to \infty} \ln f(\alpha) = L$, then $\lim_{\alpha \to \infty} f(\alpha) = e^L$.) Here we have

$$f(\alpha) = \frac{(c\alpha)^{\alpha+1}}{(x+c\alpha)^{\alpha+1}} = \frac{1}{\left(\frac{x+c\alpha}{c\alpha}\right)^{\alpha+1}},$$

so

$$\ln f(\alpha) = -(\alpha+1) \cdot \ln\left(\frac{x+c\alpha}{c\alpha}\right) = \frac{\ln\left(\frac{x+c\alpha}{c\alpha}\right)}{\frac{-1}{\alpha+1}}.$$

To find $L = \lim_{\alpha \to \infty} \ln f(\alpha)$, we use L'Hospital's rule repeatedly. We have

$$L = \lim_{\alpha\to\infty}\left(\frac{\left(\frac{c\alpha}{x+c\alpha}\right)\left(\frac{(c\alpha)(c)-(x+c\alpha)(c)}{(c\alpha)^2}\right)}{\frac{1}{(\alpha+1)^2}}\right)$$

$$= \lim_{\alpha\to\infty}\left(\frac{(\alpha+1)^2(-cx)}{(c\alpha)(x+c\alpha)}\right)$$

$$= \lim_{\alpha\to\infty}\left(\frac{-x\alpha^2-2x\alpha-x}{c\alpha^2+x\alpha}\right)$$

$$= \lim_{\alpha\to\infty}\left(\frac{-2x\alpha-2x}{2c\alpha+x}\right) = \lim_{\alpha\to\infty}\left(\frac{-2x}{2c}\right) = \frac{-x}{c}.$$

Then

$$\lim_{\alpha\to\infty} f_X(x) = \frac{1}{c}\cdot e^{-x/c},$$

which is an exponential density. ❐

In similar manner, we can show that the limit of the inverse Pareto density is the inverse exponential density. The details are left to the reader as Exercise 6-21.

6.3 MODIFICATIONS OF THE LOSS RANDOM VARIABLE

In this section, we assume that the severity random variable X represents a single loss event, and we define the random variable Y to represent the *amount paid* (which we will call the *claim amount*) to offset part or all of that loss. (We assume throughout this section that $X>0$.) It is normally the case under warranties and insurance policies that Y will be strictly less than X, to discourage individuals from engaging in behavior that makes a claim more likely. That is, the insured person shares in the risk of loss with the insurer, which is achieved through *coverage modifications*. In this section we will discuss three types of coverage modifications, namely deductibles, policy limits, and coinsurance factors.

6.3.1 DEDUCTIBLES

A *deductible* is a threshold amount, denoted d, which must be exceeded by a loss in order for a claim to be paid. If the deductible is exceeded (that is, if $X>d$), then the amount paid is $Y=X-d$. Therefore the claim amount random variable Y is defined to be

$$Y = (X-d)_+ = \begin{cases} 0 & \text{for } X \le d \\ X-d & \text{for } X > d \end{cases}, \tag{6.24}$$

where the notation $(X-d)_+$ is read "the excess of X over d, if positive."[3] From Equation (6.24) it is clear that Y has a mixed distribution, as reviewed in Section 1.1.3. That is, $Y=0$ if $X\le d$ so we have the discrete part of the distribution of Y as

[3] In some texts (see, for example, Klugman, Panjer, and Willmot [21]), the random variable $Y=(X-d)_+$ is called the *left censored and shifted variable.*

$$p_Y(0) = Pr(Y=0) = Pr(X \leq d) = F_X(d). \tag{6.25a}$$

The continuous part of the distribution of Y is given by

$$f_Y(y) = f_X(d+y), \tag{6.25b}$$

for $y>0$, since $Y=y$ if $X=y+d$. The relationship between the random variables X and Y is illustrated in the following diagram.

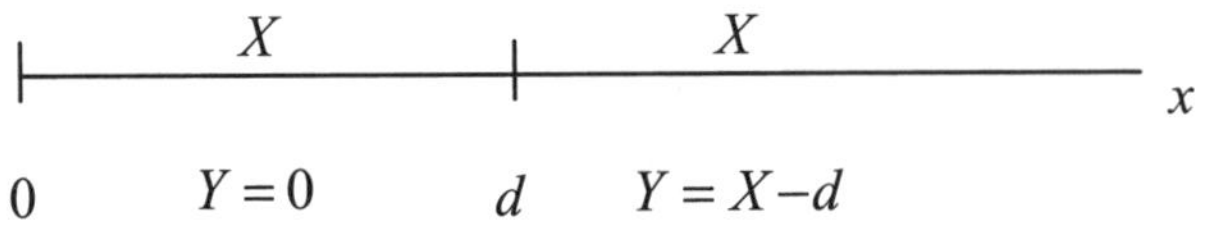

Relationship of X and Y with a Deductible

FIGURE 6.4

The moments of the random variable Y are given by

$$E[Y^k] = E\left[(X-d)_+^k\right] = \int_d^\infty (x-d)^k \cdot f_X(x)\, dx \tag{6.26a}$$

if X is continuous, and by

$$E[Y^k] = E\left[(X-d)_+^k\right] = \sum_{x>d} (x-d)^k \cdot p_X(x) \tag{6.26b}$$

if X is discrete. This represents the kth moment of the payment amount random variable per loss event (or per loss incurred).

Note that when a deductible is present, there will be fewer payments than losses since any loss for an amount less than the deductible will not result in a claim. It is important to understand that Y is the random variable for the *amount paid per loss event*. We need also to examine the idea of the *amount paid per payment event*, for which we need to define a third random variable Z. To clearly understand the difference between the random variables Y and Z, consider their expected values. $E[Y]$ is the expected amount paid on a *loss*, and is influenced by the fact that some losses (those for which $X \leq d$) do not produce a payment at all. On the other hand, $E[Z]$ is the expected amount paid on a *payment*, and would therefore exceed $E[Y]$. In some texts, the expected payment per payment event is called the *mean excess loss*.[4]

Note that Z is the same as Y whenever there is, in fact, a payment (i.e., if $Y>0$). Thus we can write

$$Z = Y \mid Y>0 \tag{6.27a}$$

[4] As mentioned at the end of Section 6.1.3, the mean excess loss is often used as a measure of the right-hand tail weight of a distribution. This is further pursued in Section 6.4.1.

or

$$Z \;=\; Y \mid X > d, \tag{6.27b}$$

since $Y > 0$ and $X > d$ are equivalent events. The kth moment of Z is given by

$$E[Z^k] \;=\; E[Y^k \mid Y > 0] \;=\; E\left[(X-d)^k \mid X > d\right]$$

$$= \frac{\int_d^\infty (x-d)^k \cdot f_X(x)\,dx}{1-F_X(d)} \tag{6.28a}$$

if X is continuous, and by

$$E[Z^k] \;=\; E\left[(X-d)^k \mid X > d\right] \;=\; \frac{\sum_{x>d} (x-d)^k \cdot p_X(x)}{1-F_X(d)} \tag{6.28b}$$

if X is discrete. It is worth repeating that $E[Z^k]$ is the kth moment of the payment amount *per payment event*. Note from Equations (6.26b) and (6.28b) that

$$E[Z^k] \;=\; \frac{E[Y^k]}{1-F_X(d)}, \tag{6.29}$$

reflecting the fact that the random variable Z is conditional on $X > d$, the probability of which is $1-F_X(d)$. Equations (6.26b) and (6.28b) show that Equation (6.29) also holds in the discrete case.[5]

6.3.2 POLICY LIMITS

In the case of a *policy limit*, a loss is fully compensated only to the extent that it does not exceed some fixed number u. That is, if $X \leq u$ the payment is $Y = X$, but if $X > u$ the payment is $Y = u$. This is illustrated in the following diagram.

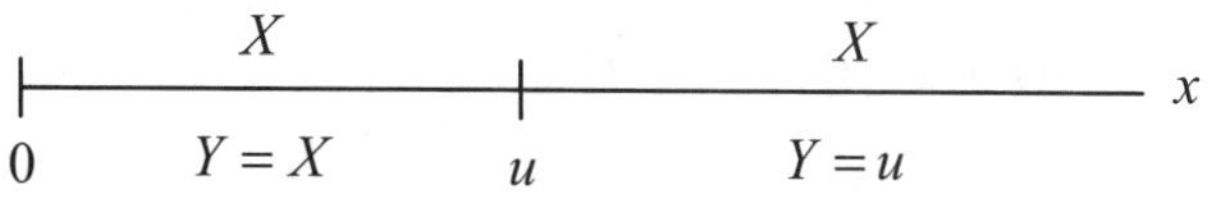

Relationship of X and Y with a Policy Limit

FIGURE 6.5

It is clear that Y will be the *smaller* of X or u, for which we write $Y = \min(X, u)$. Another notation used for this concept is $Y = (X \wedge u)$. Thus we can formally write

---

[5] Note the similarity here of $E[Z] = E[X-d \mid X > d]$ with $\mathring{e}_x = E[T_x] = E[T_0 - x \mid T_0 > x]$, as given by Equation (5.47) of Cunningham, et al. [7]. Here Z denotes the random excess (beyond d) of the loss amount variable X; in the survival model context, T_x denotes the random excess (beyond x) of the age-at-failure variable T_0.

$$Y = (X \wedge u) = \begin{cases} X & \text{for} \quad X \leq u \\ u & \text{for} \quad X > u \end{cases}. \tag{6.30}$$

Just as in the case of a deductible, it is clear that *Y* has a mixed distribution in the presence of a policy limit. Its continuous part is

$$f_Y(y) = f_X(y) \tag{6.31a}$$

for $y < u$, and its discrete part is

$$p_Y(u) = 1 - F_X(u). \tag{6.31b}$$

In the absence of a deductible there will be a payment associated with every loss event, so the random variable for amount of payment per *payment* event, denoted *Z*, will be the same as the random variable for the amount of payment per *loss* event, which is *Y*. Thus we have

$$Z = Y = (X \wedge u). \tag{6.32}$$

The moments of *Y* (or *Z*) are given by

$$E[Y^k] = \int_0^u x^k \cdot f_X(x)\, dx + \int_u^\infty u^k \cdot f_X(x)\, dx \tag{6.33}$$

in the continuous case. In particular the expected value of *Y* is given by

$$\begin{aligned} E[Y] &= \int_0^u x \cdot f_X(x)\, dx + \int_u^\infty u \cdot f_X(x)\, dx \\ &= \int_0^u x \cdot f_X(x)\, dx + u[1 - F_X(u)]. \end{aligned}$$

The first integral can be evaluated using integration by parts to obtain $u \cdot F_X(u) - \int_0^u F_X(x)\, dx$, which, when added to $u[1 - F_X(u)]$, leads to

$$\begin{aligned} E[Y] &= u - \int_0^u F_X(x)\, dx \\ &= \int_0^u [1 - F_X(x)]\, dx \\ &= \int_0^u S_X(x)\, dx. \end{aligned} \tag{6.34}$$

The random variable $Y = (X \wedge u)$ is often called the *limited loss variable*, and its expected value is called the *limited expected value* (LEV).

TABLE 6.2

Limited Expected Value (LEV) for Selected Distributions		
Distribution	**Reference**	$E[X \wedge x]$
Uniform	Section 1.3.1	$x - \frac{x^2}{2\omega}$
Exponential	Section 1.3.3	$\theta(1-e^{-x/\theta})$
Gamma	Section 1.3.4 and Exercise 6-5	$\alpha\theta \cdot \Gamma(\alpha+1; x/\theta) + x[1-\Gamma(\alpha; x/\theta)]$
Pareto	Section 6.1.2	$\frac{\theta}{\alpha-1}\left[1-\left(\frac{\theta}{x+\theta}\right)^{\alpha-1}\right]$, for $\alpha > 1$ $\theta \cdot \ln\left(\frac{x+\theta}{\theta}\right)$, for $\alpha = 1$
Inverse Exponential	Example 6.3	$\beta\int_{\beta/x}^{\infty} t^{-1}e^{-t}\,dt + x(1-e^{-\beta/x})$
Weibull (Transformed Exponential)	Example 6.4	$\theta \cdot \Gamma(1+\frac{1}{\tau}) \cdot \Gamma[1+\frac{1}{\tau}; (x/\theta)^{\tau}] + x \cdot e^{-(x/\theta)^{\tau}}$
Inverse Weibull	Exercise 6-10	$\theta \cdot \Gamma(1-\frac{1}{\tau}) - \theta \cdot \Gamma(1-\frac{1}{\tau}) \cdot \Gamma[1-\frac{1}{\tau}; (x/\theta)^{\tau}] + x - x \cdot e^{-(\theta/x)^{\tau}}$
Inverse Pareto	Exercise 6-12	$\theta\alpha\int_{0}^{x/(x+\theta)} y^{\alpha}(1-y)^{-1}\,dy + x\left[1-\left(\frac{x}{x+\theta}\right)^{\alpha}\right]$
Lognormal	Section 6.2.4	$e^{\mu+\sigma^2/2} \cdot \Phi\left(\frac{\ln x-\mu-\sigma^2}{\sigma}\right) + x\left[1-\Phi\left(\frac{\ln x-\mu}{\sigma}\right)\right]$

The LEV's for the exponential and Pareto distributions are derived in Example 6.11 and Exercise 6-26, respectively. Those for the gamma, inverse exponential, Weibull, and inverse Weibull distributions are derived in Appendix K.

6.3.3 RELATIONSHIPS BETWEEN DEDUCTIBLES AND POLICY LIMITS

There are several interesting connections between deductibles and policy limits, which we will explore in this section.

Consider two policies, one with a deductible of d (but no policy limit) and the other with a policy limit of d (but no deductible). Then if $X \leq d$ the first policy will pay $Y = 0$ and the second policy will pay $Y = X$, and if $X > d$ the first policy will pay $Y = X-d$ and the second policy will pay $Y = d$. Together the total payment will be $Y = X$ in all cases, so the two policies taken together are equivalent to one policy with neither deductible nor policy limit. Recall that Y is denoted by $(X-d)_+$ in the first case and by $(X \wedge d)$ in the second case. Since the sum of the two Y's is X, then we have

$$X = (X-d)_+ + (X \wedge d) \tag{6.35}$$

and therefore

$$E[X] = E\big[(X-d)_+\big] + E[X \wedge d]. \tag{6.36}$$

This equation shows us that $E[(X-d)_+]$ can be obtained from $E[X]$ and $E[X \wedge d]$, and conversely. Since, for most distributions, $E[X \wedge d]$ is more easily obtained than is $E[(X-d)_+]$, we will develop the LEV for many of the severity distributions summarized in Table 6.2 and then find $E[(X-d)_+]$ when needed from Equation (6.36).

EXAMPLE 6.11

Find expressions for each of the following when X has an exponential distribution:

(a) The limited expected value $E[X \wedge u]$.

(b) The expected payment per loss event $E[(X-d)_+]$.

(c) The mean excess loss.

SOLUTION

(a) From Equation (6.34) we find

$$\begin{aligned} E[Y] &= E[X \wedge u] \\ &= \int_0^u S_X(x)\,dx \\ &= \int_0^u e^{-\beta x}\,dx \\ &= \frac{1-e^{-\beta u}}{\beta} \\ &= \theta[1-e^{-u/\theta}], \end{aligned}$$

using the scale parameter form of the exponential.

(b) Then the expected payment per loss event is found from Equation (6.36) as

$$E[(X-d)_+] = E[X] - E[X \wedge d] = \theta - \theta[1-e^{-d/\theta}] = \theta \cdot e^{-d/\theta}.$$

(c) The mean excess loss is

$$E[Z] = \frac{E[(X-d)_+]}{1-F_X(d)} = \frac{\theta \cdot e^{-d/\theta}}{e^{-d/\theta}} = \theta.$$

❐

The concept of $(a \wedge b) = \min(a,b)$, developed in connection with a policy limit, also has an interesting application in connection with a deductible. If a deductible of d is added to a policy that did not previously have one, some amount of payment will be saved on a loss of X as a result of the deductible. If the loss is $X \leq d$ the amount saved will be X, since the payment will now be $Y = 0$ rather than $Y = X$; if the loss is $X > d$ the amount saved will be d, since the payment will now be $Y = X - d$ rather than $Y = X$. Thus the amount saved will be the smaller of X or d. If we let A denote the random variable for the amount saved, we have

$$A = \min(X,d) = (X \wedge d) \tag{6.37}$$

and the expected amount saved is

$$E[A] = E[X \wedge d]. \tag{6.38}$$

Without the deductible the payment is $Y = X$ so the expected payment is $E[X]$. Then the expected savings (due to the deductible) expressed as a fraction of the expected payment (in the absence of a deductible) is

$$LER = \frac{E[X \wedge d]}{E[X]}, \tag{6.39}$$

which is called the *loss elimination ratio* due to a deductible of d.

If a policy contains both a deductible and a policy limit, it is then important to distinguish between the two concepts of *maximum covered loss* and *maximum payment amount*. If m is the maximum amount of loss covered by the policy, then the maximum payment amount will be $m - d$ after the imposition of the deductible. If there is no deductible, then the maximum payment amount and the maximum covered loss will be the same.

EXAMPLE 6.12

A health maintenance organization (HMO) currently pays the full cost of any emergency room care of any of its clients. The company is evaluating the possible savings that could result from imposing a deductible of 250 per emergency room visit to be paid by the client. Assume the cost of an emergency room visit is exponentially distributed with mean 1000. By what percent are claims expected to be reduced by the imposition of the deductible?

SOLUTION

Without the deductible the expected payment is the same as the expected loss, which implies $E[Y] = E[X] = 1000$. The expected savings is given by Equation (6.38) as $E[S] = E[X \wedge 250]$, which, from Example 6.11, is

$$E[X \wedge 250] = 1000[1 - e^{-250/1000}] = 221.20.$$

The expected percentage reduction is the loss elimination ratio given by Equation (6.39) as

$$\frac{E[X \wedge 250]}{E[X]} = \frac{221.20}{1000} = 22.12\%.$$ ❒

6.3.4 COINSURANCE FACTORS

In the case of a *coinsurance factor* α, where $0 < \alpha < 1$, loss amounts are multiplied by α to arrive at claim amounts. In the absence of a deductible, each loss will produce a payment so we again have $Z = Y$, where

$$Z = Y = \alpha \cdot X, \tag{6.40}$$

for $0 < \alpha < 1$. The PDF of Y is given by

$$f_Y(y) = f_X\left(\frac{y}{\alpha}\right) \cdot \frac{1}{\alpha}. \tag{6.41}$$

It is also clear that

$$E[Z] = E[Y] = \alpha \cdot E[X]. \tag{6.42}$$

For policies with deductibles and/or policy limits along with coinsurance factors, we adopt the convention that the coinsurance factor is applied *after* the application of any deductible or limit. Then for a policy with limit u, deductible d, and coinsurance factor α, the amount paid per loss random variable Y is given by

$$Y = \alpha\big[(X \wedge u) - (X \wedge d)\big]. \tag{6.43}$$

This is illustrated in the following example.

EXAMPLE 6.13

The HMO described in Example 6.12 has decided to impose a per loss deductible of 250 per emergency room visit, along with a coverage limit of 5000 on the cost of visits. Additionally, a coinsurance factor of .80 will be applied to any resulting payment amounts. Assuming the cost of an emergency room visit is exponentially distributed with mean 1000, what are the expected payment amount per visit to the emergency room (i.e., per loss event) and the expected payment amount per payment made by the HMO?

SOLUTION

The expected payment per visit, from Equation (6.43), is

$$E[Y] = (.80)\big(E[X \wedge 5000] - E[X \wedge 250]\big).$$

We calculated the value $E[X \wedge 250] = 221.20$ in Example 6.12; a similar calculation produces $E[X \wedge 5000] = 993.26$. Then the expected payment amount per visit is

$$E[Y] = (.80)(993.26 - 221.20) = 617.65.$$

The expected payment amount per payment event is

$$E[Z] = \frac{E[Y]}{1 - F_X(d)} = \frac{617.65}{e^{-.25}} = 793.08. \qquad \square$$

6.3.5 THE EFFECT OF INFLATION

Assume that inflation occurs uniformly at a rate of $100r\%$ per year. When there is uniform inflation of $100r\%$, all loss amounts are magnified by a factor of $(1+r)$, but the impact on payment amounts for policies with deductibles is greater than $100r\%$. There are two reasons for this.

(1) More claims now exceed the deductible, so the number of claims requiring payment will increase.

(2) The deductible is not increased for inflation, so those claim amounts that exceeded the deductible even before the inflation will increase by more than the rate of inflation. For example, suppose annual inflation is 10% so that all loss amounts in Year 2 are 1.10 times any loss amounts in Year 1. If the deductible amount is 250 and a loss in Year 1 is 1000, the payment amount in Year 1 will be 750. However, that same loss-causing event in Year 2 will produce a loss amount (due to inflation) of 1100, and a resulting payment of $1100 - 250 = 850$. The result is that the payment amount has increased by 13.33%.

The effect of inflation on the expected payment per loss event in the presence of deductibles, policy limits, or coinsurance is quickly evaluated by replacing the pre-inflation loss amount random variable X with the post-inflation loss amount random variable $X^* = (1+r)X$. This is a case of scalar multiplication, as described in Section 6.2.2.

Note that if X belongs to a scale family of distributions, then a uniform inflation factor produces X^* within the same family. This is one advantage of choosing to model loss amounts using scale families. In the case where X belongs to a scale family with a scale parameter, the implementation of inflation factors is even more straightforward.

Therefore, in the presence of uniform inflation at rate r, the expected payment per loss event for a policy with deductible d is given by

$$E[Y] = E\big[(1+r)X\big] - E\big[(1+r)X \wedge d\big]. \tag{6.44a}$$

The reader may verify that for any scalars $a > 0$ and $b > 0$, and random variable $X > 0$, it will be true that

$$(a \cdot X \wedge b) = a\left(X \wedge \frac{b}{a}\right). \tag{6.45}$$

Then the expression for $E[Y]$ given by Equation (6.44a) may be written as

$$E[Y] = (1+r)\left(E[X] - E\left[X \wedge \frac{d}{1+r}\right]\right). \tag{6.44b}$$

The probability of the loss (after inflation) exceeding the deductible, and therefore producing a claim, is equal to

$$Pr\left[(1+r)X > d\right] = Pr\left(X > \frac{d}{1+r}\right) = 1 - F_X\left(\frac{d}{1+r}\right), \tag{6.46}$$

so the expected payment amount per payment made is then given by

$$E[Z] = \frac{(1+r)\left(E[X] - E\left[X \wedge \frac{d}{1+r}\right]\right)}{1 - F_X\left(\frac{d}{1+r}\right)}. \tag{6.47}$$

Similar adjustments can be made in the presence of coverage limits and/or coinsurance factors, and these are pursued in the exercises.

EXAMPLE 6.14

Again consider the HMO described in Example 6.13, with a 250 deductible, 5000 coverage limit, and 80% coinsurance factor. In the presence of 5% uniform inflation, what will now be the expected payment amounts per loss event and per payment?

SOLUTION

The expected payment per visit is now

$$\begin{aligned} E[Y] &= (.80)\left(E[(1.05)X \wedge 5000] - E[(1.05)X \wedge 250]\right) \\ &= (.80)(1.05)\left(E[X \wedge 4761.90] - E[X \wedge 238.10]\right). \end{aligned}$$

We calculate

$$E[X \wedge 4761.90] = 1000[1 - e^{-4761.90/1000}] = 991.45$$

and

$$E[X \wedge 238.10] = 1000[1 - e^{-238.10/1000}] = 211.88,$$

leading to

$$E[Y] = (.80)(1.05)(991.45 - 211.88) = 654.84.$$

The expected payment amount per payment event is

$$E[Z] = \frac{E[Y]}{1-F_X\left(\frac{250}{1.05}\right)} = \frac{654.84}{e^{-.2381}} = 830.89. \qquad \square$$

6.3.6 EFFECT OF COVERAGE DEDUCTIBLES ON FREQUENCY MODELS

In Section 6.3.1 we discussed the distinction between losses and claim payments in the presence of a coverage deductible. If there is no deductible, then each loss produces a claim payment, so the random variables for number of losses and number of claims would have the same distribution. On the other hand, if an insurance coverage has a deductible of *d*, then only losses in excess of *d* will produce claims and the distribution of number of claims will be different from the distribution of number of losses.

Let N_0 denote the frequency-of-loss random variable, and therefore also the frequency-of-claim random variable in the absence of a deductible (i.e., with $d=0$), and let N_d denote the frequency-of-claim random variable in the presence of a deductible of $d>0$, as illustrated in the following diagram.

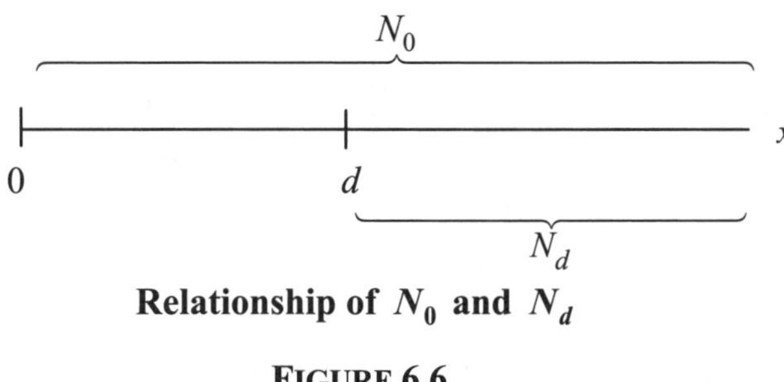

Relationship of N_0 and N_d

FIGURE 6.6

In Figure 6.6, N_0 counts the number of losses in the amount interval $(0,\infty)$ and N_d counts the number of losses in the amount interval (d,∞). In this section we will see how to derive the distribution of N_d from the distribution of N_0.

We already know the answer to this in the case where N_0 has a Poisson distribution, due to its decomposition property (see Section 5.1.2). Each loss for which $X>d$ produces a claim, and the probability that a loss is of this type is $Pr(X>d)=1-F_X(d)=k$, say. Then if N_0 is Poisson with parameter λ, it follows that the random variable for number of claims, N_d, is also Poisson with parameter $\lambda^*=k\cdot\lambda$.

We will now more formally derive the distribution of N_d from that of N_0. We can then use the result to verify the above conclusion in the Poisson case and apply it to other frequency models as well.

For the jth loss, we define the indicator variable I_j to be

$$I_j = \begin{cases} 0 & \text{if } X_j \le d \\ 1 & \text{if } X_j > d \end{cases}, \qquad (6.48)$$

where

$$Pr(I_j = 1) = Pr(X_j > d) = 1 - F_{X_j}(d) = k. \qquad (6.49)$$

Recall from probability theory that such a random variable has a Bernoulli distribution, which is the special case of the binomial distribution with $n = 1$. Then the Bernoulli random variable has expected value given by

$$E[I_j] = k,$$

variance given by

$$Var(I_j) = k(1-k),$$

and MGF given by

$$M_{I_j}(t) = 1 - k + ke^t.$$

(See Equations (1.27), (1.28), and (1.29), with $n = 1$ and p replaced by k.) Then if the number of losses is N_0, it follows that the number of claims, N_d, is given by the compound distribution

$$N_d = I_1 + I_2 + \cdots + I_{N_0}. \qquad (6.50)$$

(See Section 1.6 for a review of the compound distribution.)[6] In particular, recall that a compound distribution assumes that the I_j random variables are mutually independent, and identically distributed, and that each I_j is also independent of N_0. Then from Equation (1.67) we know that the MGF of N_d is given by

$$M_{N_d}(t) = M_{N_0}[\ln M_I(t)] = M_{N_0}[\ln(1-k+ke^t)]. \qquad (6.51)$$

Now suppose N_0 has a Poisson distribution with parameter λ, so

$$M_{N_0}(z) = e^{\lambda(e^z-1)}.$$

Then the MGF of N_d is

$$\begin{aligned} M_{N_d}(t) &= e^{\lambda(e^z-1)}\Big|_{z=\ln(1-k+ke^t)} \\ &= e^{\lambda(1-k+ke^t-1)} \\ &= e^{k\cdot\lambda(e^t-1)} = e^{\lambda^*(e^t-1)}, \end{aligned} \qquad (6.52)$$

showing that N_d has a Poisson distribution with parameter $\lambda^* = k\cdot\lambda$, as already known.

[6] Since N_d is compound, then $E[N_d] = E[N_0]\cdot E[I]$. Since $E[I] = k = 1 - F_X(d)$ by Equation (6.49), we have $E[N_d] = E[N_0]\cdot[1 - F_X(d)]$.

EXAMPLE 6.15

Find the distribution of N_d if N_0 has a binomial distribution.

SOLUTION

In this case we have a portfolio with n risks, each with probability p of producing a loss, so the number of losses, N_0, is binomial with MGF given by

$$M_{N_0}(z) = (q+pe^z)^n,$$

where $q=1-p$. Then the MGF of N_d is

$$\begin{aligned}
M_{N_d}(t) &= (q+pe^z)^n\Big|_{z=\ln(1-k+ke^t)} \\
&= [q+p(1-k+ke^t)]^n \\
&= (1-p+p-kp+kp\cdot e^t)^n \\
&= (1-p^*+p^*\cdot e^t)^{n^*} \\
&= (q^*+p^*\cdot e^t)^{n^*}, \qquad (6.53)
\end{aligned}$$

where $q^*=1-p^*$, $p^*=k\cdot p$, and $n^*=n$. Therefore N_d has a binomial distribution with parameters $n^*=n$ and $p^*=k\cdot p$. ❐

Finding the distribution of N_d when N_0 has a negative binomial distribution is left to the reader as Exercise 6-37.

The above analysis also applies to the zero-modified distributions introduced in Section 5.2.3. For example, if the distribution of losses (and hence of claims in the absence of a deductible) is zero-modified Poisson, its MGF is

$$M_{N_0}^{ZM}(z) = \frac{p_{ZM}(0)-e^{-\lambda}}{1-e^{-\lambda}} + \left(\frac{1-p_{ZM}(0)}{1-e^{-\lambda}}\right)\cdot e^{\lambda(e^z-1)},$$

from Equation (5.33a). Then the MGF of N_d is

$$M_{N_d}(t) = M_{N_0}^{ZM}(z)\Big|_{z=\ln(1-k+ke^t)} = \frac{p_{ZM}(0)-e^{-\lambda}}{1-e^{-\lambda}} + \left(\frac{1-p_{ZM}(0)}{1-e^{-\lambda}}\right)\cdot e^{k\lambda(e^t-1)}.$$

To show that N_d is also zero-modified Poisson, we need to rearrange both the constant term and the coefficient of the exponential term. For the first term, we multiply both numerator and denominator by $(1-e^{-k\lambda})$ to obtain

$$\frac{(p_{ZM}(0)-e^{-\lambda})(1-e^{-k\lambda})}{(1-e^{-\lambda})(1-e^{-k\lambda})} = \frac{p_{ZM}(0)-e^{-\lambda}-p_{ZM}(0)\cdot e^{-k\lambda}+e^{-\lambda}\cdot e^{-k\lambda}}{(1-e^{-\lambda})(1-e^{-k\lambda})},$$

and then add and subtract $e^{-k\lambda}$ in the numerator to obtain

$$\frac{p_{ZM}(0)-e^{-\lambda}+e^{-k\lambda}-p_{ZM}(0)\cdot e^{-k\lambda}-e^{-k\lambda}+e^{-\lambda}\cdot e^{-k\lambda}}{(1-e^{-\lambda})(1-e^{-k\lambda})}.$$

Next we divide both numerator and denominator by $(1-e^{-\lambda})$ to obtain

$$\frac{\dfrac{p_{ZM}(0)-e^{-\lambda}+e^{-k\lambda}-p_{ZM}(0)\cdot e^{-k\lambda}}{1-e^{-\lambda}}-e^{-k\lambda}}{1-e^{-k\lambda}} = \frac{p_{ZM}^{*}(0)-e^{-\lambda^*}}{1-e^{-\lambda^*}},$$

where $\lambda^* = k\cdot\lambda$ and $p_{ZM}^{*}(0) = \dfrac{p_{ZM}(0)-e^{-\lambda}+e^{-k\lambda}-p_{ZM}(0)\cdot e^{-k\lambda}}{1-e^{-\lambda}}$.

A similar rearrangement of the coefficient of the exponential term produces the new coefficient $\frac{1-p_{ZM}^{*}(0)}{1-e^{-\lambda^*}}$, with λ^* and $p_{ZM}^{*}(0)$ defined as above. (The details are left as Exercise 6-39.) This shows that N_d has a zero-modified Poisson distribution with parameters λ^* and $p_{ZM}^{*}(0)$ as defined.

The results developed thus far can be generalized to the case where the distribution of N_d, the random variable for number of losses in excess of *d*, is known, and the deductible is then increased from *d* to d', where $d' > d$. Let $N_{d'}$ denote the frequency-of-claim random variable in the presence of a deductible of d'. This is illustrated in Figure 6.7.

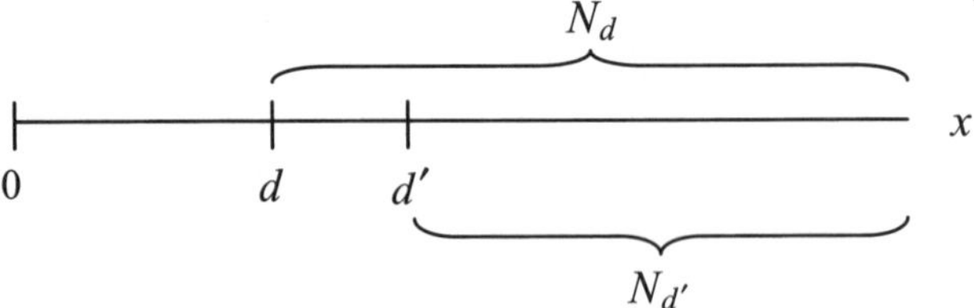

Relationship of N_d and $N_{d'}$

FIGURE 6.7

We can derive the distribution of $N_{d'}$ from that of N_d in the same manner as we earlier derived the distribution of N_d from that of N_0. However, since the distribution of N_d relates to losses in excess of *d*, this derivation is conditional on $X > d$. Thus the indicator variable I_j will equal 1 if $X_j > d'_j$, *given that* $X_j > d$. Equation (6.49) now becomes

$$Pr(I_j = 1) = Pr(X_j > d' \mid X_j > d) = \frac{1 - F_X(d')}{1 - F_X(d)} = k. \tag{6.54}$$

I_j is still a Bernoulli random variable with parameter k, but with k defined by Equation (6.54) rather than Equation (6.49). Equations (6.50) and (6.51) still hold, with N_0 replaced by N_d and N_d replaced by $N_{d'}$.

We note that the Figure 6.6 case, that of imposing a deductible of d where none previously existed, is a special case of the more general Figure 6.7 case with $d = 0$ and $d' = d$.

Finally, suppose the distribution of N_d is known, presumably having been deduced from data on number of claims in light of a deductible of d. From this distribution of N_d, can we deduce the distribution of N_0, the random variable for number of losses (or number of claims) if the deductible were removed?

Referring to Figure 6.6, we can see that the distribution of N_d provides us with information about the number of occurring losses that exceed d, but no information about the number of losses that do not exceed d. Thus to derive the distribution of N_0 from that of N_d we must make some inherent assumption regarding the number of losses less than d.

Recall Equation (6.51), which expresses the MGF of N_d in terms of the MGF of N_0. Note that the left side of Equation (6.51) is a function of t, and the right side is a function of a function of t, namely $\ln(1-k+ke^t)$. Therefore Equation (6.51) is of the general form

$$f(t) = g[h(t)],$$

and it follows that

$$g(y) = f[h^{-1}(y)]$$

provided the function h is invertible. In this case

$$y = h(t) = \ln(1-k+ke^t),$$

so

$$t = \ln(1-\tfrac{1}{k}+\tfrac{1}{k}e^y).$$

Thus we can conclude that if the assumptions underlying Equation (6.51) hold, then it follows that

$$M_{N_0}(y) = M_{N_d}[\ln(1-k^{-1}+k^{-1}e^y)]. \tag{6.55}$$

For example, if N_d is known to have a Poisson distribution with parameter λ^*, so that

$$M_{N_d}(z) = e^{\lambda^*(e^z-1)},$$

then the MGF of N_0 is

$$
\begin{aligned}
M_{N_0}(t) &= e^{\lambda^*(e^z-1)}\Big|_{z=\ln(1-k^{-1}+k^{-1}e^t)} \\
&= e^{\lambda^*(1-k^{-1}+k^{-1}e^t-1)} \\
&= e^{k^{-1}\lambda^*(e^t-1)} = e^{\lambda(e^t-1)},
\end{aligned}
$$

showing that N_0 has a Poisson distribution with parameter $\lambda = k^{-1} \cdot \lambda^*$.

6.4 TAIL WEIGHT REVISITED; RISK MEASURES

The important notion of right-hand tail weight was introduced earlier in Section 6.1.3, where three analytic measures of tail weight were defined and applied to the exponential and Pareto distributions. In this section we will define several more such measures and apply them, as well as the earlier three, to some of the additional distributions developed in Section 6.2 and summarized in Table 6.1.

In recent years, both the insurance industry and the banking industry have begun to discuss the concept of *risk measures*, methods to summarize the level of risk associated with some loss distribution. Two such risk measures, the *value at risk* (often abbreviated as VaR) and the *conditional tail expectation* (CTE), are really in the nature of additional measures of tail weight, and are therefore included in this section as well.[7]

The determination of measures of tail weight and risk measures by stochastic simulation is discussed in Example 6.19.

6.4.1 THE MEAN EXCESS LOSS FUNCTION

The discussion regarding coverage modifications in Section 6.3 gives rise to several additional measures of tail weight. One such measure is the *mean excess loss function* (MELF), defined in Section 6.3.1 as the expected amount paid per payment event. Given that the loss exceeds some deductible *d*, the expected excess loss, denoted by $E[Z]$ in Section 6.3.1, is given by

$$
E[Z] = E[(X-d) \mid X > d] = \frac{E[(X-d)_+]}{Pr(X>d)} = \frac{E[X]-E[X \wedge d]}{1-F_X(d)}. \tag{6.56}
$$

As a measure of tail weight, which is independent of the concept of a deductible, we prefer the notation $E[(X-x) \mid X > x]$, the expected amount by which the loss exceeds *x*, given that it does exceed *x*. As noted in Footnote 5 in Section 6.3.1, the mean excess loss function is mathematically equivalent to $\mathring{e}_x$ in the context of a survival model. In light of this, the MELF is sometimes called the *mean excess life function* or *mean residual life function*. For

---

[7] In some texts, such as Klugman, et al. [21], the conditional tail expectation (CTE) is referred to as the *tail value at risk* (TVaR). Others prefer the term *expected shortfall* (ES) for this concept. We prefer the CTE name, as it is more descriptive of what is being measured, and we will use it throughout this text.

convenience we will generally use the simpler $\overset{\circ}{e}_x$ symbol in place of the longer $E[(X-x)\,|\,X>x]$.

Viewed as a function of x, an increasing $\overset{\circ}{e}_x$ implies a heavier right-hand tail and a decreasing $\overset{\circ}{e}_x$ implies a lighter tail. In Section 6.1.3 it was established that a decreasing HRF implies a heavier tail and an increasing HRF implies a lighter tail. Together these suggest that a decreasing HRF implies an increasing MELF (heavy tail) and an increasing HRF implies a decreasing MELF (light tail).[8]

To show this relationship between $\overset{\circ}{e}_x$ and $\lambda_X(x)$, we make use of the survival distribution function $S_X(x)$. Starting with Equation (6.56), we substitute for $E[X]$ from Equation (5.18) of [7] and for $E[X \wedge d]$ from Equation (6.34), obtaining

$$\begin{aligned}
\overset{\circ}{e}_x &= E[(X-x)\,|\,X>x] \\
&= \frac{\int_0^\infty S_X(y)\,dy - \int_0^x S_X(y)\,dy}{1-F_X(x)} \\
&= \frac{\int_x^\infty S_X(y)\,dy}{S_X(x)} && \text{(6.57a)} \\
&= \int_0^\infty \frac{S_X(x+t)}{S_X(x)}\,dt. && \text{(6.57b)}
\end{aligned}$$

Next we substitute for the SDF in terms of the HRF from Equation (5.14) of [7], obtaining

$$\begin{aligned}
\overset{\circ}{e}_x &= \int_0^\infty \left[\frac{\exp\left[-\int_0^{x+t} \lambda_X(u)\,du\right]}{\exp\left[-\int_0^x \lambda_X(u)\,du\right]}\right] dt \\
&= \int_0^\infty \exp\left[-\int_x^{x+t} \lambda_X(u)\,du\right] dt, && \text{(6.58)}
\end{aligned}$$

where $t>0$. Now for a fixed interval of length t, if $\lambda_X(u)$ is a decreasing function of u it follows that $\int_x^{x+t} \lambda_X(u)\,du$ is a decreasing function of x, as revealed by Figure 6.8 on the following page, and, in turn, the integrand in Equation (6.58) is an increasing function of x so $\overset{\circ}{e}_x$ is an increasing function of x as well.

By similar argument, an increasing $\lambda_X(u)$ implies a decreasing $\overset{\circ}{e}_x$, as expected.

[8] Note that the converse implication does not necessarily hold. That is, an increasing MELF does not always imply a decreasing HRF, and a decreasing MELF does not always imply an increasing HRF.

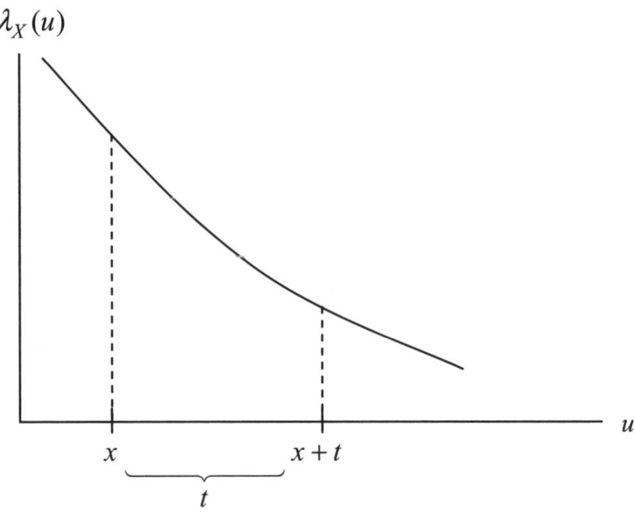

Decreasing Hazard Rate

FIGURE 6.8

EXAMPLE 6.16

Find an expression for $\overset{\circ}{e}_x$ for the Pareto distribution with $\alpha > 1$. Show that it is an increasing function of x, implying a heavy tail for this distribution (as already known).

SOLUTION

For the Pareto distribution, $E[(X-x)_+]$ is given in Exercise 6-26(c) and $S_X(x)$ is given by Equation (6.2). Then from Equation (6.56) we have

$$\begin{aligned}\overset{\circ}{e}_x &= \frac{E[(X-x)_+]}{S_X(x)} \\ &= \frac{\theta^\alpha}{(\alpha-1)(x+\theta)^{\alpha-1}} \div \frac{\theta^\alpha}{(x+\theta)^\alpha} = \frac{x+\theta}{\alpha-1},\end{aligned}$$

which is clearly an increasing function of x. □

6.4.2 CONDITIONAL TAIL EXPECTATION

Closely related to the mean excess loss function of Section 6.4.1 is the *conditional tail expectation* (CTE). Whereas the MELF gives the conditional expected *excess* of the loss over a fixed amount x, given that the loss does exceed x, the CTE gives the conditional expected amount of the loss itself, again given that the loss exceeds x. Then as a function of x we have

$$CTE_x = E[X \mid X > x]. \tag{6.59a}$$

Clearly the expected amount of loss is the expected excess of loss over x plus x itself, so we have

$$CTE_x = x + E[(X-x) \mid X > x] = x + \overset{\circ}{e}_x. \tag{6.59b}$$

Substituting for $\overset{\circ}{e}_x$ from Equation (6.56) we have

$$\begin{aligned} CTE_x &= x + \frac{E[X] - E[X \wedge x]}{S_X(x)} \\ &= \frac{1}{S_X(x)} \left[E[X] - E[X \wedge x] + x \cdot S_X(x) \right]. \end{aligned} \tag{6.59c}$$

EXAMPLE 6.17

Find an expression for CTE_x for the Pareto distribution with $\alpha > 1$.

SOLUTION

Using Equation (6.59b) and the result of Example 6.16, we have

$$\begin{aligned} CTE_x &= x + \overset{\circ}{e}_x = x + \frac{x+\theta}{\alpha-1} \\ &= \frac{x\alpha+\theta}{\alpha-1}. \end{aligned}$$

❐

6.4.3 VALUE AT RISK

Another simple measure of tail weight, often quoted as a risk measure in both insurance and banking contexts, is the value at risk (VaR). A VaR value is associated with a given probability value α, and is defined as the value for which the probability of the loss being less than that value is α so the probability of the loss exceeding that value is $1-\alpha$. Then denoting the VaR value by x_α, we have

$$Pr(X \le x_\alpha) = F_X(x_\alpha) = \alpha \tag{6.60a}$$

or

$$Pr(X > x_\alpha) = S_X(x_\alpha) = 1 - \alpha. \tag{6.60b}$$

We recognize that the VaR value x_α is simply the αth percentile of the distribution of X, assuming that X has a continuous distribution. (The case of X having a discrete distribution is discussed in Section 6.4.5.)

EXAMPLE 6.18

Find the 95th VaR for each of the (a) exponential, (b) Pareto, (c) Weibull, and (d) lognormal distributions.

SOLUTION

In all cases we seek the value of x, denoted $x_{.95}$, such that $S_X(x) = .05$.

(a) For exponential, we have

$$S_X(x) = e^{-\beta x} = .05,$$

so

$$x = x_{.95} = \frac{-\ln .05}{\beta}.$$

(b) For Pareto, we have

$$S_X(x) = \left(\frac{\theta}{x+\theta}\right)^{\alpha} = .05,$$

so

$$x = x_{.95} = \theta(.05)^{-1/\alpha} - \theta = \theta[(.05)^{-1/\alpha} - 1].$$

(c) For Weibull, we have

$$S_X(x) = e^{-(x/\theta)^{\tau}} = .05,$$

so

$$x = x_{.95} = \theta \cdot (-\ln .05)^{1/\tau}.$$

(d) For lognormal, we have

$$F_X(x) = \Phi\left(\frac{\ln x - \mu}{\sigma}\right) = .95.$$

From the table of standard normal values we find

$$\frac{\ln x - \mu}{\sigma} = 1.645,$$

so

$$x = x_{.95} = e^{\mu + 1.645\sigma}.$$ ❐

It should be noted that the conditional tail expectation measure described in Section 6.4.2 is also generally determined with respect to a probability value α such as .90, .95 or .99. In this context, with $S_X(x_\alpha) = 1-\alpha$, Equation (6.59c) would be written as

$$CTE_{x_\alpha} = \frac{1}{1-\alpha}\left[E[X] - E[X \wedge x_\alpha] + x_\alpha(1-\alpha)\right]. \tag{6.59d}$$

We use the notation CTE_α, rather than CTE_{x_α}, since the value of α implies the value of x_α.

EXAMPLE 6.19 (Simulation Illustration)

Use simulation to estimate the CTE and the VaR, at the 95% level, for the Pareto distribution with $\alpha = 20$ and $\theta = 2,000,000$.

SOLUTION

From Equation (6.2) we find the 95th percentile of this distribution to be $x_{.95} = 323,172.70$; using Example 6.17 we can find the actual value of the CTE to be

$$CTE_{323,172.70} = \frac{(323,172.70)(20) + 2,000,000}{19} = 445,444.95.$$

To estimate the same measure by simulation, we first simulated 10,000 trials of the negative binomial distribution (see Section 1.2.3) with $r = 3$ and $p = 60$, using the modified table-look-up approach of Section 4.4.4. The result of this simulation suggested the occurrence of 45,364 total claims. We then simulated 45,364 claim amounts from our Pareto distribution, and retained only the (.05)(45,364) = 2268 largest of the 45,364 simulated claim amounts. Finally, we took our estimate of the 95th CTE to be the average of these 2268 claim amounts, which turned out to be 447,048.40. (Note the closeness of the simulated result to the actual value.)

We simulated 1000 values from the distribution, and took our estimate of the 95th percentile to be the 951st order statistic within the 1000 simulated values. We performed this simulation 100 times, and found the mean of the 100 values of the 951st order statistic to be 323,882.80. (Compare this with the exact value of 323,172.70.) The sample standard deviation (or standard error) of the 100 estimated 95th percentile values was 17,116.30. ❒

6.4.4 DISTORTION RISK MEASURES

Here we consider a family of risk measures called *distortion risk measures.* We consider a continuous loss random variable X in terms of its survival distribution function $S_X(x)$, for $0 \le x < \infty$, and recall that $S_X(0) = 1$ and $S_X(x) \to 0$ as $x \to \infty$.

Next we define an increasing function $g(t)$, for $0 \le t \le 1$, where $g(0) = 0$ and $g(1) = 1$. The function $g(t)$ is called the *distortion function.* Then we define

$$S_X^*(x) = g[S_X(x)], \tag{6.61}$$

for $0 \le x < \infty$. Note that at $x = 0, S_X(x) = 1$ and, since $g(1) = 1$, then $S_X^*(x) = 1$ at $x = 0$ as well. Similarly, as $x \to \infty$, $S_X(x) \to 0$ and since $g(0) = 0$, then $S_X^*(x) \to 0$ as $x \to \infty$ as well. Therefore $S_X^*(x)$, a distortion of $S_X(x)$, is also a survival distribution function. Finally we define the distortion risk measure to be

$$DRM = \int_0^\infty S_X^*(x)\,dx = \int_0^\infty g[S_X(x)]\,dx. \tag{6.62}$$

For a given loss random variable X, a family of distortion risk measures can be produced by using different $g(t)$ distortion functions.

One characteristic of distortion risk measures is that the distorted survival function $S_X^*(x)$ might be the SDF for a random variable of the same family as the original loss random variable X. This is illustrated in the following example.

EXAMPLE 6.20

Let X be a loss random variable with a Pareto distribution, and let the distortion function be $g(t)=t^n$, for $0 \le t \le 1$. Show that the distortion risk measure in this case is the expected value of another Pareto random variable.

SOLUTION

The SDF of X, from Equation (6.2), is $S_X(x)=\left(\frac{\theta}{x+\theta}\right)^{\alpha}$. Then the distorted SDF is

$$S_X^*(x) = g[S_X(x)] = [S_X(x)]^n = \left(\frac{\theta}{x+\theta}\right)^{n\alpha},$$

which is the SDF for a Pareto distribution with α replaced by $n\alpha$. Finally, the distortion risk measure is

$$DRM = \int_0^{\infty} S_X^*(x)\,dx = E[X^*] = \frac{\theta}{n\alpha-1},$$

provided $n\alpha > 1$. ❒

By suitably selecting the distortion function $g(t)$, we can show that the two risk measures defined in Sections 6.4.2 and 6.4.3 belong to the family of distortion risk measures.

EXAMPLE 6.21

Show that if $g(t)$ is defined as $g(t) = \begin{cases} 0 & \text{for } 0 \le t \le 1-\alpha \\ 1 & \text{for } 1-\alpha < t \le 1 \end{cases}$, the resulting distortion risk measure is the VaR risk measure described in Section 6.4.3.

SOLUTION

Figure 6.9 will be useful in this analysis.

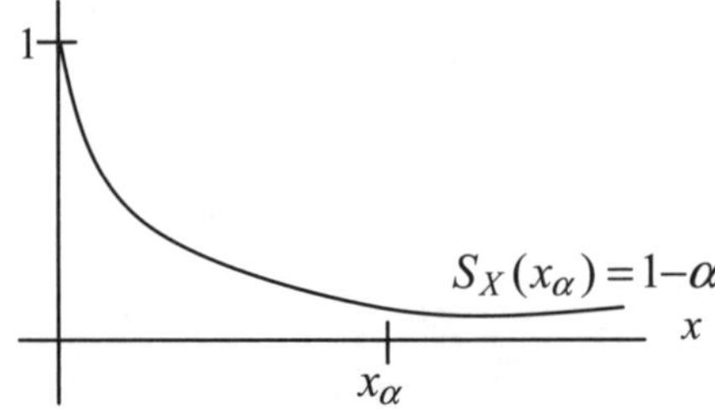

Value of the Survival Function at x_α

FIGURE 6.9

For all $x \geq x_\alpha$ we have $S_X(x) \leq 1-\alpha$, so

$$S_X^*(x) = g[S_X(x)] = 0$$

for $x \geq x_\alpha$. Similarly, for $0 \leq x < x_\alpha$ we have $S_X(x) > 1-\alpha$, so

$$S_X^*(x) = g[S_X(x)] = 1$$

for $0 \leq x < x_\alpha$. Then the distortion risk measure is

$$DRM = \int_0^\infty S_X^*(x)\,dx = \int_0^{x_\alpha} 1\,dx + \int_{x_\alpha}^\infty 0\,dx = x_\alpha,$$

which is the value of the VaR risk measure. ❒

The demonstration that the CTE risk measure of Section 6.4.2 is also a distortion risk measure is left as Exercise 6-47.

6.4.5 RISK MEASURES USING DISCRETE DISTRIBUTIONS

When the loss distribution is discrete, in whole or in part, there is often no unique value of x for which $F_X(x) = \alpha$. In this case we define the αth percentile of the distribution to be the *smallest* value of X for which $F_X(x) \geq \alpha$. A numerical example will make this clear.

EXAMPLE 6.22

Find the 90th VaR for the discrete Poisson distribution with $\lambda = 2$.

SOLUTION

We have $p(0) = .13534$, $p(1) = .27061$, $p(2) = .27061$, $p(3) = .18045$, $p(4) = .09020$, and so on. The values of the CDF are $F(0) = .13534$, $F(1) = .40595$, $F(2) = .67656$, $F(3) = .85701$, and $F(4) = .94721$. We observe that $F_X(x) \geq .90$ for all $x \geq 4$. We take $x_{.90} = 4$ as the 90th VaR since it is the smallest value of X satisfying $F_X(x) \geq .90$. ❒

Similarly, Equation (6.59d) for finding the value of CTE_α with a continuous distribution must be modified in the case where the distribution of X is discrete. First we find the value of x_α as defined for discrete distributions earlier in this section. Secondly we observe the largest value of α (call this value β) for which $x_\beta = x_\alpha$. Thirdly we calculate $E[X \mid X > x_\alpha]$. Finally we take a weighted average of x_α and $E[X \mid X > x_\alpha]$ using weights of $\frac{\beta-\alpha}{1-\alpha}$ and $\frac{1-\beta}{1-\alpha}$, respectively. Again a numerical example will make the process clearer.

EXAMPLE 6.23

Find the 95th CTE for the discrete distribution with $p(0) = .77$, $p(50) = .20$, $p(100) = .02$, $p(200) = .01$.

SOLUTION

The CDF of X is $F(0) = .77,\ F(50) = .97,\ F(100) = .99,\ F(200) = 1.00$. The value of $x_{.95}$ is 50, the smallest value of x satisfying $F_X(x) \geq .95$. Then we observe that $x_{.96}$ and $x_{.97}$ are also 50, since 50 is the smallest value of x satisfying $F_X(x) \geq .96$ and $F_X(x) \geq .97$. Therefore we have $\beta = .97$. Next we calculate

$$E[X \mid X > 50] = \frac{(100)(.02) + (200)(.01)}{.03} = 133.3\dot{3}.$$

Finally we have

$$CTE_{.95} = \left(\frac{.97 - .95}{1 - .95}\right)(50) + \left(\frac{1 - .97}{1 - .95}\right)(133.3\dot{3}) = (.40)(50) + (.60)(133.3\dot{3}) = 100.00. \quad \square$$

6.5 EMPIRICAL LOSS DISTRIBUTIONS

For well-established lines of business offering ample credible loss data, directly using an empirical distribution may serve more effectively than fitting a parametric model to those data. The random variable X is treated as discrete with the observed loss amounts treated as equally likely.[9] This makes the calculation of the PDF, CDF, and moments of X relatively simple to do. Also, simulation of claim experience over a variety of scenarios is quite straightforward.

Along with these advantages, there are two principal disadvantages to the use of models that are solely empirical.

(1) The physics of the underlying phenomenon are ignored. For example, suppose it is true that claim amounts for an automobile insurer really do follow a Pareto distribution for logically identifiable reasons. When using an empirical model, that information is lost to some extent. Without that type of information, there is less chance the insurer may discover some action or policy change that may be taken in order to change the claim amount distribution to one that is more favorable to both insurer and insured.

(2) Parametric models more easily facilitate the development of completely new products for which little or no claim data exists. The first computer manufacturers to provide repair warranties may have priced those warranties using parametric models based on warranty experience from other types of electronics.

In Example 6.23 below we discuss the use of empirical distributions, using an example that includes only 16 data points. This data set is far too small to make this approach appropriate, but the techniques of calculation presented in the example are effective for larger, more realistic data sets. For some risk products, such as warranties, insurance, or default protections, we can expect the availability of data sets involving many thousands of observations. In this type of scenario, empirical distributions can be both more effective and much simpler to use than parametric models.

---

[9] The implication of this is that the mean of X is then taken as the average of the data values.

EXAMPLE 6.24

A manufacturer of washing machines provides a repair warranty on each new machine it sells. Under the warranty, all repairs are paid by the company except for a deductible of 50 per repair that is paid by the customer. The historical total repair costs are shown in the following table.[10]

TABLE 6.3

Data for Example 6.24	
Event	**Loss Amount (x)**
1	150
2	85
3	25
4	200
5	72
6	182
7	52
8	332
9	141
10	281
11	171
12	253
13	33
14	197
15	273
16	96

Determine each of the following:

(a) The probability function and cumulative distribution function for X.

(b) The expected payment amount made by the company per loss event and the expected payment amount per payment event.

(c) The variance in the amount paid by the company per loss event.

(d) The impact of 20% uniform inflation on the expected payment amount per loss event.

SOLUTION

(a) From the raw historical data we calculate the values shown in Table 6.4. The probability function is exhibited in Column (2) and the CDF in Column (3). Columns (4) and (5) are used in parts (b) and (c), respectively, and Columns (6) and (7) are used in part (d).

---

[10] To provide for a tractable analysis, we use only 16 data points in this example. Similar analysis is easily applied to very large data sets using spreadsheets or other computer software. The reader should keep in mind that this approach is only appropriate for large sets of data.

TABLE 6.4

Results for Example 6.24						
x (1)	$p_X(x)$ (2)	$F_X(x)$ (3)	$(x-d)_+$ (4)	$(x-d)_+^2$ (5)	$1.20x$ (6)	$(1.20x \wedge 50)$ (7)
25	.0625	.0625	0	0	30.0	30.0
33	.0625	.1250	0	0	39.6	39.6
52	.0625	.1875	2	4	62.4	50.0
72	.0625	.2500	22	484	86.4	50.0
85	.0625	.3125	35	1,225	102.0	50.0
96	.0625	.3750	46	2,116	115.2	50.0
141	.0625	.4375	91	8,281	169.2	50.0
150	.0625	.5000	100	10,000	180.0	50.0
171	.0625	.5625	121	14,641	205.2	50.0
182	.0625	.6250	132	17,424	218.4	50.0
197	.0625	.6875	147	21,609	236.4	50.0
200	.0625	.7500	150	22,500	240.0	50.0
253	.0625	.8125	203	41,209	303.6	50.0
273	.0625	.8750	223	49,729	327.6	50.0
281	.0625	.9375	231	53,361	337.2	50.0
332	.0625	1.0000	282	79,524	398.4	50.0
			1,785	**322,107**	**3,051.6**	**769.6**

(b) The expected payment per loss event is

$$E[Y] = E\left[(X-50)_+\right] = \sum_{x>50} (x-50) \cdot p_X(x).$$

Since our data points are equally likely, this is equal to the sum of the elements in Column (4) of Table 6.4 divided by the number of elements, producing

$$E[Y] = E\left[(X-50)_+\right] = \frac{1{,}785}{16} = 111.56.$$

The expected payment per payment event is

$$E[Z] = \frac{E[Y]}{1-F_X(50)} = \frac{111.56}{\frac{14}{16}} = 127.50.$$

(c) We have

$$E[Y^2] = \frac{322{,}107}{16} = 20{,}131.69.$$

Then the variance in the payment amount per loss is

$$Var(Y) = E[Y^2]-\left(E[Y]\right)^2 = 20{,}131.69-(111.56)^2 = 7{,}686.06.$$

(d) Here we have

$$E[(1.20X-50)_+] = E[1.20X]-E[1.20X\wedge 50].$$

Using the data in Columns (6) and (7) of Table 6.4, we can calculate $E[1.20X]=190.73$ and $E[1.20X\wedge 50]=48.10$. Thus we have

$$E[(1.20X-50)_+] = 190.73-48.10 = 142.63.$$

Note that 20% inflation causes a greater than 20% increase in the expected payment per loss, as expected. ❐

6.6 SUMMARY

In this chapter we have thoroughly reviewed a wide range of continuous distributions that might be used to model claim severity. Starting with the fundamental distributions of normal, exponential, and Pareto, we went on to generate a number of additional distributions. All such distributions are summarized in Appendix A. We also examined mixture distributions, frailty models, spliced distributions, and limiting distributions.

A major topic examined in this chapter was the effect of coverage modifications, such as deductibles, policy limits, and coinsurance. The effect of inflation was also explored.

Next we defined and analyzed a series of risk measures, including mean excess loss, conditional tail expectation, value at risk, and distortion risk measures.

We concluded the chapter with a brief examination of empirical loss distributions.

6.7 EXERCISES

6.1 Introduction

6-1 Derive Equation (6.2).

6-2 Derive Equation (6.3a).

6-3 Derive Equation (6.3b).

6-4 Show that $\lim_{x\to\infty}\frac{S_X(x)}{S_Y(x)} = \lim_{x\to\infty}\frac{f_X(x)}{f_Y(x)}$. Then show that $\lim_{x\to\infty}\frac{S_X(x)}{S_Y(x)} = \infty$, if X has a Pareto distribution and Y has an exponential distribution.

6.2 Generating Additional Distributions

6-5 In Section 1.3.3 the exponential density was written in its traditional form (see Equation (1.50a)) and in an alternative form (see Equation (1.50b)). Similarly, the traditional form of the gamma density, given by Equation (1.55), can be written as

$$f_X(x) = \frac{(x/\theta)^{\alpha} \cdot e^{-x/\theta}}{x \cdot \Gamma(\alpha)},$$

by substituting $\beta = \frac{1}{\theta}$. Express the (a) mean, (b) variance, (c) MGF, and (d) CDF of the gamma distribution using this alternative parameterization.

6-6 Show that the set of normal distributions forms a scale family.

6-7 Show that the Pareto distribution family has a scale parameter.

6-8 Show that the gamma distribution, when reparameterized as in Exercise 6-5, forms a scale family with a scale parameter. (This is the primary reason for doing the reparameterization.)

6-9 Show that the Weibull distribution forms a scale family with a scale parameter.

6-10 Find the CDF and the PDF of the inverse Weibull distribution.

6-11 Find the expected value of the (a) Weibull and (b) inverse Weibull distributions.

6-12 Find the CDF and the PDF of the inverse Pareto distribution.

6-13 Let $\Phi(z)$ denote the CDF for the standard normal distribution. Show that the CDF for a lognormal random variable X with parameters μ and σ is

$$F_X(x) = \Phi\left(\frac{\ln x - \mu}{\sigma}\right).$$

6-14 Show that the lognormal distribution forms a scale family, but does not possess a scale parameter.

6-15 A loss severity random variable X is exponentially distributed with parameter β, where β is a realization of the random variable B. That is, $f_{X|B}(x\,|\,\beta) = \beta \cdot e^{-\beta x}$. For the entire population, B is uniformly distributed over (1, 11). Find the value of $Pr(X > .50)$.

6-16 Let X be a random variable with parameter λ, where λ is a realization of a discrete random variable Λ. Show that, for any integer k,

$$E[X^k] \;=\; \sum_{\Lambda} p_{\Lambda}(\lambda) \cdot E[X^k \,|\, \Lambda = \lambda].$$

6-17 A manufacturer provides a warranty on its washers and dryers. Repair costs for washers are exponentially distributed with mean 60, and those for dryers are uniformly distributed on (0, 150). 30% of the machines under warranty are dryers. Find each of the following:

(a) The expected cost per repair.

(b) The variance of repair cost over all repairs.

(c) The probability that the repair cost will be less than 60, for a repair chosen at random.

6-18 A loss severity distribution is a two-point Pareto mixture. With probability .80 the distribution is Pareto with $\alpha = 2$ and $\theta = 100$, and with probability .20 the distribution is Pareto with $\alpha = 4$ and $\theta = 3000$. Find the probability that the loss severity is less than 200.

6-19 (a) Let X have a normal distribution with mean θ and variance σ_1^2, but where θ is the realization of a normal random variable with mean μ and variance σ_2^2. That is, the overall distribution is a mixture of normals with mixing on the mean parameter using a normal mixing distribution. Show that the marginal (unconditional) distribution of X is normal with mean μ and variance $\sigma_1^2 + \sigma_2^2$.

(b) On a certain exam, the scores are normally distributed with mean θ and standard deviation 8, where θ is the outcome of a normal random variable with mean 75 and standard deviation 6. The passing score is 65. For an exam candidate selected at random, find the probability that the score is less than 90, given that the score is a passing score.

6-20 The random variable X is originally believed to have an exponential distribution with mean 4. Recent data now suggests that a better model would be a spliced distribution whose density is constant over $(0,3)$, proportional to the original exponential density over $(3,\infty)$, and continuous at the junction of the two components. Calculate $Pr(X<3)$ according to the spliced model.

6-21 Show that the limit of the inverse Pareto density, as $\theta \to 0$, $\alpha \to \infty$, $\alpha\theta \to c$, a constant, is the inverse exponential density.

6.3 Modifications of the Loss Random Variable

6-22 Find the expected payment per payment event for a deductible of 100 under each of the following distributions:

(a) The uniform distribution over (0, 500).

(b) A Pareto distribution with mean of 500 and scale parameter $\theta = 1000$.

(c) The discrete distribution given by $p(50)=.20$, $p(150)=.30$, $p(250)=.20$, $p(350)=.20$, and $p(500)=.10$.

6-23 A severity distribution is exponential with mean 1000. An insurer will pay the amount of each loss in excess of a deductible of 100. Calculate the variance of the insurer's payment on one loss.

6-24 Find the mean excess loss under an insurance with a deductible of 4 per loss with loss severity distribution given by $f(x)=.02x$, for $0<x<10$.

6-25 Find the variance of the claim payment per payment event under an insurance with a deductible of 150 per loss and a discrete loss severity distribution where losses can be 100, 200 or 300 with probabilities .20, .20 and .60, respectively.

6-26 Consider a Pareto distribution with shape parameter α and scale parameter θ. Let $d>0$.

(a) Show that $E[X \wedge d] = \dfrac{\theta}{\alpha-1}\left[1-\left(\dfrac{\theta}{d+\theta}\right)^{\alpha-1}\right]$, for $\alpha>1$.

(b) Find the appropriate expression for $E[X \wedge d]$ when $\alpha=1$.

(c) Show that $E[(X-d)_+] = \dfrac{\theta^\alpha}{(\alpha-1)(d+\theta)^{\alpha-1}}$, for $\alpha>1$.

6-27 A loss distribution is Pareto with $\alpha = 2.$ Given that

$$E[X-100 \mid X>100] = \frac{5}{3} \cdot E[X-50 \mid X>50],$$

find the value of $[X-150 \mid X>150]$.

6-28 An auto liability insurance policy will pay 100% of a claim amount up to a limit of 1000 per claim. The claim severity distribution is given by its CDF as

$$F_X(x) = 1 - .80e^{-.02x} - .20e^{-.001x},$$

for $x \geq 0$. Calculate the expected payment for one claim.

6-29 Determine the loss elimination ratio for each of the following severity distributions and deductibles:

(a) Pareto with $\alpha = 2$ and $\theta = 2000$, and deductible of 500.

(b) $f_X(x) = .01$ for $0 < x \leq 80$, $f_X(x) = .00025(120-x)$ for $80 < x \leq 120$, and $f_X(x) = 0$ otherwise, and deductible of 20.

6-30 An exponential severity model produces a loss elimination ratio of 70% with a deductible of *d*. Find the LER if the deductible is increased by one-third but the severity distribution remains the same.

6-31 An insurance pays 80% of the amount of a loss in excess of a deductible of 20, subject to a maximum payment of 60 per loss. The CDF of the loss severity distribution is $F_X(x) = (.01x)^2$, for $0 \leq x \leq 100$. Find the conditional expected claim payment, given that a payment has been made.

6-32 The amount of loss under a certain risk has a Poisson distribution with mean 3. The risk is insured under a policy with a deductible of 2. It is proposed to replace the deductible with a coinsurance factor of α, such that the expected insurance payment remains the same. Find the value of α.

6-33 A prescription drug plan provides that the insured has the following annual payment responsibilities:

(i) All costs up to a deductible of 250.
(ii) 25% of costs between 250 and 2250.
(iii) All costs above 2250 until the total insured's payment reaches 3600.
(iv) 5% of all remaining costs.

The plan's costs are modeled by a Pareto distribution with $\alpha = 2$ and $\theta = 2000$. Find the expected annual payment made by the plan.

6-34 An incentive plan to control hospitalization costs will pay a physician a bonus of B, determined as c times the amount by which total hospital claims are under 400, where $0 \leq c \leq 1$. It is assumed that total hospital claims follow a Pareto distribution with $\alpha = 2$ and $\theta = 300$. Given that $E[B] = 100$, find the value of c.

6-35 Loss amounts in Year Z have a discrete uniform distribution on the points 1000, 2000, 3000, 4000, 5000, and 6000. A contingent payment contract calls for a deductible of 1500, and inflation at 5% will impact all claims from Year Z to Year Z+1. Without changing the deductible, determine the percentage increase in the expected payment from Year Z to Year Z+1.

6-36 Loss amounts in Year Z are normally distributed with mean 1000 and standard deviation 100. If inflation increases all loss amounts by 5% from Year Z to Year Z+1, determine the distribution of loss amounts in Year Z+1.

6-37 Repeat Example 6.15 if N_0 has a negative binomial distribution.

6-38 Some texts[11] use an alternate parameterization for the negative binomial distribution by substituting $p = \frac{1}{1+\beta}$, so $1-p = \frac{\beta}{1+\beta}$, resulting in a probability function of

$$p(x) = \binom{x+r-1}{r-1}\left(\frac{1}{1+\beta}\right)^r\left(\frac{\beta}{1+\beta}\right)^x,$$

for $x = 0,1,2,\cdots$. Using this alternate parameterization, show each of the following:

(a) $E[X] = r\beta$

(b) $Var(X) = r\beta(1+\beta)$

(c) $M_X(t) = [1-\beta(e^t-1)]^{-r}$

(d) $P_X(s) = [1-\beta(s-1)]^{-r}$

(e) $M_{N_d}(t) = [1-\beta^*(e^t-1)]^{-r^*}$, where $r^* = r$ and $\beta^* = k \cdot \beta$ [12]

[11] See, for example, Klugman, Panjer, and Willmot [21].

[12] Compare this result with that obtained in Exercise 6-33. Again we see that when N_0 has a negative binomial distribution, then N_d is also negative binomial with parameter $\beta^* = k \cdot \beta$. Under the alternate parameterization, the negative binomial frequency distribution adjusts to the imposition of a deductible in the same manner as do the Poisson and binomial distributions.

6-39 Complete the derivation of $M_{N_d}(t)$ in the zero-modified Poisson case by showing that

$$\frac{1-p_{ZM}(0)}{1-e^{-\lambda}} = \frac{1-p_{ZM}^*(0)}{1-e^{-\lambda^*}},$$

where $\lambda^* = k \cdot \lambda$ and

$$p_{ZM}^*(0) = \frac{p_{ZM}(0) - e^{-\lambda} + e^{-k\lambda} - p_{ZM}(0) \cdot e^{-k\lambda}}{1-e^{-\lambda}}.$$

6-40 Suppose the severity of loss distribution is Pareto with $\alpha = 2$ and $\theta = 1000$. In the presence of a deductible of 100, the frequency-of-claim random variable has a Poisson distribution with $\lambda = 6$. Find the probability of exactly five claims if the deductible is increased to 150.

6.4 Tail Weight Revisited; Risk Measures

6-41 Show that

$$\lim_{x\to\infty} \overset{\circ}{e}_x = \lim_{x\to\infty} \frac{1}{\lambda_X(x)},$$

provided the limits exist.

6-42 Find expressions for $\overset{\circ}{e}_x$ for the (a) exponential and (b) Weibull distributions.

6-43 Find a general expression for the conditional tail expectation (CTE) for the continuous uniform distribution.

6-44 Repeat Exercise 6-43 for the lognormal distribution.

6-45 Find the 90th VaR for the inverse exponential distribution.

6-46 A risk measure for the loss random variable X could be simply its expected value $E[X]$. What would the distortion function $g(t)$ be in order to produce the expected value of X as a distortion risk measure?

6-47 Show that if $g(t)$ is defined as

$$g(t)=\begin{cases}\frac{t}{1-\alpha} & \text{for } 0\le t\le 1-\alpha \\ 1 & \text{for } 1-\alpha<t\le 1\end{cases},$$

the resulting distortion risk measure is the CTE risk measure defined by Equation (6.59d).

6-48 Let the distortion function be $g(t)=1-(1-t)^k$. Find an expression for the distortion risk measure if X has a continuous uniform distribution on $(0,\omega)$.

6-49 Using the distortion function $g(t)=\sqrt{t}$, calculate the distortion risk measure for losses that follow a Pareto distribution with $\theta=1000$ and $\alpha=4$.

6-50 Find the 90th CTE for the Poisson distribution of Example 6.21.

6.5 Empirical Loss Distributions

6-51 A loss random variable X has the following characteristics:

X	$F_X(x)$	$E[X\wedge x]$
0	.00	0
100	.20	91
200	.60	153
1000	1.00	331

Calculate the expected payment per payment event for a deductible of 100.

CHAPTER SEVEN

MODELS FOR AGGREGATE PAYMENTS

7.1 INTRODUCTION

In this chapter we provide a framework for analyzing aggregate loss amounts or aggregate payments for a portfolio of individual contingent risks. We assume that our portfolio consists of a collection of n contracts, each of which may experience one or more claims per period. We also assume that the experience under any contract is independent of the experience under all other contracts.

7.2 INDIVIDUAL RISK VERSUS COLLECTIVE RISK

There are two standard approaches for developing a model for the sum S of all losses or claims during a period.

The first approach is to treat each contingent contract individually and develop a claim amount distribution by contract. For Contract i, where $i=1,2,\cdots,n$, a severity distribution is chosen to model the loss amount, denoted by X_i, for that contract during the period. Note that many of the X_i will turn out to be zero, indicating that no loss or claim occurs under that contract during the period. The aggregate loss amount for the period over the entire portfolio is then given by

$$S = \sum_{i=1}^{n} X_i. \tag{7.1}$$

This model is called the *individual risk model*. Some of the mathematical concepts associated with this model were covered in Section 1.5. There we saw that the mathematics of convolutions was necessary to find exact probabilities for S, although the first two moments of S can be easily calculated as

$$E[S] = \sum_{i=1}^{n} E[X_i] \tag{7.2a}$$

and

$$Var(S) = \sum_{i=1}^{n} Var(X_i), \tag{7.2b}$$

since we have assumed mutual independence among the X_i's. Higher moments of S can also be calculated so that an approximating distribution may be employed if we wish to calculate probabilities of S.

Note that under the individual risk model, it is not necessary that claim amounts be *identically distributed* under the various contracts. If they are, however, the moments of S then become

$$E[S] = n \cdot E[X] \tag{7.3a}$$

and

$$Var(S) = n \cdot Var(X), \tag{7.3b}$$

where $E[X]$ and $Var(X)$ denote the common mean and variance of X_i, respectively.

The second approach is to keep track of losses by claim incurred, rather than by policy. A frequency random variable N is chosen to model the number of claims produced *by the entire portfolio*, and it is assumed that all claim amounts X_i, for $i = 1, 2, \cdots, N$, are independent and identically distributed. Then the aggregate claim amount for the entire portfolio is given by

$$S = \sum_{i=1}^{N} X_i. \tag{7.4a}$$

This approach is called the *collective risk model.* It requires the assumption that claim amounts are identically distributed between, as well as within, individual contracts. The collective risk model for S produces a compound distribution with primary distribution N and secondary distribution X, as introduced in Section 1.6. We recall from the double expectation theorem presented in that section that

$$E[S] = E[N] \cdot E[X] \tag{7.5a}$$

and

$$Var(S) = E[N] \cdot Var(X) + Var(N) \cdot (E[X])^2. \tag{7.5b}$$

Higher moments of S can be found by further application of the double expectation theorem. As with the individual risk model, we observe that evaluating probability statements about S exactly will require the mathematics of convolutions, and will be very computationally intensive. Accordingly, in the past, the moments of S, along with an approximating distribution, were often used to arrive at approximate probabilities in practice. In light of our modern computing capabilities, however, there is less reason to use this approximation today.

A third approach is possible, although not recommended, whereby a model is developed for the distribution of S without regard to the component distributions of N and X. The compound distribution model given by Equation (7.4a), however, is more flexible than this third approach in that it more easily accommodates changes in the portfolio (such as additional policies) or changes in the severity distribution due to inflation or policy modifications such as changing deductibles or policy limits. (See Section 6.4)

EXAMPLE 7.1

A bond investor uses an actuarial model to analyze default risk on a portfolio consisting of 450 corporate bonds, each with face amount 1000. Each bond is the obligation of a separate corporation, and the investor assumes that during any given year a particular bond will default with probability .005. Whether a given bond defaults is independent of the default status of any other bond. In the event of default, a loss event occurs that is uniformly distributed on the interval (0, 1000).

(a) Using the individual risk model, calculate the expected aggregate loss and the variance in aggregate loss for a given year.

(b) Using the collective risk model with the Poisson approximation to the binomial distribution (see Section 5.1.2) as the primary distribution, calculate the expected aggregate loss and the variance in aggregate loss.

SOLUTION

(a) Since the probability of default is .005, the loss amount random variable X_i has a probability distribution that is a discrete two-point mixture of $X_i = 0$ (if there is no default) with probability .995, and $X_i = U(0,1000)$ with probability .005, where $U(0,1000)$ denotes the uniform distribution on $(0,1000)$. Then the first two moments of X_i are

$$E[X_i] = 0 + .005\int_0^{1000} .001x\,dx = 2.50$$

and

$$E[X_i^2] = 0 + .005\int_0^{1000} .001x^2\,dx = 1{,}666.6\dot{6},$$

so

$$Var(X_i) = E[X_i^2] - \left(E[X_i]\right)^2 = 1{,}666.6\dot{6} - (2.50)^2 = 1{,}660.42.$$

Then

$$E[S] = n \cdot E[X_i] = (450)(2.50) = 1{,}125$$

and

$$Var(S) = n \cdot Var(X_i) = (450)(1{,}660.42) = 747{,}187.$$

(b) We assume defaults occur at a Poisson rate of $\lambda = (450)(.005) = 2.25$ per year, and that each resulting loss is uniformly distributed over $(0,1000)$. Since N is Poisson, then

$$E[N] = Var(N) = \lambda = 2.25.$$

We also have

$$E[X] = 500$$

and

$$Var(X) = \frac{(1000)^2}{12} = 83{,}333.3\dot{3}.$$

Then from Equations (7.5a) and (7.5b) we have

$$E[S] = (2.25)(500) = 1{,}125$$

and

$$Var(S) = (2.25)(83{,}333.3\dot{3}) + (2.25)(500)^2 = 750{,}000.$$ ❐

We make the following two observations on Example 7.1:

(1) In a more realistic scenario, in which the size of bond holdings varies greatly among corporations, only the individual risk model would be appropriate since the X_i would very likely be far from identically distributed.

(2) Example 7.1 provides a good demonstration of the Poisson approximation to a binomial random variable. The aggregate means are equal, and the aggregate variance is the same to within .40%.

The remainder of this chapter will focus on the collective risk model.

7.3 SELECTION OF FREQUENCY AND SEVERITY DISTRIBUTIONS

Under the collective risk model, the actuary is required to select both an optimal frequency distribution for N and an optimal severity distribution for X. We concern ourselves here with the question of which families of distributions are most appropriate. The problem of selecting optimal parameters for a chosen parametric model is outside the scope of this text.

7.3.1 FREQUENCY

For the frequency distribution, it is good to choose a random variable that responds well to changes in the number of contracts in the portfolio or to changes in the period of time over which the portfolio is under observation. For this reason, it is useful to choose a frequency distribution for which the expected number of claims is proportional both to the number of policies in the portfolio and to the length of period of observation. For example, if the size of the portfolio were doubled, we would like the expected number of claims per period to double. Similarly, if the initial model and parameters are fitted using data from a portfolio of 1000 policies over a five-year period, we say the *exposure* of the portfolio during the observation period is $(5)(1000) = 5000$ policy-years. We would like the expected number of claims during a one-year period to be one-fifth of the expected number for five years.

In short, if we view the exposure m as the number of policy-years for an observation period, then we would like the expected number of claims to be proportional to m. Distributions with this property are said to be *infinitely divisible*. Examples of infinitely divisible frequency distributions that we considered in Chapter 5 are the Poisson and negative binomial distributions.[1] In fact, to achieve infinite divisibility was the main reason we pointed out the extension of the negative binomial distribution to non-integer values of the parameter r (see Section 5.1.3). The binomial distribution fails to be infinitely divisible because its parameter n must be an integer (see Exercise 7-30). Therefore, in light of our criterion of infinite divisibility, the Poisson and negative binomial distributions turn out to be ideal candidates for frequency distributions.

7.3.2 SEVERITY

With regard to the choice of the severity distribution, it is advantageous if the severity distribution (a) fits the experience data well and (b) can easily incorporate inflation in loss amounts or changes in reporting currency. Scale families (see Section 6.3.2) do this well, since uniform inflation or currency changes are represented through scalar multiplication of the severity random variable X. For scale families, scalar multiplication preserves the distribution type and results only in a change of parameters. Examples of scale families are the normal, Pareto, exponential, and lognormal distributions.

7.3.3 FREQUENCY-SEVERITY INTERACTION

Modifications of the severity distribution can occasionally have implications for the frequency distribution. For example, if the severity distribution is being used to model claim payments for an insurance company and a deductible is introduced, the frequency distribution is then impacted since fewer claims will be paid. The introduction of a deductible can be modeled either through a modified frequency distribution, as we saw in Section 6.3.6, or by keeping the frequency distribution intact and modifying the severity distribution to include a positive probability mass at $X=0$. This is illustrated in the following example.

EXAMPLE 7.2

Company A provides default insurance to the bond investor of Example 7.1. For any default, Company A agrees to pay the amount by which any loss exceeds a deductible amount $d=200$. Using the collective risk model from Example 7.1, describe the frequency and severity distributions that result from each of the following:

(a) Changing only the severity distribution, leaving the frequency distribution unchanged.

(b) Modifying both frequency and severity so that the frequency reflects only positive claim events.

[1] See Section 7.6 for a formal mathematical definition of infinite divisibility, and a proof that the Poisson and negative binomial distribution families are infinitely divisible.

SOLUTION

(a) Since N is unchanged it is still Poison with parameter $\lambda = 2.25$. The severity distribution will now be a discrete two-point mixture of the distribution $X_i = 0$, with probability .20 (the probability that the default loss is less than the deductible), and the uniform distribution on the interval $(0,800)$, with probability .80 (the probability that the default loss results in a claim). Thus we have

$$f_X(x) = (.20)(0) + (.80) f_U(x),$$

where

$$f_U(x) = \begin{cases} .00125, & 0 < x < 800 \\ 0 & \text{otherwise.} \end{cases}$$

(b) In this case only 80% of the loss events will result in claims, so the modified frequency distribution is also Poisson with parameter $\lambda = (.80)(2.25) = 1.80$. Furthermore, any claim amount will be uniform over $(0,800)$, so we directly have $f_X(x) = .00125$ for $0 < x < 800$. The two compound distributions in parts (a) and (b) are, of course, identical, each with mean 720 and variance 384,000. ❐

7.4 MORE ON THE COLLECTIVE RISK MODEL

Now that the reader has a good understanding of the components of the collective risk model, we return to a discussion of the mathematics involved in developing the distribution of S.

7.4.1 CONVOLUTIONS OF THE PROBABILITY FUNCTION OF *X*

As stated in Section 7.1, the aggregate claim amount random variable is given by

$$S = X_1 + X_2 + \cdots + X_N, \tag{7.4b}$$

where N is the discrete frequency random variable and the random variables X_i are mutually independent and identically distributed. It is also assumed that the X_i's are mutually independent of N. To discuss the distribution of S, we first need to formalize the discussion of convolutions introduced in Section 1.5.3.

For $i = 1, 2, \cdots, N$, let the X_i's be identically distributed *discrete* random variables with probability function given by $p_X(x)$. We are interested in finding the probability function of $X_1 + \cdots + X_N$. We start by finding the PF of $X_1 + X_2$, which is called the *two-fold convolution* of $p_X(x)$ with itself, and is denoted by $p_X{}^{*(2)}(x)$. (Note that $p_X{}^{*(2)}(x)$ is the *conditional* probability that $S = x$, *given that* $N = 2$.) We illustrate the calculation of $p_X{}^{*(2)}(x)$ in the following example.

EXAMPLE 7.3

Let the independent random variables X_1 and X_2 both have the following probability function:

TABLE 7.1

Data for Example 7.3	
x	$p_X(x)$
1	.20
2	.30
3	.40
4	.10

Find $p_X^{*(2)}(x)$, the PF for the random variable $S = X_1+X_2$.

SOLUTION

For each value of x, we find the probability that $X_1+X_2 = x$. Note that $X_1 + X_2$ is at least 2 and at most 8, since each of X_1 and X_2 is bounded between 1 and 4. By calculations similar to those demonstrated in Section 1.5.3, we find the probability function for $X_1 + X_2$ to be as given in Table 7.2, which the reader should verify.

TABLE 7.2

Results for Example 7.3	
x	$p_X^{*(2)}(x)$
2	.04
3	.12
4	.25
5	.28
6	.22
7	.08
8	.01
	1.00

❒

The formula used to calculate the entries in Table 7.2 can be written as

$$p_X^{*(2)}(x) = \sum_{t=0}^{x} p_X(t) \cdot p_X(x-t). \tag{7.6a}$$

For sums with three terms, we use the fact that $S = X_1 + X_2 + X_3 = (X_1+X_2) + X_3$, so the probability function for S, which is denoted by $p_X^{*(3)}(x)$, can be found as the convolution of $p_X^{*(2)}(x)$ with $p_X(x)$. That is,

$$p_X^{*(3)}(x) = \sum_{t=0}^{x} p_X(t) \cdot p_X^{*(2)}(x-t). \tag{7.6b}$$

We can continue in this recursive way to find, in general,

$$p_X^{*(k)}(x) = \sum_{t=0}^{x} p_X(t) \cdot p_X^{*(k-1)}(x-t). \tag{7.6c}$$

(Again, we note that $p_X^{*(3)}(x)$ is the conditional probability that $S=x$, given that $N=3$, and, in general, $p_X^{*(k)}(x)$ is the conditional probability that $S=x$, given that $N=k$, which we write as $Pr(S=x\,|\,N=k)$.) It should be clear that $p_X^{*(1)}(x)=p_X(x)$, and we define the special initial value $p_X^{*(0)}(x)$ to be

$$p_X^{*(0)}(x) = \begin{cases} 1 & \text{for } x=0 \\ 0 & \text{for } x>0 \end{cases}. \tag{7.7}$$

EXAMPLE 7.4

Extend Example 7.3 to exhibit $p_X^{*(k)}(x)$ for $k=0,1,2,3,4$.

SOLUTION

Using the recursion formula given by Equation (7.6c), we obtain the following values of $p_X^{*(k)}(x)$, which the reader should verify.

TABLE 7.3

Results for Example 7.4						
x	$p_X^{*(0)}(x)$	$p_X^{*(1)}(x)$	$p_X^{*(2)}(x)$	$p_X^{*(3)}(x)$	$p_X^{*(4)}(x)$
0	1	.00	.00	.000	.0000
1	0	.20	.00	.000	.0000
2	0	.30	.04	.000	.0000
3	0	.40	.12	.008	.0000
4	0	.10	.25	.036	.0016
5	0	.00	.28	.102	.0096
6	0	.00	.22	.183	.0344
7	0	.00	.08	.240	.0824
8	0	.00	.01	.219	.1473
9	0	.00	.00	.142	.1992
10	0	.00	.00	.057	.2084
11	0	.00	.00	.012	.1656
12	0	.00	.00	.001	.0982
13	0	.00	.00	.000	.0408
14	0	.00	.00	.000	.0108
15	0	.00	.00	.000	.0016
16	0	.00	.00	.000	.0001
	1	**1.00**	**1.00**	**1.000**	**1.0000**

❒

In Examples 7.3 and 7.4 we have treated the severity distribution as discrete. Then, since N is discrete as well, so will be the aggregate claims distribution S, with probability function given by

$$\begin{aligned} p_S(x) = Pr(S=x) &= \sum_{k=0}^{\infty} Pr(N=k)\cdot Pr(S=x\,|\,N=k) \\ &= \sum_{k=0}^{\infty} p_N(k)\cdot p_X{}^{*(k)}(x). \end{aligned} \tag{7.8}$$

Note that whereas $p_X{}^{*(k)}(x)$ denotes the *conditional* $Pr(S=x\,|\,N=k)$, $p_S(x)$ denotes the *unconditional* $Pr(S=x)$.

EXAMPLE 7.5

Using the severity distribution of Examples 7.3 and 7.4, along with a Poisson frequency distribution with $\lambda=3$, calculate $Pr(S\geq 3)$.

SOLUTION

First we note that

$$Pr(S\geq 3) = 1-Pr(S=0)-Pr(S=1)-Pr(S=2).$$

We have

$$Pr(S=0) = Pr(N=0) = \left(\frac{e^{-3}\cdot 3^0}{0!}\right) = .04979$$

and

$$Pr(S=1) = Pr(N=1)\cdot p_X{}^{*(1)}(1) = \left(\frac{e^{-3}\cdot 3^1}{1!}\right)(.20) = .02987.$$

There are two ways to end up with $S=2$. Either we have one claim with loss amount 2, or two claims each with loss amount 1. Thus we have

$$\begin{aligned} Pr(S=2) &= Pr(N=1)\cdot p_X{}^{*(1)}(2)+Pr(N=2)\cdot p_X{}^{*(2)}(2) \\ &= \left(\frac{e^{-3}\cdot 3^1}{1!}\right)(.30)+\left(\frac{e^{-3}\cdot 3^2}{2!}\right)(.04) = .05377. \end{aligned}$$

Then

$$Pr(S\geq 3) = 1-.04979-.02987-.05377 = .8666.$$ ❐

From Examples 7.3, 7.4, and 7.5 we can see that, even with modern computers, considerable computation is required to obtain values of $p_S(x)$ via Equation (7.8). However, in the special case where the severity random variable is discrete and assumes only integral values, as is the case in these three examples, and if the frequency distribution is a member of the $(\alpha,\beta,0)$

class (see Section 5.2.5), then values of $p_S(x)$ can be generated recursively since S has a compound distribution.

The recursive approach was developed in Section 5.3.1 in the context of a compound frequency model. Now we can simply adapt the results presented there to our current application. We rewrite Equation (5.28) as

$$p_S(x) = \frac{1}{1-\alpha \cdot p_X(0)} \cdot \sum_{k=1}^{x}\left(\alpha+\frac{\beta k}{x}\right) \cdot p_X(k) \cdot p_S(x-k). \tag{7.9}$$

In the particular case where N is Poisson, with $\alpha=0$ and $\beta=\lambda$, then Equation (7.9) becomes

$$p_S(x) = \sum_{k=1}^{x} \frac{\lambda k}{x} \cdot p_X(k) \cdot p_S(x-k). \tag{7.10}$$

(See also Exercise 5-9.) The initial value of the recursion, $p_S(0)$, is given by Equation (5.29) as $M_N\left[\ln p_X(0)\right]$. In the compound Poisson case this leads to

$$\begin{aligned} p_S(0) &= M_N(t)\Big|_{t=\ln p_X(0)} \\ &= e^{\lambda(e^t-1)}\Big|_{t=\ln p_X(0)} \\ &= e^{-\lambda[1-p_X(0)]}. \end{aligned} \tag{7.11}$$

EXAMPLE 7.6

For the compound Poison distribution described in Example 7.5, use the recursion method to find $p_S(x)$, for $x=0,1,2,3,4,5$.

SOLUTION

We use Equation (7.11) to initialize the recursion at $x=0$, obtaining

$$p_S(0) = e^{-\lambda[1-p_X(0)]} = e^{-\lambda} = e^{-3} = .04979.$$

(The reason $p_S(0)=e^{-\lambda}$ is because the severity distribution is never zero, so the only way to have a zero aggregate claim amount is to have no claims.) Then for $x=1$ we find

$$p_S(1) = \sum_{k=1}^{1} \frac{\lambda k}{1} \cdot p_X(k) \cdot p_S(1-k) = (3)(.20)(.04979) = .02987.$$

Repeated application of the recursion formula produces the results shown in the following table

TABLE 7.4

Results for Example 7.6	
x	$p_S(x)$
0	.04979
1	.02987
2	.05377
3	.08842
4	.07928
5	.08723

❐

7.4.2 CONVOLUTIONS OF THE CDF OF X

In the prior section we saw how to convolute the probability function of the discrete severity random variable X to obtain the conditional PF of S, given $N=k$, and eventually the unconditional PF of S after assuming a distribution for the frequency random variable N. We could then easily obtain the conditional CDF of S, given $N=k$, and the unconditional CDF of S by summation of the appropriate PF values.

Alternatively, we could begin with the CDF of X and convolute it to directly obtain the conditional CDF of S, given $N=k$, and eventually the unconditional CDF of S. We let $F_X(x)$ denote the CDF of X. Then the *two-fold convolution* of $F_X(x)$, denoted $F_X^{*(2)}(x)$, represents the conditional probability $Pr(S \leq x \mid N=2)$.

EXAMPLE 7.7

Using the severity distribution of Example 7.3, find the values of $F_X^{*(2)}(x)$.

SOLUTION

The CDF of X is given in the following table:

TABLE 7.5

Data for Example 7.7	
x	$F_X(x)$
1	.20
2	.50
3	.90
4	1.00

In general, given two claims we will have $S \leq x$ if the first claim is t and the second claim is less than or equal to $x-t$, where there could be several different values of t. For example, we will have $S \leq 4$ if the first claim is 1 with the second less than or equal to 3, or the first is

2 with the second less than or equal to 2, or the first is 3 with the second less than or equal to 1. That is,

$$\begin{aligned} F_X^{*(2)}(4) &= Pr(S \le 4 \mid N=2) \\ &= \sum_{t=0}^{4} p_X(t) \cdot F_X(4-t) \\ &= (0)(1.00) + (.20)(.90) + (.30)(.50) + (.40)(.20) + (.10)(0) \\ &= .41. \end{aligned}$$

(The case of $t=0$ is included for generality, although $p_X(0)=0$ in this example.) In similar manner we find the complete distribution of $F_X^{*(2)}(x)$ shown in the following table, which the reader should verify.

TABLE 7.6

Results for Example 7.7	
x	$F_X^{*(2)}(x)$
2	.04
3	.16
4	.41
5	.69
6	.91
7	.99
8	1.00

❐

The general formula used to calculate the entries in Table 7.6 is

$$F_X^{*(2)}(x) = Pr(S \le x \mid N=2) = \sum_{t=0}^{x} p_X(t) \cdot F_X(x-t). \qquad (7.12a)$$

Similarly, given three claims we have

$$F_X^{*(3)}(x) = Pr(S \le x \mid N=3) = \sum_{t=0}^{x} p_X(t) \cdot F_X^{*(2)}(x-t), \qquad (7.12b)$$

and, in general, given $N=k$ we have

$$F_X^{*(k)}(x) = Pr(S \le x \mid N=k) = \sum_{t=0}^{x} p_X(t) \cdot F_X^{*(k-1)}(x-t). \qquad (7.12c)$$

EXAMPLE 7.8

Extend Example 7.7 to exhibit $F_X^{*(k)}(x)$ for $k=0,1,2,3,4$.

SOLUTION

We use Equation (7.12c) recursively to obtain the values shown in Table 7.7, with the values for $k=0,1,2$ already known. The reader should practice using Equation (7.12c) to verify the results for $k=3$ and $k=4$.

TABLE 7.7

Results for Example 7.8

x	$F_X^{*(0)}(x)$	$F_X^{*(1)}(x)$	$F_X^{*(2)}(x)$	$F_X^{*(3)}(x)$	$F_X^{*(4)}(x)$
0	1	.00	.00	.000	.0000
1	1	.20	.00	.000	.0000
2	1	.50	.04	.000	.0000
3	1	.90	.16	.008	.0000
4	1	1.00	.41	.044	.0016
5	1	1.00	.69	.146	.0112
6	1	1.00	.91	.329	.0456
7	1	1.00	.99	.569	.1280
8	1	1.00	1.00	.788	.2753
9	1	1.00	1.00	.930	.4745
10	1	1.00	1.00	.987	.6829
11	1	1.00	1.00	.999	.8485
12	1	1.00	1.00	1.000	.9467
13	1	1.00	1.00	1.000	.9875
14	1	1.00	1.00	1.000	.9983
15	1	1.00	1.00	1.000	.9999
16	1	1.00	1.00	1.000	1.0000

❐

Finally, we can find the unconditional CDF of *S*, denoted $F_S(x)$, from the conditional CDF's, given $N=k$, as

$$F_S(x) = Pr(S \le x) = \sum_{k=0}^{\infty} Pr(N=k) \cdot Pr(S \le x \mid N=k)$$

$$= \sum_{k=0}^{\infty} p_N(k) \cdot F_X^{*(k)}(x). \tag{7.13}$$

EXAMPLE 7.9

Repeat Example 7.5 by using Equation (7.13).

SOLUTION

The result is more direct than in Example 7.5. We have

$$
\begin{aligned}
Pr(S \geq 3) &= 1 - Pr(S \leq 2) \\
&= 1 - \sum_{k=0}^{\infty} p_N(k) \cdot F_X^{*(k)}(2) \\
&= 1 - p_N(0) \cdot F_X^{*(0)}(2) - p_N(1) \cdot F_X^{*(1)}(2) - p_N(2) \cdot F_X^{*(2)}(2) \\
&= 1 - \left(\frac{e^{-3} \cdot 3^0}{0!}\right)(1) - \left(\frac{e^{-3} \cdot 3^1}{1!}\right)(.50) - \left(\frac{e^{-3} \cdot 3^2}{2!}\right)(.04) \\
&= 1 - .04979 - .07468 - .00896 \;=\; .86657,
\end{aligned}
$$

as already known. ❐

7.4.3 CONTINUOUS SEVERITY DISTRIBUTIONS

In the previous two sections we have seen how to tabulate the discrete distribution of S when the severity random variable X is discrete, including the special case where X assumes only integral values. Now we consider the case where X has a continuous distribution.

In the continuous case we convolute the density function of X with itself. The two-fold convolution of the PDF, denoted by $f_X^{*(2)}(x)$ and given by

$$f_X^{*(2)}(x) \;=\; f_S(x \mid N{=}2) \;=\; \int_0^x f_X(t) \cdot f_X(x-t)\, dt, \tag{7.14a}$$

represents the conditional density of S at x, given that $N = 2$. Similarly,

$$f_X^{*(3)}(x) \;=\; f_S(x \mid N{=}3) \;=\; \int_0^x f_X(t) \cdot f_X^{*(2)}(x-t)\, dt \tag{7.14b}$$

represents the conditional density of S at x, given that $N = 3$, and, in general,

$$f_X^{*(k)}(x) \;=\; f_S(x \mid N{=}k) \;=\; \int_0^x f_X(t) \cdot f_X^{*(k-1)}(x-t)\, dt, \tag{7.14c}$$

the k-fold convolution of the PDF, represents the conditional density of S at x, given that $N = k$. (Note the similarity of Equations (7.6a), (7.6b), and (7.6c) in the discrete case with Equations (7.14a), (7.14b), and (7.14c) in the continuous case.) Note also that $f_X^{*(1)}(x) = f_X(x)$, and the recursion is initialized by defining

$$f_X^{*(0)}(x) \;=\; \begin{cases} 1 & \text{for } x = 0 \\ 0 & \text{for } x > 0 \end{cases}, \tag{7.15}$$

the counterpart of Equation (7.7) in the discrete case. Then the unconditional density of S at x is a discrete mixture of the conditional densities given by

$$f_S(x) = \sum_{k=0}^{\infty} p_N(k) \cdot f_X^{*(k)}(x). \tag{7.16}$$

Note that, although X is continuous, S has a mixed distribution because there is a probability mass at $S=0$ equal to $Pr(N=0) = p_N(0)$. To make this clear, we could rewrite Equation (7.16) as

$$p_S(0) = p_N(0) \tag{7.16a}$$

and

$$f_S(x) = \sum_{k=1}^{\infty} p_N(k) \cdot f_X^{*(k)}(x), \tag{7.16b}$$

for $x > 0$.

EXAMPLE 7.10

Find the k-fold convolution of the PDF if X has an exponential distribution.

SOLUTION

We already know, from both Section 1.5.2 and Section 6.2.1, that the k-fold convolution of identically-distributed exponential random variables is a gamma random variable with $\alpha = k$. Here we have

$$\begin{aligned} f_X^{*(2)}(x) &= \int_0^x f_X(t) \cdot f_X(x-t)\, dt \\ &= \int_0^x \left(\beta \cdot e^{-\beta t}\right)\left(\beta \cdot e^{-\beta(x-t)}\right) dt \\ &= \beta^2 \int_0^x e^{-\beta x}\, dt = \beta^2 \cdot x \cdot e^{-\beta x} \end{aligned}$$

and

$$\begin{aligned} f_X^{*(3)}(x) &= \int_0^x f_X(t) \cdot f_X^{*(2)}(x-t)\, dt \\ &= \int_0^x \left(\beta \cdot e^{-\beta t}\right)\left(\beta^2 (x-t) \cdot e^{-\beta(x-t)}\right) dt \\ &= \beta^3 \int_0^x (x-t) \cdot e^{-\beta x}\, dt \\ &= \frac{\beta^3}{2} \cdot x^2 \cdot e^{-\beta x}, \end{aligned}$$

which can be written as $\frac{\beta^\alpha}{\Gamma(\alpha)} \cdot x^{\alpha-1} \cdot e^{-\beta x}$, where $\alpha = 3$. Continuing in this way we obtain

$$f_X^{*(k)}(x) = \frac{\beta^k}{\Gamma(k)} \cdot x^{k-1} e^{-\beta x},$$

as already known. ❐

As an alternative to using the PDF, we could convolute the CDF of X, as we did in Section 7.3.2 in the discrete case. Analogous to Equations (7.12a), (7.12b), and (7.12c) we now have

$$F_X^{*(2)}(x) = Pr(S \leq x \mid N=2) = \int_0^x f_X(t) \cdot F_X(x-t)\, dt, \tag{7.17a}$$

$$F_X^{*(3)}(x) = Pr(S \leq x \mid N=3) = \int_0^x f_X(t) \cdot F_X^{*(2)}(x-t)\, dt, \tag{7.17b}$$

and, in general,

$$F_X^{*(k)}(x) = Pr(S \leq x \mid N=k) = \int_0^x f_X(t) \cdot F_X^{*(k-1)}(x-t)\, dt. \tag{7.17c}$$

Then we find the unconditional CDF of S from the conditional CDF's as

$$F_S(x) = Pr(S \leq x) = \sum_{k=0}^{\infty} p_N(k) \cdot F_X^{*(k)}(x), \tag{7.18}$$

which is the same as Equation (7.13) except that here X is understood to be continuous.

Generally speaking, most continuous severity distributions do not lead to tractable results under the convolution approach. The notable exception to this would be for distributions that are closed under convolution (see Section 1.5.2), such as the gamma distribution (including its special case the exponential distribution).

A particularly convenient result is obtained for the distribution of S in the following example.

EXAMPLE 7.11

Find the distribution of S when X is exponential and N is geometric.

SOLUTION

Since N is geometric we have $p_N(k) = p \cdot q^k$ and $p_N(0) = p$. (See Section 5.1.4.) The discrete part of the distribution of S is

$$p_S(0) = p_N(0) = p. \tag{7.19a}$$

The continuous part of the distribution of S has PDF given by Equation (7.16b) as

$$\begin{aligned} f_S(x) &= \sum_{k=1}^{\infty} p_N(k) \cdot f_X^{*(k)}(x) \\ &= \sum_{k=1}^{\infty} p \cdot q^k \cdot \frac{\beta^k}{\Gamma(k)} \cdot x^{k-1} e^{-\beta x}, \end{aligned}$$

for $x > 0$, since $f_X^{*(k)}(x)$ has a gamma distribution (see Example 7.10). Note also that we start the summation at $k = 1$ since $f_X^{*(0)}(x) = 0$ for $x > 0$. The expression for $f_S(x)$ then becomes

$$\begin{aligned} f_S(x) &= \sum_{k=1}^{\infty} p \cdot q^k \cdot \frac{\beta^k}{\Gamma(k)} \cdot x^{k-1} e^{-\beta x} \\ &= pq\beta \cdot e^{-\beta x} \sum_{k=1}^{\infty} \frac{(xq\beta)^{k-1}}{(k-1)!}, \end{aligned}$$

where $\Gamma(k) = (k-1)!$ because k is an integer. We recognize the summation as the series expansion of $e^{xq\beta}$, so the PDF of S becomes

$$\begin{aligned} f_S(x) &= pq\beta \cdot e^{-\beta x} \cdot e^{xq\beta} \\ &= pq\beta \cdot e^{-\beta x} \cdot e^{\beta x(1-p)} \\ &= pq\beta \cdot e^{-p\beta x}, \end{aligned} \tag{7.19b}$$

for $x > 0$. Note that the PDF in the continuous part of the distribution of S integrates to q, as it must, so that when added to the discrete probability mass of p at $S = 0$ we have total probability of 1, as required. ❐

The CDF of the distribution of S developed in Example 7.11 is given by

$$\begin{aligned} F_S(x) &= p + \int_0^x f_S(y)\, dy \\ &= p + q \int_0^x p\beta \cdot e^{-p\beta y}\, dy \\ &= p + q\left(1 - e^{-p\beta x}\right) \\ &= 1 - q \cdot e^{-p\beta x}. \end{aligned} \tag{7.20}$$

Finding the density function of S when X is exponential and N is Poisson is left to the reader as Exercise 7-13.

An alternative approach to finding the continuous part of the distribution of S would be to use the CDF. Again if X has an exponential distribution, then its k-fold convolution is gamma with integral $\alpha = k$. From Section 1.3.4 we know that the CDF of the gamma distribution is given by the incomplete gamma function $\Gamma(\alpha; \beta x) = \Gamma(k; \beta x)$ in this case. Then from Equation (7.18) we have

$$F_S(x) = p_N(0) + \sum_{k=1}^{\infty} p_N(k) \cdot \Gamma(k; \beta x). \tag{7.21a}$$

But from Appendix K we know that when $\alpha = k$ is integral, the incomplete gamma function can be evaluated by Equation (K.3). Thus we have

$$\begin{aligned} F_S(x) &= p_N(0) + \sum_{k=1}^{\infty} p_N(k) \left[1 - e^{-\beta x} \sum_{r=0}^{k-1} \frac{(\beta x)^r}{r!} \right] \\ &= 1 - e^{-\beta x} \sum_{k=1}^{\infty} p_N(k) \cdot \sum_{r=0}^{k-1} \frac{(\beta x)^r}{r!}, \end{aligned} \tag{7.21b}$$

since $\sum_{k=1}^{\infty} p_N(k) = 1 - p_N(0)$. Next we reverse the order of the double summation, leading to

$$\begin{aligned} F_S(x) &= 1 - e^{-\beta x} \sum_{r=0}^{\infty} \frac{(\beta x)^r}{r!} \cdot \sum_{k=r+1}^{\infty} p_N(k) \\ &= 1 - e^{-\beta x} \sum_{r=0}^{\infty} \frac{(\beta x)^r}{r!} \left(1 - \sum_{k=0}^{r} p_N(k) \right). \end{aligned} \tag{7.21c}$$

A numerical example will be helpful in understanding the application of Equation (7.21c).

EXAMPLE 7.12

Approximate the value of $F_S(100)$ if X has an exponential distribution with mean 100 and N has a Poisson distribution with mean 5.

SOLUTION

Here $\beta = .01$ so Equation (7.21c) becomes

$$F_S(100) = 1 - e^{-1} \sum_{r=0}^{\infty} \frac{1}{r!} \left(1 - \sum_{k=0}^{r} p_N(k) \right).$$

The first nine values of $p_N(k)$ with $\lambda = 5$ are as follows:

k	$p_N(k)$	k	$p_N(k)$	k	$p_N(k)$
0	.00674	3	.14037	6	.14622
1	.03369	4	.17547	7	.10444
2	.08422	5	.17547	8	.06528

Then we have

$$
\begin{aligned}
F_S(100) &= 1-e^{-1}\Big[(1-p_N(0))+\frac{1}{1!}(1-p_N(0)-p_N(1)) \\
&\qquad +\frac{1}{2!}(1-p_N(0)-p_N(1)-p_N(2))+\cdots\Big] \\
&= 1-.36788\Big[.99326+.95957+\frac{1}{2!}(.87535)+\frac{1}{3!}(.73498) \\
&\qquad +\frac{1}{4!}(.55951)+\frac{1}{5!}(.38404)+\frac{1}{6!}(.23782) \\
&\qquad +\frac{1}{7!}(.13338)+\cdots\Big] \\
&= .06563.
\end{aligned}
$$

(Note that the first neglected term would deduct only an additional

$$
(.36788)\left[\frac{1}{8!}(.06810)\right] = .00000062,
$$

which does not change our value of $F_S(100)$ within five places.) ❐

Finally, we note that if N has a binomial distribution, with parameter n, then the values of $p_N(k)$ become zero for $k>n$ so

$$
\sum_{k=r+1}^{\infty} p_N(k) = 0
$$

for $r \geq n.$ Therefore the upper limit on the first summation in Equation (7.21c) is $r=n-1$, and the expression for $F_S(x)$ can be evaluated exactly. This is illustrated in Exercise 7-14.

7.4.4 A FINAL THOUGHT REGARDING CONVOLUTIONS

A large portfolio may have thousands of individual contracts, requiring 1000-fold convolutions in order to calculate exact probabilities for the aggregate claims distribution. In the case of either discrete or continuous severity distributions, this is an onerous task even with modern computers. For this reason, it is more common to calculate the moments of S using the formulas of Section 7.1, and then to estimate probabilities about S using a more tractable approximating distribution. This is illustrated in the following example.

EXAMPLE 7.13

Two types of claims are made to an insurance company. The number of Type A claims follows a Poisson distribution with $\lambda=12$, and the amount of a Type A claim is uniformly distributed over $(0,1)$. The number of Type B claims follows a Poisson distribution with $\lambda=4$, and the amount of a Type B claim is uniformly distributed over $(0,5)$. All claim numbers and claim amounts are mutually independent. Use the normal approximation to determine the probability that the total of claim amounts exceeds 18.

SOLUTION

We can model total claims as

$$S = S_A + S_B = (X_1 + X_2 + \cdots + X_N) + (Y_1 + Y_2 + \cdots + Y_M),$$

where N is the number of Type A claims and M is the number of Type B claims. The assumed distributions tell us that $E[N] = Var(N) = 12$, $E[M] = Var(M) = 4$, $E[X] = \frac{1}{2}$, $Var(X) = \frac{1}{12}$, $E[Y] = \frac{5}{2}$, $Var(Y) = \frac{25}{12}$. Then from Equations (7.5a) and (7.5b) we have

$$E[S_A] = E[X] \cdot E[N] = \left(\tfrac{1}{2}\right)(12) = 6,$$

$$E[S_B] = E[Y] \cdot E[M] = \left(\tfrac{5}{2}\right)(4) = 10,$$

$$Var(S_A) = Var(X) \cdot E[N] + Var(N) \cdot (E[X])^2 = 12\left(\frac{1}{12} + \frac{1}{4}\right) = 4,$$

and

$$Var(S_B) = Var(Y) \cdot E[M] + Var(M) \cdot (E[Y])^2 = 4\left(\frac{25}{12} + \frac{25}{4}\right) = \frac{100}{3}.$$

Then

$$E[S] = E[S_A] + E[S_B] = 6 + 10 = 16$$

and, due to independence,

$$Var(S) = Var(S_A) + Var(S_B) = 4 + \frac{100}{3} = \frac{112}{3}.$$

Finally,

$$Pr(S > 18) = Pr\left(Z > \frac{18-16}{\sqrt{112/3}}\right)$$

$$= Pr(Z > .327) = 1 - \Phi(.327) = .3727,$$

from a table of standard normal values.[2] ❐

Another approach to making probability statements about S is to use simulation; this is further pursued in Examples 7.19 and 7.20.

---

[2] Note that the normal approximation continuity correction is not needed in this case, since the severity distribution is continuous.

7.5 EFFECT OF COVERAGE MODIFICATIONS

In Section 6.3 we explored the effect of coverage modifications, such as deductibles and policy limits, on the distribution of individual claim amounts. Now we consider, in Section 7.5.1, the effect of such individual coverage modifications on aggregate claims. Alternatively, the modifications, particularly deductibles, can be applied to the aggregate loss, rather than to the underlying individual losses. This arrangement is explored in Section 7.5.2.

7.5.1 MODIFICATIONS APPLIED TO INDIVIDUAL LOSSES

Under the collective risk model, the X_i's of Equation (7.4b) denote the individual claim payments after the application of any coverage modifications. When the distribution of S is approximated from the moments of X and N, as in Example 7.13, the moments of X are found as shown in Section 6.3. (Note that X in the collective risk model denotes the claim payment amount, given that a claim is incurred, so it is the same as Z in Section 6.3; it is *not* the same as X in Section 6.3 which denotes the amount of loss before application of any coverage modifications.)

If loss amounts are discrete, so claim payment amounts (after applying any coverage modifications) are also discrete, then we can convolute the discrete distribution of claim amounts to tabulate the discrete distribution of S.

The following two examples illustrate the effect of individual coverage modifications on the moments of aggregate payments.

EXAMPLE 7.14

The number of losses is Poisson with $\lambda = 5$, and the size of each loss is Pareto with $\theta = 10$ and $\alpha = 2.50$. An insurance for losses has a deductible of 5 for each individual loss. Find the expected value of the aggregate payments under this insurance.

SOLUTION

With an individual deductible of 5, the expected payment per loss event is

$$E[Y] = E[(X-5)_+] = \frac{\theta^\alpha}{(\alpha-1)(5+\theta)^{\alpha-1}} = \frac{10^{2.5}}{(1.5)(15)^{1.5}} = 3.62887,$$

using the notation of Section 6.3.1 and the result of Exercise 6-26(c). The expected payment per payment event is

$$E[Z] = \frac{E[Y]}{1-F_X(d)} = \frac{3.62887}{\left(\frac{10}{15}\right)^{2.5}} = 10.$$

In the collective risk model, the random variable N denotes the *number of payments*, so it is the number of losses in excess of the deductible (so as to produce a claim). Here the expected number of *losses* is 5, so the expected number of *claims* is $5 \cdot Pr(X>5) = 5\left(\frac{10}{15}\right)^{2.5} = 1.81444$. Finally the expected aggregate payment is

$$E[S] = E[N] \cdot E[Z] = (1.81444)(10) = 18.14440.$$ ❒

EXAMPLE 7.15

The number of annual losses is Poisson with $\lambda = 10$. The distribution of loss amounts is uniform over $(0,10)$, with a deductible of 4 per loss. Assuming independence of loss amounts and number of losses, find the variance of annual aggregate payments.

SOLUTION

The independence assumptions of the collective risk model hold, so we can write

$$S = Z_1 + Z_2 + \cdots + Z_N,$$

where Z_i denotes the ith payment per payment event and N denotes the number of payments. Here the probability that a loss produces a payment is $Pr(X > 4) = .60$, since X is uniform over $(0,10)$. Therefore the number of payments is Poisson with $\lambda = (10)(.60) = 6$, so $E[N] = Var(N) = 6$. Then from Equation (7.5b) we have

$$Var(S) = E[N] \cdot Var(Z) + Var(N) \cdot (E[Z])^2 = 6 \cdot E[Z^2].$$

We find the second moment of Z from Equation (6.28a) as

$$E[Z^2] = \frac{\int_4^{10} (x-4)^2 \cdot f_X(x)\,dx}{1 - F_X(x)} = \frac{.10 \int_4^{10} (x-4)^2\,dx}{.60},$$

since X is uniform over $(0,10)$. Then

$$E[Z^2] = \frac{(.10)\left(\frac{1}{3}(x-4)^3\right)\Big|_4^{10}}{.60} = \frac{(.10)\left(\frac{1}{3}\right)(6^3)}{.60} = 12$$

and finally

$$Var(S) = (6)(12) = 72.$$

❐

7.5.2 MODIFICATIONS APPLIED TO THE AGGREGATE LOSS (STOP-LOSS REINSURANCE)

In Chapter 6 we discussed contingent contracts with a per-contract deductible d, with payment amount per loss event given by Equation (6.24) as

$$Y = (X-d)_+ = \begin{cases} 0 & \text{for } X \le d \\ X-d & \text{for } X > d \end{cases}.$$

Now we consider an arrangement whereby the deductible is applied not on an individual contract basis, but rather to the block of contracts as a whole. That is, the deductible d will be applied to S instead of to X. This arrangement is called *stop-loss reinsurance*, and results in an aggregate claim amount equal to

$$(S-d)_+ = \begin{cases} 0 & \text{for } S \le d \\ S-d & \text{for } S > d \end{cases}. \tag{7.22}$$

Just as in the case of individual deductibles (see Section 6.3.3), it will be true that

$$S = (S \wedge d) + (S-d)_+, \tag{7.23}$$

and if S is continuous (i.e., if the severity distribution X is continuous), then

$$E[(S-d)_+] = \int_d^\infty (x-d) \cdot f_S(x)\,dx = \int_d^\infty [1-F_S(x)]\,dx. \tag{7.24a}$$

In the case where S is discrete, the situation is a bit more complicated. Here we have

$$E[(S-d)_+] = \sum_{x>d} (x-d) \cdot p_S(x). \tag{7.24b}$$

If d and x are integral, Equation (7.24b) is then equal to $p(d+1) + 2 \cdot p(d+2) + 3 \cdot p(d+3), \cdots,$ which can be written as

$$E[(S-d)_+] = \sum_{x=d}^{\infty} [1-F_S(x)]. \tag{7.25}$$

From Equation (7.25) we find the recursive relationship

$$E[(S-d)_+] = [1-F_S(d)] + E[(S-d-1)_+], \tag{7.26}$$

which can then be used to calculate successive values of $E[(S-d)_+]$ starting with

$$E[(S-0)_+] = E[S]. \tag{7.27}$$

The reader will have an opportunity to explore this recursion further in the exercises.

For the case where d is non-integral, we can use the following more general result that applies to continuous as well as discrete aggregate distributions.

Let the deductible d satisfy $a < d < b$, where $Pr(a < S < b) = 0$. Then $E[(S-d)_+]$ is obtained by linear interpolation between $E[(S-a)_+]$ and $E[(S-b)_+]$, producing

$$E[(S-d)_+] = \frac{b-d}{b-a} \cdot E[(S-a)_+] + \frac{d-a}{b-a} \cdot E[(S-b)_+]. \tag{7.28}$$

To derive Equation (7.28) we start with Equation (7.24a). We have

$$E[(S-d)_+] = \int_d^\infty [1-F_S(x)]\,dx$$

$$= \int_a^\infty [1-F_S(x)]\,dx - \int_a^d [1-F_S(x)]\,dx. \tag{7.29}$$

Since $Pr(a<S<b)=0$, we know that $F_S(x)=F_S(a)$, for $a<x<b$, so the rightmost term in Equation (7.29) becomes

$$\int_a^d [1-F_S(a)]\,dx = (d-a)\cdot[1-F_S(a)].$$

Then Equation (7.29) itself becomes

$$E[(S-d)_+] = E[(S-a)_+]-(d-a)\cdot[1-F_S(a)]. \tag{7.30}$$

Similar analysis leads to

$$E[(S-b)_+] = E[(S-a)_+]-(b-a)\cdot[1-F_S(a)]. \tag{7.31}$$

We rearrange Equation (7.31) to read

$$1-F_S(a) = \frac{E[(S-a)_+]-E[(S-b)_+]}{b-a}. \tag{7.32}$$

Finally we substitute the right side of Equation (7.32) for the $1-F_S(a)$ term in Equation (7.30) and rearrange to obtain Equation (7.28).

EXAMPLE 7.16

For the compound Poisson distribution described in Example 7.5, find the expected value of a stop-loss reinsurance payment with an aggregate deductible of 2.

SOLUTION

One approach to this problem is to use recursion. Starting with Equation (7.27) we have

$$\begin{aligned} E[(S-0)_+] &= E[S] \\ &= E[N]\cdot E[X] \\ &= (3)[(1)(.20)+(2)(.30)+(3)(.40)+(4)(.10)] \\ &= 7.20. \end{aligned}$$

Then from Equation (7.26) we find

$$E[(S-1)_+] = E[(S-0)_+]-[1-F_S(0)] = 7.20-(1-.04979) = 6.2498,$$

where we use the fact that $F_S(0) = p_S(0) = .04979$. Next we find

$$E[(S-2)_+] = E[(S-1)_+]-[1-F_S(1)] = 6.2498-.9203 = 5.3295,$$

where we use the fact that $F_S(1) = p_S(0)+p_S(1) = .0797$.

Alternatively we could calculate $E[(S-2)_+]$ by modifying Equation (7.24b) as

$$E[(S-d)_+] = \sum_{x=d+1}^{\infty} (x-d)\cdot p_S(x) = E[S]-d+\sum_{x=0}^{d-1}(d-x)\cdot p_S(x),$$

which the reader should verify. Substituting $d=2$ will then lead to $E[(S-2)_+] = 5.3295$, as before. ❐

EXAMPLE 7.17

For the compound Poisson distribution described in Example 7.5, find the expected value of a stop-loss reinsurance payment with an aggregate deductible of 1.70.

SOLUTION

We use Equation (7.28) and linear interpolation in the interval (1,2) to obtain

$$\begin{aligned} E[(S-1.70)_+] &= (.30)\cdot E[(S-1)_+]+(.70)\cdot E[(S-2)_+] \\ &= (.30)(6.2498)+(.70)(5.3295) = 5.6056. \end{aligned}$$ ❐

The above examples are manually tractable because the deductible d is small enough that we only need values of $p_S(x)$ for very small values of x. For more realistic contingent payment arrangements with meaningful portfolio sizes and meaningful group deductibles, such calculations could be prohibitively time consuming. In this scenario, the moments of the compound distribution are used to evaluate an approximating distribution. According to the Central Limit Theorem, a good candidate for the approximating distribution is the normal distribution with mean and variance equal to those of S. For small numbers of policyholders, or for distributions of S with significant skewness, a different approximating distribution may be needed and can be chosen using higher moments of S along with the mean and variance.

EXAMPLE 7.18

A corporation provides health insurance to its 100 employees, and has purchased stop-loss reinsurance with a deductible of 330,000 to limit its liability for health care payments. The number of medical care visits per employee per year has a Poisson distribution with parameter $\lambda = 6$. The cost of each visit has an exponential distribution with mean 500. The number of visits and costs per employee are independent of the experience of the other employees.

Using the normal distribution to approximate the distribution of annual aggregate claims, calculate the probability that the reinsurer will make a payment to the corporation at year-end (i.e., that aggregate claims will exceed the deductible of 330,000).

SOLUTION

Since a normal distribution is uniquely determined by its mean and variance, we need to first find $E[S]$ and $Var(S)$. Since N is Poisson we know that $E[N] = Var(N) = (100)(6) = 600$, and since X is exponential we know that $E[X] = 500$ and $Var(X) = 250{,}000$. Then we use Equation (7.5a) to find

$$E[S] \;=\; E[N]\cdot E[X] \;=\; (600)(500) \;=\; 300{,}000$$

and Equation (7.5b) to find

$$\begin{aligned} Var(S) &= E[N]\cdot Var(X) + Var(N)\cdot (E[X])^2 \\ &= (600)(250{,}000) + (600)(250{,}000) \\ &= 300{,}000{,}000. \end{aligned}$$

Then assuming that S has a normal distribution we find

$$\begin{aligned} Pr(S > 330{,}000) &= Pr\left[Z > \frac{330{,}000 - 300{,}000}{\sqrt{300{,}000{,}000}}\right] \\ &= 1 - \Phi(1.732) \;=\; .0416. \end{aligned}$$ ❐

EXAMPLE 7.19 (Simulation Illustration)

Let N denote the random variable for number of accidents in a year, with probability function

$$p_N(n) \;=\; .90(.10)^{n-1},$$

for $n = 1, 2, \cdots$. Let X_i denote the random variable for the claim amount of the ith accident, with PDF

$$f(x_i) \;=\; .01e^{-.01x_i},$$

for $x_i > 0$ and $i = 1, 2, \cdots$. Let U and $V_1, V_2, \cdots$ be independent random variables on the uniform distribution over $[0, 1)$. Given the random numbers $\{.05, .30, .22, .52, .46\}$, calculate the total amount of claims during the year where U is used to simulate N and V_i is used to simulate X_i, in that order.

SOLUTION

First we observe that $p_N(1) = F_N(1) = .90$. Then since $u = .05$ falls in the interval $[0, .90)$, the simulated number of accidents in the year is $n = 1$. Since X_i has an exponential distribution, then the second random number .30 implies a simulated claim amount for this accident of

$$x_i = \frac{-\ln(1-v_1)}{\beta} = \frac{-\ln(1-.30)}{.01} = 35.67. \quad \square$$

EXAMPLE 7.20 (Simulation Illustration)

Annual dental claims are modeled as a compound Poisson distribution, where the number of claims has mean 2 and the loss amounts follow a Pareto distribution with $\theta = 500$ and $\alpha = 2$. An insurance pays 80% of the first 750 of annual losses and 100% of annual losses in excess of 750.

We use the random number .80 to simulate the number of claims, and the sequence of random numbers {.60, .25, .70, .10, .80} to simulate the claim amounts. What is the total simulated amount of claims for one year?

SOLUTION

The values of the CDF of a Poisson distribution with mean $\lambda = 2$ are $F(0) = .135$, $F(1) = .406$, $F(2) = .677$, $F(3) = .857, \cdots$. The output value .80 falls in the interval $[.677, .857)$, so the simulated number of claims is 3. The simulated claim amounts are obtained from the output values (see Equation (4.6c)) as

$$x = \frac{\theta}{(1-u)^{1/\alpha}} - \theta = \frac{500}{(1-u)^{.50}} - 500.$$

Then $u_1 = .60$ simulates $x_1 = 290.57$, $u_2 = .25$ simulates $x_2 = 77.35$, and $u_3 = .70$ simulates $x_3 = 412.87$. The simulated aggregate loss is

$$290.57 + 77.35 + 412.87 = 780.79,$$

so the simulated amount of claim payment is

$$.80(750.00) + (780.79 - 750.00) = 630.79. \quad \square$$

7.6 INFINITELY DIVISIBLE DISTRIBUTIONS

In this section we enlarge on the discussion of infinite divisibility that was introduced in Section 7.3.1, and demonstrate that the Poisson and negative binomial distributions possess this property.

7.6.1 DEFINITION OF INFINITE DIVISIBILITY

The distribution of a random variable X is said to be infinitely divisible if, for every positive integer k, the MGF of X can be written as

$$M_X(t) = [M_Y(t)]^k,$$

where $M_Y(t)$ is the MGF for some random variable.

7.6.2 THE POISSON DISTRIBUTION

If X has a Poisson distribution (see Section 1.2.5), its MGF is $M_X(t) = e^{\lambda(e^t-1)}$. Then for any positive integer k we can write

$$M_X(t) = e^{\lambda(e^t-1)} = \left[e^{(\lambda/k)(e^t-1)}\right]^k = [M_Y(t)]^k,$$

where $M_Y(t)$ is the MGF for a Poisson random variable with parameter $\frac{\lambda}{k}$.

7.6.3 THE NEGATIVE BINOMIAL DISTRIBUTION

If X has a negative binomial distribution (see Section 1.2.3), its MGF is $M_X(t) = \left(\frac{p}{1-q\cdot e^t}\right)^r$. Then for any positive integer k we can write

$$M_X(t) = \left(\frac{p}{1-q\cdot e^t}\right)^r = \left[\left(\frac{p}{1-q\cdot e^t}\right)^{r/k}\right]^k = [M_Y(t)]^k,$$

where $M_Y(t)$ is the MGF for a negative binomial random variable with parameters p and $\frac{r}{k}$. (Note that in both the Poisson and negative binomial cases, the division preserves the family of the distribution.)

7.7 SUMMARY

We have explored here both the individual and collective approaches to modeling aggregate loss amounts, with emphasis on the convolution method. The effect of coverage modifications on aggregate claims was also examined.

7.8 EXERCISES

7.1 Introduction
7.2 Individual Risk versus Collective Risk

7-1 If S is the aggregate claim amount random variable having a compound Poisson distribution with parameter λ, show that

$$E[S] = \lambda \cdot E[X]$$

and

$$Var(S) = \lambda \cdot E[X^2].$$

7-2 Let S represent aggregate claims under a collective risk model, where the frequency distribution is $p_N(0) = .50$, $p_N(1) = .30$, and $p_N(2) = .20$, and the severity distribution is Pareto (see Section 6.1.2) with parameters $\alpha = 3$ and $\theta = 5000$. Calculate the coefficient of variation of S.

7-3 A farmer models the amount of rainfall per day as follows:

(i) The probability of rain in any day is .10.
(ii) The daily amounts of rain are independent of rain amounts on other days, as is the event of rain itself.
(iii) If rain occurs on a given day, the amount of rain has a gamma distribution with mean .50 and variance .50.

Let S represent the total rainfall in a month of 30 days. Find each of the following:

(a) $E[S]$ (b) $Var(S)$ (c) $M_S(t)$

7-4 Individual members of an insured group have independent claim distributions. Males and females have distinct severity distributions with the following properties:

Gender	Mean	Variance
Male	2	4
Female	4	10

(a) Find the mean and variance of the aggregate claim distribution for a group of 40 males and 60 females.

(b) For a group of n members for which the genders are unknown, the number of males is treated as a binomial random variable with parameters n and $p = .40$. Find the mean and variance of aggregate claims for a group of 100 members for which the genders are unknown.

7-5 A company insures oil-carrying ships. The insurer's actuary makes the following assumptions:

(i) The probability of a claim for a single ship is .01.
(ii) There will be at most one claim per ship.
(iii) The claim amount has a gamma distribution with mean 500 and variance 2500.

Determine the mean and variance of aggregate claims for a portfolio of 10 policies.

7-6 Hospital charges for an individual have the following characteristics:

Charges	Mean	Standard Deviation
Room	1000	500
Other	500	300

The covariance between an individual's Room Charges and Other Charges is 100,000. An insurer issues a policy that reimburses 100% for Room Charges and 80% for Other Charges. The number of hospital admissions has a Poisson distribution with parameter 4. Determine the variance of the insurer's total payment under the policy.

7-7 The repair costs for boats in a marina have the following characteristics:

Type of Boat	Number of Boats	Probability of Repair	Mean Repair Cost, Given Repair	Variance of Repair Cost, Given Repair
Power	100	.30	300	10,000
Sail	300	.10	1000	400,000
Yacht	50	.60	5000	2,000,000

At most one repair is required per boat each year, and all boats are independent with regard to repair needs. The marina's annual budget for repairs is the mean plus one standard deviation of aggregate repair costs. Calculate the annual repair cost budget.

7-8 A new insurance sales person has ten friends, all age 22, each of whom is considering the purchase of a whole life insurance policy of 1000, payable at the end of the year of death. Each friend has probability .10 of buying a policy, and all future lifetimes and purchase decisions are independent. Given the values $A_{22} = .07135$ and ${}^2A_{22} = .01587$, find the variance of the present value at issue of total payments made to those who purchase the insurance.

7.3 Selection of Frequency and Severity Distributions
7.4 More on the Collective Risk Model

7-9 A claim severity distribution is given by $p_x(0)=.30$, $p_x(1)=.30$, and $p_x(3)=.40$. Calculate $p_X^{*(k)}(x)$, for $k=0,1,2,3$.

7-10 An aggregate claims distribution S has PF given by

$$p_S(x) = \sum_{k=0}^{\infty} p_X^{*(k)}(x) \cdot \frac{e^{-50}(50)^k}{k!},$$

with a severity distribution given by $p_X(1)=.40$, $p_X(2)=.50$, and $p_X(3)=.10$. Find the value of $Var(S)$.

7-11 A compound Poisson aggregate claims distribution S has parameter $\lambda=.60$ and severity distribution given by $p_X(1)=.20$, $p_X(2)=.30$, and $p_X(3)=.50$. Determine $Pr(S \geq 3)$.

7-12 The number of claims made on an insurance portfolio follows the distribution $p_N(0)=.70$, $p_N(1)=.20$, and $p_N(2)=.10$. If a claim occurs, the benefit is 0 (due to certain coverage restrictions) or 10, with probability .80 and .20, respectively. The number of claims and the claim amounts are independent. Find the probability that actual aggregate claim benefits will exceed expected aggregate benefits by more than two standard deviations.

7-13 Let X have an exponential distribution with mean 100, and let N have a Poisson distribution with mean 5. Approximate the value of $f_S(100)$.

7-14 Four separate and independent buildings are insured against fire for one year. Each building can have at most one fire in a year, the probability of which is .05. If a fire occurs, the distribution of damage amount is exponential with mean 1000. Find the probability that the aggregate damage amount for the four buildings will exceed 2000.

7-15 For a compound Poisson aggregate claims distribution, the expected number of claims is 2 and the claim severity distribution is given by $X=e^Y$, where Y is normally distributed with mean 1 and standard deviation 2. Find the coefficient of variation of aggregate claims.

7-16 An aggregate claims distribution S has a continuous uniform severity distribution over (0, 100), and frequency distribution given by $p_N(1) = .60$ and $p_N(2) = .40$. Calculate $Pr(S > 75)$.

7-17 An aggregate loss random variable S has a negative binomial frequency distribution with mean 3 and variance 3.60. The common distribution of the independent individual loss amounts is uniform over $(0, 20)$. Use the normal distribution to approximate the 95th percentile of the distribution of S.

7-18 A dam is proposed for a river currently used for salmon breeding.

(i) For each hour the dam is open, the number of salmon passing through has a distribution with mean 100 and variance 900.

(ii) The number of eggs released by each salmon has a distribution with mean 5 and variance 5.

(iii) The number of salmon passing through the dam and the number of eggs released are independent.

Using the normal approximation for the aggregate number of eggs released, how many hours must the dam be open so the probability of at least 10,000 eggs being released is at least .95?

7.5 Effect of Coverage Modifications

7-19 For a certain fleet of vehicles, aggregate property damage losses has a compound Poisson distribution with $\lambda = 20$ and an exponential distribution of loss severity with $\beta = .005$. To reduce the cost of insurance, coverage modifications are made whereby a certain type of vehicle will no longer be insured (which will reduce loss frequency by 20%) and a deductible of 100 will be imposed on each individual loss. Find the expected aggregate insurance payment after the modifications are made.

7-20 For a certain collective risk model, the number of losses has a Poisson distribution with $\lambda = 20$. The distribution of the individual loss random variable X has the following characteristics:

$$E[X] = 70 \qquad E[X \wedge 30] = 25$$

$$Pr(X > 30) = .75 \qquad E[X^2 \mid X > 30] = 9000$$

An insurance covers aggregate losses subject to a deductible of 30 per individual loss. Calculate the variance of the aggregate payment under the insurance.

7-21 An aggregate claim distribution S has the severity distribution given in Exercise 7-9 and frequency distribution given by $p_N(1) = .60$, $p_N(2) = .30$ and $p_N(3) = .10$. Find each of the following:

(a) The PF and CDF of S.

(b) The expected value of a reinsurer's stop-loss payment under a group deductible of 3.00.

(c) The expected value of a reinsurer's stop-loss payment under a group deductible of 2.70.

(d) The deductible d that produces an expected value of stop-loss coverage equal to 1.00.

7-22 An investment bank insures three loans with a group deductible of 8 million. The distribution of possible aggregate claim amounts S for the three guarantees is as follows:

S	$p_S(x)$
0	.90
5 million	.05
10 million	.03
15 million	.02

Find the expected total payment amount for the investment bank.

7-23 One way to establish the market view of probabilities is to consider the market price placed on contingent events in an efficient market. For example, suppose we have the following values from a competitive market:

$$E[S-5{,}000)_+] = 2000$$
$$E[(S-10{,}000)_+] = 1500$$

Suppose also that loss amounts between 5,000 and 10,000 are impossible. According to this information, what is the probability that total losses will exceed 5,000?

7-24 A random loss has the following probability function:

x	0	1	2	3	4	5	6	7	8	9
$p_X(x)$	.05	.06	.25	.22	.10	.05	.05	.05	.05	.12

Given that $E[X] = 4$ and $E[(X-d)_+] = 2$, find the value of d.

7-25 The aggregate claims S for a block of business has PDF given by

$$f_S(x) = \beta \cdot e^{-\beta x},$$

for $\beta > 0$. In terms of β and d, find the expected claim payment to be made by a reinsurer under a stop-loss arrangement with deductible d.

7-26 An employer self-insures a life insurance program with the following characteristics:

(i) Given that a claim has occurred, the claim amount will be 2000 with probability .30 or 3000 with probability .70.

(ii) The claim frequency distribution is given by $p_N(0) = .35$, $p_N(1) = .35$, $p_N(2) = .20$, and $p_N(3) = .10$.

The employer purchases aggregate stop-loss coverage to limit its annual claim cost to 4000. The cost of the coverage is 750. Find the employer's total expected annual cost, including the retained claim cost and the cost of the stop-loss coverage.

7-27 A stop-loss reinsurance pays 80% of the amount by which aggregate claims exceed 1000, subject to a maximum payment of 300. Given the following information, find the total amount of claims the reinsurer expects to pay:

(i) $E[(S-1000)_+] = 400$

(ii) $E[(S-1500)_+] = 200$

(iii) The probability of an aggregate claim amount between 1000 and 1500 is zero.

7-28 A stop-loss insurance covers a three-person group with a group deductible of 1. The distribution of loss amounts per person in the group is $p_X(0) = .40$, $p_X(1) = .30$, $p_X(2) = .20$, and $p_X(3) = .10$, and loss amounts are independent among persons. Calculate the expected insurance payment.

7-29 For a certain collective risk model the number of losses is Poisson with $\lambda = 2$ and the common distribution of individual losses is $p_X(1) = .60$ and $p_X(2) = .40$. Calculate the expected aggregate payment made by an insurance that covers aggregate losses subject to a deductible of 3.

7.6 Infinitely Divisible Distributions

7-30 Show that the binomial distribution does not posses the property of infinite divisibility.

CHAPTER EIGHT

SURPLUS PROCESS MODELS (RUIN THEORY)

8.1 INTRODUCTION

In Sections 5.2 and 5.3 we discussed the role of the discrete random variable as a *counting random variable* for the number of losses under a collection (or portfolio) of contingent contracts over a fixed unit interval of time, and in Section 5.3 we extended this to the concept of a *counting process* for the number of losses over the general time interval from 0 to t. In particular we considered the Poisson counting random variable N and, more generally, the Poisson counting process $N(t)$. Note that $N(1)=N$, the random variable for the number of losses in unit time, so the former is included within the latter as a special case.

Then in Chapter 7 we discussed the distribution of the aggregate loss amount, under a portfolio of contingent contracts, over a fixed interval of time. Under the collective risk model, the random variable for the aggregate loss amount over unit time, which we denoted by S, has a compound distribution with primary distribution N and secondary distribution X for the individual loss severity. Now we extend the aggregate loss random variable S to the concept of an *aggregate loss process*, denoted $S(t)$, for the aggregate loss amount over the general time interval from 0 to t.

The effect of interest, or the time value of money, is ignored throughout this chapter.

8.2 THE COMPOUND POISSON PROCESS

Let the aggregate loss process $S(t)$ be modeled by

$$S(t) = X_1 + X_2 + \cdots + X_{N(t)}, \tag{8.1}$$

where $N(t)$ denotes a counting process for the number of losses over $(0,t]$, the several X_i are independent and identically distributed loss severity random variables, and the loss severity is independent of the loss frequency process represented by $N(t)$. Under these assumptions, the aggregate loss process $S(t)$ is a *compound process* with primary distribution $N(t)$ and secondary distribution X. In particular, if $N(t)$ is a Poisson counting process, then we say that $S(t)$ is a *compound Poisson process*.

8.2.1 MOMENTS OF THE COMPOUND POISSON PROCESS

Recall from Section 5.3.2 that the mean and variance of a Poisson counting process are given by

$$E[N(t)] = Var[N(t)] = \lambda t. \tag{8.2}$$

Then if $S(t)$ is a compound Poisson process defined by Equation (8.1) we have, from the double expectation theorem,

$$E[S(t)] = E[N(t)] \cdot E[X] = \lambda t \cdot E[X] \tag{8.3a}$$

and

$$\begin{aligned} Var[S(t)] &= E[N(t)] \cdot Var(X) + Var[N(t)] \cdot (E[X])^2 \\ &= \lambda t \cdot [Var(X) + (E[X])^2] \\ &= \lambda t \cdot E[X^2]. \end{aligned} \tag{8.3b}$$

Recall from Equation (1.67) that if S has a compound distribution, with primary distribution N and secondary distribution X, then the MGF of S is given by

$$M_S(r) = M_N[\ln M_X(r)]. \tag{8.4a}$$

Now if $S(t)$ is a compound process, with primary distribution $N(t)$ and secondary distribution X, it follows that the MGF of $S(t)$ is given by

$$M_{S(t)}(r) = M_{N(t)}[\ln M_X(r)]. \tag{8.4b}$$

In particular if $N(t)$ is a Poisson process with rate (mean) λt, then we have

$$M_{S(t)}(r) = e^{\lambda t(e^u - 1)}\Big|_{u = \ln M_X(r)} = e^{\lambda t[M_X(r) - 1]}. \tag{8.4c}$$

8.2.2 OTHER PROPERTIES OF THE COMPOUND POISSON PROCESS

The properties of independent and stationary increments, described in Section 5.3.1 for the Poisson counting process, extend to the compound Poisson process defined by Equation (8.1). Therefore $S(t)$ can denote the aggregate loss amount over *any* interval of length t, and not just the interval from time 0 to time t. That is, if we let

$${}_tS_r = S(r+t) - S(r) \tag{8.5a}$$

denote the aggregate loss amount over the interval $(r, r+t]$, then ${}_tS_r$ has the same compound Poisson distribution as does $S(t)$. More generally, if

$${}_hS_r = S(r+h) - S(r) \tag{8.5b}$$

denotes the aggregate loss amount over the interval $(r, r+h]$ for any r and h, then ${}_hS_r$ has a compound Poisson distribution with parameter λh.

EXAMPLE 8.1

Automobiles go past a certain billboard according to a Poisson process at rate $\lambda = 3$ per minute. The number of passengers in each car is an independent random variable with probability function $p(1) = .50$, $p(2) = .30$, $p(3) = .12$, $p(4) = .06$, and $p(5) = .02$. Find the mean, variance, and MGF for the process representing the number of passengers going past the billboard in an hour.

SOLUTION

Unit time is measured in minutes, so we seek information about the random process $S(60)$. First we note that $\lambda t = 180$ and

$$E[X] = (1)(.50)+(2)(.30)+(3)(.12)+(4)(.06)+(5)(.02) = 1.80,$$

$$E[X^2] = (1)(.50)+(4)(.30)+(9)(.12)+(16)(.06)+(25)(.02) = 4.24,$$

and

$$M_X(r) = E[e^{Xr}] = .50e^r + .30e^{2r} + .12e^{3r} + .06e^{4r} + .02e^{5r}.$$

Then

$$E[S(60)] = (180)(1.80) = 324,$$

$$Var[S(60)] = (180)(4.24) = 756.20,$$

and

$$M_{S(60)}(r) = e^{180[M_X(r)-1]},$$

where $M_X(r)$ is given above. ❐

8.3 THE SURPLUS PROCESS MODEL

An interesting application of the aggregate loss process is in the area of *surplus process models*. The general form of such a model assumes an initial supply of some commodity, a mechanism for augmenting the supply, and a loss process for reducing the supply. Generally the supply is augmented in a deterministic fashion but reduced according to a stochastic process model. For convenience we assume the supply is augmented continuously at constant rate c per unit time and reduced according to a compound Poisson loss process of amount $S(t)$ over the interval $(0,t]$. Then the supply at time t is given by

$$U(t) = u + ct - S(t), \tag{8.6}$$

for $t \geq 0$, where $U(0) = u$ denotes the initial supply of the commodity.[1]

[1] If $U(t)$ is defined for all $t \geq 0$, then it represents a *continuous-time* surplus process and $S(t)$ is a continuous-time loss process. If $U(t)$ is defined only for certain discrete values of t, such as $t = 0,1,2,\ldots$, then $U(t)$ represents a *discrete-time* process. In this chapter we consider mainly continuous-time processes, with the discrete-time process explored in Section 8.6.

One example of a surplus process model is the *inventory model*. Let u denote the number of units of a product in inventory at time 0, and let c denote the rate at which units are continuously being added to the inventory. Sales events occur according to a Poisson process with rate λ, and each sale is for a random number X of units. If the independence conditions for a compound process are met, then $S(t)$ denotes the cumulative sales over $(0,t]$ and the size of the inventory at time t is $U(t)$ as given by Equation (8.6).

A second example, and a common actuarial problem within an insurance context, would consider u to be an initial fund of money associated with a particular portfolio of contingent contracts. The fund is incremented by continuous premium income at fixed rate c per unit time and decremented by insurance claims occurring according to the aggregate claims process $S(t)$. Then $U(t)$ represents the balance in the fund at time t, which we call the *surplus* at time t.

In practice, the premium rate c will exceed the expected claim amount per unit time. The random variable for aggregate claims over one time unit is $S(1)$, so we will have $c > E[S(1)]$. In particular, we write

$$c = (1+\theta)\cdot E[S(1)], \tag{8.7}$$

for $\theta > 0$, and refer to θ as the *relative security loading*.

If the claims experience is large enough to overcome the initial surplus plus the increase in surplus due to premium income, then the surplus will become negative, and we say that *ruin* has occurred to this portfolio. A major portion of this chapter is devoted to the analysis of the event of ruin and the probability of its occurrence. For a continuous-time surplus process, we can define the event of ruin as $U(t) < 0$ at any time t. (Note that since $U(0) = u$, ruin at time 0 is not possible.) The event of ruin and the relationship among u, c, and $S(t)$ are illustrated in the following figure.

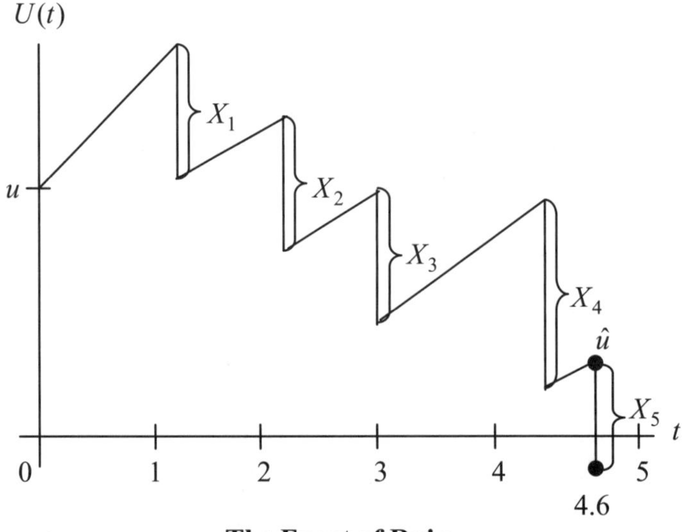

The Event of Ruin

FIGURE 8.1

The surplus grows at constant rate c until the occurrence of the first claim, at which point it drops by X_1, the amount of the claim. Then it grows again until it drops by X_2, the amount of the second claim, and so on. In the experience illustrated in Figure 8.1, the surplus grows after the fourth claim to the level denoted as $\hat{u}$, and then drops by X_5, the amount of the fifth claim, to a level less than zero at time 4.6, which is then the time of ruin.

EXAMPLE 8.2

A continuous-time surplus process begins with initial surplus of 100 and is incremented by premium income received at continuous rate 110 per unit time. The experience shows that claims occur at the following times and in the following amounts:

Time of Claim	Amount of Claim
0.3	100
0.7	50
1.2	80
1.5	10
1.9	70
2.2	60

At what time does ruin occur?

SOLUTION

The experience of this process is shown on the following graph.

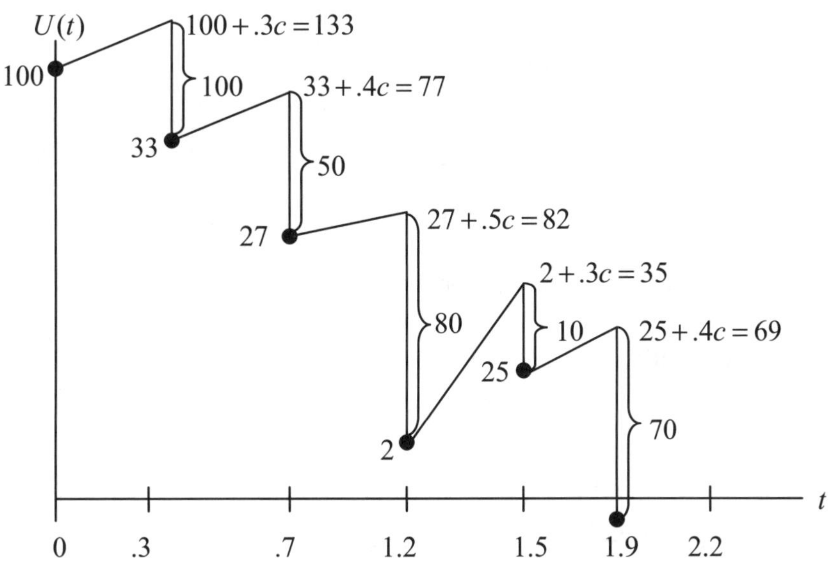

The Event of Ruin for Example 8.2 Data

FIGURE 8.2

The graph shows that ruin occurs with the fifth claim at time $t = 1.9$. ❐

8.4 THE PROBABILITY OF RUIN

Now that we have an understanding of the surplus process model and the concept of ruin, we will next consider how to evaluate the probability of ruin. Two subcases are considered. We can investigate the probability of ruin occurring within the finite time interval $(0,\tau]$, which we denote by $\psi(u,\tau)$, or within the unlimited time interval $(0,\infty)$, which we denote by $\psi(u)$. The probability of ruin will be a function of the initial surplus u, and we incorporate that fact into our notation. Most of the presentation in this chapter considers the probability of ruin over the infinite interval, with the finite interval considered in Section 8.6.

8.4.1 THE ADJUSTMENT COEFFICIENT

As background to investigating the probability of ruin, we first note that we are assuming $S(t)$ to be a compound Poisson process. Then the expected aggregate claims over one unit of time is given by

$$E[S(1)] = \lambda \cdot E[X], \tag{8.8}$$

which we will denote by $\lambda\mu$ for notational convenience. From Equation (8.7) we are also assuming that $c=(1+\theta)\lambda\mu$, where $\theta>0$ so that $c>\lambda\mu$, the expected claims in unit time.

Now we consider the net claim payment (net loss) over the interval $(0,t]$, defined by

$$Z(t) = S(t)-ct. \tag{8.9}$$

The MGF of $Z(t)$ is given by

$$\begin{aligned} M_{Z(t)}(r) &= E\left[e^{r[S(t)-ct]}\right] \\ &= E\left[e^{r\cdot S(t)}\cdot e^{-rct}\right] \\ &= e^{-rct}\cdot M_{S(t)}(r) \\ &= e^{-rct}\cdot e^{\lambda t[M_X(r)-1]}, \end{aligned} \tag{8.10}$$

from Equation (8.4c) since $S(t)$ is a compound Poisson process.

Next we consider the equation $M_{Z(t)}(r)=1$, which, from Equation (8.10), can be written as

$$e^{-rct}\cdot e^{\lambda t[M_X(r)-1]} = 1. \tag{8.11a}$$

Taking the log of both sides of Equation (8.11a) we have

$$-rct+\lambda t[M_X(r)-1] = 0$$

or

$$rc = \lambda[M_X(r)-1].$$

Substituting $c=(1+\theta)\lambda\mu$ this becomes

$$r(1+\theta)\lambda\mu = \lambda[M_X(r)-1]$$

or

$$M_X(r) = 1+r(1+\theta)\mu. \tag{8.11b}$$

Clearly Equation (8.11b) is satisfied at $r=0$. We wish to also find a value of $r>0$, which we denote by r^*, that satisfies Equation (8.11b). For convenience of notation we use $g(r)$ for $1+r(1+\theta)\mu$. The problem is illustrated in Figure 8.3.

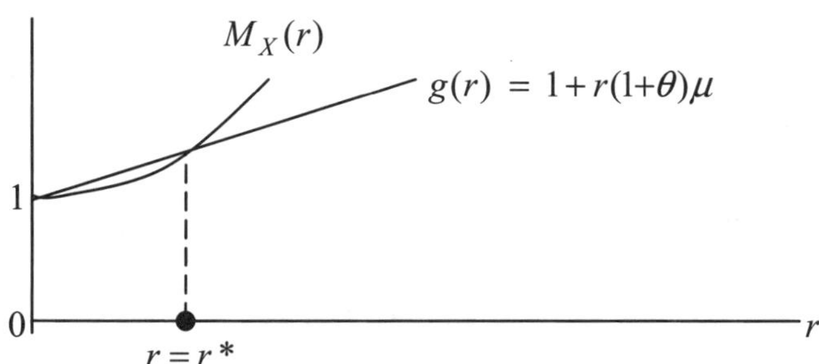

Illustration of the Adjustment Coefficient

FIGURE 8.3

Note that $M_X(0)=g(0)=1$. The slope of $M_X(r)$ at $r=0$ is given by $M'_X(0)= E[X]=\mu$, and the slope of the line $g(r)$ is $g'(0)=(1+\theta)\mu$. Since $\theta>0$, then $g'(0)>M'_X(0)$, so $g(r)$ at $r=0$ starts out higher than $M_X(r)$. But $M_X(r)$ is concave up, so, for most claim amount distributions, $M_X(r)$ eventually crosses $g(r)$ again. The value of r at which this occurs, if in fact it does, is called the *adjustment coefficient*, and is denoted by $r=r^*$.[2]

It should be clear that r^* depends on the distribution of X and on the relationship between c and $E[S(1)]=\lambda\mu$, which is expressed by the value of θ in the relationship $c=(1+\theta)\lambda\mu$. Observe from the graph in Figure 8.3 that as θ increases, $g(r)$ moves up more steeply, but $M_X(r)$ is not affected, so the crossover point $r=r^*$ moves upward and to the right. Therefore r^* is an increasing function of θ. On the other hand, as $\theta\to 0$, the slope of $g(r) = 1+r(1+\theta)\mu$, which is $g'(r)=(1+\theta)\mu$, approaches μ, so $g(r)$ becomes tangent to $M_X(r)$ at $r=0$. Then $g(r)$ and $M_X(r)$ never cross again, so $r^*\to 0$ as $\theta\to 0$.

If the distribution of X is sufficiently simple, we may be able to find the value of r^*. One special case is where the individual claim amount X is fixed at $X=x$, so the expected value is

$$E[X] = \mu = x \tag{8.12}$$

and the MGF is

[2] For some distributions of X (e.g., inverse Gaussian), $M_X(r)$ is not defined at $r\geq\gamma$. If $\lim_{r\to\gamma} M_X(r)<g(\gamma)$, then $M_X(r)$ does not cross $g(r)$ again, so the adjustment coefficient is not defined in this case.

$$M_X(r) = E[e^{Xr}] = E[e^{xr}] = e^{xr}. \tag{8.13}$$

Then Equation (8.11b) for defining r^* becomes

$$M_X(r) = e^{xr} = 1+r(1+\theta)x, \tag{8.14}$$

which can be solved for r^* by iteration.

If X has an exponential distribution (see Section 1.3.3), then its expected value is

$$E[X] = \mu = \frac{1}{\beta} \tag{8.15}$$

and the MGF is

$$M_X(r) = \frac{\beta}{\beta - r}, \tag{8.16}$$

and Equation (8.11) for defining r^* becomes

$$\frac{\beta}{\beta - r} = 1+r(1+\theta)\cdot\frac{1}{\beta}$$

or

$$\beta^2 = \beta^2 - \beta r + \beta r(1+\theta) - r^2(1+\theta)$$

or

$$r^2(1+\theta) = \beta r(1+\theta) - \beta r = \beta r\theta$$

and finally

$$r^* = \frac{\beta\theta}{1+\theta}. \tag{8.17}$$

EXAMPLE 8.3

A surplus process with a compound Poisson claims process has all claim amounts fixed at $X=1$. Determine the relative security loading θ such that the adjustment coefficient will be $r^*=.50$.

SOLUTION

From Equation (8.14) we have

$$e^{xr} = 1+r(1+\theta)x,$$

which becomes

$$e^{.50} = 1+.50(1+\theta)$$

in this case. This equation is easily solved for $\theta=.29744$. ❐

8.4.2 THE PROBABILITY OF RUIN

For a continuous-time surplus process, the probability of ruin over an infinite time interval is given by

$$\psi(u) = \frac{e^{-r^*u}}{E[e^{-r^* \cdot U(T)}\,|\,T<\infty]}, \tag{8.18}$$

where T denotes the (random) time of ruin and $U(T)$ denotes the random variable for the surplus position at time of ruin.[3] Note that $U(T)$ is necessarily a negative quantity, so $Y = -U(T)$ is positive and denotes the random variable for the (positive) surplus deficit at the instant of ruin. The denominator of Equation (8.18) gives the conditional expected value of e^{r^*Y}, given that ruin occurs, which is notated as $|\,T<\infty$.[4] The denominator can be interpreted as $M_Y(r^*)$, the MGF for the random variable Y evaluated at the adjustment coefficient r^*.

We make several observations about $\psi(u)$ as given by Equation (8.18).

(1) As $\theta \to 0$, $r^* \to 0$ as well, so $\psi(u) \to 1$ indicating that ruin is certain. That is, as $\theta \to 0$ we find c approaching the expected claim amount, suggesting that if we charge only the expected claim payment amount for the insurance then ruin is (eventually) inevitable.

(2) Since both Y and r^* are positive, then the denominator of Equation (8.18) exceeds 1 and $\psi(u)$ is therefore less that its numerator. That is, $\psi(u) < e^{-r^*u}$, establishing an upper bound on the probability of ruin.

(3) A lower bound can be established on $\psi(u)$ as well if there is a maximum value for the individual loss amount X. If m is the maximum value for X, then m is the maximum value for Y as well, since the surplus deficit at time of ruin cannot exceed the size of the claim that caused the ruin event. Then we have $Y \le m$, so $r^*Y \le r^*m$, so $e^{r^*Y} \le e^{r^*m}$, and therefore $E[e^{r^*Y}] \le e^{r^*m}$. This shows that

$$\psi(u) \ge \frac{e^{-r^*u}}{e^{r^*m}} = e^{-r^*(u+m)},$$

which establishes $e^{-r^*(u+m)}$ as a lower bound on $\psi(u)$.

(4) Clearly $\psi(u) \to 0$ as $u \to \infty$, indicating that ruin is not possible if we begin with a "sufficiently large" initial surplus.

---

[3] For a derivation of Equation (8.18), see Section 13.4 of Bowers et al. [4].

[4] It is important to note that we are not asserting that ruin does, in fact, occur, since in that case the probability of its occurrence would be 1. Rather we are finding the conditional expectation of e^{r^*Y} under the condition that ruin occurs.

EXAMPLE 8.4

Find an expression for the probability of ruin if X has an exponential distribution.

SOLUTION

To evaluate the denominator of Equation (8.18), we first need the conditional distribution of Y, given the occurrence of ruin, which is denoted as $|\,T<\infty$. Let $\hat{u}$ denote the surplus position just before time T and let X denote the amount of the claim causing ruin. It follows that $X = Y+\hat{u}$, and therefore $f_Y(y)=f_X(y+\hat{u})$. The condition "given ruin" means that $X>\hat{u}$, so we seek the conditional PDF

$$f_X(y+\hat{u}\,|\,X>\hat{u}) = \frac{f_X(y+\hat{u})}{Pr(X>\hat{u})} = \frac{f_X(y+\hat{u})}{S_X(\hat{u})}.$$

But X has an exponential distribution, so we have

$$f_X(y+\hat{u}\,|\,X>\hat{u}) = \frac{\beta\cdot e^{-\beta(y+\hat{u})}}{e^{-\beta\hat{u}}} = \beta\cdot e^{-\beta y},$$

as expected from the memoryless property of the exponential distribution. Then

$$E[e^{-r^*\cdot U(T)}\,|\,T<\infty] = E[e^{r^*Y}\,|\,X>\hat{u}].$$

Since the conditional distribution of Y, given $X>\hat{u}$, is the same exponential distribution as for X, then the denominator is simply the MGF of Y evaluated at r^*, which is $\frac{\beta}{\beta-r^*}$. Recall from Equation (8.17) that $r^*=\frac{\theta\beta}{1+\theta}$ in the exponential case. Substituting this for r^* in the expression $\frac{\beta}{\beta-r^*}$, the denominator of Equation (8.18) simplifies to $1+\theta$. Substituting for r^* in the numerator of Equation (8.18) we have

$$\exp\left[-\frac{\theta\beta u}{1+\theta}\right] = \exp\left[-\frac{\theta u}{(1+\theta)\mu}\right],$$

since $\beta=\frac{1}{E[X]}=\frac{1}{\mu}$. Thus we have

$$\psi(u) = \frac{1}{1+\theta}\cdot\exp\left[-\frac{\theta u}{(1+\theta)\mu}\right]. \qquad (8.19)$$

❐

8.5 THE DISTRIBUTION OF SURPLUS DEFICIT

In Example 8.4 we developed the probability of ruin $\psi(u)$ in the case where $N(t)$ is a Poisson counting process, so that $S(t)$ is a compound Poisson claims process, and the individual claim amount *X* has an exponential distribution. As part of that derivation we considered the conditional density of *Y*, the random variable for the positive surplus deficit when $U(t)$ first becomes negative, given that the event of $U(t)$ becoming negative does occur. Now in this section we extend that analysis to consider the distribution of *Y* without requiring that *X* have an exponential distribution. The requirement that $S(t)$ be a compound Poisson process does continue to hold, however.

8.5.1 THE EVENT OF $U(t) < u$

Recall that the event of ruin means $U(t) < 0$. Before getting to the event of ruin, and its probability, consider first the event of $U(t)$ becoming less than *u*, the initial surplus position. We let Event A denote the event $\{U(t) < u\}$, and illustrate this event in the following figure.

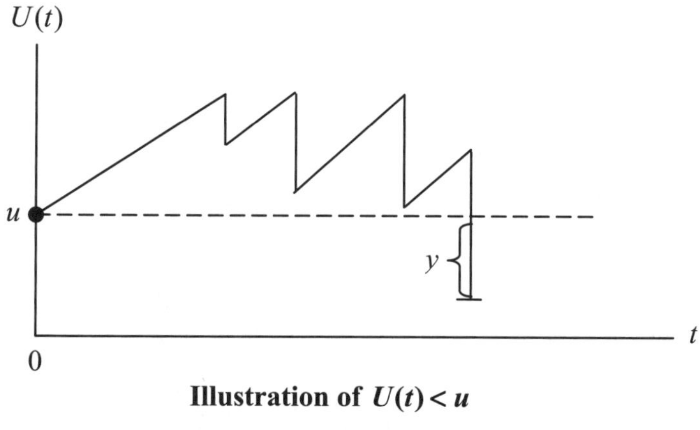

Illustration of $U(t) < u$

FIGURE 8.4

It is important to keep in mind that Event A is the event of $U(t)$ dropping below *u*, whereas *Y* denotes the (continuous) random variable for the amount by which $U(t)$ has dropped below *u*. That is, $Y = u - U(t)$ at the time *t* at which Event A first occurs.

We begin our analysis by considering the event $\{Y = y\}$, the event of *y* being the amount by which $U(t)$ has dropped below *u*. We let B denote the event $\{Y = y\}$. Note that since *Y* is continuous we must refer to the differential probability (or probability density) associated with Event B, rather than the probability of Event B. Now we consider the differential probability of the joint event $\{A \cap B\}$, which is given by

$$Pr(A \cap B) = \frac{\lambda}{c}[1 - F_X(y)]\, dy, \tag{8.20a}$$

where $F_X(y)$ is the CDF of the random variable X for individual claim amount, λ is the rate of the underlying Poisson counting process $N(t)$, and c is the continuous rate of premium income.[5] Recall that $c=(1+\theta)\lambda\mu$, so $\frac{\lambda}{c}=\frac{1}{(1+\theta)\mu}$ where $\mu=E[X]$. Then Equation (8.20a) can be written as

$$Pr(A \cap B) \;=\; \frac{S_X(y)\,dy}{(1+\theta)\mu}, \tag{8.20b}$$

where $S_X(y)=1-F_X(y)$ is the SDF of X.

If we integrate this joint density over all values of y, we get the marginal probability of Event A, which is the probability that $U(t)$ ever drops below u. We have

$$Pr(A) \;=\; \frac{1}{(1+\theta)\mu}\int_0^\infty S_X(y)\,dy \;=\; \frac{1}{1+\theta}, \tag{8.21a}$$

since

$$\int_0^\infty S_X(y)\,dy \;=\; E[X] \;=\; \mu.$$

Note that $Pr(A)$, the probability of $U(t)$ dropping below u, does not involve u so it holds for any value of u. In particular, if $u=0$ then Event A is the event of $U(t)$ dropping below zero, which is the event of ruin. Thus the probability of ruin if $u=0$ is

$$\psi(0) \;=\; Pr(A) \;=\; \frac{1}{1+\theta}. \tag{8.21b}$$

Note that this result does not depend on the distribution of X, although it does require that $S(t)$ be a compound Poisson process.

Next we consider

$$Pr(B \mid A) \;=\; \frac{Pr(A \cap B)}{Pr(A)}. \tag{8.22a}$$

Taking $Pr(A \cap B)$ from Equation (8.20b) and $Pr(A)$ from Equation (8.21a) we have

$$Pr(B \mid A) \;=\; \frac{S_X(y)\,dy}{(1+\theta)\mu} \div \frac{1}{1+\theta} \;=\; \frac{S_X(y)\,dy}{\mu}. \tag{8.22b}$$

This conditional differential probability follows from the conditional density of Y, the amount by which the surplus position is below u when this first happens, given that Event A does occur, so we may write

$$f_Y(y) \;=\; \frac{S_X(y)}{\mu}. \tag{8.22c}$$

[5] For a derivation of Equation (8.20a), see Section 13.5 of Bowers et al. [4].

EXAMPLE 8.5

Evaluate $f_Y(y)$ for the case where X has an exponential distribution.

SOLUTION

If X is exponential, then $\mu = E[X] = \frac{1}{\beta}$ and $S_X(y) = e^{-\beta y}$. Equation (8.22c) becomes

$$f_Y(y) = \frac{e^{-\beta y}}{\frac{1}{\beta}} = \beta \cdot e^{-\beta y},$$

so we see that Y has the same exponential distribution as does X. (Recall that we saw this same result in Example 8.4.) ❐

The MGF of Y can be found as

$$\begin{aligned} M_Y(r) = E[e^{ry}] &= \int_0^\infty e^{ry} \cdot f_Y(y)\, dy \\ &= \frac{1}{\mu} \int_0^\infty e^{ry} \cdot S_X(y)\, dy \\ &= \frac{1}{r\mu}[M_X(r) - 1]. \end{aligned} \tag{8.23}$$

(The details of the integration are left to the reader as Exercise 8-21.) From the MGF we can find the first two moments of Y as

$$E[Y] = \frac{E[X^2]}{2 \cdot E[X]} \tag{8.24a}$$

and

$$E[Y^2] = \frac{E[X^3]}{3 \cdot E[X]} \tag{8.24b}$$

(which the reader should verify), from which the variance of Y follows.

8.5.2 THE CUMULATIVE LOSS OF SURPLUS

Recall that the random variable Y analyzed in Section 8.5.1 represents the amount by which $U(t)$ drops below u when this event (Event A) first occurs. We denote the time at which Event A occurs as time t_1. If we let y_1 denote the realized value of Y, then the surplus is at amount $u - y_1$ at time t_1. Now suppose $U(t)$ eventually drops below this surplus level $u - y_1$ by an amount $Y = y_2$ at time t_2, dropping the surplus level to amount $u - y_1 - y_2$. Continuing in this way, we define $L = L(t)$ to be the *cumulative surplus loss*, the cumulative amount by which $U(t)$ drops below the initial amount u over the interval $(0, t]$. The meaning of L is illustrated in Figure 8.5.

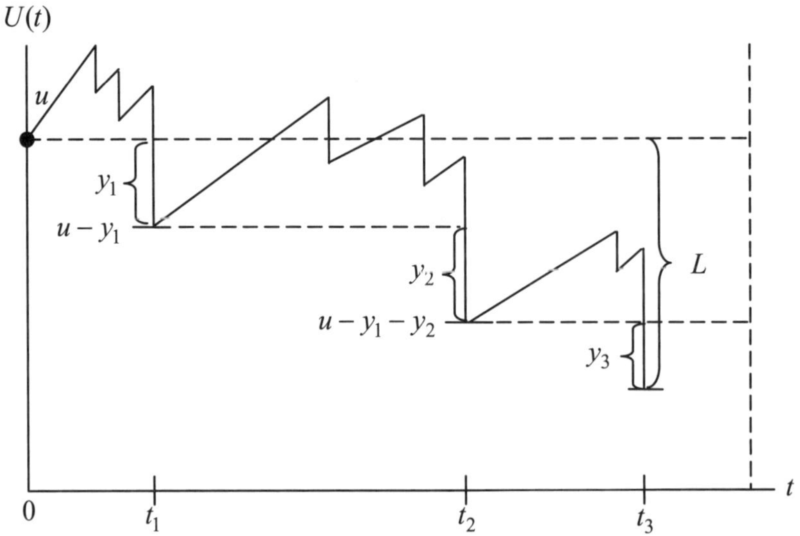

The Cumulative Surplus Loss
FIGURE 8.5

If $U(t)$ never drops below u, then the cumulative surplus loss is $L=0$. But the event $\{L=0\}$ is the event A′, so we have

$$Pr(L=0) \quad = \quad Pr(A') \quad = \quad 1-\frac{1}{1+\theta} \quad = \quad \frac{\theta}{1+\theta}. \tag{8.25}$$

On the other hand, if Event A does occur then we have $L>0$. Furthermore, if $L>u$ ruin occurs, so the event $\{L>u\}$ is the event of ruin and therefore $Pr(L>u)$ is the probability of ruin, already denoted by $\psi(u)$. Thus we have

$$Pr(L>u) \quad = \quad S_L(u) \quad = \quad \psi(u) \tag{8.26a}$$

and

$$Pr(L \leq u) \quad = \quad F_L(u) \quad = \quad 1-\psi(u). \tag{8.26b}$$

By differentiating Equation (8.26b) we obtain

$$f_L(u) \quad = \quad -\psi'(u), \tag{8.26c}$$

for $u>0$. Note that this is the PDF for the continuous part of the random variable L. Because it also has a probability mass of $\frac{\theta}{1+\theta}$ at $L=0$, it follows that L has a mixed distribution.

We can express the MGF of L as

$$M_L(r) \;=\; E[e^{rL}] \;=\; e^{r\cdot 0}\cdot Pr(L=0)+\int_0^\infty e^{ru}\cdot f_L(u)\,du \;=\; \frac{\theta}{1+\theta}+\int_0^\infty e^{ru}\cdot -\psi'(u)\,du. \tag{8.27}$$

Now we consider the MGF of L from a different perspective. From Figure 8.5 and the definition of L it follows that

$$L = Y_1 + Y_2 + \cdots + Y_{N(t)}, \tag{8.28}$$

where each Y_i is the random variable for the amount by which the surplus drops below the previously established level. As a consequence of $S(t)$ being a compound Poisson process, each Y_i is distributed the same as Y_1 (which we called just Y back in Section 8.5.1), and furthermore the Y_i's are mutually independent.

The random variable $N(t)$[6] in Equation (8.28) denotes the number of sequential drops in the surplus level over $(0,t]$. The probability of another drop in the previously lowest surplus level is $\frac{1}{1+\theta}$ and the probability of not having another such drop is $\frac{\theta}{1+\theta}$. Therefore the random variable N has a geometric distribution, with

$$Pr(N=n) = \left(\frac{1}{1+\theta}\right)^n \left(\frac{\theta}{1+\theta}\right) = \theta\left(\frac{1}{1+\theta}\right)^{n+1} \tag{8.29}$$

giving the probability of n sequential drops and then no further drop after the nth drop and before time t.

Recall that the MGF of a geometric random variable with these parameter values is

$$M_N(r) = \frac{\frac{\theta}{1+\theta}}{1-\frac{1}{1+\theta}\cdot e^r} = \frac{\theta}{1+\theta-e^r}. \tag{8.30}$$

Next note that L, as given by Equation (8.28), has a compound distribution with primary distribution N and secondary distribution Y. Then it follows that

$$M_L(r) = M_N\left[\ln M_Y(r)\right] = \frac{\theta}{1+\theta-M_Y(r)} = \frac{\theta}{1+\theta-\frac{1}{r\mu}[M_X(r)-1]},$$

using Equation (8.23) to substitute for $M_Y(r)$. This can be written as

$$M_L(r) = \frac{\theta r\mu}{1+(1+\theta)r\mu - M_X(r)}.$$

If we multiply both numerator and denominator by $(1+\theta)$ and then add and subtract the quantity $\theta[M_X(r)-1]$ in the numerator and rearrange, we obtain

$$M_L(r) = \frac{\theta}{1+\theta} + \frac{\theta[M_X(r)-1]}{(1+\theta)[1+(1+\theta)r\mu - M_X(r)]}. \tag{8.31}$$

[6] Hereinafter we use just N for $N(t)$.

Why did we do this? Recall our earlier expression for $M_L(r)$ given by Equation (8.27). By equating the two expressions for $M_L(r)$ we obtain

$$\int_0^\infty e^{ru} \cdot -\psi'(u)\,du \quad = \quad \frac{\theta[M_X(r)-1]}{(1+\theta)[1+(1+\theta)r\mu - M_X(r)]}. \tag{8.32}$$

The importance of this result is that it gives a direct relationship between $\psi(u)$ and $M_X(r)$, and might enable us to find $\psi(u)$ from $M_X(r)$ in certain cases.

8.6 PROBABILITY OF RUIN IN FINITE TIME

Here we consider the problem of finding the probability that ruin will occur within the finite time interval $(0,\tau]$, given a discrete-time loss process $S(t)$, for $t=1,2,\cdots$. Such a probability can be calculated numerically from the assumptions of the model, without involving a complex analytical formulation. This notion is best illustrated as an example.

EXAMPLE 8.6

An insurance fund pays an annual claim at the end of each year of possible amounts 3, 5, or 7, with probabilities $p(3)=.75$, $p(5)=.15$, and $p(7)=.10$. The fund collects a premium at the beginning of each year equal to the expected claim plus a relative security loading of 30%. Expenses and interest can be ignored. If the fund starts with an initial surplus of 3, find the probability of ruin within the first two years, which we have denoted by $\psi(3,2)$.

SOLUTION

The premium is

$$1.30E[X] \;=\; (1.30)[3(.75)+5(.15)+7(.10)] \;=\; 4.81,$$

so the fund is 7.81 at the end of the first year. After paying the first year claim, the fund is either 4.81, 2.81, or 0.81, with probabilities .75, .15, and .10, respectively. (Note that ruin by the end of the first year is not possible.) The fund at the end of the second year, including the second year premium, is then either 9.62, 7.62, or 5.62. Since the maximum possible second year claim is 7, the only way for ruin to occur at the end of the second year is with a claim of 7 against a fund of 5.62. In turn, a fund of 5.62 results only if the claim is also 7 in the first year. Therefore the probability of ruin is

$$\Psi(3,2) \;=\; (.10)(.10) \;=\; .01,$$

since the probability of a claim of 7 is $p(7)=.10$. ❒

As the number of years increases, the calculation becomes more extensive but can be made in a similar manner.

EXAMPLE 8.7 (Simulation Illustration)

A casualty insurance company selling earthquake insurance has a reserve of 1 billion to pay claims arising under this insurance. We make the following assumptions:

(1) At the beginning of each month the insurer receives 100 million of premium income.

(2) Each month there is a 1% chance of a significant earthquake, in which case the insurer's claim cost will be 1 billion. The chance of two or more earthquakes in a month is negligibly small, and the occurrence of an earthquake in any month is independent of any other month.

(3) The insurer has no other significant income or expense.

(a) Calculate the exact probability that the reserves will become negative during a two-month period.

(b) Calculate the exact probability that the reserves will become negative during a six-month period.

(c) Use simulation to estimate the probability that the reserves will become negative during a twelve-month period.

SOLUTION

(a) Because of the premium income, it will require earthquakes in each of the two months to overdraw the reserves, so the probability is $(.01)(.01) = .0001$.

(b) Again, because of the 600 million in premium income over the six-month period, it will require two or more earthquakes in the six-month period to overdraw the reserves. Then the probability is

$$Pr(X \geq 2) \quad = \quad 1 - Pr(X = 0) - Pr(X = 1),$$

where X has a binomial distribution with $n = 6$ and $p = .01$, which evaluates to .00146. If we consider an n-month period instead of a six-month period, for any integer $1 \leq n \leq 9$, it will still require two or more earthquakes to overdraw the reserve, which occurs with probability

$$1 - (.99)^n - \binom{n}{1}(.99)^{n-1}(.01)^1.$$

(c) As the time frame increases, the exact calculation becomes more complex (although not impossible). Accordingly, for the 12-month period we will use simulation to obtain an estimate of this probability. We choose to simulate 10,000 trials (i.e., years) of the experiment which entails a sequence of $(12)(10,000) = 120,000$ independent Bernoulli trials, one for each month. For each month, we draw a value from the uniform distribution over $[0,1)$. If this value is in the interval $[0,.01)$, we say there is a significant earthquake; otherwise, there is not. Following this process we found that the reserve became overdrawn in 29 of these 10,000 trials (years), yielding an estimated probability of .0029. ❐

8.7 SUMMARY

The topic of surplus process models, or "ruin theory" in traditional actuarial language, has long been an area for interesting actuarial research.

In this chapter we have reviewed the Poisson counting process for number of losses in the time interval $(0,t]$, and then explored the properties of the compound Poisson process for the aggregate amount of loss in $(0,t]$. In turn, the compound process for aggregate loss is the major component of the surplus process.

From the surplus process model we can, in simplified cases, define the probability of ruin (i.e., of surplus falling below zero) and the distribution of the surplus deficit once it does so.

Of greater interest is the probability of ruin in finite time, which is discussed briefly in Section 8.6.

8.8 EXERCISES

8.1 Introduction
8.2 The Compound Poisson Process

8-1 A compound Poisson process $S(t)$ is based on a Poisson counting process $N(t)$ with rate $\lambda = 2$. The MGF of $S(t)$ is

$$M_{S(t)}(r) = \exp\left[\frac{8t}{(r-2)^2} - 2t\right],$$

for $r < 2$. Determine the variance of the individual claim amount distribution.

8-2 A compound Poisson process $S(t)$ is based on a Poisson counting process with rate λ and a uniform individual claim amount distribution over the interval $(1,10)$. Determine the ratio of the variance of $S(t)$ to the expected value of $S(t)$.

8-3 For a certain compound Poisson claims process, the probability that the waiting time until the next claim will be at least two years is .60. Find the probability that exactly four claims will occur within a five-year period.

8.3 The Surplus Process Model

8-4 A continuous-time surplus process begins with initial surplus of 250 and receives premium income at continuous rate 120 per unit time. The experience shows that claims occur at the following times and in the following amounts:

Time of Claim	Amount of Claim
0.5	X
1.2	100
1.8	250
3.0	150
3.6	50

Determine the maximum value of X such that ruin does not occur in the time interval (0, 3.6).

8-5 A surplus process begins with initial surplus of 200. The expected aggregate claim payment per unit time is 80. The experience shows that claims occur at the following times and in the following amounts:

Time of Claim	Amount of Claim
0.5	100
1.2	75
1.8	200
3.0	200
3.6	50

Determine the minimum relative security loading such that ruin does not occur in the time interval (0, 3.6).

8-6 A surplus process begins with initial surplus of 10. The experience shows that claims occur at the following times and in the following amounts:

Time of Claim	Amount of Claim
0.5	8
1.6	4
1.9	6
2.5	10
3.8	7

Determine the minimum premium rate per unit time such that ruin does not occur in the time interval (0, 3.8).

8-7 A portfolio contains only one risk that can become a claim of amount 100 with probability .60 or amount 200 with probability .40. The probability that the claim has not yet occurred by time t is $(1+t)^{-1}$. The surplus process for the portfolio is given by

$$U(t) = 60 + 20t - S(t).$$

Calculate the probability of ruin for this portfolio.

8.4 The Probability of Ruin

8-8 A surplus process has a compound Poisson claims process in which all claim amounts are equal to $\ln 2$. The relative security loading is $\frac{3-\ln 4}{\ln 4}$. Find the adjustment coefficient.

8-9 A surplus process has a compound Poisson claims process, with an exponential claim amount distribution with mean $\frac{1}{\beta}$ and a positive relative security loading. Which of the following statements are true?

I. The adjustment coefficient will never exceed β.

II. The adjustment coefficient increases as the relative security loading increases.

III. The probability of ruin is independent of β.

8-10 A surplus process has a compound Poisson claims process, with an exponential claim amount distribution with mean .50 and an adjustment coefficient of 1. Determine the amount of initial surplus required to make the probability of ruin equal to .10.

The following information relates to Exercises 8-11 and 8-12.

A portfolio consists of a single risk, which can become a claim with probability .10. If the claim does occur, it can be of amount 1000 with probability .80 or amount 5000 with probability .20. If the claim does occur, its time of occurrence is uniformly distributed over $(0, 50)$. Premium income is received continuously at rate 100 per unit time.

8-11 Given an initial surplus of 900, calculate the probability of ruin.

8-12 Determine the initial surplus required to make the probability of ruin equal to .02.

8-13 A surplus process has a compound Poisson claims process with $\lambda = 10n$ and an exponential individual claim amount distribution with mean 100,000. The relative security loading is .10 and the initial surplus amount is 1,100,000. Let r_n^* denote the adjustment coefficient and $\psi_n(u)$ denote the probability of ruin. Which of the following statements are true?

I. $\psi_{10}(1{,}100{,}000) < e^{-1}$

II. $r_{20}^* < 10^{-6}$

III. $\psi_{10}(1{,}100{,}000) < (.95) \cdot \psi_{20}(1{,}100{,}000)$

8-14 A surplus process has a compound Poisson claims process, with an exponential claim amount distribution with mean 5. The relative security loading is .20 and the initial surplus amount is 10. Determine the amount of *additional* surplus required to reduce the probability of ruin by 50%.

8.5 The Distribution of Surplus Deficit

8-15 A surplus process has a compound Poisson claims process, with a gamma claim amount distribution with mean 2 and variance 2. Determine $E[Y]$.

8-16 A compound Poisson surplus process has a claim amount distribution with all claim amounts of size 5. The initial surplus amount is 10. Determine the conditional probability that the new surplus level will be less than 8 when the surplus first drops below 10, given that this event does occur.

8-17 A compound Poisson surplus process has an exponential claim amount distribution with mean 2. Let Y denote the amount by which $U(t)$ drops below u when the surplus first drops below u, given that this event does occur. Determine the initial surplus u such that $Pr(Y>u) = e^{-2}$.

8-18 A compound Poisson surplus process has a uniform claim amount distribution over $(0,30)$, a relative security loading of .50, and no initial surplus. Find the expected value of the surplus deficit at time of ruin, given that ruin does occur.

8-19 For a compound Poisson surplus process, Y denotes the amount by which $U(t)$ drops below the initial surplus level when this event first occurs, and L denotes the cumulative amount by which $U(t)$ has dropped below the initial surplus level over the time interval $(0,t]$. Given that the MGF of Y is $M_Y(r)=\frac{e^r-1}{r}$, for $r\neq 0$, determine the MGF of L.

8-20 A compound Poisson surplus process has an underlying Poisson counting process with $\lambda=4$ and a gamma claim amount distribution with $\alpha=1$ and $\beta=2$. The relative security loading is .20. Which of the following statements are true, where L and Y are as defined in Exercise 8-19?

I. $M_L(r) = \frac{2-r}{2-3r}$, for $r<\frac{2}{3}$

II. $M_Y(r) = \frac{2}{2-r}$, for $r<2$

III. The adjustment coefficient is $r^*=\frac{1}{3}$.

8-21 Derive Equation (8.23).

8-22 Show that Equation (8.32) is satisfied when X has an exponential distribution, using the expression for $\psi(u)$ found in Example 8.4 (see Equation (8.19)).

8.6 Probability of Ruin in Finite Time

8-23 A simple insurance fund has surplus of 3 at time 0. Each year it collects a premium of 2 (at the beginning of the year), and pays a random claim amount with the following distribution:

x	0	1	2	4
$p(x)$	.15	.25	.40	.20

At the end of each year, if the surplus exceeds 3 a dividend equal to the amount of surplus in excess of 3 is paid. If claims cannot be paid, or surplus falls to 0, the fund goes out of business. Assuming no interest or administrative expenses, find the probability that the fund is still in business at time $t=3$.

8-24 A simple insurance fund has initial surplus of 1, collects a premium at the beginning of each year of 2, and credits interest on the fund at 10%. The annual claim distribution, paid at year end, is as follows:

x	0	2	6
$p(x)$	.60	.30	.10

Find the probability that the fund is ruined by time $t=3$.

PART III

ESTIMATION OF TABULAR MODELS

The primary organization of the estimation topics covered in this text is with regard to the two fundamental types of models, namely *tabular* (presented here in Part III) and *parametric* (presented in Part IV). The description of a model as "tabular" comes from the fact that such a model appears as a *table of numbers*, whereas a parametric model appears as a mathematical function. A simple example will make the distinction clear.

Suppose a discrete random variable can take on only the positive integer values $x=0,1,2$ and 3. A tabular model would present the probability distribution of this random variable as a table of numbers, such as the following:

x	$Pr(X=x)$
0	.20
1	.30
2	.40
3	.10

A parametric model, on the other hand, would present the distribution as a mathematical function, such as

$$Pr(X=x) = p(x) = \binom{3}{x} p^x(1-p)^{3-x},$$

for $x=0,1,2,3$. Of course a parametric model can, in some cases, be presented in tabular form by calculating, and then listing, each $p(x)$ value. The converse cannot necessarily be said of the tabular model.

Note that a tabular model is necessarily discrete, whereas a parametric model can be discrete (such as the binomial model mentioned above), or continuous, with the probability density given by the continuous function $f(x)$. (Try listing the density for all possible values of a continuous random variable in a table of numbers!)

Various synonyms are sometimes used for what we call a tabular model in this text. A common one is *nonparametric*, a natural term to use to distinguish tabular models from parametric models.[1]

Another term sometimes used as a synonym for tabular is *data-dependent*, presumably because the values appearing in the model depend directly on observed sample data. However, the values of the parameters in parametric models are normally estimated from sample data, so these models are "data-dependent" in some sense of the term as well. To avoid the need to distinguish between these two usages of the term data-dependent, we prefer not to use that term in this text.

In general, the values appearing in a tabular model are estimated from the information supplied by a sample of data. In most cases, the nature of the data is such that an estimation process must be adopted, often along with some simplifying assumptions, in order to produce

[1] Technically speaking, every probability value listed in a tabular model is, in some sense, a "parameter" of the model. For this reason, we prefer to use the term tabular, rather than nonparametric, in this text.

the estimated value. In the general case, we will refer to the process as an *estimator*, the resulting value as an *estimate*, and the entire tabular model as an *estimated model*. A special case, described in Section 9.2, arises when the estimation process and the form of the data are so uncomplicated that the entire estimated model can simply be *observed* directly from the data. In this special case we might refer to the estimated tabular model as an *observed model*. The term *empirical model* is often used as a synonym for observed model.

A very important distinction applies to sample data that are *complete* versus *incomplete*. Tabular models estimated from complete data are explored in Chapter 9, and those estimated from incomplete data in Chapters 10 and 11. The meanings of complete and incomplete will be made clear in the later chapters.

Finally, as noted in the preface to this text, we address all three of the major actuarial models of loss frequency, loss severity, and survival. Loss frequency and loss severity models are *primarily* parametric models, so most of the attention paid to them will be in Part IV of the text. The extent to which they might be presented in tabular form is explored in Chapters 9 and 10 of this part.

Survival models can be expressed in either parametric or tabular forms, with the parametric form used primarily for models arising in clinical, economic, or social science applications. (This will be discussed in Part IV of the text.) On the other hand, traditional actuarial survival models arising in life insurance or pension fund applications are nearly always tabular in form; the estimation of such models from sample data is pursued extensively in Chapters 11 and 12.

CHAPTER NINE

ESTIMATION FROM COMPLETE DATA

9.1 INTRODUCTION

In this chapter we consider the estimation of frequency, severity, and survival models from sample data that is available to us in a simplified form that we refer to as *complete data*. (A fuller understanding of the concept of complete data will emerge in the next chapter when we explore the circumstances that can cause data to be not complete.) For now, we might interpret "complete" to mean "no loss of information."

We consider two sub-cases of complete data. The first sub-case, in which the *precise value* of each individual observation is recorded, is referred to as *exact data*, or *individual data*. If the population under observation is very large, so that the number of different exact individual values is also large, it might be more practical to record the observations in a suitable number of value intervals, producing the sub-case of *grouped data*. Note that although less information is available to us in the case of grouped data than in the case of exact data, we will nonetheless still consider the estimation circumstance to be one of complete data.

The exact data sub-case is explored in Section 9.2 and the grouped data sub-case in Section 9.3.

9.2 COMPLETE EXACT DATA

In this section we consider the estimation of frequency, severity, and survival models from *complete exact* (or *complete individual*) data. Although certain mathematical and statistical similarities exist among the three kinds of models, we prefer to treat them separately in this first approach to estimation due, in part, to the use of different descriptive wording. The meaning of this will become clearer as we proceed.

9.2.1 FREQUENCY MODELS

Consider a block of business of 100 family health insurance policies, with at least three persons covered under each policy. Over a one-year period we observe and record the number of policies that submitted no claims, one claim, two claims, and so on. Table 9.1 on the following page summarizes this hypothetical set of data.

TABLE 9.1

Frequency-of-Claim Data	
Number of Claims	**Number of Policies**
0	10
1	21
2	37
3	18
4	9
5	5

EXAMPLE 9.1

Use the complete exact data in Table 9.1 to estimate a claim frequency model for this class of health insurance business.

SOLUTION

This is a good example of our earlier description of an observed (or empirical) model. (See page 221.) The data show the proportion of policies producing each of 0, 1, 2, 3, 4, or 5 claims. If we take the observed proportion as our estimate of the corresponding probability, we directly find the following results.

TABLE 9.2

Observed Frequency Model						
x	0	1	2	3	4	5
$p_{100}^o(x)$ [1]	.10	.21	.37	.18	.09	.05

In the observed model, each individual observation (or data point) is assigned probability $\frac{1}{n}$, where there are n observations in the total data set. Then if observation x occurs n_x times, so that $\sum_x n_x = n$, the observed (estimated) probability is

$$p_n^o(x) = \frac{n_x}{n}, \tag{9.1}$$

for $x = 0,1,2,3,4,5$ in this illustration. ❐

EXAMPLE 9.2

Find the observed (or empirical) cumulative distribution function (CDF) corresponding to the observed probability function of Example 9.1.

---

[1] Note the notational choice to denote the estimate of $p(x)$ by $p_{100}^o(x)$, where the "upper o" stands for "observed," and the subscript indicates the underlying sample size.

SOLUTION

By simple summation we obtain the following results.

TABLE 9.3

Observed Frequency Distribution Function						
x	0	1	2	3	4	5
$F_{100}^{o}(x)$	.10	.31	.68	.86	.95	1.00

❐

In general, for a complete exact data set as described in this section, with n_x observations of size x, the observed distribution function is given by

$$F_n^o(x) = \frac{1}{n} \cdot \sum_{y \leq x} n_y, \tag{9.2}$$

where $n = \sum_x n_x$ is the total number of observations.

9.2.2 SEVERITY MODELS

The definitions of the observed probability function and the observed distribution function will be the same in the case of claim severity data as in the case of claim frequency data, although different language might be used to describe the data. Furthermore, whereas observations of claim frequency (data points) are naturally going to be 0, 1, 2, and so on, observations of claim severity would not be so restricted.

EXAMPLE 9.3

Claim amounts for automobile property damage on a certain block of business in a certain time period were 456, 981, 1042, 1266, 1856, 2020, 2356, and 2792 (rounded to the nearer dollar amount). Construct the observed probability and distribution functions implied by this data.

SOLUTION

Unlike with the frequency data of Examples 9.1 and 9.2, this time no precise value occurs more than once. Since each data point gets probability $\frac{1}{n}$ in the observed model, and $n = 8$ in this case, then the observed PF is $p_8^o(x) = .125$ for each of the eight values of x in the sample. The observed CDF is shown in Table 9.4 on the following page.

TABLE 9.4

Observed Severity Distribution Function	
x	$F_8^o(x)$
456	.125
981	.250
1042	.375
1266	.500
1856	.625
2020	.750
2356	.875
2792	1.000

As well, $F_8^o(x)=0$ for all $x<456$ and $F_8^o(x)=1$ for all $x>2792$. ❒

9.2.3 SURVIVAL MODELS

The estimation of a survival model from complete exact data is mathematically similar to the estimation of a severity model, but presented in different language. Here the data represent exact times of failure of the members of a cohort group, all of whom exist (are "alive") at time $t=0$. We can follow the cohort across time, observing the time point where each unit fails and observing the proportion still surviving at any time. The observed surviving proportion at time t, denoted $S_n^o(t)$, constitutes the *observed survival distribution* (or *empirical survival distribution*) implied by the data of a sample of size n.

Suppose a cohort of five study units is observed, with failures occurring at ordered times $t_1, t_2, t_3, t_4,$ and t_5. The observed surviving proportion at any value of t is shown in the following figure.

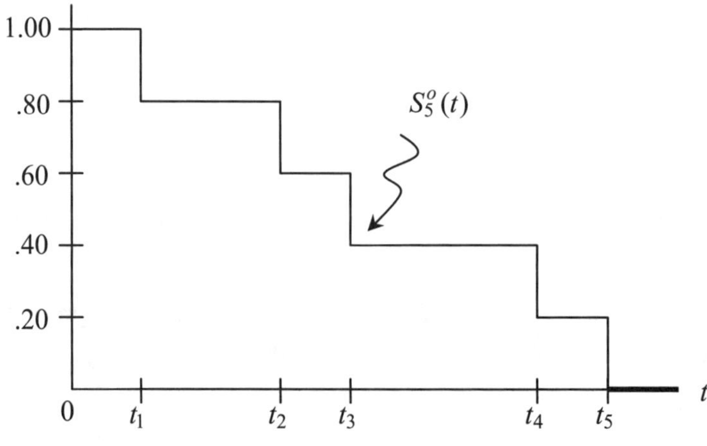

Observed Surviving Proportion

FIGURE 9.1

Values of $S_5^o(t)$ are easily read from the graph. For all $t<t_1$, the proportion surviving to that t is 1.00, which we take as our estimate of $S(t)$. It is important to note that we are not saying failure prior to time t is *impossible*, but rather that $S_5^o(t)=1.00$ is the estimate of $S(t)$ which results from this particular data and estimation procedure.

Similarly, we take our estimate of $S(t)$ to be $S_5^o(t)=.80$ for all t such that $t_1 \le t < t_2$, since .80 is the observed surviving proportion at all such t. In like manner we take $S_5^o(t)=.60$ for all t such that $t_2 \le t < t_3$, and so on.

What about for all $t \ge t_5$? Since our estimation procedure is defined to be simply the observed proportion surviving, it follows that we take $S_5^o(t)=0$ for all such t. We are not saying that survival beyond t_5 is *impossible*, but rather that $S_5^o(t)=0$ is the estimate of $S(t)$ from *this* data, according to *this* procedure.

In summary, for an initial cohort of size n, the observed (or empirical) survival function is

$$S_n^o(t) = \begin{cases} 1.00 & \text{for } t<t_1 \\ \frac{n-i}{n} & \text{for } t_i \le t < t_{i+1}, \\ 0 & \text{for } t \ge t_n \end{cases} \tag{9.3}$$

for $i=1,2,\cdots,n-1$.

We have assumed here that time of failure is recorded with sufficient accuracy such that there is no more than one failure at each time point. If the recording unit (e.g., week or day) is not sufficiently fine, or if the sample is sufficiently large, or both, then *multiple failures* will occur at one time point. When this occurs, our step graph of $S_n^o(t)$ will merely step down $\frac{2}{n}$ if there are two failures at that point, or, in general, $\frac{k}{n}$ for k failures at the same time point. This is illustrated in the following example.

EXAMPLE 9.4

A cohort of eight individuals is observed from time $t=0$ until all have failed. Only the day of failure is recorded. The observed failure durations are 3, 4, 5, 5, 7, 10, 10, and 12. The observed survival function is used to estimate the operative (but unknown) $S(t)$. What are the estimates of $S(2)$, $S(5)$, and $S(12)$? Draw the graph of $S_8^o(t)$.

SOLUTION

First we find $S_8^o(2)=1.00$, the proportion still surviving at $t=2$. Four of the eight failures have occurred by time 5, so the observed proportion surviving at $t=5$ is $S_8^o(5)=.50$. Since $t=12$ is the time of the last failure, then $S_8^o(12)=0$.

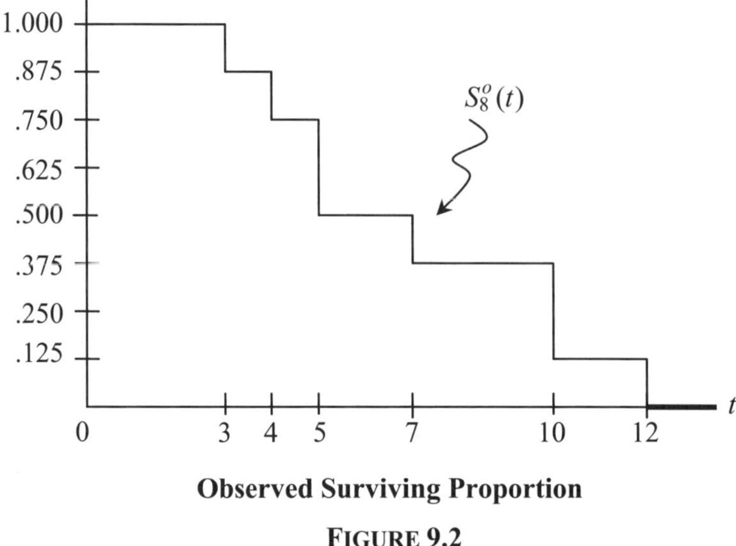

Observed Surviving Proportion

FIGURE 9.2

9.2.4 ANALYSIS OF THE OBSERVED (EMPIRICAL) SURVIVAL FUNCTION

Recall that $S_n^o(t)$ is an estimate of the underlying, operative survival function $S(t)$, with the estimate depending on the *random* occurrence of failures prior to (and therefore also following) time t. For any value of t, we have defined $S_n^o(t)$ as

$$S_n^o(t) = \frac{\textit{number of survivors at time } t}{n} = \frac{N(t)}{n}, \tag{9.4}$$

where $N(t)$ denotes the random variable for the number of survivors at time t. Equation (9.4) defines $S_n^o(t)$ as the *estimator* for $S(t)$. In general, an estimator is a random variable depending, usually, on one or more other random variables. In this case it depends on the random variable for number of survivors at time t.

If failure times are independent among the cohort of n study units, and all are subject to the same underlying $S(t)$, then $N(t)$ is a binomial random variable with parameters n and $p = S(t)$. Then it follows that

$$E[N(t)] = n \cdot S(t) \tag{9.5a}$$

and

$$Var[N(t)] = n \cdot S(t) \cdot F(t), \tag{9.5b}$$

where $F(t) = 1 - S(t)$. Since $N(t)$ is binomial, then the estimator $S_n^o(t)$ defined by Equation (9.4) is a *binomial proportion* random variable with

$$E[S_n^o(t)] = \frac{1}{n}\cdot E[N(t)] = S(t) \tag{9.6a}$$

and

$$Var[S_n^o(t)] = \frac{1}{n^2}\cdot Var[N(t)] = \frac{S(t)\cdot F(t)}{n}. \tag{9.6b}$$

Equations (9.6a) and (9.6b) show that $S_n^o(t)$ is an *unbiased* and *consistent* estimator of $S(t)$. (The concepts of unbiasedness and consistency were reviewed in Chapter 2.)

Of course the true value of $S(t)$ is not known, so if we want a numerical value of $Var[S_n^o(t)]$ we must approximate it by using $S_n^o(t)$ in place of $S(t)$. This produces the *estimated variance* given by

$$Est.Var[S_n^o(t)] = \frac{S_n^o(t)\cdot F_n^o(t)}{n}, \tag{9.6c}$$

where $F_n^o(t) = 1 - S_n^o(t)$. The estimated variance is sometimes denoted by $\widehat{Var}[S_n^o(t)]$.

EXAMPLE 9.5

Suppose it is "known" that the operative survival distribution to which our sample in Example 9.4 is actually subject is uniform on $(0,15]$. Find the variance of the random variable $S_8^o(6)$. If the uniform distribution assumption is not made, how would we estimate $Var[S_8^o(6)]$?

SOLUTION

If T is uniform on $(0,15]$, then $S(6) = .60$ and, from Equation (9.6b),

$$Var[S_8^o(6)] = \frac{(.60)(.40)}{8} = .03.$$

If $S(6) = .60$ is not known, then Equation (9.6c) gives

$$Est.Var[S_8^o(6)] = \frac{(.50)(.50)}{8} = .03125,$$

by using $S_8^o(6) = .50$ in place of the true value $S(6) = .60$.[2] ❐

Since $S_n^o(t)$ is a binomial proportion random variable, its distribution is approximately normal if n is sufficiently large. In turn, it follows that

[22] Note that the data of this sample could be used to test the hypothesis that the applicable distribution is uniform on $(0,15]$. This issue is reviewed in Chapter 2 and further pursued in Part IV of this text.

$$Z = \frac{S_n^o(t) - E[S_n^o(t)]}{\sqrt{Var[S_n^o(t)]}} \tag{9.7a}$$

is approximately a unit normal random variable. Using Equations (9.6a) and (9.6b) this can be written as

$$Z = \frac{S_n^o(t) - S(t)}{\sqrt{S(t) \cdot F(t)/n}}. \tag{9.7b}$$

Under this assumption of normality, we can construct a confidence interval for our estimate of $S(t)$. For example, to find a 95% symmetric confidence interval we write

$$.95 = Pr(-1.96 < Z < 1.96).$$

Substituting for Z, the inequality becomes

$$-1.96 < \frac{S_n^o(t) - S(t)}{\sqrt{S(t) \cdot F(t)/n}} < 1.96,$$

so

$$S(t) > S_n^o(t) - 1.96\sqrt{\frac{S(t) \cdot F(t)}{n}} \tag{9.8a}$$

and

$$S(t) < S_n^o(t) + 1.96\sqrt{\frac{S(t) \cdot F(t)}{n}}. \tag{9.8b}$$

Finally, we can use the estimated value of $S(t)$ to approximate the unknown $S(t)$ and $F(t)$, giving us an interval within which we are 95% confident that the true value of $S(t)$ lies.

EXAMPLE 9.6

Use the data of Example 9.4 to construct an approximate 95% confidence interval for the value of $S(5)$. (Note that here $n = 8$, which would not be considered "large," so the normal approximation is not particularly good.)

SOLUTION

Our estimate of $S(5)$ is $S_8^o(5) = .50$ and the variance of the estimator is approximately $\frac{(.50)(.50)}{8} = .03125$. Then

$$S_8^o(5) - 1.96\sqrt{Var[S(5)]} = .50 - 1.96\sqrt{.03125} = .15352$$

and

$$S_8^o(5) + 1.96\sqrt{Var[S(5)]} = .50 + 1.96\sqrt{.03125} = .84648.$$

That is, we are 95% confident that $.15352 < S(5) < .84648$. ❑

Confidence intervals can be similarly constructed for other estimated values. Several examples of this are pursued in the exercises (see Exercises 9-5 and 9-11).

9.2.5 INTERVAL ESTIMATES

In the simplified world of complete exact data, we saw in Section 9.2.3 how easy it is to estimate $S(t)$ using the observed proportion surviving, denoted by $S_n^o(t)$. Now we consider a different approach to estimating $S(t)$, by first estimating the conditional probabilities of survival over a sequence of subintervals from time 0 to time t.

We introduce these ideas by referring to Figure 9.1 on page 226. Let p_1 denote the probability of survival from time 0 to time t_1, p_2 denote the *conditional* probability of survival from time t_1 to time t_2, *given survival to time* t_1, p_3 denote the conditional probability of survival from time t_2 to time t_3, given survival to time t_2, and so on. Then it follows from basic survival model theory (as well as from the basic multiplication rule of probability) that, for example,

$$S(t_3) = p_1 \cdot p_2 \cdot p_3. \tag{9.9a}$$

(Note that, using survival model notation, $p_1 = S(t_1)$, $p_2 = \frac{S(t_2)}{S(t_1)}$, and $p_3 = \frac{S(t_3)}{S(t_2)}$, so that Equation (9.9a) is easily verified.)

It follows from Equation (9.9a) that an alternative way to estimate $S(t_3)$ would be to first estimate p_1, p_2 and p_3, and then to estimate $S(t_3)$ as

$$S_n^o(t_3) = p_1^o \cdot p_2^o \cdot p_3^o, \tag{9.9b}$$

where p_i^o is the estimate of p_i. In turn, p_i is naturally estimated by the observed proportion surviving the ith subinterval, *given the number surviving at the beginning of that subinterval.* We refer to the number surviving at the beginning of the ith subinterval as the *risk set* for the ith subinterval, and denote it by r_i.[3] Then conditional on the risk set r_i, p_i^o is an unbiased binomial proportion estimator.

For an initial cohort group of size n, we have $r_1 = n, r_2 = n-1$, $r_3 = n-2$, and so on, as long as there is just one failure at each failure time point. If there are multiple failures at a time point, then the risk set is reduced accordingly. In general, if there are k_i failures at time t_i, the time point at the end of the ith subinterval, then the observed proportion surviving the ith subinterval is

$$p_i^o = \frac{r_i - k_i}{r_i}. \tag{9.10}$$

[3] With no failures (or other activity) *within* the subinterval, the risk set is the same at the *end* of the subinterval, just before the failure, as it is at the beginning.

We can see that, under complete exact data, if p_i is estimated by p_i^o as defined by Equation (9.10), and then $S_n^o(t_i)$ is estimated as

$$\begin{aligned} S_n^o(t_i) &= p_1^o \cdot p_2^o \cdot \dots \cdot p_i^o \\ &= \left(\frac{r_1-k_1}{r_1}\right)\left(\frac{r_2-k_2}{r_2}\right)\cdots\left(\frac{r_i-k_i}{r_i}\right) \\ &= \prod_{j=1}^{i}\left(\frac{r_j-k_j}{r_j}\right), \end{aligned} \tag{9.11}$$

the same value for $S_n^o(t_i)$ will result as in Section 9.2.3 where $S_n^o(t_i)$ was directly observed as the proportion surviving at time t_i. Furthermore, since there are no failures at time t for $t_i < t < t_{i+1}$, then the estimate of $S(t)$ is also $S_n^o(t_i)$ for all $t_i < t < t_{i+1}$.

EXAMPLE 9.7

Using the data of Example 9.4, estimate $S(8)$ by the procedure described in this section.

SOLUTION

Referring to Figure 9.2 we observe that the risk sets for the first four subintervals are $r_1 = 8, r_2 = 7, r_3 = 6,$ and $r_4 = 4$. Then the interval estimates are $p_1^o = \frac{7}{8}$, $p_2^o = \frac{6}{7}$, $p_3^o = \frac{4}{6}$, and $p_4^o = \frac{3}{4}$, and the estimate of $S(7)$ is

$$\begin{aligned} S_8^o(7) &= p_1^o \cdot p_2^o \cdot p_3^o \cdot p_4^o \\ &= \left(\frac{7}{8}\right)\left(\frac{6}{7}\right)\left(\frac{4}{6}\right)\left(\frac{3}{4}\right) = \frac{3}{8}. \end{aligned}$$

With no failures again until time 10, we have $S_8^o(8) = S_8^o(7) = .375$, as already known from Figure 9.2. ❐

The process of estimating $S(t)$ by the product of the estimates of survival over the sequence of subintervals preceding time t is called *product-limit estimation*. It has been suggested by several writers, but is mainly attributed to Kaplan and Meier [19], and is therefore often referred to as Kaplan-Meier estimation.

It should be clear that the two-step process of first estimating the several p_i's and then estimating $S(t)$ from them is not needed in the simplified world of complete exact data. However we prefer to introduce it at this early point of our presentation so that it is familiar to our readers when encountered again under more complex estimation situations.

Equation (9.6a) established that the binomial proportion estimator $S_n^o(t_i)$ is unbiased. When $S(t_i)$ is estimated by Equation (9.11), where each p_i^o is an unbiased binomial proportion estimator conditional on the risk set r_i, it can be shown that $S_n^o(t_i)$ is unbiased in that case as well. (See Exercise 9-6.) However, the variance of $S_n^o(t_i)$, when determined by the interval estimates approach of Equation (9.11), is not the same as when $S_n^o(t_i)$ is determined directly as a binomial proportion itself. The latter variance is given by Equation (9.6b); the variance in the former case will be derived in Section 10.4.2.

9.2.6 ESTIMATION OF $S(t)$ USING CUMULATIVE HAZARD

Recall from survival model theory (see, for example, Section 5.1.4 of Cunningham, et al. [7]) that the *cumulative hazard function* (CHF) over the interval $(0,t]$ is defined as

$$\Lambda(t) = \int_0^t \lambda(r)\,dr = -\ln S(t), \tag{9.12a}$$

so that

$$S(t) = e^{-\Lambda(t)}. \tag{9.12b}$$

Then it would be reasonable to estimate $S(t)$ by first estimating $\Lambda(t)$ and then defining

$$\hat{S}(t) = e^{-\hat{\Lambda}(t)}, \tag{9.13a}$$

where we use the common carat (or hat) symbol to denote an estimator. If we write Equation (9.13a) as

$$\hat{\Lambda}(t) = -\ln \hat{S}(t) \tag{9.13b}$$

and substitute the estimate of $S(t)$ produced by the product-limit procedure, as given by Equation (9.11), we have

$$\begin{aligned} \hat{\Lambda}(t) &= -\ln\left[\prod_{j=1}^{i}\left(\frac{r_j-k_j}{r_j}\right)\right] \\ &= -\sum_{j=1}^{i}\ln\left(1-\frac{k_j}{r_j}\right), \end{aligned} \tag{9.13c}$$

for all t such that $t_i \le t < t_{i+1}$. Recall that

$$-\ln\left(1-\frac{k_j}{r_j}\right) = \frac{k_j}{r_j}+\frac{1}{2}\left(\frac{k_j}{r_j}\right)^2+\cdots.$$

By ignoring quadratic and higher order terms, we obtain the approximation

$$-\ln\left(1-\frac{k_j}{r_j}\right) \approx \frac{k_j}{r_j}, \tag{9.14}$$

thereby estimating the cumulative hazard by

$$\hat{\Lambda}(t) = \sum_{j=1}^{i} \frac{k_j}{r_j}, \tag{9.15a}$$

for $t_i \leq t < t_{i+1}$, and, in turn, estimating the survival function by

$$\hat{S}(t) = \exp\left(-\sum_{j=1}^{i} \frac{k_j}{r_j}\right), \tag{9.16}$$

for $t_i \leq t < t_{i+1}$. This is called the *Nelson-Aalen estimator* (see [32]).

When there is only one failure at any failure point, so that $k_j = 1$ for all j, then the Nelson-Aalen estimator is particularly easy to calculate under complete data. In that case $r_j = n - j + 1$, so

$$\hat{\Lambda}(t) = \sum_{j=1}^{i} \frac{1}{r_j} = \frac{1}{n} + \frac{1}{n-1} + \cdots + \frac{1}{n-i+1}, \tag{9.17}$$

for $t_i \leq t < t_{i+1}$.

Note that, although our estimate of $S(t)$ from Equation (9.11) is the observed survival function $S_n^o(t)$, the estimate of $\Lambda(t)$ given by Equation (9.15a) cannot be called "observed" due to the approximation (given by Equation (9.14)) used in its derivation. Accordingly, the estimate of $S(t)$ given by Equation (9.16), the Nelson-Aalen estimate, is not the same as the estimate of $S(t)$ given by Equation (9.11), the product-limit estimate. Since the Nelson-Aalen estimate is *not* $S_n^o(t)$, we use the more generic notation $\hat{S}(t)$ for it.

EXAMPLE 9.8

Consider a newborn litter of five mice. As a result of the poor health of the mother, they fail at times 2, 3, 6, 9, and 12. Estimate $S(10)$ by both the product-limit and the Nelson-Aalen methods.

SOLUTION

We have complete exact data, so the product-limit estimate of $S(10)$ is

$$S_5^o(10) = \left(\frac{4}{5}\right)\left(\frac{3}{4}\right)\left(\frac{2}{3}\right)\left(\frac{1}{2}\right) = .20,$$

the observed proportion surviving at time 10. The Nelson-Aalen estimate of the CHF, from Equation (9.18), is

$$\hat{\Lambda}(10) = \frac{1}{5} + \frac{1}{4} + \frac{1}{3} + \frac{1}{2} = 1.2833\dot{3},$$

so the Nelson-Aalen estimate of $S(10)$ is

$$\hat{S}(10) = e^{-1.2833\dot{3}} = .27711. \qquad \square$$

It can be shown (see Exercise 9-10) that the product-limit estimate of $S(t)$ is always less than the Nelson-Aalen estimate, for all $t \geq t_1$.

When the Nelson-Aalen estimator is viewed as a random variable, Equation (9.15a) for the cumulative hazard estimator at failure point t_i becomes

$$\hat{\Lambda}(t_i) = \sum_{j=1}^{i} \frac{K_j}{r_j}, \tag{9.15b}$$

where K_j is the random variable for number of failures at time t_j. A standard way to approximate the mean and variance of $\hat{\Lambda}(t_i)$ is to assume that K_j has a Poisson distribution with rate $\lambda_j = r_j \cdot \lambda(t_j)$, where $\lambda(t_j)$ denotes the force of failure (or hazard rate) at time t_j. We also assume that, given the risk sets $r_1, r_2, \cdots, r_i$, the random variables $K_1, K_2, \cdots, K_i$ are mutually independent. Under these assumptions, the expected value of the estimator random variable $\hat{\Lambda}(t_i)$ is given by

$$E[\hat{\Lambda}(t_i)] = \sum_{j=1}^{i} \frac{E[K_j]}{r_j} = \sum_{j=1}^{i} \frac{r_j \cdot \lambda(t_j)}{r_j} = \sum_{j=1}^{i} \lambda(t_j), \tag{9.18a}$$

since the expected value of a Poisson random variable is equal to its rate parameter. For the variance of $\hat{\Lambda}(t_i)$ we have

$$Var[\hat{\Lambda}(t_i)] = \sum_{j=1}^{i} \frac{Var(K_j)}{r_j^2},$$

by the assumption of independence. Since K_j is Poisson, we have $Var(K_j) = \lambda_j = r_j \cdot \lambda(t_j)$ as well, so we have

$$Var[\hat{\Lambda}(t_j)] = \sum_{j=1}^{i} \frac{r_j \cdot \lambda(t_j)}{r_j^2} = \sum_{j=1}^{i} \frac{\lambda(t_j)}{r_j}. \tag{9.18b}$$

In practice, the values of $\lambda(t_j)$ in Equations (9.18a) and (9.18b) are not known. To estimate the variance of $\hat{\Lambda}(t_i)$ numerically we approximate $\lambda(t_j)$ by the observed value $\frac{k_j}{r_j}$. Then the variance is estimated as

$$Est.Var[\hat{\Lambda}(t_j)] = \sum_{j=1}^{i} \frac{k_j}{r_j^2}. \tag{9.18c}$$

The cumulative hazard estimator is further pursued in Exercises 9-11 and 9-12.

Throughout this section we have focused on using the Nelson-Aalen estimate of $\Lambda(t)$ as a stepping-stone to reach an estimate of $S(t)$. The converse process is also available to us. That is, we can first estimate $S(t)$ by product-limit (or otherwise) and then use that estimate to find an estimate of $\Lambda(t)$ from Equation (9.13b).

As we have seen, under complete exact data the product-limit estimate of $S(t)$ is the same as $S_n^o(t)$, the observed (or empirical) proportion surviving. Then if our estimate of $\Lambda(t)$ is found from $S_n^o(t)$ by Equation (9.13b), we can call this estimate observed (or empirical) as well, and denote it by $\Lambda_n^o(t)$, since no other approximation is involved. This is illustrated in the following example using insurance claim amounts.

EXAMPLE 9.9

A portfolio of policies produces the set of claim amounts

$$\{100, 100, 100, 200, 300, 300, 300, 400, 500, 600\}.$$

Find the empirical estimate of $\Lambda(300)$ and the Nelson-Aalen estimate of $S(300)$.

SOLUTION

Since the data set is complete and exact, the empirical estimate of $S(300)$ is the "surviving proportion" $S_{10}^o(300) = .30.$[4] Then the empirical estimate of $\Lambda(300)$ is

$$\Lambda_{10}^o(300) \;=\; -\ln S_{10}^o(300) \;=\; -\ln .30 \;=\; 1.20397.$$

By contrast, the Nelson-Aalen estimate of $\Lambda(300)$ is

$$\hat{\Lambda}(300) \;=\; \frac{3}{10}+\frac{1}{7}+\frac{3}{6} \;=\; .94286,$$

and the corresponding Nelson-Aalen estimate of $S(300)$ is

$$\hat{S}(300) \;=\; e^{-.94286} \;=\; .38951. \qquad \square$$

Finally, it should be noted that we might use Nelson-Aalen simply to estimate $\Lambda(t)$ as our final goal, and not as a step in the process of estimating $S(t)$.

---

[4] In the case of claim amounts, the concept of "surviving proportion" is the proportion of the data elements that *exceed* the given value, rather than the proportion of study units "still alive" at the given value. The interpretation is different, but the mathematical concept is the same.

9.3 COMPLETE GROUPED DATA

Now we consider the case where our data does not show the exact value of each observation, but, perhaps because the number of observations is very large, shows only the interval on the real number axis into which each observation falls. It is convenient, but not necessary, if the several intervals are of equal length. We first present the general case, in which the intervals may be of unequal length, with the understanding that it can pertain to any of our three kinds of models (frequency, severity, or survival). Then in Sections 9.3.2 and 9.3.3 we consider the more specific case of survival model estimation using equal intervals.

9.3.1 THE GENERAL CASE

We begin by partitioning the axis into k (not necessarily equal) intervals, as illustrated in Figure 9.3.

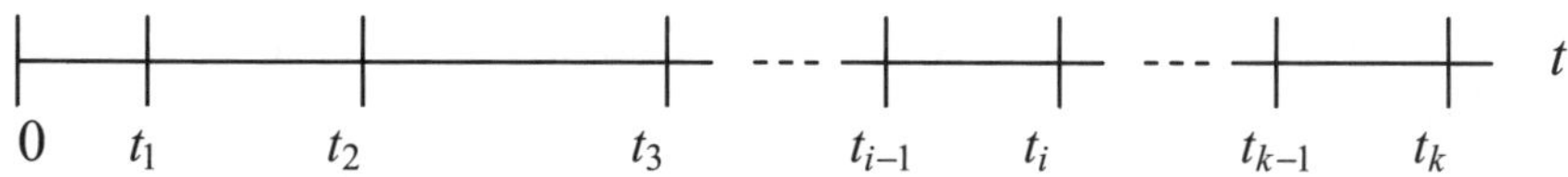

General Model for Grouped Data

FIGURE 9.3

The value of t_k is selected so that it equals or exceeds the largest value of the observations. We also adopt the rule that any observation falling precisely at an interval boundary is assigned to the interval to the *left* of that boundary.

As before, we have a data set of n observations. We let n_j denote the number of observations falling in the jth interval, which is denoted by $(t_{j-1}, t_j]$ to indicate that an observation of precisely t_j belongs to this interval. Then $\sum_{j=1}^{i} n_j$ is the number of observations prior to (or at) t_i and $\sum_{j=i+1}^{k} n_j$ is the number of observations after t_i, where $\sum_{j=1}^{k} n_j = n$. Then the observed (or empirical) distribution function at the upper boundary of the ith interval is

$$F_n^o(t_i) = \frac{1}{n} \cdot \sum_{j=1}^{i} n_j, \tag{9.19}$$

and the corresponding observed survival function is

$$S_n^o(t_i) = 1 - F_n^o(t_i) = \frac{1}{n} \cdot \sum_{j=i+1}^{k} n_j. \tag{9.20}$$

Note the special cases of $F_n^o(t_k) = 1$, so that $S_n^o(t_k) = 0$, and $F_n^o(0) = 0$, so that $S_n^o(0) = 1$.

It is important to note that values of $F_n^o(t)$ can be observed *only* at interval boundaries. To estimate $F(t)$ at values of t *between* interval boundaries, we need to impose an additional assumption on our estimation process. We choose to define our estimate of $F(t)$ as that obtained by *linear interpolation* between the observed estimates at the interval boundaries. Then for all t such that $t_{i-1} < t < t_i$, we have

$$\hat{F}(t) = \frac{t_i - t}{t_i - t_{i-1}} \cdot F_n^o(t_{i-1}) + \frac{t - t_{i-1}}{t_i - t_{i-1}} \cdot F_n^o(t_i). \tag{9.21}$$

(Note that the estimate of $F(t)$ in this case cannot properly be called an "observed" value, so we use the generic estimator notation $\hat{F}(t)$ rather than the specific observed notation $F_n^o(t)$.)

The overall $\hat{F}(t)$ function is piecewise linear, so it is continuous and differentiable everywhere except at interval boundaries. The derivative of $\hat{F}(t)$ gives us an estimate of the density function (PDF), which is

$$\begin{aligned} \hat{f}(t) = \frac{d}{dt}\hat{F}(t) &= \frac{-1}{t_i - t_{i-1}} \cdot F_n^o(t_{i-1}) + \frac{1}{t_i - t_{i-1}} \cdot F_n^o(t_i) \\ &= \frac{F_n^o(t_i) - F_n^o(t_{i-1})}{t_i - t_{i-1}}, \end{aligned} \tag{9.22}$$

for $t_{i-1} < t < t_i$. Note that the estimated PDF is a step function that is constant for all t within a particular interval. The piecewise-linear CDF is called an *ogive*, and the step-function PDF is called a *histogram*.

EXAMPLE 9.10

A generic data set contains $n = 500$ observations recorded in five amount intervals as shown in Table 9.5.

TABLE 9.5

Generic Grouped Data	
Amount Interval	**Number of Observations**
0 – 2,000	178
2,000 - 5,000	142
5,000 - 20,000	82
20,000 - 50,000	50
50,000 - 100,000	48

We wish to use the results of this section to estimate (a) $F_{500}^o(5{,}000)$, (b) $S_{500}^o(20{,}000)$, (c) $\hat{F}(12{,}000)$, and (d) $\hat{f}(30{,}000)$.

SOLUTION

(a) $t_2 = 5{,}000$ is an interval boundary; the observed proportion prior to (or at) 5,000 is

$$F_{500}^{o}(5{,}000) = \frac{178+142}{500} = .640.$$

(b) Similarly, $t_3 = 20{,}000$ is an interval boundary; the observed proportion surviving at 20,000 is

$$S_{500}^{o}(20{,}000) = \frac{50+48}{500} = .196.$$

(c) $t = 12{,}000$ is not an interval boundary; we use Equation (9.21) to find

$$\begin{aligned}\hat{F}(12{,}000) &= \left(\frac{20{,}000-12{,}000}{20{,}000-5{,}000}\right)(.640)+\left(\frac{12{,}000-5{,}000}{20{,}000-5{,}000}\right)(.804)\\ &= \left(\frac{8}{15}\right)(.640)+\left(\frac{7}{15}\right)(.804) = .71653.\end{aligned}$$

(d) Note that $F_{500}^{o}(20{,}000) = .804$ and $F_{500}^{o}(50{,}000) = .904$, so, from Equation (9.22), we have

$$\hat{f}(30{,}000) = \frac{.904-.804}{50{,}000-20{,}000} = .00000\dot{3}\dot{3}.$$ ❐

To analyze the mean and variance of the estimator of the CDF in the grouped data case, we first define the binomial random variable $N(t_i)$ to denote the number of observations *after* time t_i, which is an interval boundary. It is clear that

$$F_n^{o}(t_i) = 1-\frac{N(t_i)}{n} = \frac{n-N(t_i)}{n} \tag{9.23}$$

is again a binomial proportion estimator whose properties are by now well understood.

We now consider the estimator $\hat{F}(t)$, given by Equation (9.21), where t is not an interval boundary. Substituting for $F_n^{o}(t_i)$ and $F_n^{o}(t_{i-1})$ in Equation (9.21) in terms of the random variable $N(t)$ we have

$$\hat{F}(t) = \left(\frac{t_i-t}{t_i-t_{i-1}}\right)\left(\frac{n-N(t_{i-1})}{n}\right)+\left(\frac{t-t_{i-1}}{t_i-t_{i-1}}\right)\left(\frac{n-N(t_i)}{n}\right). \tag{9.24}$$

Next we let $D_1 = n-N(t_{i-1})$ denote the number of observations in the interval $(0, t_{i-1}]$ and $D_2 = N(t_{i-1})-N(t_i)$ denote the number of observations in the interval $(t_{i-1}, t_i]$. (Along with

D_3, the number of observations in the interval $(t_i, t_k]$, the random variables D_1, D_2, D_3 have a joint multinomial distribution[5] with $D_1+D_2+D_3 = n$.) Substituting into Equation (9.24) we have

$$\hat{F}(t) = \left(\frac{t_i - t}{t_i - t_{i-1}}\right)\left(\frac{D_1}{n}\right) + \left(\frac{t - t_{i-1}}{t_i - t_{i-1}}\right)\left(\frac{D_1 + D_2}{n}\right) = \frac{D_1(t_i - t_{i-1}) + D_2(t - t_{i-1})}{n(t_i - t_{i-1})}. \quad (9.25)$$

Then the expected value of the estimator $\hat{F}(t)$ is

$$\begin{aligned} E[\hat{F}(t)] &= \frac{(t_i - t_{i-1}) \cdot E[D_1] + (t - t_{i-1}) \cdot E[D_2]}{n(t_i - t_{i-1})} \\ &= \frac{(t_i - t_{i-1}) \cdot (n \cdot F(t_{i-1})) + (t - t_{i-1}) \cdot \left[n\left(F(t_i) - F(t_{i-1})\right)\right]}{n(t_i - t_{i-1})}, \end{aligned}$$

using properties of the multinomial distribution (see Section 1.2.2) to substitute for $E[D_1]$ and $E[D_2]$. This simplifies to

$$E[\hat{F}(t)] = \frac{(t - t_{i-1}) \cdot F(t_i) + (t_i - t) \cdot F(t_{i-1})}{t_i - t_{i-1}}, \quad (9.26)$$

by combining the two terms involving $F(t_{i-1})$. Since $F_n^o(t_i)$ is unbiased, then it follows that $E[F_n^o(t_i)] = F(t_i)$ and Equation (9.26) can be obtained directly from Equation (9.21), without resorting to the random variables $N(t)$, D_1, and D_2.

The usefulness of expressing $\hat{F}(t)$ in terms of the multinomial random variables D_1 and D_2 arises in finding the variance of $\hat{F}(t)$. From Equation (9.25) we have

$$Var[\hat{F}(t)] = \frac{\begin{array}{r}(t_i - t_{i-1})^2 \cdot Var(D_1) + (t - t_{i-1})^2 \cdot Var(D_2) \\ + 2(t_i - t_{i-1})(t - t_{i-1}) \cdot Cov(D_1, D_2)\end{array}}{n^2 (t_i - t_{i-1})^2}.$$

Again we use the properties of the multinomial distribution to substitute for $Var(D_1)$, $Var(D_2)$, and $Cov(D_1, D_2)$, obtaining

$$Var[\hat{F}(t)] = \frac{\begin{array}{l}(t_i - t_{i-1})^2 \cdot \left[n \cdot F(t_{i-1}) \cdot (1 - F(t_{i-1}))\right] \\ \quad + (t - t_{i-1})^2 \cdot \left[n\left(F(t_i) - F(t_{i-1})\right)\left(1 - F(t_i) + F(t_{i-1})\right)\right] \\ \quad + 2(t_i - t_{i-1})(t - t_{i-1}) \cdot \left[-n \cdot F(t_{i-1}) \cdot \left(F(t_i) - F(t_{i-1})\right)\right]\end{array}}{n^2 (t_i - t_{i-1})^2}. \quad (9.27)$$

[5] See Section 1.2.2 for a review of the multinomial distribution.

Finding the mean and variance of the estimator of the PDF, given by Equation (9.22), is left as Exercise 9-18.

9.3.2 SURVIVAL MODEL ESTIMATION USING EQUAL INTERVALS

Now we will customize the general complete grouped data model to one with equal intervals which we will analyze in the context of a survival model. We again have a cohort of n individuals existing at time $t=0$. We observe them surviving across time until all have failed (so that we have complete data), but we can observe only the interval of failure. The length of each failure interval is arbitrary; it could be a day, week, month, year, or m-year period. For our analysis we consider the interval to be one time unit, whatever that may be. This is illustrated in the following figure, where the value of k is set large enough so that survival to time k is not possible.

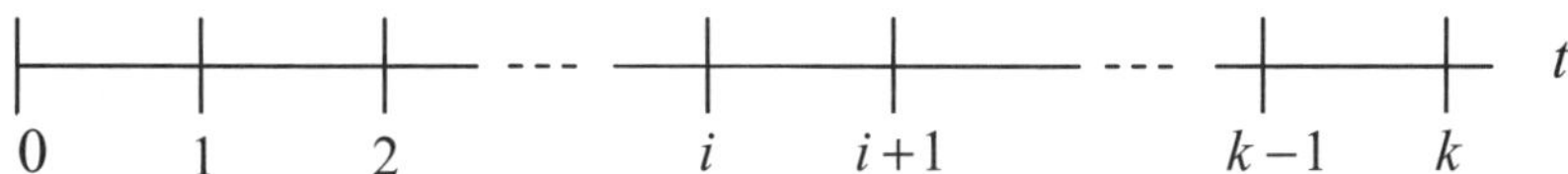

Time Line for Complete Grouped Data with Equal Interval Length

FIGURE 9.4

There are three quantities of interest that we may wish to estimate from the data.

(1) The (unconditional) probability of survival to time i, $i=1,2,\ldots k-1$, denoted by $S(i)$.

(2) The (unconditional) probability of failure in the $(i+1)^{st}$ interval, denoted in standard actuarial notation by ${}_{i|}q_0 = S(i)-S(i+1)$.

(3) The (conditional) probability of failure in the $(i+1)^{st}$ interval, given survival to the beginning of that interval, denoted in standard actuarial notation by q_i.

Note that the unconditional probability of failure prior to time i, denoted $F(i)$, and the conditional probability of survival through the $(i+1)^{st}$ interval, given survival to the beginning of that interval, denoted p_i, are the complements of $S(i)$ and q_i, respectively, and are therefore estimated by the complements of the estimates of $S(i)$ and q_i, respectively.

9.3.3 ESTIMATION OF $S(i)$, ${}_{i|}q_0$, AND q_i

Let N_i denote the random variable for the number of survivors at time i, and let D_i denote the random variable for the number of failures occurring in the $(i+1)^{st}$ interval. Let n_i and d_i represent the realized values of N_i and D_i, respectively, in an actual study. Note that $n=\sum_{i=0}^{k-1} d_i$. As already mentioned, each N_i is a binomial random variable with parameters n and $S(i)$, with mean and variance given by Equations (9.5a) and (9.5b), respectively, with t replaced by i.

Together the set of random variables $\{D_0, D_1, \dots, D_{k-1}\}$ has a joint multinomial distribution, with multinomial probability ${}_{i|}q_0$ for D_i. We recall that the multinomial distribution has joint probability function

$$p(d_0, d_1, \dots, d_{k-1}) = \frac{n!}{d_0!\,d_1!\dots d_{k-1}!} \cdot \prod_{i=0}^{k-1} ({}_{i|}q_0)^{d_i}, \tag{9.28}$$

with expected values given by

$$E[D_i] = n \cdot {}_{i|}q_0, \tag{9.29}$$

variances given by

$$Var(D_i) = n({}_{i|}q_0)(1 - {}_{i|}q_0), \tag{9.30}$$

and covariances given by

$$Cov(D_i, D_j) = -n({}_{i|}q_0)({}_{j|}q_0), \tag{9.31}$$

where the means, variances, and covariances are all unconditional (i.e., given only n study units existing at time $t = 0$).

Conditional on $N_i = n_i$ actual survivors at time i, however, the random variable D_i has a binomial distribution with parameters n_i and q_i, with conditional mean $n_i \cdot q_i$ and conditional variance $n_i \cdot q_i \cdot p_i$.

With the relevant random variables clearly understood, we can now define the estimators of our three quantities of interest.

As before, $S(i)$ is estimated by the observed proportion surviving to time i, so

$$\hat{S}(i) = \frac{N_i}{n} \tag{9.32}$$

is a binomial proportion random variable with mean and variance given by Equations (9.6a) and (9.6b), respectively, with $S_n^o(t)$ replaced by $\hat{S}(i)$.

Similarly, ${}_{i|}q_0$ is naturally estimated by the observed relative frequency of failures between i and $i+1$. Thus we have

$${}_{i|}\hat{q}_0 = \frac{D_i}{n}, \tag{9.33}$$

for $i = 0, 1, \dots, k-1$, which is a multinomial proportion random variable with mean given by

$$E[{}_{i|}\hat{q}_0] = \frac{1}{n} \cdot E[D_i] = {}_{i|}q_0 \tag{9.34}$$

and variance given by

$$Var({}_{i|}\hat{q}_0) = \frac{1}{n^2}\cdot Var(D_i) = \frac{({}_{i|}q_0)(1-{}_{i|}q_0)}{n}. \tag{9.35}$$

Equations (9.34) and (9.35) show us that the multinomial proportion estimator is unbiased and consistent.

Finally, the conditional probability q_i is estimated by

$$\hat{q}_i = \frac{D_i}{n_i}. \tag{9.36}$$

Conditional on their being n_i survivors at time i, D_i is binomial so $\hat{q}_i$, given by Equation (9.36), is conditionally a binomial proportion estimator with conditional mean given by

$$E[\hat{q}_i \mid n_i] = \frac{1}{n_i}\cdot E[D_i] = q_i \tag{9.37}$$

and conditional variance given by

$$Var(\hat{q}_i \mid n_i) = \frac{1}{n_i^2}\cdot Var(D_i) = \frac{q_i(1-q_i)}{n_i}. \tag{9.38}$$

Furthermore, the estimator for p_i, namely

$$\hat{p}_i = 1-\hat{q}_i = \frac{N_{i+1}}{n_i}, \tag{9.39}$$

is also conditionally a binomial proportion, so

$$E[\hat{p}_i \mid n_i] = p_i \tag{9.40}$$

and

$$Var(\hat{p}_i \mid n_i) = \frac{p_i(1-p_i)}{n_i}. \tag{9.41}$$

Since $q_i = 1-p_i$, then clearly $Var(\hat{q}_i \mid n_i) = Var(\hat{p}_i \mid n_i)$, as expected.

EXAMPLE 9.11

Consider a sample of 20 individuals existing at $t=0$. All fail within five weeks, and only the week of failure is recorded. The observed outcome of this sample is that two individuals failed in the first week, three in the second, eight in the third, six in the fourth, and one in the fifth. Using the data of this sample, estimate (a) ${}_{2|}q_0$, (b) $S(3)$, and (c) q_3.

SOLUTION

The data are summarized in Figure 9.5 on the following page.

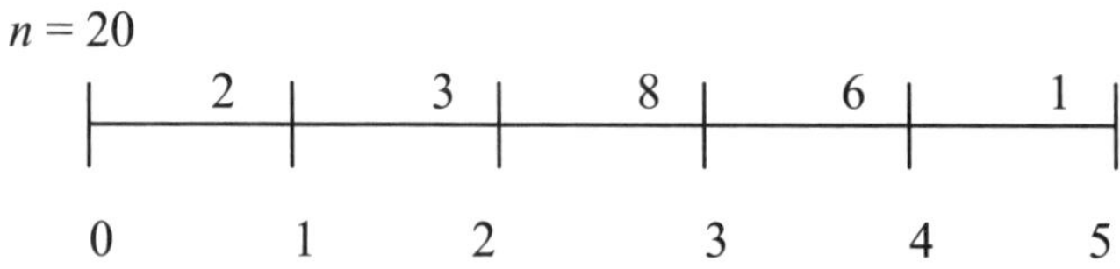

Time Line for Example 9.11

FIGURE 9.5

SOLUTION

(a) ${}_{2|}q_0$ is estimated by the multinomial proportion of failures in the third interval, so ${}_{2|}\hat{q}_0 = \frac{d_2}{n} = \frac{8}{20} = .40.$

(b) $S(3)$ is estimated by the proportion surviving to $i = 3$, producing $S_{20}^o(3) = \frac{7}{20} = .35.$

(c) q_3, a conditional probability, is estimated by the binomial proportion of failures in the fourth interval, out of those surviving to the beginning of that interval, so $\hat{q}_3 = \frac{d_3}{n_3} = \frac{6}{7}.$ ❐

EXAMPLE 9.12

Suppose our sample in Example 9.11 is known to be subject to a survival distribution that is uniform on $(0, 5]$. (a) Calculate the variance of ${}_{2|}\hat{q}_0$ and the conditional variance of $\hat{p}_3$. (b) Estimate these variances if no distribution is assumed.

SOLUTION

(a) ${}_{2|}q_0 = F(3) - F(2) = .20$, under the uniform distribution. Then by Equation (9.35), $Var({}_{2|}\hat{q}_0) = \frac{(.20)(.80)}{20} = .008.$ $p_3 = \frac{S(4)}{S(3)} = .50$, and $n_3 = 7$, so, from Equation (9.41), we find $Var(\hat{p}_3 \mid n_3) = .03571.$

(b) In this case we use ${}_{2|}\hat{q}_0$ in place of ${}_{2|}q_0$, and $\hat{p}_3$ in place of p_3, obtaining the results $Est.Var({}_{2|}\hat{q}_0) = .012$ and $Est.Var(\hat{p}_3 \mid n_3) = .01749.$ ❐

9.3.4 ESTIMATION OF $S(i)$ FROM $\{\hat{p}_j\}$

In Section 9.2, we observed that $S(t_i)$ could be estimated by the directly-observed $S_n^o(t_i)$, using Equation (9.4), or by first estimating the probability of surviving the jth subinterval, using Equation (9.10), and then using Equation (9.11) to estimate $S(t_i)$. The two-step procedure produced the same estimate of $S(t_i)$, namely $S_n^o(t_i)$, as did the direct procedure.

The same idea holds for complete grouped data as well. We can estimate $S(i)$ directly as $\hat{S}(i) = S_n^o(i)$, where i is an interval boundary, by Equation (9.32). Alternatively, we can estimate each *conditional* interval survival probability by Equation (9.39), and estimate $S(i)$ by

$$\hat{S}(i) = \hat{p}_0 \cdot \hat{p}_1 \cdot \cdots \cdot \hat{p}_{i-1}. \tag{9.42}$$

This estimation approach follows logically from the conceptual relationship

$$S(i) = p_0 \cdot p_1 \cdot \cdots \cdot p_{i-1}. \tag{9.43}$$

For a given sample of complete data, we see that the same value of $\hat{S}(i)$ will result from both the (unconditional) Equation (9.32) approach and the (conditional) Equation (9.42) approach, provided each $\hat{p}_j$ in Equation (9.42) is obtained by Equation (9.39). (The demonstration of this is left as Exercise 9-26.) The same comments made at the end of Section 9.2.5 regarding the mean and variance of $S_n^o(t_i)$ determined by the conditional Equation (9.11) approach apply here for $\hat{S}(i)$ determined by the conditional Equation (9.42) approach.

In studies which are not restricted to an initial cohort, or which allow for termination of observation before all have failed (incomplete data), the Equation (9.32) approach to $\hat{S}(i)$ will not be possible and the Equation (9.42) approach will be used instead.

9.4 SUMMARY

Several important points made in this chapter should be reemphasized in summary.

In practice, frequency and severity models are generally in parametric form, and the estimation of them will therefore be discussed extensively in Part IV of this text. Estimation of tabular frequency and severity models was briefly covered in this chapter (when estimated from complete data), and will be similarly briefly considered in Chapter 10 in the presence of incomplete data.

On the other hand, survival models are primarily tabular in nature. The estimation of tabular survival models from incomplete data is pursued in Chapter 10 in a primarily clinical setting, and in Chapter 11 in a traditional actuarial setting.

The estimation of $S(t)$ by the observed survival pattern of a sample, denoted by $S_n^o(t)$, is a special result that can occur only with complete data. (Recall that $S_n^o(t)$ is defined for all t with complete exact data, but only for values of t at interval boundaries with complete grouped data.)

We gave some emphasis in this chapter (see Sections 9.2.5 and 9.3.4) to the notion of estimating $S(t)$ by the product of the estimates of survival over a sequence of time intervals prior to time t. When we consider survival model estimation from incomplete data in the next two chapters, we will find that estimating $S(t)$ in this manner will be the standard approach, and it is for this reason that we included it here.

We derived the mean and variance for most of the estimators described in this chapter, with several derivations left to the exercises and two derivations deferred to the next chapter. The results are summarized in Table 9.6 on the following page.

TABLE 9.6

Summary of Chapter 9 Estimators			
Estimator	**Nature of Estimator**	**Mean**	**Variance**
Complete Exact Data			
$F_n^o(t)$ or $S_n^o(t)$	(Unconditional) Binomial Proportion (Equation (9.4))	$F(t)$ or $S(t)$ (Equation (9.6a))	$\frac{F(t)\cdot S(t)}{n}$ (Equation (9.6b))
p_i^o	Binomial Proportion, conditional on the risk set r_i (Equation (9.10))	p_i (Exercise 9-6)	$\frac{p_i\cdot q_i}{r_i}$ (Exercise 9-6)
$S_n^o(t_i)$	Product-Limit, conditional on the risk sets $r_1, r_2, \ldots, r_i$ (Equation (9.11))	$S(t_i)$ (Exercise 9-6)	Deferred to Chapter 10
$\hat{\Lambda}(t_i)$	Nelson-Aalen, conditional on the risk sets $r_1, r_2, \ldots, r_i$ (Equation (9.16))	$\sum_{j=1}^{i}\lambda(t_j)$ (Equation (9.18a))	$\sum_{j=1}^{i}\frac{\lambda(t_j)}{r_j}$ (Equation (9.18b))
Complete Grouped Data			
$F_n^o(t_i)$ or $S_n^o(t_i)$	(Unconditional) Binomial Proportion (Equations (9.19) and (9.20))	$F(t_i)$ or $S(t_i)$	$\frac{F(t_i)\cdot S(t_i)}{n}$
$\hat{F}(t)$ $(t_{i-1} < t < t_i)$	Linear interpolation between $F_n^o(t_{i-1})$ and $F_n^o(t_i)$ (Equation (9.21))	See Equation (9.26)	See Equation (9.27)
$\hat{f}(t)$ $(t_{i-1} < t < t_i)$	Differentiation of $\hat{F}(t)$ (Equation (9.22))	See Exercise 9-18(a)	See Exercise 9-18(b)
${}_{i\|}\hat{q}_0$	(Unconditional) Multinomial Proportion (Equation (9.33))	${}_{i\|}q_0$ (Equation (9.34))	$\frac{({}_{i\|}q_0)(1-{}_{i\|}q_0)}{n}$ (Equation (9.35))
$\hat{q}_i$ or $\hat{p}_i$	Binomial Proportion, conditional on n_i survivors at time i (Equations (9.36) and (9.39))	q_i or p_i (Equations (9.37) and (9.40))	$\frac{p_i\cdot q_i}{n}$ (Equations (9.38) and (9.41))
$\hat{S}(i)$	Product-Limit, conditional on the interval samples $n_0, n_1, \ldots, n_{i-1}$ (Equation (9.42))	$S(i)$ (Exercise 9-28)	Deferred to Chapter 10

9.5 EXERCISES

9.1 Introduction
9.2 Complete Exact Data

9-1 Let $\hat{e}_0$ represent the observed average lifetime of a cohort whose times at failure are recorded exactly. Find $\hat{e}_0$ for the sample described in Example 9.4.

9-2 Let $\hat{e}_t$ be the observed average remaining lifetime for those in the cohort who survive to time t. Find $\hat{e}_6$ for the sample of Example 9.4.

9-3 Suppose the cohort of Example 9.4 is actually subject to a uniform survival distribution on the interval $(0,15]$. Compare the observed average lifetimes $\hat{e}_0$ and $\hat{e}_6$ to the expected, according to the assumed distribution.

9-4 The following values are taken from a standard life table:

$$\ell_{70}=80{,}000 \qquad \ell_{83}=42{,}000 \qquad \ell_{84}=37{,}000$$

Four individuals, each exact age 70, are observed until failure. The failures occur at exact ages 83.30, 83.34, 83.36, and 83.47. Assuming that the operative survival model for these individuals is given by the standard table, determine the probability that the number of individuals whose lifetimes exceed their expected median future lifetimes is greater than the number actually observed.

9-5 Out of 2000 policies, 1600 experienced no claims and 400 experienced one or more claims. Using a normal approximation, find the upper bound of the symmetric 95% confidence interval for the probability of one or more claims on a single policy.

9-6 Let $S_n^o(t_i)$ be estimated by the conditional interval estimates approach of Section 9.2.5.

(a) What are $E[p_j^o]$ and $Var(p_j^o)$?

(b) Conditional on the risk sets $r_1, r_2, \ldots, r_i$, the estimators $p_1^o, p_2^o, \ldots, p_i^o$ are mutually independent. Show that this implies the unbiasedness of the estimator $S_n^o(t_i)$.

9-7 In a complete data study, with only one failure at each failure point, $\Lambda(t)$ is estimated by the Nelson-Aalen method. Given $\hat{\Lambda}(t_i)=.3101$ and $\hat{\Lambda}(t_{i+1})=.3726$, find $\hat{\Lambda}(t_{i+2})$.

9-8 In a complete data study, with only one failure at each failure point, the Nelson-Aalen estimate of $\Lambda(t_2)$ is $\frac{11}{30}$. Find the Nelson-Aalen estimate of $\Lambda(t_4)$.

9-9 In a complete data study with $n=10$ and with only one failure at each failure point, the product-limit estimate of $S(12)$ is .70. Find the Nelson-Aalen estimate of $S(12)$.

9-10 If ${}^{PL}\hat{S}(t)$ and ${}^{NA}\hat{S}(t)$ represent the product-limit and Nelson-Aalen estimators of $S(t)$, respectively, show that ${}^{PL}\hat{S}(t) < {}^{NA}\hat{S}(t)$, for all $t \geq t_1$.

9-11 Twelve policyholders were monitored from the start of their policies to the time of first claim. The following results were observed:

Time of First Claim, *t*	1	2	3	4	5	6	7
Number of Claims at Time *t*	2	1	2	2	1	2	2

Find the approximate 95% confidence interval for the Nelson-Aalen estimate of $\Lambda(4.5)$.

9-12 A complete data sample of four observations is subject to a distribution with median value y. Let $\hat{\Lambda}(y)$ denote the Nelson-Aalen estimator of the cumulative hazard at value y. Find the value of $E[\hat{\Lambda}(y)]$, without approximation.

9.3 Complete Grouped Data

9-13 A data set contains n observations recorded in six amount intervals as follows:

Amount Interval	Number of Observations
$(0,50]$	36
$(50,150]$	x
$(150,250]$	y
$(250,500]$	84
$(500,1000]$	80
$(1000,\infty)$	0

Using the interpolation approach of Equation (9.21), we find the values $\hat{F}(90)=.21$ and $\hat{F}(210)=.51$. Find the value of x.

9-14 (a) Using Equation (9.19) to substitute for $F_n^o(t_i)$ and $F_n^o(t_{i-1})$ in Equation (9.22), derive the result $\hat{f}(t) = \frac{n_i}{n(t_i - t_{i-1})}$.

(b) Give a verbal interpretation of this result.

9-15 Using the data of Example 9.10, draw the graphs of $\hat{F}(t)$ and $\hat{f}(t)$, for $0 \leq t \leq 100{,}000$.

9-16 Consider the grouped data of Example 9.10 and the ogive defined by Equation (9.21). Let y denote the 90th percentile of the estimated distribution.

(a) What is the value of $\hat{F}(y)$?

(b) What is the value of $\hat{S}(y)$?

(c) What is the value of y?

9-17 For the general grouped data case, show that

$$E[\hat{S}(t)] = \frac{(t-t_{i-1})\cdot S(t_i)+(t_i-t)\cdot S(t_{i-1})}{t_i - t_{i-1}}.$$

9-18 Find the (a) mean and (b) variance of the estimator of the PDF, given by Equation (9.22), in the grouped data case.

9-19 Find a general expression for $Est.Var[\hat{S}(i)]$, when the sample estimate is used to estimate $S(i)$.

9-20 Find $Cov({}_t|\hat{q}_0, {}_r|\hat{q}_0)$.

9-21 Find $Cov[\hat{S}(t), \hat{S}(r)]$, where $t<r$. Hint: Consider the trinomial distribution of the random variables (1) observations before t, (2) observations between t and r, and (3) observations beyond r.

9-22 A cohort of n study units is observed until all fail, with failures grouped in fixed intervals. If $Var[\hat{S}(t)] = .0009$, $Var[\hat{S}(r)] = .0016$, and their covariance is $Cov[\hat{S}(t), \hat{S}(r)] = .0008$, find $E[\hat{S}(t)]$.

9-23 Let $n = 500$. If $Var[\hat{S}(t)] = .000420$, $Var[\hat{S}(r)] = .000255$, and if $S(t) > 2\cdot S(r)$, where $t<r$, then find $Cov[\hat{S}(t), \hat{S}(r)]$.

9-24 Demonstrate that, if each value of $\hat{p}_j$ is determined by Equation (9.39), then the estimated value $\hat{S}(i)$ will be the same whether obtained by the unconditional approach of Equation (9.32) or by the conditional approach of Equation (9.42).

9-25 A complete data survival study is made from a sample of seven lives. The cohort is believed to be subject to the survival pattern given by the following life table.

t	0	1	2	3
ℓ_t	100	?	10	0

The value of ℓ_1 in the table is not given, but it is known that the unconditional variance of D_1, the random variable for the number of failures in $(1,2]$ for this sample is 1.68. It is also known that, in the life table, $d_0 > d_1$. Find the probability that the outcome for this sample will be one failure in $(0,1]$, one failure in $(1,2]$, and five failures in $(2,3]$.

9-26 A complete data survival study was made of $n = 1000$ persons all exact age 100. The following is a partially completed record of results, by duration since age 100.

Duration (t)	**Observed Failures (d_t)**	**Observed Survivors (n_t)**	**Estimated Conditional Probability ($\hat{q}_t$)**	**Estimated Survival Function [$\hat{S}(t)$]**
0		1000	.200	1.000
1	150			
2				
3			.100	
4	50			
5			.250	
6	100			
7		200		
8		100		

Complete the missing entries in the table.

9.4 Summary

9-27 Show that ${}_{i|}\hat{q}_0$, as defined by Equation (9.33), is a maximum likelihood estimator.

9-28 Repeat Exercise 9-6, this time to show that the estimator $\hat{S}(i)$, determined by the conditional Equation (9.42) approach, is unbiased.

CHAPTER TEN

ESTIMATION FROM INCOMPLETE DATA

10.1 INTRODUCTION

In the previous chapter we saw how to estimate the survival function (and therefore also the cumulative distribution function), as well as conditional interval probabilities, in the simplified estimation environment of complete data, both exact and grouped. Now we complicate the situation by introducing the notion of *incomplete data*, which is the most common estimation environment encountered in practice.

First we describe the kinds of circumstances that create an incomplete data environment, in the context of both severity and survival models. We then extend both the product-limit and the Nelson-Aalen estimators, introduced in Chapter 9 under complete data, to the incomplete data case, and present an analysis of these estimators in the presence of incomplete data.

10.2 CAUSES OF INCOMPLETE DATA

For the estimation of models work discussed in this text, two causes of incomplete data, namely *truncation* and *censoring*, are considered.

It can occur, in the design of an estimation exercise, that there are values below which, or above which, it is not possible to observe data outcomes. Consider the following representation of the real number axis.

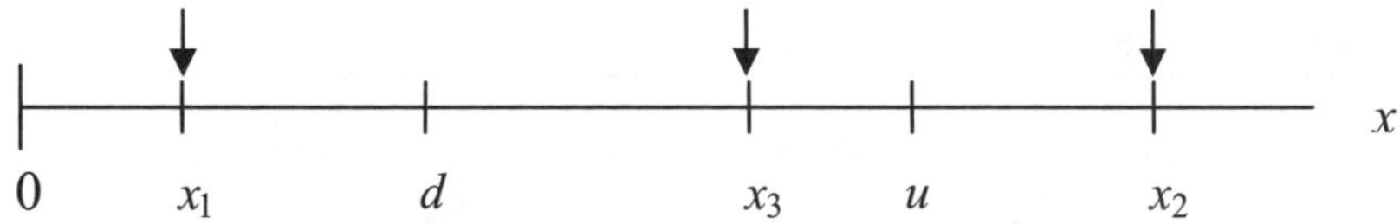

Minimum and Maximum Values of Observations

FIGURE 10.1

10.2.1 TRUNCATION OF DATA

In certain circumstances, an observation that is less than some value d is simply not, or cannot be, observed and is therefore excluded from the data set. This can occur, for example, if an insured loss amount is less than a per-loss deductible of d. The loss would not be reported to the insurer and would therefore be excluded from a data set used to estimate a loss severity model. In the context of survival model estimation, with a study design that uses a defined observation period, failure at an age earlier than the attained age at the beginning of the observation period would result in that study unit being excluded from the data set.[1]

In each of these cases of exclusion from the data set, we say that the excluded data point has been *left truncated*, or *truncated from below*. Data point x_1 in Figure 10.1 represents such truncation.

Similarly, if a data point is excluded from a study's data set because it exceeds some value u, we say the data point has been *right truncated*, or *truncated from above*. Data point x_2 is Figure 10.1 illustrates the idea of right truncation.

In the kind of actuarial model estimation considered in this text, a study design that would produce right truncation is quite unlikely to occur. Therefore we consider *only* truncation from below (left truncation) in this text.

EXAMPLE 10.1

A life insurance company experience study observes inforce policies from their respective policy anniversaries in 2000 to those in 2005. Policies A and B were both issued on April 15, 1980. Policyholder A died on October 15, 1998 and Policyholder B died on October 15, 2002. What roles do these policies play in this experience study?

SOLUTION

Policy A would have attained duration 20 at the start of observation on April 15, 2000, but it failed before that time and is therefore excluded from the data set by left truncation.

Policy B does attain duration 20 on April 15, 2000, so it is included in the data set as coming under observation at that time. It leaves observation as a failure at duration 22.5 on October 15, 2002. ❐

10.2.2 CENSORING OF DATA

We say that a data point has been *left censored*, or *censored from below*, if the data point is less than d but is reported and included in the data set at value d. Note the important difference between left censoring and left truncation. In both cases the actual value of the data point is less than d; under left censoring it is recorded as d, but under left truncation it is simply excluded from the data set. In both cases its actual value is unknown (although known to be less than d). Note also that the number of left censored data points is known, since they are reported and included, but the number of left truncated data points is generally not known since they are not reported.

Data point x_1 in Figure 10.1 would be reported at value d under left censoring. However, as was the case with right truncation, we will find that left censoring seldom arises in the estimation work considered in this text, and will therefore not be discussed further.

---

[1] Data truncation caused by the interaction of date of failure with the beginning date of an observation period is further discussed in Chapter 11.

Right censoring, or *censoring from above*, occurs if a data point greater than the value u is included in the data set at value u. It would be known that the observation exceeds u, but its actual value would not be known. This can arise under an insurance coverage with a policy maximum of amount u; any loss in excess of u, such as one of amount x_2 in Figure 10.1, would be reported as u in a data set used to estimate a loss severity model.

In the context of survival model estimation, all study units still surviving at the close of an observation period will fail at ages in excess of their respective attained ages when last observed. Their actual ages at failure are not known; it is only known that each age at failure exceeds some value u. This value, along with the understanding that the value has been right censored, will be recognized in the estimation process.

An additional cause of right censoring is also present in most cases of actuarial survival model estimation. It is generally possible for study units to *withdraw* from the sample under observation prior to failure, so that the actual value of the age at failure is not known. If withdrawal occurs at age u, and failure occurs at age $x_2 > u$ (as in Figure 10.1), the study unit is recorded at value u as a right censored observation.

It is important to note the distinction between an observation that is right censored due to the end of an observation period and one that is right censored due to withdrawal from the study. The former is referred to as *planned censoring* (or *scheduled censoring*), and the latter is referred to as *random censoring*, since the censored value u depends on the random event of withdrawal. Under scheduled censoring, the potential censored value is known in advance and is realized if survival to the end of the observation period occurs.

In the estimation procedures considered in this chapter, these two types of right censoring are treated the same, so we have no need to distinguish them in the estimation work. In Chapter 11, however, we will find it advantageous to treat them separately for reasons to be explained at that time.

Finally, we note that data point x_3 in Figure 10.1 is neither truncated nor censored, and is reported at its actual value.

EXAMPLE 10.2

For the study described in Example 10.1, Policies C and D were also both issued on April 15, 1980. Policy C was terminated for nonpayment of premium on its anniversary in 2003; Policy D was still in force on its anniversary in 2005. What roles do these policies play in the experience study?

SOLUTION

Policy C is an example of random censoring at duration 23. Policy D is an example of scheduled censoring at duration 25. The eventual failure dates for the two policyholders are not known, although they are known to be greater than their respective censored values. ❐

10.3 ESTIMATION PROCEDURES

In this section we will show how two of the estimation procedures introduced in Chapter 9 under complete data can be applied in the presence of incomplete data as well. These procedures can be used to estimate both severity and survival models. We will first discuss them in the context of survival models, because we believe that application to be more easily understood, and then show how they apply to severity models as well.

10.3.1 PRODUCT-LIMIT ESTIMATION WITH INCOMPLETE DATA

Recall that complete exact data, as defined in Chapter 9 in the context of survival model estimation, means that n study units come under observation at time (or age) 0 and remain under observation until all have failed, and the exact time (age) of failure is recorded. With incomplete data, there are two possible modifications of this simple observation environment.

The presence of left truncation in the design of a study means that study units can come under observation at a time (age) greater than 0, and the presence of right censoring means that study units can leave observation prior to failure, either planned or at random. (With the estimation procedures of this chapter, no distinction need be made between planned and random censoring when estimating the failure (survival) distribution.) We will use the term *migration* to refer both to study units entering observation and those leaving observation for a reason other than failure.

Product-limit estimation is widely used in clinical studies and also those conducted by social scientists and reliability engineers. It is less commonly used in traditional actuarial survival studies in the context of life insurance company or pension fund data. Furthermore, there is some variation between the clinical and actuarial versions of the product-limit estimator. (We will describe the clinical version in this section, and the actuarial version in Section 10.5.) The reader will notice the similarity here to the discussion in Section 9.2.5.

As before, we partition the real number axis at each observed failure time, and order these times as $t_1, t_2, \ldots, t_n$, where there are n distinct failure times. (Note that there may be more than n failures, due to multiple failures at one or more of the failure times.) Let k_i denote the number of failures at the ith failure time, where generally $k_i = 1$.

For the jth study unit, let y_j denote the time of coming under observation and let z_j denote the time of leaving observation if due to censoring of any kind (i.e., *not* a failure). Note that any study units not subject to the possibility of truncation will have $y_j = 0$. Let r_i denote the risk set for the ith subinterval, defined as the number of units under observation *immediately preceding* the ith failure time.[2] It is important to note that in Section 9.2.5, under complete data, the risk set for the ith subinterval was defined as the number surviving at the *beginning* of the ith subinterval. But under complete data there is no migration within the subinterval, so the same number will be surviving at the end of the subinterval (*just before* the failure) as at the beginning. Under incomplete data this is not the case, so it is important to note which definition (beginning or end of the subinterval) is used to define the risk set.

[2] The determination of the risk sets from the sequence of z_j and y_j values is explained in Section 10.3.3.

Using the product-limit estimation approach, we then estimate the conditional probability of failure for the ith subinterval as

$$\hat{q}_i = \frac{k_i}{r_i}, \tag{10.1}$$

and the conditional probability of survival for the ith subinterval as

$$\hat{p}_i = 1-\hat{q}_i = \frac{r_i-k_i}{r_i}. \tag{10.2}$$

(Note that $\hat{q}_i$ and $\hat{p}_i$ estimate the conditional probability of failure and survival, respectively, over the ith subinterval, which ends at the ith failure time, given survival at the beginning of that subinterval. They are *not* probabilities applying to an interval which begins at time i, as would be suggested by standard actuarial notation.)

Then

$$\hat{S}(t_i) = \prod_{j=1}^{i}\hat{p}_j = \prod_{j=1}^{i}\left(\frac{r_j-k_j}{r_j}\right) \tag{10.3}$$

estimates the probability of survival from $t=0$ to $t=t_i$, the ith failure time. Furthermore, for all t such that $t_i \le t < t_{i+1}$, the estimate of $S(t)$ is also $\hat{S}(t_i)$, since there are no failures in the sample between t_i and t_{i+1}. Thus

$$\hat{S}(t) = \prod_{j=1}^{i}\left(\frac{r_j-k_j}{r_j}\right), \tag{10.4}$$

for $t_i \le t < t_{i+1}$ and for $i=1,2,\cdots,n-1$. As a special case, of course, $\hat{S}(t)=1$ for all $t<t_1$.

Special attention is required at values of $t \ge t_n$, where t_n is the time of the last failure in the sample. If $k_n = r_n$, which means that *all* units still in the risk set just before the nth failure time fail at that time, then Equation (10.2) shows that $\hat{p}_n = 0$ and Equation (10.3) shows that $\hat{S}(t_n)=0$ as well. Then clearly $\hat{S}(t)=0$ for all $t>t_n$. If $k_n < r_n$, so that some study units survive the nth failure point and are eventually censored out of the sample, the process will produce a value of $\hat{S}(t_n)>0$. However, no values of $\hat{S}(t)$ for $t>t_n$ are implied unless additional assumptions are imposed on the estimation process. One common approach is to select an arbitrary time point beyond which survival is deemed to be impossible, which we denote by ω, and then connect the estimated value $\hat{S}(t_n)$ to the value $\hat{S}(\omega)=0$ by some continuous function, such as an exponential, linear, or quadratic function. (See Exercise 10-8.)

Finally, we establish the rule that if any migration occurs at the same time as a failure (i.e., if any y_j or z_j value is the same as any t_i value), we deem that the failure occurs *first*. Thus if a unit migrates *into* the sample (due to truncation) simultaneously with a failure, we deem that the failure came first so the risk set associated with that failure *excludes* the migrating unit. Similarly, if a unit migrates *out of* the sample (due to censoring) simultaneously with a failure, we deem that the failure came first so the risk set associated with that failure *includes* the migrating unit.

EXAMPLE 10.3

A clinical study with n study units at $t=0$, has no left truncation mechanism. There was one failure at time t_7, two failures at time t_8, and one failure at time t_9. The product-limit estimate of $S(t)$ is found to be $\hat{S}(t_7)=.75$, $\hat{S}(t_8)=.60$, and $\hat{S}(t_9)=.50$. Determine the number of observations censored from the study between times t_8 and t_9.

SOLUTION

We are given

$$\hat{S}(t_7) = \prod_{j=1}^{7}\left(\frac{r_j-k_j}{r_j}\right) = .75$$

and

$$\hat{S}(t_8) = \prod_{j=1}^{8}\left(\frac{r_j-k_j}{r_j}\right) = .60,$$

which together tell us that

$$\frac{r_8-k_8}{r_8} = \frac{.60}{.75} = .80.$$

We also know that $k_8=2$, which tells us that $r_8=10$. Similarly,

$$\frac{\hat{S}(t_9)}{\hat{S}(t_8)} = \frac{.50}{.60} = \frac{5}{6} = \frac{r_9-k_9}{r_9}.$$

Since $k_9=1$, we can then find $r_9=6$. The risk set $r_8=10$ is reduced by $k_8=2$. To reach $r_9=6$, there must have been two censored observations between t_8 and t_9. ❐

10.3.2 NELSON-AALEN ESTIMATION WITH INCOMPLETE DATA

The derivation of the Nelson-Aalen estimator from the product-limit estimator, in the presence of incomplete data, is identical to its derivation under complete data, which was given in Section 9.2.6. The general result is given by Equation (9.16), for $t_i \le t < t_{i+1}$ and for $i=1,2,\cdots,n-1$. For all $t<t_1$, where $\hat{S}(t)=1$, we naturally have $\hat{\Lambda}(t)=0$ since no failures have been observed.

EXAMPLE 10.4

A survival study contains right censored data but no left truncated data. Failures occur at times 3, 5, 6, and 10. The numbers of failures at each failure point are $k_1=1$ (at time 3), $k_2=3$ (at time 5), $k_3=5$ (at time 6), and $k_4=7$ (at time 10), with respective risk sets $r_1=50$, $r_2=49$, $r_3=x$, and $r_4=21$. The Nelson-Aalen estimate of $S(10)$ is .575. Find the value of r_4.

SOLUTION

We are given

$$\hat{S}(10) = e^{-\hat{\Lambda}(10)} = \exp\left[-\left(\frac{1}{50}+\frac{3}{49}+\frac{5}{x}+\frac{7}{21}\right)\right] = .575,$$

so

$$\frac{1}{50}+\frac{3}{49}+\frac{5}{x}+\frac{7}{21} = -\ln .575 = .55339,$$

which solves for $x=36$. ❐

The approximations for the mean and variance of the Nelson-Aalen estimator of cumulative hazard, as well as the estimated values of them using sample data, as developed in Section 9.2.6, can apply in the case of incomplete data as well. (See Exercise 10-12.)

10.3.3 DETERMINATION OF THE RISK SET

For the estimation methods of this section, we assume that we have exact data (rather than grouped), so that the precise entry and exit times are known for all study units. The risk set at time t_i, which we denote by r_i, is then easily found by adding all entrants that occur prior to t_i (i.e., all study units with $y_j < t_i$), and subtracting all exits (both failures and censored units) that occur prior to t_i (i.e., all study units with $z_j < t_i$ or $t_j < t_i$). This is reviewed in Exercise 10-13. Even for a study with a very large sample size, it would not be difficult to write a computer algorithm to calculate each value of r_i.

10.3.4 APPLICATION TO SEVERITY MODEL ESTIMATION

We have chosen to present the estimation methods of this section in the context of survival model estimation, because it is convenient to speak of units "coming under observation" and units "leaving observation." When applied in the context of severity model estimation, the mathematics is the same even if the descriptive wording is different. In that case the t_i values are the values of non-censored observations (each of which is an observed loss amount), the z_j values are the values of censored observations (which are, for example, payment amounts less than the actual loss amounts due to a policy limit), and the y_j values are left truncation values.

For example, if a loss amount data set has been collected from experience on policies with a per-loss deductible of *d*, it would not be possible for any y_j value to be less than *d*. As we think from left to right on the real number axis, starting at 0, we cannot observe any data values until we get to *d*. As we move to the right of *d*, we could begin to encounter observation values. In light of this, we could stretch the language used for survival model studies and say that loss amount values "come under observation" at *d*. The number of values in our data that arose from policies with left truncation (i.e., deductibles) at *d* must be shown as joining the risk set at $y_j = d$.

A numerical example will make this discussion more clear.

EXAMPLE 10.5

Let $\{3, 3^*, 5, 5, 5^*, 8, 10, 10^*, 12, 15\}$ be a sample of ten loss amounts, where five of them occurred under policies with no deductible and the other five occurred under policies with a deductible of 4. The values marked with (*) are right-censored values. Find the product-limit estimate of $F(10)$ for this data.

SOLUTION

Five values "come under observation" at 0, since, with no deductible, losses are possible immediately "to the right" of 0, and five additional values "come under observation" at 4, since the observed loss values cannot be less than 4. The data are represented on the following diagram, where the X's represent the location of non-censored observations.

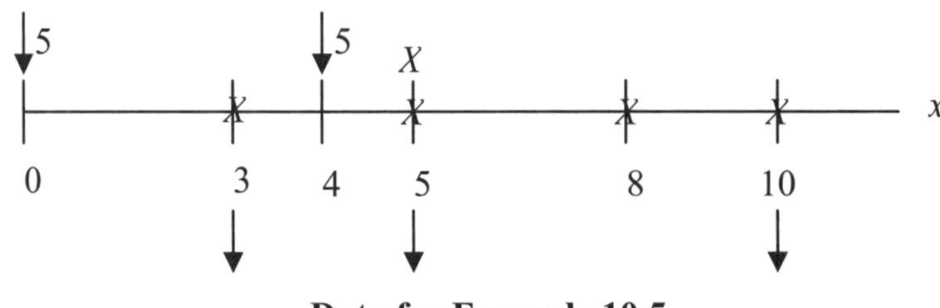

Data for Example 10.5

FIGURE 10.2

The risk sets at the several non-censored observation points are $r_1 = 5$ (at $x = 3$), $r_2 = 8$ (at $x = 5$), $r_3 = 5$ (at $x = 8$), and $r_4 = 4$ (at $x = 10$). Recall that the risk set is measured *just before* the "failures" (which are non-censored observations in this case) and the "withdrawals" (the censored observations). Then the product-limit estimate of $F(10)$ is

$$\begin{aligned}\hat{F}(10) = 1 - \hat{S}(10) &= 1 - \left(1 - \tfrac{1}{5}\right)\left(1 - \tfrac{2}{8}\right)\left(1 - \tfrac{1}{5}\right)\left(1 - \tfrac{1}{4}\right) \\ &= 1 - \left(\tfrac{4}{5}\right)\left(\tfrac{6}{8}\right)\left(\tfrac{4}{5}\right)\left(\tfrac{3}{4}\right) = .64000.\end{aligned}$$ ❐

For a severity study, although the methods discussed here naturally estimate the SDF of the severity distribution, it would be usual to summarize the results in terms of the CDF instead. The estimate of the CDF is naturally taken to be the complement of the estimate of the SDF.

10.4 PROPERTIES OF THE PRODUCT-LIMIT ESTIMATOR

The product-limit estimator of the survival function at a failure point, t_i, is unbiased and consistent. To find the expected value and variance of $\hat{S}(t_i)$, we make two important assumptions:

(1) We assume each $\hat{q}_i$ and $\hat{p}_i$, given by Equations (10.1) and (10.2), respectively, are approximately unbiased binomial proportion estimators, with means q_i and p_i, respectively, and common variance $\frac{p_i q_i}{r_i}$, where r_i is the associated risk set. Note that the risk set is interpreted as an approximate binomial sample.

(2) We assume that, conditional on the set $\{r_i\}$ of all risk sets, the $\hat{p}_i$'s are mutually independent.

The first assumption implies that $E[\hat{p}_i \mid r_i] = p_i$, and the second assumption implies that the conditional expected value of a product of $\hat{p}_i$'s, being conditionally independent, will equal the product of their conditional expected values.

10.4.1 EXPECTED VALUE OF $\hat{S}(t_i)$

It is important to note that this expected value is conditional on the set of risk sets (approximate binomial samples) underlying the estimation of the $\hat{p}_i$'s. We reflect this by using the notation $E[\hat{S}(t_i) \mid \{r_i\}]$. Then with $\hat{S}(t_i)$ given by Equation (10.3), we have

$$E[\hat{S}(t_i) \mid \{r_i\}] = E[\hat{p}_1 \cdot \hat{p}_2 \cdot \cdots \cdot \hat{p}_i \mid \{r_i\}] = \prod_{j=1}^{i} E[\hat{p}_j \mid \{r_i\}], \tag{10.5}$$

as a consequence of the independence assumption. Then from the assumption of unbiasedness, we have

$$E[\hat{S}(t_i) \mid \{r_i\}] = p_1 \cdot p_2 \cdot \cdots \cdot p_i = S(t_i), \tag{10.6}$$

establishing the unbiasedness of $\hat{S}(t_i)$ under these assumptions.

10.4.2 VARIANCE OF $\hat{S}(t_i)$

Again we note that this variance is conditional on the risk sets, and we reflect this in the notation $Var[\hat{S}(t_i) \mid \{r_i\}]$. Proceeding from first principles,

$$\begin{aligned} Var[\hat{S}(t_i) \mid \{r_i\}] &= E[\hat{S}(t_i)^2 \mid \{r_i\}] - \left(E[\hat{S}(t_i) \mid \{r_i\}]\right)^2 \\ &= E[\hat{p}_1^{\,2} \cdot \hat{p}_2^{\,2} \cdot \cdots \cdot \hat{p}_i^{\,2} \mid \{r_i\}] - \left(E[\hat{p}_1 \cdot \hat{p}_2 \cdot \cdots \cdot \hat{p}_i \mid \{r_i\}]\right)^2. \end{aligned} \tag{10.7}$$

The conditional independence assumption then allows us to write Equation (10.7) as

$$Var[\hat{S}(t_i) \mid \{r_i\}] = \prod_{j=1}^{i} E[\hat{p}_j^{\,2} \mid \{r_i\}] - \left(\prod_{j=1}^{i} E[\hat{p}_j \mid \{r_i\}]\right)^2. \tag{10.8}$$

Now for each $\hat{p}_j$,

$$Var(\hat{p}_j \mid r_j) = E[\hat{p}_j^{\,2} \mid r_j] - \left(E[\hat{p}_j \mid r_j]\right)^2,$$

so

$$E[\hat{p}_j^{\,2} \mid r_j] = Var(\hat{p}_j \mid r_j) + \left(E[\hat{p}_j \mid r_j]\right)^2.$$

But since $\hat{p}_j$ is taken to be an unbiased binomial proportion, the first moment is

$$E[\hat{p}_j \mid r_j] = p_j \tag{10.9}$$

and the second moment is

$$E[\hat{p}_j^{\,2} \mid r_j] = \frac{p_j q_j}{r_j} + p_j^{\,2} = (p_j^{\,2}) \cdot \left(\frac{q_j}{p_j r_j} + 1\right). \tag{10.10}$$

Substituting Equations (10.9) and (10.10) into Equation (10.8), we have

$$\begin{aligned} Var[\hat{S}(t_i) \mid \{r_i\}] &= \prod_{j=1}^{i} (p_j^{\,2}) \cdot \left(\frac{q_j}{p_j r_j} + 1\right) - \left(\prod_{j=1}^{i} p_j\right)^2 \\ &= \left(\prod_{j=1}^{i} p_j\right)^2 \cdot \prod_{j=1}^{i} \left(\frac{q_j}{p_j r_j} + 1\right) - \left(\prod_{j=1}^{i} p_j\right)^2 \\ &= [S(t_i)]^2 \cdot \left[\prod_{j=1}^{i} \left(\frac{q_j}{p_j r_j} + 1\right) - 1\right], \end{aligned} \tag{10.11}$$

since $S(t_i) = p_1 \cdot p_2 \cdot \cdots \cdot p_i = \prod_{j=1}^{i} p_j$.

The exact expression for the conditional variance of $\hat{S}(t_i)$, given by Equation (10.11), is often approximated as follows. Expanding the product of the binomial terms, we obtain

$$\begin{aligned} \prod_{j=1}^{i} \left(\frac{q_j}{p_j r_j} + 1\right) &= \left(1 + \frac{q_1}{p_1 r_1}\right)\left(1 + \frac{q_2}{p_2 r_2}\right) \cdots \left(1 + \frac{q_i}{p_i r_i}\right) \\ &= 1 + \frac{q_1}{p_1 r_1} + \frac{q_2}{p_2 r_2} + \cdots + \frac{q_i}{p_i r_i} + (\textit{higher order terms}). \end{aligned}$$

These second and higher order terms are quite small, so we ignore them and approximate $\prod_{j=1}^{i} \left(\frac{q_j}{p_j r_j} + 1\right)$ by $1 + \sum_{j=1}^{i} \frac{q_j}{p_j r_j}$. Then Equation (10.11) is approximated as

$$Var[\hat{S}(t_i) \mid \{r_i\}] \approx [S(t_i)]^2 \cdot \sum_{j=1}^{i} \frac{q_j}{p_j r_j}, \tag{10.12}$$

which is known as *Greenwood's Formula* (see Greenwood [10]). Since the terms we ignored were all positive, Greenwood's approximation *understates* the true value of this variance. This is unfortunate; given a choice, we would prefer variance *overstatement* in order to be taking a conservative approach in our estimation work.

As usual, with all p_i and q_i unknown, we estimate the value of the approximate variance by using the values of $\hat{q}_i$ and $\hat{p}_i$, from Equations (10.1) and (10.2), respectively, in place of the true values of q_i and p_i, and the estimated value $\hat{S}(t_i)$ in place of the true value of $S(t_i)$. The summand in Equation (10.12) becomes

$$\frac{q_j}{p_j r_j} = \frac{\hat{q}_j}{\hat{p}_j r_j} = \frac{\frac{k_j}{r_j}}{\frac{r_j - k_j}{r_j} \cdot r_j} = \frac{k_j}{r_j(r_j - k_j)},$$

and Equation (10.12) itself becomes

$$Est.Var[\hat{S}(t_i) \mid \{r_i\}] = [\hat{S}(t_i)]^2 \cdot \sum_{j=1}^{i} \left(\frac{k_j}{r_j(r_j - k_j)} \right). \tag{10.13}$$

EXAMPLE 10.6

Following is a sample of ten insurance payments:

$$\{4, 4, 5^+, 5^+, 5^+, 8, 10^+, 10^+, 12, 15\}$$

The payments marked with (+) are right-censored observations, where the actual loss exceeded the policy limit. Determine Greenwood's approximation to the variance of the product-limit estimate of $S(11)$.

SOLUTION

The data are represented on the following diagram. There is no left truncation, so all observations begin at $t = 0$.

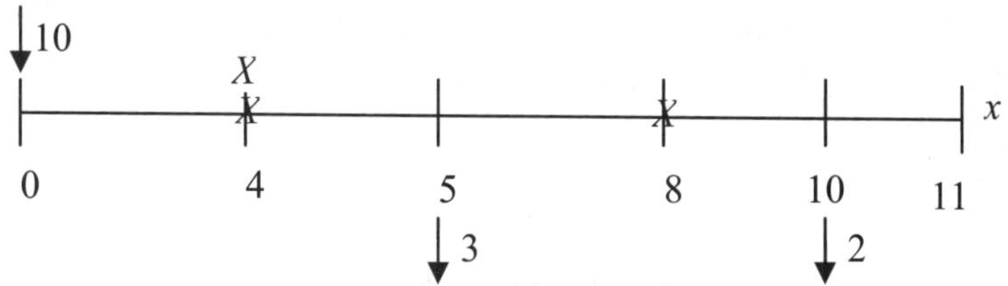

Time Line for Example 10.6

FIGURE 10.3

The uncensored observations ("failures") are represented by X's, and the censored observations are represented by the arrows below the axis. The relevant risk sets, which are measured immediately before each failure point, are $r_1 = 10$ (at $x = 4$) and $r_2 = 5$ (at $x = 8$), reflecting the two "failures" at time 4 and the three censored observations at time 5. Then we find

$$\hat{S}(8) = \left(1-\frac{2}{10}\right)\left(1-\frac{1}{5}\right) = .64,$$

and $\hat{S}(11) = .64$ as well since there are no failures (uncensored observations) between times 8 and 11. Using Equation (10.13) we have

$$\begin{aligned} Est.Var[\hat{S}(11)] &= [\hat{S}(11)]^2 \cdot \left[\left(\frac{k_4}{r_4(r_4-k_4)}\right)+\left(\frac{k_8}{r_8(r_8-k_8)}\right)\right] \\ &= (.64)^2 \cdot \left(\frac{2}{(10)(8)}+\frac{1}{(5)(4)}\right) = .03072. \end{aligned}$$

❐

10.5 APPLICATION TO ACTUARIAL SURVIVAL STUDIES

We saw in Section 10.3 that the product-limit procedure, in a clinical setting, is generally used to estimate $S(t_i)$, where t_i is a failure time point, with the same estimate then extended to all $t_i \leq t < t_{i+1}$. In the traditional actuarial setting with life insurance or pension fund data, the primary goal is to estimate the conditional probabilities p_x and q_x, given survival to age x, for integral x.[3] Then the survival function is estimated as

$$\hat{S}(x) = \hat{p}_0 \cdot \hat{p}_1 \cdot \dots \cdot \hat{p}_{x-1}, \tag{10.14}$$

now using standard actuarial notation.[4]

We again assume exact data, so the precise age of coming under observation and the precise age of leaving observation, for whatever reason, are known. Recall that scheduled withdrawals and random withdrawals are treated alike under the product-limit estimation method.

The method is easily explained by an example. Suppose a sample of $n_x = 20$ study units alive at age x is augmented by 2 additional entrants and decremented by 3 withdrawals and 5 failures prior to age $x+1$. Figure 10.4 illustrates this data, using arrows to locates the entrants and withdrawals and X's to locate the failures.

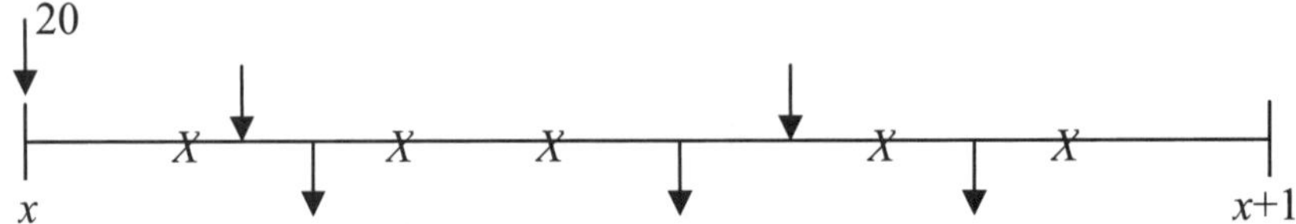

Data for Product-Limit Estimation of q_x

FIGURE 10.4

---

[3] The reader should be familiar with the standard form of the actuarial life table, as described in Chapter 6 of Cunningham, et al. [7] and briefly reviewed in Section 3.3 of this text.

[4] Recall that we use $\hat{p}_i$ to denote the conditional probability of survival over the ith subinterval, of whatever length. In this section, and in the next chapter, $\hat{p}_x$ denotes the conditional probability of survival from age x to age $x+1$, where x is generally an integer.

We have not bothered to indicate the ages within $(x, x+1]$ at which the events of failure, entry and withdrawal occur, since this information is not used in computing $\hat{q}_x$. It is only necessary to indicate the events *in order of occurrence*, but not the precise ages at which they occur.

We now break our basic estimation interval into six subintervals by partitioning $(x, x+1]$ at each point where an entry or withdrawal occurs, as shown in Figure 10.5.

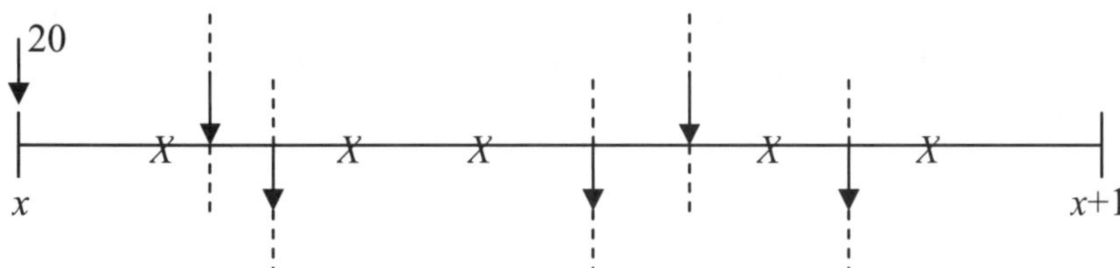

Partitioned Interval for Product-Limit Estimation of q_x

FIGURE 10.5

We recognize that each of the six subintervals is a complete data situation, since there are no events *within* the subinterval except (possibly) failures. If q_i is the conditional probability of failure in the ith subinterval, given alive at the beginning of that subinterval, then the natural estimator of q_i is the binomial proportion

$$\hat{q}_i = \frac{k_i}{n_i}, \tag{10.15}$$

where k_i is the number of observed failures in the ith subinterval, and n_i is the binomial sample size for that subinterval. Clearly if $k_i = 0$, as is true for $i = 2$ and $i = 4$, then $\hat{q}_i = 0$ as well.

The product-limit estimator of q_x is then defined as

$$\hat{q}_x = 1 - \prod_{i=1}^{m}(1-\hat{q}_i) = 1 - \prod_{i=1}^{m}\left(\frac{n_i - k_i}{n_i}\right), \tag{10.16}$$

where m is the number of subintervals in $(x, x+1]$. (In this example, $m = 6$.)

To complete the example, we first note that the subinterval sample sizes are $n_1 = n_x = 20$, $n_2 = 20$, $n_3 = 19$, $n_4 = 16$, $n_5 = 17$, and $n_6 = 15$. Thus we have

$$\hat{q}_x = 1 - \left(\frac{19}{20}\right)\left(\frac{20}{20}\right)\left(\frac{17}{19}\right)\left(\frac{16}{16}\right)\left(\frac{16}{17}\right)\left(\frac{14}{15}\right) = 1 - \frac{(16)(14)}{(20)(15)} = .25333.$$

The occurrence of a failure at the same age as an entrant or withdrawal raises the question of the subinterval to which such failure belongs. The usual rule is to consider a failure that coincides with an entrant or withdrawal as belonging to the subinterval *preceding* such event. That is, a failure at a subinterval boundary is deemed to belong to the subinterval closing at the boundary, rather than the one opening there. This is consistent with our general notation $(x, x+1]$.

There is an important distinction here from our earlier presentation of the product-limit estimator in Section 10.3. There we partitioned the real number axis at each *failure point*, and defined the risk set for each subinterval as the number surviving *immediately before* the failure. In this section we partition the axis at each *migration point*, and use the number surviving at the *beginning* of the subinterval as our binomial sample for estimating $\hat{q}_i$ for that subinterval. It can be shown, however, that the same estimate value will result if we partition at each failure point.

EXAMPLE 10.7

Repeat the estimation of q_x for the data given above, this time partitioning the axis at each failure point as in Section 10.3.

SOLUTION

We again have six subintervals, with risk sets $r_1 = 20,\ r_2 = 19,\ r_3 = 18,\ r_4 = 17,$ and $r_5 = 15.$ Then, with only one failure at each failure point, the estimates of q_i are $\hat{q}_1 = \frac{1}{20},\ \hat{q}_2 = \frac{1}{19},$ $\hat{q}_3 = \frac{1}{18}.\ \hat{q}_4 = \frac{1}{17},\ \hat{q}_5 = \frac{1}{15},$ and $\hat{q}_6 = 0$ since there are no failures in the final subinterval. Then our estimate of q_x is

$$\hat{q}_x = 1-\left(\frac{19}{20}\right)\left(\frac{18}{19}\right)\left(\frac{17}{18}\right)\left(\frac{16}{17}\right)\left(\frac{14}{15}\right) = .25333,$$

as before. □

The primary reason for preferring the partition-at-migration approach over the partition-at-failure approach is that under the former the random variable for failures in the subinterval is precisely binomial, with parameters n_i and q_i, so $\hat{q}_i$ is precisely a binomial proportion estimator. Under the partition-at-failure approach, the model is not precisely binomial since the risk set r_i does not apply throughout the entire subinterval. Being a precise binomial proportion, the unbiasedness and consistency of each $\hat{q}_i$ is more clearly established than in the case of Equation (10.1) where $\hat{q}_i$ is only approximately a binomial proportion estimator.

By reasoning analogous to that employed in Section 10.4 for the estimator $\hat{S}(t_i)$, we can now show that

$$E[\hat{q}_x \mid \{n_i\}] = q_x, \tag{10.17}$$

$$E[\hat{p}_x \mid \{n_i\}] = p_x, \tag{10.18}$$

and

$$Var(\hat{q}_x \mid \{n_i\}) = Var(\hat{p}_x \mid \{n_i\}) = (p_x)^2 \cdot \left[\prod_{i=1}^{m}\left(\frac{q_i}{p_i n_i}+1\right)-1\right]. \tag{10.19}$$

Furthermore, by steps parallel to those leading from Equation (10.11) to Equation (10.12) we find

$$Var(\hat{q}_x \mid \{n_i\}) = Var(\hat{p}_x \mid \{n_i\}) \approx (p_x)^2 \cdot \sum_{i=1}^{m} \frac{q_i}{p_i n_i}. \tag{10.20}$$

The details of deriving these results are left as Exercises 10-18, 10-19, and 10-20.

The Nelson-Aalen estimator can also be adapted to the actuarial study format. Recall that the basic idea with Nelson-Aalen is to estimate $\Lambda(t)$, the cumulative hazard over the interval $(0, t]$, and then estimate $S(t)$ as $\hat{S}(t) = e^{-\hat{\Lambda}(t)}$. In the actuarial setting, where we are estimating the conditional probability p_x, the cumulative hazard would be measured over $(x, x+1]$ only, and denoted by $\hat{\Lambda}_x$. Then p_x would be estimated as

$$\hat{p}_x = e^{-\hat{\Lambda}_x}. \tag{10.21}$$

To be consistent with our earlier definition of Nelson-Aalen, however, we would need to revert to the earlier partitioning-at-failure approach using the risk set at the end of each subinterval. Because we prefer the partitioning-at-migration approach in the actuarial setting, for reasons described above, Nelson-Aalen is seldom used to estimate p_x and q_x.

10.6 SUMMARY

Incomplete data results from either left truncation or right censoring, or both. With the causes of incomplete data understood, we went on in this chapter to define the concept of the risk set, and then proceeded to define the product-limit estimator of the survival function $S(t_i)$, where t_i is the ith failure time, with extension to all values of t such that $t_i \leq t < t_{i+1}$.

Next we developed exact expressions for the mean and variance of the product-limit estimator of $S(t_i)$, along with an approximation to the variance (Greenwood's Formula) and an expression for the estimated value of the Greenwood variance.

The steps of product-limit estimation were then reviewed in the context of actuarial survival model estimation. The results here are expressed in different notation, but no new theory was involved in this review.

The Nelson-Aalen estimators of both the survival function (see Equation (9.16)) and the cumulative hazard function (see Equation (9.15a)), along with the mean and variance of the Nelson-Aalen estimator of cumulative hazard (see Equations (9.18a) and (9.18b)), were developed in Chapter 9 in the context of complete data. These results are the same in the presence of incomplete data, and consequently were not derived anew in this chapter.

The product-limit results developed in this chapter are summarized in Table 10.1 below.

TABLE 10.1

Summary of Product-Limit Estimators			
Function to be Estimated	Estimator	Mean	Variance
$S(t_i)$	$\prod_{j=1}^{i}\left(\frac{r_j-k_j}{r_j}\right)$	(Conditional on $\{r_i\}$): $S(t_i)$ (Conditionally Unbiased)	Exact, (conditional on $\{r_i\}$): $[S(t_i)]^2\cdot\left[\prod_{j=1}^{i}\left(\frac{q_j}{p_jr_j}+1\right)-1\right]$ Approximate, (conditional on $\{r_i\}$): $[S(t_i)]^2\cdot\sum_{j=1}^{i}\frac{q_j}{p_jr_j}$

10.7 EXERCISES

10.1 Introduction
10.2 Causes of Incomplete Data

10-1 Eight people join an exercise program on the same day, with no prior experience in such a program. They remain in the program until they reach their weight loss goals, or choose to switch to a diet program to achieve weight loss.

Member	Time (in weeks) of Reaching Weight Loss Goal	Time (in weeks) of Switching to Diet Program
1	--	4
2	--	8
3	8	--
4	12	--
5	--	12
6	12	--
7	22	--
8	36	--

The variable we wish to model is the time to reach the weight loss goal.

(a) Is this data set complete or incomplete?

(b) If incomplete, is it due to truncation, planned censoring, or random censoring?

10-2 Suppose the exercise program of Exercise 10-1 had always been planned as a 30-week program only. Which members have their roles changed from what they were in Exercise 10-1?

10-3 Suppose an identical exercise program had started on the same day but at another location of the same health club. That program closed after four weeks due to insufficient interest, and several of its active members transferred to the location described in Exercise 10-1. What role do they play in our study?

10-4 A particular insurance coverage has a per-loss deductible of 500 and a per-loss coverage maximum of 5000. The following is a set of loss amounts incurred by a group of policyholders:

$$\{2000, 6000, 7000, 200, 3000, 400\}$$

(a) Which losses produce truncation of claim payment data?

(b) Which losses produce censoring of claim payment data?

10.3 Estimation Procedures

10-5 Ten nuclear power plant workers were accidentally exposed to a significant dosage of radiation. A worker died at each of times 2 and 4 following the accident. At time 3, x workers moved to Australia for treatment and were lost from observation. The product-limit estimate of $S(5)$ is $\hat{S}(5) = .75$. Find the value of x.

10-6 All members of a survival study are observed from time 0, but some members are censored out of the sample. One failure was observed at the third failure time, and three failures were observed at the fourth failure time. Between the fourth and fifth failure times, six members were censored from the sample. Given the product-limit estimates $\hat{S}(t_3) = .65$, $\hat{S}(t_4) = .50$, and $\hat{S}(t_5) = .25$, find the value of k_5, the number of failures at the fifth failure time.

10-7 Show that the right side of Equation (10.3) reduces to the right side of Equation (9.4) if there is no migration.

10-8 Refer to Example 10.3. Suppose $t_9 = 15$ is the last time point of an observed failure so the five study units surviving past time 15 are all censored out. $\hat{S}(15) = .50$ is the last value of $S(t)$ that can be estimated from the given data. If we arbitrarily declare that $\omega = 20$ is the maximum survival age for these study units, and connect $\hat{S}(15) = .50$ to $\hat{S}(20) = 0$ by a linear function, what is the value of $\hat{S}(18)$?

10-9 In the data set {200, 300, 100, 400, X}, the value of X is known to be the same as one of the other four observations but not 200 or 400. Determine the value of X, given the Nelson-Aalen estimate $\hat{\Lambda}(410) > 2.15$.

10-10 Consider the following data set of loss amounts:

{2500, 2500, 2500, 3617, 3662, 4517, 5000, 5000, 6010, 6932, 7500, 7500}

The Nelson-Aalen estimate $\hat{\Lambda}_1(7000)$ is calculated by assuming that all observations are uncensored, and the Nelson-Aalen estimate $\hat{\Lambda}_2(7000)$ is calculated by assuming that all observed values 2500, 5000, and 7500 have been censored. Find the value of $|\hat{\Lambda}_1(7000) - \hat{\Lambda}_2(7000)|$.

10-11 For a certain data set, the product-limit estimate of $S(x)$ is as follows:

$$\hat{S}(x) = \begin{cases} 1 & \text{for } 0 \le x < a \\ \frac{49}{50} & \text{for } a \le x < b \\ \frac{1{,}911}{2{,}000} & \text{for } b \le x < c \\ \frac{36{,}309}{40{,}000} & \text{for } c \le x < d \end{cases}$$

Determine the Nelson-Aalen estimate of $S(c)$.

10-12 Use the data of Exercise 10-1 to estimate the symmetric 90% confidence interval for the Nelson-Aalen estimate of $\Lambda(12)$.

10-13 Find the value of each of the risk sets needed to do product-limit or Nelson-Aalen estimation, given the following data.

Study Unit	Left Truncation Point	Time of Uncensored Observation	Time of Censored Observation
1	0	0.9	--
2	0	--	1.2
3	0	1.5	--
4	0	--	1.5
5	0	--	1.6
6	0	1.7	--
7	0	--	1.7
8	1.3	2.1	--
9	1.5	2.1	--
10	1.6	--	2.3

10-14 Consider the following set of incomplete severity data, where both left truncation and right censoring have been present:

Study Unit	Value at First Observation (Left Truncation Value)	Value at Last Observation (Right Censored Value)	Value as an Uncensored Observation
1	0	6	--
2	0	27	--
3	0	--	42
4	0	--	42
5	5	--	60
6	10	--	24
7	15	50	--
8	20	23	--

Calculate the expected value of the distribution estimated from this data by the product-limit method.

10-15 A survival study is based on the following data:

Failure Time	Number of Failures	Risk Set
5	2	15
7	1	12
10	1	10
12	2	6

Determine the Nelson-Aalen estimate of $S(12)$.

10.4 Properties of the Product-Limit Estimator

10-16 In a study of 200 auto accident claims, it is found that claims are submitted t months after the accident occurs, for $t = 0,1,2,\cdots$, and there are no censored observations. $\hat{S}(t)$ is determined by the product-limit method, and its variance is estimated by Greenwood's formula. Find the number of claims submitted at time $t = 10$, given the following values:

$$\hat{S}(8) = .22 \qquad Est.Var[\hat{S}(9)] = .000672$$

$$\hat{S}(9) = .16 \qquad \frac{Est.Var[\hat{S}(10)]}{[\hat{S}(10)]^2} = .04045$$

10-17 A survival study is based on a sample of $n=50$ units observed from time zero. The failure times are $t_1=15$, $t_2=25$, and $t_3=32$. The respective numbers of failures are $k_1=2$, $k_2=4$, and $k_3=8$. In addition, 3 units are censored out at time 17 and c units are censored out at time 30. Determine the value of c, given that

$$\frac{Est.Var[\hat{S}(35)]}{[\hat{S}(35)]^2} = .011467,$$

where $\hat{S}(35)$ denotes the product-limit estimate of $S(35)$ and $Est.Var[\hat{S}(35)]$ denotes the estimated variance of the $\hat{S}(35)$ estimator random variable using Greenwood's approximation.

10.5 Application to Actuarial Survival Studies

10-18 Repeat the presentation of Section 10.4.1 to derive Equation (10.18).

10-19 Repeat the presentation of Section 10.4.2 to derive Equation (10.19).

10-20 Derive Equation (10.20) from Equation (10.19) by duplicating the derivation of Equation (10.12) from Equation (10.11).

10-21 One hundred annuitants are observed from attainment of age 75 for part or all of the following year of age. There are four failures, one at the end of each quarter year of age. At the end of the observation period, there were ten surviving annuitants at age 75⅔, and the other survivors had all attained age 76 or greater.

(a) Find the product-limit estimate of q_{75}.

(b) Estimate the variance of $\hat{q}_{75}$ by using $\hat{q}_i$ in place of each q_i.

10-22 At each age x, n_x lives are observed for one year of age with no migration within each annual estimation interval. There are k_x failures in $(x, x+1]$. Calculate Greenwood's estimate of the standard deviation of ${}_3\hat{p}_{48}$, given the following data.

x	n_x	k_x
48	200	2
49	200	4
50	196	7

CHAPTER ELEVEN

ACTUARIAL SURVIVAL MODEL ESTIMATION

11.1 INTRODUCTION

In this chapter we expand on the idea introduced in Section 10.5 to consider in depth traditional actuarial approaches to the estimation of tabular survival models. For the most part, this type of survival model estimation is carried out in the context of a life insurance company or pension fund setting.

There are three important ways in which the estimation work of this chapter differs from that presented in Chapters 9 and 10.

(1) The earlier studies, particularly the complete data studies of Chapter 9, utilized a *longitudinal study design*, whereby an initial cohort of n study units existed at time (or age) 0 and were followed across time until all had failed (complete data) or were censored out of the study group (incomplete data). In actuarial studies of healthy human beings, such a study design is not feasible due to the length of time required for all to fail. Instead, these studies use a *cross-sectional study design*, in which a *period of observation* is chosen and the members of the study sample are observed only during that period. The sample members are various ages when the observation period begins, and come under observation at those respective ages. (These were referred to as left-truncated observations in the terminology of Chapter 10.) When the observation period ends, most sample members are still alive and observation terminates for them at their respective ages at that time. (These were called scheduled right-censored observations in Chapter 10.)

(2) As mentioned in Section 10.5, the goal in actuarial survival studies is to determine an estimate of the conditional probability of failure over the age interval $(x, x+1]$, given survival to age x, such estimate denoted by $\hat{q}_x$. From the sequence $\{\hat{q}_x\}$ for all x, the tabular actuarial survival model (generally called a *life table*) is derived.[1] This approach stands in contrast to the clinical studies that were the focus of Chapters 9 and 10, whereby the primary estimated functions were $\hat{F}(t)$ and its complement $\hat{S}(t)$.

(3) Traditional actuarial studies in the life insurance or pension fund context will tend to have very large data bases, especially in the case where several insurance companies have pooled their data to achieve greater statistical reliability in the results.[2]

[1] For a review of the properties and notation of the traditional actuarial life table, see Section 3.3.

[2] These are appropriately referred to as *intercompany studies*.

As a consequence of the large data sets involved in these studies, actuaries have historically employed various ways of grouping the data to minimize calculation. That is, the exact individual data approaches used in Chapters 9 and 10 were deemed to be impractical due to excessive data sorting and classification, and rules for grouping data to reduce calculation were sometimes quite imaginative.[3]

In light of today's high speed computing capabilities, however, a return to the use of exact individual data is no longer impractical and is frequently done. The product-limit procedure described in Section 10.5 makes use of exact data. In Section 11.2 we present another approach using exact data, one that is often employed in modern actuarial studies.

Sections 11.3 – 11.5 then deal with some degree of data grouping and/or other features of study design intended to simplify the calculation of the estimate and the analysis of the associated estimators. Section 11.3 addresses a modification of the product-limit approach, and Sections 11.4 and 11.5 deal more directly with insurance company and pension fund estimation environments.

11.2 ESTIMATION OF q_x FROM EXACT DATA

Suppose a survival study is to be conducted over the five-year observation period running from January 1, M to December 31, M+4. The group whose survival is being observed constitutes a sample from which the underlying population survival model is to be estimated. Any persons leaving the defined group before 1/1/M or joining the defined group after 12/31/M+4 are not part of the study sample. Persons in the study group on 1/1/M (traditionally called *starters*) and those joining the study group during the observation period (traditionally called *new entrants*) are included in the study sample. Both starters and new entrants are treated the same in the estimation approach that follows. We let y_i denote the exact age at which person i enters the study (comes under observation), which is the age when the observation period opens or on the date person i joins the study group, whichever is later.

11.2.1 DECIMAL YEARS

A convenient way to obtain exact ages is to first express dates of events in terms of decimal years. These, in turn, are easily obtained from a day-of-the-year table, illustrated by Table 11.1 on the following page, which has been stored in the computer. We assume that sufficient accuracy can be obtained by ignoring leap years, so that any events occurring on a February 29 will be presumed to have occurred on February 28. The decimal part of a decimal year is then obtained by dividing the day of the year by 365.

EXAMPLE 11.1

Find the decimal year for October 11, 1963.

[3] For a detailed description of some of these elaborate grouping rules, see Batten [3].

SOLUTION

October 11 is day 284 of the year, so the decimal year would be

$$1963+\frac{284}{365} = 1963.78.$$

(In the examples and exercises for this chapter, decimal years will be rounded to two places.)

❐

TABLE 11.1

Days of the Year												
Date	**Jan**	**Feb**	**Mar**	**Apr**	**May**	**Jun**	**Jul**	**Aug**	**Sep**	**Oct**	**Nov**	**Dec**
1	1	32	60	91	121	152	182	213	244	274	305	335
2	2	33	61	92	122	153	183	214	245	275	306	336
3	3	34	62	93	123	154	184	215	246	276	307	337
4	4	35	63	94	124	155	185	216	247	277	308	338
5	5	36	64	95	125	156	186	217	248	278	309	339
6	6	37	65	96	126	157	187	218	249	279	310	340
7	7	38	66	97	127	158	188	219	250	280	311	341
8	8	39	67	98	128	159	189	220	251	281	312	342
9	9	40	68	99	129	160	190	221	252	282	313	343
10	10	41	69	100	130	161	191	222	253	283	314	344
11	11	42	70	101	131	162	192	223	254	284	315	345
12	12	43	71	102	132	163	193	224	255	285	316	346
13	13	44	72	103	133	164	194	225	256	286	317	347
14	14	45	73	104	134	165	195	226	257	287	318	348
15	15	46	74	105	135	166	196	227	258	288	319	349
16	16	47	75	106	136	167	197	228	259	289	320	350
17	17	48	76	107	137	168	198	229	260	290	321	351
18	18	49	77	108	138	169	199	230	261	291	322	352
19	19	50	78	109	139	170	200	231	262	292	323	353
20	20	51	79	110	140	171	201	232	263	293	324	354
21	21	52	80	111	141	172	202	233	264	294	325	355
22	22	53	81	112	142	173	203	234	265	295	326	356
23	23	54	82	113	143	174	204	235	266	296	327	357
24	24	55	83	114	144	175	205	236	267	297	328	358
25	25	56	84	115	145	176	206	237	268	298	329	359
26	26	57	85	116	146	177	207	238	269	299	330	360
27	27	58	86	117	147	178	208	239	270	300	331	361
28	28	59	87	118	148	179	209	240	271	301	332	362
29	29		88	119	149	180	210	241	272	302	333	363
30	30		89	120	150	181	211	242	273	303	334	364
31	31		90		151		212	243		304		365

11.2.2 EXACT AGES

It is easy to see that the exact age at which an event takes place is found by subtracting the decimal year of birth from the decimal year of the event.

EXAMPLE 11.2

If person i was born on October 11, 1963, and comes under observation on August 1, 2002, find y_i, the exact age that observation begins.

SOLUTION

August 1, 2002 is decimal year $2002+213/365 = 2002.58$. Then

$$y_i \;=\; 2002.58-1963.78 \;=\; 38.80. \qquad \square$$

Example 11.2 illustrates the general approach to finding the exact age at which an event occurs. For each person in the study, three ages are important: y_i, the age into the study; z_i, the scheduled age out of the study; and the actual age out of the study, due to failure or withdrawal, before age z_i, if this does, in fact, occur. We denote the exact age at failure by θ_i and the exact age at withdrawal by ϕ_i, and adopt the convention that $\theta_i = 0$ if person i is not a study failure and $\phi_i = 0$ if person i is not a study withdrawal.

Each person in a study is then assigned an *age vector* defined by $\mathbf{v}_i = [y_i, z_i, \theta_i, \phi_i]^T$, where T denotes the transpose of the vector. The age vector contains all the information needed to process person i's contribution to our estimation work.

EXAMPLE 11.3

An observation period runs from August 1, 2002 to December 31, 2007. Person i was born on October 11, 1963 and fails on April 12, 2006. Find the age vector $\mathbf{v}_i$ for this person.

SOLUTION

The age into the study is $y_i = 38.80$ from Example 11.2. December 31, 2007 is decimal year $2007+365/365 = 2008.00$, so $z_i = 2008.00-1963.78 = 44.22$ is the scheduled age out of the study. April 12, 2006 is decimal year $2006+102/365 = 2006.28$, so the age at failure is found to be $\theta_i = 2006.28-1963.78 = 42.50$. The age at withdrawal (or random censoring) is recorded as $\phi_i = 0$. Then $\mathbf{v}_i = [38.80, 44.22, 42.50, 0]^T$. $\square$

The vector $\mathbf{v}_i$ summarizes person i's contribution to the study as a whole. To estimate q_x over the interval $(x, x+1]$, we must first determine person i's contribution, if any, to that interval. We note first that if $y_i \geq x+1$, then person i enters the study beyond age $x+1$ and does not contribute to $(x, x+1]$. Similarly, if $z_i \leq x$, then person i leaves the study before age x and does not contribute to $(x, x+1]$. Even if $y_i < x+1$ and $z_i > x$, which implies that person i is *scheduled* to contribute to $(x, x+1]$, the occurrence of failure or random censoring (withdrawal) before age x would prevent this scheduled contribution from being realized. This would be evidenced either by $0 < \theta_i \le x$ or by $0 < \phi_i \le x$.

Once the age vectors for persons who do not contribute to $(x, x+1]$ have been eliminated from consideration, the next step is to convert each age vector $\mathbf{v}_i$ into a *duration vector* for the interval $(x, x+1]$, showing the fractional duration within $(x, x+1]$ at which observation begins, is scheduled to end, or actually does end due to failure or withdrawal prior to scheduled ending. We denote the duration vector by $\mathbf{u}_{i,x} = [r_i, s_i, \iota_i, \kappa_i]^T$, where, necessarily, at least one of ι_i or κ_i must be zero. The double subscript on $\mathbf{u}$ identifies both the person and the estimation interval to which it relates.

The reader should verify the following conversion relationships for person i known to contribute to $(x, x+1]$.

$$r_i = \begin{cases} 0 & \text{for } y_i \le x \\ y_i - x & \text{for } x < y_i \le x+1 \end{cases} \tag{11.1a}$$

$$s_i = \begin{cases} z_i - x & \text{for } x < z_i \le x+1 \\ 1 & \text{for } z_i > x+1 \end{cases} \tag{11.1b}$$

$$\iota_i = \begin{cases} 0 & \text{for } \theta_i = 0 \\ \theta_i - x & \text{for } x < \theta_i \le x+1 \\ 0 & \text{for } \theta_i > x+1 \end{cases} \tag{11.1c}$$

$$\kappa_i = \begin{cases} 0 & \text{for } \phi_i = 0 \\ \phi_i - x & \text{for } x < \phi_i \le x+1 \\ 0 & \text{for } \phi_i > x+1 \end{cases} \tag{11.1d}$$

EXAMPLE 11.4

Convert the age vector of Example 11.3 into duration vectors for the estimation intervals (38,39], (39,40], and (42,43].

SOLUTION

For (38,39], we have $r_i = y_i - 38 = .80$, $s_i = 1$ (since $z_i > 39$), $\iota_i = 0$ (since $\theta_i > 39$), and $\kappa_i = 0$ (since $\phi_i = 0$); then $\mathbf{u}_{i,38} = [.80, 1, 0, 0]^T$.

For $(39, 40]$, $r_i = 0$ (since $y_i < 39$), $s_i = 1$ (since $z_i > 40$), $\iota_i = 0$ (since $\theta_i > 40$), and $\kappa_i = 0$ (since $\phi_i = 0$); then $\mathbf{u}_{i,39} = [0, 1, 0, 0]^T$.

For $(42, 43]$, $r_i = 0$ (since $y_i < 42$), $s_i = 1$ (since $z_i > 43$), $\iota_i = \theta_i - 42 = .50$, and $\kappa_i = 0$ (since $\phi_i = 0$); then $\mathbf{u}_{i,42} = [0, 1, .50, 0]^T$.

(Note that $\mathbf{u}_{i,39} = \mathbf{u}_{i,40} = \mathbf{u}_{i,41}$, and $\mathbf{u}_{i,x}$ is not defined for $x < 38$ nor for $x > 42$, since person i does not contribute to any such intervals.) ❐

With person i's contribution to the estimation interval $(x, x+1]$ summarized in the duration vector $\mathbf{u}_{i,x}$, at least three different approaches to estimating q_x are available to us. One is the method of moments and another is an older traditional actuarial approach. (Both approaches are extensively described in London [26], and are not included in this text.) The third approach is described in the following section.

11.2.3 ESTIMATION OF q_x

To estimate the conditional probability q_x over the interval $(x, x+1]$ we assume that the hazard rate (often called the *force of mortality* in an actuarial context) is constant over that interval. In that case, the (constant) hazard rate is equal to the *central rate of failure*, denoted in standard actuarial notation by m_x, and they are related to the conditional probability of failure by

$$q_x = 1 - e^{-m_x} = 1 - e^{-\mu}, \tag{11.2}$$

where μ denotes the constant hazard rate over $(x, x+1]$. In turn, the central rate is defined as

$$m_x = \frac{d_x}{L_x}, \tag{11.3}$$

where d_x denotes the number of failures in $(x, x+1]$ and L_x denotes the number of *life years lived* (or *exposure*) by the survivorship group within $(x, x+1]$. (See Section 3.3 for a review of the life table functions q_x, m_x, L_x, and μ_x, and the relationships among them.)

In light of the relationships among these functions in the life table model, it is reasonable to estimate m_x by the ratio of number of sample failures in $(x, x+1]$, which we denote by k_x, to the *exact exposure of the sample*, which we denote by $(EE)_x$. That is, since $m_x = \frac{d_x}{L_x}$ in the underlying, operative survival model, it is natural to estimate m_x by

$$\hat{m}_x = \frac{k_x}{(EE)_x} \tag{11.4}$$

and to then estimate q_x by

$$\hat{q}_x = 1 - e^{-\hat{m}_x} = 1 - e^{-k_x/(EE)_x}. \tag{11.5}$$

The number of sample failures k_x is easily determined as the number of $\mathbf{v}_i$ age vectors with $x < \theta_i \leq x+1$ (or the number of $\mathbf{u}_{i,x}$ duration vectors for which $\iota_i \neq 0$), and the exact exposure over $(x, x+1]$ is determined as

$$(EE)_x = \sum_i (EE)_{i,x} = \sum_i \begin{bmatrix} s_i \\ \iota_i \\ \kappa_i \end{bmatrix} - r_i, \tag{11.6}$$

where $(EE)_{i,x}$ denotes the exact exposure over $(x, x+1]$ contributed by person i, and $\begin{bmatrix} s_i \\ \iota_i \\ \kappa_i \end{bmatrix}$ represents the minimum of s_i, ι_i, κ_i that exceed zero.

In other words, if $\iota_i = \kappa_i = 0$, so that person i neither fails nor withdraws in $(x, x+1]$, then we have $(EE)_{i,x} = s_i - r_i$. But if person i fails in $(x, x+1]$, $(x, x+1]$, so that $\iota_i < s_i$ and $\kappa_i = 0$, then $(EE)_{i,x} = \iota_i - r_i$. Finally, if person i withdraws (is randomly censored) in $(x, x+1]$, so that $\kappa_i < s_i$ and $\iota_i = 0$, then we have $(EE)_{i,x} = \kappa_i - r_i$.

EXAMPLE 11.5

Consider the age vector $\mathbf{v}_i = [39.85,\ 40.75,\ 40.25,\ 0]^T$. Find the value of $(EE)_{i,40}$.

SOLUTION

First we convert $\mathbf{v}_i$ to $\mathbf{u}_{i,40} = [0,.75,.25,0]^T$. Then $(EE)_{i,40} = \iota_i - r_i = .25$ (since $\iota_i < s_i$). ❒

11.3 MODIFIED PRODUCT-LIMIT ESTIMATION

The estimation of the conditional probability q_x by the product-limit approach, presented in Section 10.5, used the exact times (or ages) at which each study unit came under observation or left observation, either by failure or censoring. As the number of study units contributing to an estimation interval becomes very large, we might wish to reduce the level of calculation by using some degree of data grouping.

For the approach described in this section, we need only to count the *number* of migrants into (due to truncation) or out of (due to censoring) the sample during $(x, x+1]$, as well as the *number* of failures in $(x, x+1]$, but we do not need to know the precise ages at which they do so. We then make the simplifying assumptions that (1) all failures occur at one common failure point (possibly the center) within $(x, x+1]$, (2) all in migration occurs *before* the common failure point, and (3) all out migration occurs *after* the common failure point. Note that the estimation intervals are predetermined before considering the data; they are often defined by consecutive integral ages.

As before, we let n_x denote the size of the study sample at age x and k_x denote the number of failures. In addition, let d_x denote the number of in migrants and u_x denote the number of out migrants. Under the assumptions stated above, the risk set at the common failure point would be

$$r_x = n_x + d_x \tag{11.7}$$

and the estimate of q_x would be

$$\hat{q}_x = \frac{k_x}{r_x} = \frac{k_x}{n_x + d_x}. \tag{11.8}$$

Note that n_x, in turn, would be found by adding all the in migrants, and subtracting all the out migrants and failures, that occur in estimation intervals prior to $(x, x+1]$. That is,

$$n_x = \sum_{t=0}^{x-1}(d_t - u_t - k_t). \tag{11.9}$$

Since d_x is added to n_x to reach r_x, the risk set associated with k_x, it then follows that

$$r_x = \sum_{t=0}^{x} d_t - \sum_{t=0}^{x-1}(u_t + k_t). \tag{11.10}$$

EXAMPLE 11.6

Recalculate the estimate of q_x in Section 10.5 (see Figure 10.3) using the simplifying assumptions above.

SOLUTION

From Figure 10.3 we see that $n_x = 20$, $d_x = 2$, $u_x = 3$, and $k_x = 5$. Under the assumptions described above, we have $r_x = n_x + d_x = 22$ and

$$\hat{q}_x = \frac{k_x}{r_x} = \frac{5}{22} = .22727.$$ ❐

It is not surprising that the result is less than the value of .25333 obtained in Section 10.5. By presuming all in migration to precede the failures, and all out migration to follow the failures, we have biased the risk set upward and therefore biased the estimate downward. It would be more realistic to assume that a proportion, say α, of the d_x in migrants enter before the common failure point (so that $1-\alpha$ enter after) and, similarly, a proportion, say β, of the u_x out migrants leave before the common failure point (so that $1-\beta$ leave after). Then the risk set would be

$$r_x = n_x + \alpha \cdot d_x - \beta \cdot u_x \tag{11.11}$$

in this more general case, and the special case presented above follows with $\alpha = 1$ and $\beta = 0$.

11.4 INSURING AGE STUDIES

Since most people do not purchase individual insurance policies on their actual birthdays, it follows that they are various fractional attained ages when their policies are issued. The insurance company, on the other hand, will not calculate a premium rate for the policy that depends on the insured's actual fractional age at issue. Instead an integral *insuring age* is substituted for the insured's actual age as of the policy issue date. Most commonly this insuring age will be the insured's actual age on the birthday nearest the policy issue date. In other words,

$$IA = Actual\ Age\ Nearest\ Birthday, \tag{11.12}$$

where IA denotes the insuring age.

Less commonly, the insuring age could be taken as the actual age on the birthday preceding the policy issue date, in which case we say that IA is the actual age last birthday. The examples and exercises of this section all use the age nearest birthday basis.

11.4.1 VALUATION YEAR OF BIRTH

Assigning an integral insuring age to the insured as of the policy issue date implies that a hypothetical date of birth, called the *insuring date of birth*, has been substituted for the actual date of birth. Clearly the month and day of this insuring date of birth are the same as the policy issue date. The hypothetical year of birth, called the *valuation year of birth*, is then found as

$$VYB = CYI - IA, \tag{11.13}$$

where CYI is the calendar year of policy issue. It should be recognized that VYB will frequently be the same as CYB, the actual calendar year of birth, but it can also be one year earlier or one year later than CYB.

EXAMPLE 11.7

An insurance policy is issued on August 22, 2008. Find IA and VYB if the actual date of birth is (a) January 12, 1988, or (b) July 4, 1987.

SOLUTION

(a) As of August 22, 2008, the nearest birthday is the one coming up on January 12, 2009, when this person will be $IA = 21$. Then we have $VYB = 2008 - 21 = 1987$, which is one year less than the actual CYB.

(b) As of August 22, 2008, the nearest birthday is the one just passed on July 4, 2008, and again $IA = 21$. Then $VYB = 2008 - 21 = 1987$, the same as the actual CYB. ❐

11.4.2 ANNIVERSARY-TO-ANNIVERSARY STUDIES

When insuring ages are used, a natural choice for the observation period is one that opens on the policy anniversary in a designated calendar year for each insured person involved in the study. Similarly, the observation period would close on the policy anniversary in a later year. For example, an observation period might be defined as running from policy anniversaries in 2004 to those in 2008. Note that each person involved in the study has his or her own observation period.

Observation periods that run from a fixed date to a later fixed date *can* be used with insuring ages, but generally are not since there are significant advantages to the anniversary-to-anniversary observation period when insuring ages are involved. In this text we consider only anniversary-to-anniversary observation periods with insuring ages.

The major convenient consequence of an anniversary-to-anniversary observation period with insuring ages is that all persons enter the study at an integral age y_i. This is true whether the person enters the study as a new entrant (by joining the study sample via policy issue during the observation period) or as a starter (by already being in the study sample when the observation period opens). In the latter case, entry is at a policy anniversary which is always the attainment of an integral (insuring) age. Since y_i is an integer, it follows that $r_i = 0$ for any estimation interval $(x, x+1]$ since x is an integer.

Similarly, with the observation period ending on a policy anniversary, all scheduled out migration (censoring) ages z_i are integers, from which it follows that $s_i = 1$ for all estimation intervals $(x, x+1]$. Therefore all $\mathbf{u}_{i,x}$ vectors are of the convenient form $[0, 1, \iota_i, \kappa_i]^T$.

If there are no withdrawals (random censoring), then the estimate of q_x is naturally taken as

$$\hat{q}_x = \frac{k_x}{n_x}, \tag{11.14}$$

the unbiased and consistent binomial proportion estimator encountered several times earlier in this text. The value of n_x is found by counting the number of $\mathbf{u}_{i,x}$ vectors with $r_i = 0$, and the value of k_x is found by counting the $\mathbf{u}_{i,x}$ vectors with $\iota_i \neq 0$.

If there are withdrawals, the number of them in $(x, x+1]$, say w_x, is found by counting the $\mathbf{u}_{i,x}$ vectors with $\kappa_i \neq 0$. If the modified product-limit estimator of Section 11.3 is being used, where the out migrants denoted u_x in that section are here called withdrawals and denoted w_x, then a value of β would be chosen to distribute some of the withdrawals before the common failure point and the rest after it. (Note that there can be no in migrants, denoted d_x in Section 11.3, in the estimation interval $(x, x+1]$ in an anniversary-to-anniversary study using insuring ages.)

In practice, with this study design a different approach is taken with respect to the withdrawals. Rather than grouping together those that occur in $(x, x+1]$, which is a grouping by *age last birthday*, the standard practice is to group together those that occur in $(x-\frac{1}{2}, x+\frac{1}{2}]$, which is a grouping by *age nearest birthday*. This group of withdrawals would include those in any $\mathbf{u}_{i,x-1}$ vector with $\kappa_i > \frac{1}{2}$ and those in any $\mathbf{u}_{i,x}$ vector with $\kappa_i \leq \frac{1}{2}$.[4] We again denote this group of withdrawals by w_x, where here x is the age nearest insuring birthday.[5]

---

[4] Alternatively, we could count all $\mathbf{v}_i$ vectors with $x - \frac{1}{2} < \phi_i \leq x + \frac{1}{2}$.

[5] Historically, it was common practice to use the easier approach of grouping the withdrawals by *calendar insuring age x*, which was found by subtracting *VYB* from the calendar year of withdrawal, rather than by age nearest insuring birthday. Today, with all such large sample studies totally computerized, the age nearest birthday grouping is no more difficult to achieve than the calendar age grouping.

The w_x withdrawals are then assumed to all occur at age x, an averaging of their actual withdrawal ages which are spread over $(x-\frac{1}{2}, x+\frac{1}{2}]$. The usefulness of this assumption is that the out migration then occurs at the estimation interval boundary, and no migration of either type occurs *within* the estimation interval. We then simply count the risk set, n_x, moving forward into the $(x, x+1]$ estimation interval, and once again estimate q_x by the familiar and convenient binomial proportion estimator

$$\hat{q}_x = \frac{k_x}{n_x}. \tag{11.14}$$

Note that assuming withdrawals to occur only at integral ages, which are policy anniversaries, is quite reasonable, since withdrawal from an insured group often means policy surrender or expiry. These events do indeed often occur on policy anniversaries.

EXAMPLE 11.8

For the sample of ten policyholders shown in Table 11.2, estimate q_{30} by assuming (1) an observation period from anniversaries in 2003 to those in 2008, (2) insuring ages are used, and (3) withdrawals are grouped by insuring age nearest birthday.

SOLUTION

Each person is first assigned an *IA* by Equation (11.12) and a *VYB* by Equation (11.13). Then the *VYB*, Date of Policy Issue, and dates of the observation period imply an integral y_i and z_i for all persons involved in the study. The age nearest birthday grouping for withdrawals implies that an integral ϕ_i replaces the exact, fractional ϕ_i shown in Table 11.3.

TABLE 11.2

Basic Data for Example 11.8				
Person	Date of Birth	Date of Policy Issue	Date of Failure	Date of Withdrawal
1	Mar 17, 1974	Jun 20, 2002	--	--
2	May 6, 1974	Aug 6, 2002	Jun 12, 2003	--
3	Aug 12, 1974	Dec 18, 2002	--	Jul 18, 2005
4	Oct 27, 1974	Jan 4, 2003	--	--
5	Jan 4, 1975	Apr 28, 2003	Aug 29, 2006	--
6	Apr 18, 1975	Jun 16, 2003	--	Dec 12, 2005
7	May 20, 1975	Oct 29, 2003	Apr 21, 2006	--
8	Jul 4, 1975	Feb 16, 2004	--	--
9	Sep 16, 1975	Aug 22, 2004	--	Feb 22, 2007
10	Dec 11, 1975	Mar 6, 2005	Feb 17, 2007	--

Exact ages at failure, θ_i, are fractional. The data are summarized in Table 11.3.

TABLE 11.3

Expanded Data for Example 11.8						
Person	*IA*	*VYB*	y_i	z_i	θ_i	ϕ_i
1	28	1974	29	34	0	0
2	28	1974	--	--	--	--
3	28	1974	29	34	0	30.59
4	28	1975	28	33	0	0
5	28	1975	28	33	31.34	0
6	28	1975	28	33	0	30.49
7	28	1975	28	33	30.48	0
8	29	1975	29	33	0	0
9	29	1975	29	33	0	31.51
10	29	1976	29	32	30.95	0

Note that Persons 2 and 6 do not contribute to $(30, 31]$. Person 2 is not even in the study, since failure precedes the start of the observation period. Under the age nearest grouping assumption, Person 6 withdraws at age 30, rather than at age 30.49, so does not enter $(30, 31]$. The remaining $n_{30} = 8$ persons all enter $(30, 31]$ at age 30, and stay until age 31, except for the $k_{30} = 2$ failures (Persons 7 and 10). Note that Person 3, who actually does withdraw within $(30, 31]$, is considered to withdraw at age 31 under the grouping assumption. As expected, this study design produces a binomial proportion estimation situation. Using Equation (11.14) we find $\hat{q}_{30} = \frac{2}{8} = .25$. ❐

11.4.3 SELECT STUDIES

In a life insurance context, we often wish to estimate the survival distribution for persons approved for insurance at a particular age x, generally an integer. We denote this issue age by $[x]$, and refer to it as the *select age*, or *age at selection*. (For a review of the select mortality model, see Section 6.6 of Cunningham, et al. [7].) Then the variable of interest in our survival study is the *duration since selection*, denoted t. As before, we proceed by estimating the conditional probability of failure over $(t, t+1]$, given survival to duration t, and denote the estimate by $\hat{q}_{[x]+t}$.

We again normally choose an anniversary-to-anniversary observation period, so all policies in the study group when the observation period opens will come under observation at an integral duration. Any persons joining the study group during the observation period, by issue of new policies, will come under observation at duration $t = 0$. As with insuring ages, we would likely group withdrawals by duration nearest anniversary, and assume those who withdraw in $(t-½, t+½]$ do so at duration t. This creates the familiar binomial proportion estimation model yet again.

An example will show the similarity of select studies to insuring age studies.

EXAMPLE 11.9

Consider the policies of Example 11.8 with $IA = 28$. Estimate $q_{[28]+2}$ using an observation period from anniversaries in 2004 to those in 2009, grouping withdrawals by duration nearest anniversary.

SOLUTION

In Example 11.8, Policies 1 through 7 have $IA = 28$, and Policy 2 is not involved in the study due to failure before the observation period opens. The other policies have duration vectors $\mathbf{v}_i$ for the study as follows.

TABLE 11.4

Expanded Data for Example 11.9

Policy	y_i	z_i	θ_i	ϕ_i
1	2	7	0	0
3	2	7	0	2.60
4	1	6	0	0
5	1	6	3.34	0
6	1	6	0	2.49
7	1	6	2.48	0

For estimation interval (2,3], all policies enter at $t = 2$, except Policy 6 which does not contribute to (2,3] due to the duration nearest anniversary grouping of withdrawals. (Policy 6 leaves observation at duration 2 under the assumption.) All policies which enter are scheduled to complete (2,3], and all do so except Policy 7. Then we have our usual binomial proportion estimation model, and $\hat{q}_{[28]+2} = \frac{1}{5} = .20$. ❐

11.5 FISCAL AGE STUDIES

The discussion in Section 11.4 regarding insuring age studies is particularly applicable when our study sample is a group of persons insured under individual insurance policies or annuities. Now we consider the case where the study sample is a large number of individual persons covered under a single policy or plan, as with a group insurance policy or group pension plan.

There will exist a key date for such a plan, called the *plan anniversary* or *plan valuation date*. On such a date it will be necessary to calculate premium rates, actuarial present values of accrued benefits, or other financial values. For this purpose it will be convenient for all members of the plan to be an integral age on this date. This integral age is called the *fiscal age*.

Note that this situation is similar to that under insuring ages, where each individual insured was an integral insuring age on that person's policy anniversary. Here the same idea holds, with the further condition that the policy anniversary is the same date for all persons. It is traditional to refer to this date as the *T-date*.

Historically the terms T-date and fiscal age were adopted to indicate that the T-date was the *terminal* date of the fiscal year of an enterprise. In this text the major application of the fiscal age concept is to studies of mortality under group insurance or pension plans. Thus the T-date is the plan anniversary. The term fiscal age is not particularly descriptive, but we will retain it for the sake of actuarial tradition.

11.5.1 FISCAL YEAR OF BIRTH

Analogous to the definitions of insuring age and valuation year of birth in Section 11.4, we now assign each person in a group plan a fiscal age (FA) as of some particular T-date, say the T-date in calendar year Z. This fiscal age would likely be the actual age nearest birthday, or possibly actual age last birthday, on that date. Regardless of how it is assigned, we would then define a fiscal year of birth as

$$FYB = Z - FA. \tag{11.15}$$

Just as was true for VYB under insuring ages, FYB could be the same as the person's actual CYB, or it could be one year less or one year greater. Once FYB has been assigned, the T-date in the FYB is then the hypothetical date of birth for each person in the group plan.

EXAMPLE 11.10

A pension plan has its anniversary on March 31. A new employee becomes a member of the plan on March 31, 2008. This employee's actual date of birth is November 17, 1976. If the fiscal age is assigned as *actual age last birthday*, find this employee's FYB.

SOLUTION

The actual age last birthday as of March 31, 2008, is 31, which was attained on November 17, 2007. Then $FYB = 2008-31 = 1977$. Note that $FYB = CYB+1$. ❐

11.5.2 OBSERVATION PERIODS FOR FISCAL AGE STUDIES

The natural choice of an observation period is one that runs from the T-date in a certain year to the T-date in a later year. (Note that the T-date is the anniversary for all members in the group plan, so a T-to-T study is really both a date-to-date study and an anniversary-to-anniversary study.)

The principal benefit of using a T-to-T observation period is that all members of the plan when the observation period opens enter the study at an integral age y_i, and all members in the study sample will have an integral scheduled exit age z_i. Although dates other than T-dates can be used in fiscal age studies, there is no particular advantage to this and only T-to-T studies will be considered in this section.

11.5.3 NEW MEMBERS AND WITHDRAWALS

If new employees can only join the group plan under study on a T-date, then such new employees would enter the study at integral fiscal ages, just as was true under insuring ages.

However such a restriction does not usually hold, so persons joining the group during the observation period could do so at any fractional fiscal age. Similarly, persons might withdraw from the group plan by terminating employment at any date, and hence at any fractional fiscal age.

The procedures using exact actual ages described in Section 11.2 can be used with fiscal ages as well. On the other hand, grouping procedures could be used for the new members and withdrawals. If *fiscal age nearest T-date* grouping is used, then an integral fiscal age is substituted for the exact fractional fiscal ages. It is customary to use the same grouping for both new members and withdrawals.

EXAMPLE 11.11

A group life insurance plan has a June 30 anniversary date. From the following sample data, estimate q_{40} using an observation period that runs from June 30, 2000, to June 30, 2005. Group new members and withdrawals by fiscal age nearest T-date.

TABLE 11.5

Basic Data for Example 11.11				
Member	***FYB***	**Date of Plan Membership**	**Date of Failure**	**Date of Withdrawal**
1	1962	May 12, 1999	--	Sep 30, 2003
2	1962	Aug 24, 1999	--	--
3	1961	Oct 3, 1999	Mar 17, 2004	--
4	1961	Jan 30, 2000	--	Apr 30, 2000
5	1961	May 18, 2000	--	--
6	1960	Jan 3, 2001	--	--
7	1961	Jul 15, 2000	--	Feb 15, 2002
8	1961	Dec 7, 2001	Jun 22, 2002	--
9	1963	Sep 15, 2004	--	--
10	1963	Jul 1, 2005	--	--

SOLUTION

Note that Member 4 withdrew from the plan before the observation period opened, and Member 10 did not join the plan until after the observation period closed, so neither member is involved in this study. Members 6 through 9 are new members during the observation period, whereas the others all come under observation on June 30, 2000. The table on the following page gives the usual $\mathbf{v}_i$ vector information for the eight members involved in the study, both before (and after) applying the grouping rule to the new members and withdrawals.

TABLE 11.6

Expanded Data for Example 11.11				
Member	y_i	z_i	θ_i	ϕ_i
1	38	43	0	41.25 (41)
2	38	43	0	0
3	39	44	42.71	0
5	39	44	0	0
6	40.51 (41)	45	0	0
7	39.04 (39)	44	0	40.63 (41)
8	40.43 (40)	44	40.97	0
9	41.21 (41)	42	0	0

Member 9 does not contribute to $(40, 41]$, by joining the plan after age 41. Member 6 *appears* to contribute to $(40, 41]$, based on its fractional age at entry to the plan, but the grouping assumption treats it as joining the plan at age 41. Member 8 joins the plan at age 40, under the grouping assumption. Both Members 1 and 7 withdraw at age 41, under the grouping assumption, so both contribute to $(40, 41]$. Only Member 8 fails in the estimation interval $(40, 41]$. Therefore the risk set is $n_{40} = 6$, and the estimate of q_{40} is $\hat{q}_{40} = \frac{1}{6} = .16\dot{6}$. ❐

11.6 WITHDRAWAL OR DOUBLE-DECREMENT STUDIES[6]

In the studies considered thus far in this chapter, our goal has been to estimate the rate of failure, which is also the probability of failure in an environment where only failure can occur. In decrement theory this rate (or probability) is referred to as a *single-decrement rate* (or *single-decrement probability*), and is denoted by $q_x'^{(j)}$, where the superscript identifies the decrement. When the decrement under discussion is clearly known, such as the decrement of failure, then the prime and the superscript (j) are generally deleted. Thus far in this text, where it has been clear that we were discussing the single-decrement rate of failure, we have used the simpler symbol q_x.

In the complete data estimation environment of Chapter 9, failure was the only decrement available to members of the study sample. Under incomplete data, however, we considered that both failure and withdrawal (also called random censoring) were available. When we estimate the single-decrement rate for decrement (1) from sample data containing both decrements, we neutralize the effect of decrement (2) by treating it as a censored observation.

Suppose we wished to estimate the single-decrement rate for decrement (2) from this same (incomplete) data where both decrements were present. We would simply reverse the roles of decrements (1) and (2), now treating decrement (2) as our decrement of interest, and therefore as uncensored observations, and treating decrement (1) as censored observations. No other adjustments need be made in our estimators.

---

[6] For a brief review of double-decrement theory, see Section 3.4. For a more detailed review, see Chapter 13 of Cunningham, et al. [7].

Finally, we might wish to use sample data containing both decrements to estimate the *double-decrement probability* for each decrement. In decrement theory these probabilities are denoted $q_x^{(1)}$ and $q_x^{(2)}$, for decrements (1) and (2), respectively. (There is no prime on the double-decrement probability symbol.)

The following example illustrates these ideas.

EXAMPLE 11.12

Consider the age estimation interval $(x, x+1]$, where $n_x = 10$ persons come under observation at age x. (Any persons joining the study group have been grouped by age nearest birthday at entry, and therefore do so at an integral age.) We observe a decrement (1) at age $x+.10$ and another at age $x+.70$, and we observe a decrement (2) at age $x+.60$. We wish to estimate $q_x'^{(1)}$, $q_x'^{(2)}$, $q_x^{(1)}$, and $q_x^{(2)}$, using age nearest grouping for the censoring decrement.

Solution

The data are illustrated on the following diagram.

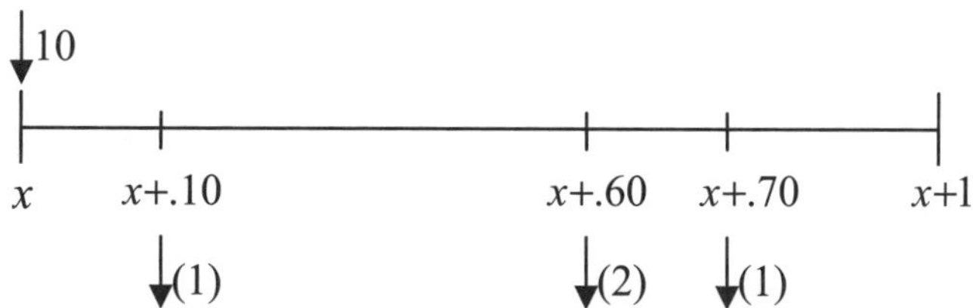

Time Line for Example 11.12

FIGURE 11.1

To estimate $q_x'^{(1)}$, we place the decrement (2) actually occurring at age $x+.60$ at the nearest integral age, which is $x+1$. Then we have $\hat{q}_x'^{(1)} = \frac{2}{10} = .20$.

To estimate $q_x'^{(2)}$, we place the decrements (1) actually occurring at ages $x+.10$ and $x+.70$ at the nearest integral ages, which are x and $x+1$, respectively. Then the risk set for the estimation interval becomes $n_x = 9$, and we have $\hat{q}_x'^{(2)} = \frac{1}{9} = .11111$.

For the double-decrement probabilities, the concept of neutralizing the effect of the opposite decrement (by treating it as a censored observation) does not apply. The risk set of $n_x = 10$ applies to both decrements, so we directly have $\hat{q}_x^{(1)} = \frac{2}{10} = .20$ and $\hat{q}_x^{(2)} = \frac{1}{10} = .10$. ❐

As an alternative to grouping the opposite decrements and placing them at estimation interval boundaries, we could use the product-limit approach of Chapter 10 or the exact data approach of Section 11.2. These alternative approaches are pursued in the exercises.

11.7 SUMMARY

In this chapter we have considered large sample studies, primarily in the actuarial setting of life insurance companies or pension funds, from which we seek to estimate the conditional probability q_x over the estimation interval $(x, x+1]$. This orientation stands in contrast with the content of Chapters 9 and 10, where we sought an estimate of the overall survival function $S(x)$.

By taking advantage of modern computing capabilities, we showed in Section 11.2 how to organize the data processing steps to allow the use of exact ages throughout the estimation process. To summarize, for the estimation interval $(x, x+1]$ we can identify the duration point within the interval (often at 0) at which each study unit comes under observation, and the duration at which each study unit leaves observation, whether as a failure (uncensored observation), scheduled censored observation, or random censored observation. Subtracting the "duration in" from the "duration out" gives the exact amount of exposure (to the risk of failure) contributed by that unit, and summing over all units gives the exposure of the entire sample. Dividing the sample exposure into the number of observed failures gives the sample central rate, which we take as an estimate of the underlying population central rate. Finally the estimate of the underlying failure probability is found from the central rate estimate by the relationship

$$\hat{q}_x = 1-e^{-\hat{m}_x},$$

which assumes a constant force of failure over the $(x, x+1]$ interval.

The modified product-limit estimation approach of Section 11.3 has been suggested by other texts[7], and is reminiscent of older actuarial approaches. As we have shown, it is negatively biased. In light of our ability to make more precise calculations in the modern computer world, there would seem to be little to recommend this approach.

Grouping approaches, rather than exact data approaches, are still widely used in the insurance and pension fields, however. When the age nearest grouping technique is used with insuring ages, insuring durations, or fiscal ages, as described in Sections 11.4 and 11.5, the convenient binomial proportion estimator is obtained. The binomial sample size in the denominator of this estimator is also referred to as "exposure" in traditional actuarial estimation, although of a different nature from the exact exposure described in Section 11.2.

Finally we considered, in Section 11.6, how our estimation procedures could easily be altered to estimate single-decrement withdrawal (random censoring) probabilities or double-decrement probabilities. A good understanding of multiple decrement theory is essential background knowledge for this topic.

---

[7] See, for example, Chapter 14 of Klugman, et al. [21].

11.8 EXERCISES

11.1 Introduction

11.2 Estimation of q_x from Exact Data

Authors' Note: The content of Section 11.2 can be summarized in the following six steps: (1) Express the date of each event in decimal years; (2) Find the exact age vector $\mathbf{v}_i$ for each person i contributing to a study; (3) Convert person i's age vector into duration vectors $\mathbf{u}_{i,x}$ for each interval $(x, x+1]$ to which person i contributes; (4) Calculate $(EE)_{i,x}$, and therefore $(EE)_x$, from Equation (11.6); (5) Count k_x, the number of observed failures in $(x, x+1]$; (6) Calculate $\hat{q}_x$ from Equation (11.5).

The five examples presented in that section illustrate most of these steps, and little educational benefit would result from additional exercises that essentially duplicated the examples. Instead, we present here an opportunity for the reader to deal with this topic in a macro, rather than micro, sense. Logically the exercises presented here would be performed with the aid of a computer.

On pages 298 and 299 the basic data are given for a sample of 70 persons, showing Date of Birth, Date of Entry, Date of Withdrawal (random censoring), and Date of Failure. For Exercises 11-1 through 11-4, consider the data to refer to members of a fraternal organization, where the Date of Entry is the date of membership in the organization. Values of q_x are to be estimated from this sample data using an observation period of January 1, 2000 to December 31, 2009.

11-1 Determine the exact age vector $\mathbf{v}_i$ for each member of the sample, indicating any members who are not involved in the study. Round decimal years to two decimal places.

11-2 Find the values of k_x, the number of observed failures in $(x, x+1]$, for all values of x for which $k_x \neq 0$.

11-3 Use the age vectors from Exercise 11-1 to find $(EE)_x$ for all values of x for which exposure exists.

11-4 Use Equation (11.5) to estimate q_x for all x for which $k_x \neq 0$.

11.3 Modified Product-Limit Estimation

11-5 Let $\alpha = \beta = .50$ in Equation (11.11). Show that

$$r_x = .50(n_x + n_{x+1} + k_x).$$

Person Number	Date of Birth	Date of Entry	Date of Withdrawal	Date of Failure
1	Apr 12, 1970	Jan 16, 1998	--	--
2	Jul 2, 1966	Mar 29, 1998	--	Jan 4, 2000
3	Jun 11, 1968	Aug 1, 1998	Dec 1, 2000	--
4	Feb 28, 1964	Aug 20, 1998	Aug 27, 1999	--
5	Nov 28, 1971	Jan 11, 1999	--	Dec 25, 2001
6	Jun 6, 1961	Jan 6, 1999	May 3, 1999	--
7	Mar 15, 1967	Dec 9, 1998	--	--
8	Aug 24, 1968	May 3, 1999	Mar 4, 2000	--
9	Jun 25, 1970	Jan 31, 2000	Dec 31, 2000	--
10	Feb 23, 1969	Sep 22, 1999	--	May 10, 2008
11	Dec 15, 1967	Oct 8, 1999	May 16, 2001	--
12	Jul 6, 1968	Feb 18, 2000	Aug 10, 2009	--
13	Jun 10, 1970	Apr 5, 2000	--	--
14	Feb 19, 1969	Jun 2, 2000	--	Apr 14, 2006
15	Oct 15, 1970	Nov 24, 2000	May 10, 2008	--
16	Apr 14, 1971	Feb 10, 2001	--	--
17	Aug 10, 1968	Dec 20, 2000	--	Oct 10, 2007
18	Oct 8, 1971	Jul 7, 2001	Apr 6, 2006	--
19	Oct 26, 1969	May 26, 2001	--	--
20	Feb 5, 1970	Dec 16, 2001	Aug 25, 2004	--
21	Dec 14, 1971	Dec 12, 2001	--	Mar 6, 2007
22	Dec 10, 1970	May 2, 2002	--	--
23	Jul 31, 1972	Apr 22, 2002	--	--
24	Jan 24, 1971	Sep 9, 2002	Sep 9, 2003	--
25	Jul 18, 1973	Jan 28, 2003	Nov 16, 2009	--
26	Oct 2, 1972	Oct 14, 2002	--	Nov 14, 2004
27	Sep 5, 1970	Aug 24, 2002	Jun 4, 2007	--
28	Mar 21, 1971	Nov 12, 2002	--	Dec 2, 2007
29	Apr 10, 1973	Mar 4, 2003	--	--
30	May 25, 1972	Dec 30, 2002	Jun 21, 2005	--
31	Aug 6, 1972	May 26, 2003	--	--
32	Nov 20, 1973	Jun 13, 2003	--	--
33	Dec 10, 1971	Apr 6, 2003	--	Feb 15, 2008
34	Aug 4, 1973	Sep 2, 2003	Aug 19, 2004	--
35	Sep 10, 1973	Feb 28, 2004	--	--

Person Number	Date of Birth	Date of Entry	Date of Withdrawal	Date of Failure
36	Jun 30, 1972	Nov 1, 2003	Mar 10, 2008	--
37	Feb 28, 1973	Jul 15, 2004	--	Jul 16, 2007
38	Jan 31, 1974	Aug 8, 2004	--	--
39	Sep 5, 1972	Nov 2, 2004	Aug 6, 2006	--
40	Nov 2, 1973	Jan 21, 2005	--	--
41	Jul 15, 1975	Mar 16, 2005	--	--
42	Apr 20, 1974	May 4, 2005	--	Jan 20, 2006
43	Jul 27, 1975	Sep 17, 2005	Jul 6, 2008	--
44	Dec 3, 1975	Apr 10, 2006	--	--
45	Jan 4, 1974	Dec 23, 2005	--	--
46	Nov 6, 1974	Mar 10, 2006	Jun 21, 2006	--
47	May 19, 1976	Jul 12, 2006	Jul 12, 2007	--
48	Aug 16, 1976	Jul 6, 2006	Jul 6, 2009	--
49	Jan 4, 1975	Aug 19, 2006	--	--
50	Mar 10, 1976	Jun 25, 2006	--	Sep 24, 2008
51	Sep 24, 1976	Feb 7, 2007	Dec 21, 2008	--
52	Nov 15, 1976	Apr 14, 2007	--	--
53	Sep 6, 1974	Dec 8, 2006	--	Jun 4, 2008
54	Sep 14, 1977	May 21, 2007	Sep 21, 2007	--
55	Nov 21, 1975	Aug 27, 2007	--	--
56	Aug 19, 1977	Sep 16, 2007	--	--
57	Jan 6, 1977	Aug 9, 2007	--	--
58	Apr 6, 1977	Nov 30, 2007	--	Aug 19, 2008
59	Aug 4, 1975	Oct 23, 2007	Nov 23, 2007	--
60	Feb 3, 1976	Dec 4, 2007	--	--
61	Apr 27, 1978	Jan 4, 2008	Jun 4, 2008	--
62	Feb 26, 1977	May 10, 2008	--	--
63	Aug 13, 1978	Jul 25, 2008	--	Sep 5, 2009
64	Jul 6, 1976	Sep 16, 2008	Nov 19, 2009	--
65	May 21, 1979	Feb 3, 2009	--	--
66	Sep 15, 1976	Dec 12, 2008	Dec 12, 2009	--
67	Nov 8, 1977	Apr 27, 2009	--	--
68	Jul 21, 1979	Aug 5, 2009	Jan 10, 2010	--
69	Feb 16, 1978	Oct 18, 2009	--	--
70	Nov 13, 1976	Jan 14, 2010	--	--

11-6 Rework Example 11.6 using $\alpha = \beta = .50$.

11-7 Although the method of Section 11.3 was presented in the context of survival model estimation, it can be applied to severity model estimation as well. Recall that left truncations (in migrants) result from policy deductibles, and right censorings (out migrants) result from policy limits, in the severity model context. A sample of $n = 19$ policies produced the following data:

Amount Interval $(x, x+1]$	**Number of Left Truncation Amounts** d_x	**Number of Right Censored Amounts** u_x	**Number of Uncensored Amounts** k_x
(250, 500]	6	0	1
(500, 1000]	6	0	2
(1000, 2750]	7	1	4
(2750, 5500]	0	1	7
(5500, 6000]	0	1	1

Make the simplifying assumption that, within each interval, all in migrant amounts are less than the uncensored amounts and all out migrant amounts are greater than the uncensored amounts. (Recall that this is denoted as $\alpha = 1$ and $\beta = 0$ in Section 11.3.) Use the data to estimate the probability that a policy with a deductible of 500 will incur a claim payment in excess of 5500.

11.4 Insuring Age Studies

For Exercises 11-8 through 11-10, consider the data to refer to a sample of individual life insurance policyholders, and the Date of Entry is the date of policy issue. Insuring age is defined as actual age nearest birthday at issue. The observation period will be policy anniversaries in 2000 to those in 2009. Group withdrawals by age nearest insuring birthday.

11-8 Find the insuring age vector $\mathbf{v}_i$ for each policyholder, indicating those not involved in the study. Use the age nearest insuring birthday, rather than exact insuring age, for ϕ_i.

11-9 Recall that this study design produces the binomial proportion estimator $\hat{q}_x = \frac{k_x}{n_x}$. Calculate k_x and n_x for all x for which $n_x \neq 0$.

11-10 For each of issue ages 30, 31 and 32 separately, a select study is to be performed. Use the observation period of anniversaries in 2000 to those in 2009 and group withdrawals by duration nearest anniversary, so the binomial proportion estimation model again results. Calculate $k_{[x]+t}$ and $n_{[x]+t}$, for $x = 30, 31, 32$, for all t for which $n_{[x]+t} \neq 0$.

11.5 Fiscal Age Studies

For Exercises 11-11 through 11-13, consider the data to refer to the members of a group insurance plan with policy anniversary on June 30. The Date of Entry is the date of employment, at which time insurance coverage begins. A fiscal age is assigned as the actual age nearest birthday as of the June 30 *following* Date of Entry. (E.g., for Date of Entry November 18, 2005, the following June 30 is June 30, 2006. If the member's actual birthday is April 4, 1974, then the fiscal age is the actual age nearest birthday on June 30, 2006, which is 32. Then $FYB = 2006 - 32 = 1974$.) Values of q_x are to be estimated over an observation period of June 30, 2002 to June 30, 2010.

11-11 Find the set of exact fiscal age vectors $\mathbf{v}_i$ for all persons who are involved in this study.

11-12 From the exact fiscal age vectors of Exercise 11-11, calculate the exact exposure, the values of k_x, and the values of $\hat{q}_x$ for all x for which $k_x \neq 0$.

11-13 Group new members and withdrawals by age nearest fiscal birthday, and estimate q_x for all x for which $k_x \neq 0$.

11.6 Withdrawal or Double-Decrement Studies

11-14 Consider the model of Section 11.2, which uses exact data in the presence of two decrements. The exact exposure over the interval $(x, x+1]$, which we have denoted by $(EE)_x$, is the same regardless of the decrement whose rate is being estimated. Repeat Exercise 11-4, but this time to estimate $q_x'^{(w)}$ rather than $q_x'^{(f)}$ as was done in Exercise 11-4.

11-15 Consider the insuring age study of Exercises 11-8 and 11-9. Retain the exact insuring age at withdrawal for each withdrawal, rather than grouping them at integral insuring ages as in Exercises 11-8 and 11-9. Calculate the number of observed withdrawals, $k_x^{(w)}$, in each age interval $(x, x+1]$, and the risk set, n_x, at each value of x.

11-16 The number of observed failures, $k_x^{(f)}$, was determined in Exercise 11-9. Use the results of Exercises 11-9 and 11-15 to calculate estimated values of the double-decrement probabilities $q_x^{(f)}$ and $q_x^{(w)}$.

CHAPTER TWELVE

REVISION OF TABULAR MODELS

12.1 INTRODUCTION

The final version of a tabular actuarial model estimated from sample data, whether a frequency, severity, or survival model, must possess some degree of smooth regularity in order to be appropriate for actual use. The initial estimate of a model, directly from the sample data, may or may not meet this requirement. If it does not, a process of *revision* of the initial estimate is undertaken. In traditional actuarial terminology, the process of revising the initial estimate of a model is called *graduation*. A thorough treatment of graduation can be found in London [25].

It should be noted that if we estimate a *continuous parametric* model directly from the sample data, then generally no further revision is required, since our model will possess the intrinsic smoothness of the fitted parametric form. (Parametric estimation of models is pursued in Part IV of this text.) Therefore the revision methods described in this chapter are understood to apply to discrete tabular models only.

In Section 12.2 we consider the special case of revising an empirical (or observed) model of the type described in Section 9.2, where we revise a discrete empirical severity model into a continuous one by a process known as *kernel density estimation*. This would normally be used only for severity models; although the process could be applied to survival model estimation as well, this is generally not done in practice.

Methods for revising an initial estimated tabular survival model are then presented in Sections 12.3 and 12.4. Those of Section 12.3, called *graduation by splines*, are designed to revise the initial tabular model into a continuous one, if that is desired. *Whittaker graduation*, presented in Section 12.4, revises the initial tabular survival model into a new tabular model, but one with a greater degree of smooth regularity than was contained in the initial estimated model.

An additional method, called *Bayesian graduation*, also addresses tabular models. Our presentation of it is deferred to Section 15.6, following the development of Bayesian techniques earlier in Chapter 15.

12.2 KERNEL DENSITY ESTIMATION

As stated in the previous section, *kernel density estimation* is a technique for replacing a discrete empirical distribution with a piecewise continuous one, denoted by $\hat{f}(x)$. The density function of the selected continuous replacement distribution is called the *kernel*, and is denoted by $k_t(x)$. Several different continuous replacement distributions are considered in the remainder of this section. The general relationship is

$$\hat{f}(x) = \sum_t p_n^o(t) \cdot k_t(x), \tag{12.1a}$$

where $p_n^o(t)$ is the empirical estimate at $x=t$, as defined earlier. The logic of Equation (12.1a) will become clearer as we proceed.

12.2.1 THE UNIFORM KERNEL DENSITY ESTIMATOR

In the *uniform kernel density* estimation process, each discrete mass of probability in the empirical distribution is replaced by a continuous uniform distribution with mean equal to the observed value it replaces. The following overly-simplified example will illustrate the procedure.

Suppose a sample of ten observed loss amounts contains the value 5 three times, the value 7 five times, and the value 10 two times. Then the discrete empirical estimate of the (presumed continuous) underlying loss distribution is $p_{10}^o(5)=.30$, $p_{10}^o(7)=.50$, and $p_{10}^o(10)=.20$. This is illustrated in Figure 12.1a on the following page.

Recall that the mean of a uniform distribution is the midpoint of its domain. In order that the mean of the first replacement kernel equals the observation value of 5, the domain of that uniform random variable must be centered at $t=5$. The length of the domain will be $2b$, where the parameter b is called the *bandwidth* of the kernel. Then it follows that the kernel density function, which we denote by $k_5(x)$, will be $k_5(x)=\frac{1}{2b}$, for $5-b \le x \le 5+b$, and $k_5(x)=0$ elsewhere. Similar remarks hold for the other two replacement kernels (those centered at $t=7$ and $t=10$), which we denote by $k_7(x)$ and $k_{10}(x)$, respectively. (The notational principle is to subscript the kernel density function for the observation value that it replaces.)

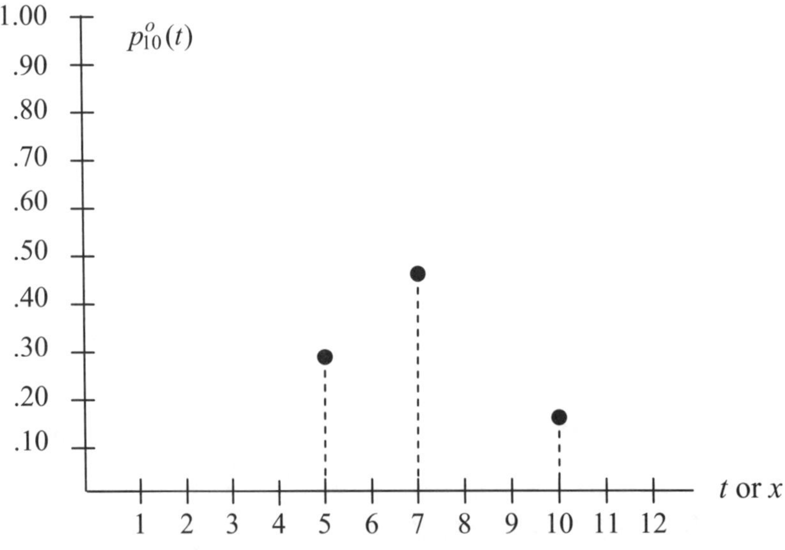

Discrete Empirical Estimated Loss Distribution

FIGURE 12.1a

The kernel density is represented by a rectangle of length of $2b$, centered at $t = 5$. The total probability in the kernel (i.e., in the rectangle) must be .30, to match the probability at $x = 5$ in the empirical distribution. Therefore the height of the rectangle must be $\frac{.30}{2b}$, since its area, which represents its total probability, must be .30. Similarly, the rectangular densities centered at $x = 7$ and $x = 10$, also of length $2b$, must have heights of $\frac{.50}{2b}$ and $\frac{.20}{2b}$, respectively.

To illustrate, suppose we select the bandwidth $b = 1$, so the kernel density is $k_t(x) = \frac{1}{2b} = \frac{1}{2}$, for $t = 5,7,10$. Each rectangular density is then $p_n^o(t) \cdot k_t(x)$, again for $t = 5,7,10$, giving us

$$p_{10}^o(5) \cdot k_5(x) = .15,$$

$$p_{10}^o(7) \cdot k_7(x) = .25,$$

and

$$p_{10}^o(10) \cdot k_{10}(x) = .10.$$

The three rectangular densities define the kernel density estimator that replaces the three discrete empirical values shown in Figure 12.1a. The PDF of the replacement distribution is piecewise constant. It is given by

$$\hat{f}(x) = \begin{cases} .15 & \text{for } 4 \le x < 6 \\ .25 & \text{for } 6 \le x \le 8 \\ .10 & \text{for } 9 \le x \le 11 \end{cases}, \tag{12.2}$$

as illustrated in Figure 12.1b.

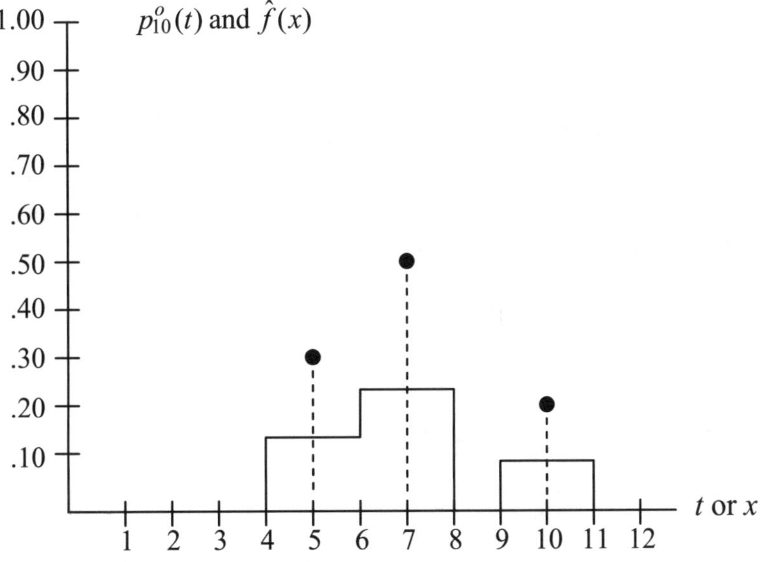

Uniform Kernel Density Estimator, with $b = 1$

FIGURE 12.1b

Several important observations can be made regarding these results.

(1) The density function $\hat{f}(x)$ integrates to

$$\int_4^6 .15\,dx + \int_6^8 .25\,dx + \int_9^{11} .10\,dx \;=\; 1,$$

as required.

(2) The result includes the values $\hat{f}(x)=0$ for $x<4$, $8<x<9$, and $x>11$. Although it might be reasonable to accept $\hat{f}(x)=0$ for $x<4$ and $x>11$, the result $\hat{f}(x)=0$ for $8<x<9$ would not seem to be appropriate.

(3) Because of the step-function nature of $\hat{f}(x)$, an arbitrary rule must be adopted to determine if $\hat{f}(6)=.15$ or $\hat{f}(6)=.25$. We have chosen to let $\hat{f}(6)=.25$ in Equation (12.2), but the other choice would have been just as reasonable.

Note that a bandwidth of $b=1$ (or less) produces no overlap of the several kernel densities. On the other hand, suppose we use $b=2$, so that $k_t(x)=\frac{1}{2b}=\frac{1}{4}$. Then we *appear to have*

$$\hat{f}(x) \;=\; \begin{cases} \frac{.30}{2b}=.075 & \text{for } 3\le x\le 7 \\ \frac{.50}{2b}=.125 & \text{for } 5\le x\le 9 \\ \frac{.20}{2b}=.050 & \text{for } 8\le x\le 12 \end{cases}. \tag{12.3a}$$

Again we find that $\hat{f}(x)$, as given by Equation (12.3a), integrates to

$$\int_3^7 .075\,dx + \int_5^9 .125\,dx + \int_8^{12} .050\,dx \;=\; 1,$$

as required. But, because of the overlap, Equation (12.3a) does not correctly state the density function of the uniform kernel density estimator. Rather we have

$$\hat{f}(x) \;=\; \begin{cases} .075 & \text{for } 3\le x<5 \\ .075+.125=.200 & \text{for } 5\le x<7 \\ .125 & \text{for } 7\le x<8 \\ .125+.050=.175 & \text{for } 8\le x<9 \\ .050 & \text{for } 9\le x\le 12 \end{cases}. \tag{12.3b}$$

Again we see that the correct $\hat{f}(x)$, given by Equation (12.3b), integrates to one (see Exercise 12-1). It is illustrated in Figure 12.2.

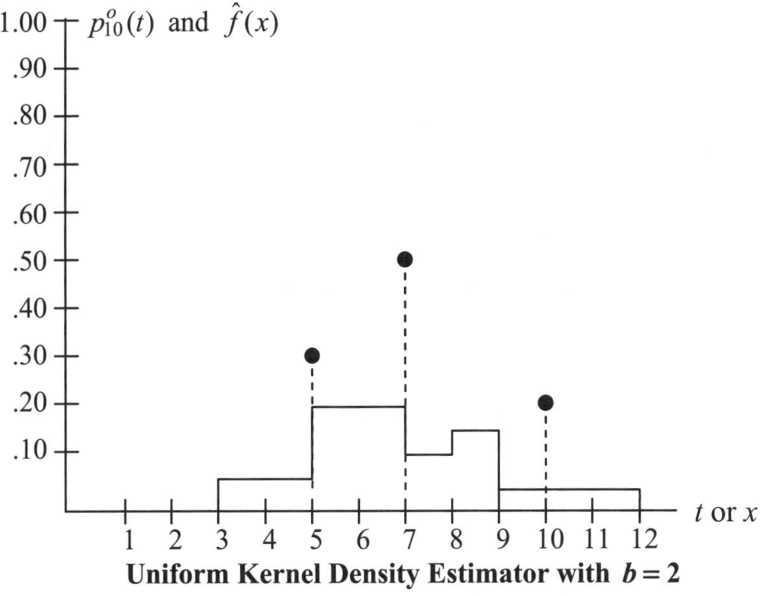

Uniform Kernel Density Estimator with $b = 2$

FIGURE 12.2

With $b=2$ we have no "holes" in $\hat{f}(x)$, as we did for $8<x<9$ with $b=1$ where $\hat{f}(x)=0$. In general, a larger bandwidth will produce greater smoothness and a smaller bandwidth will produce lesser smoothness.

Note that we must still adopt a rule to assign the value of $\hat{f}(x)$ at values of x where the step function has a jump or a drop. Arbitrarily, we have chosen to use the value to the right, as shown in Equation (12.3b).

EXAMPLE 12.1

The uniform kernel density estimator, with bandwidth $b=50$, is used to replace the empirical distribution of workers compensation loss payments based on the sample $\{82, 126, 161, 294, 384\}$. Determine both the empirical and the kernel density estimates of $F(150)$.

SOLUTION

Two loss amounts are less than 150, so the empirical estimate of $F(150)$ is $F_5^o(150)=.40$. Each loss amount appears only once, so the empirical probabilities are $p_5^o(t)=.20$, for $t=82,126,161,294,384$. With $b=50$, the kernel density is $k_t(x)=\frac{1}{2b}=.01$, so each piece of $\hat{f}(t)$ is

$$p_5^o(t)\cdot k_t(x) \ = \ (.20)(.01) \ = \ .002.$$

These values are illustrated in Figure 12.3 on the following page.

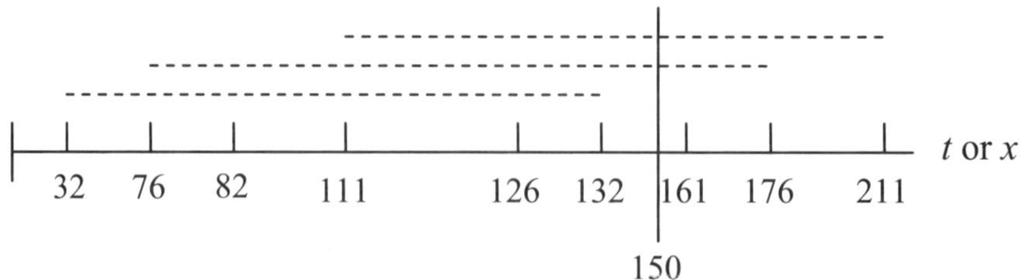

Uniform Kernel Density Estimator, with $b = 50$

FIGURE 12.3

The .20 probability centered at t = 82, spread from x = 32 to x = 132, is all contained in $\hat{F}(150)$. Of the .20 probability centered at t = 126, spread from x = 76 to x = 176, we find $\frac{150-76}{100} = .74$ of it contained in $\hat{F}(150)$. Of the .20 probability centered at t = 161, spread from x = 111 to x = 211, we find $\frac{150-111}{100} = .39$ of it contained in $\hat{F}(150)$. The probability centered at t = 294 and at t = 384 does not spread as far left as $x = 150$, so none of it is contained in $\hat{F}(150)$ and is not shown in Figure 12.3. Then we have

$$\hat{F}(150) \;=\; .20 + (.20)(.74) + (.20)(.39) \;=\; .426. \qquad \square$$

Further practice with this estimator is provided by Exercises 12-2, 12-3, and 12-12.

12.2.2 THE TRIANGULAR KERNEL DENSITY ESTIMATOR

The process described in Section 12.2.1 replaces the empirical probability mass at $x = t$ by a rectangular density, with length $2b$ and height $\frac{p_n^o(t)}{2b}$, containing probability of amount $p_n^o(t)$. Alternatively, we could let the replacement density be a *triangular kernel density* with base $2b$ centered at $x = t$. (Again the parameter b is called the bandwidth.) As before, the area of the triangle must be $p_n^o(t)$, so its height must be $\frac{p_n^o(t)}{b}$. (Recall that the area of a triangle is one-half the base times the height.)

The triangular kernel density is not constant, as it was in the uniform case. Rather it increases linearly from zero at $x = t-b$ to $\frac{p_n^o(t)}{b}$ at $x = t$, and then decreases linearly back to zero at $x = t+b$. The kernel density itself, again denoted $k_t(x)$, would increase linearly from zero at $x = t-b$ to $\frac{1}{b}$ at $x = t$, and then decrease linearly back to zero at $x = t+b$. The equation of a continuous function with these properties is

$$k_t(x) \;=\; \begin{cases} \dfrac{x-t+b}{b^2} & \text{for } t-b \le x \le t \\[2ex] \dfrac{t+b-x}{b^2} & \text{for } t \le x \le t+b \end{cases}, \tag{12.4}$$

and $k_t(x)=0$ elsewhere. (See Exercise 12-4.) The replacement triangle, which we call the *triangular kernel density estimator*, is given by $\hat{f}(x)=\sum_t p_n^o(t)\cdot k_t(x)$, already given as Equation (12.1a).

We illustrate the triangular process with the same three-point empirical distribution used in Section 12.2.1. Again we use a bandwidth of $b = 1$, so there is no overlap of the triangles. Further, with $b = 1$ the height of each triangle is $p_{10}^o(t)$, for $t = 5, 7, 10$. Then the triangular kernel density estimator is

$$\hat{f}(x) = \begin{cases} .30(x-4) & \text{for } 4 \le x < 5 \\ .30(6-x) & \text{for } 5 \le x < 6 \\ .50(x-6) & \text{for } 6 \le x < 7 \\ .50(8-x) & \text{for } 7 \le x \le 8 \\ .20(x-9) & \text{for } 9 \le x < 10 \\ .20(11-x) & \text{for } 10 \le x \le 11 \end{cases}, \tag{12.5}$$

which is illustrated in Figure 12.4.

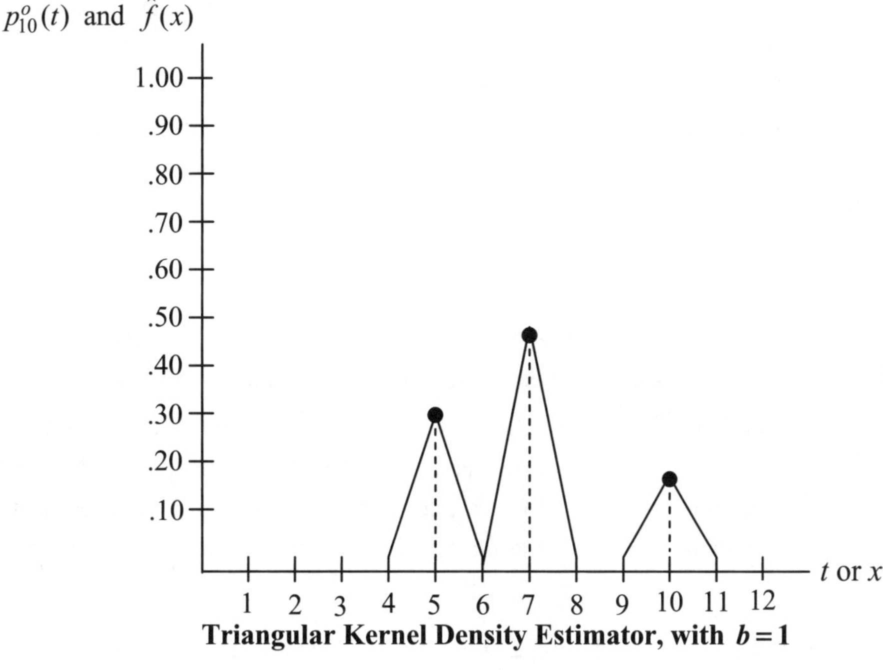

Triangular Kernel Density Estimator, with $b=1$

FIGURE 12.4

With a bandwidth of $b = 2$, the triangles overlap (just as the rectangles did in Section 12.2.1), so greater smoothness can be attained and the determination of $\hat{f}(x)$ is more involved. This is left as Exercise 12-5.

EXAMPLE 12.2

A sample of five lives was observed from the onset of a disease until death. The observed times of death were $\{2, 3, 3, 3, 7\}$. Use a triangular kernel density estimator with bandwidth $b=2$ to estimate $f(2.5)$.

SOLUTION

The observed values are $p_5^o(2)=.20$ and $p_5^o(3)=.60$. (The observed value at $t=7$ does not contribute to $\hat{f}(2.5)$ with bandwidth $b=2$.) The triangular kernel centered at $t=2$ has $k_2(2.5)=\frac{2+2-2.5}{4}=.375$, from the "down-slope" line of Equation (12.4); the one centered at $t=3$ has $k_3(2.5)=\frac{2.5-3+2}{4}=.375$, from the "up-slope" line of Equation (12.4). Then the estimate of $f(2.5)$ is

$$\begin{aligned}\hat{f}(2.5) &= p_5^o(2)\cdot k_2(2.5)+p_5^o(3)\cdot k_3(2.5)\\ &= (.20)(.375)+(.60)(.375) = .30.\end{aligned}$$

❒

Note that the value $k_2(2.5)=.375$ can be obtained in an intuitive manner. With $b=2$ the triangle at $t=2$ has base 4 and height .50. Then $k_2(2)=.50$ and $k_2(4)=0$, so we can find $k_2(2.5)=.375$ by linear interpolation. The value of $k_3(2.5)$ can also be obtained in this intuitive manner.

12.2.3 OTHER KERNEL DENSITY ESTIMATORS

The essential feature of the uniform and triangular kernel density estimators of the past two sections is that the probability mass at $x=t$ is spread over the interval from $x=t-b$ to $x=t+b$. Then if t_1 is the smallest observed value and t_n is the largest observed value, we will have $\hat{f}(x)=0$ for all $x<t_1-b$ and all $x>t_n+b$. If we believe that the domain of the true underlying $f(x)$ should be all positive values of x, as we are assuming if we let the distribution of X be exponential, gamma, or Pareto, for example, then the estimate of $f(x)$ produced by the uniform or triangular kernel density estimator might be viewed as unsatisfactory.

As an alternative approach, we could spread the probability mass at $x = t$ over all positive values by selecting a kernel density with that domain. As stated earlier, we want the mean of the kernel to match the empirical point it replaces. Suppose we let the kernel have an exponential density of the form $f(x)=\frac{1}{\theta}\cdot e^{-x/\theta}$ (see Section 1.3.3). The mean of this distribution is θ, so we use $\theta = t$ for the exponential density that replaces the probability mass at $x = t$. Then the kernel density is

$$k_t(x) = \frac{1}{t}\cdot e^{-x/t}. \tag{12.6}$$

Of course the total probability in this kernel is one, so we must multiply it by $p_n^o(t)$ so that we are spreading the probability mass $p_n^o(t)$ over the interval $(0, \infty)$.

This is repeated for all values of t, so each value of t contributes to the estimate of the total density at each value of x. (Contrast this with the uniform and triangular estimators where a particular value of t contributes only to values of x in the interval $(t-b, t+b)$.) Then the total estimated density at x is

$$\hat{f}(x) = \sum_t p_n^o(t) \cdot k_t(x) = \sum_t \frac{p_n^o(t) \cdot e^{-x/t}}{t}, \tag{12.1b}$$

a specific application of Equation (12.1a). We recognize the final form of $\hat{f}(x)$ as a mixture of exponential densities. Since the mean of each kernel is the value of t whose probability mass it replaces, it follows that the mean of the overall estimated distribution is the same as the mean of the initial empirical distribution it replaces.

EXAMPLE 12.3

Determine the value of $\hat{f}(6)$ for the exponential kernel density estimator used to replace the three-point empirical distribution of Section 12.2.1.

SOLUTION

We have

$$\begin{aligned}\hat{f}(6) &= \frac{p_{10}^o(5) \cdot e^{-6/5}}{5} + \frac{p_{10}^o(7) \cdot e^{-6/7}}{7} + \frac{p_{10}^o(10) \cdot e^{-6/10}}{10} \\ &= \frac{(.30)(.30119)}{5} + \frac{(.50)(.42437)}{7} + \frac{(.20)(.54881)}{10} \\ &= .01807 + .03031 + .01098 = .05936.\end{aligned}$$

❐

For the Pareto kernel density estimator, where we have two parameters (see Section 6.1.2), the shape parameter α controls the overall shape of the final estimated distribution. Recall that the mean of each kernel is to equal the observation point whose probability mass it replaces. Since the observation point is t, and the Pareto mean is $E[X] = \frac{\theta}{\alpha-1}$, provided $\alpha > 1$, then we require $\frac{\theta}{\alpha-1} = t$, so $\theta = t(\alpha-1)$.

EXAMPLE 12.4

Repeat Example 12.3, this time using a Pareto kernel density estimator with α=2.

SOLUTION

The Pareto kernel density, with $a = 2$ and $\theta = t(\alpha-1) = t$, is

$$k_t(x) = \frac{2t^2}{(x+t)^3}.$$

Then the Pareto kernel density estimator of $f(6)$ is

$$\begin{aligned}
\hat{f}(6) &= p_{10}^o(5) \cdot k_5(6) + p_{10}^o(7) \cdot k_7(6) + p_{10}^o(10) \cdot k_{10}(6) \\
&= (.30)\left(\frac{(2)(25)}{(11)^3}\right) + (.50)\left(\frac{(2)(49)}{(13)^3}\right) + (.20)\left(\frac{(2)(100)}{(16)^3}\right) \\
&= (.30)(.03757) + (.50)(.04461) + (.20)(.04883) \\
&= .04334.
\end{aligned}$$

❒

In the case of the gamma kernel density estimator, again using the scale parameter form given in Appendix A.1.2, we retain the parameter α and let the parameter θ be $\frac{t}{\alpha}$ so that the mean of the kernel will be $\alpha\theta = \alpha\left(\frac{t}{\alpha}\right) = t$, as required. Practice with the gamma kernel density estimator is provided by Exercises 12-10 and 12-11.

12.2.4 SUMMARY OF THE KERNEL DENSITY ESTIMATOR

With the overall goal of revising an empirical distribution being the attainment of greater smoothness in the estimated distribution, it is easy to see that both the uniform and triangular options are not ideal. If adjacent observations (i.e., adjacent values of t) are further apart than $2b$, then the revised estimated distribution will have "holes" in it where $\hat{f}(x) = 0$ for no apparent reason. In revising an empirical (therefore discrete) severity distribution into a continuous one, a kernel density of the type described in Section 12.2.3 is recommended.

It should be noted, however, that the uniform and triangular versions still produce a final estimated density of the form $\hat{f}(x) = \sum_t p_n^o(t) \cdot k_t(x)$, as given by Equation (12.1a), just as in the case of the Section 12.2.3 versions. If the bandwidth parameter b is small enough so there is no overlap of rectangular or triangular densities, then only one term in the sum will contribute to $\hat{f}(x)$, since $k_t(x) = 0$ for all x outside of $(t-b, t+b)$.

Finally, the development in this section focused on the estimated density function $\hat{f}(x)$. From this we can develop expressions for the kernel density estimator of $F(x)$ or $S(x)$, which is pursued in Exercise 12-12. The general relationship is

$$\hat{F}(x) = \sum_t p_n^o(t) \cdot K_t(x), \tag{12.1c}$$

where $K_t(x)$ is the CDF of the kernel function. (The reader should verify that the answer to Example 12.1, which was reached by using the CDFs intuitively, can also be obtained by using Equation (12.1c).

12.3 PIECE-WISE PARAMETRIC REVISION

As stated in Chapter 11, the estimation of a tabular survival model produces, from sample data, a sequence of estimates of conditional failure probabilities over successive age intervals $(x, x+1]$. We denote the initial sequence of estimates by $\{\hat{q}_x\}$. Before we use $\{\hat{q}_x\}$ to construct a tabular survival model, by the steps described in Section 3.3.4, we need to feel confident that $\{\hat{q}_x\}$ constitutes an acceptable representation of the underlying operative survival model that gave rise to the sequence of estimates. As a minimum, we would expect the sequence to exhibit a pattern of smooth regularity when considered as a function of x.[1]

Consequently, this process of revision of the initial estimates $\{\hat{q}_x\}$, which actuaries call *graduation*, has long been viewed as primarily one of improving the degree of smoothness in the sequence, while simultaneously retaining some degree of fit to the initial estimates.

It has already been mentioned that fitting the sequence of initial estimates to a parametric function, as we explore in Part IV of the text, will automatically achieve a degree of smooth regularity. In many cases, however, especially if the range of the data is fairly broad, fitting a *single* functional form over the entire initial sequence will not achieve a satisfactory revision. As an alternative we might fit parametric functions over subranges of the data, with special attention paid to the manner in which adjacent fitted functions meet each other. The general name for this approach is graduation by *splines*.[2]

12.3.1 BASIC PROPERTIES OF GRADUATION BY SPLINES

A fundamental characteristic of graduation by splines is that the sub-range fitted functions can be of simpler mathematical form than might be the case for a function fitted over the entire range. In this section we use only third degree polynomials for the subrange fitted functions, and therefore refer to the process as graduation by cubic splines.[3] We will fit our cubic spline to the sequence of initial estimates by the familiar least-squares approach, of which we presume the reader to be aware.[4]

It is important to understand that the term spline refers to the *overall* function fitted to the data, and the spline is comprised of two or more successive cubic curves, called *arcs*, which will join each other smoothly. To simplify notation, we use u_x to denote the initial estimate $\hat{q}_x$, and v_x to denote the revised estimate. Viewed as a function of x, v_x also denotes the entire sequence of revised estimates; that is, v_x denotes the revising spline. We denote the ith cubic arc of v_x by $p_i(x)$.

---

[1] This requirement of "smooth regularity" is based on practical, as well as theoretical, reasoning. The final model will be used to determine premiums, reserves, and other financial values in an insurance or pension operation. Using a survival model lacking this property of smooth regularity would result in illogical financial values, and would, according to Miller [31], "tend to arouse an entirely justifiable skepticism."

[2] For a review of spline theory in general, and its application to graduation, see DeBoor [8], Greville [11], and McCutcheon [29]and [30].

[3] Note that a quadratic spline is used in Exercise 12-18. Although the mathematics is simpler in that case, cubic splines are more flexible and generally produce better results than do quadratics. Higher degree polynomials are harder to manage, without necessarily producing better results than do cubics.

[4] The technique of fitting by least-squares is covered in any statistics textbook.

The value of x at which adjacent cubic arcs meet is called a *knot*. If the spline is comprised of two arcs, there will be one knot at $x=k$. If the spline contains three arcs, there will be two knots, one at $x=k_1$ and the other at $x=k_2$. In general, a spline with n cubic arcs will require $n-1$ knots. Note that a knot need not be a value of x for which a value of u_x exists and/or a value of v_x is desired.

Graduation by splines does not require that $v_x=u_x$ at any particular value of x. By freeing the spline from the initial estimates, the desired improved smoothness is obtained. In fact, values of u_x need not be available at all values of x for which v_x is desired. When this is the case, the spline then functions as an *interpolant* as well as a revision of initial u_x values.

12.3.2 THE TWO-ARC CUBIC SPLINE

In the case of only two arcs, the revised estimates are given by

$$v_x = \begin{cases} p_1(x) & \text{for } a \le x \le k \\ p_2(x) & \text{for } k \le x \le b \end{cases}, \tag{12.7}$$

where a and b are the lowest and highest values of x, respectively, for which u_x values exist. Then the sum of squares is given by

$$SS = \sum_a^h w_x[u_x - p_1(x)]^2 + \sum_{h+1}^b w_x[u_x - p_2(x)]^2, \tag{12.8}$$

where h is the greatest value of x less than (or equal to) k at which a value of u_x exists, and w_x is a suitably chosen weight.

To obtain the desired smooth junction of $p_1(x)$ and $p_2(x)$, we require that they meet with equal ordinates and equal first and second derivatives. That is,

$$p_1(k) = p_2(k), \tag{12.9a}$$

$$p_1'(k) = p_2'(k), \tag{12.9b}$$

and

$$p_1''(k) = p_2''(k). \tag{12.9c}$$

Since $p_1(x)$ and $p_2(x)$ are cubics, they are internally twice differentiable; the conditions imposed by Equations (12.9a), (12.9b), and (12.9c) assure that the entire spline is twice differentiable.

We let

$$p_1(x) = c_1 + c_2x + c_3x^2 + c_4x^3 \tag{12.10a}$$

and

$$p_2(x) = c_1 + c_2x + c_3x^2 + c_4x^3 + c_5(x-k)^3. \tag{12.10b}$$

Substituting Equations (12.10a) and (12.10b) into Equation (12.8) produces

$$SS = \sum_{a}^{h} w_x[u_x - c_1 - c_2x - c_3x^2 - c_4x^3]^2 + \sum_{h+1}^{b} w_x[u_x - c_1 - c_2x - c_3x^2 - c_4x^3 - c_5(x-k)^3]^2. \tag{12.11}$$

EXAMPLE 12.5

Show that Equations (12.10a) and (12.10b) satisfy the conditions stated by Equations (12.9a), (12.9b), and (12.9c).

SOLUTION

At $x = k$, the fifth term in $p_2(x)$ disappears, and the remaining $p_2(k)$ clearly equals $p_1(k)$. The fifth term in $p_2'(x)$ is $3c_5(x-k)^2$, which again disappears at $x = k$; clearly the remaining $p_2'(k)$ equals $p_1'(k)$. Similarly, the fifth term in $p_2''(k)$ is $6c_5(x-k)$, which again disappears at $x = k$, and the remaining $p_2''(k)$ clearly equals $p_1''(k)$. ❐

Now we seek the values of c_j, for $j = 1, 2, 3, 4, 5$, that minimize SS as given by Equation (12.11). By differentiating SS with respect to each of c_1, c_2, c_3, c_4, c_5, and equating each derivative to zero, we obtain the set of normal equations

$$c_1\sum_{a}^{b} w_x + c_2\sum_{a}^{b} xw_x + c_3\sum_{a}^{b} x^2w_x + c_4\sum_{a}^{b} x^3w_x + c_5\sum_{h+1}^{b} (x-k)^3 w_x = \sum_{a}^{b} w_xu_x, \tag{12.12a}$$

$$c_1\sum_{a}^{b} xw_x + c_2\sum_{a}^{b} x^2w_x + c_3\sum_{a}^{b} x^3w_x + c_4\sum_{a}^{b} x^4w_x + c_5\sum_{h+1}^{b} x(x-k)^3 w_x = \sum_{a}^{b} xw_xu_x, \tag{12.12b}$$

$$c_1\sum_{a}^{b} x^2w_x + c_2\sum_{a}^{b} x^3w_x + c_3\sum_{a}^{b} x^4w_x + c_4\sum_{a}^{b} x^5w_x + c_5\sum_{h+1}^{b} x^2(x-k)^3 w_x = \sum_{a}^{b} x^2w_xu_x, \tag{12.12c}$$

$$c_1\sum_a^b x^3 w_x + c_2\sum_a^b x^4 w_x + c_3\sum_a^b x^5 w_x$$
$$+ c_4\sum_a^b x^6 w_x + c_5\sum_{h+1}^b x^3(x-k)^3 w_x = \sum_a^b x^3 w_x u_x, \tag{12.12d}$$

and

$$c_1\sum_{h+1}^b (x-k)^3 w_x + c_2\sum_{h+1}^b x(x-k)^3 w_x + c_3\sum_{h+1}^b x^2(x-k)^3 w_x$$
$$+ c_4\sum_{h+1}^b x^3(x-k)^3 w_x + c_5\sum_{h+1}^b (x-k)^6 w_x = \sum_{h+1}^b (x-k)^3 w_x u_x. \tag{12.12e}$$

(The details are left to the reader as Exercise 12-13.)

It is convenient to represent the set of normal equations in matrix-vector notation. We define the matrix **x** to be

$$\mathbf{x} = \begin{vmatrix} 1 & a & a^2 & a^3 & 0 \\ \vdots & \vdots & \vdots & \vdots & \vdots \\ 1 & h & h^2 & h^3 & 0 \\ 1 & h+1 & (h+1)^2 & (h+1)^3 & (h+1-k)^3 \\ \vdots & \vdots & \vdots & \vdots & \vdots \\ 1 & b & b^2 & b^3 & (b-k)^3 \end{vmatrix} \tag{12.13}$$

and define the diagonal matrix **w** to be

$$\mathbf{w} = \begin{vmatrix} w_a & 0 & \cdots & 0 & 0 \\ 0 & w_{a+1} & \cdots & 0 & 0 \\ \vdots & \vdots & \ddots & \vdots & \vdots \\ 0 & 0 & \cdots & w_{b-1} & 0 \\ 0 & 0 & \cdots & 0 & w_b \end{vmatrix}. \tag{12.14}$$

Then the set of normal equations given by Equations (12.12a) through (12.12e) is represented by the matrix equation

$$\mathbf{x}^T\mathbf{wxc} = \mathbf{x}^T\mathbf{wu}, \tag{12.15}$$

where $\mathbf{x}^T$ denotes the transpose of the matrix **x**, and **c** and **u** are column vectors with elements c_1 to c_5 and u_a to u_b, respectively. (See Exercise 12-14.)

12.3.3 THE THREE-ARC CUBIC SPLINE

In the three-arc case, the total $[a,b]$ range of the data is divided into three subranges by two internal knots located at $x=k_1$ and $x=k_2$. Then the spline is defined as

$$v_x = \begin{cases} p_1(x) & \text{for} \quad a \le x \le k_1 \\ p_2(x) & \text{for} \quad k_1 \le x \le k_2 \\ p_3(x) & \text{for} \quad k_2 \le x \le b \end{cases}. \tag{12.16}$$

In addition to the conditions given by Equations (12.9a), (12.9b), and (12.9c), with k replaced by k_1, we also require

$$p_2(k_2) = p_3(k_2), \tag{12.17a}$$

$$p_2'(k_2) = p_3'(k_2), \tag{12.17b}$$

and

$$p_2''(k_2) = p_3''(k_2). \tag{12.17c}$$

In the three-arc case, $p_1(x)$ remains as defined by Equation (12.10a) and $p_2(x)$ remains as defined by Equation (12.10b), except that k is replaced by k_1. We define $p_3(x)$ to be

$$p_3(x) = c_1 + c_2 x + c_3 x^2 + c_4 x^3 + c_5 (x-k_1)^3 + c_6 (x-k_2)^3. \tag{12.18}$$

(The verification that $p_2(x)$ and $p_3(x)$ satisfy Conditions (12.17a), (12.17b), and (12.17c) is left as Exercise 12-15.) Then the sum of squares is given by

$$\begin{aligned} SS = & \sum_{a}^{h_1} w_x [u_x - c_1 - c_2 x - c_3 x^2 - c_4 x^3]^2 \\ & + \sum_{h_1+1}^{h_2} w_x [u_x - c_1 - c_2 x - c_3 x^2 - c_4 x^3 - c_5 (x-k_1)^3]^2 \\ & + \sum_{h_2+1}^{b} w_x [u_x - c_1 - c_2 x - c_3 x^2 - c_4 x^3 - c_5 (x-k_1)^3 - c_6 (x-k_2)^3]^2, \end{aligned} \tag{12.19}$$

where h_1 is the greatest value of x less than (or equal to) k_1 at which a value of u_x exists, and h_2 is similarly defined with respect to k_2. This time there will be six normal equations, which can again be expressed in matrix-vector notation as $\mathbf{x}^T \mathbf{wxc} = \mathbf{x}^T \mathbf{wu}$, with the matrix $\mathbf{x}$ suitably defined. (See Exercise 12-16). Note that the column dimension of $\mathbf{x}$ equals the number of the c_j's, and the row dimension equals the number of data values in the $[a, b]$ range.

12.3.4 THE GENERAL CASE

In the general case, the spline is comprised of n cubic arcs, denoted $p_1(x),\ p_2(x), \ldots, p_n(x)$, with $n-1$ internal knots located at $x = k_1, k_2, \ldots, k_{n-1}$. Each adjacent pair of arcs is required to meet with equal ordinates and equal first and second derivatives. The form of each $p_i(x)$, for $i = 1, 2, \ldots, n$, the form of the SS expression, and the form of the matrix $\mathbf{x}$ in the general case should be clear by extension.

12.3.5 THE KNOTS

There are no fixed rules for determining the number and location of the knots. Scrutinizing a graph of u_x for major changes of shape can give some guidance in this matter. In general, as the number of knots increases, the revised sequence v_x approaches the original sequence u_x, which is the no-graduation case.

Judicious relocation of the knots can sometimes be more effective in reducing the magnitude of SS than would be obtained by adding another knot. It might also be possible to consider SS as a function of the knot values, as well as the parameters of v_x, and make the selection of the knots part of the minimization process. Of course it would be necessary to specify that the knots lie in the interval $[a,b]$.

12.3.6 SUMMARY OF GRADUATION BY SPLINES

A characteristic of graduation by splines is that revised values are available at *all* x, even if only desired at, say, integral values of x. Therefore we can obtain values of v_x at ages intermediate to those for which u_x values originally existed. In turn, this means that we could start with values of u_x at, say, quinquennial ages, and obtain values of v_x at all integral ages. In this context, graduation by splines is really an exercise in *interpolation*.

Note that *all* values of u_x in the entire $[a, b]$ range are considered when determining the values of v_x. An alternative approach would be to consider only a small number (usually an even number such as four or six) of u_x values, and interpolate for v_x values in the central interval defined by the four or six values. In this approach, we usually combine original observed data to produce initial u_x values at quinquennial ages, and then interpolate in the central interval for revised values of v_x at each integral age.

As with splines, the adjacent interpolating arcs would be required to meet with equal ordinates and (at least) equal first derivatives. This type of *smooth-junction interpolation* is discussed in many standard textbooks on numerical analysis; its application to graduation in particular is presented in Chapter 7 of London [25].

12.4 WHITTAKER GRADUATION

The Whittaker graduation method was developed by E.T. Whittaker[5] in 1923, and has been frequently used by actuaries to revise discrete tabular survival models over the ensuing years. It is based on the traditional view of graduation as a process to improve the smoothness of a sequence of discrete values while simultaneously adhering to some degree of fit to the initial set of estimates. It approaches this dual goal by defining a composite measure of fit and smoothness,

[5] See Whittaker [40]. Following Whittaker's initial work, Henderson [13] and [14] made a significant contribution by showing how Whittaker's theory could be put into practice. Consequently, actuaries have often referred to the method as Whittaker-Henderson graduation.

denoted M, allowing for emphasis to be directed toward one or the other of these two competing attributes.

12.4.1 THE BASIC GRADUATION FORMULA

The Whittaker composite measure of fit and smoothness is defined as

$$M = F + hS = \sum_{x=1}^{n} w_x (v_x - u_x)^2 + h \sum_{x=1}^{n-z} (\Delta^z v_x)^2, \tag{12.20}$$

where, as in Section 12.3, we use u_x and v_x to denote the initial estimate and revised estimate, respectively. The sequence $\{v_x\}$ that minimizes the composite measure M is then taken as the set of revised estimates. Several observations on Equation (12.20) are in order:

(1) Although x is frequently age, so that the range in Equation (12.20) might be, say, 30 to 75, we prefer to use 1 to n for convenience.

(2) The parameter z establishes a standard of smoothness, by constraining the revised estimates toward a polynomial of degree $z-1$.[6] In applying the Whittaker method, z is generally taken as 3 or 4.

(3) Note that there are z fewer terms in S than in F.

(4) $\{w_x\}$ is a sequence of suitably chosen weights.[7] In the context of revising a tabular survival model, greater weight would be applied to the ages where the initial estimates were based on greater amounts of data.

(5) The parameter h is a positive real number that controls the relative emphasis given to F and S. It should be clear that $h = 0$ produces the no-graduation result of $v_x = u_x$ for all x, so smaller values of h emphasize fit and larger values emphasize smoothness.

12.4.2 THE MINIMIZATION OF M

The sequence of v_x values which minimizes M can be obtained by solving the n equations resulting from equating the partial derivative of M, with respect to each v_x, to zero. Although this standard calculus technique will locate the unique global minimum of M, we prefer to approach our minimization problem using a matrix-vector formulation of M. As in Section 12.3, we use bold letters to denote vectors and matrices, and primes to denote transposes.

Let $\mathbf{u}$ denote the n-element column vector of the u_x initial estimates, $\mathbf{v}$ denote the n-element column vector of the v_x revised estimates, and $\mathbf{w}$ denote the $n \times n$ diagonal matrix of weights. Let $\mathbf{k_z}$ be a special matrix containing the binomial coefficients of order z, with due regard for sign, such that the matrix product $\mathbf{k_z v}$ is the vector containing the values of

---

[6] Readers unfamiliar with the forward finite difference operator Δ can review its properties in Appendix D.

[7] Historically the minimization of M was facilitated by using $w_x = 1$ for all x, and this was referred to as Whittaker Type A graduation. The general case was referred to as Whittaker Type B graduation. Today we need make no such distinction.

$\Delta^z v_x$. If there are n values of v_x, so $\mathbf{v}$ is an $n\times 1$ vector, then $\mathbf{k_z}$ will be dimension $(n-z)\times n$ and $\mathbf{k_z v}$ will be an $(n-z)\times 1$ vector. (See Exercises 12-19 and 12-20.)

With **u**, **v**, **w**, and $\mathbf{k_z}$ defined, we see that the function *M*, given by Equation (12.20), can be written as

$$\begin{aligned} M &= (\mathbf{v}-\mathbf{u})^T \mathbf{w}(\mathbf{v}-\mathbf{u}) + h(\mathbf{k_z v})^T \mathbf{k_z v} \\ &= (\mathbf{v}-\mathbf{u})^T \mathbf{w}(\mathbf{v}-\mathbf{u}) + h\mathbf{v}^T (\mathbf{k_z}^T \mathbf{k_z})\mathbf{v}, \end{aligned} \tag{12.21}$$

since $\mathbf{y}^T\mathbf{y}$ will produce the sum of the squares of the elements in a column vector **y**. (See Exercise 12-21.)

Then it can be shown[8] that the vector **v** of v_x values that minimizes *M*, as given by Equation (12.21), is the vector that solves the matrix-vector equation

$$(\mathbf{w}+h\mathbf{k_z}^T\mathbf{k_z})\mathbf{v} = \mathbf{wu}, \tag{12.22}$$

which we write as $\mathbf{cv} = \mathbf{wu}$ for convenience, where $\mathbf{c} = \mathbf{w}+h\mathbf{k_z}^T\mathbf{k_z}$. It is not difficult to solve Equation (12.22) with the use of modern computer software. Exercises 12-22 through 12-25 provide a review of this process in simplified settings.

12.4.3 VARIATIONS ON THE STANDARD WHITTAKER FORM

A number of variations on the standard Whittaker form have been presented over the years. Here we will identify four such variations, without developing the mathematics of them. The interested reader can pursue a further study of them in Section 4.6 of London [25] or in the original papers.

Spoerl [39] proposed the use of a linear combination of two (or more) smoothness measures, so the composite measure *M* would be of the form

$$\begin{aligned} M &= \sum_{x=1}^{n} w_x(v_x-u_x)^2 + h_1\sum_{x=1}^{n-1}(\Delta v_x)^2 \\ &\qquad + h_2\sum_{x=1}^{n-2}(\Delta^2 v_x)^2 + \cdots + h_z\sum_{x=1}^{n-z}(\Delta^z v_x)^2. \end{aligned} \tag{12.23}$$

Equation (12.23) might be used, for example, with $h_2 > 0$, $h_3 > 0$, and all other $h_j = 0$. The steps to minimize *M* are analogous to those of the standard form.

Camp [6] proposed a smoothness measure that would constrain the revised estimates toward the mathematical form of a low degree polynomial plus an exponential function. At the time of

---

[8] See Appendix E.

Camp's writing, the Makeham distribution[9] was popular as a model for human mortality. If the graduation was of a sequence of initial estimates of hazard rates, Camp's smoothness measure in the Whittaker form would constrain the revised estimates toward the Makeham form.

Lowrie [27] expanded on the Camp proposal of a "polynomial plus exponential" form for the smoothness measure S by suggesting a two-term fit measure as well. In addition to the traditional Whittaker term that fits the revised estimates to the initial estimates, Lowrie proposed that a second fit measure be included that fit the revised estimates to values from a standard table. Parameter values could be assigned to give relative emphasis to one or the other of the two fit measures.

Schuette [38] proposed replacing the squared fit and smoothness measures in the standard Whittaker form with absolute values. This form allows the revised estimates to be less influenced by statistical outliers, making the estimation procedure more robust. The mathematics of minimizing M when absolute values are used is more complicated. Schuette approaches the minimization of M by making use of the theory of linear programming.

12.5 SUMMARY

The discussion of graduation of tabular models in this chapter has been intentionally brief, considering only the kernel density method for revising a discrete empirical distribution into a continuous one, the piece-wise continuous method of cubic splines (or more general smooth-junction interpolation), and the traditional Whittaker method for tabular-to-tabular revision. Other methods are described in the text by London [25], and the extensive bibliography included in that text provides ample opportunity for further study.

12.6 EXERCISES

12.1 Introduction
12.2 Kernel Density Estimation

12-1 Show that the uniform kernel density estimator given by Equation (12.3b) integrates to one.

12-2 Using a uniform kernel with bandwidth $b=10$, determine the kernel density estimate of the probability of survival to age 40, given the following sample of observed times of failure:

$$\{25, 30, 35, 35, 37, 39, 45, 47, 49, 55\}$$

[9] For a review of the Makeham distribution, see Section 3.2.4 or the original paper by Makeham [28].

12-3 Using a uniform kernel with bandwidth $b=1.4$, determine the kernel density estimate of $F(4)$, given the following sample of observed data:

$$\{2.0, 3.3, 3.3, 4.0, 4.0, 4.7, 4.7, 4.7\}$$

12-4 Derive the kernel density $k_t(x)$ given by Equation (12.4).

12-5 Repeat the determination of the triangular kernel density estimator given by Equation (12.5), this time using a bandwidth of $b=2$.

12-6 Verify that the triangular kernel density estimator of Exercise 12-5 integrates to one.

12-7 Consider the following sample of observed failure times:

$$\{1, 2, 3, 3, 3, 3, 3, 3, 3, 3\}$$

The observed distribution is to be revised using each of the uniform kernel and triangular kernel methods, with bandwidth $b=1$ in both cases.

(a) Find the values of $\hat{F}_U(x)$, for $x=1,2,3,4$.

(b) Find the values of $\hat{F}_T(x)$, for $x=1,2,3,4$.

(c) Show that $\hat{F}_U(x)=\hat{F}_T(x)$ for all x in the interval $1 \leq x \leq 2$.

12-8 Determine the exponential kernel density estimate of $F(150)$ based on the sample of workers compensation loss payments in Example 12.1.

12-9 Determine the Pareto kernel density estimate of $f(2.50)$ based on the sample of five lives given in Example 12.2, using shape parameter $\alpha=2.50$.

12-10 Show that the gamma kernel density, using the scale parameter form with $\alpha=3$, is

$$k_t(x) = \frac{\left(\frac{3x}{t}\right)^3 \cdot e^{-3x/t}}{2x}.$$

12-11 Determine the gamma kernel density estimate of $f(2.50)$ based on the sample of five lives given in Example 12.2, using shape parameter $\alpha=3$.

12-12 (a) Derive the CDF of the scale parameter form of the exponential kernel density estimator.

(b) Derive the SDF of the Pareto kernel density estimator.

12.3 Piece-Wise Parametric Revision

12-13 Verify the normal equations given by Equations (12.12a) through (12.12e) by differentiating *SS*, as given by Equation (12.11), with respect to each of c_1, c_2, c_3, c_4, and c_5, respectively.

12-14 Show that the matrix equation given by Equation (12.15) represents the set of normal equations given by Equations (12.12a) through (12.12e).

12-15 Show that $p_2(x)$, given by Equation (12.10b) with k replaced by k_1, and $p_3(x)$, given by Equation (12.18), satisfy Conditions (12.17a), (12.17b), and (12.17c).

12-16 (a) Define the matrix **x** for the three-arc case.

(b) Show that the six normal equations that result from differentiation the *SS* given by Equation (12.19) can again be represented as $\mathbf{x}^T\mathbf{wxc} = \mathbf{x}^T\mathbf{wu}$.

12-17 A two-arc cubic spline is being fit to initial estimates u_x, for $x = 1, 2, \cdots, 10$. The first arc is

$$p_1(x) = 100 + 50x + 10x^2 + 5x^3,$$

for $x = 1, 2, \cdots, 5$. The second arc meets the first arc with equal ordinates and equal first and second derivatives. Given the value $p_2(10) = 9100$, find the value of $p_2(9)$.

12-18 A two-arc *quadratic* spline is fit to initial estimates u_x, for $x = 1, 2, \cdots, 20$, with the knot at $x = 10$. Given $p_2(15) = 3 \cdot p_1(5)$, $p_1(x) = 100 + c_2x + x^2$, and $p_2(20) = 800$, find the value of $p_2(15)$.

12.4 Whittaker Graduation

12-19 If $z = 2$ and $n = 6$, write the matrix $\mathbf{k}_2$.

12-20 If $z = 3$ and $n = 7$, write the matrix $\mathbf{k}_3$.

12-21 Show that the function *M*, given by Equation (12.20), can be written as the matrix equation given by Equation (12.21).

12-22 In a Whittaker graduation, the matrix-vector equation to be solved for the vector **v** of revised estimates is $\mathbf{cv} = \mathbf{wu}$, where

$$\mathbf{c} = \begin{vmatrix} 8 & -12 & 12 & -4 & 0 \\ -12 & 43 & -48 & 24 & -4 \\ 12 & -48 & 73 & -48 & 12 \\ -4 & 24 & -48 & 45 & -12 \\ 0 & -4 & 12 & -12 & 6 \end{vmatrix}$$

and

$$[\mathbf{w}(\mathbf{u}-\mathbf{v})]^T = [-4, 6, 0, -15, 2].$$

Determine the value of the fit measure

$$F = \sum_{x=1}^{5} w_x (v_x - u_x)^2.$$

12-23 A Whittaker graduation uses the parameters $z=3, h=3, n=5,$ and $w_x = 4$ for all x. When written as a linear combination of v_x values,

$$u_4 = a_1 v_1 + a_2 v_2 + a_3 v_3 + a_4 v_4 + a_5 v_5.$$

Find the value of a_4.

12-24 A Whittaker graduation uses the parameters $z=1, h=2,$ and $n=3$. The initial estimates are $u_1 = 0, u_2 = 1,$ and $u_3 = 3$. The weights are $w_1 = 1, w_2 = 2,$ and $w_3 = 3$. Find the value of v_1.

12-25 A Whittaker graduation uses the Spoerl two-term smoothness measure, with

$$M = \sum_{x=1}^{4} w_x (v_x - u_x)^2 + 2 \cdot \sum_{x=1}^{2} \left(\Delta^2 v_x\right)^2 + 2 \cdot \sum_{x=1}^{3} \left(\Delta v_x\right)^2.$$

Given the values $w_1 = 4, u_1 = 3, v_1 = 6,$ and $v_2 = 8$, find the value of v_3.

PART IV

ESTIMATION OF PARAMETRIC MODELS

As indicated in the introduction to Part III, the primary organization of the estimation topics covered in this text is with regard to two fundamental types of models, namely *tabular* and *parametric*. The former are the focus of Part III, and the latter are the focus of Part IV.

A tabular model is based on observations (i.e., sample data) obtained from real-world phenomena that can be quantified. In the development of a tabular model, the sample data become the foundation for the entire model itself. The model is typically expressed in tabular form (hence the name).

By way of contrast, in applying a parametric model the first step in the process is the selection of the model to be used. The model typically is a probability distribution of some type. Various approaches will be discussed in Part IV for selecting and testing appropriate models.

The second step in the process is the calibration of the model. In this step the sample data obtained are utilized to estimate the parameters in the probability distribution being considered to be the model. There are several different techniques for estimating parameters that will be presented in Part IV.

The third step in the process is to assess how well the model is expected to perform. This is normally accomplished through one or more statistical tests of fit. The purpose of these tests of fit is to assess how accurately the model chosen represents the information contained in the sample data. Based on these tests of fit and other considerations, the modeler decides whether or not the model should be adopted.

The fourth and final step is to monitor how well the model performs over time. As additional data are obtained, trends are observed. Perhaps the original model continues to perform satisfactorily. Perhaps the basic model chosen continues to be appropriate, but the parameters need to be updated (e.g. due to inflation). Or perhaps the underlying process being sampled has changed to such an extent that a new model is needed.

The above four steps are not done independently in isolation, but rather form an iterative modeling process. Effective modeling is not a destination, but rather a journey of continuous improvement.

Parametric models can be either discrete or continuous. Loss frequency models are usually discrete, while loss severity models are usually continuous. Also, models that are partly discrete and partly continuous may be appropriate, e.g., in modeling aggregate losses involving both frequency and severity. Fortunately, the various techniques for estimating parameters to be presented in Part IV can readily be adapted for all these situations.

Similar to the tabular models discussed in Part III, parametric models may be based on *complete* data or *incomplete* data. The various techniques will first be developed using complete data and then adaptations are developed for situations with incomplete data.

As noted in the introduction to Part III, in traditional actuarial applications parametric models are used much more widely in modeling claim frequency and claim severity, while tabular models are in much more widespread use for survival models. This phenomenon occurs since excellent parametric models exist in many practical applications involving claim frequency and severity. However, the complexities of data patterns that often exist in survival models have been difficult to represent using parametric distributions with only a few parameters.

The following are some additional comparative comments between the two different approaches:

(1) Parametric models tend to be simpler to develop and apply than tabular models, since they follow specified mathematical formulas with few parameters. However, greater accuracy is often possible with tabular models in view of the ability of tabular models to represent the underlying sample data more accurately.

(2) The size of the data set may be a factor in some cases. Although either approach can be successfully applied with either large or small data sets, there often is some tendency to prefer parametric models for smaller data sets and tabular methods for larger data sets.

(3) As covered in Part III, tabular models usually require some type of graduation or smoothing in view of the "lumpiness" of tabular empirical data. However, parametric models are inherently "smooth" due to their mathematical formula representation.

(4) Parametric models can often be readily adjusted to reflect changes in coverage such as deductibles (truncation) or changes in policy limits (censoring) in modeling loss processes. Tabular models can also be adjusted for these types of changes, but the process may be somewhat more complex.

Chapters 13 and 14 develop three basic and widely-applied methods of estimating parameters: (1) method of moments, (2) percentile matching, and (3) maximum likelihood.[1] In Chapter 15 a more complex method, Bayesian estimation, is developed that involves the blending of existing known prior information together with the new sample data obtained. Chapter 16 then turns to the testing and selection of models, the other key components of the parametric modeling process.

[1] For readers interested in further broadening their knowledge of estimation, two additional methods of parameter estimation, namely minimum chi-square and minimum distance, are briefly discussed in Appendix I.

CHAPTER THIRTEEN

PARAMETER ESTIMATION USING MOMENTS OR PERCENTILES

13.1 INTRODUCTION

In this chapter we introduce two basic methods of estimating parameters that are widely used and relatively simple to apply in practice. The basic approach is straightforward. Selected statistical measures are applied to both the sample data obtained and to the model being fitted. These measures are then equated between the sample and the model being fitted. The estimated values of the unknown parameters in question are then determined from these equations.

The concept behind these methods is that if the chosen model replicates the values of these measures existing in the sample data, then the model may be an acceptable approximation to, or representation of, the population from which the sample is drawn. Of course, there is no guarantee that the chosen model will prove to be a good one, but at least there is a reasonably good chance that it will be.

The first of these methods is called the *method of moments*. In this method, parameter values are chosen such that low-order moments in the fitted model will equal corresponding moments in the sample data. The second of these methods is called *percentile matching*. In this method, parameter values are chosen such that certain percentiles in the fitted model will match those in the sample data.

These two methods are often used in practice to get a basic idea of the general magnitude of the unknown parameters in the fitted model. In some situations, these parameter estimates may be good enough; in other situations, more sophisticated methods, to be developed in succeeding chapters, are required.

13.2 METHOD OF MOMENTS - COMPLETE EXACT DATA

We first consider the method of moments applied with *complete exact data* in the sample. The meaning of "complete exact data" is the same as that described in Chapter 9. The technique will first be demonstrated for continuous distributions (which often are used for severity models), and will then be demonstrated for discrete distributions (which are used for frequency models and occasionally for severity models).[1]

---

[1] As noted in Part III of the text, survival models are usually tabular models. However, the techniques in Part IV of the text can readily be applied to those less common situations in which parametric survival models are being utilized.

13.2.1 CONTINUOUS DISTRIBUTIONS

Consider a proposed fitted model distribution that has k unknown parameters $\theta_1, \theta_2, ..., \theta_k$. The basic approach using the method of moments is to equate the first k low-order moments in the sample distribution to the corresponding first k low-order moments in the model distribution. We then have k equations in k unknowns that must be solved to produce the k parameter estimates for the fitted model.

The k equations in k unknowns will not necessarily be linear, and some type of ad hoc algebraic approach might be required. The algebraic manipulations required to solve these k simultaneous equations will depend on the formulas for the moments of the model distribution involved. Thus, it is not possible to develop general algebraic formulas that work in all cases. The required algebraic manipulations will differ from distribution to distribution.

We may choose to equate moments about the origin. Let $E[X^m]$ be the mth moment about the origin in the model and $E_n[X^m]$ be the mth moment about the origin in a sample of size n.[2] Then the system of equations that must be solved for the k unknown parameters is

$$\begin{aligned} E[X] &= E_n[X], \\ E[X^2] &= E_n[X^2], \\ &\vdots \\ E[X^k] &= E_n[X^k]. \end{aligned} \tag{13.1}$$

The reader may wonder if it possible to use moments around points other than the origin. For example, what about using variances rather than second moments about the origin? Fortunately, the same answer will be obtained if this is done, which can easily be seen from the standard variance formula $\sigma_X^2 = E[X^2] - E[X]^2$. Just be careful to use the same type of moments in the model as are used in the sample to maintain consistency.

One other question may also occur to readers. Sample variances are sometimes computed on an unbiased basis with $n-1$ in the denominator, but at other times are computed with n in the denominator.[3] In this text, when using method of moments, we will assume that sample variances are defined with n in the denominator, unless specifically stated to the contrary.

EXAMPLE 13.1

We are given the following sample of 10 claim amounts: 1, 1, 1, 2, 2, 3, 5, 7, 8, 10. Estimate the parameters μ and σ using the method of moments if the normal distribution is being fit to the given sample data.

---

[2] When $m=1$ the random variable for the sample mean will be denoted by $\overline{X}$ instead of $E_n[X]$. The actual realized value of the sample mean will be denoted by $\overline{x}$.

[3] These two different approaches to calculating the sample variance are discussed at greater length in Sections 2.2 and 2.3.

SOLUTION

In this case, we need not apply Equations (13.1), since the two parameters in the normal distribution are directly the first two moments of the distribution, namely the mean and the standard deviation. We first compute the sample statistics $\sum_{i=1}^{10} x_i = 40$ and $\sum_{i=1}^{10} x_i^2 = 258$. Under the method of moments, the parameter estimate for μ is the sample mean $\bar{x}$ and the parameter estimate for σ is the sample standard deviation s_n. We denote the parameter estimates by $\hat{\mu}$ and $\hat{\sigma}$. Thus we have

$$\hat{\mu} = \frac{40}{10} = 4$$

and

$$\hat{\sigma} = \sqrt{\frac{258}{10} - 4^2} = \sqrt{9.80} = 3.13.$$ ❐

The astute reader may question whether the normal distribution is an appropriate model to fit to this data. Indeed, a visual inspection of the data seems to indicate positive skewness, since most of the data is less than the sample mean (i.e., the mean exceeds the median), so there is a significant right-hand tail. Also, the standard deviation is fairly large relative to the mean, and the absolute minimum value of $x = 0$ is only 1.28 standard deviations below the mean. These observations may lead the reader to consider a different model, as in Example 13.2.

EXAMPLE 13.2

Rework Example 13.1 using the gamma distribution.

SOLUTION

The gamma distribution (see Section 1.3.4) has positive skewness and may provide a better fit to the data than the normal distribution. In this case we will utilize Equations (13.1). Equating first and second moments about the origin between the model and sample, we have

$$E[X] = \alpha\theta = \frac{40}{10} = 4$$

and

$$E[X^2] = \alpha(\alpha+1)\theta^2 = \frac{258}{10} = 25.80,$$

where we have used the scale-parameter version of the gamma moments given in the first table of Appendix A.1.2.

This is a system of two non-linear equations in two unknowns that must be solved. We can algebraically determine the solution by first taking

$$\frac{E[X^2]}{E[X]^2} = \frac{\alpha(\alpha+1)\theta^2}{\alpha^2\theta^2} = \frac{\alpha+1}{\alpha} = \frac{25.80}{4^2} = 1.6125.$$

This is now one equation in one unknown and can be solved for the parameter $\hat{\alpha} = 1.63265$. The other parameter can easily be solved from the equation for $E[X]$ to give $\hat{\theta} = \frac{4}{\hat{\alpha}} = \frac{4}{1.63265} = 2.45$. ❒

We might surmise that the gamma distribution will prove to be superior to fitting these data than the normal distribution. However, we have not yet run any tests to establish that result. Furthermore, even if the gamma distribution proves to be superior to the normal distribution, there may be other positively skewed distributions that might even be superior to the gamma. The various tests that might be used to select among different competing models fit to sample data are the subject of Chapter 16.

EXAMPLE 13.3

A sample of 10 laboratory mice produces the times of death $t = 3, 4, 5, 7, 7, 8, 10, 10, 10, 12$ where t is measured in days. Assuming that the underlying survival model is exponential (see Section 1.3.3), estimate the parameter θ by the method of moments.

SOLUTION

In this example, we illustrate a simple parametric survival model. The exponential distribution involves a constant failure rate over time and can be used to measure the time until failure of each study unit. From the data the sample mean is $\bar{t} = \sum_{i=1}^{10} \frac{t_i}{10} = 7.60$. The mean of the exponential distribution is the parameter θ, so the method of moments estimate is $\hat{\theta} = \bar{t} = 7.60$. ❒

13.2.2 DISCRETE DISTRIBUTIONS

In this section we consider the method of moments for discrete distributions. A good application for this procedure is the modeling of claim frequency. Since the number of claims in any finite period of time will be a non-negative integer, the appropriateness of using a discrete distribution should be obvious. The use of discrete distributions is not limited to models for claim frequency but has other applications as well.

Fortunately, the method of moments for discrete distributions is the same as for continuous distributions. The concepts and techniques are largely identical. With discrete distributions defined on the non-negative integers (e.g., claim frequency) a certain notation is sometimes used. Let n_0 denote the number of outcomes with 0 claims, n_1 the number of outcomes with 1 claim, and so on. The total number in the sample is denoted by n so that $n = \sum_i n_i$. Figure 13.1 clarifies this notational system.

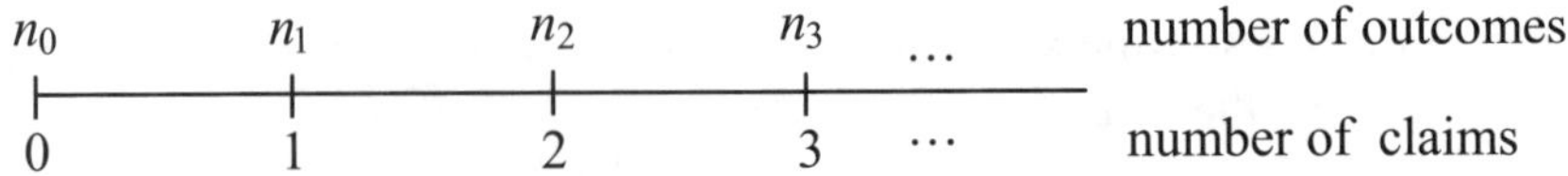

Notation for Claim Frequency

FIGURE 13.1

With this notation we then have

$$\bar{x} = \frac{\sum_{k=0}^{\infty} k \cdot n_k}{\sum_{k=0}^{\infty} n_k} = \frac{\sum_{k=0}^{\infty} k \cdot n_k}{n} \tag{13.2}$$

and, in general,

$$E_n[X^m] = \frac{\sum_{k=0}^{\infty} k^m \cdot n_k}{\sum_{k=0}^{\infty} n_k} = \frac{\sum_{k=0}^{\infty} k^m \cdot n_k}{n}. \tag{13.3}$$

Note that the upper limit in the summation is actually the largest number of claims for the sample in question, but is written as ∞ for convenience.

EXAMPLE 13.4

Table 13.1 provides accident data from 25 insurance policies.

TABLE 13.1

Observed Accident Data	
Number of Accidents	**Number of Policies**
0	7
1	5
2	4
3	3
4	3
5	2
6	1

We wish to fit a Poisson distribution (see Section 1.2.5) to model this claim data. Find the method of moments estimate for the Poisson parameter λ.

SOLUTION

The Poisson distribution has only one parameter. Using the method of moments, that parameter is estimated by equating the model mean to the sample mean. Thus, using Equation (13.2) we have

$$\hat{\lambda} = \bar{x} = \frac{\sum_{k=0}^{\infty} k \cdot n_k}{n} = \frac{7 \cdot 0 + 5 \cdot 1 + 4 \cdot 2 + 3 \cdot 3 + 3 \cdot 4 + 2 \cdot 5 + 1 \cdot 6}{25} = \frac{50}{25} = 2. \quad \square$$

EXAMPLE 13.5

Rework Example 13.4 using the negative binomial distribution (see Section 1.2.3).

SOLUTION

We can express the probability function for the negative binomial distribution as

$$p(x) = \binom{x+r-1}{r-1} p^r (1-p)^x = \binom{x+r-1}{r-1}\left(\frac{1}{1+\beta}\right)^r \left(\frac{\beta}{1+\beta}\right)^x$$

(see Equation (1.30a) and Exercise 6-38), for $x = 0, 1, 2, \cdots$. The mean and variance are

$$E[X] = \frac{rq}{p} = r\beta$$

and

$$Var(X) = \frac{rq}{p^2} = r\beta(1+\beta).$$

Note that the variance for the negative binomial distribution is greater than the mean. From the sample data we obtain

$$\bar{x} = \frac{\sum_{k=0}^{6} k \cdot n_k}{25} = \frac{50}{25} = 2$$

and

$$s_{25}^2 = \frac{\sum_{k=0}^{6} k^2 \cdot n_k}{25} - \bar{x}^2 = \frac{182}{25} - 2^2 = 3.28.$$

Since the sample variance is greater than the sample mean, the negative binomial distribution can be applied. In fact, the negative binomial distribution might well produce a better fit to this sample data than the Poisson distribution, since with the Poisson distribution the variance is equal to the mean. We now equate the model mean to the sample mean and the model variance to the sample variance to obtain

$$r\beta = 2$$

and

$$r\beta(1+\beta) = 3.28.$$

These equations can be readily solved by simply dividing to obtain the parameter estimates

$$\hat{\beta} = .64$$

and

$$\hat{r} = 3.125.$$

❐

13.2.3 SPECIAL HANDLING FOR THE BINOMIAL

The method of moments can be applied as described above for any discrete distribution. However, the binomial distribution usually requires special handling when this is done. The binomial distribution (see Section 1.2.2) has probability function

$$p(x) = \binom{n}{x} p^x (1-p)^{n-x},$$

for $x = 0, 1, 2, \cdots, n$. The mean and variance are

$$E[X] = np$$

and

$$Var(X) = np(1-p).$$

Note that the variance for the binomial distribution is smaller than the mean.

Assume that the parameter n is unknown. When the method of moments is applied to the binomial distribution, the two parameters being estimated are then n and p. The problem is that the binomial distribution is only defined when n is a positive integer. However, the estimated value of n obtained using the method of moments is quite unlikely to be an integer.

There are several ways to deal with this problem. The simplest method is to round off the estimated value of n to the nearest integer. The value of p is then adjusted so that the mean is unchanged, i.e., that the sample mean will still be reproduced by the model.

The reader should note that this problem does not exist for the two other distributions commonly used to model claim frequency, namely the Poisson and the negative binomial. Neither of these distributions restricts parameter choices only to positive integers.

EXAMPLE 13.6

Table 13.2 provides accident data from 1000 insurance policies.

TABLE 13.2

Observed Accident Data	
Number of Accidents	**Number of Policies**
0	100
1	267
2	311
3	208
4	87
5	23
6	4

We wish to fit a binomial distribution to model this claim data. Find the method of moments estimates for the binomial parameters n and p.

SOLUTION

Since the binomial distribution has two parameters, the method of moments equates the model mean to the sample mean and the model variance to the sample variance.

From the sample data using Equations (13.2) and (13.3) we obtain

$$\overline{x} = \frac{\sum_{k=0}^{6} k \cdot n_k}{1000} = \frac{2000}{1000} = 2$$

and

$$s_{1000}^2 = \frac{\sum_{k=0}^{6} k^2 \cdot n_k}{1000} - \overline{x}^2 = \frac{5494}{1000} - 2^2 = 1.494.$$

Since the sample variance is smaller than the sample mean, the binomial distribution can be applied. We now equate the model mean to the sample mean and the model variance to the sample variance to obtain the equations

$$np = 2$$

and

$$np(1-p) = 1.494.$$

These equations can be readily solved by simply dividing to obtain the parameter estimates

$$\hat{p} = .253$$

and

$$\hat{n} = 7.905.$$

However, the binomial model cannot be applied unless $\hat{n}$ is a positive integer. We can arbitrarily round off $\hat{n}$ the nearest integer and then recompute the value of $\hat{p}$ to preserve the sample mean $\overline{x} = 2$. This gives us the adjusted parameter estimates

$$\hat{p} = .250$$

and

$$\hat{n} = 8.$$ ❐

13.3 METHOD OF MOMENTS – EXTENSIONS

In this section we consider some extensions of the basic method of moments technique described in Section 13.2. We first consider the case for complete grouped data, and then consider extensions for incomplete data including both censoring and truncation.

13.3.1 COMPLETE GROUPED DATA

We now consider the case where the sample data do not show the exact value of each observation, but only the interval into which each observation falls. The comparison of the cases with complete individual data and complete grouped data is quite analogous to the same two cases considered in Chapter 9.

Complete grouped data can be encountered in any application. However, among typical actuarial applications, complete grouped data is quite common in tabulating claim amounts, particularly for large data sets. The boundary points for the intervals are usually established ahead of time, rather than being determined by the sample data actually obtained.

We will consider the general case in which the intervals are not necessarily equal. The definitions and notation we use are quite analogous to the framework developed in Section 9.3.1, except that we use the letter c for the boundary points of the intervals rather than the letter t as used in Section 9.3.1. With parametric models the intervals are usually defined by something other than "time," so a different letter might be less ambiguous or confusing.[4]

We divide the x-axis into the k intervals defined by the k+1 values $c_0, c_1, c_2, \cdots, c_k$, where $c_0 < c_1 < c_2 < \cdots < c_k$. The value of c_0 is often zero, but does not have to be. For example, if the data consist of loss amounts above some threshold, then c_0 would not be zero, but would be this threshold amount. Similarly, at the right-hand end c_k might be infinite or it might be some finite maximum value.

As in Section 9.3.1, we have a total of n observations in the sample. We let n_j denote the number of observations falling in the jth interval which is defined by $(c_{j-1}, c_j]$. (Note that the left end of the first interval may need to be closed depending upon the situation, such as if $c_0 > 0$. Similarly, the right end of the last interval may need to be open depending upon the situation, such as if $c_k = \infty$.) It must be true that $\sum_{j=1}^{k} n_j = n$. Figure 13.2 is similar to Figure 9.3, and illustrates these definitions and notational system.

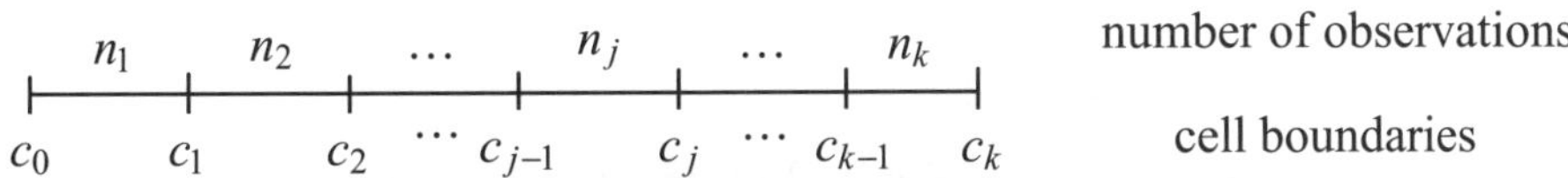

General Model for Grouped Data

FIGURE 13.2

In using the method of moments for complete grouped data, no change in procedure is needed for the model being fitted. However, in determining the sample moments an approximation is required, since exact values of the sample observations are not known. The best approximation will vary from situation to situation, and must be chosen by the modeler to provide a reasonable approximation for the situation at hand.

A common approximation that works well in many cases is to assume that the sample observations in each interval are uniformly distributed across that interval. In this situation the average value in each interval would simply be the midpoint of the interval. We could then compute a weighted average of these midpoints across all intervals, using the number of observations in each interval as the weights. We can then use

---

[4] The letter c could stand for "cell" or for "category."

$$\bar{x} = \frac{1}{n}\left(\sum_{j=1}^{k} \frac{c_j + c_{j-1}}{2} \cdot n_j\right) \tag{13.4}$$

to calculate the sample mean for complete grouped data under these assumptions.

If the sample observations are not uniformly distributed across each interval, then the modeler may need to modify Equation (13.4) accordingly. For example, in a particular interval if the sample observations are concentrated on average three-quarters of the way through the interval, then the term $\frac{c_j + c_{j-1}}{2}$ would be replaced by $\frac{3c_j + c_{j-1}}{4}$.

Higher-order moments present another challenge. For purposes of discussion, suppose we wish to fit a two-parameter distribution to the data and therefore need the second sample moment. It might be natural to modify Equation (13.4) by squaring the $\frac{c_j + c_{j-1}}{2}$ term to obtain a second moment about the origin for the sample. This procedure would be consistent with the assumption that all sample observations in each interval are located at the midpoint. Unfortunately, we know this procedure is not consistent with the assumption of a uniform distribution across each interval. (The latter assumption is pursued in Exercise 13-11.)

Yet another complication arises if the last interval goes to infinity, since the final interval then has no midpoint! Some appropriate value is needed for the mean of that interval, but it cannot be the midpoint.

What would seem at first glance to be a rather simple generalization of a basic technique from complete individual data to complete grouped data has unexpected pitfalls.

EXAMPLE 13.7

Table 9.5 contains data for a sample of $n = 500$ observations grouped into five amount intervals. We wish to fit an exponential distribution to this data using the method of moments. Use Equation (13.4) to estimate the value of the parameter θ in the exponential distribution.

SOLUTION

From Equation (13.4) the sample mean is computed to be

$$\begin{aligned}
\bar{x} &= \frac{1}{n}\left(\sum_{j=1}^{k} \frac{c_j + c_{j-1}}{2} \cdot n_j\right) \\
&= \frac{1}{500}\Bigg[\left(\frac{2000+0}{2}\right)(178) + \left(\frac{5000+2000}{2}\right)(142) \\
&\qquad + \left(\frac{20{,}000+5{,}000}{2}\right)(82) + \left(\frac{50{,}000+20{,}000}{2}\right)(50) + \left(\frac{100{,}000+50{,}000}{2}\right)(48)\Bigg] \\
&= 14{,}100.
\end{aligned}$$

Since the parameter θ is equal to the mean of the exponential distribution (see Section 1.3.3), the method of moments gives

$$\hat{\theta} = \bar{x} = 14{,}100. \qquad \square$$

The astute reader might observe that the sample observations are monotonically decreasing as amounts increase, and likewise the fitted exponential distribution follows this same pattern. Overall, this is a desirable result, but there may be another issue to consider. A monotonically decreasing pattern is not really compatible with using the midpoint assumption, particularly when the intervals are as broad as they are in this example. This pattern suggests that perhaps the average value in each interval occurs somewhere below the midpoint.

13.3.2 INCOMPLETE DATA – CENSORING

We now turn to situations involving incomplete data. The first case we consider is that of censored data. The general concept of censoring data was covered at some length in Chapter 10 and will not be extensively described again here. The applications in Chapter 10 mostly involved survival models. Recall that Section 10.2.2 drew a distinction between *planned* censoring and *random* censoring. In this chapter, all censoring is random.

In applications involving loss models, the most common type of censoring is right censoring due to the existence of policy limits. For example, if a liability insurance policy has a policy limit (maximum benefit) of \$1 million and a loss of \$1.5 million is incurred, the insurance company will pay only the policy limit of \$1 million. Calling this loss a \$1 million event is an example of right censoring, the recording of a loss as something other than its true value.

There are other situations involving censoring that may be encountered. However, the following discussion will be structured around the situation described immediately above. The same technique used here can easily be adapted to other situations involving censored data.

The key concept in modifying the method-of-moments technique for censored data is that the sample distribution and the model distribution must both be censored consistently. The expected value of claim payments in the presence of a policy limit is given by the *limited expected value* (LEV) function, denoted by $E[X \wedge u]$, where u is the value above which values are censored (i.e., the policy limit). The reader will recall[5] that the limited expected value function is defined by

$$\begin{aligned} E[X \wedge u] &= \int_0^u x \cdot f(x)\,dx + \int_u^\infty u \cdot f(x)\,dx \\ &= \int_0^u x \cdot f(x)\,dx + u[1-F(u)]. \end{aligned} \qquad (13.5)$$

Equation (13.5) has a straightforward explanation. The limited expected value function is the same as a "regular" expected value function for losses below the policy limit, but is "limited" to the policy limit for losses above the policy limit.

[5] For a review of the LEV function, see Section 6.3.2.

Higher order moments can also be defined and will be needed in applying the method of moments to situations where two or more unknown parameters are being estimated. The kth moment about the origin would be given by

$$E\left[(X\wedge u)^k\right] = \int_0^u x^k\cdot f(x)\,dx + \int_u^\infty u^k\cdot f(x)\,dx$$
$$= \int_0^u x^k\cdot f(x)\,dx + u^k\left[1-F(u)\right]. \quad (13.6)$$

We now turn to the sample of n observations. Assume that we have complete exact data below the point of censoring. Let n_u be the number of sample observations that are not censored and n_c be the number of sample observations that are censored, so that $n_u + n_c = n$. For the sample, the formula corresponding to Equation (13.5) would be

$$E_n\left[X\wedge u\right] = \frac{1}{n}\left(\sum_{n_u} x + \sum_{n_c} u\right) = \frac{1}{n}\left(\sum_{n_u} x + n_c\cdot u\right), \quad (13.7)$$

and the formula corresponding to Equation (13.6) would be

$$E_n\left[(X\wedge u)^k\right] = \frac{1}{n}\left(\sum_{n_u} x^k + \sum_{n_c} u^k\right) = \frac{1}{n}\left(\sum_{n_u} x^k + n_c\cdot u^k\right). \quad (13.8)$$

The method of moments then equates the sample moments to the moments of the fitted model, and solves the resulting simultaneous equations.

In the case of complete grouped data, we need a formula for the limited expected value function in the sample that would be a generalization of Equation (13.4) for the unrestricted sample mean. Assume that the policy limit is located at one of the boundary points, so that $u = c_m$ in the grouped data where m is a positive integer such that $1 < m < k$. This generalized formula would be

$$E_n[X\wedge u] = \frac{1}{n}\left(\sum_{j=1}^{m}\frac{c_j + c_{j-1}}{2}\cdot n_j + u\sum_{j=m+1}^{k} n_j\right). \quad (13.9)$$

The idea is to use midpoint estimates for all intervals below the policy limit and the policy limit u for all intervals above the policy limit. Figure 13.3 illustrates this definition.

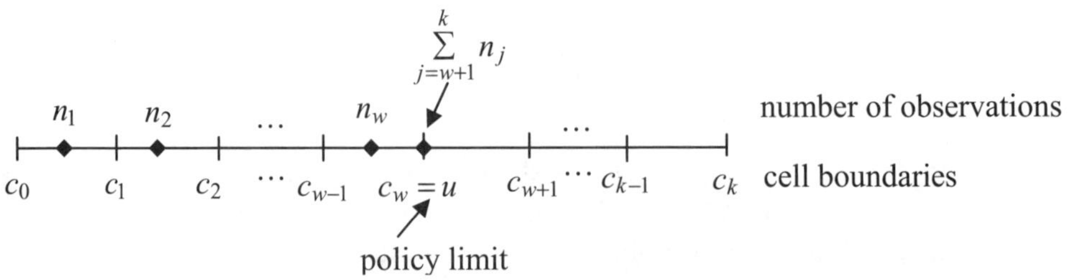

LEV Function for Complete Grouped Data

FIGURE 13.3

The reader should note that the solution of equations involving censored data often will involve algebraic complexity and may be difficult to solve with analytical methods. This complexity arises due to the algebraic form of the LEV function for many of the basic distributions used in this text. Iteration techniques may be required to obtain a numerical solution. (See Appendix F for a review of various iteration methods from numerical analysis.)

EXAMPLE 13.8

We wish to fit a Pareto distribution (see Section 6.1.2) with parameters $\alpha = 2$ and unknown θ to sample claims data that have been censored at $u = 1000$ due to a policy limit. For a sample of size $n = 7$, we are given the observations $200, 200, 400, 600, 800, 1000^*, 1000^*$, where * indicates a censored observation. We wish to estimate the value of the unknown parameter θ using the method of moments.

SOLUTION

The limited expected value for the sample distribution is

$$\begin{aligned} E_7[X \wedge 1000] &= \frac{200+200+400+600+800+1000+1000}{7} \\ &= \frac{4200}{7} = 600. \end{aligned}$$

The limited expected value function for the Pareto distribution[6] is

$$E[X \wedge 1000] = \frac{\theta}{\alpha-1}\left[1-\left(\frac{\theta}{1000+\theta}\right)^{\alpha-1}\right] = \theta\left(\frac{1000}{1000+\theta}\right),$$

with $\alpha = 2$. We then equate the above two expressions to obtain

$$1000\theta = 600(1000+\theta),$$

which solves for

$$\hat{\theta} = 1500. \qquad \square$$

Note that Example 13.8 can be solved analytically for the unknown parameter, but often an iteration of some type is required to obtain a numerical answer in this type of problem.

EXAMPLE 13.9

Use Equation (13.9) to calculate $E_{500}[X \wedge 20{,}000]$ for the sample data given in Example 13.7.

Solution

We have

---

[6] See Table 6.2.

$$E_{500}[X \wedge u] = \frac{1}{500}\left(\sum_{j=1}^{m} \frac{c_j + c_{j-1}}{2} \cdot n_j + u \sum_{j=m+1}^{k} n_j\right)$$

$$= \frac{1}{500}\left[\left(\frac{2000+0}{2}\right)(178) + \left(\frac{5000+2000}{2}\right)(142)\right.$$

$$\left. + \left(\frac{20{,}000+5{,}000}{2}\right)(82) + (20{,}000)(50+48)\right]$$

$$= 7320.$$

□

13.3.3 INCOMPLETE DATA – TRUNCATION

The second case involving incomplete data we consider is that of truncated data. As with censoring discussed above, the general concept of truncating data was covered at some length in Chapter 10 and will not be extensively described again here. The applications in Chapter 10 mostly involved survival models.

In applications involving loss models, the most common type of truncation is left truncation due to the existence of deductibles. For example, if a property insurance policy has a deductible of \$1000 and a loss of \$500 is incurred, the insurance company will not be obligated to pay anything and likely will not even know that the loss has occurred. Ignoring losses below the deductible is an example of left truncation, i.e., completely eliminating this portion of the loss distribution.

There are other situations involving truncation that may be encountered. However, the following discussion will be structured around the situation described immediately above. The same technique used here can easily be adapted to other situations involving truncated data.

As was the case with censoring, the key concept in modifying the method of moments for truncated data is that the sample distribution and the model distribution must both be truncated consistently. Eliminating a portion of the distribution creates a conditional distribution in statistics. The *expected payment per payment* for a loss greater than a deductible of d is given by[7]

$$E[X-d \mid X>d] = \frac{\int_d^{\infty}(x-d)\cdot f(x)\,dx}{\int_d^{\infty} f(x)\,dx}$$

$$= \frac{\int_d^{\infty}(x-d)\cdot f(x)\,dx}{1-F(d)}. \tag{13.10}$$

Equation (13.10) has a straightforward explanation. The numerator is the expected amount of claim payment, i.e., the amount of loss minus the deductible, across the portion of the distribution on which something positive is paid. The denominator arises from conditional proba-

[7] See Section 6.3.1.

bility theory; intuitively, the effect is to ratio the area under the truncated density function back up to one.

The term "expected payment per payment" is in contrast to the term *expected payment per loss*. The "expected payment per loss" is the numerator of Equation (13.10) and represents an unconditional mean across the entire loss distribution. This unconditional mean is *smaller* than the conditional mean given by Equation (13.10), since the net effect is to average in zeroes for all losses below the deductible.

The reader may encounter a variety of terms in the literature that are synonymous with the term "expected payment per payment." One common term is *mean excess loss* and another is *mean residual life*. In the context of survival models, the term *expectation of life* or *life expectancy* is often used.

Higher order moments can also be defined and will be needed in applying the method of moments to situations where two or more unknown parameters are being estimated. The kth moment about the origin would be given by

$$E\left[(X-d)^k \mid X>d\right] = \frac{\int_d^\infty (x-d)^k \cdot f(x)\,dx}{\int_d^\infty f(x)\,dx}$$

$$= \frac{\int_d^\infty (x-d)^k \cdot f(x)\,dx}{1-F(d)}. \tag{13.11}$$

We now turn to the sample of n observations. The process of truncation means that if we have any losses in the sample below the deductible, they must be eliminated from consideration. Assume that we have complete exact data above the point of truncation. We would then compute moments in the sample above the point of truncation in the usual fashion, remembering to subtract d from each value if these sample moments are to be used as estimates for model moments calculated from Equation (13.11). No special formulas would be required for this purpose.

It is important to correctly interpret parameter estimates using the method of moments with truncated distributions. The answers obtained are estimates for the parameters in the original untruncated distribution. A new distribution with different parameters is not being created by the process of truncation. We are simply using truncated sample data along with a truncated fitted model for consistency, but we are still estimating parameters for the original distribution.

EXAMPLE 13.10

A random variable X has probability density function

$$f(x;\theta) = \theta + 2(1-\theta)x,$$

for $0 \le x \le 1$ and $0 \le \theta \le 2$. A sample of size $n=6$ contains the values .50, .55, .70, .75, .80, .80. Using the method of moments, what is the estimate for the parameter θ in a distribution which is truncated from below at $x=.60$?

SOLUTION

Note that in this example truncated distributions are to be used, but there is no mention of a deductible. In particular, the value of .60 is not to be subtracted from the values of x in either the sample distribution or in the fitted model distribution. We have one unknown parameter and therefore will only need to work with first moments in both the sample and model distributions.

In the sample, we have two observations, namely .50 and .55, that are below .60, the point of truncation. Under the concept of truncation, these two sample observations must be completely ignored. Then the sample mean for the four remaining sample observations is

$$E_4[X \mid X > .60] = \frac{.70 + .75 + .80 + .80}{4} = .7625.$$

For the fitted model, we must adapt Equation (13.11) to not include subtraction of the quantity d, so we have

$$E[X \mid X > .60] = \frac{\int_{.60}^{1} x \cdot f(x;\theta)\, dx}{\int_{.60}^{1} f(x;\theta)\, dx}.$$

At this point we have a routine, although somewhat tedious, calculus problem to integrate both the numerator and denominator of this expression. When we do these two integrations we obtain $.5227 - .2027\theta$ in the numerator and $.64 - .24\theta$ in the denominator. Equating the sample mean to the fitted model mean we have

$$\frac{.5227 - .2027\theta}{.64 - .24\theta} = .7625,$$

which is easily solved to give the method of moments parameter estimate $\hat{\theta} = 1.76$. ❐

13.4 PERCENTILE MATCHING

The second technique for estimating unknown parameters in parametric distributions considered in this chapter is the technique of *percentile matching*. Conceptually, this technique is quite similar to the method of moments. In a nutshell, the technique is based on matching percentiles between the sample data and the fitted model, rather than matching moments, as is done with the method of moments. Although the concepts underlying the two methods are similar, the details of implementing them will differ.

We use the symbol π_p to denote the $100p^{th}$ percentile in a population or model distribution. Thus, for example, the median, or 50th percentile, would be denoted by $\pi_{.50}$. We can express percentiles directly in terms of the cumulative distribution function, where, by definition, $F(\pi_p) = p$. Similarly, we use x_p to denote the $100p^{th}$ percentile in an observed or empirical distribution. Then it follows that $F_n^o(x_p) = p$.

13.4.1 SMOOTHED EMPIRICAL PERCENTILES

Before demonstrating the actual technique of percentile matching, we need to develop a type of adjusted percentile to use for the empirical sample distribution. The sample distribution is necessarily a discrete distribution, and percentiles in a discrete distribution are not always well defined.

The reader will recall from probability theory that the cumulative distribution function $F_n^o(x)$ for a discrete sample distribution has the familiar "upward stair-step" pattern, since empirical sample values come into the distribution in discrete pieces each with probability $1/n$. This pattern is illustrated in Figure 2.1.

When the cumulative distribution function looks like this, it is clear that a unique value for each percentile does not exist. Therefore the meaning of percentiles in a discrete distribution is a matter of convention and definition, and should be specified in any particular application.

The *smoothed empirical percentile* procedure is a technique that produces a unique and distinct value for each percentile. It achieves this outcome by performing an interpolation between adjacent sample values at which exact values of the percentile are known.

Consider a sample of size n. We denote the n sample values of the random variable X in ascending order as $x_1 \le x_2 \le \ldots \le x_n$. The smoothed empirical percentile x_p is then defined by the following procedure:

(1) Let $k = (n+1)p$, where p is the percentile in question.

(2) Let l be the greatest integer in k, where l can be equal to any of $1, 2, \cdots, n-1$.

(3) Let m be the fractional part of k, where $0 \le m < 1$. (Note that $m = 0$ if k is an integer.)

(4) Then we define

$$x_p = (1-m) \cdot x_l + m \cdot x_{l+1}. \tag{13.12}$$

These definitions and formulas need some explanation along with an example. Assume that we have a sample of size $n = 7$. The seven observations ranked in ascending order are displayed in Figure 13.4.

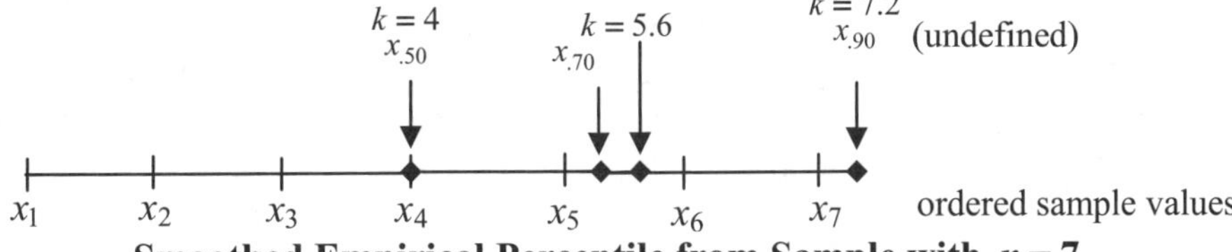

Smoothed Empirical Percentile from Sample with $n = 7$

FIGURE 13.4

Assume that we want the smoothed empirical percentile for the median, which is the 50th percentile, denoted by $x_{.50}$. We apply Step (1) above to obtain $k=(7+1)(.50)=4$. The value of k refers to the subscripts on the x_i's. In this case $l=4$ and $m=0$, which gives a smoothed empirical percentile, using Equation (13.12), of $x_{.50}=x_4$. This should be an intuitively comfortable result, since x_4 is the middle value of the seven observations. Note that this answer results from using the factor $n+1$ in calculating k. Note also that this answer would not be given by elementary statistics, since $F_7^o(x_4)=\frac{4}{7}$.

We now continue this example to develop the smoothed empirical percentile for the 70th percentile, denoted $x_{.70}$. This time $k=(7+1)(.70)=5.60$, so that $l=5$ and $m=.60$. In this case k is not an integer, as it was for the 50th percentile. Equation (13.12) determines the smoothed empirical percentile using linear interpolation, obtaining $x_{.70}=.40x_5+.60x_6$.

Note that Step (2) above imposes a condition on the value of k such that $1\leq k\leq n$. This restriction is to ensure that we are in the range of sample values so that Equation (13.12) can be applied. If $k<1$ or if $k>n$, then the smoothed empirical percentile is not defined. Continuing our illustration on to the 90th percentile will produce this result, since

$$k=(7+1)(.90)=7.20$$

which lies to the right of the last sample value.

Algebraically, we can express the ranges for which the smoothed empirical percentile does not exist by the conditions $k<\frac{1}{n+1}$ or $k>\frac{n}{n+1}$. In our illustration with $n=7$, this means that any percentiles below the 12.5^{th} or above the 87.5^{th} are undefined. This seems reasonable. Since our illustration has only $n=7$ sample values, there simply is not enough information to make a reasonable estimate of the 90th percentile.

It is also possible to use the binomial distribution to provide a non-parametric (i.e., not dependent on the particular model distribution being used) estimate for the probability of a particular distribution percentile being in any of the intervals displayed in Figure 13.4. The technique is similar to one first introduced in Chapter 9, when analyzing the cumulative distribution function or the survival distribution function for a survival model.[8]

The rationale for this technique is that percentiles are obtained from the cumulative distribution function that inherently partitions a distribution into two intervals, namely those below and above the percentile. This is a binomial outcome. If we draw repeated sample values, the probability of being above or below a particular percentile value is constant from trial to trial and the trials are independent, so all the conditions for using the binomial distribution are satisfied. This technique will be illustrated in Example 13.11.

[8] See Equations (9.5) and (9.6) in Section 9.2.4.

EXAMPLE 13.11

Consider the following sample of size 10, drawn from a continuous distribution, in ascending order:

$$\{1, 2, 10, 20, 25, 30, 40, 45, 55, 65\}$$

We wish to find the smoothed empirical percentile for the 60th percentile, and find the probability that the 60th percentile of the underlying distribution lies in the interval $[25,45)$.

SOLUTION

The smoothed empirical percentile is obtained from

$$k = (10+1)(.60) = 6.60,$$

so that $l = 6$ and $m = .60$. Applying Equation (13.12) we have

$$x_{.60} = .40x_6 + .60x_7 = (.40)(30) + (.60)(40) = 36.$$

(One way to conceptualize this answer is to think of it as a point estimate for the 60th percentile of the underlying distribution, $\pi_{.60}$.)

The second part of the example asks for the probability that the value of $\pi_{.60}$ falls into some range. (This could be considered as a type of confidence interval for the point estimate just obtained.) The interval $[25,45)$ actually consists of three subintervals. For each of the three subintervals we must find the number of sample values less than the percentile and the number greater than the percentile. These results are displayed in Table 13.3. ❒

TABLE 13.3

Binomial Probabilities for Smoothed Empirical Percentiles	
Interval	**Needed Outcomes**
$[25,30)$	5 less than, 5 greater than
$[30,40)$	6 less than, 4 greater than
$[40,45)$	7 less than, 3 greater than

The probability that $\pi_{.60}$ lies in the interval $[25,45)$ is the sum of the three binomial probabilities implied in Table 13.3, which is

$$\binom{10}{5}(.60)^5(.40)^5 + \binom{10}{6}(.60)^6(.40)^4 + \binom{10}{7}(.60)^7(.40)^3 = .666.$$

In essence, we could say that, based on this technique, the interval $[25,45)$ is a 66.6^{th} confidence interval for $\pi_{.60}$ around the point estimate 36.

13.4.2 COMPLETE EXACT DATA

We now turn to consideration of the percentile matching method for estimating parameters. In this section we apply the method in a situation in which the fitted model is continuous and the sample has complete exact data. These conditions make the percentile matching method of estimating parameters relatively straightforward to apply, and would usually need to exist for the method to be of practical use.

Consider a proposed fitted model that has the k unknown parameters $\theta_1, \theta_2, ..., \theta_k$. The basic approach using percentiles is to equate k different percentiles in the sample to the corresponding k percentiles in the model. We then have k equations in k unknowns that must be solved to produce the k parameter estimates for the fitted model.

The k equations in k unknowns will not generally be linear and some type of ad hoc algebraic approach will be required. The algebraic manipulations required to solve these k simultaneous equations will depend on the formula for the cumulative distribution function of the model distribution involved, so it is not possible to develop general algebraic formulas that work in all cases. The required algebraic manipulations will differ from distribution to distribution.

There is one significant conceptual difference between the method of moments and percentile matching. With the method of moments the parameter estimates will be the same regardless of which *type* of moments (e.g., moments about the origin or moments about the mean) are used. However, there is an infinite number of different percentiles, and the choice of percentiles to be used will affect the answer, often materially. Therefore, percentile matching allows the modeler a great deal of latitude in deciding what percentiles to use, which may be both an advantage and disadvantage of the method.

Let π_{p_i}, for $i = 1, 2, \cdots, k$, be k percentiles in the model distribution, and let x_{p_i} be the corresponding k percentiles in the sample distribution. Then the system of equations that must be solved for the k unknown parameters is

$$\begin{aligned} F(\pi_{p_1}) &= F_n^o(x_{p_1}) = p_1, \\ F(\pi_{p_2}) &= F_n^o(x_{p_2}) = p_2, \\ &\vdots \\ F(\pi_{p_k}) &= F_n^o(x_{p_k}) = p_k, \end{aligned} \tag{13.13}$$

where $F(\pi_{p_i})$, the cumulative distribution function of the model distribution is expressed in terms of the k parameters $\theta_1, \theta_2, \cdots, \theta_k$. The percentiles used in the sample distribution are typically the smoothed empirical percentiles developed in the prior section. These percentiles will produce a unique value for each percentile chosen, provided each smoothed empirical percentile is in the range where it is defined.

One possible complication that may arise with percentile matching is that an algebraic solution of the system of equations given by Equation (13.13) requires that the fitted model cumulative distribution function possesses a closed form expression. However, not all the distributions that we use possess closed form expressions for the cumulative distribution function. For example, the normal, lognormal, and gamma[9] distributions do not possess such closed form expressions.

EXAMPLE 13.12

Rework Example 13.3 using percentile matching based on matching medians.

SOLUTION

The sample has 10 observations. The smoothed empirical percentile for the median will be the value halfway between the 5th and 6th values in the ordered sample, which is $x_{.50} = .50(7+8) = 7.50$.

The exponential distribution has a cumulative distribution function given by $F(x) = 1 - e^{-x/\theta}$. At the median, $F(x) = .50$ and $x = \pi_{.50}$. Then

$$F(\pi_{.50}) = 1 - e^{-\pi_{.50}/\theta} = .50,$$

so

$$-\frac{\pi_{.50}}{\theta} = \ln(.50)$$

and

$$\pi_{.50} = .69315\theta.$$

We then equate the sample median to the model median to obtain $.69315\theta = 7.50$, which gives the percentile matching parameter estimate $\hat{\theta} = 10.82$. ❐

EXAMPLE 13.13

We wish to estimate the parameters in a Weibull distribution (see Equations (6.12a) and 6.12b)) using percentile matching, given the sample percentiles $x_{.50} = 10{,}000$ and $x_{.90} = 100{,}000$. What is the estimate for the parameter τ?

SOLUTION

In this example the sample percentiles are directly provided and do not need to be calculated using the smoothed empirical percentile procedure. The CDF of the Weibull distribution is $F(x) = 1 - e^{-(x/\theta)^{\tau}}$, which has two parameters, so we need to solve two equations in two unknowns. We have

$$F_n^o(x_{.50}) = .50 = 1 - e^{-(10{,}000/\theta)^{\tau}} = F(\pi_{.50})$$

and

$$F_n^o(x_{.90}) = .90 = 1 - e^{-(100{,}000/\theta)^{\tau}} = F(\pi_{.90}),$$

from which we obtain

[9] The gamma distribution does have a closed form CDF if α is a positive integer.

$$e^{-(10{,}000/\theta)^{\tau}} = .50$$

and

$$e^{-(100{,}000/\theta)^{\tau}} = .10.$$

Taking natural logarithms we have

$$\left(\frac{10{,}000}{\theta}\right)^{\tau} = -\ln(.50) = .69315$$

and

$$\left(\frac{100{,}000}{\theta}\right)^{\tau} = -\ln(.10) = 2.30259.$$

Finally, we divide to obtain

$$10^{\tau} = \frac{2.30259}{.69315} = 3.32192,$$

which gives

$$\hat{\tau} = \frac{\ln 3.32192}{\ln 10} = .521.$$ ❐

EXAMPLE 13.14

Rework Example 13.1 using percentile matching based on percentiles that are one standard deviation above and one standard deviation below the mean.

SOLUTION

This example uses the normal distribution which does not have a closed form expression for the cumulative distribution function. However, the normal distribution tables contain values of the cumulative distribution function, often denoted as $\Phi(z)$ for a standard normal variable with $\mu=0$ and $\sigma=1$. From the tables these two values for the standard normal distribution are

$$\Phi(-1) = .1587$$

and

$$\Phi(1) = .8413.$$

The smoothed empirical percentiles from the sample are

$$(10+1)(.1587) = 1.7457$$

and

$$(10+1)(.8413) = 9.2543,$$

so that

$$x_{.1587} = (.2543)(1)+(.7457)(1) = 1$$

and

$$x_{.8413} = (.7457)(8)+(.2543)(10) = 8.5086.$$

Equating the percentiles we have

$$\mu - \sigma = 1$$

and

$$\mu + \sigma = 8.5086,$$

which has the solution $\hat{\mu} = 4.7543$ and $\hat{\sigma} = 3.7543$. ❐

13.4.3 EXTENSIONS

Following the approach taken with method of moments, the reader might assume we would now turn to applications of percentile matching in other situations such as discrete model distributions, complete grouped data, censored distributions, and truncated distributions. It is possible to develop approaches for percentile matching in such situations. However, we will find that the approaches become complicated, may require additional assumptions, and may not be able to be solved analytically.

Model distributions that are discrete will have definitional problems for percentiles similar to the empirical sample distribution that led us to develop smoothed empirical percentile estimates. Censored distributions are partially continuous and partially discrete, raising a challenge in the discrete part of the distribution.

Complete grouped data in the sample would require us to develop a variation of the smoothed empirical percentile estimation procedure. Truncated distributions have a denominator from conditional probability theory that may lead to formulas that cannot be solved analytically and require a numerical solution.

All these complexities can be solved, but only at the cost of considerable effort. We must remember that percentile matching is inherently not a very sophisticated method in the first place. The main purpose of using percentile matching is to apply a relatively simple, straightforward procedure to get quick estimates for unknown parameters in situations where the percentiles are important.

For these reasons, percentile matching is rarely applied to situations other than those for which the sample has complete exact data and the model distribution is continuous. The challenge of adapting the method to other situations may be interesting mathematically, but is probably just not worth the trouble in most practical applications. The method of moments is usually easier to apply as a basic method in such situations. Also, more sophisticated estimation methods are available, as we shall see in Chapters 14 and 15.

13.5 SOME ADVANCED ILLUSTRATIONS

In this final section we present three illustrative examples of more advanced applications of the method of moments and percentile matching. These examples are in no way comprehensive, but they do illustrate the application of these two methods of parameter estimation in settings other than the basic ones illustrated previously in this chapter.

The first example illustrates using the method of moments in a situation involving inflation. The second example illustrates the method of moments with a discrete mixture distribution, and the third illustrates percentile matching for a parametric survival model.

EXAMPLE 13.15

An insurance company had the experience shown in Table 13.4 over a three-year period.

TABLE 13.4

Three Years of Claim Experience		
Year	**Number of Insureds**	**Total Claim Payments**
1	500	550,000
2	650	780,000
3	800	1,000,000

The company wishes to use a model in which claim severity per insured each year is based on an exponential distribution that reflects inflation. The parameter of the exponential distribution for Year 1 is θ, for Year 2 it is $c\theta$, and for Year 3 it is $c^2\theta$. The parameter c is to reflect the average compound rate of inflation from Year 1 to Year 3. The parameter θ is to be estimated by the method of moments applied to the entire block of business over the three-year period. Find estimates for the parameters c and θ using this model.

SOLUTION

This example has several new features not seen in earlier examples in this chapter. First, it includes recognition of inflation. Recall that the parameter θ in the exponential distribution is an example of a *scale parameter* (see Section 6.2.2) that can be used to capture the effects of inflation. Second, this example has multi-year data with variable numbers of insureds each year. Third, the method of moments is to be applied on an aggregate basis rather than on an individual basis.

We first focus on estimating the parameter c. The average claim severity per insured over the three-year experience period is

$$\frac{550{,}000}{500} = 1100$$

in Year 1,

$$\frac{780{,}000}{650} = 1200$$

in Year 2, and

$$\frac{1{,}000{,}000}{800} = 1250$$

in Year 3.

The rate of inflation experienced varies over the period, but is to be modeled by a level value c calculated on a compound basis. Thus we have

$$c^2 = \frac{1200}{1100} \cdot \frac{1250}{1200} = 1.13636$$

so that

$$\hat{c} = 1.066,$$

or 6.6% per year on average.

We now turn to estimating the parameter θ. Applying the method of moments on an aggregate basis is intended to ensure that the model will reproduce the total amount of claims actually paid over the three-year period. The total amount of claims in the sample is

$$550{,}000 + 780{,}000 + 1{,}000{,}000 = 2{,}330{,}000.$$

The model total claims are

$$500\theta + 650c\theta + 800c^2\theta = 500\theta + 692.9\theta + 909.088\theta = 2101.988\theta,$$

using the estimate for c already determined. Equating the two values and solving for θ gives

$$\hat{\theta} = \frac{2{,}330{,}000}{2101.988} = 1108.47.$$ ❐

EXAMPLE 13.16

We wish to model a claim process as a mixture of two independent distributions, A and B. Distribution A is exponential with mean 1, and Distribution B is exponential with mean 10. Positive weight p is assigned to Distribution A. The standard deviation of the mixture distribution is equal to 2. Determine p using the method of moments.

SOLUTION

This example involves the method of moments in a mixture distribution. For the exponential distribution, $E[X] = \theta$ and $E[X^2] = 2\theta^2$, so we have the values shown in Table 13.5.

TABLE 13.5

Moments in a Discrete Mixture of Exponentials

Distribution	**Parameter**	$E[X]$	$E[X^2]$
A	$\theta = 1$	1	2
B	$\theta = 10$	10	200

For the mixture distribution, we then have

$$E[X] = 1 \cdot p + 10(1-p) = 10 - 9p$$

and

$$E[X^2] = 2 \cdot p + 200(1-p) = 200 - 198p.$$

We then calculate

$$Var[X] = (200-198p)-(10-9p)^2 = 100-18p-81p^2,$$

and set this equal to 2^2. We now have a quadratic in p, whose positive root gives the parameter estimate $\hat{p}=.983$. ❐

EXAMPLE 13.17

A sample of 9 laboratory rats produces the times of death $t=3,4,5,7,7,8,10,10,$ and 12, where time is measured in days. Estimate the Gompertz survival model parameters B and c using percentile matching of the 25th and 65th percentiles.

SOLUTION

The Gompertz survival model[10] is defined by a force of mortality (hazard rate) of the form $\mu_x = Bc^x$, which then leads to the survival function

$$S(x) = \exp\left[\frac{B}{\ln c}(1-c^x)\right].$$

The cumulative distribution function is $F(x)=1-S(x)$. The 25th and 65th percentiles in the fitted model are

$$\pi_{.25} = \frac{\ln\left[1-\frac{\ln(.75)\cdot\ln c}{B}\right]}{\ln c}$$

and

$$\pi_{.65} = \frac{\ln\left[1-\frac{\ln(.35)\cdot\ln c}{B}\right]}{\ln c},$$

respectively. The smoothed empirical percentiles from the sample are $x_{.25}=4.50$ and $x_{.65}=9$. Equating the model percentiles to the smoothed empirical percentiles and solving the resulting two equations in two unknowns gives the parameter estimates $\hat{B}=.03777$ and $\hat{c}=1.24173$. ❐

13.6 SUMMARY

In Chapter 13 we began the consideration of parametric models, following the discussion of tabular models in Part III of the text. Parametric models are widely used in practice for modeling both frequency and severity of loss processes. Parametric models also are occasionally utilized for survival models, but less frequently in practice than the tabular models presented in Part III.

---

[10] See Section 3.2.3.

Two basic techniques were introduced in Chapter 13: the method of moments and percentile matching. The two techniques are similar in concept. Both are based on matching selected measures (i.e., low-order moments or percentiles) in the sample to the comparable measures in the fitted model. Unknown parameters in the fitted model are then estimated by solving simultaneous equations.

The method of moments was first illustrated with complete exact data for both continuous and discrete distributions. The technique was then extended to complete grouped data and to incomplete data due to censoring and/or truncation. We saw that grouping data into intervals requires an assumption regarding the distribution of sample data across each interval. We also saw that special handling was necessary for the binomial distribution, since its parameter n must be a positive integer.

With percentile matching a complication arises, since the sample distribution is discrete. The graph of the CDF for a discrete distribution is a "stair-step" pattern and thus all percentiles over each vertical "step" in the graph of the CDF are equal to each other. The smoothed empirical percentile technique was developed to produce a unique and distinct value for each percentile. These values, rather than unadjusted percentile values, are typically utilized in percentile matching.

We saw that percentile matching works well in the case of complete exact data drawn from a continuous distribution. However, we then discovered that significant complications arise in other situations, so that percentile matching is usually not applied in situations involving discrete distributions, grouped data, or incomplete data due to censoring or truncation.

13.7 EXERCISES

13.1 Introduction
13.2 Method of Moments – Complete Exact Data

13-1 Rework Example 13.1 using the lognormal distribution.

13-2 Explain why the method of moments estimation technique will fail if we attempt to rework Example 13.4 (Poisson) and Example 13.5 (negative binomial) using the binomial distribution.

13-3 The following is a sample of five claims:

$$\{4, 5, 21, 99, 421\}$$

Determine the 95th percentile of the Pareto distribution fit to the data by the method of moments.

13-4 Consider the following table of accident data from 30 insurance policies:

Number of Accidents	Number of Policies
0	8
1	12
2	7
3	2
4	1

We wish to fit a binomial distribution to this claim data. Find the method of moments estimates for the binomial parameters n and p, using the special handling technique described in Section 13.2.3.

13-5 A sample of size 10 is drawn from the two-point mixture of exponential distributions with PDF given by

$$f(x) = \frac{1}{2}\left[\frac{1}{\theta}\cdot e^{-x/\theta} + \frac{1}{\sigma}\cdot e^{-x/\sigma}\right],$$

for $0 < x < \infty$. Given the values $\sum x_i = 150$ and $\sum x_i^2 = 5000$, and the fact that $\theta > \sigma$, estimate θ using the method of moments to first and second moments.

13-6 Consider the following probability function for a population:

x	0	1	2	3
$p(x)$	.50	.30	.10	.10

The method of moments is used to estimate the population mean μ and variance σ^2 by the sample values $\bar{x}$ and s_n^2, respectively. Calculate the bias of the random variable S_n^2, given that $n = 4$. (The definition of bias is given in Section 2.3.1.)

13-7 Rework Example 13.3 using a modified method of moments procedure in which the second moment about the origin is matched between the sample distribution and the fitted model distribution. Calculate the absolute value of the difference in the estimate of the parameter θ when using this procedure rather than matching first moments as in Example 13.3.

13.3 Method of Moments – Extensions

13-8 Rework Example 13.7 assuming that the average sample value in each interval is located one-third of the way through each interval, rather than at the midpoint of each interval. (Note: This type of adjustment might be made by the modeler to reflect the monotonically decreasing volume of sample data across all the intervals. The value of one-third is arbitrary and is used here for illustrative purposes only.)

13-9 Consider the following summary statistics for a sample of 100 losses:

Interval	Number of Losses	Sum of Loss Amounts	Sum of Squares of Loss Amounts
0 – 2,000	39	38,065	52,170,078
2,000 – 4,000	22	63,816	194,241,387
4,000 – 8,000	17	96,447	572,753,313
8,000 – 15,000	12	137,595	1,628,670,023
15.000 – ∞	10	331,831	17,906,839,238
Total	100	667,754	20,354,674,039

Calculate the value of $E_{100}[X \wedge 15{,}000]$, the empirical limited expected value function.

13-10 A Pareto distribution is fit to the table of data in Exercise 13-9 using the method of moments. Determine the two Pareto parameter estimates.

13-11 Consider the following grouped claim data:

Claim Size	Number of Claims
0 – 25	30
25 – 50	32
50 – 100	20
100 – 200	8

Assume a uniform distribution of claim sizes within each interval. Determine the second moment about the origin in the claim size distribution.

13-12 For the data given in Exercise 13-11, determine $E_{90}\left[(X \wedge 150)^2\right]$, the second moment in the claim size distribution subject to a policy limit of 150.

13-13 Suppose losses are uniformly distributed on $(0, \omega)$, with $\omega > 150$, and there is a policy limit of 150. The following is a sample of claim payments:

$$\{14, 33, 72, 94, 120, 135, 150, 150\}$$

Estimate ω by matching the average sample payment to the expected payment per loss.

13-14 The expected payment per payment for the Pareto distribution is given by

$$E\left[X-d \mid X>d\right] = \frac{d+\theta}{\alpha-1}.$$

For a sample of six claims on which a positive amount is paid, each with a deductible of $d=10$, the total *loss* amounts for each claim are as follows:

$$\{13, 16, 22, 48, 106, 365\}$$

It is believed that these losses arise from a Pareto distribution with parameters $\alpha=3$ and unknown θ. Estimate θ by matching the average sample *claim* payment to the expected payment per payment in the fitted model.

13.4 Percentile Matching

13-15 Consider the following claim data for automobile policies:

$$\{200, 255, 295, 320, 360, 420, 440, 490, 500, 520, 1020\}$$

Calculate the smoothed empirical estimate of the 45th percentile of the underlying distribution.

13-16 For the claim data given in Exercise 13-15, use the binomial distribution to calculate the probability that the 45th percentile of the underlying distribution lies in the interval [320, 440).

13-17 For a sample of individual claims, the 20th percentile is equal to 18.25 and the 80th percentile is equal to 35.80. Estimate the parameters μ and σ of a lognormal distribution fit to the data by percentile matching. Then use the fitted lognormal distribution to estimate the probability that a new claim will be greater than 30.

13-18 Losses follow a Weibull distribution with parameters θ and τ. The following is a sample of 16 losses:

$$\{54, 70, 75, 81, 84, 88, 97, 105, 109,$$
$$114, 122, 125, 128, 139, 146, 153\}$$

The parameters are to be estimated by percentile matching, using the 20th and 70th smoothed empirical percentiles. Determine the estimate of θ.

13-19 Losses follow an exponential distribution with mean θ. A random sample of losses is distributed as follows:

Loss Range	Number of Losses
0 – 100	32
100 – 200	21
200 – 400	27
400 – 750	16
750 – 1000	2
1000 – 1500	2
Total	100

Estimate θ by matching at the 80th percentile level. (Do not use smoothed empirical percentiles.)

13-20 Consider the following sample of claim counts:

$$\{0, 0, 1, 2, 2\}$$

We wish to fit a binomial (n, p) model such that there is a match between the sample mean and the fitted model mean, and also a match between the $33\frac{1}{3}^{rd}$ smoothed empirical percentile in the sample and the $33\frac{1}{3}^{rd}$ percentile in the fitted model. Determine the smallest estimate of n that satisfies these requirements.

13.5 Some Advanced Illustrations

13-21 Losses on a certain warranty product in Year i follow a lognormal distribution with parameters μ_i and σ_i. The parameters μ_i vary in such a way that there is an annual inflation rate of 10% for losses, but the parameters σ_i have a constant value of σ for all years. The following is a sample of seven losses:

Year 1: $\{20, 40, 50\}$
Year 2: $\{30, 40, 90, 120\}$

Using sample losses inflated to Year 3, determine the method of moments estimate of μ_3.

13-22 We wish to model aggregate losses involving both frequency and severity, using a mixed discrete-continuous distribution with a point mass at zero in the event there are no claims and a continuous distribution to the right of zero in the event there is at least one claim. The point mass at zero has probability k. The continuous part of the distribution has PDF

$$f(x) = \frac{1-k}{\theta} \cdot e^{-x/\theta},$$

for $0 < x < \infty$. The following sample of ten aggregate losses is available:

$$\{0, 0, 0, 3, 6, 9, 17, 26, 31, 48\}$$

Obtain unbiased estimates for the parameters k and θ, using the method of moments to first moments.

13-23 A random sample of observations is taken from a shifted exponential distribution with PDF

$$f(x) = \frac{1}{\theta} \cdot e^{-(x-\delta)/\theta},$$

for $\delta < x < \infty$. The sample mean and median are 300 and 240, respectively. Estimate δ by matching these two sample quantities to the corresponding population statistics.

13-24 The random variables $X_1, X_2, \cdots, X_n$ are independent and identically exponentially distributed with mean θ. Determine $E[\overline{X}^2]$ as a function of n and θ.

CHAPTER FOURTEEN

PARAMETER ESTIMATION USING MAXIMUM LIKELIHOOD

14.1 INTRODUCTION

In this chapter we introduce *maximum likelihood estimation*, perhaps the most popular and significant method of estimating parameters in statistics. Maximum likelihood estimation is denoted by the abbreviation "MLE" by many authors. It is a more sophisticated method for estimating parameters than either the method of moments or percentile matching.

The basic concept underlying maximum likelihood estimation is relatively straightforward. As with the two methods described in Chapter 13, we have a population with an unknown distribution from which a sample of size n is drawn, and we wish to fit a model distribution with one or more parameters to this population. The estimated value of any unknown parameter in the model distribution is based on the sample observations. The maximum likelihood estimate for any unknown parameter is that value which maximizes the *likelihood*, as measured by the density function or the probability, of obtaining the sample outcomes actually obtained. Hence, the name is quite descriptive of the method.

Although maximum likelihood is a relatively sophisticated method, the basic technique can often be readily applied in many different situations. Also, the method has relatively straightforward generalizations to situations involving complete grouped data, and to situations involving incomplete data, including censoring and/or truncation.

Finally, maximum likelihood estimation possesses some quite attractive properties for producing parameter estimates with an optimal confidence interval around the point estimate obtained. The dispersion of parameter estimates around a point estimate was not covered in Chapter 13, but will be addressed in Chapter 14.

14.2 COMPLETE EXACT DATA – ONE PARAMETER

We consider first the use of maximum likelihood estimation for one parameter in a situation involving a sample with complete exact data. Extensions for complete grouped data and incomplete data involving censoring and/or truncation will be covered in Sections 14.3.1 through 14.3.3. Maximum likelihood with more than one parameter becomes considerably more complex than for one parameter; it will be addressed in Section 14.3.4.

We will first apply the technique for continuous distributions and then for discrete distributions. As we shall see, the basic technique is virtually identical with either type of distribution.

14.2.1 CONTINUOUS DISTRIBUTIONS

Consider a proposed fitted model distribution that has one unknown parameter θ. We will denote the density function of this model by $f(x\,|\,\theta)$. A sample of n independent observations is drawn from the population, with the sample values denoted by x_i, for $i=1,2,\cdots,n$. The reader will note that the notation x_i used in Chapter 14 for maximum likelihood estimation does not imply that the sample values are arranged in ascending order, as it did in Chapter 13 for percentile matching.

We then define the *likelihood function*, denoted by $L(\theta)$, as

$$L(\theta) = \prod_{i=1}^{n} f(x_i\,|\,\theta). \tag{14.1}$$

The likelihood function $L(\theta)$ can be interpreted as the joint density of obtaining the n values in the sample. Since the sample observations are independent, the joint density function can be factored into the product of n individual density functions, one for each sample value. The estimated value of the parameter is denoted by $\hat{\theta}$, and is that value of θ that will maximize $L(\theta)$. Remember that the x_i's are a set of known values, so that θ is the only unknown in Equation (14.1).

The parameter estimate $\hat{\theta}$ can be obtained using standard calculus techniques for finding the relative maximum (or minimum) of a given function. In the absence of unusual restrictions on θ, the maximum value for $L(\theta)$ generally does not occur at some boundary point and can be found using standard calculus techniques.

Therefore we might proceed to take the first derivative and set it equal to zero, obtaining $L'(\theta)=0$. This is often difficult to do, however, since it involves differentiating a product with n factors. A much simpler approach, which will make the differentiation more manageable, is to take the natural logarithm of both sides of Equation (14.1), since that will convert the product to a sum.

The rationale for this approach is based on the fact that a function taking on only positive values (as for a density function) and its logarithm are directly related, so that maximizing the logarithm of a function will maximize the function itself, and conversely.[1] The reader should remember that taking logs is an optional step to facilitate the calculus, but is not an inherent part of the method itself.

We define the *log likelihood function*, denoted $\ell(\theta)$, as

$$\ell(\theta) = \ln L(\theta) = \sum_{i=1}^{n} \ln f(x_i\,|\,\theta). \tag{14.2}$$

---

[1] The logarithms are generally negative, since all the factors in Equation (14.1) are probability densities which are generally less than one.

Finally, we maximize $\ell(\theta)$ using standard calculus techniques by setting

$$\ell'(\theta) = 0 \tag{14.3}$$

and solving for θ. Although the solution of Equation (14.3) may prove difficult in some cases, for most common statistical distributions an analytical solution is feasible.

EXAMPLE 14.1

Rework Example 13.3 using maximum likelihood estimation.

SOLUTION

In Example 13.3 we assume that time until death follows an exponential distribution, so we have

$$f(t \mid \theta) = \frac{1}{\theta} \cdot e^{-t/\theta}.$$

Then the likelihood function becomes

$$L(\theta) = \prod_{i=1}^{n} \frac{1}{\theta} \cdot e^{-t_i/\theta} = \left(\frac{1}{\theta}\right)^n \cdot \exp\left[-\frac{1}{\theta} \sum_{i=1}^{n} t_i\right].$$

We now take logs to obtain

$$\ell(\theta) = \ln L(\theta) = -n \cdot \ln \theta - \frac{1}{\theta} \cdot \sum_{i=1}^{n} t_i.$$

Finally, taking the derivative of the log likelihood function with respect to θ, setting it equal to zero, and solving for θ, we have

$$\ell'(\theta) = -\frac{n}{\theta} + \frac{1}{\theta^2} \cdot \sum_{i=1}^{n} t_i = 0,$$

so that

$$\hat{\theta} = \frac{1}{n} \cdot \sum_{i=1}^{n} t_i = \bar{t} = \frac{76}{10} = 7.60.$$

The reader should note that the maximum likelihood estimate is identical to the method of moments estimate. Upon reflection, this should not be a surprise. The exponential distribution has a mean equal to its parameter, so the method of moments estimate will be the sample mean by definition. Maximum likelihood estimation will not produce a parameter estimate that changes the estimate of the population mean from being equal to the sample mean. ❐

EXAMPLE 14.2

Using a sample of size n, find the general formula for the maximum likelihood estimator of the population variance σ^2 in a normal distribution with mean $\mu = 0$.

SOLUTION

Letting $\mu = 0$ simplifies the application of the method, but still provides a general formula. The density function for this normal distribution is given by

$$f(x \mid \mu = 0, \sigma) = \frac{1}{\sigma\sqrt{2\pi}} \cdot e^{-x^2/2\sigma^2},$$

so the likelihood function becomes

$$L(\sigma) = \left(\frac{1}{\sigma\sqrt{2\pi}}\right)^n \cdot \exp\left[-\frac{1}{2\sigma^2}\sum_{i=1}^{n} x_i^2\right].$$

We now take logs to obtain

$$\ell(\sigma) = -n \cdot \ln\sigma - n \cdot \ln\sqrt{2\pi} - \frac{1}{2\sigma^2}\sum_{i=1}^{n} x_i^2.$$

Then taking the derivative of the log likelihood function with respect to σ, setting it equal to zero, and solving for σ^2, we have

$$\ell'(\sigma) = -\frac{n}{\sigma} + \frac{1}{\sigma^3}\sum_{i=1}^{n} x_i^2 = 0,$$

so that

$$\hat{\sigma}^2 = \frac{1}{n}\sum_{i=1}^{n} x_i^2. \tag{14.4}$$

There are two interesting observations to make about the development of Equation (14.4). First, notice that the term $-n \cdot \ln\sqrt{2\pi}$ drops out when differentiating, since it does not involve the parameter σ. This happens fairly often in maximum likelihood estimation, where constants that multiply the density function are irrelevant. If the density function without the constant is maximized, then the density function with the constant will also be maximized. Thus, the factor $1/\sqrt{2\pi}$ in the original density function could have been dropped from the very beginning since it does not involve σ. Some authors prefer to write the likelihood function in this case as

$$L(\sigma) \propto \sigma^{-n} \cdot \exp\left[\frac{1}{2\sigma^2}\sum_{i=1}^{n} x_i^2\right].$$

The symbol $\propto$ is read as "is proportional to." The reader should verify that if the factor $1/\sqrt{2\pi}$ is dropped from the beginning the same answer is obtained.

Second, note that the maximum likelihood estimate can be interpreted as a sample variance (assuming $\overline{X} = 0$, its expected value when $\mu = 0$) with n in the denominator. This example sheds considerable light on the quandary facing authors of statistics texts. Those authors wishing to use unbiased estimators will define the sample variance with $n-1$ in the denominator. Those authors wishing to use maximum likelihood estimators will define the sample variance with n in the denominator. This has been a source of perennial confusion for students, but it is a good example of the old adage, "You can't have your cake and eat it too." An estimator for the population variance cannot be both unbiased and maximum likelihood at the same time. Of course, for large samples, whether we define the sample variance with n or $n-1$ in the denominator makes little difference. ❐

14.2.2 DISCRETE DISTRIBUTIONS

The maximum likelihood technique for discrete distributions is the same as for continuous distributions. There is nothing in the development and examples in Section 14.2.1 that is unique to continuous distributions. As long as there are no restrictions on the parameters, the technique is identical in both cases.

However, if there are restrictions on one or more parameters, then the technique may need to be modified. A good example of such a restriction was discussed in Section 13.2.3, where we discussed special handling for the binomial distribution that might be needed. The purpose of this special handling is to modify unrestricted parameter estimates to ensure that the parameter n is a positive integer. The same adjustment discussed in that section for the method of moments would also be necessary when using maximum likelihood estimation to estimate binomial distribution parameters.

EXAMPLE 14.3

Rework Example 13.4 using maximum likelihood estimation.

SOLUTION

In Example 13.4 we were estimating the parameter λ in a Poisson distribution, where

$$p(x \mid \lambda) = \frac{e^{-\lambda} \cdot \lambda^{x}}{x!},$$

for $x = 1, 2, 3, \cdots$. Then the likelihood function becomes

$$L(\lambda) = \prod_{i=1}^{n} \frac{e^{-\lambda} \cdot \lambda^{x_i}}{x_i\,!}$$

or

$$L(\lambda) \propto \prod_{i=1}^{n} e^{-\lambda} \cdot \lambda^{x_i} = e^{-n\lambda} \cdot \lambda^{(x_1 + x_2 + \cdots + x_n)},$$

since the $x_i!$ terms do not involve the parameter λ. We now take logs to obtain

$$\ell(\lambda) = \ln L(\lambda) = -n\lambda + \ln\lambda \cdot \sum_{i=1}^{n} x_i.$$

Finally, taking the derivative of the log likelihood function with respect to λ, setting it equal to zero, and solving for λ, we have

$$\ell'(\lambda) = -n + \frac{1}{\lambda}\sum_{i=1}^{n} x_i = 0$$

and

$$\hat{\lambda} = \frac{1}{n}\sum_{i=1}^{n} x_i = \bar{X} = 2.$$

As with the exponential distribution in Example 14.1, we see in this example that the maximum likelihood estimate is identical to the method of moments estimate. Again this should not be a surprise, for the same reasons cited in Example 14.1. ❐

EXAMPLE 14.4

Assume that sample data is obtained in which n_x lives are alive at age x and d_x of them die in the interval $(x, x+1]$. Find the maximum likelihood estimate of q_x, the conditional probability that a life aged x will die in the next year.

SOLUTION

The binomial distribution is the appropriate model for this situation, since we have a two-way outcome with independent trials and constant probability of "success" from trial to trial. The likelihood function can be written as

$$L(q_x \,|\, n_x, d_x) = \frac{n_x!}{d_x!(n_x - d_x)!}(q_x)^{d_x}(1-q_x)^{n_x - d_x}.$$

Note that the coefficient involving the factorial terms is a constant that will not affect the maximum likelihood estimate. Temporarily suppressing the subscripts x to simplify the notation, we have

$$L(q) \propto q^d (1-q)^{n-d}$$

so that

$$\ell(q) = \ln L(q) = d \cdot \ln q + (n-d) \cdot \ln(1-q)$$

and

$$\ell'(q) = \frac{d}{q} - \frac{n-d}{1-q} = 0.$$

Replacing the subscripts x and solving the last equation for q_x, we obtain the familiar estimator seen in Part III of the text.[2]

$$\hat{q}_x = \frac{d_x}{n_x}, \tag{14.5}$$

now seen to be a maximum likelihood estimator. ❐

14.3 EXTENSIONS

In Section 14.3 we consider four extensions of maximum likelihood estimation beyond the basic case of complete exact data covered above. Extensions for complete grouped data and incomplete data with censoring and/or truncation will be covered in Sections 14.3.1 through 14.3.3. Maximum likelihood with more than one parameter will be addressed in Section 14.3.4.

14.3.1 COMPLETE GROUPED DATA

Our first extension is for complete grouped data. The notational system will be identical to that used in Section 13.3.1 when considering the same extension for the method of moments. In particular, we partition the x-axis into k intervals that are defined by the $k+1$ values $c_0, c_1, c_2, \cdots, c_k$, where $c_0 < c_1 < c_2 < \cdots < c_k$. The number of observations in each interval is denoted by n_j, for $j=1,2,\cdots,k$, respectively, and $\sum_{j=1}^{k} n_j = n$. The reader is encouraged to review Figure 13.2 for an illustration of this notational system.

The main challenge we face with grouped data is immediately apparent. The likelihood function defined by Equation (14.1) is a product of density functions with one factor for each sample observation. However, with complete grouped data we do not have an exact value for each observation and thus cannot use density functions. The corresponding measure in a grouped data situation would be the probability mass within each of the k intervals. The probability mass in the jth interval is given by the difference between the cumulative distribution function at the end of the interval and at the beginning of the interval, which is $F(c_j) - F(c_{j-1})$, for $j=1,2,\cdots,k$.

We then apply one factor in each interval for each observation, so that our likelihood function will have n factors. Then the extended version of Equation (14.1) for complete grouped data becomes

$$L(\theta) = [F(c_1)-F(c_0)]^{n_1}[F(c_2)-F(c_1)]^{n_2}\cdots[F(c_k)-F(c_{k-1})]^{n_k}. \tag{14.6}$$

Each of the cumulative distribution functions in Equation (14.4) is a function of θ, so we could write $F(c_j \mid \theta)$ in place of $F(c_j)$, for $j=1,2,\cdots,k$, but we choose not to do that so as to avoid unnecessary clutter in the notation.

---

[2] See, for example, Equations (9.36), (10.15), and (11.14), among others.

The rest of the maximum likelihood procedure follows the same steps as for complete individual data discussed in Section 14.2. One complication that often arises with complete grouped data is that an analytical solution may be quite difficult, or even impossible, to reach, so it is not unusual to find we must use iteration techniques from numerical analysis in order to obtain numerical answers.[3]

EXAMPLE 14.5

We wish to fit a model of the form $f(x)=\lambda e^{-\lambda x}$, for $x>0$, to a sample of size $n=2$, where the observations have been grouped into two intervals. One sample observations falls in the interval $(0,2]$ and the other falls in the interval $(2,\infty]$. Find the maximum likelihood estimate for the parameter λ.

SOLUTION

The given distribution is exponential with parameter $\lambda=\frac{1}{\theta}$ from the version we have used earlier. (The reader should be comfortable in using the exponential distribution in either formulation, since both versions are frequently encountered in practice.) The cumulative distribution function for this version of the exponential distribution is given by $F(x)=1-e^{-\lambda x}$.

The likelihood function given by Equation (14.6) then becomes

$$\begin{aligned} L(\lambda) &= [F(2)-F(0)]\cdot[F(\infty)-F(2)] \\ &= (1-e^{-2\lambda})(e^{-2\lambda}) = e^{-2\lambda}-e^{-4\lambda}. \end{aligned}$$

In this example there is no advantage to using the log likelihood function $\ell(\theta)$. Remember that this is an optional step; in this example it is actually easier to just differentiate the likelihood function directly! We then have

$$L'(\lambda) = -2e^{-2\lambda}+4e^{-4\lambda} = 0,$$

so that

$$e^{-2\lambda} = .50,$$

which solves for

$$\hat{\lambda} = \frac{\ln .50}{-2} = .34657.$$

In this example an analytical solution is possible, but the reader can readily see that an example with more intervals and sample values would likely be of a form for which a numerical solution would be required. ❐

---

[3] Interestingly, maximum likelihood estimation with complete grouped data does not require the types of arbitrary assumptions needed for the method of moments (see, for example, Equation (13.4)).

14.3.2 INCOMPLETE DATA – CENSORING

Our second extension is for incomplete data due to censoring. We will again use the notational system developed in Chapter 13 where we considered this extension for the method of moments. As the reader will recall, the process of censoring creates an interval with grouped data in it.

To illustrate the technique for a familiar and common application, we consider an insurance policy with a policy limit (maximum benefit) equal to u. Below u we have n_u uncensored (exact) observations and above u we have n_c censored (grouped) observations. The total sample size is $n = n_u + n_c$.

The key concept in applying maximum likelihood estimation in this situation is that the likelihood function can be constructed using the density function for each of the n_u exact values below the censoring point and the survival distribution function (the complement of the CDF) for the n_c censored values above the censoring point. Thus, we can construct a composite likelihood function using techniques already developed.

The likelihood function under these conditions is then given by

$$\begin{aligned} L(\theta) &= \prod_{i=1}^{n_u} f(x_i \mid \theta) \cdot \prod_{i=1}^{n_c} \left[1 - F(u \mid \theta)\right] \\ &= \prod_{i=1}^{n_u} f(x_i \mid \theta) \cdot \left[1 - F(u \mid \theta)\right]^{n_c} \end{aligned} \tag{14.7}$$

The rest of the maximum likelihood procedure follows the same steps as for complete individual data discussed in Section 14.2. Again, it is not unusual to be required to use iteration techniques from numerical analysis to obtain numerical answers to problems involving maximum likelihood estimation with censored data.

EXAMPLE 14.6

We wish to use a distribution with density function given by

$$f(x) = \frac{\alpha}{x^{\alpha+1}},$$

for $x > 1$,[4] to model losses on a policy that is right-censored at $u = 5$. A sample of three observations is obtained. One loss is equal to 2, one loss is equal to 3, and the final loss exceeds the censoring point of 5. Estimate the value of α using maximum likelihood estimation.

---

[4] This is also referred to as a single-parameter Pareto distribution, with the Pareto parameter θ preestablished at $\theta = 1$. This distribution is summarized in Appendix A.1.1.

SOLUTION

The cumulative distribution function for this distribution is

$$F(x) = 1-\left(\frac{1}{x}\right)^{\alpha},$$

for $x > 1$. The likelihood function is

$$\begin{aligned} L(\alpha) &= f(2)\cdot f(3)\cdot[1-F(5)] \\ &= \frac{\alpha}{2^{\alpha+1}}\cdot\frac{\alpha}{3^{\alpha+1}}\cdot\left(\frac{1}{5}\right)^{\alpha} = \frac{\alpha^2}{6\cdot 30^{\alpha}}. \end{aligned}$$

We then have

$$\ell(\alpha) = \ln L(\alpha) \propto 2\cdot\ln\alpha - \alpha\cdot\ln 30,$$

so that

$$\ell'(\alpha) = \frac{2}{\alpha} - \ln 30 = 0,$$

which solves for

$$\hat{\alpha} = \frac{2}{\ln 30} = \frac{2}{3.4012} = .588.$$

In this example an analytical solution is possible, but the reader can readily see that a different example could easily be of a form for which a numerical solution would be required. ❐

14.3.3 INCOMPLETE DATA – TRUNCATION

Our third extension is for incomplete data due to truncation. To illustrate the technique for a common application, we consider an insurance policy with a deductible equal to d. We assume that exact values for losses above the deductible in the sample are known.

The key concept in applying maximum likelihood estimation in this situation is to recognize that the process of left truncating a distribution creates a conditional distribution. Thus, for each value in the sample, a factor will enter the likelihood function that is a conditional density function for the portion of the distribution above the point of truncation.

However, we have a complication in how the value of x is tabulated in constructing the likelihood function. If the amount of the deductible is not subtracted in tabulating the sample data, then x can be considered to be the amount of the *loss*. Under this definition, for a sample of size n the likelihood function is given by

$$L(\theta) = \frac{\prod_{i=1}^{n} f(x_i\,|\,\theta)}{\left[1-F(d\,|\,\theta)\right]^n}, \tag{14.8}$$

where $x_i > d$, for $i = 1, 2, \cdots, n$.

From conditional probability theory, one factor is needed in the denominator for each factor in the numerator so that the likelihood function will be the product of n conditional density functions.

On the other hand, if the amount of the deductible is subtracted in tabulating the sample data, then x can be considered to be the amount of the *claim payment*. Under this definition, for a sample of size n the likelihood function is given by

$$L(\theta) = \frac{\prod_{i=1}^{n} f(x_i+d \mid \theta)}{\left[1-F(d \mid \theta)\right]^n}, \tag{14.9}$$

where $x_i > 0$, for $i = 1, 2, \cdots, n$.

It is necessary to add d to the amount of the claim payment in order to determine the amount of the loss that led to the claim. Remember that we are estimating parameters in the original loss distribution, so it is necessary to use values of x that represent the original losses before any adjustments are made to determine the amount actually paid.

The rest of the maximum likelihood procedure follows the same steps as for complete individual data discussed in Section 14.2. Again, it is not unusual to be required to use iteration techniques from numerical analysis to obtain numerical answers to problems involving maximum likelihood estimation with truncated data.

EXAMPLE 14.7

Table 14.1 presents claim frequencies during a year for 100 insurance policies on which at least one claim occurred during the year.

Table 14.1

Claim Frequency Data	
Number of Claims	**Number of Policies**
1	54
2	28
3	12
4	6

We wish to fit this data with a Poisson distribution. Use the technique developed in this section to estimate the parameter λ of the Poisson distribution.

SOLUTION

In this example we are estimating the parameter of a discrete distribution rather than a continuous one. Since policies with no claims during the year are excluded, the sample data has been truncated and we will use a truncated Poisson distribution in our parameter estimation procedure.

The probability function for the Poisson distribution is

$$p(x) = \frac{e^{-\lambda} \cdot \lambda^x}{x!},$$

for $x = 0,1,2,3,\cdots$, and the probability of at least one claim during the year is equal to $1-p(0) = 1-e^{-\lambda}$. Since x is the number of claims with no adjustment, we apply Equation (14.8) rather than Equation (14.9) to obtain the likelihood function

$$L(\lambda) = \frac{\left[\frac{e^{-\lambda}\lambda^1}{1!}\right]^{54}\left[\frac{e^{-\lambda}\lambda^2}{2!}\right]^{28}\left[\frac{e^{-\lambda}\lambda^3}{3!}\right]^{12}\left[\frac{e^{-\lambda}\lambda^4}{4!}\right]^{6}}{[1-e^{-\lambda}]^{100}}$$

$$\propto \frac{e^{-100\lambda}\lambda^{54+56+36+24}}{[1-e^{-\lambda}]^{100}} = \frac{e^{-100\lambda}\lambda^{170}}{[1-e^{-\lambda}]^{100}},$$

since the factorial terms are constants and will not affect the maximization procedure.

We then have

$$\ell(\lambda) = -100\lambda + 170\ln\lambda - 100\ln(1-e^{-\lambda}),$$

so that

$$\ell'(\lambda) = -100 + \frac{170}{\lambda} - \frac{100e^{-\lambda}}{1-e^{-\lambda}} = -100 + \frac{170}{\lambda} - \frac{100}{e^{\lambda}-1} = 0.$$

Multiplying by the denominators leads to the equation

$$g(\lambda) = -100\lambda(e^{\lambda}-1) + 170(e^{\lambda}-1) - 100\lambda = 0$$

or

$$g(\lambda) = e^{\lambda}(170-100\lambda) - 170 = 0.$$

We define $g(\lambda)$ as the function of λ that must equal 0. We have an equation that does not have an analytical solution and must be solved numerically, which, as we have seen above, is quite common in extensions of maximum likelihood estimation. There are several well-known iteration techniques in numerical analysis for solving equations of this type. Several of these are summarized in Appendix F.

Here we will just use rudimentary successive approximation on a hand calculator. The results are summarized in Table 14.2 on the following page.

TABLE 14.2

Successive Approximations for λ	
λ	$g(\lambda)$
1	20.28
1.1	10.25
1.2	−3.99
1.17	.77
1.18	−.77
1.175	.00

Our maximum likelihood estimate, accurate to three decimal places, is $\hat{\lambda} = 1.175$. It is important to emphasize that this parameter estimate is for the original non-truncated Poisson distribution. To further underscore this point, note that the sample mean of the truncated sample data is $\bar{X} = \frac{170}{100} = 1.70$ which is greater than the estimated mean for the non-truncated Poisson distribution. ❒

14.3.4 MULTIPLE PARAMETERS

Thus far in Chapter 8 we have considered maximum likelihood estimation only for the situation in which we have one unknown parameter to estimate. However, we frequently have two or even more unknown parameters to estimate. Many of the most common distributions used in practice have two parameters and some of the more general and complex distributions have three or even four parameters. Thus it is important to define the maximum likelihood technique with multiple parameters.

Consider a proposed fitted model distribution that has k unknown parameters $\theta_1, \theta_2, \cdots, \theta_k$. The technique of constructing the likelihood function is the same as already described above; it will be a function involving these k unknown parameters and is written as $L(\theta_1, \theta_2, \cdots, \theta_k)$. The corresponding log likelihood function is written as $\ell(\theta_1, \theta_2, \cdots, \theta_k)$. These symbols are often abbreviated to just L and ℓ for convenience when there is no possibility for ambiguity.

The maximum likelihood estimation procedure then takes k partial derivatives of the log likelihood function, once with respect to each parameter, sets all these equations equal to zero, and solves the k equations for the k unknown parameters. Symbolically we write

$$\begin{aligned} \frac{\partial \ell}{\partial \theta_1} &= 0, \\ \frac{\partial \ell}{\partial \theta_2} &= 0, \\ &\vdots \\ \frac{\partial \ell}{\partial \theta_k} &= 0. \end{aligned} \tag{14.10}$$

Although this procedure appears quite straightforward and logical, solving these k equations in k unknowns may be quite difficult, or even impossible, using standard algebraic approaches and a pocket calculator. The equations are typically nonlinear, so that ad hoc methods will be required. Also, the form of some, or all, of these partial derivatives may be rather complex, depending on the model distribution being fitted. In many cases, computer software with numerical algorithms to solve nonlinear systems of equations may be the only practical means of obtaining numerical answers.

The reader will recall that we faced this same challenge in Chapter 13 when using the method of moments or percentile matching for multiple parameters. However, the form of the equations that need to be solved when using those two methods usually is much better suited for standard algebraic manipulation by hand than are the equations that result when using maximum likelihood estimation.

EXAMPLE 14.8

We wish to fit the two parameters k and n of a distribution whose density function is given by $f(t) = kt^n \cdot e^{-kt^{n+1}/(n+1)}$ to the 10 survival times given in Example 13.3, using maximum likelihood estimation. Develop the formulas from which a numerical answer can be obtained.

SOLUTION

The likelihood and log likelihood functions are

$$L(k,n) = \prod_{i=1}^{10} f(t_i) = \prod_{i=1}^{10} kt^n \cdot e^{-kt^{n+1}/(n+1)}$$

and

$$\ell(k,n) = \ln L(k,n) = 10 \ln k + n\sum_{i=1}^{10} \ln t_i - \frac{k}{n+1}\sum_{i=1}^{10} t_i^{n+1}.$$

We now take the two partial derivatives of the log likelihood, with respect to each to the two parameters, and set each to zero, obtaining

$$\frac{\partial \ell(k,n)}{\partial n} = \sum_{i=1}^{10} \ln t_i - \frac{k}{(n+1)^2}\left[(n+1)\sum_{i=1}^{10}(\ln t_i)t_i^{n+1} - \sum_{i=1}^{10} t_i^{n+1}\right] = 0$$

and

$$\frac{\partial \ell(k,n)}{\partial k} = \frac{10}{k} - \frac{1}{n+1}\sum_{i=1}^{10} t_i^{n+1} = 0.$$

From the second equation we obtain

$$k = \frac{10(n+1)}{\sum_{i=1}^{10} t_i^{n+1}}.$$

This expression for k is then substituted into the first equation which is then solved numerically for $\hat{n}$. Finally, this value of $\hat{n}$ is substituted back into the formula for k to solve for $\hat{k}$.

❐

The fitted model is actually a Weibull distribution that has been parameterized in a different form from that given in Section 6.2.3. The Weibull distribution is often parameterized in this form when it is used in a survival analysis context rather than in a loss models context. When the Weibull distribution is parameterized in this manner, the hazard rate (force of mortality) is the nth degree polynomial $\lambda(t) = kt^n$. Thus in the Weibull distribution the hazard rate increases by age as an nth degree polynomial, whereas in the Gompertz distribution it increases as an exponential function.

14.4 VARIANCES OF PARAMETER ESTIMATORS

In all of Chapter 13, and so far in Chapter 14, we have developed parameter estimates by a variety of techniques, and in all cases we have obtained one specific numerical estimate for each parameter being estimated.

Consider now that if we were to obtain a second sample from the same population, and use it to obtain the parameter estimates rather than using the original sample, we almost certainly will obtain a different answer. Continuing this process using a different sample each time will lead to a collection of different parameter estimates. Thus, a parameter estimator is itself a random variable and will have its own distribution.

In the language of statistics, the parameter estimates we have obtained, using any of the techniques discussed in Chapters 13 and 14, represent *point estimates* for the true (unknown) value of the parameter. The fact that we do not always obtain the same estimate in repeated sampling indicates that the collection of estimates also has *dispersion*.

Then the question arises that if we have a point estimate, and a measure of dispersion, can we obtain a confidence interval? These questions will be explored in Sections 14.4 and 14.5.

We will state a number of key results in the remainder of this chapter without derivation or proof, as such derivation and proof would involve an extensive amount of space and graduate-level knowledge of mathematical statistics. Appendix G contains a mathematical development of some of the theory underlying the remainder of this chapter and is provided for the benefit of mathematically-inclined readers.

14.4.1 ONE PARAMETER

We consider first the situation in which we use maximum likelihood estimation for one unknown parameter. As background for the discussion to come, the reader is encouraged to review the properties of parameter estimators covered in Section 2.3. In particular, there are three primary properties of estimators that are addressed in mathematical statistics. These are the properties of *bias*, *consistency*, and *efficiency*.

Maximum likelihood estimators may have *bias*. For example, as we saw in Example 14.2, the maximum likelihood estimator for σ^2 in the normal distribution is S_n^2, the sample variance defined with n in the denominator. However, as we know from basic statistics, the unbiased estimator for σ^2 is S_{n-1}^2, the sample variance defined with $n-1$ in the denominator. This initially sounds like a possible weakness of maximum likelihood estimation, but it is not. As we shall see, maximum likelihood estimation has other desirable properties that more than offset any problems arising from bias that may exist in the estimation process.

Furthermore, as the sample size $n \to \infty$, it can be shown that maximum likelihood estimators are asymptotically unbiased. In symbols, if $\hat{\theta}_n$ denotes the maximum likelihood estimator of the parameter θ with a sample of size n, then

$$\lim_{n\to\infty} E\left[\hat{\theta}_n\right] = \theta. \qquad (2.13/14.11)$$

Again, using the sample variance illustration above, as n becomes larger, the sample variance defined with either n or $n-1$ in the denominator is essentially the same value.

Maximum likelihood estimators can be shown to have *consistency*. In symbols, this means that, for any $\varepsilon > 0$,

$$\lim_{n\to\infty} \Pr\left(|\hat{\theta}_n - \theta| > \varepsilon\right) = 0. \qquad (2.16/14.12)$$

Consistency is not a particularly stringent property, since other widely- used parameter estimation techniques also have this property. However, if maximum likelihood estimation did *not* have this property, it would be a major weakness of the method.

Perhaps the most significant advantage of maximum likelihood estimations lies with the third property of *efficiency*. This property deals with the dispersion of parameter estimates around the true (unknown) value of the parameter. A parameter estimation technique with maximum efficiency is one that has *minimum mean square error* (MSE). The reader will recall from Chapter 2 that

$$MSE(\hat{\theta}) = Var(\hat{\theta}) + \left(Bias(\hat{\theta})\right)^2. \qquad (2.19/14.13)$$

Note that an unbiased parameter estimator will therefore have the property that $MSE(\hat{\theta}) = Var(\hat{\theta})$.

Parameter estimators that are efficient have low mean square error, and thus the dispersion of parameter estimates around the true value of the parameter is relatively low. As we shall see later in this section, maximum likelihood estimators are inherently quite efficient.

There is an important theorem in mathematical statistics that provides the asymptotic distribution of a maximum likelihood estimator as the sample size $n \to \infty$. We will describe this theorem rather informally in the upcoming discussion. A more precise mathematical formulation of the theorem and a reference for its proof, are provided in Appendix G.

In essence, the theorem states that (in all but quite unusual situations) as $n \to \infty$ the distribution of a maximum likelihood estimator $\hat{\theta}_n$ approaches a normal distribution with mean equal to θ and variance equal to $I^{-1}(\theta)$, where $I^{-1}(\theta)$ can be written in any of the four ways

$$I^{-1}(\theta) = \frac{1}{n \cdot E\left[\left(\frac{d}{d\theta} \ln f(X;\theta)\right)^2\right]}, \tag{14.14a}$$

$$I^{-1}(\theta) = \frac{-1}{n \cdot E\left[\frac{d^2}{d\theta^2} \ln f(X;\theta)\right]}, \tag{14.14b}$$

$$I^{-1}(\theta) = \frac{1}{E\left[\left(\frac{d}{d\theta} \ell(X;\theta)\right)^2\right]}, \tag{14.14c}$$

or

$$I^{-1}(\theta) = \frac{-1}{E\left[\frac{d^2}{d\theta^2} \ell(X;\theta)\right]}, \tag{14.14d}$$

where $\ell(X;\theta)$ is the log likelihood function and the expectation is taken with respect to the random variable X. The theorem establishes the results that a maximum likelihood estimator is asymptotically unbiased and consistent. The equivalence of the four formulas for $I^{-1}(\theta)$ is demonstrated in Appendix G.

The notation $I^{-1}(\theta)$ may seem a bit unusual at first. The motivation for this notation will become clearer in Section 14.4.2, where we discuss the generalization of the theorem for multiple parameters. The function $I(\theta)$, which denotes the reciprocal in each of Equations (14.14a) through (14.14d), is called the *information*, or *Fisher's information.*

The four expressions for $I^{-1}(\theta)$ all produce the same result if applied consistently, as we will see in Example 14.9. Note carefully the similarities and differences in these formulas. Equations (14.14a) and (14.14b) are expressed in terms of the log of the density function, whereas Equations (14.14c) and (14.14d) are expressed in terms of the log likelihood function. Equations (14.14a) and (14.14c) involve the square of a first derivative, whereas Equations (14.14b) and (14.14d) involve a second derivative and also have a negative sign.

One complication that can arise in applying any of the four formulas is that, in some cases, the expectations are quite difficult to obtain. In these situations an approximate technique that is sometimes used is to simply calculate the values from the sample directly rather than to take their expectation. If the information is obtained in this manner, it is called *observed information*. This technique will be illustrated in the Equation (14.14a) part of Example 14.9.

The above development is quite important and useful, but we have not yet directly discussed the efficiency of a maximum likelihood estimator. An analysis of that property comes from another key result in mathematical statistics, called the Cramer-Rao inequality.

Again, speaking in descriptive terms rather than precise mathematical terms, the Cramer-Rao inequality essentially states that the expressions in Equation (14.14) for $I^{-1}(\theta)$ are a lower bound on the variance of a parameter estimator in general. The implication is that maximum likelihood estimation achieves the Cramer-Rao lower bound so that the inequality becomes an equality. Thus, the variance of a parameter estimator obtained by any other parameter estimation method can be no smaller than it is for maximum likelihood, and is often larger. Thus, maximum likelihood estimates are inherently quite efficient.

This property is one of the fundamental reasons why maximum likelihood estimation methods are so widely used in statistics. Many statisticians would maintain that the gain in efficiency by using maximum likelihood estimators more than offsets any disadvantage arising from bias (if any exists).

EXAMPLE 14.9

We wish to fit an exponential distribution of the form $f(x;\lambda) = \lambda e^{-\lambda x}$ to the following ten sample values:

$$\{.001, .003, .053, .062, .127, .131, .377, .382, .462, .481\}$$

Using maximum likelihood estimation, find the point estimate of the parameter λ, an expression for the variance of the parameter estimator, and the estimated value of this variance. Verify that all four versions of Equation (14.14) produce the same variance expression.

SOLUTION

We first obtain the following values and expressions which will be used in the solution:

$$\sum_{i=1}^{10} x_i = 2.079 \qquad \sum_{i=1}^{10} x_i^2 = .773$$

$$\ln f(x;\lambda) = \ln\lambda - \lambda x$$

$$\frac{d}{d\lambda}\ln f(x;\lambda) = \frac{1}{\lambda} - x \qquad \frac{d^2}{d\lambda^2}\ln f(x;\lambda) = -\frac{1}{\lambda^2}$$

$$L(\lambda) = \lambda^{10} e^{-2.079\lambda} \qquad \ell(\lambda) = 10\ln\lambda - 2.079\lambda$$

$$\frac{d}{d\lambda}\ell(\lambda) = \frac{10}{\lambda} - 2.079 \qquad \frac{d^2}{d\lambda^2}\ell(\lambda) = -\frac{10}{\lambda^2}$$

To determine the point estimate we proceed as usual. We have

$$\frac{d}{d\lambda}\ell(\lambda) = \frac{10}{\lambda} - 2.079 = 0,$$

which solves for

$$\begin{aligned}\hat{\lambda} &= \frac{10}{2.079} \\ &= 4.81.\end{aligned}$$

Note that we could also have obtained this answer by using the result observed in Example 14.1, namely that the maximum likelihood estimate and the method of moments estimate are the same. Both estimates equal the reciprocal of the sample mean, which gives us

$$\begin{aligned}\hat{\lambda} = \frac{1}{\bar{X}} &= \frac{1}{2.079/10} \\ &= 4.81.\end{aligned}$$

For the variance of the estimator, using Equation (14.14a), we have

$$\begin{aligned}Var(\hat{\lambda}) &= I^{-1}(\lambda) \\ &= \frac{1}{n \cdot E\left[\left(\frac{d}{d\lambda}\ln f(X;\lambda)\right)^2\right]} \\ &= \frac{1}{10E\left[\left(\frac{1}{\lambda} - X\right)^2\right]} \\ &= \frac{1}{10E\left[\frac{1}{\lambda^2} - \frac{2X}{\lambda} + X^2\right]} \\ &= \frac{1}{10\left[\frac{1}{\lambda^2} - \frac{2}{\lambda^2} + \frac{2}{\lambda^2}\right]} \\ &= \frac{\lambda^2}{10}.\end{aligned}$$

Note that the expectations are being taken with respect to the random variable X, and λ is a constant with respect to these expectations. Recall also that $E[X^2] = \frac{2}{\lambda^2}$ for this exponential distribution. Furthermore, as first noted in Footnote 6 in Section 2.3, we are using $\hat{\lambda}$ for both the parameter estimator and a realized value of it. We can then find a numerical estimate of $Var(\hat{\lambda})$ by substituting $\hat{\lambda} = 4.81$ for the unknown value of λ, obtaining

$$Est.Var(\hat{\lambda}) = \frac{(4.81)^2}{10} = 2.314.$$

Although a direct application of Equation (14.14) works quite well in this simple example, since regular expectations can readily be taken, the example does present us an opportunity to demonstrate the technique of "observed information." In this approximate technique, sample observations are used directly rather than taking expectations. For the first moment about the origin, the same answer is obtained either way (see discussion at the end of Example 14.1). However, a different answer will be obtained for the second moment about the origin, and it is instructive to compare these two quantities. The second moment about the origin based on true expectations, as used above, is $\frac{2}{\lambda^2}$, which we can then estimate numerically by using $\hat{\lambda}=4.81$ in place of λ, obtaining $\frac{2}{(4.81)^2}=.0864$. If the observed information technique had been applied, and the second moment of the sample used instead, this quantity would have been $\frac{.773}{10}=.0773$.

When we use Equation (14.14b), we have

$$\begin{aligned} Var(\hat{\lambda}) &= I^{-1}(\lambda) \\ &= \frac{-1}{n \cdot E\left[\frac{d^2}{d\lambda^2} \ln f(X;\lambda)\right]} \\ &= \frac{-1}{10\left(-\frac{1}{\lambda^2}\right)} = \frac{\lambda^2}{10}, \end{aligned}$$

as expected. Note that in this case we are taking the expectation of the constant $-\frac{1}{\lambda^2}$ only, since all terms involving X have dropped out in obtaining the second derivative. Equation (14.14b) is generally superior to Equation (14.14a) in most applications. Not only does a second differentiation sometimes simplify results, as it did in this case, but also Equation (14.14a) involves squaring a multi-term expression whereas Equation (14.14b) does not. Again we can substitute $\hat{\lambda}=4.81$ for λ to obtain $Est.Var(\hat{\lambda})=2.314$.

The derivation using Equation (14.14c) is similar to that using Equation (14.14a), and is left as Exercise 14-13(a).

The derivation using Equation (14.14d) is similar to that using Equation (14.14b), and is left as Exercise 14-13(b). Again, the reader will discover that using the formula involving a second derivative entails less work than using the formula involving the square of a first derivative.

In summary, we might consider Equation (14.14b) to be the "standard" formula when working problems given only the density function. Equation (14.14d) provides an attractive alternative when the log likelihood function is already available. ❐

14.4.2 MULTIPLE PARAMETERS

In this section we extend the theory presented in the prior section to parameter estimates for more than one parameter. We present results for two parameters, which covers many of the distributions used in this text. The generalization to three or more parameters should be obvious once we cover the two-parameter case.

The underlying theory in this section follows quite closely the development in the prior section for one variable. Consider a distribution that has two unknown parameters, θ_1 and θ_2, being estimated by maximum likelihood. There is a generalization of the major theorem presented in the prior section which shows that the asymptotic distribution of the two maximum likelihood estimators approaches a bivariate normal distribution as $n \to \infty$.[5] The point estimates for the two parameters are the two means of this bivariate normal distribution. The procedure by which these point estimates are obtained was covered in Section 14.3.4.

The remaining issue is the determination of the variances of the estimators for the two parameters, which we denote by $Var(\hat{\theta}_1)$ and $Var(\hat{\theta}_2)$. There also is a covariance term in the bivariate normal distribution which we denote by $Cov(\hat{\theta}_1, \hat{\theta}_2)$.

The determination of the two variances and the covariance requires the use of matrix algebra. In the two-parameter case, we make use of two-by-two matrices; there are two matrices required to determine these quantities.

The first is the *information matrix* $\mathbf{I}(\boldsymbol{\theta})$, which is defined analogously to the information function $I(\theta)$ in the one parameter case.[6] It is defined as

$$\mathbf{I}(\boldsymbol{\theta}) = -\begin{pmatrix} E\left[\dfrac{\partial^2}{\partial\theta_1^2}\ell(X;\theta_1,\theta_2)\right] & E\left[\dfrac{\partial^2}{\partial\theta_1\theta_2}\ell(X;\theta_1,\theta_2)\right] \\ E\left[\dfrac{\partial^2}{\partial\theta_1\theta_2}\ell(X;\theta_1,\theta_2)\right] & E\dfrac{\partial^2}{\partial\theta_2^2}\ell(X;\theta_1,\theta_2) \end{pmatrix}, \tag{14.15}$$

which is a matrix of expected values of second derivatives of the log likelihood function $\ell(X;\theta_1,\theta_2)$, where the expectation is taken with respect to the random variable X. The similarity of Equation (14.15) with Equation (14.14d) in the one parameter case should be apparent.

The second is the *variance-covariance matrix*, containing the desired two variances and one covariance (appearing twice in the matrix), and is given by

$$\mathbf{I}^{-1}(\boldsymbol{\theta}) = \begin{vmatrix} Var(\hat{\theta}_1) & Cov(\hat{\theta}_1,\hat{\theta}_2) \\ Cov(\hat{\theta}_1,\hat{\theta}_2) & Var(\hat{\theta}_2) \end{vmatrix}. \tag{14.16}$$

The rationale for the notation $I^{-1}(\theta)$ for the variance of the parameter estimator in the single-parameter case, used in the prior section, should now be clear.

The information matrix and the variance-covariance matrix are inverses of each other. There are a number of different matrix algebra techniques for inverting matrices. Appendix H presents an efficient algorithm for inverting a 2×2 matrix by hand.

---

[5] The bivariate normal distribution is reviewed in Appendix A.2.

[6] $\mathbf{I}(\boldsymbol{\theta})$ is sometimes referred to as the *Fisher information matrix*. Notationally, we adopt the convention, first introduced in Chapter 11, of denoting vectors and matrices in bold type.

EXAMPLE 14.10

A sample of ten observations comes from a two-parameter distribution, with density function $f(x;\theta_1,\theta_2)$, so the log likelihood function is $\ell=\ell(x;\theta_1,\theta_2)=\sum_{i=1}^{10}\ln f(x_i;\theta_1,\theta_2)$. The structure of the density function and the values of the ten observations are such that the log likelihood function becomes

$$\ell(\theta_1,\theta_2) = -2.5\theta_1^2 - 3\theta_1\theta_2 - \theta_2^2 + 5\theta_1 + 2\theta_2 + k,$$

where k is a constant, when the observed values of x_i are inserted. Determine the estimated variance-covariance matrix.

SOLUTION

We have the following set of first and second partial derivatives of the log likelihood function with data values inserted:

$$\frac{\partial \ell}{\partial \theta_1} = -5\theta_1 - 3\theta_2 + 5 \qquad \frac{\partial^2 \ell}{\partial \theta_1^2} = -5$$

$$\frac{\partial \ell}{\partial \theta_2} = -3\theta_1 - 2\theta_2 + 2 \qquad \frac{\partial^2 \ell}{\partial \theta_2^2} = -2$$

$$\frac{\partial^2 \ell}{\partial \theta_1 \partial \theta_2} = -3$$

Applying Equation (14.15), with data values inserted so that no expectations need be taken, the information matrix is

$$\mathbf{I}(\boldsymbol{\theta}) = -\begin{vmatrix} -5 & -3 \\ -3 & -2 \end{vmatrix} = \begin{vmatrix} 5 & 3 \\ 3 & 2 \end{vmatrix}.$$

The variance-covariance matrix is the inverse of the information matrix. Using the algorithm provided in Appendix H, we have

$$\mathbf{I}^{-1}(\boldsymbol{\theta}) = \frac{\begin{vmatrix} 2 & -3 \\ -3 & 5 \end{vmatrix}}{\det\begin{vmatrix} 5 & 3 \\ 3 & 2 \end{vmatrix}} = \begin{vmatrix} 2 & -3 \\ -3 & 5 \end{vmatrix}.$$ ❒

14.4.3 CONFIDENCE INTERVALS

We have now characterized maximum likelihood estimates as point estimates, and we have determined the variance of the process by which they were obtained. The final step in this chain of results is the construction of confidence intervals.

The fact that the distribution of parameter estimators is asymptotically normal as $n \to \infty$ raises the obvious question of whether a typical normal distribution confidence interval is justifiable. Fortunately, the answer is yes, although we will not prove this result mathematically. The mathematically-inclined reader can refer to any standard textbook in mathematical statistics for such a proof.[7]

EXAMPLE 14.11

Construct the two-tailed 95% confidence interval for the maximum likelihood estimation presented in Example 14.9.

SOLUTION

The maximum likelihood point estimate obtained was $\hat{\lambda} = 4.81$, and the estimated variance of the estimator was $Est.Var(\hat{\lambda}) = 2.314$. Then the 95% normal distribution confidence interval is

$$4.81 \pm 1.96\sqrt{2.314} = 4.81 \pm 2.98 = (1.83, 7.99). \qquad \square$$

EXAMPLE 14.12

Use the results of Example 14.10 to find the two-tailed 90% confidence interval for the parameter θ_1, using the marginal normal distribution for this parameter.

SOLUTION

Example 14.10 did not provide the point estimates for either θ_1 or θ_2, so we will first have to obtain them. Setting the two first derivatives in the solution of Example 14.10 equal to zero gives the equations

$$\frac{\partial \ell}{\partial \theta_1} = -5\theta_1 - 3\theta_2 + 5 = 0$$

and

$$\frac{\partial \ell}{\partial \theta_2} = -3\theta_1 - 2\theta_2 + 2 = 0.$$

We now have two linear equations in two unknowns, which solve for the maximum likelihood estimates $\hat{\theta}_1 = 4$ and $\hat{\theta}_2 = -5$. From the variance-covariance matrix in Example 14.10 we have $Est.Var(\hat{\theta}_1) = 2$. Therefore the 90% normal distribution confidence interval is

$$4 \pm 1.645\sqrt{2} = 4 \pm 2.33 = (1.67, 6.33). \qquad \square$$

[7] See, for example, Hogg and Tanis [18].

14.5 VARIANCES OF FUNCTIONS OF PARAMETER ESTIMATORS

In Section 14.4 we considered variances of the parameter estimators themselves. In some cases, it is important to consider the variance of some function of the parameter estimators, and that is the subject of this section. The technique demonstrated in this section is called the *delta method*. It will be demonstrated first for one parameter and then extended to multiple parameters.

14.5.1 ONE PARAMETER

Assume that we have a distribution with one parameter θ, to be estimated by maximum likelihood, and we have obtained $\hat{\theta}$ as its maximum likelihood estimate. We now have some function of θ, denoted by $g(\theta)$, that we wish to analyze. The point estimate for this function is simply $g(\hat{\theta})$, but what is the variance of this function of the parameter estimator?[8]

The delta method provides a simple approximation for this variance as

$$Var\left[g(\hat{\theta})\right] \approx [g'(\theta)]^2 \cdot Var(\hat{\theta}). \tag{14.17}$$

This formula will often be straightforward to apply in practice. It says in words that the variance of the function g can be approximated by taking the first derivative of g, squaring it, and multiplying the result by the variance of the parameter estimator itself given by Equation (14.14).

Equation (14.17) can be derived by using a Taylor series expansion for $g(\hat{\theta})$ around $g(\theta)$, carried to first derivatives only, producing

$$g(\hat{\theta}) \approx g(\theta)+(\hat{\theta}-\theta)\cdot g'(\theta).$$

We now take the variance of both sides, remembering that only terms involving $\hat{\theta}$ have dispersion since θ is constant (even if unknown). Also, the term $g'(\theta)$ is a multiplicative constant with respect to the variance and is therefore squared. With these observations, Equation (14.17) is immediately obtained.

EXAMPLE 14.13

The random variable X follows an exponential distribution with parameter θ. A maximum likelihood estimate $\hat{\theta}$ is obtained based on a large sample of data. The probability that X is greater than k is obtained from the estimator $e^{-k/\theta}$. Determine an approximate expression for the variance of the estimator for the probability that X is greater than k.

---

[8] As noted several places earlier, we use the same notation, $g(\hat{\theta})$, for both the estimator random variable and a realized value (point estimate) of it.

SOLUTION

The density function and cumulative distribution function of this exponential distribution are given by

$$f(x) = \frac{1}{\theta} \cdot e^{-x/\theta}$$

and

$$F(x) = 1 - e^{-x/\theta},$$

respectively. The given estimator follows as

$$\Pr(X > k) = 1 - F(k) = e^{-k/\theta}.$$

Then we have

$$g(\theta) = e^{-k/\theta}$$

and

$$g'(\theta) = \frac{k}{\theta^2} \cdot e^{-k/\theta}.$$

Substituting into Equation (14.17), we have

$$\begin{aligned} Var\left[g(\hat{\theta})\right] &\approx [g'(\theta)]^2 \cdot Var(\hat{\theta}) \\ &= \frac{k^2}{\theta^4} \cdot e^{-2k/\theta} \cdot Var(\hat{\theta}). \end{aligned}$$

The value of $Var(\hat{\theta})$, found by applying Equation (14.14), is $\frac{\theta^2}{n}$ (see Exercise 14-19). Then we finally have

$$\begin{aligned} Var[g(\hat{\theta})] &\approx \frac{k^2}{\theta^4} \cdot e^{-2k/\theta} \cdot \frac{\theta^2}{n} \\ &= \frac{k^2}{n \cdot \theta^2} \cdot e^{-2k/\theta}. \end{aligned}$$

❐

14.5.2 MULTIPLE PARAMETERS

The delta method can be generalized for more than one parameter. As before, we will present results for two parameters, with the generalization to three or more parameters then implied.

As expected, the solution involves matrices and vectors. Consider a function of the two parameters denoted by $g = g(\theta_1, \theta_2)$. We take the two partial derivatives $\frac{\partial g}{\partial \theta_1}$ and $\frac{\partial g}{\partial \theta_2}$, and put them in a 1×2 row vector denoted by $\mathbf{\partial g} = \left(\frac{\partial g}{\partial \theta_1}, \frac{\partial g}{\partial \theta_2}\right)$. The generalized version of Equation (14.17) is then

$$Var\left[g\left(\hat{\theta}_1,\hat{\theta}_2\right)\right] = \partial\mathbf{g} \times \mathbf{I}^{-1}(\boldsymbol{\theta}) \times \partial\mathbf{g}^T, \qquad (14.18)$$

where $\times$ denotes matrix multiplication, $\mathbf{I}^{-1}$ is the variance-covariance matrix, and $\partial\mathbf{g}^T$ is the 2×1 column vector that is the transpose of $\partial\mathbf{g}$.

The reader should note that when the matrix product is taken, we then have a 1×1 matrix containing the desired variance. The reader should also note that if we have only one parameter, then the variance-covariance matrix becomes a 1×1 matrix and Equation (14.18) simplifies to Equation (14.17).

EXAMPLE 14.14

We wish to model a loss process with a lognormal distribution. The maximum likelihood estimates of the two parameters are obtained as $\hat{\mu}=4.215$ and $\hat{\sigma}=1.093$. The estimated variance-covariance matrix is obtained as

$$\begin{pmatrix} .1195 & 0 \\ 0 & .0597 \end{pmatrix}.$$

Estimate the variance of the maximum likelihood estimator of the mean of the lognormal distribution, using the delta method.

SOLUTION

This is an excellent illustration of the importance of the delta method, since the mean of the lognormal distribution is a function of both parameters. The presence of the two zeroes in the variance-covariance matrix is not a coincidence. The two parameters in the lognormal distribution are independent, and therefore have no covariance. (Many of the other two-parameter distributions we commonly encounter, however, do have a non-zero covariance.)

The g function is the formula for the mean of the lognormal distribution, so we have

$$g = g(\mu,\sigma) = e^{\mu+\sigma^2/2},$$

$$\frac{\partial g}{\partial \mu} = e^{\mu+\sigma^2/2} = e^{4.215+(1.093)^2/2} = 123.017,$$

and

$$\frac{\partial g}{\partial \sigma} = \sigma \cdot e^{\mu+\sigma^2/2} = 1.093e^{4.215+(1.093)^2/2} = 134.458,$$

when both $\frac{\partial g}{\partial \mu}$ and $\frac{\partial g}{\partial \sigma}$ are numerically estimated by using the point estimates for μ and σ. A direct application of Equation (14.18) then gives

$$Est.Var[g(\hat{\mu},\hat{\sigma})] = (123.017, 134.458)\begin{pmatrix} .1195 & 0 \\ 0 & .0597 \end{pmatrix}\begin{pmatrix} 123.017 \\ 134.458 \end{pmatrix}$$

$$= 2888.$$

❐

14.6 SOME ADVANCED ILLUSTRATIONS

In this final section we present four illustrative examples of more advanced applications of maximum likelihood estimation. These examples are in no way comprehensive, but they do illustrate the application of this important technique in settings other than the basic ones presented earlier in this chapter.

The first example illustrates maximum likelihood involving both censoring and truncation. The second example illustrates maximum likelihood with a restriction imposed on the parameters. The third example illustrates maximum likelihood in which calculus is not used as a maximization technique. The fourth example actually does not involve maximum likelihood, but rather seeks the variance of a method of moments estimator.

EXAMPLE 14.15

A health insurance policy has an ordinary deductible of 250, coinsurance of 20% paid by the insured, and a policy coverage limit of 1000 (before application of the deductible and coinsurance). In the past year, the following claim payments were made:

$$\{40, 120, 160, 280, 600^*, 600^*\}$$

The two payments marked with (*) were made on losses that exceeded the policy coverage limit. Find an expression for the likelihood function for estimating parameters in the loss distribution prior to imposing any of the coverage limitations.

SOLUTION

The first step is to convert the claim amounts to loss amounts. If we denote the loss amount by x and the claim amount paid by the insurer by y, then the formula connecting the two is

$$y = .80(x-250),$$

where $x \leq 1000$, so that

$$x = \frac{y}{.80} + 250.$$

The loss amounts are computed using this formula and are displayed in Table 14.3 on the following page.

TABLE 14.3

Claim and Loss Amounts for Example 14.15	
Claim Amount y	**Loss Amount x**
40	300
120	400
160	450
280	600
600	≥ 1000
600	≥ 1000

It is important to note that when more than one coverage limitation exists, the order in which the limitations are imposed may make a difference. In particular, if the policy limit were imposed after the deductible and the coinsurance rather than before, then the maximum claim amount would be 1000 instead of only 600.

The likelihood function must reflect the mix of exact values, censored values, and the fact that we have a truncated distribution. It is appropriate to construct composite likelihood functions with more than one of the individual types of adjustments we considered on a one-by-one basis earlier in the chapter. The answer is

$$L = \frac{f(300)\cdot f(400)\cdot f(450)\cdot f(600)\cdot[1-F(1000)]^2}{[1-F(250)]^6}.$$ ❐

EXAMPLE 14.16

Phil and Sylvia are competitors in the light bulb business. Sylvia advertises that her light bulbs burn twice as long as Phil's. We were able to test 20 of Phil's bulbs and 10 of Sylvia's. We assume that the distribution of the lifetime (in hours) of a light bulb is exponential, and have separately estimated Phil's parameter as $\hat{\theta}_P = 1000$ and Sylvia's parameter as $\hat{\theta}_S = 1500$ using maximum likelihood estimation. Determine θ^*, the maximum likelihood estimate of θ_P restricted by Sylvia's claim that $\theta_S = 2\theta_P$.

SOLUTION

This example has an interesting feature in that it contains a restriction that the maximum likelihood estimate must satisfy. For convenience in notation, we will denote Phil's parameter by θ and Sylvia's parameter by 2θ in setting up the likelihood function. This will reflect the stated restriction. The likelihood function is constructed as the product of 20 frequency functions for Phil and 10 for Sylvia.

Another complication is that we do not have exact sample values provided for either Phil or Sylvia. However, we do know the two sample means which is sufficient information, since $\sum_{i=1}^{n} X_i = n\bar{X}$. Thus we have the likelihood function

$$\begin{aligned} L(\theta) &= \left[\prod_{i=1}^{20} \frac{e^{-x_i/\theta}}{\theta}\right]\left[\prod_{j=1}^{10} \frac{e^{-x_j/2\theta}}{2\theta}\right] \\ &= 2^{-10}\theta^{-30} \cdot \exp\left[-\tfrac{1}{\theta}\sum_{i=1}^{20} x_i\right] \cdot \exp\left[-\tfrac{1}{2\theta}\sum_{j=1}^{10} x_j\right] \\ &= 2^{-10}\theta^{-30} \cdot e^{-(20)(1000)/\theta} \cdot e^{-(10)(1500)/2\theta} \\ &= 2^{-10}\theta^{-30} \cdot e^{-27,500/\theta}. \end{aligned}$$

The rest of the estimation process continues in the usual fashion. The log likelihood function is

$$\ell(\theta) = \ln L(\theta) = \ln 2^{-10} - 30\ln\theta - \frac{27,500}{\theta},$$

and its derivative, set equal to zero, gives

$$\frac{\partial \ell(\theta)}{\partial \theta} = -\frac{30}{\theta} + \frac{27,500}{\theta^2} = 0,$$

from which we find

$$\theta^* = \frac{27,500}{30} = 917.$$

❐

EXAMPLE 14.17

Two research teams studied five diseased cows. We are given the following information:

(1) The survival function is $S(t) = \frac{\omega - t}{\omega}$, for $0 \le t \le \omega$.

(2) Each cow came under observation at time $t = 0$.

(3) The times of death were $t = 1, 3, 4, 4, 6$.

(4) Research Team X, impatient to publish results, terminated its observations at time $t = 5$ and estimated ω using the maximum likelihood method with incomplete data.

(5) Research Team Y waited for the last cow to die, and estimated ω using the maximum likelihood method with complete data.

Compute the absolute value of the difference between Research Team X's and Research Team Y's maximum likelihood estimates of ω.

SOLUTION

In this example we are doing maximum likelihood estimation in a survival models context. Since $S(t) = \frac{\omega - t}{\omega}$, then

$$f(t) = -S'(t) = \frac{1}{\omega}.$$

Team X Estimate:

$$L_X = \prod_{i=1}^{4} f(t_i) \cdot [1 - F(5)]$$

$$= \prod_{i=1}^{4} f(t_i) \cdot S(5)$$

$$= \left(\frac{1}{\omega}\right)^4 \left(\frac{\omega - 5}{\omega}\right) = \frac{\omega - 5}{\omega^5}$$

Then

$$\ell_X = \ln L_X = \ln(\omega - 5) - 5 \ln \omega,$$

so that

$$\frac{\partial \ell_X}{\partial \omega} = \frac{1}{\omega - 5} - \frac{5}{\omega} = 0,$$

which solves for

$$\hat{\omega} = 6.25.$$

Team Y Estimate:

$$L_Y = \prod_{j=1}^{5} f(t_j) = \left(\frac{1}{\omega}\right)^5$$

By inspection, L_Y is maximized when $\omega = 6$. A smaller value of ω is impossible, since one cow lived to time $t = 6$, and a larger value of ω produces a smaller value of L_Y. This is one of those unusual problems in which the maximum of a function occurs at a boundary point and cannot be determined as a relative maximum by differentiation. Furthermore, this particular maximum likelihood estimation does not satisfy the conditions for the theorem given in Section 14.4.1, so the variance of this estimator cannot be obtained from Equation (14.14).

The absolute value of the difference in estimates is $|6.25 - 6| = .25$. ❐

EXAMPLE 14.18

Losses are modeled using a Pareto distribution with parameters $\alpha = 3$ and θ unknown. A sample consisting of 300 losses is obtained. Determine the variance of $\hat{\theta}$, the method of moments estimator of θ. The answer will be a function of θ.

SOLUTION

This example seeks the variance of a method of moments estimator, a quantity we have not previously discussed. Our prior discussion did identify the Cramer-Rao inequality as a lower bound for such a variance, but we did not discuss how to obtain an exact value for it. Thus, in order to solve this example, we will have to develop some new approach not seen before.

For the Pareto distribution, we have

$$E[X] = \frac{\theta}{\alpha-1} = \frac{\theta}{2},$$
$$E[X^2] = \frac{2\theta^2}{(\alpha-1)(\alpha-2)} = \theta^2,$$

and

$$\begin{aligned} Var(X) &= E[X^2]-E[X]^2 \\ &= \theta^2 - \left(\frac{\theta}{2}\right)^2 = \frac{3\theta^2}{4}. \end{aligned}$$

From the first of these equations we see that $\theta = 2 \cdot E[X]$. However, under the method of moments, we would have the corresponding relationship $\hat{\theta} = 2\bar{X}$. Taking variances, and using Equation (2.7b) for the variance of a sample mean random variable, we have

$$\begin{aligned} Var(\hat{\theta}) &= 4 \cdot Var(\bar{X}) \\ &= \frac{4\sigma^2}{n} \\ &= \frac{4}{300} \cdot \frac{3\theta^2}{4} = \frac{\theta^2}{100}. \end{aligned}$$ ❐

14.7 SUMMARY

In Chapter 14 we developed the maximum likelihood estimation (MLE) technique for estimating parameters of the fitted model distribution. This technique is widely used in practice and has a number of attractive properties.

The technique was first illustrated for the case of complete exact data with one parameter. The technique for continuous distributions and for discrete distributions is identical. The first step in the technique is the construction of the likelihood function $L(\theta)$. This function is the product of probabilities (discrete case) or densities (continuous case) of obtaining the sample values actually obtained. The concept of the technique is to find the value of θ, denoted $\hat{\theta}$, that maximizes $L(\theta)$, and to then use this value of $\hat{\theta}$ as the parameter estimate.

The second step in the technique is usually to obtain the log of the likelihood function, $\ell(\theta) = \ln L(\theta)$. Finally, the third step is to then take the first derivative to find the relative maximum of $\ell(\theta)$ and then solve for $\hat{\theta}$. Although this is by far the most common situation in practice, on rare occasions the second step is omitted (it is optional) and on rare occasions the third step involves finding the maximum value at a boundary point.

Extensions of the basic technique were then developed for grouped data and for incomplete data due to censoring or truncation. In all cases, we saw that it was relatively straightforward to develop an adjusted likelihood function to handle each of these situations.

We then turned to a consideration of the dispersion of the parameter estimation process. The MLE technique produces parameter estimators with the minimum possible variance. Thus, the technique produces parameter estimators that are inherently efficient, so that they have low mean square error (MSE).

The one-parameter case was then extended to the two-parameter case which can easily be generalized to more than two parameters. The technique in this case requires the use of matrix algebra and the definition of two key matrices, the information matrix and the variance-covariance matrix.

Two important extensions were then presented. The first was to use the MLE point estimate for the parameter, together with the estimator's variance, and then apply a version of the Central Limit Theorem to obtain confidence intervals. The second was to obtain the variance of some function of the estimator rather than just the estimator itself. The delta method was developed as a technique for doing this. Both the one-parameter and multi-parameter cases were considered and illustrated.

14.8 EXERCISES

14.1 Introduction
14.2 Complete Exact Data – One Parameter

14-1 Consider the following five observations:

$$\{521, 658, 702, 819, 1217\}$$

Assume these sample values are drawn from a single-parameter Pareto distribution, with CDF given by

$$F(x) = 1-\left(\frac{500}{x}\right)^{\alpha},$$

for $x > 500$ and $\alpha > 0$. Calculate the maximum likelihood estimate of the parameter α.

14-2 Consider the following claim severities:

$$\{11.0, 15.2, 18.0, 21.0, 25.8\}$$

The distribution with PDF given by

$$f(x) = \frac{1}{\sqrt{2\pi x}}\cdot\exp\left[-\frac{1}{2x}(x-\mu)^2\right],$$

for $x > 0$ and $\mu > 0$, is fit to the data. Determine the maximum likelihood estimate of μ.

14-3 A sample of 10 losses has the following statistics:

$$\sum_{i=1}^{10} x_i^{-2} = .00033674 \qquad \sum_{i=1}^{10} x_i^{.50} = 488.97$$

$$\sum_{i=1}^{10} x_i^{-1} = .023999 \qquad \sum_{i=1}^{10} x_i = 31{,}939$$

$$\sum_{i=1}^{10} x_i^{-.50} = .34445 \qquad \sum_{i=1}^{10} x_i^{2} = 211{,}498{,}983$$

Assuming that the losses come from a Weibull distribution with $\tau = .50$, determine the maximum likelihood estimate of the Weibull parameter θ.

14-4 The number of claims follows a negative binomial distribution, with known parameter r and unknown parameter β. (See Exercise 6-38 for the r, β parameterization of the negative binomial distribution.) We wish to estimate β based on n observations, where $\bar{x}$ is the mean of these observations. Find the maximum likelihood estimate of β, expressing the answer as a function of r and $\bar{x}$.

14-5 Consider the following study of low-hazard, medium-hazard, and high-hazard risks:

(i) Low-hazard risks have an exponential claim size distribution with mean θ.

(ii) Medium-hazard risks have an exponential claim size distribution with mean 2θ.

(iii) High-hazard risks have an exponential claim size distribution with mean 3θ.

(iv) No claims from low-hazard risks are observed.

(v) Three claims from medium-hazard risks are observed, of sizes 1, 2, 3.

(vi) One claim from a high-hazard risk is observed, of size 15.

Determine the maximum likelihood estimate of θ.

14-6 We wish to fit the distribution with PDF given by

$$f(x) = (p+1)\cdot x^p,$$

for $0 < x < 1$ and $p > -1$, to the data set $\{.74, .81, .95\}$ by maximum likelihood. Determine the MLE of p.

14.3 Extensions

14-7 Losses under a certain dental policy follow an exponential distribution with mean θ. For each loss over 50, there is a deductible of 50 and a policy limit of 350 (applied after the deductible), and losses under 50 are not reported to the insurer.

The following is a random sample of five claim payments under this policy, where + indicates that the original loss exceeds 400:

$$\{50, 150, 200, 350^+, 350^+\}$$

Determine the likelihood function $L(\theta)$.

14-8 Losses follow an exponential distribution with mean θ. A random sample of twenty losses is distributed as follows:

Loss Range	Frequency
0 – 1000	7
1000 – 2000	6
2000 – ∞	7

Calculate the maximum likelihood estimate of θ.

14-9 Personal auto property damage claims in a certain region are known to follow the Weibull distribution with CDF given by

$$F(x) = 1 - e^{-(x/\theta)^{.20}},$$

for $x > 0$. A sample of four claims is $\{130, 240, 300, 540\}$, plus two additional claims known to exceed 1000. Determine the maximum likelihood estimate of θ.

14-10 An insurance company records the following loss amounts, which are generated by a policy with a deductible of 100:

$$\{120, 180, 200, 270, 300, 1000, 2500\}$$

Losses less than 100 are not reported to the company. Losses are modeled by a Pareto distribution with parameters $\theta = 400$ and unknown α. Use the maximum likelihood estimate of α to estimate the expected loss with no deductible.

14-11 The random variable X has the survival function

$$S(x) = \frac{\theta^4}{(\theta^2+x^2)^2}.$$

Two values of X are observed to be 2 and 4, and one other value is known to exceed 4. Calculate the maximum likelihood estimate of θ.

14-12 Consider the following twenty bodily injury losses (before the deductible is applied):

Loss	Number of Losses	Deductible	Policy Limit
750	3	200	∞
200	3	0	10,000
300	4	0	20,000
> 10,000	6	0	10,000
400	4	300	∞

Past experience indicates that these losses follow a Pareto distribution with parameters $\theta = 10{,}000$ and unknown α. Determine the maximum likelihood estimate of α.

14.4 Variances of Parameter Estimators

14-13 (a) Continue Example 14.9 by verifying that Equation (14.14c) produces the same answer as do Equations (14.14a) and (14.14b).

(b) Complete Example 14.9 by verifying that Equation (14.14d) produces the same answer as do Equations (14.14a) and (14.14b).

14-14 We wish to find the maximum likelihood estimates of the parameters α and θ in a Pareto distribution, using complete exact data from a sample of size n. Develop the two equations in two unknowns that will need to be solved simultaneously for $\hat{\alpha}$ and $\hat{\theta}$.

14-15 The following are the numbers of claims over a ten-year period under a hospital liability policy:

$$\{10, 2, 4, 0, 6, 2, 4, 5, 4, 2\}$$

The numbers of claims are independent from year to year. We wish to fit the data to a Poisson distribution. Use the data to estimate the coefficient of variation of the maximum likelihood estimator of the Poisson parameter.

14-16 A random sample of size n is drawn from a distribution with PDF

$$f(x) = \frac{\theta}{(\theta+x)^2},$$

for $0<x<\infty$ and $\theta>0$. Determine the asymptotic variance of the maximum likelihood estimator of θ, as a function of θ and n.

14-17 The random variable X has an exponential distribution with mean θ. Calculate the mean square error (MSE) of X^2 as an estimator of θ^2; the answer will be a function of θ.

14.5 Variances of Functions of Parameter Estimators

14-18 The time until an accident occurs follows an exponential distribution. A random sample of size two has a mean time of 6. Let Y denote the mean of a new sample of size two. Use the delta method to approximate the variance of the maximum likelihood estimator of $F_Y(10)$.

14-19 Show that $Var(\hat{\theta}) = \frac{\theta^2}{n}$, for the exponential distribution of Example 14.13.

14-20 Fifty claims have been observed from a lognormal distribution with unknown parameters μ and σ. The maximum likelihood estimates of these parameters are $\hat{\mu}=6.84$ and $\hat{\sigma}=1.49$. The estimated variance-covariance matrix of $\hat{\mu}$ and $\hat{\sigma}$ is

$$\mathbf{I}^{-1} = \begin{vmatrix} .0444 & 0 \\ 0 & .0222 \end{vmatrix}.$$

The partial derivatives of the lognormal CDF are

$$\frac{\partial F}{\partial \mu} = \frac{-\phi(z)}{\sigma}$$

and

$$\frac{\partial F}{\partial \sigma} = \frac{-z\cdot\phi(z)}{\sigma},$$

where $\phi(z)$ is the PDF of the unit normal distribution. An approximate 95% equal-tailed confidence interval for the probability that the next claim will be less than or equal to 5000 is (L,U). Determine the value of L.

14-21 Loss payments for a group health policy follow an exponential distribution with unknown mean. The following is a sample of six losses:

$$\{100, 200, 400, 800, 1400, 3100\}$$

Use the delta method to approximate the variance of the maximum likelihood estimator of $S(1500)$.

14-22 A survival study produced (.283, 1.267) as the symmetric linear 95% confidence interval for the cumulative hazard function $\Lambda(5)$. Using the delta method, determine the symmetric linear 95% confidence interval for the associated $S(5)$.

14.6 Some Advanced Illustrations

14-23 The number of claims follows a Poisson distribution with mean λ. Observations other than 0 or 1 have been deleted from the data, which contain an equal number of observations 0 and 1. Determine the maximum likelihood estimate of λ.

14-24 The following are ten total loss amounts, not adjusted by any deductibles or policy limits, observed in Year Z:

$$\{18, 78, 125, 168, 250, 313, 410, 540, 677, 1100\}$$

Losses are modeled by an exponential distribution with parameter estimated by maximum likelihood. Inflation at a compound rate of 5% is expected each year. All policies written in Year Z+2 have an ordinary deductible of 100 and a policy limit of 1000, so the maximum payment per loss is 900. Determine the expected amount paid per loss in Year Z+2.

14-25 Losses come from a mixture of an exponential distribution with mean 100 (with probability p), and an exponential distribution with mean 10,000 (with probability $1-p$). Losses of 100 and 2000 are observed. Determine an algebraic expression for the likelihood function $L(p)$.

14-26 The following three loss amounts have been observed:

$$\{186, 91, 66\}$$

Seven other loss amounts are known to be less than or equal to 60. Losses follow an inverse exponential distribution with CDF given by

$$F(x) = e^{-\theta/x},$$

for $x > 0$. The mode of the inverse exponential is $\frac{\theta}{2}$. Calculate the maximum likelihood estimate of the population mode.

14-27 For a sample of fifteen losses, the following data is collected:

Interval	Number of Losses
0 – 2	5
2 – 5	5
5 – ω	5

Losses follow the uniform distribution on $(0,\omega)$. Estimate ω by minimizing the function $\sum_{j=1}^{3}\frac{(E_j - O_j)^2}{O_j}$, where E_j is the expected number of losses in the jth interval and O_j is the observed number of losses in the jth interval.

CHAPTER FIFTEEN

BAYESIAN TECHNIQUES

15.1 INTRODUCTION

In this chapter we introduce the reader to *Bayesian techniques*, a different type of approach than encountered previously in Part IV of this text. Bayesian techniques constitute a family of techniques used in statistics for a variety of different situations and applications. However, all Bayesian techniques are based on the fundamental concept of blending together prior information, that we already possess from some source, with new information obtained from a sample. The result is a revised estimate, for one or more values, from those that existed prior to obtaining the sample.

The Bayesian approach is fundamentally different from the classical statistical approaches followed earlier in the text. These classical approaches do not assume that we already possess relevant information, and thus they base estimates strictly on the sample data. The primary emphasis in this chapter is on *Bayesian parameter estimation*, and, in that context, Chapter 15 can be considered to be a continuation of Chapters 13 and 14. However, Bayesian techniques also can be used for a variety of purposes other than estimation of parameters in parametric distributions. For example, such techniques can be adapted for revising estimates of tabular models as discussed in Part III of the text. In this chapter we will introduce another important application in this family of techniques, called *Bayesian graduation*, that is used for smoothing empirical estimates obtained from data.

Bayesian techniques are based on *Bayes' Theorem*, a well-known and fundamental probability theorem that readers should have encountered previously in basic courses in probability and statistics. Because of the importance of thoroughly understanding the foundation upon which Bayesian techniques are based, however, we provide a review of Bayes' Theorem in Section 15.2.

Another important application of Bayesian techniques in the actuarial literature is the subject of *credibility theory*. This text does not address this important topic, since credibility theory is an extensive topic and is the subject of full texts in its own right.[1] However, readers who have been exposed to material on credibility theory will recognize many similarities between material covered in that subject and material covered in this chapter.

[1] See, for example, Herzog [5].

15.2 BAYES' THEOREM

In Section 15.2.1 we present a discrete version of Bayes' Theorem as a fundamental probability theorem. This is the version that most readers first encountered in basic courses in probability and statistics. This is followed in Section 15.2.2 with a more sophisticated continuous version, in which density functions are being revised based on new sample information being obtained. This version will be used for Bayesian parameter estimation and is also widely used in credibility theory.

15.2.1 DISCRETE CASE

Since we are assuming that readers are already familiar with Bayes' Theorem, we will not present a detailed development. Readers with no background in Bayes' Theorem are referred to any standard textbook in basic probability, if they feel that additional background would be helpful.[2]

The discrete version of Bayes' Theorem, derived in basic probability texts, is given by

$$Pr(A_i \mid B) = \frac{Pr(A_i) \cdot Pr(B \mid A_i)}{\sum_i Pr(A_i) \cdot Pr(B \mid A_i)}, \tag{15.1}$$

where (1) $Pr(A_i)$ is the *prior probability* of some possible state before obtaining a new sample, (2) $Pr(B \mid A_i)$ is the conditional probability of getting the sample outcome B, conditional on A_i being the true state, and (3) $Pr(A_i \mid B)$ is the *posterior probability* of the same state A_i after obtaining the sample outcome B.

Some observations about Equation (15.1) are in order.

(1) $Pr(A_i \mid B)$ is the probability for the same state as is $Pr(A_i)$. The only difference is that $Pr(A_i \mid B)$ is *after* the sample whereas $Pr(A_i)$ is *before* the sample.

(2) The denominator comes from conditional probability theory and is that constant necessary to make the sum of the posterior probabilities be equal to one.

(3) The A_i's as a group constitute all possible states. Therefore, we have

$$\sum_i Pr(A_i) = \sum_i Pr(A_i \mid B) = 1.$$

(4) In summary, Bayes' Theorem revises prior probabilities, and turns them into posterior probabilities reflecting the sample outcome actually obtained. Some of the prior probabilities will increase and some will decrease, but the sum of the probabilities for all possible states, prior and posterior, must still equal one.

---

[2] See, for example, Hassett and Stewart [12].

Bayes' Theorem can be applied to a wide variety of problems and applications in statistics and related fields. We now illustrate the discrete version with three diverse examples. The first example is a basic, straightforward application to a survival models problem. The second and third are somewhat more involved examples that illustrate how problems involving Bayes' Theorem can be embedded in different types of loss models questions.

EXAMPLE 15.1

A group of laboratory rats born with a serious genetic impairment is being used to test the effectiveness of a proposed new technique for genetic engineering. The density function for the time-until-death random variable T is given by a continuous uniform distribution with $f(t)=1/10,$ for $0<t\leq 10,$ where time t is measured in weeks. A group of three rats, denoted as $R_1, R_2,$ and $R_3,$ is being observed with attained survival times of $t=2, 5,$ and 8 weeks, respectively. If exactly one of these three rats dies during the next week, find the probability that it was Rat $R_3,$ the one with attained survival time $t=8.$

SOLUTION

The cumulative distribution function and survival function for this distribution are

$$F(t) = \int_0^t f(r)\,dr = \frac{t}{10}$$

and

$$S(t) = 1-F(t) = \frac{10-t}{10},$$

respectively, for $0\leq t\leq 10.$ The prior probabilities of the three possible states (i.e., a selected rat) for use in Bayes' Theorem are

$$Pr(R_1) = Pr(R_2) = Pr(R_3) = \frac{1}{3},$$

since all three states are equally likely prior to obtaining any sample information. The conditional probabilities of obtaining the sample outcome of one death $(\text{denoted by } D=1)$ are

$$Pr(D=1\,|\,R_1) = q_2 = \frac{S(2)-S(3)}{S(2)} = \frac{8-7}{8} = \frac{1}{8},$$

$$Pr(D=1\,|\,R_2) = q_5 = \frac{S(5)-S(6)}{S(5)} = \frac{5-4}{5} = \frac{1}{5},$$

and

$$Pr(D=1\,|\,R_3) = q_8 = \frac{S(8)-S(9)}{S(8)} = \frac{2-1}{2} = \frac{1}{2}.$$

We now apply Equation (15.1) to obtain the answer for the posterior probability being sought, which is

$$Pr(R_3 \mid D=1) = \frac{Pr(R_3) \cdot Pr(D=1 \mid R_3)}{\sum_i Pr(R_i) \cdot Pr(D=1 \mid R_i)}$$

$$= \frac{\left(\frac{1}{3}\right)\left(\frac{1}{2}\right)}{\left(\frac{1}{3}\right)\left(\frac{1}{8}\right)+\left(\frac{1}{3}\right)\left(\frac{1}{5}\right)+\left(\frac{1}{3}\right)\left(\frac{1}{2}\right)}$$

$$= \frac{\left(\frac{1}{2}\right)}{\left(\frac{1}{8}\right)+\left(\frac{1}{5}\right)+\left(\frac{1}{2}\right)} = \frac{20}{33}.$$ ❐

Bayes' Theorem has revised the prior probability $Pr(R_3)=1/3$ to the posterior probability $Pr(R_3 \mid D=1)=20/33$, based on the sample data obtained. The reader should note that if the other two posterior probabilities were calculated, the sum of the three posterior probabilities would equal one.

Another observation about this example is also pertinent. Note that the equal prior probabilities in the numerator and denominator cancel each other out. Thus, in a discrete Bayes' Theorem problem with equal prior probabilities, the prior probabilities can be ignored.

EXAMPLE 15.2

A portfolio consists of 150 independent risks with identical claim count distributions. 100 of the risks have a policy with a \$100,000 per claim policy limit, and 50 of the risks have a policy with a \$1,000,000 per claim policy limit. Prior to censoring by policy limits, the claim size distribution for each risk is as follows:

Claim Size	Probability
\$ 10,000	1/2
50,000	1/4
100,000	1/5
1,000,000	1/20

A claims report is available that shows actual claim sizes incurred for each policy after censoring by policy limits, but does not identify the policy limit associated with each policy. The claims report shows exactly three claims for a policy selected at random. Two of the claims are \$100,000 each, but the amount of the third claim is illegible. Given this information, determine the expected value of this illegible number.

SOLUTION

This example illustrates several features not encountered in Example 15.1. We denote the event of censoring at \$100,000 by C (for "censored") and the event of censoring at \$1,000,000 by U (for "uncensored" since no claim can exceed \$1,000,000). We then construct the probability function for the censored case by combining the probabilities for claim sizes \$100,000 and \$1,000,000, since they would pay the same amount with a policy limit of \$100,000. This is summarized in Table 15.1.

TABLE 15.1

Probability Functions for Example 15.2		
Claim Size x	**Probability Function for Uncensored Case** $p_U(x)$	**Probability Function for Censored Case** $p_C(x)$
\$ 10,000	1/2	1/2
50,000	1/4	1/4
100,000	1/5	1/4
1,000,000	1/20	---

We now apply Bayes' Theorem. The prior probabilities are

$$Pr(U) = \frac{50}{150} = \frac{1}{3}$$

and

$$Pr(C) = \frac{100}{150} = \frac{2}{3}.$$

Note that in this case the prior probabilities are not equal to each other and will not cancel out, as they did in the prior example.

The sample has three observations, but only two values can be read. This is equivalent to a sample of size two, since the third observation contains no usable information. We let Y denote the event of having the two legible claims both be equal to \$100,000, and we let X denote the amount of the third (illegible) claim. We then have

$$Pr(Y\,|\,U) = \left(\frac{1}{5}\right)^2 = \frac{1}{25}$$

and

$$Pr(Y\,|\,C) = \left(\frac{1}{4}\right)^2 = \frac{1}{16}.$$

Applying Equation (15.1) we obtain the posterior probabilities

$$Pr(U\,|\,Y) = \frac{\frac{1}{3}\cdot\frac{1}{25}}{\frac{1}{3}\cdot\frac{1}{25}+\frac{2}{3}\cdot\frac{1}{16}} = \frac{8}{33}$$

and

$$Pr(C\,|\,Y) = \frac{25}{33}.$$

(There was no need to independently calculate the second posterior probability, since the sum of the two posterior probabilities must be one.)[3]

We are now finished with Bayes' Theorem, but not with the example. We must use the two posterior probabilities to obtain the expected value of the illegible claim amount. We first compute the two conditional means

$$\begin{aligned} E[X \mid U] &= \tfrac{1}{2}(10{,}000) + \tfrac{1}{4}(50{,}000) + \tfrac{1}{5}(100{,}000) + \tfrac{1}{20}(1{,}000{,}000) \\ &= 87{,}500 \end{aligned}$$

and

$$E[X \mid C] = \tfrac{1}{2}(10{,}000) + \tfrac{1}{4}(50{,}000) + \tfrac{1}{4}(100{,}000) = 42{,}500.$$

The expected value of X is still conditional on event Y having occurred, so, using the law of total expectation, we finally have

$$\begin{aligned} E[X \mid Y] &= E[X \mid U] \cdot Pr(U \mid Y) + E[X \mid C] \cdot Pr(C \mid Y) \\ &= \tfrac{8}{33}(87{,}500) + \tfrac{25}{33}(42{,}500) = 53{,}409. \end{aligned}$$ ❐

EXAMPLE 15.3

A car manufacturer is testing the ability of safety devices to limit damages in car accidents. We are given the following information:

(1) A test car has either front airbags or side airbags (but not both), with each type being equally likely.

(2) The test car will be driven into either a wall or a lake, with each accident type being equally likely.

(3) The manufacturer randomly selects 1, 2, 3, or 4 crash test dummies to put into a car with front airbags.

(4) The manufacturer randomly selects 2 or 4 crash test dummies to put into a car with side airbags.

(5) Each crash test dummy in a wall-impact accident suffers random damage of either .50 or 1, with equal probability, with damage to each dummy being independent of damage to the others.

(6) Each crash test dummy in a lake-impact accident suffers random damage of either 1 or 2, with equal probability, with damage to each dummy being independent of damage to the others.

One test car is selected at random, and the test accident produces total damage of 1. Determine the expected value of the total damage from the second test accident, given that the kind of safety device (front or side airbags) and accident type (wall or lake) remain the same.

[3] Nonetheless, the reader might wish to independently calculate this probability as a check on our accuracy.

SOLUTION

This is a rather elaborate Bayes' Theorem problem with a large number of different cases. Due to the large number of cases we organize the solution in tabular form, which is presented in Table 15.2. We use the following notation:

(1) F denotes front airbags and S denotes side airbags.

(2) W denotes wall test and L denotes lake test.

(3) X_i denotes the total damage from the ith test, for $i = 1, 2$.

(4) The number of testing dummies is denoted by 1, 2, 3, 4 for the various cases.

TABLE 15.2

Solution for Example 15.3

(1) Possible Case	(2) Prior Probability	(3) Conditional Probability of X_1=1, Given Case	(4) Product (2) x (3)	(5) Posterior Probability
*FW*1	1/16	1/2	1/32	2/7
*FW*2	1/16	1/4	1/64	1/7
*FW*3	1/16	0		
*FW*4	1/16	0		
*FL*1	1/16	1/2	1/32	2/7
*FL*2	1/16	0		
*FL*3	1/16	0		
*FL*4	1/16	0		
*SW*2	1/8	1/4	1/32	2/7
*SW*4	1/8	0		
*SL*2	1/8	0		
*SL*4	1/8	0		

Column (1) contains every possible case using the defined coding. Column (2) is the prior probability for each case listed in Column (1). Column (3) is the conditional probability of obtaining the sample observation $X_1 = 1$ for each case. Each entry in Column (4) is the product of the entries in Columns 2 and 3 and forms the numerator in Equation (15.1). Finally, Column (5) is proportional to the entries in Column (4), such that the sum of the entries is one. These are the Bayesian posterior probabilities given by Equation (15.1).

Similar to the prior example, we are not yet finished. We use these posterior probabilities to find the expected value of the total damage from the second test accident. We first obtain the conditional expected values of damage per person for a wall event and a lake event, which are

$$E[X_2 \mid W] = .50(.50+1) = .75$$

and

$$E[X_2 \mid L] = .50(1+2) = 1.50.$$

We next compute the conditional expected value of X_2, the damage from the second test, for each of the three cases *FW*, *FL* and *SW*, obtaining

$$E[X_2 \mid FW] = .25(.75+1.50+2.25+3) = 1.875,$$
$$E[X_2 \mid FL] = .25(1.50+3+4.50+6) = 3.75,$$

and

$$E[X_2 \mid SW] = .50(1.50+3) = 2.25.$$

Finally, the answer is the weighted average of these three conditional expected values (all of which are also conditional on $X_1 = 1$), using the posterior probabilities, so we have

$$E[X_2 \mid X_1{=}1] = \frac{3}{7}(1.875)+\frac{2}{7}(3.75)+\frac{2}{7}(2.25) = 2.518.$$ ❐

The reader has now been exposed to a variety of illustrative applications of the discrete version of Bayes' Theorem.

15.2.2 CONTINUOUS CASE

The continuous version of Bayes' Theorem involves an infinite number of outcomes rather than a finite number of outcomes, as in the discrete version discussed in the prior section. These outcomes are modeled by assuming they follow some continuous probability distribution. However, before we can state the continuous version of Bayes' Theorem and demonstrate how it is used, we first need to provide some further background and definitions.

We consider first the basic case with one random variable that has a distribution with one parameter. In some cases the distribution is continuous, and $f(x \mid \theta)$ denotes the density function of the random variable X with parameter θ. In other cases, the distribution is discrete (e.g., Poisson), but the continuous version of Bayes' Theorem can still be used in the analysis of discrete distributions, such as claim frequency distributions. In these cases we will use $p(x \mid \theta)$ instead of $f(x \mid \theta)$, as in Example 15.4.

The parameter θ, in turn, is the outcome of a second distribution with density function $\pi(\theta)$. The distribution of θ must be continuous. (If θ's distribution were discrete, then we would have to use a discrete version of Bayes' Theorem, rather than the continuous version we are developing in this section.)

It may not yet be clear just how Bayes' Theorem is to be used in this situation. The distribution with PDF $\pi(\theta)$ is called the *prior distribution*, since no sample has yet been taken. (The term "prior distribution" is analogous to the term "prior probability" for the discrete case.) The mean of this prior distribution is typically used as the *prior estimate* $\hat{\theta}$ for the parameter

θ. Although this is a commonly used point estimate for the parameter θ, we do have the entire distribution of θ specified by $\pi(\theta)$.

We now obtain a sample of size n which is denoted $\{x_1, x_2, \cdots, x_n\}$. The concept is to modify the prior distribution of θ to reflect the new information contained in the sample. This will give us the conditional density function $\pi(\theta \mid x_1, x_2, \cdots, x_n)$, which is the PDF of the *posterior distribution* of θ. (The term "posterior distribution" is analogous to the term "posterior probability" for the discrete case.) As expected, the mean of the posterior distribution is typically used as the *posterior estimate* $\hat{\theta}$ for the parameter θ.

The continuous version of Bayes' Theorem is the mechanism by which the prior distribution is modified by the sample to become the posterior distribution. The continuous version of Bayes' Theorem is given by

$$\pi(\theta \mid x_1, x_2, \cdots, x_n) = \frac{\pi(\theta) \cdot f(x_1, x_2, \cdots, x_n \mid \theta)}{\int_\theta \pi(\theta) \cdot f(x_1, x_2, \cdots, x_n \mid \theta)\, d\theta}. \tag{15.2}$$

Although Equation (15.2) may appear complicated at first glance, upon examination it is seen to be quite analogous to Equation (15.1). The term $\pi(\theta)$ is analogous to $Pr(A_i)$, the term $f(x_1, x_2, \cdots, x_n \mid \theta)$ is analogous to $Pr(B \mid A_i)$, and the term $\pi(\theta \mid x_1, x_2, \cdots, x_n)$ is analogous to $Pr(A_i \mid B)$. The denominator in Equation (15.2) is the integral of the numerator, rather than the sum, since this is a continuous version. The limits on the integral are the range of values of θ in the domain of $\pi(\theta)$.

It is possible to write Equation (15.2) in a more compact fashion, with less clutter in the notation, as

$$\pi(\theta \mid x_1, x_2, \cdots x_n) = k \cdot \pi(\theta) \cdot L(\theta). \tag{15.3}$$

In Equation (15.3) the reciprocal of the integral in the denominator is expressed as a *normalizing constant k*. This integral takes on a numerical value after performing the integration with respect to θ, since all the sample values x_i have numerical values. The purpose of the normalizing constant is to ensure that the sum of the posterior probabilities will equal one. As we shall see in the examples in this and the next sections, in some cases the normalizing constant can be determined without performing the integration, but in other cases it cannot be.

Continuing the description of Equation (15.3), the expression $\pi(\theta)$ is unchanged from Equation (15.2). Finally, the remainder of the numerator can be expressed as $L(\theta)$, the likelihood function in maximum likelihood estimation. This can be seen directly from Equation (14.1). In the continuous version of Bayes' Theorem we are not actually performing a maximum likelihood estimation, but we can utilize its notation to simplify the expression.

EXAMPLE 15.4

We are given that annual claim frequency follows a Poisson distribution with parameter λ. The prior distribution of λ is believed to follow a uniform distribution on [0,2]. We then take a sample of two independent observations. During the next year the first insured has no claims, and the second insured has one claim. Based on this information, let us use the continuous version of Bayes' Theorem to obtain the posterior distribution of λ.

SOLUTION

We know that for the Poisson distribution $p(x\,|\,\lambda)=\frac{e^{-\lambda}\lambda^x}{x!}$. The parameter λ has a prior uniform distribution with PDF $\pi(\lambda)=.50,$ since the domain of λ is $0\leq\lambda\leq 2$. The two sample values are independent, so we have

$$\Pr(X_1=0\cap X_2=1\,|\,\lambda) \;=\; p(0\,|\,\lambda)\cdot p(1\,|\,\lambda) \;=\; e^{-\lambda}\cdot\lambda e^{-\lambda} \;=\; \lambda e^{-2\lambda}.$$

We then apply Equation (15.2) to obtain

$$\pi(\lambda\,|\,0,1) \;=\; \frac{\pi(\lambda)\cdot p(0\,|\,\lambda)\cdot p(1\,|\,\lambda)}{\int_0^2 \pi(\lambda)\cdot p(0\,|\,\lambda)\cdot p(1\,|\,\lambda)\,d\lambda} \;=\; \frac{.50\lambda e^{-2\lambda}}{\int_0^2 .50\lambda e^{-2\lambda}\,d\lambda}.$$

The .50 constants in the numerator and the denominator cancel. We then perform an integration by parts in the denominator to obtain

$$\pi(\lambda\,|\,0,1) \;=\; \frac{\lambda e^{-2\lambda}}{\int_0^2 \lambda e^{-2\lambda}\,d\lambda} \;=\; \frac{4\lambda e^{-2\lambda}}{1-5e^{-4}},$$

for $0\leq\lambda\leq 2$. As we see in this example, the simple uniform prior distribution has turned into a rather complex posterior distribution. Also, note that the domain of the posterior distribution must be the same as that of the prior distribution. ❐

The reader may rightly sense from this simple example that the mechanics of applying the continuous version of Bayes' Theorem can become rather complex. Fortunately, as we shall see in the next section, simple results do occur in several common situations in practice. However, the required calculus manipulations can become rather onerous in other situations.

15.3 BAYESIAN PARAMETER ESTIMATION

In Section 15.3.1 we extend the discussion of Section 15.2.2 to a more comprehensive treatment of continuous mixture models. We then have sufficient background to demonstrate the technique of parameter estimation using Bayesian techniques in Section 15.3.2.

Throughout Section 15.3 we consider estimating only one parameter by Bayesian techniques. Estimating more than one parameter simultaneously by Bayesian techniques requires some fairly sophisticated matrix techniques, and is beyond the scope of this book.

15.3.1 CONTINUOUS MIXTURE MODELS

In this section we use the continuous version of Bayes' Theorem to develop continuous mixture models which have many important applications in Bayesian statistics.[4] We start with a distribution with PDF $f(x\,|\,\theta)$, which is called the *model distribution*, or *likelihood*. The model distribution is the distribution from which sample values are drawn.

As stated above, the parameter θ contained in the model distribution is a realization of the random variable Θ, whose PDF is denoted by $\pi_\Theta(\theta)$ or simply $\pi(\theta)$ for convenience. The distribution of Θ is called the *prior distribution* for the parameter θ. We now appeal to basic probability theory and note that $f(x;\theta)$ is the *joint density function* of the *joint distribution* of the two random variables X and Θ, so that

$$f(x;\theta) = f\left(x\,|\,\theta\right)\cdot\pi(\theta). \tag{15.4}$$

The *marginal density function* of the random variable X is then given by

$$f(x) = \int_\theta f(x\,|\,\theta)\cdot\pi(\theta)\,d\theta, \tag{15.5}$$

where the range of integration in Equation (15.5) is the domain of the values of θ. All these definitions and results pertain prior to taking any sample values.

There are two more important results of interest after the sample values are obtained. The first of these we have encountered in the prior section. It is the *posterior distribution* and is the revised distribution of the parameter θ based on the sample values obtained. For convenience, we will express the posterior density function with a more compact version of Equation (15.2) as

$$\pi(\theta\,|\,\mathbf{x}) = \frac{\pi(\theta)\cdot f(\mathbf{x}\,|\,\theta)}{\int_\theta \pi(\theta)\cdot f(\mathbf{x}\,|\,\theta)\,d\theta}. \tag{15.6}$$

In this formula we let $\mathbf{x}$ denote the vector of sample values previously denoted by $\{x_1, x_2, \cdots, x_n\}$.

Finally, we come to the *predictive distribution*. This distribution is used to model the outcome for a new observation taken after the sample values have been obtained. More precisely, it is the conditional distribution for a new value, which we call y, based on the vector $\mathbf{x}$ of

[4] For an alternative explanation of this topic, see Section 5.2.2.

sample values that have already been obtained. As such, it is based on the model distribution and the posterior distribution. The PDF of the predictive distribution is given by

$$f(y\,|\,\mathbf{x}) = \int_{\theta} f(y\,|\,\theta)\cdot\pi(\theta\,|\,\mathbf{x})\,d\theta. \tag{15.7}$$

Intuitively, the predictive distribution can be interpreted as a mixture distribution in which the model distribution, conditional on θ, is weighted by the posterior distribution of θ, conditional on the set of sample values obtained.

The reader should note that Equation (15.7) provides the probability density function for the entire predictive distribution. In some cases, obtaining the full distribution may be required. In other cases, however, it may be sufficient to obtain a predictive estimate for some measure of the distribution, such as a particular moment, percentile, or probability. In such cases, obtaining a predictive estimate for this one particular measure may be possible without first obtaining the complete predictive distribution.

As an example of this, consider the case where all that is required is a predictive estimate for the mean of the next value to be drawn. An adaptation of Equation (15.7) to fit this common situation is given by

$$E[Y\,|\,\mathbf{x}] = \int_{\theta} E[Y\,|\,\theta]\cdot\pi(\theta\,|\,\mathbf{x})\,d\theta. \tag{15.8}$$

Similar formulas for obtaining other measures from the predictive distribution can be developed by analogy.

It is also interesting to observe that a predictive distribution exists prior to drawing the original sample values. In this case, the predictive distribution is based on the prior distribution of θ rather than the posterior distribution of θ. This predictive distribution is itself the distribution of the original sample values to be drawn.

If the reader is beginning to get the idea that obtaining predictive estimates is more of an approach that can be adapted to fit a variety of different situations, rather than one formula that is always applied in the same manner, then the reader is on the right track.

Continuing along these lines, consider the common situation in which all that is required is the mean and variance of the predictive distribution. These can be obtained by applying the well-known "double-expectation" formulas from probability theory, which are

$$E[Y] = E\big[E[Y\,|\,X]\big] \tag{15.9}$$

and

$$Var(Y) = E[Var(Y\,|\,X)] + Var(E[Y\,|\,X]).^{5} \tag{15.10}$$

[5] For a derivation of this result, see, for example, page 55 of Herzog, [15].

One additional attribute of continuous mixture models is important to discuss, which is the *conjugate property*. If the prior and posterior distributions belong to the same family, albeit with different parameters, then the distributions are said to be *conjugates*. In some cases the conjugate property holds and in some cases it does not. It depends on the combination of the model distribution and the prior distribution. Some combinations of model and prior distributions produce a conjugate property and some do not.

Those situations in which the conjugate property holds are usually relatively easy to work with and involve simple, attractive results. Moreover, the distributions can be periodically updated merely by changing the parameters, but not the underlying distributions themselves. If the conjugate property does not hold, then the results are usually much more difficult to work with and periodic updating may become quite complex.

Example 15.4 in the prior section illustrated a situation in which the conjugate property did not hold. Although the prior distribution in that example was a simple uniform distribution, we saw that after only one updating involving two sample values the posterior distribution had already become rather complex. The following examples involve situations in which the conjugate property holds, and the reader will see a marked difference in the ease of expressing the posterior distribution and making the ensuing computations.

EXAMPLE 15.5

We are given that annual claim frequency follows a Poisson distribution with parameter λ. The prior distribution of λ is believed to follow a gamma distribution with parameters α and β, with PDF given by Equation (1.55). We then take a sample of n insureds. During the next year the number of claims from this group of insureds is equal to $\sum_{i=1}^{n} x_i$, where x_i is the number of claims experienced by the ith insured.

(a) Develop the general formula for the posterior distribution of λ.

(b) Identify the type of the posterior distribution.

(c) Identify the parameters of the posterior distribution.

SOLUTION

(a) The model distribution is Poisson, with probability function given by $p(x\,|\,\lambda)=\frac{e^{-\lambda}\lambda^x}{x!}$. In turn, the parameter λ has a prior distribution with PDF $\pi(\lambda)=\frac{\beta^\alpha}{\Gamma(\alpha)}\cdot\lambda^{\alpha-1}e^{-\beta\lambda}$. We now apply the continuous version of Bayes Theorem, as given by Equation (15.3), to obtain

$$\begin{aligned}\pi(\lambda\,|\,x_1,x_2,\cdots,x_n) &= k\cdot\pi(\lambda)\cdot L(\lambda)\\ &= k\cdot\frac{\beta^\alpha}{\Gamma(\alpha)}\cdot\lambda^{\alpha-1}e^{-\beta\lambda}\cdot\prod_{i=1}^{n}\frac{e^{-\lambda}\lambda^{x_i}}{x_i!}.\end{aligned}$$

At first glance, this expression appears complicated. However, upon reflection, we see there is only one unknown, namely λ, in this expression. All the other components of this expression, i.e., α, β, k, x_i, have numerical values. Thus, despite the apparent clutter, all factors not involving λ can essentially be consolidated into one overall constant that will be the right value to produce a probability density function at the end. Moreover, we will not need to even do all this calculation, if we can identify the distribution, since the distribution will specify its constant term.

(b) If we now examine the terms involving λ, we see that the two factors in the numerator after the product sign match up exactly with the two factors immediately prior to the product sign. In other words, we can transfer the values from the Poisson distribution directly into corresponding terms in the gamma distribution. We can then see by inspection that the posterior will be a gamma distribution, since the information from the sample can be directly reflected as parameter changes in the prior gamma without changing the underlying distribution itself. Thus, with the Poisson/gamma combination, the conjugate property holds.

(c) The prior gamma distribution has parameters α and β. We will denote the corresponding parameters in the posterior gamma distribution by α^* and β^*. We then have

$$\alpha^* = \alpha + \sum_{i=1}^{n} x_i, \tag{15.11}$$

since the product of factors becomes a sum in the exponent, and

$$\beta^* = \beta + n. \tag{15.12}$$

These results have an insightful and attractive interpretation. The parameter α is updated by the total number of claims, and the parameter β is updated by the number of exposures (insureds).

Note that if we had used the scale-parameter form of the gamma distribution, with PDF given in Appendix A.1.2, then we would need to use the reciprocal of θ all the way through the above development. The results would have been equivalent, but clumsier to express algebraically. ❐

EXAMPLE 15.6

Continue Example 15.5 to develop the predictive distribution of original sample values (as described in the second paragraph following Equation (15.8)) for the Poisson/gamma combination, identifying the type of the predictive distribution and its parameters.

SOLUTION

We adapt the general formula for developing a predictive distribution, given by Equation (15.7), to reflect the assumptions of Example 15.5, where the model distribution is discrete. We have

$$\begin{aligned} p(x) &= \int_{\lambda} p(x \mid \lambda) \cdot \pi(\lambda)\, d\lambda \\ &= \int_0^{\infty} \frac{e^{-\lambda}\lambda^x}{x!} \cdot \frac{\beta^{\alpha}}{\Gamma(\alpha)} \cdot \lambda^{\alpha-1} e^{-\beta\lambda}\, d\lambda \\ &= \frac{\beta^{\alpha}}{x! \cdot \Gamma(\alpha)} \int_0^{\infty} e^{-\lambda(1+\beta)} \lambda^{x+a-1}\, d\lambda. \end{aligned}$$

We now make the variable change $\kappa = \lambda(1+\beta)$, so that $\lambda = \frac{\kappa}{1+\beta}$ and $d\lambda = \frac{d\kappa}{1+\beta}$. This gives us

$$\begin{aligned} p(x) &= \frac{\beta^{\alpha}}{x! \cdot \Gamma(\alpha)} \cdot \int_0^{\infty} e^{-\kappa} \left(\frac{\kappa}{1+\beta}\right)^{(x+\alpha)-1} \cdot \frac{d\kappa}{1+\beta} \\ &= \frac{\beta^{\alpha}}{x! \cdot \Gamma(\alpha)} \left(\frac{1}{1+\beta}\right)^{x+\alpha} \cdot \int_0^{\infty} e^{-\kappa} \kappa^{(x+\alpha)-1} d\kappa \\ &= \frac{\beta^{\alpha}}{x! \cdot \Gamma(\alpha)} \left(\frac{1}{1+\beta}\right)^{x} \left(\frac{1}{1+\beta}\right)^{\alpha} \cdot \Gamma(x+\alpha), \end{aligned}$$

from the definition of the gamma function. We note that x is a non-negative integer, so that $\Gamma(x+1) = x!$. Then we have

$$p(x) = \frac{\Gamma(x+\alpha)}{\Gamma(x+1) \cdot \Gamma(\alpha)} \cdot \left(\frac{\beta}{1+\beta}\right)^{\alpha} \left(\frac{1}{1+\beta}\right)^{x}. \tag{15.13a}$$

It can be shown[6] that the gamma-function expression $\frac{\Gamma(x+\alpha)}{\Gamma(x+1) \cdot \Gamma(\alpha)}$ is equal to the combinatorial factor $\binom{x+\alpha-1}{\alpha-1}$. Further, if we let $p = \frac{\beta}{1+\beta}$, so that $1-p = \frac{1}{1+\beta}$, we then have

$$p(x) = \binom{x+\alpha-1}{\alpha-1} p^{\alpha}(1-p)^x, \tag{15.13b}$$

which we recognize as a negative binomial distribution (see Section 1.2.3 and Equation (1.30a), with r replaced by α). Thus the Poisson/gamma mixture produces a negative binomial as the predictive distribution.

If we further let $\theta = \frac{1}{\beta}$, so that $p = \frac{\beta}{1+\beta} = \frac{1}{1+\theta}$ and $1-p = \frac{1}{1+\beta} = \frac{\theta}{1+\theta}$, then we have

$$p(x) = \binom{x+\alpha-1}{\alpha-1} \cdot \left(\frac{1}{1+\theta}\right)^{\alpha} \left(\frac{\theta}{1+\theta}\right)^{x}, \tag{15.13c}$$

[6] See Section 5.1.3.

which is the alternative form of the negative binomial probability function as given by Exercise 6-38, with r replaced by α and β replaced by θ. In this form, the negative binomial parameter r is equal to the prior gamma parameter α, and the negative binomial parameter θ is equal to the reciprocal of the prior gamma parameter β. ❒

EXAMPLE 15.7

Continuing Examples 15.5 and 15.6, use the double-expectation formulas, given by Equations (15.9) and (15.10), to find the mean and variance of the predictive distribution of original sample values.

SOLUTION

We seek $E[X]$ and $Var(X)$, where X is the random variable for original sample values. Since the distribution of X is conditional on the random variable Λ, we have

$$E[X] = E_\Lambda\left[E_X[X \mid \Lambda]\right] \tag{15.14a}$$

and

$$Var(X) = E_\Lambda\left[Var_X(X \mid \Lambda)\right] + Var_\Lambda\left(E_X[X \mid \Lambda]\right). \tag{15.14b}$$

But X is conditionally Poisson, so $E_X[X \mid \Lambda] = Var_X(X \mid \Lambda) = \Lambda$. In turn, the prior distribution of the parameter Λ is gamma, so $E[\Lambda] = \frac{\alpha}{\beta} = \alpha\theta$ and $Var(\Lambda) = \frac{\alpha}{\beta^2} = \alpha\theta^2$. Then

$$E[X] = E_\Lambda[\Lambda] = \frac{\alpha}{\beta} = \alpha\theta$$

and

$$Var(X) = E_\Lambda[\Lambda] + Var_\Lambda(\Lambda) = \frac{\alpha}{\beta} + \frac{\alpha}{\beta^2} = \alpha\theta + \alpha\theta^2 = \alpha\theta(1+\theta).$$

Recall that the unconditional (or marginal) distribution of X, which is the predictive distribution for original sample values, is negative binomial. The results here for $E[X]$ and $Var(X)$ agree with Exercises 6-38(a) and 6-38(b) under the alternative negative binomial parameterization, with α replacing r and θ replacing β. ❒

15.3.2 ESTIMATING PARAMETERS

In the last section we developed several useful and important results arising from the Poisson/gamma mixture. We see from the relative simplicity of the results that having a mixture in which the conjugate property holds is quite attractive. In particular, the same process can be repeated over and over again in successive periods with the underlying distributions remain unchanged; only the parameters change.

There are a number of other mixtures in which similar results occur, including the conjugate property. Among many possible mixtures, the following three have proven to be particularly important and useful in many applications:

(1) Binomial/beta (and negative binomial/beta)

(2) Normal/normal (where the parameter μ in the model distribution in turn follows another normal distribution)

(3) Exponential/gamma (also exponential/inverse gamma)

Note that Poisson/gamma and binomial/beta involve discrete model distributions commonly used to model claim frequency. In contrast, normal/normal and exponential/gamma involve continuous model distributions and could be used to model claim severity.

The above mixtures are explored in the exercises at the end of this chapter. These mixtures also appear in credibility theory and are more completely developed in various texts on that subject.

We return now to our original objective, which was to develop a Bayesian approach for parameter estimation. In essence, we have already developed all the theory necessary to accomplish this objective. The basic approach is summarized in the following steps:

(1) Specify an appropriate model distribution, with a parameter for the process in question.

(2) Specify an appropriate prior distribution for this parameter, whose mean is the current estimate of the parameter in the model distribution obtained from a source such as prior experience, published results, or an educated guess.

(3) Obtain additional experience through a sampling process.

(4) Use the continuous version of Bayes' Theorem to update the prior distribution into a posterior distribution.

(5) Then the parameter estimate, using Bayesian estimation, is the mean of the posterior distribution.

Although our Bayesian parameter estimation is now complete, we may also wish to obtain the predictive distribution to make estimates of future outcomes of the underlying process.

EXAMPLE 15.8

Suppose the number of annual claims per insured automobile follows a Poisson distribution with parameter λ, where λ, in turn, follows a gamma distribution with prior parameters $\alpha_1 = 50$ and $\beta_1 = \theta_1^{-1} = 500$. Over a two-year period the following experience is obtained:

	Year 1	Year 2
Number of claims	75	210
Number of autos insured	600	900

The company expects to insure 1100 autos in Year 3.

(a) What is the estimated annual claim frequency per insured auto at the beginning of Year 1?

(b) What is the estimated annual claim frequency per insured auto at the beginning of Year 2?

(c) What is the estimated annual claim frequency per insured auto at the beginning of Year 3?

(d) What is the expected number of claims that will occur during Year 3?

SOLUTION

(a) The estimated annual claim frequency per insured auto at the beginning of Year 1 (denoted by λ_1) is taken to be the mean of the prior gamma distribution, which is

$$\lambda_1 = \frac{\alpha_1}{\beta_1} = \frac{50}{500} = .1000.$$

(b) We need to update the parameters by the experience during Year 1, using Equations (15.11) and (15.12), giving us

$$\alpha_2 = \alpha_1 + \sum_{i=1}^{600} x_i = 50+75 = 125$$

and

$$\beta_2 = \beta_1 + n_1 = 500+600 = 1100.$$

Then the estimated annual claim frequency per insured auto at the beginning of Year 2 (denoted by λ_2) is the mean of the posterior gamma distribution for Year 1, which is

$$\lambda_2 = \frac{\alpha_2}{\beta_2} = \frac{125}{1100} = .1136.$$

(c) Notice how the posterior gamma distribution for Year 1 becomes the prior gamma distribution for Year 2. We again need to update the parameters by the experience during Year 2. Repeating the process in part (b), we obtain

$$\alpha_3 = \alpha_2 + \sum_{i=1}^{900} x_i = 125+210 = 335$$

and

$$\beta_3 = \beta_2 + n_2 = 1100+900 = 2000.$$

Then the estimated annual claim frequency per insured auto at the beginning of Year 3 (denoted by λ_3) is the mean of the posterior gamma distribution for Year 2, which is

$$\lambda_3 = \frac{\alpha_3}{\beta_3} = \frac{335}{2000} = .1675.$$

(d) The expected number of claims to occur during Year 3 is simply the expected annual claim frequency per insured auto for that year times the number of insured autos, which is $(1100)(.1675) = 184$. ❐

An important observation about Example 15.8 is that part (d) is really a question involving the predictive distribution rather than the posterior distribution, since it is asking for an expected future outcome, not a parameter. As we have seen earlier, the predictive distribution for the Poisson/gamma mixture is the negative binomial distribution. However, the mean of the negative binomial is equal to the mean of the posterior gamma, since the parameter λ in the Poisson distribution is also its mean. Thus, we can go directly to an answer as above. However, the reader needs to be careful. If we were interested in some estimated value other than the mean, then it would be necessary to use the negative binomial to answer such a question.

15.4 LOSS FUNCTIONS

As we have seen above, a full Bayesian analysis will develop a complete posterior distribution for a parameter. However, in many cases, such as in Example 15.8, we really do not use the entire distribution, but rather we simply use some point value, such as the mean, to estimate the parameter. Bayesian statisticians have developed the approach of using a *loss function* to measure the impact of the error when using a point estimate in place of the true value of the parameter. The loss function *could* be considered with respect to the prior distribution of a parameter, but is generally used with respect to the posterior distribution.

It should be noted that the term "loss function" might be ambiguous to many readers. The term "loss" in this context means something quite different from the more general use of that term in analyzing insurance and related risk management techniques throughout the rest of this text. In Bayesian statistics, the term is intended to be interpreted as some type of *penalty*, or magnitude of impact, associated with making an error of estimation. In other words, a loss function attempts to answer the question "If we make an error in estimating the value of the unknown parameter using a Bayesian technique, how serious is the error?"

More precisely, we define a *loss function* $\ell(\hat{\theta},\theta)$ to be the penalty associated with using a parameter estimate $\hat{\theta}$ when the true (but unknown) value of the parameter is actually θ. The basic concept is that we should use the *Bayesian estimate* that minimizes the expected value of the given posterior loss function. The following three sections present the three loss functions most commonly used in Bayesian statistics.

15.4.1 SQUARED ERROR LOSS

Our first Bayesian loss function is *squared error loss*. It is defined by

$$\ell(\hat{\theta},\theta) = (\hat{\theta}-\theta)^2, \tag{15.15}$$

and is displayed in Figure 15.1 on the following page. The Bayesian estimate that minimizes the expected value of the posterior squared error loss function is the *mean* of the posterior distribution of θ.

To prove this assertion, consider first a generic random variable X, and a function of that random variable given by $g(X)=(X-k)^2$, where k is a constant. Then

$$\begin{aligned} E[g(X)] = E[(X-k)^2] &= \int_x (x-k)^2 \cdot f(x)\ dx \\ &= \int_x (x^2-2xk+k^2)\cdot f(x)\ dx = E[X^2]-2k\cdot E[X]+k^2, \end{aligned}$$

since $\int_x f(x)\,dx = 1$. Clearly $E[(X-k)^2]$ is a function of *k*. To find the value of *k* that minimizes this function we set

$$\frac{d}{dk}\left(E[X^2] - 2k \cdot E[X] + k^2\right) = -2 \cdot E[X] + 2k = 0,$$

which is easily solved for $k = E[X]$.

Our application here is a special case of this generic result, where Bayesian estimates of the parameter θ are summarized in the posterior distribution of the random variable Θ, given the vector of data $\mathbf{x}$, with PDF $\pi(\theta \mid \mathbf{x})$. Using the posterior PDF to determine the expected value of $(\Theta - \hat{\theta})^2$, it follows that $E\left[(\Theta - \hat{\theta})^2\right]$ is minimized by the mean of that posterior distribution.

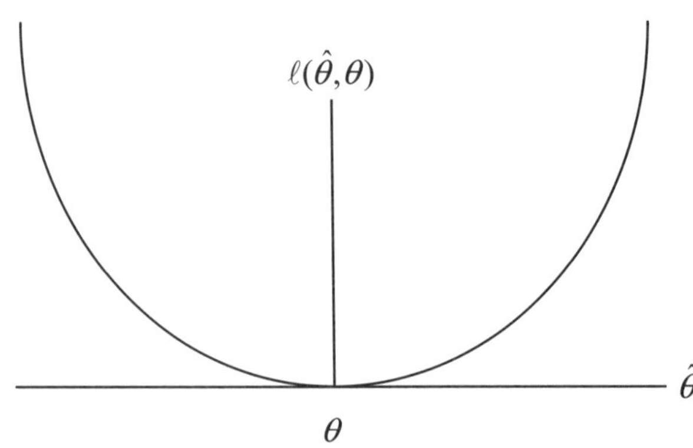

Squared Error Loss Function

FIGURE 15.1

The squared error Bayesian loss function is perhaps a different way to conceptualize the relationship between the mean and the variance than the usual way the reader probably learned about these measures in a basic statistics course. However, upon reflection, it does make intuitive sense. The reader can easily verify that the expected value of squared deviations around any value other than the mean will be larger than it will be around the mean.

EXAMPLE 15.9

A Bayesian estimation produces a posterior distribution for θ which is lognormal with $\mu = 5$ and $\sigma = 2$. Find the Bayesian estimate for θ that will minimize the squared error loss function.

SOLUTION

The required estimate is the mean of the posterior lognormal distribution (see Equation (6.16a)), which gives us

$$\hat{\theta} = E[\Theta] = e^{\mu+\sigma^2/2} = e^{5+2^2/2} = e^7. \qquad \square$$

15.4.2 ABSOLUTE LOSS

Our second Bayesian loss function is *absolute loss*. It is defined by

$$\ell(\hat{\theta},\theta) = |\hat{\theta}-\theta|. \tag{15.16}$$

The Bayesian estimate that minimizes the expected value of the absolute loss function is the *median* of the posterior distribution of θ.[7] This loss function is displayed in Figure 15.2.

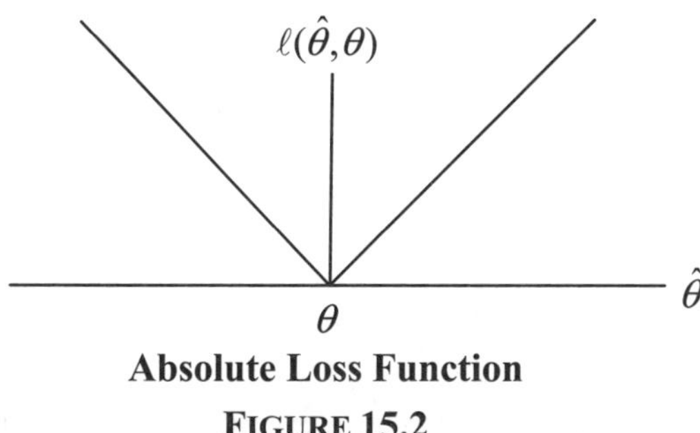

Absolute Loss Function

FIGURE 15.2

One possible motivation for using absolute loss is the belief that squared-error loss extracts too harsh a penalty for values far from the mean. A more moderate approach might be to say that the penalty should be proportional to the absolute size of the error, rather than to its square. This concept would lead to use of the absolute loss method.

Again, the reader should verify that the absolute loss function will be increased for any value other than the 50th percentile. For example, going to the 60th percentile would exchange values between .40 and .50 on one side of the distribution for values between .50 and .60 on the other side, leading to an overall increase.

EXAMPLE 15.10

For the posterior distribution of θ given in Example 15.9, find the Bayesian estimate for θ that will minimize the absolute loss function.

SOLUTION

This time we use the median of the posterior lognormal distribution, which we denote by $\pi_{.50}$. At this value we have

$$F(\pi_{.50}) = \Phi\left(\frac{\ln \pi_{.50}-\mu}{\sigma}\right) = .50,$$

so that

$$\ln \pi_{.50} - \mu = 0$$

[7] For a proof of this assertion, see page 35 of Herzog, [15].

and therefore

$$\hat{\theta} = \pi_{.50} = e^{\mu} = e^{5}.$$ ❐

15.4.3 ALMOST CONSTANT LOSS

Our third, and final, Bayesian loss function is *almost constant loss*.[8] It is defined by

$$\ell(\hat{\theta},\theta) = \begin{cases} 0 & \text{if } \hat{\theta}=\theta \\ c & \text{if } \hat{\theta}\neq\theta \end{cases}. \tag{15.17}$$

The Bayesian estimate that minimizes the expected value of the almost constant loss function is the *mode* of the posterior distribution of θ.[9] This loss function is displayed in Figure 15.3.

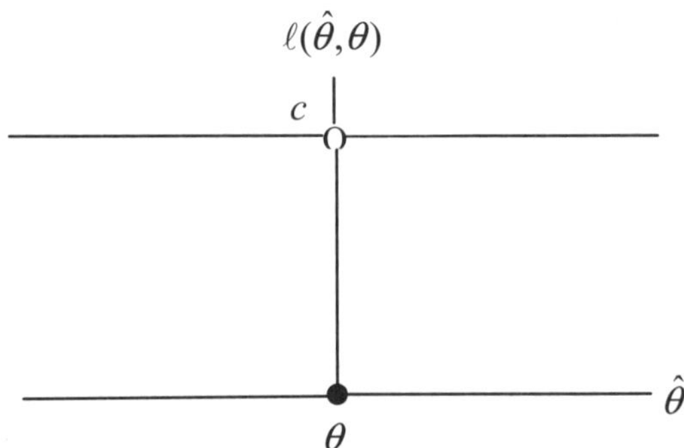

Almost Constant Loss Function

FIGURE 15.3

The almost constant Bayesian loss function has a straightforward explanation. If all errors are equally significant, then the loss function will be minimized if we make the fewest possible errors. This will happen when we use the mode of the posterior distribution as our estimate of θ.

EXAMPLE 15.11

Again using the posterior distribution for θ from Examples 15.9 and 15.10, find the Bayesian estimate for θ that will minimize the almost constant loss function.

SOLUTION

This time we use the mode of the posterior lognormal distribution (see Appendix A), giving

$$\hat{\theta} = e^{\mu-\sigma^2} = e^{5-2^2} = e.$$ ❐

---

[8] Other texts use other names for this loss function. Klugman, et al. [21], for example, set $c = 1$ and call it *zero-one loss* (see page 407).

[9] For a proof of this assertion, see page 37 of Herzog [15].

As a side comment on Examples 15.9, 15.10, and 15.11, it is interesting to compare the numerical values of the mean, median, and mode. They are quite far apart from each other. Moreover, they have the relationship mode < median < mean. These are the relationships that occur in a highly right-skewed distribution, such as the lognormal.

15.5 CONFIDENCE (CREDIBILITY) INTERVALS

We now turn to the development of confidence intervals for parameters estimated by a Bayesian technique. These confidence intervals will be determined from the posterior distribution that has been generated by the continuous version of Bayes' Theorem, as described in Section 15.3.

At this point, we encounter another semantic ambiguity in terminology, not unlike the special meaning of the word "loss" in the definition of loss function in Section 15.4. The standard term used in Bayesian statistics for a confidence interval is *credibility interval*. Unfortunately, this term might be ambiguous to many readers, since the word "credibility" has a different meaning here than it does in the term *credibility theory* used in the actuarial literature. Over the years, Bayesian statistics has developed a particular vernacular that does not always transfer cleanly into certain application areas of the theory.

It turns out that there is more than one type of credibility interval used in Bayesian statistics. Three different approaches to constructing confidence intervals will be presented in the following three subsections.

15.5.1 EQUAL PROBABILITY

The first type of credibility interval is the *equal probability interval*. This type of credibility interval is the one that would likely occur first to most readers. An equal probability credibility interval has two tails with equal probability in each tail. This type of credibility interval can be immediately constructed by obtaining the appropriate percentiles from the cumulative distribution function of the posterior distribution.

EXAMPLE 15.12

Bayesian parameter estimation for an unknown parameter λ results in a posterior distribution which is chi-square with $n=4$ degrees of freedom. Find three different point estimates of λ, using the three methods of Section 15.4. Then find the 90% equal probability credibility interval.

SOLUTION

The chi-square distribution is a special case of the gamma distribution in which the two parameters are $\alpha=\frac{n}{2}=2$ and $\beta=\frac{1}{2}$ (or $\theta=2$). When the squared error loss function is the one selected to be minimized, the point estimate for the parameter is the mean of its posterior distribution, which, in this case, is

$$E[\Lambda] = \frac{\alpha}{\beta} = \alpha\theta = 2 \cdot 2 = 4.$$

In some cases, however, we might use the median as the point estimate. The median of a chi-square distribution with 4 degrees of freedom is $\pi_{.50} = 3.357$. This value is determined from the cumulative distribution function of the associated gamma distribution, which involves an incomplete gamma function (see Equation (1.59)). (Values of the chi-square CDF can readily be determined using the CHIINV function in Excel. For the reader's convenience, selected values are shown in the chi-square table in Appendix C.)

Finally, we might choose to use the mode as the point estimate. The mode of the gamma distribution (see Appendix A) is given by $\theta(\alpha-1)$, which is $2(2-1) = 2$ in this case.

We again see the familiar pattern, mode < median < mean, that characterizes a positively skewed distribution.

A 90% equal probability credibility interval will run from the 5th to the 95th percentile. By inspection of the $n = 4$ chi-square table, or by using the incomplete gamma function, we find these percentiles to be $\pi_{.05} = .711$ and $\pi_{.95} = 9.488$. The length of this credibility interval is $9.488 - .711 = 8.777$. ❐

15.5.2 HIGHEST POSTERIOR DENSITY

Another type of credibility interval often used in Bayesian statistics is the *highest posterior density* (HPD) *interval*. The concept underlying this type of credibility interval is to find the shortest possible interval containing the requisite amount of probability mass.

Consider first the common situation in which we have a positively skewed distribution that is unimodal (i.e., heaped in the middle with tails running off at both ends). Many of the continuous distributions in Appendix A fit this basic profile with commonly used parameter values. We will state two intuitively appealing properties of such distributions without formal proof:

(1) The HPD credibility interval is shifted to the left from the equal probability credibility interval.

(2) If the two boundary points of the HPD credibility interval are denoted by λ_L on the left and λ_R on the right, then the values of the probability density function at these two boundary points will be equal. That is

$$f(\lambda_L) = f(\lambda_R) \tag{15.18}$$

Both of these properties are illustrated in Figure 15.4. The validity of the second property should be graphically obvious by considering the area gained or lost under the density curve as the boundary points are shifted one way or the other. Note also that the area to the left of the dotted line in the left tail is equal to the area to the right of the dotted line in the right tail.

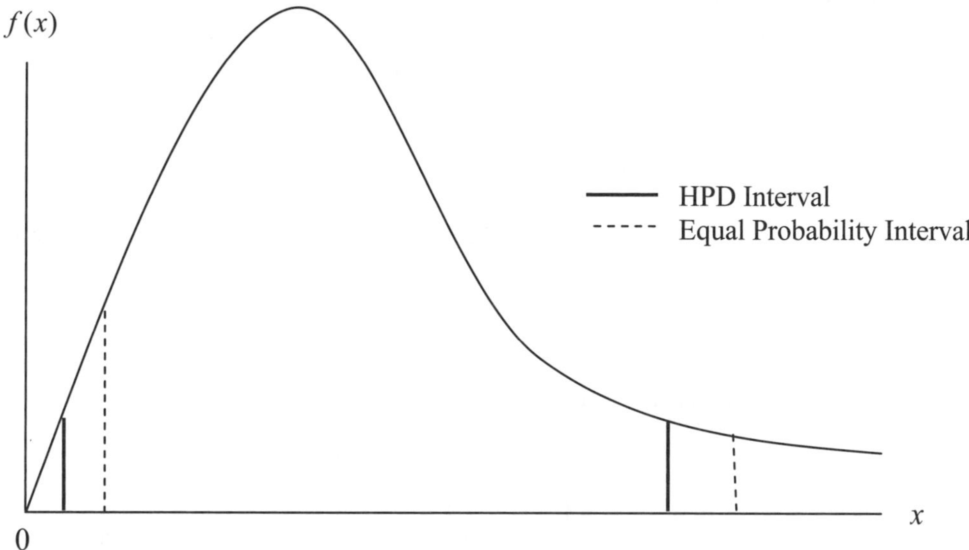

Bayesian Credibility Intervals – Unimodal Skewed Distribution

FIGURE 15.4

Consider next the situation in which the probability density function is monotonically decreasing over its entire domain. Two frequently-used distributions fitting this profile are the exponential distribution and the Pareto distribution. For this category of distribution, the HPD confidence interval is simply that interval shifted as far left as possible. This property should be clear from a visual inspection of Figure 15.5, since the further we go to the left in the distribution, the greater is the probability mass included over successive intervals along the x-axis.

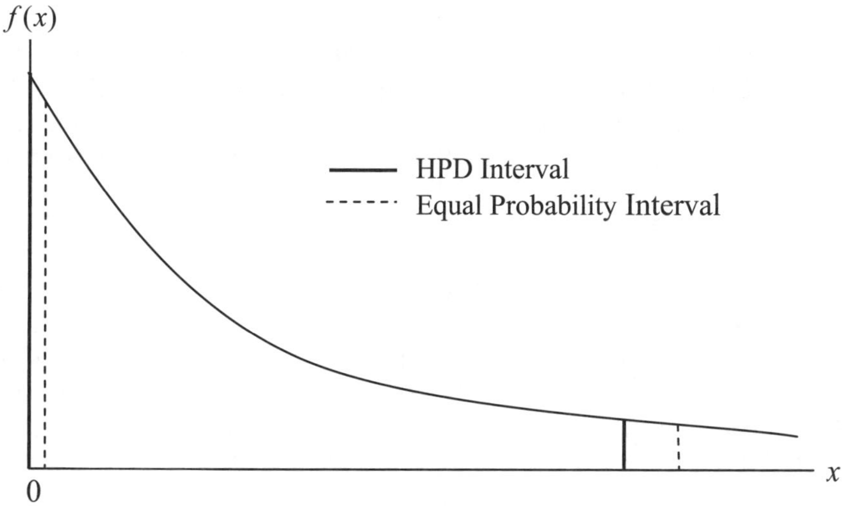

Baysian Credibility Intervals – Monotonically Decreasing Distribution

FIGURE 15.5

HPD credibility intervals for distributions that fit neither of the two common patterns described above also can be obtained. We will not consider such cases in more detail, however, since such distributions are not often encountered in typical applications of primary interest in this text.

EXAMPLE 15.13

Repeat Example 15.12, this time to find the 90% highest posterior density (HPD) credibility interval.

SOLUTION

The HPD credibility interval must have a length such that 90% of the probability mass lies within the interval. This requirement implies that

$$F(\lambda_R) - F(\lambda_L) = .90.$$

Furthermore, Equation (15.18) requires that $f(\lambda_L) = f(\lambda_R)$. We therefore have two equations in the two unknowns λ_L and λ_R. Solving these two equations is not straightforward. The second equation can be expressed in closed algebraic form, but the first equation involves two values of the incomplete gamma function. Thus, some type of numerical solution technique is required.

Using the CHIINV function in Excel leads to the solution $\lambda_{.0034} = 0.1696$ and $\lambda_{.9034} = 7.8663$.

As an independent verification, we can confirm that Equation (15.18) is satisfied, since

$$f(.1696) = f(7.8663) = .039.$$

The length of this credibility interval is $7.8663 - .1696 = 7.6967$. As expected, the length of the HPD credibility interval is shorter than the length of the equal probability credibility interval, which was calculated in the prior section to be 8.777. Also, note that the HPD credibility interval is shifted left in comparison with the equal probability credibility interval. ❐

15.5.3 BAYESIAN CENTRAL LIMIT THEOREM

As we saw above, the numerical calculation of HPD credibility intervals may be difficult. An alternative approach is to appeal to a Bayesian version of the Central Limit Theorem. There is valid statistical theory to support such an application of the Central Limit Theorem, although the details are beyond the scope of this text. This will be an attractive option if the moments of the distribution are easier to obtain than are the percentiles, which is often the case in practice. All that we need to calculate a normal credibility interval is the mean and variance.

EXAMPLE 15.14

Repeat Example 15.12, this time to find the 90% credibility interval using the Bayesian Central Limit Theorem.

SOLUTION

In Example 15.12, we already calculated the mean to be $E[\Lambda]=4$. The variance of this chi-square (gamma) distribution is

$$Var(\Lambda) = \alpha\theta^2 = 2\cdot 2^2 = 8.$$

The 90% credibility interval using the normal approximation is given by

$$\mu \pm 1.645\sigma = 4\pm 1.645\sqrt{8} = (-.653, 8.653).$$

The length of this credibility interval is $8.653-(-.653)=9.306$, which is longer than either of the other two credibility intervals. It also goes slightly below zero.

We should not expect a close fit when using the normal distribution to approximate a chi-square distribution with only 4 degrees of freedom. However, as the degrees of freedom increase in a chi-square distribution, the distribution becomes much more symmetrical and the normal distribution would provide a better and better approximation. (This can easily be seen from a simple inspection of the chi-square tables. The chi-square with only 20 degrees of freedom is already fairly symmetrical.)

One rationale for using the Bayesian Central Limit Theorem as an easy approximation in this situation goes back to the continual updating process involved in using Bayesian parameter estimation. As new data keep coming in, and parameters keep getting updated, the posterior distributions will approach the normal distribution over time.

15.6 BAYESIAN GRADUATION

In this section we introduce the topic of Bayesian graduation, which can be considered as another option for smoothing data along with those presented in Chapter 12. It is included in Chapter 15 because, as the title suggests, it is based on Bayesian techniques.

The specific technique presented in this section is called the *Kimeldorf-Jones method* in tribute to the two authors who originally presented it in a paper in 1967.[10] The technique is based on the multi-normal distribution. (The bivariate version of this distribution is reviewed in Appendix A.2.) We will present the method in this section utilizing the notation used by Kimeldorf and Jones.

---

[10] See Kimeldorf and Jones [20].

The specific application for which the technique was illustrated in the original paper was the graduation of a set of mortality rates (i.e., q_x for various ages x) as presented in Chapter 11. Since mortality rates can be estimated using a binomial proportion estimator (see Equation (11.14)), the use of a multi-normal distribution as an approximation seems reasonable. However, the technique is not limited to this application and should be considered as a general one available in other contexts in which the multi-normal distribution is a reasonable model.

The reader should not be surprised that the Kimeldorf-Jones method requires the use of vectors and matrices. We will continue our practice in this book of using bold notation to denote vectors and matrices. We will denote the n underlying random variables that we wish to estimate, $W_1, W_2, \cdots, W_n$, by the column vector **W**, where **W** is defined by

$$\mathbf{W} = [W_1, W_2, \cdots, W_n]^T, \tag{15.19}$$

where T denotes the transpose of the vector.

In classical statistics the underlying values being estimated are usually thought of as fixed, but unknown, values. By contrast, in Bayesian statistics these underlying values are thought of as random variables. We will not pursue the nuances of this conceptual, even philosophical, distinction in this book. The mathematics is the same either way. We merely want the reader to be alert to the different concepts that are used in estimating underlying values in this situation.

In similar fashion, we define the n corresponding estimator random variables of the sample values by the column vector

$$\mathbf{U} = [U_1, U_2, \cdots, U_n]^T, \tag{15.20a}$$

and the corresponding realizations of those estimator random variables (i.e., the observed sample values) by the column vector

$$\mathbf{u} = [u_1, u_2, \cdots, u_n]^T. \tag{15.20b}$$

Finally, the n graduated values (which are the Bayesian estimates of the W_i's) are contained in the column vector

$$\mathbf{v} = [v_1, v_2, \cdots, v_n]^T. \tag{15.21}$$

The Bayesian graduation technique can be described by the following four steps:

(1) Formulate a prior probability distribution for each random variable W_i, the sequence we wish to estimate.

(2) Select the model for the experiment, which is an expression for the conditional distribution of the observed data u_i, given the sequence w_i.

(3) Use Bayes' Theorem to solve for the posterior distribution of w_i, given the observed data u_i.

(4) Select the vector of graduated values $\mathbf{v}$ from the posterior distribution, in light of the objective of the graduation problem.

For Step (1), we will utilize the multi-normal distribution as mentioned above. The reader will recall that the PDF for the single variable normal distribution with mean m and variance a is given by

$$f_W(w) = (2\pi a)^{-1/2} \cdot \exp\left[-\frac{1}{2}a^{-1}(w-m)^2\right]. \tag{15.22}$$

For the multi-normal distribution, the term $(w-m)$ is replaced by the column vector $(\mathbf{w}-\mathbf{m})$ and the variance a is replaced by the variance-covariance matrix $\mathbf{A}$. Then the joint PDF for the multi-normal distribution is given by

$$f_{\mathbf{W}}(\mathbf{w}) = k_1 \cdot \exp\left[-\frac{1}{2}(\mathbf{w}-\mathbf{m})^T \mathbf{A}^{-1}(\mathbf{w}-\mathbf{m})\right]. \tag{15.23}$$

The constant $k_1 = \left[(2\pi)^n \,|\, \mathbf{A} \,|\right]^{-1/2}$ is the first in a series of constants k_i where the subscript will increase whenever the constant changes.

The reader might ask what the multi-normal parameters $\mathbf{m}$ and $\mathbf{A}$ in Equation (15.23) are, and where they come from. The specification of these parameters is a key step in the application of this technique. However, it will be deferred until later in the section, so that we can continue the presentation of the four steps in the method without interruption.

For Step (2), we will assume that the appropriate conditional distribution for U_i, given w_i, is the binomial proportion distribution for each value of i, which we will approximate for all variables collectively using the multi-normal distribution. Since $E[U_i] = w_i$ for each value of $i = 1, 2, \ldots, n$, it follows that the mean vector for our conditional multi-normal distribution is $\mathbf{w}$. If we assume independence of the U_i random variables, then the covariances are all equal to zero and the variance-covariance matrix $\mathbf{B}$ for the conditional distribution becomes a diagonal $n \times n$ matrix containing only the variances of the random variables U_i on the main diagonal.

The above considerations lead us to the conditional density

$$f_{\mathbf{U}|\mathbf{W}}(\mathbf{u}|\mathbf{w}) = k_2 \cdot \exp\left[-\frac{1}{2}(\mathbf{u}-\mathbf{w})^T \mathbf{B}^{-1}(\mathbf{u}-\mathbf{w})\right], \tag{15.24}$$

where the constant $k_2 = \left[(2\pi)^n \,|\, \mathbf{B} \,|\right]^{-1/2}$.

For Step (3), we apply Bayes' Theorem to develop the posterior density $f_{\mathbf{W}|\mathbf{U}}(\mathbf{w}|\mathbf{u})$. We first note that $f_{\mathbf{U}}(\mathbf{u})$ is constant with respect to $\mathbf{w}$, so it can be combined with k_1 and k_2. This leads us to define k_3 as

$$k_3 = \frac{k_1 \cdot k_2}{f_{\mathbf{U}}(\mathbf{u})}.$$

We then apply Bayes' Theorem to obtain

$$f_{\mathbf{W}|\mathbf{U}}(\mathbf{w}|\mathbf{u}) = k_3 \cdot \exp\left\{-\frac{1}{2}\left[(\mathbf{w}-\mathbf{m})^T \mathbf{A}^{-1}(\mathbf{w}-\mathbf{m}) + (\mathbf{u}-\mathbf{w})^T \mathbf{B}^{-1}(\mathbf{u}-\mathbf{w})\right]\right\}. \qquad (15.25)$$

It is possible to simplify the exponent in this expression to obtain

$$f_{\mathbf{W}|\mathbf{U}}(\mathbf{w}|\mathbf{u}) = k_4 \cdot \exp\left[-\frac{1}{2}(\mathbf{w}-\mathbf{v})^T \mathbf{C}^{-1}(\mathbf{w}-\mathbf{v})\right], \qquad (15.26)$$

where k_4 does not involve $\mathbf{w}$. The new parameters $\mathbf{v}$ and $\mathbf{C}$ are defined by

$$\mathbf{v} = (\mathbf{A}^{-1} + \mathbf{B}^{-1})^{-1}(\mathbf{B}^{-1}\mathbf{u} + \mathbf{A}^{-1}\mathbf{m}) \qquad (15.27)$$

and

$$\mathbf{C} = (\mathbf{A}^{-1} + \mathbf{B}^{-1})^{-1}. \qquad (15.28)$$

The details of the derivation of Equation (15.26) from (15.25) are left as Exercise 15-24(a), with step-by-step guidance.

This is a very nice result. We see that the posterior density given by Equation (15.26) is a multi-normal distribution with mean vector $\mathbf{v}$ and variance-covariance matrix $\mathbf{C}$. Thus the conjugate property holds, which we know produces quite desirable results in applications of Bayesian statistics (see Section 15.3).

Finally, for Step (4), we observe that all three of the mean, median, and mode are the same for the multi-normal distribution, so it is convenient to take the vector $\mathbf{v}$ as our graduated values. Then from Equation (15.27) we have the graduation formula

$$\mathbf{v} = (\mathbf{A}^{-1} + \mathbf{B}^{-1})^{-1}(\mathbf{B}^{-1}\mathbf{u} + \mathbf{A}^{-1}\mathbf{m}). \qquad (15.27)$$

Equation (15.27) has an important verbal interpretation. The vector $\mathbf{u}$ contains our sample information and the vector $\mathbf{m}$ contains part of our prior information about $\mathbf{W}$ ($\mathbf{A}$ being the other part). Equation (15.27) can be viewed as a weighted average of $\mathbf{u}$ and $\mathbf{m}$ in which each is weighted by the inverse of the appropriate variance-covariance matrix.

It is possible to obtain two other equivalent expressions for the vector $\mathbf{v}$ from Equation (15.27). The first (see Exercise 15-24(b)) expresses $\mathbf{v}$ as the observed data $\mathbf{u}$ modified by the prior opinion $\mathbf{m}$, and can be written as

$$\mathbf{v} = \mathbf{u}+(\mathbf{I}+\mathbf{AB}^{-1})^{-1}(\mathbf{m}-\mathbf{u}), \tag{15.29a}$$

where **I** is the identity matrix of order n. This is an attractive formula for computational purposes. Since **B** is diagonal, it is easily inverted, so Equation (15.29a) involves only one difficult matrix inversion whereas Equation (15.27) involves two. Of course, with the ready availability of computer software to invert matrices, this advantage may be less significant than in the past.

The second (see Exercise 15-24(c)) expresses **v** as the prior opinion **m** modified by the observed data **u**, and can be written as

$$\mathbf{v} = \mathbf{m}+(\mathbf{I}+\mathbf{BA}^{-1})^{-1}(\mathbf{u}-\mathbf{m}). \tag{15.29b}$$

Equation (15.29b) does not produce the same computational advantages as does Equation (15.29a), but conceptually complements Equation (15.29a) by providing an interesting companion formula going in the opposite direction. The derivations of Equations (15.29a) and (15.29b) are left as exercises.

Our presentation of the Bayesian graduation technique is now complete. However, we need to discuss the specification of the three matrices **m**, **A**, and **B**. These specifications, along with the sample values **u**, are the inputs necessary to perform a Bayesian graduation.

There is considerable latitude available to the modeler in the specification of these three matrices. We will briefly present some basic considerations to help guide the selection of appropriate values. However, it is possible to have a deeper and more detailed discussion of this topic.[11]

The mean vector **m** consists of the prior estimates in the Bayesian estimation. Commonly used options for **m** would be prior estimates for the group in question (if they exist) or published tables. In connection with the mortality illustration of Kimeldorf and Jones, the use of published mortality tables for values of **m** would be quite common.

The specification of the matrix **A** is, beyond a doubt, the most difficult and subjective aspect of performing a Bayesian graduation. The elements a_{ii} on the positive diagonal are the variances of the random variables contained in the vector **W**. These should be selected first by the modeler using whatever available insight and experience the modeler believes is appropriate for the problem at hand.

Once the variances are specified, the covariances a_{ij}, where $i \neq j$ can be chosen. Since the matrix **A** is symmetric, we know that $a_{ij} = a_{ji}$. One substitution that is often helpful is to consider the correlation coefficient between W_i and W_j, denoted by c_{ij} and given by

$$a_{ij} = c_{ij}\sqrt{a_{ii}a_{jj}}\,. \tag{15.30}$$

[11] For a more extensive discussion the reader is referred to [20], the original paper by Kimeldorf and Jones, or to Chapter 5 of London [25].

The rationale for using this formula is that correlation coefficients have an intuitive interpretation that is lacking with covariances.

Typically, the modeler would expect that correlations between values of W_i and W_j would be larger when i is close to j and would diminish as i and j move further apart. Thus, if j is closer to i than is k, we are suggesting that $c_{ij} > c_{ik}$. This does not imply that $a_{ij} > a_{ik}$, but rather that

$$\frac{a_{ij}}{\sqrt{a_{jj}}} > \frac{a_{ik}}{\sqrt{a_{kk}}}. \qquad (15.31)$$

One simple formula suggested by Kimeldorf and Jones based on constant variances and correlation coefficients is

$$a_{ij} = p^2 \cdot r^{|i-j|}, \qquad (15.32)$$

where $p > 0$ and $0 \le r < 1$. In Equation (15.32) p^2 is the variance of W_i, which is assumed to be constant for all i. The value r is the (constant) correlation coefficient between W_i and W_j when $|i-j| = 1$. Then if $|i-j| = 2$, for example, the correlation coefficient between W_i and W_j would be r^2, and so on.

Two straightforward generalizations of Equation (15.32) are possible. The first is to allow the correlation coefficients to vary between each adjacent pair of values, which gives the formula

$$a_{ij} = p^2 \cdot r_i \cdot r_{i+1} \cdot \cdots \cdot r_{j-1}. \qquad (15.33)$$

The second generalization is to remove the constant variance assumption in Equation (15.32), which gives the formula

$$a_{ij} = p_i \cdot p_j \cdot r^{|i-j|}. \qquad (15.34)$$

Finally, we come to the specification of the matrix **B**. Recall that **B** is diagonal, reflecting the independence assumption, and the element b_{ii} is the variance of U_i in the conditional distribution of **U** given **w**. As we saw several times in Chapters 9 and 10, the variance of the binomial proportion estimator can be written as

$$Var(U_i) = \frac{w_i(1-w_i)}{n_i},$$

where n_i is the number of trials in the binominal process. However, in the Kimeldorf-Jones method, **B** must be free of **w**, so a reasonable alternative formula would be

$$b_{ii} = \frac{m_i(1-m_i)}{n_i}, \tag{15.35}$$

since **m** is our prior "best estimate" of **W**.

EXAMPLE 15.15

We wish to perform a Bayesian graduation for retirement mortality rates at ages 65, 75, 85, and 95, using the information displayed in Table 15.3 on the following page.

We make the following assumptions concerning the elements in the variance-covariance matrix **A**: (1) The coefficient of variation (C.V.) in the prior rates varies as shown in Table 15.3. (2) The correlation coefficient is .60 for each pair of rates one unit apart, $(.60)^2$ for each pair of rates two units apart, and so on, where each unit is ten years.

We will perform a Bayesian graduation based on this information using Equations (15.27), (15.34), and (15.35), to obtain the graduated values v_i at the four given ages. Then we calculate the ratio v_i / m_i at each age and compare it with the ratio u_i / m_i.

TABLE 15.3

Input Data for Example 15.15					
Age i	**Prior Rate**[12] m_i	**Sample Rate** u_i	**Ratio** u_i / m_i	**Sample Size** n_i	**C.V.Prior** $\sqrt{a_{ii}} / m_i$
65	.0172	.0516	3.00	200	.40
75	.0413	.0620	1.50	120	.30
85	.1080	.2160	2.00	60	.20
95	.2779	.3335	1.20	20	.10

SOLUTION

We first construct the variance-covariance matrix **A**. We use the given coefficient of variation information to compute the standard deviations, obtaining $\sigma_{65} = .00688$, $\sigma_{75} = .01239$, $\sigma_{85} = .02160$, and $\sigma_{95} = .02779$. These values, when squared, are the variances a_{ii} on the main diagonal of **A**.

[12] The prior rates in this example are taken from the 2006 Life Table for males (rounded to four decimals), available on the website of the Social Security Administration Office of the Actuary at the time this textbook was being written. As noted, the use of published mortality tables as the source for prior information is quite common in Bayesian graduation. In this example, the sample data has apparently been drawn from a group with substantially higher mortality than the published table, but also with an element of "lumpiness" of excess mortality by age that would be typical of sample data.

We next use Equation (15.34), with the above standard deviations and the correlation coefficient $r = .60$, to compute the covariances. The result of these calculations gives us the matrix **A** (values $\times 10^{-3}$) as

$$\mathbf{A} = \begin{vmatrix} .0473 & .0511 & .0535 & .0413 \\ .0511 & .1535 & .1606 & .1240 \\ .0535 & .1606 & .4666 & .3602 \\ .0413 & .1240 & .3602 & .7723 \end{vmatrix}.$$

Next we use Equation (15.35) to compute the matrix **B** (values $\times 10^{-3}$), obtaining

$$\mathbf{B} = \begin{vmatrix} .0845 & 0 & 0 & 0 \\ 0 & .3300 & 0 & 0 \\ 0 & 0 & 1.6056 & 0 \\ 0 & 0 & 0 & 10.0336 \end{vmatrix}.$$

We now have all the ingredients needed to calculate the values of **v** from Equation (15.27). We need to invert several 4 × 4 matrices, which we accomplish using freely available internet software possessing matrix inversion functionality.

Not all steps in the solution are presented here due to space considerations, but three intermediate results are shown to provide the reader with some of the key steps in the solution. The first intermediate result is the calculation of the matrix $(\mathbf{A}^{-1} + \mathbf{B}^{-1})^{-1}$, which is (values $\times 10^{-4}$)

$$(\mathbf{A}^{-1} + \mathbf{B}^{-1})^{-1} = \begin{vmatrix} 0.27693 & 0.22019 & 0.19166 & 0.14099 \\ 0.22019 & 0.89858 & 0.78144 & 0.57526 \\ 0.19166 & 0.78144 & 3.16172 & 2.32652 \\ 0.14099 & 0.57526 & 2.32652 & 6.42226 \end{vmatrix}.$$

The second intermediate result is the calculation of the vector $\mathbf{B}^{-1}\mathbf{u}$, which is

$$\mathbf{B}^{-1}\mathbf{u} = [610.634, 187.860, 134.568, 33.350]^T.$$

The third intermediate result is the calculation of the vector $\mathbf{A}^{-1}\mathbf{m}$, which is

$$\mathbf{A}^{-1}\mathbf{m} = [113.941, 3.998, -96.841, 393.472]^T.$$

Putting it all together we have the results displayed in Table 15.4 on the following page.

TABLE 15.4

Output Data for Example 15.15					
Age i	**Prior Rate** m_i	**Sample Rate** u_i	**Graduated Rate** v_i	**Ratio** u_i / m_i	**Ratio** v_i / m_i
65	.0172	.0516	.0312	3.00	1.81
75	.0413	.0620	.0615	1.50	1.49
85	.1080	.2160	.1433	2.00	1.33
95	.2779	.3335	.3065	1.20	1.10

The results of the graduation are quite interesting. The graduated rates v_i lie between the prior rates m_i and the sample rates u_i, as we would expect in any Bayesian process blending together prior information with sample information. It is also instructive to compare the two ratio columns. The final column is a smoother set of ratios than is the next-to-last column, clearly demonstrating the graduation effect that has been achieved.

15.7 SUMMARY

In Chapter 15 we introduced various Bayesian techniques, including Bayesian parameter estimation. Bayesian techniques are conceptually quite distinct from the techniques presented in Chapters 13 and 14. Bayesian techniques do not base parameter estimates strictly on the sample obtained, but instead blend together the new sample information with prior information existing before the sample was taken.

We first discussed the familiar discrete version of Bayes' Theorem covered in basic courses in probability. This was followed by detailed coverage of the more sophisticated continuous version of Bayes' Theorem. Precise definitions were given for key terms in Bayesian estimation, including model distribution or likelihood, prior distribution, posterior distribution, predictive distribution, and the conjugate property.

We then demonstrated Bayesian parameter estimation using the Poisson-gamma continuous mixture model as an extended illustration. Other continuous mixture combinations possessing the conjugate property were also noted.

Next, we covered three common Bayesian loss functions, namely square error loss, absolute loss, and almost constant loss. These three functions were illustrated graphically and with examples.

We then discussed Bayesian confidence intervals, which are usually called credibility intervals. The unfortunate ambiguity in the terms "loss function" and "credibility interval," when used in actuarial applications, was highlighted. Three types of credibility intervals were discussed. The first was the familiar equal probability interval, which has equal probability in each tail. The second was the highest posterior density (HPD) interval, which is the shortest possible interval with the requisite probability mass. The third was a description of the Bayesian Central Limit Theorem.

Finally, we presented an overview of Bayesian graduation, illustrating an application of the Bayesian principles introduced earlier in the chapter to the classical actuarial process of graduation discussed in Chapter 12.

15.8 EXERCISES

15.1 Introduction
15.2 Bayes' Theorem

15-1 A portfolio of independent risks is divided into two classes, Class A and Class B. There are twice as many risks in Class A as in Class B. The number of claims for each insured during a single year follows a Bernoulli distribution. Classes A and B have claim size distributions as follows:

Claim Size	Class A	Class B
50,000	.60	.36
100,000	.40	.64

The expected number of claims per year is .22 for Class A and .11 for Class B. One insured is chosen at random. The insured's loss for two years combined is 100,000. Calculate the probability that the selected insured belongs to Class A.

15-2 Prior to observing any claims, we believed that claim sizes followed a Pareto distribution with parameters $\theta = 10$ and $\alpha = 1, 2,$ or 3, with each value being equally likely. We then observe one claim of 20 for a randomly selected risk. Determine the posterior probability that the next claim for this risk will be greater than 30.

15-3 Two classes of policyholders have the following severity distributions:

Claim Amount x	Class 1 Probability $p_1(x)$	Class 2 Probability $p_2(x)$
250	.50	.70
2,500	.30	.20
60,000	.20	.10

Class 1 has twice as many claims as Class 2. A claim of 250 is observed. Determine the Bayesian estimate of the expected value of a second claim from the same policyholder.

15-4 An observation from a single experiment has the probability function

$$Pr(D = d \mid G = g) = g^{1-d}(1-g)^d,$$

for $d = 0,1$. The prior distribution of G is

$$Pr\left(G=\frac{1}{5}\right) = \frac{3}{5}$$

and

$$Pr\left(G=\frac{1}{3}\right) = \frac{2}{5}.$$

Calculate the value of

$$Pr\left(G=\frac{1}{3}\middle|D=0\right).$$

15-5 Consider the information in the following table:

Class	Number of Insureds	Claim Count Probabilities				
		0	1	2	3	4
1	3000	1/3	1/3	1/3	0	0
2	2000	0	1/6	2/3	1/6	0
3	1000	0	0	1/6	2/3	1/6

A randomly selected insured has one claim in Year 1. Determine the expected number of claims in Year 2 for that insured.

15-6 A portfolio consists of 100 independent risks, with an identical claim frequency distribution and the following per claim policy limits censoring the severity distribution:

Number of Risks	Policy Limit
25	5,000
25	10,000
50	20,000

Prior to censoring by policy limit, claim sizes for each risk follow a Pareto distribution with parameters $\alpha=2$ and $\theta=5000$. A claims report is available which shows the number of claims in various claim size ranges for each policy after censoring by policy limit, but does not identify the policy limit associated with each policy. The claims report shows exactly one claim for a policy selected at random. This claim falls in the claim size range from 9,000 to 11,000. Determine the probability that this policy has a 10,000 policy limit.

15-7 Rework Example 15.4 if both insureds have one claim during the next year.

15.3 Bayesian Parameter Estimation

15-8 The annual number of claims for a policyholder, N, follows a Poisson distribution with mean λ. The prior distribution of the random variable Λ is gamma with probability density function

$$f_{\Lambda}(\lambda) = \frac{4\lambda^4 e^{-2\lambda}}{3},$$

for $\lambda > 0$. An insured is selected at random and observed to have $N_1 = 5$ claims during Year 1 and $N_2 = 3$ claims during Year 2. Determine the value of the posterior expectation $E[\Lambda \mid N_1 = 5 \text{ and } N_2 = 3]$.

15-9 The number of claims per year for a given risk follows a Poisson distribution with mean λ. The prior distribution of the random variable Λ is assumed to be gamma, with coefficient of variation $\frac{1}{6}$. Determine the coefficient of variation of the posterior distribution of Λ, after 160 claims have been observed for this risk in one year.

15-10 Use the probability density function

$$f(x;\theta) = \frac{\theta e^{-\theta x^{1/2}}}{2x^{1/2}},$$

for $x > 0$ and $\theta > 0$, together with the sample observations 1, 4, 9, and 64, to find the Bayesian estimate for the parameter θ based on the mean of the posterior distribution, if the prior distribution of the random variable Θ is gamma with parameters $\alpha = .70$ and $\beta = 2$.

15-11 The number of claims during one year for an employee covered by workers' compensation follows a Poisson distribution with mean $\frac{100-p}{100}$, where p is the salary (in thousands) for the employee. The distribution of the random variable P is uniform on the interval (0, 100]. An employee is selected at random. No claims were observed for this employee during the year. Determine the posterior probability that the selected employee has salary greater than 50 thousand.

15-12 Claim size amounts follow a Pareto distribution with parameters $\alpha = 2$ and θ. The prior distribution of the random variable Θ has probability density function

$$\pi_{\Theta}(\theta) = \frac{1}{\theta^2},$$

for $1 < \theta < \infty$. One claim of size 3 is observed. Calculate the posterior probability that Θ exceeds 2.

15-13 The probability that an insured will have exactly one claim is θ. The prior distribution of the random variable Θ has probability density function

$$\pi_{\Theta}(\theta) = \frac{3}{2}\sqrt{\theta},$$

for $0<\theta<1$. A randomly chosen insured is observed to have exactly one claim. Determine the posterior probability that Θ is greater than .60.

15-14 An individual automobile insured has an annual claim frequency that follows a Poisson distribution with mean λ. The prior distribution for the random variable Λ has the mixture PDF

$$\pi_{\Lambda}(\lambda) = \frac{1}{2}\left[5e^{-5\lambda}+.20e^{-\lambda/5}\right],$$

for $\lambda>0$. In the first policy year, no claims were observed for this insured. Determine the expected number of claims in the second policy year.

15.4 Loss Functions

15-15 Determine the point estimate $\hat{\theta}$ which minimizes the expected value of the posterior squared error loss function, given the sample of loss amounts $\{1, 2, 6, 15, 21\}$. Assume that the mean of the posterior distribution of the parameter is equal to the mean of the sample.

15-16 Calculate the expected value of the squared error loss function using the parameter estimate $\hat{\theta}$ obtained in Exercise 15-15 and the probability density function for θ given by $g(\theta)=\frac{1}{6}$, for $6\leq\theta\leq 12$.

15-17 (a) Rework Exercise 15-15 using the absolute loss function, based on the median of the sample using smoothed empirical percentiles, rather than the squared error loss function.

(b) Rework Exercise 15-16 using the point estimate obtained in part (a) and the absolute loss function rather than the squared error loss function.

15-18 (a) Determine the point estimate $\hat{\theta}$ which minimizes the expected value of the posterior almost constant loss function, given the sample of claim frequencies $\{0, 0, 1, 1, 1, 3\}$. The value of c is assumed to be 3. Assume that the mode of the posterior distribution of the parameter is equal to the mode of the sample.

(b) Calculate the expected value of the almost constant loss function if the parameter θ is assumed to have the discrete distribution $p(\theta)=\frac{1}{4}$ for $\theta=0,1,2,3$.

15-19 A popular variation of the absolute loss function replaces Equation (15.16) with

$$\ell(\hat{\theta},\theta) = \left| \begin{array}{ll} a(\theta-\hat{\theta}) & \text{if } \theta>\hat{\theta} \\ b(\hat{\theta}-\theta) & \text{if } \theta<\hat{\theta} \end{array} \right|.$$

The purpose of using such a loss function is to model a lack of symmetry in the severity of estimation errors above and below the parameter's true value. It can be shown that the percentile that will minimize this loss function is given by

$$p=\frac{a}{a+b},$$

where smoothed empirical percentiles are used. (Note that if $a=b=1$, then the standard absolute loss function is obtained and the above formula gives $p=.50$, which is the median). If $a=1$ and $b=2$, find the parameter estimate that is obtained using the sample values $\{-.70, 1.10, 3.00, 3.20, 6.80\}$.

15-20 The number of claims made by an individual in any given year has a binomial distribution with parameters $n=4$ and unknown p. The prior distribution of the random variable P has probability density function

$$\pi_P(p) = 6p(1-p),$$

for $0<p<1$. Two claims are made in a given year. Find the estimate of p that will minimize the expected value of the almost constant loss function.

15.5 Confidence (Credibility) Intervals

15-21 Bayesian parameter estimation for an unknown parameter λ results in a posterior distribution which is Weibull with parameters $\theta=10$ and τ=2. Develop two equations in two unknowns, λ_L and λ_R, that must be solved in order to determine the 90% highest posterior density (HPD) credibility interval.

15-22 Bayesian parameter estimation for an unknown parameter λ results in a posterior distribution for λ which is a single parameter Pareto with $\alpha=2$ and $\theta=1$.

(a) Find the 90% equal probability confidence interval.

(b) Find the 90% highest posterior density (HPD) confidence interval.

(c) What is the ratio of the length of the confidence interval in (b) to the length of the confidence interval in (a)?

15-23 Consider the following information:

Loss Experience	Number of Policies
No claims	1600
One or more claims	400

Using the normal approximation, determine the upper bound of the symmetric 95% confidence interval for the probability that a single policy has one or more claims.

15.6 Bayesian Graduation

15-24 Complete the development of the Kimeldorf-Jones method by providing the following derivations not presented in the text:

(a) Derive Equation (15.26) from Equation (15.25) by the following steps:

(i) Multiply out the exponent in Equation (15.25), recalling that $(\mathbf{w}-\mathbf{m})^T = \mathbf{w}^T - \mathbf{m}^T$. (Keep all terms in order since commutativity does not always hold.)

(ii) Factor out two terms not involving $\mathbf{w}$, combining them with k_3.

(iii) Rearrange the six remaining terms, doing some factoring to the left, or right, or both, to obtain

$$-\frac{1}{2}\left[\mathbf{w}^T(\mathbf{A}^{-1}+\mathbf{B}^{-1})\mathbf{w}-\mathbf{w}^T(\mathbf{B}^{-1}\mathbf{u}+\mathbf{A}^{-1}\mathbf{m})-(\mathbf{u}^T\mathbf{B}^{-1}+\mathbf{m}^T\mathbf{A}^{-1})\mathbf{w}\right]$$

as the new exponent.

(iv) Substitute $\mathbf{v}$ and $\mathbf{C}$, as defined by Equations (15.27) and (15.28), into the exponent of (iii) to obtain

$$-\frac{1}{2}\left[\mathbf{w}^T\mathbf{C}^{-1}\mathbf{w}-\mathbf{w}^T\mathbf{C}^{-1}\mathbf{v}-(\mathbf{u}^T\mathbf{B}^{-1}+\mathbf{m}^T\mathbf{A}^{-1})\mathbf{w}\right]$$

as the new exponent.

(v) From Equations (15.27) and (15.28), $\mathbf{C}^{-1}\mathbf{v}=(\mathbf{B}^{-1}\mathbf{u}+\mathbf{A}^{-1}\mathbf{m})$ so that $\mathbf{v}^T\mathbf{C}^{-1}=\mathbf{u}^T\mathbf{B}^{-1}+\mathbf{m}^T\mathbf{A}^{-1}$, due to the symmetry of **A**, **B**, and **C**. Substitute this into the exponent of (iv).

(vi) Add and subtract $\mathbf{v}^T\mathbf{C}^{-1}\mathbf{v}$ in the exponent, factor out the negative term, combining it with the constant. The remaining four terms are the expansion of

$$(\mathbf{w}-\mathbf{v})^T\mathbf{C}^{-1}(\mathbf{w}-\mathbf{v}),$$

which establishes Equation (15.26).

(b) Derive Equation (15.29a) from Equation (15.27). [Hint: Add **u** and then subtract it as $(\mathbf{A}^{-1}+\mathbf{B}^{-1})^{-1}(\mathbf{A}^{-1}+\mathbf{B}^{-1})\mathbf{u}$.]

(c) Derive Equation (15.29b) from Equation 15.27). [Hint: Add **m** and then subtract it as $(\mathbf{A}^{-1}+\mathbf{B}^{-1})^{-1}(\mathbf{A}^{-1}+\mathbf{B}^{-1})\mathbf{m}$.]

15-25 Rework Example 15.15 assuming that the mortality rates at the four ages are independent, so that the covariance terms in the matrix **A** are all equal to zero. Does this increase or decrease the weighting put on the sample data compared with the original Example 15.15?

15-26 Suppose W_1, W_2, and W_3 are assumed to be independent normal random variables, with prior means and variances given by

$$\mathbf{m} = [2, 6, 16]^T$$

and

$$\mathbf{A} = \begin{vmatrix} \frac{1}{4} & 0 & 0 \\ 0 & 1 & 0 \\ 0 & 0 & 2 \end{vmatrix}.$$

An experiment produces observations given by $\mathbf{u}=[1,4,18]^T$, with $Var(\mathbf{U}\,|\,\mathbf{W})$ given by

$$\mathbf{B} = \begin{vmatrix} \frac{1}{5} & 0 & 0 \\ 0 & \frac{3}{4} & 0 \\ 0 & 0 & \frac{3}{2} \end{vmatrix}.$$

Using the Kimeldorf-Jones method, find the vector of graduated values **v**. Express the answer in fractional form rather than decimal form.

15-27 For a set of normal random variables W_i, for $i=1,2,\ldots,6$, the following have been selected:

(i) The mean vector is $\mathbf{m}=[.314,.329,.345,.360,.376,.392]^T$.

(ii) The variance of each U_i is calculated using Equation (15.35), where $\mathbf{n}=[100,70,50,30,20,10]^T$.

(iii) Each adjacent pair W_i, W_{i+1} is correlated by $r=.90$; each pair W_i, W_{i+2} is correlated by $r=.40$; each pair W_i, W_{i+3} is correlated by $r=.10$; all other pairs are uncorrelated.

Complete the matrix **A** to four decimal places.

15.7 Summary

(Authors' Note: The following three exercises illustrate the three mixtures listed at the top of page 407. The full development of these methods is not provided here, but applications of them are illustrated. Readers interested in a more complete development are referred to Section 8.3 of Herzog [15].)

15-28 In the first case, the likelihood distribution is Bernoulli with parameter p so that

$$p_N(1|p) = p$$

and

$$p_N(0|p) = 1-p.$$

In turn, the parameter p, as a random variable, follows a beta distribution with parameters a and b, so the prior distribution of P is

$$g_P(p) = \frac{\Gamma(a+b)}{\Gamma(a)\cdot\Gamma(b)}\cdot p^{a-1}(1-p)^{b-1}.$$

The posterior distribution is again a beta distribution (i.e., it possesses the conjugate property), now with parameters

$$a^* = a+\sum_{i=1}^{n} n_i \tag{15.36a}$$

and

$$b^* = b+n-\sum_{i=1}^{n} n_i\,. \tag{15.36b}$$

In words, the parameter a is updated by the total number of claims, and the parameter b is updated by the total number of non-claims in n trials. If the prior distribution is beta with $a=3$ and $b=7$, and in the next ten Bernoulli trials four claims are observed, find the mean of the posterior beta distribution (which is also the mean of the predictive distribution).

15-29 In the second case, the likelihood distribution is normal with parameters μ_1 and σ_1. The parameter μ_1 follows a prior distribution which is also normal with parameters μ_2 and σ_2. Then the posterior distribution is normal (due to the conjugate property) with parameters

$$\mu_2{}^* = \frac{\mu_2\sigma_1^2+\sigma_2^2\sum_{i=1}^{n} x_i}{\sigma_1^2+n\sigma_2^2} \tag{15.37a}$$

and

$$\sigma_2^* = \sqrt{\frac{\sigma_1^2\sigma_2^2}{\sigma_1^2 + n\sigma_2^2}}. \tag{15.37b}$$

Suppose the likelihood distribution is normal with mean μ_1 and standard deviation 3. The mean μ_1, in turn, follows another normal distribution with mean currently estimated to be 20 and standard deviation currently estimated to be 1. Three losses are observed, equal to 21, 25, and 26. Find the mean of the posterior distribution (which is also the mean of the predictive distribution).

15-30 In the third case, the likelihood distribution is exponential (as defined by Equation 1.25a) with parameter λ. The parameter λ follows a prior distribution which is gamma (as defined by Equation 1.55) with parameters α and β. The posterior distribution is gamma (conjugate property) with parameters

$$\alpha^* = \alpha + n \tag{15.38a}$$

and

$$\beta^* = \beta + \sum_{i=1}^{n} x_i. \tag{15.38b}$$

In words, the parameter α is updated by the total number of claims, and the parameter β is updated by the total amount paid on the claims. Suppose the prior density of the parameter λ is

$$\pi_\Lambda(\lambda) = \lambda e^{-\lambda},$$

and one claim of size 5 is observed. Determine the posterior density of λ.

CHAPTER SIXTEEN

TESTING AND SELECTING MODELS

16.1 INTRODUCTION

Chapter 16 brings us to the logical conclusion of Part IV of this book, which is devoted to the estimation of parametric models. The prior three chapters dealt extensively with a variety of techniques for estimating parameters of a distribution based wholly, or in part, on sample data. The remaining issue now is the important matter of actually selecting a model in which we have confidence to use for measuring frequency, severity, and aggregate losses in various loss processes.

The focus of this chapter can be summarized into three primary categories of questions:

(1) The prior three chapters dealt with a variety of methods to fit parameters to a parametric distribution. Now that we have obtained the estimated parameters, we must address the important question, "How closely does this parametric distribution reproduce the sample data obtained?" In other words, "How good is the fit?" To answer this question, we will discuss a number of different *tests of fit*.

(2) In some cases, depending on the situation, there may be a compelling case for which distribution we should use. In many other cases, however, there may be several different potential distributions that could appropriately be used. If this is the case, then typically we need to estimate parameters for each of the potential candidates. The question then becomes, "Given the array of potential distributions we could use to model the data, which one should we choose?" To answer this question, we will discuss several different criteria to use in deciding which distribution to choose.

(3) Finally, once we make the decision described in Item (2), we may discover that the chosen distribution is complicated and difficult to apply. The question then becomes, "Is there a simpler distribution that would be 'good enough,' or do we need to retain the more complex distribution to obtain sufficient accuracy?" We will present two different tests on which to base this decision.

Chapter 16 will make use of hypothesis testing and related results from statistical inference. Readers who may be a bit rusty on this material are encouraged to review Chapter 2 to strengthen their background prior to proceeding further.

16.2 GRAPHICAL COMPARISONS

Sections 16.2 and 16.3 present several different tests of fit for the parameters that have been estimated by one of the techniques covered in Chapters 13, 14, and 15. The most rudimentary tests of fit are simple *graphical comparisons* between the sample distribution and the fitted model. Four of these graphical tests are discussed in this section.

16.2.1 OVERLAYS OF PDFS AND CDFS

The two most basic graphical comparison tests of fit are (1) those between the raw sample data and the fitted PDF, and (2) those between the sample (empirical) CDF and the fitted CDF. Each test is really nothing more than a decision by the modeler, based on a visual comparison, as to whether the graphs of the sample distribution and the fitted model are "close enough" for the purpose at hand.

Obviously, these are non-rigorous tests involving considerable subjective judgment by the modeler. However, they are potentially useful in gaining a quick insight into whether or not a particular distribution might be a contender to use as the fitted model, and might therefore be useful in rejecting those that clearly are not "close enough." For those distributions showing promise, these simple visual tests could be followed by the more formal and rigorous tests to be discussed in Section 16.3.

The fitted model can be either discrete or continuous. The graphical comparison methods are more frequently used with a continuous fitted model than with a discrete one. Although they can be used with discrete model distributions, they really add little to the insight that can be gained by simply reviewing a tabular display of values.

The sample distribution is, of necessity, discrete, since the sample probability masses occur in discrete segments as each sample value is obtained. When the PDF is being used and exact values (complete data) are available in the sample, an immediate issue arises. Since the probability of equal independent outcomes from a continuous distribution is presumably zero, each sample value should be a distinct number.

If the sample is i.i.d. and of size n, then the raw sample data will be n irregularly spaced values along the x-axis, each with probability mass of $1/n$. In such cases, it is often difficult to compare such a graph with a continuous PDF and reach meaningful insights. For this reason, the sample data are often grouped in some fashion, which permits the use of a histogram to represent it. The potential for comparing a histogram with a continuous PDF and reaching some meaningful insight is often enhanced.

In order to illustrate these graphical techniques, we will use a simple example as the basis for Figures 16.1, 16.2, and 16.3. Consider a sample of $n=5$ values equal to 1, 2, 3, 5, and 9, being fitted to an exponential distribution. The parameter estimate for θ, using either the method of moments or maximum likelihood, will be the sample mean, which is

$$\hat{\theta} = \bar{x} = \frac{1}{5}(1+2+3+5+9) = 4.$$

Values of the PDF and CDF for a fitted exponential distribution with $\hat{\theta}=4$, at integer values including $x=0$, are given in Table 16.1.

Figure 16.1a presents a graphical fitted PDF overlay against the raw sample data. Figure 16.1b presents a graphical fitted PDF overlay against a histogram in which the raw data have been grouped into the five intervals $0.5 \le x < 2.5$; $2.5 \le x < 4.5$; $4.5 \le x < 6.5$; $6.5 \le x < 8.5$; and $8.5 \le x < 10.5$.

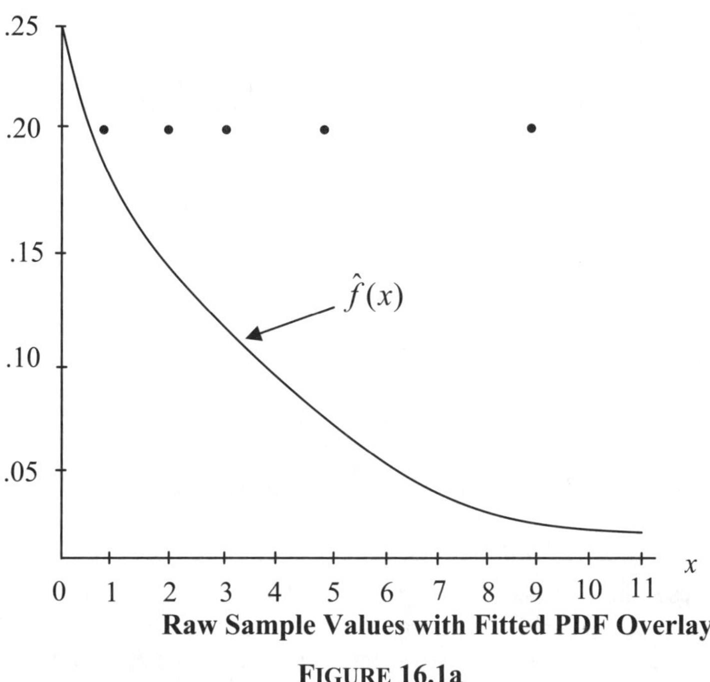

Raw Sample Values with Fitted PDF Overlay

FIGURE 16.1a

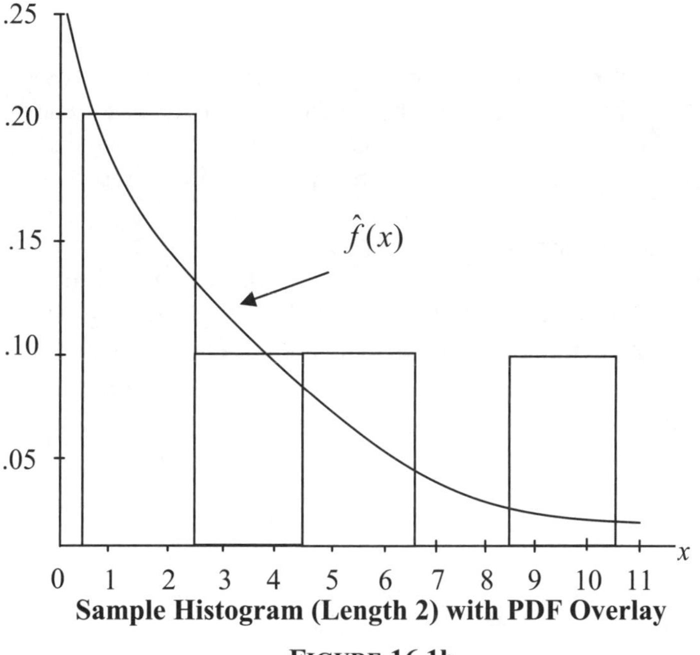

Sample Histogram (Length 2) with PDF Overlay

FIGURE 16.1b

TABLE 16.1

Fitted Exponential Distribution Values, with $\hat{\theta} = 4$		
x	$\hat{f}(x)$	$\hat{F}(x)$
0	.250	.000
1	.195	.221
2	.152	.393
3	.118	.528
4	.092	.632
5	.072	.714
6	.056	.777
7	.043	.826
8	.034	.865
9	.026	.895
10	.021	.918

In view of these challenges involving a fitted PDF overlay against the raw sample data, many modelers using graphical comparison methods tend to prefer using CDFs (although both can be reviewed in tandem, and often are). The visual comparison of the sample (or empirical) CDF and the fitted model CDF can be more readily interpreted graphically. Continuing the example, such a comparison using CDFs is given in Figure 16.2 on the following page.

Another issue to consider is the possibility of using truncated and/or censored distributions. In previous chapters, we have seen that these modifications to distributions frequently arise in many of the common applications considered in this text. Truncated and censored distributions do not present any new difficulties in applying these graphical comparison methods.

First, it is necessary for consistency that the same modification be applied to both the sample distribution and the fitted model. Next, consider the common situation of left truncation. Both the sample distribution CDF and the fitted model CDF start at some value $d > 0$ and the visual comparison proceeds as usual. The example is continued with $d = 1.5$, and is illustrated in Figure 16.3a.

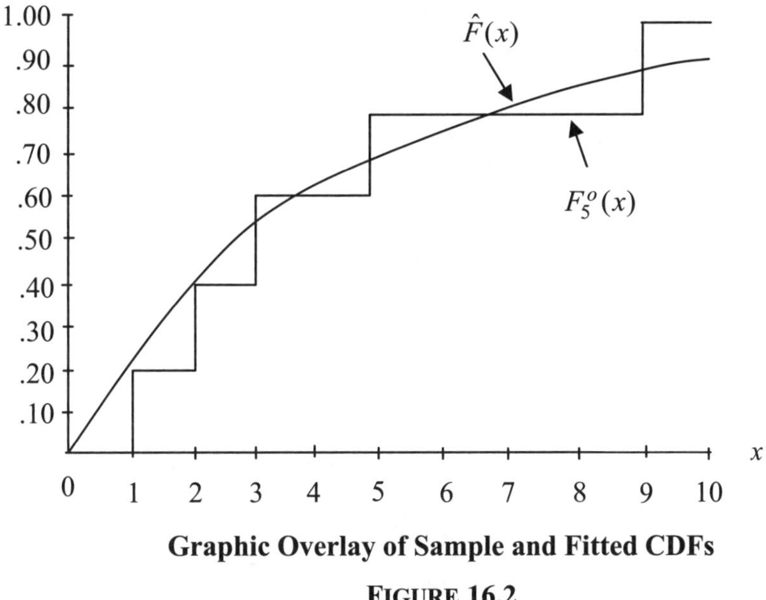

Graphic Overlay of Sample and Fitted CDFs

FIGURE 16.2

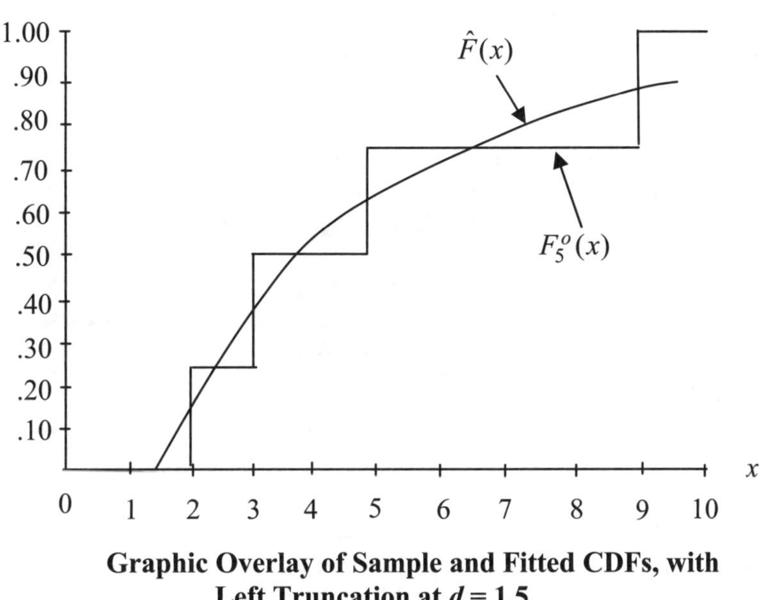

Graphic Overlay of Sample and Fitted CDFs, with Left Truncation at $d = 1.5$

FIGURE 16.3a

Finally, consider the common situation of right censoring. Both the sample distribution CDF and the fitted model CDF reach a value of one at the censoring point, and continue at that value for all $X \geq u$. The example is continued with $u = 6$, and is illustrated in Figure 16.3b.

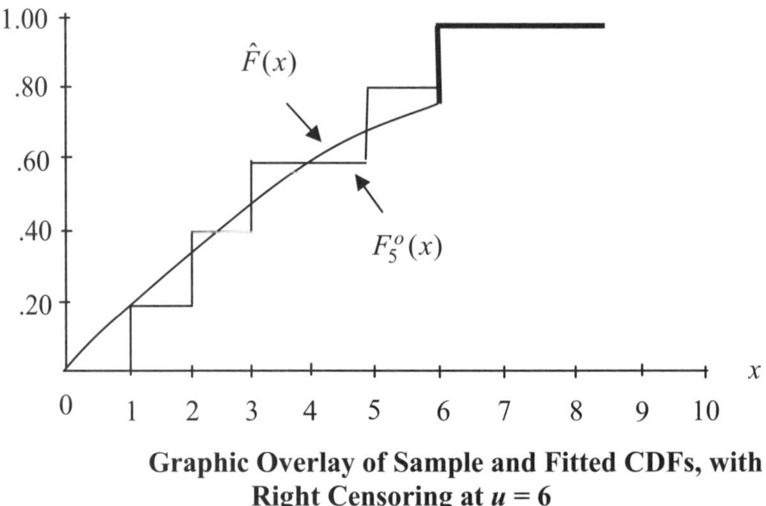

Graphic Overlay of Sample and Fitted CDFs, with Right Censoring at $u = 6$

FIGURE 16.3b

EXAMPLE 16.1

Apply a graphical comparison of the sample histogram with the fitted gamma distribution, with parameters estimated by the method of moments, from Example 13.2.

SOLUTION

The sample consists of the 10 claim amounts 1, 1, 1, 2, 2, 3, 5, 7, 8, and 16. From Example 13.2, the gamma parameter estimates are $\hat{\alpha} = 1.63265$ and $\hat{\theta} = 2.45$.

The fitted gamma distribution CDF involves the incomplete gamma function, and cannot be evaluated analytically. However, it is possible to evaluate both the gamma PDF and CDF using the GAMMADIST functionality in EXCEL. The values to three decimals are displayed in Table 10.2 for non-negative integers from 0 through 10.

TABLE 16.2

Fitted Gamma Distribution Values, with $\hat{\alpha} = 1.63265$ and $\hat{\theta} = 2.45$		
x	PDF $\hat{f}(x)$	CDF $\hat{F}(x)$
0	.000	.000
1	.172	.123
2	.177	.302
3	.152	.467
4	.121	.604
5	.093	.711
6	.069	.791
7	.051	.851
8	.037	.894
9	.026	.925
10	.019	.948

It is clear that something is unusual, and requires interpretation, with this sample data. All the sample values are positive integers and duplications exist in the data. This clearly is not the pattern that would be expected to occur if exact sample values were being used, so some type of grouping must be going on within the sample data. We choose to interpret these values as being rounded to the nearest integer, which appears to be a reasonable assumption under the circumstances. Also, this assumption will not change the original parameter estimates using the method of moments.

The graphical comparison using the sample histogram and fitted PDF is displayed in Figure 16.4, taking the fitted PDF values from the second column of Table 16.2. The histogram display uses length one, which is consistent with our assumption of round-off to the nearest integer.

In interpreting the goodness of fit, it must be kept in mind that a sample of size 10 is quite small. No graphical test of fit is likely to result in a close match for any distribution. In real-world applications, much larger sample sizes would typically be utilized in this type of analysis, if possible.

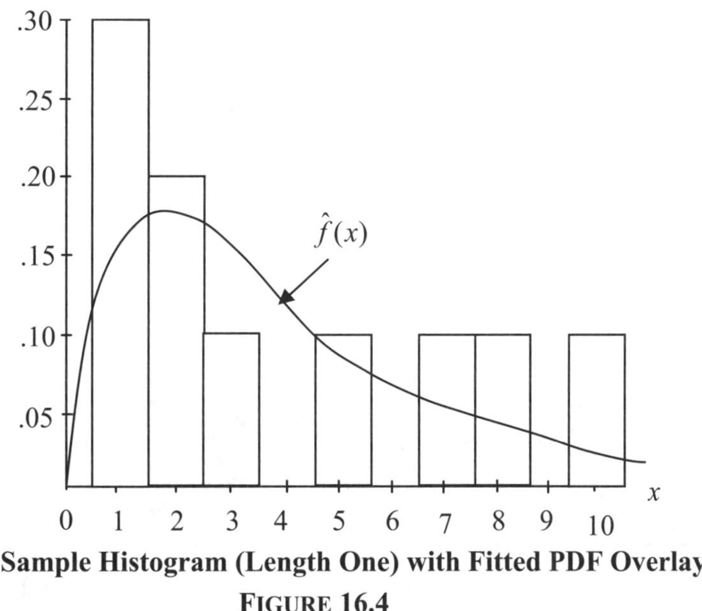

Sample Histogram (Length One) with Fitted PDF Overlay

FIGURE 16.4 ❐

EXAMPLE 16.2

Rework Example 16.1 using a graphical comparison CDF test.

SOLUTION

The graphical comparison using the CDF values is displayed in Figure 16.5 on the following page, taking the fitted CDF values from the third column of Table 16.2 and the empirical (sample) CDF values from Table 16.3.

TABLE 16.3

Empirical (Sample) Cumulative Distribution Function Values								
x	0	1	2	3	5	7	8	10
$F_{10}^{o}(x)$	0	.30	.50	.60	.70	.80	.90	1

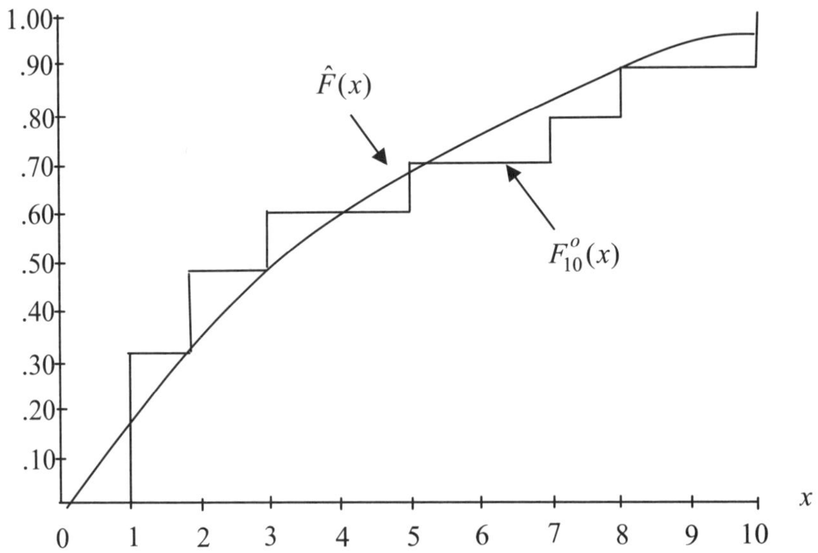

Graphic Overlay of Sample and Fitted CDFs

FIGURE 16.5

Readers should find it easier to visually interpret Figure 16.5 than Figure 16.4. Typically, CDF graphs are easier to interpret for goodness of fit than are fitted PDF overlays against either the raw sample data or a histogram of it. ❒

16.2.2 *D*(*x*) PLOT

When the empirical (sample) distribution CDF and the fitted model CDF are fairly close together, the CDF graphical comparison method, as illustrated in Figure 16.5, may be difficult to interpret. In particular, this type of graph is not very sensitive to small changes in the values of the two cumulative distribution functions.

One way of magnifying small changes so as to better interpret the fit is with the $D(x)$ *plot.* The value of $D(x)$ is defined as

$$D(x) = F_n^o(x) - \hat{F}(x), \qquad (16.1)$$

the difference between the two cumulative distribution functions, where $F_n^o(x)$ is the sample distribution CDF and $\hat{F}(x)$ is the fitted model CDF.

Values of $D(x)$ close to zero reflect close fit between $F_n^o(x)$ and $\hat{F}(x)$. Recall that $F_n^o(x)$ has the familiar stair-step pattern, whereas $\hat{F}(x)$ is continuously increasing. Therefore the graph of $D(x)$ will zigzag back and forth across the x-axis and be positive for some values of x and negative for others. Excellent fit would be characterized by frequent sign changes in $D(x)$, but with values never straying too far above or below zero. Poor fit would be characterized by few signs changes in $D(x)$, protracted intervals with either all positive or negative signs, and greater deviations away from zero.

EXAMPLE 16.3

Rework Example 16.1 using the $D(x)$ plot.

SOLUTION

The data used in the $D(x)$ plot is the same as in the CDF graphical comparison of Example 16.2, but changed into values of $D(x)$ using Equation (16.1). The values at integer points are tabulated in Table 16.4 and the results are displayed in Figure 16.6 on the following page.

Note that, necessarily, $D(0)=0$. Then $F_{10}^o(x)$ stays constant at zero for all $x<1$, but $\hat{F}(x)$ increases continuously from $\hat{F}(0)=0$ to $\hat{F}(1)=.123$. Since $D(x)=F_{10}^o(x)-\hat{F}(x)$, it follows that $D(x)$ will decrease from $D(0)=0$ to $D(1_-)=-.123$, the value of $D(x)$ just before $x=1$. At $x=1$, $F_{10}^o(x)$ jumps to $F_{10}^o(1)=.300$ whereas $\hat{F}(1)$ is still equal to .123, giving us

$$D(1) \;=\; .300-.123 \;=\; .177.$$

This pattern of discrete jumps in $F_{10}^o(x)$ and continuous increase in $\hat{F}(x)$ produces the pattern of $D(x)$ shown in Figure 16.6.

TABLE 16.4

Values of $D(x)$ for Example 16.1 Data

x	$F_{10}^o(x)$	$\hat{F}(x)$	$D(x)$
0	.000	.000	.000
1	.300	.123	.177
2	.500	.302	.198
3	.600	.467	.133
4	.600	.604	−.004
5	.700	.711	−.011
6	.700	.791	−.091
7	.800	.851	−.051
8	.900	.894	.006
9	.900	.925	−.025
10	1.000	.948	.052

The values of $D(x)$ at the left end of the distribution are rather large and all have the same sign, which may indicate a problem, but the pattern seems reasonably good thereafter. Again, when the sample size is this small deviations of this type can be expected. The gamma distribution with these parameters may not be the best possible fit to this sample data, but the $D(x)$ plot by itself certainly is not sufficiently bad to disqualify this distribution without further investigation and consideration of alternatives. ❐

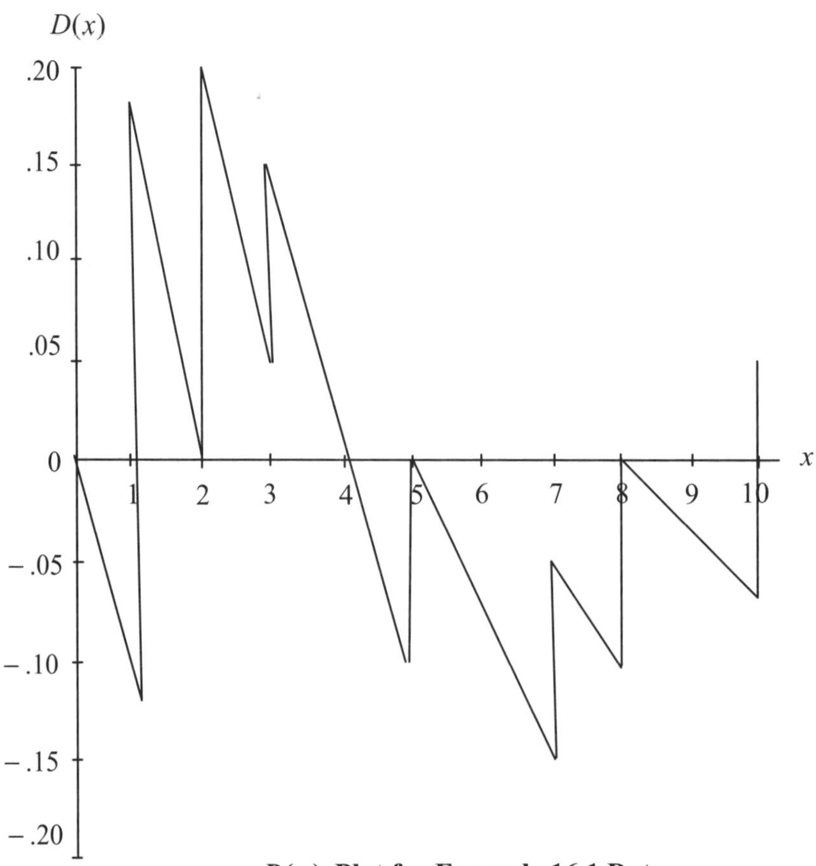

$D(x)$ Plot for Example 16.1 Data

FIGURE 16.6

16.2.3 *p-p* PLOT

The *p-p plot*, sometimes called the *probability plot*, is a second method of magnifying small changes to better interpret the goodness of fit. As such, it is an alternative to the $D(x)$ plot. The basic concept is to construct a graph that plots values for both $F_n^o(x)$ and $\hat{F}(x)$ for each sample value.

These plotted points are then compared visually with a 45° diagonal line running outward from the origin. With perfect fit, the plotted points would all lie on the 45° line, so the closer the plotted points are to the 45° line the better. The further away they are the less favorable is the fit. Also, we like to see several crossings back and forth across the 45° line, rather than extended intervals that lie either above or below the line.

To define the *p-p* plot more precisely, we order the sample of size n so that $x_1 \leq x_2 \leq \cdots \leq x_n$. A point is then plotted for each sample value with (x,y) coordinates given by

$$(x_j, y_j) = \left[F_n^o(x_j), \hat{F}(x_j)\right], \tag{16.2}$$

for $j=1,2,\cdots,n$. There are, however, two refinements to this basic approach that need to be discussed.

First, it can be shown that

$$E\left[F_n^o(x_j)\right] = F_n^*(x_j) = \frac{j}{n+1}, \tag{16.3}$$

rather than $\frac{j}{n}$. These adjusted values F_n^* should be used in constructing the sample CDF. The reader may recall the smoothed empirical percentile technique discussed in Section 13.4.1. There is a strong analogy between the definition of k in Equation (13.12), which defines the smoothed empirical percentile, and Equation (16.3).

Second, we need to have a method of dealing with multiple sample values that are equal. There are several approaches to this that have appeared in the literature. The approach that we adopt is to plot a separate x-coordinate (i.e., value of $F_n^*(x_j)$) for each of the multiple values, but use the same y-coordinate (i.e., value of $\hat{F}(x_j)$) for each.

EXAMPLE 16.4

Rework Example 16.1 using the *p-p* plot.

SOLUTION

The plotted points will be based on the same values of $\hat{F}(x_j)$ used in the prior two examples, but using the adjusted values $F_n^*(x_j)$ as defined by Equation (16.3). Each sample value, including each of the multiples, is considered individually. The results are tabulated in Table 16.5.

TABLE 16.5

Values for the *p-p* Plot for Example 16.1 Data

j	x_j	$F_{10}^*(x_j)$	$\hat{F}(x_j)$
1	1	1/11 = .091	.123
2	1	2/11 = .182	.123
3	1	3/11 = .273	.123
4	2	4/11 = .364	.302
5	2	5/11 = .455	.302
6	3	6/11 = .545	.467
7	5	7/11 = .636	.711
8	7	8/11 = .727	.851
9	8	9/11 = .818	.894
10	10	10/11 = .909	.948

The *p-p* plot is then constructed using these 10 pairs of values for the 10 sample points, placed on a graph along with the 45° line. The results are displayed in Figure 16.7.

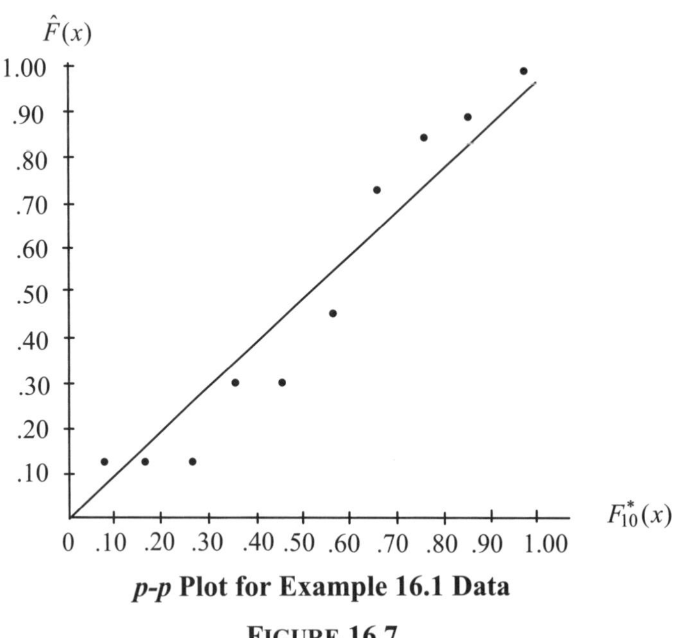

***p-p* Plot for Example 16.1 Data**

FIGURE 16.7

Values that lie above the 45° line occur when $\hat{F}(x)$ is greater than $F_{10}^*(x)$, and values that lie below the 45° line occur when $\hat{F}(x)$ is less than $F_{10}^*(x)$. Therefore an interpretation of this graph, as we move from left to right, is whether the fitted model has brought in more or less probability across a certain interval than has the adjusted empirical distribution. For example, at $j=4$ the point lies below the 45° line and at $j=7$ it lies above it. As we increase from $j=4$ to $j=7$, the fitted model has $.711-.302=.409$ probability mass, whereas the adjusted empirical distribution has only $.636-.364=.272$ probability mass. This pattern might be construed as indicating that, in the vicinity of the median, the fitted model is bringing in probability mass faster than is reflected in the adjusted empirical distribution. Similar evaluative statements could be made about the left and right tails of the distribution. ❐

16.3 FORMAL TESTS OF FIT

In Section 16.3 we discuss more formal tests of fit than the informal visually-based tests described in Section 16.2. The tests discussed in Section 16.3 all involve formal statistical development and numbers-based decision criteria, as well as formal hypothesis testing.

We will discuss tee such tests of fit, namely (a) the chi-square test, (b) the Kolmogorov-Smirnov test, and (c) the Anderson-Darling test.

A separate subsection is devoted to each.

16.3.1 CHI-SQUARE TEST

Our first formal test of fit is the *chi-square test*. Readers might be familiar with this test of fit from prior coursework in statistics, so our presentation of it will not include its development, only its application.

The chi-square test of fit, not surprisingly given the name, is based on the *chi-square distribution*, which is a special case of the gamma distribution.[1] A chi-square table is given in Appendix C.1 for reference purposes.

The chi-square test of fit can be applied directly to a discrete distribution. However, if it is to be applied to a continuous distribution, then the data must first be grouped into cells. We will use the same notation for grouped data as developed in Section 13.3.1, namely that there are k cells defined by the $k+1$ endpoints $c_0, c_1, \cdots, c_k$, where $c_0 < c_1 < \cdots < c_k$.

The null hypothesis is the assumption that the sample data comes from some specified distribution. The chi-square test is based on a comparison of the actual number from the sample that lie in each cell (or at each discrete point) with the expected number for that cell (or discrete point) based on the null hypothesis.

The chi-square statistic[2] is then calculated using the formula

$$\chi^2 = \sum_{j=1}^{k} \frac{(E_j - O_j)^2}{E_j}, \tag{16.4}$$

where E_j is the expected number in the jth cell and O_j is the observed number in the jth cell. Note that the summation has one term for each cell. It also should be noted that one constraint on this equation is the requirement that

$$\sum_{j=1}^{k} E_j = \sum_{j=1}^{k} O_j = n, \tag{16.5}$$

where n is the sample size. In words, the entire sample must be distributed across all the cells on both the expected basis and the observed basis.

The chi-square test of fit is a one-tailed test with its critical region being the right tail of the distribution. This makes sense, since the fit is extremely good in the left tail. In fact, we see that $\chi^2 = 0$ if the fit were perfect.

The chi-square distribution requires that the number of *degrees of freedom* be specified. The number of degrees of freedom in the standard chi-square test of fit is equal to $k-1$, which is one fewer than the number of cells. Intuitively, we might say that one degree of freedom is

---

[1] The gamma parameters are $\alpha = \frac{k}{2}$ and $\beta = \theta^{-1} = \frac{1}{2}$, so the mean of the chi-square distribution is k and its variance is $2k$.

[2] It should be noted that the statistic denoted here by χ^2 is only *approximately* chi-square distributed.

"lost" because Equation (16.5) must hold. Once we know the values in any $k-1$ of the cells, the values in the remaining cell are also determined.

However, there is a complicating factor the reader must remember. The conventional use of the chi-square test of fit also requires another adjustment. If the parameters in the distribution assumed as the null hypothesis were estimated from the sample data prior to running the chi-square test, then we must also reduce the number of degrees of freedom in the test by one for each unknown parameter estimated from the sample.

Another complicating convention in common usage with the chi-square test of fit is to avoid cells that have very small values in them. Typically, this involves the requirement that $E_j \geq m$ to avoid having the denominator in Equation (16.4) be too small. The choice of m is arbitrary, but the most common value in use seems to be $m=5$.

The concern is to avoid the possibility of rejecting an excellent fit due only to one cell with little data contributing an unusually high amount to the summation in Equation (16.4). Numerically, this could happen when the denominator in a fraction is small. The remedy most commonly suggested is to regroup the data by merging such very small cells into adjacent cells until all cells meet the minimum size requirement being applied.

One final consideration is the possibility of truncated or censored distributions. These modifications to the distributions do not present any significant difficulty in using the chi-square test of fit. If the distribution is left truncated at some value $d>0$, then no sample values will lie below d and the left end of the first cell for grouping the data will simply be d. If the distribution is right censored at some value $u>0$, the last cell for grouping the data will simply be $[u,\infty)$.

EXAMPLE 16.5

During a one-year period, the number of accidents tabulated each day was distributed as shown in Table 16.6.

TABLE 16.6

Illustrative Accident Data

Number of Accidents	Days
0	213
1	105
2	34
3	8
4	3
5	2

We wish to use the chi-square test to measure the fit of a Poisson distribution with parameter .60. The minimum expected number of observations in any group should be 5. The maximum possible number of groups should be used.

(a) Calculate the value of the chi-square test statistic.

(b) If the significance level of the test of fit is 10%, should we accept or reject the null hypothesis?

SOLUTION

Since the Poisson distribution is discrete, the chi-square test of fit can be used directly without creating grouped data as would be necessary with a continuous distribution. Also, as a quick check on the sample data, the summation of the days column in Table 16.6 does indeed equal 365.

The values of O_j are directly given in the table, but we need to compute the values of E_j. Under the null hypothesis of a Poisson distribution with mean .60, this is done using the formula

$$E_j = 365\left(\frac{e^{-.60}(.60)^j}{j!}\right),$$

for $j = 0, 1, 2, 3, 4, 5$. When we do these calculations, we discover that the last two values are $E_4 = 1.08$ and $E_5 = .14$ (a balancing item to ensure the total equals 365). These are both too small to permit using a separate cell, and both cells must be "rolled up" and merged with E_3. The observed values must be similarly "rolled up" for consistency, so that O_4 and O_5 must be merged with O_3. Any further merging of cells would violate the condition that the maximum possible number of groups should be used, so we conclude that four cells will be used.

We now have the values displayed in Table 16.7, where the final column is the calculation of the chi-square statistic using Equation (16.4).

TABLE 16.7

Data for Chi-Square Test

j	O_j	E_j	$\frac{(E_j - O_j)^2}{E_j}$
0	213	200.32	0.8026
1	105	120.19	1.9198
2	34	36.06	0.1177
3	13	8.43	2.4774
Total	365	365.00	5.3175

(a) The value of the chi-square statistic is the column total in the last column, which we round to 5.32.

(b) The number of degrees of freedom is $k-1 = 4-1 = 3$. The size of the critical region is 10%. From the chi-square tables, the 90th percentile of the chi-square distribution with 3 degrees of freedom is 6.251. Therefore we cannot reject the null hypothesis that this data could come from a Poisson distribution with mean .60. ❐

EXAMPLE 16.6

Rework Example 16.5 with the same null hypothesis, except that the parameter of the Poisson distribution is not assumed but rather is estimated from the sample data.

SOLUTION

In this case we calculate the sample mean of the original data, obtaining

$$\bar{x} = \frac{0\cdot 213+1\cdot 105+2\cdot 34+3\cdot 8+4\cdot 3+5\cdot 2}{365} = .60.$$

Since the sample mean is the same as the parameter assumption made in Example 16.5, all the calculations previously made can be used in this example.

(a) The value of the chi-square statistic is still 5.32.

(b) Since one unknown parameter was estimated from the sample data, the number of degrees of freedom is reduced from 3 to 2. The size of the critical region is still 10%. From the chi-square tables, the 90th percentile of the chi-square distribution with 2 degrees of freedom is 4.605. Thus, in this case, we would reject the null hypothesis that this data could come from a Poisson distribution whose parameter was estimated from the sample data. ❒

The reader should appreciate the subtle difference between Examples 16.5 and 16.6. The specific circumstances surrounding how the parameters are obtained for the distribution in the null hypothesis can be quite significant.

EXAMPLE 16.7 (Simulation Illustration)

A computer program has generated 1000 simulated values from a uniform distribution over the interval $[0,1)$. The values have been grouped into twenty intervals of equal length. The sum of the squares of the numbers of simulated observations in each interval is

$$\sum_{j=1}^{20} O_j^2 = 51{,}850.$$

We wish to test the null hypothesis that the 1000 values came from a $U[0,1)$ distribution, using a chi-square goodness-of-fit test and a .01 significance level. What can we conclude about the test results?

SOLUTION

If the values came from a $U[0,1)$ distribution, then 5% of them, or 50 values, are expected to fall into each of the twenty equal-length intervals. Then the chi-square statistic is

$$\chi^2 = \sum_{j=1}^{20} \frac{(50-O_j)^2}{50}$$
$$= .02\left[\sum_{j=1}^{20}\left(2500-100O_j+O_j^2\right)\right]$$
$$= .02[(20)(2500)-(100)(1000)+51{,}850] = 37,$$

since $\sum_{j=1}^{20} O_j = 1000$, the number of simulated observations. With nineteen degrees of freedom, the critical value at a .01 significance level is 36.191, and therefore the null hypotheses is rejected. ❐

16.3.2 KOLMOGOROV-SMIRNOV TEST

Our second formal test of fit is the *Kolmogorov-Smirnov test*, often called the *K-S test* for short. This test is based on a comparison of the CDFs for the empirical distribution and the fitted model, i.e., between $F_n^o(x)$ and $\hat{F}(x)$. The reader might recall that three of the four informal graphical tests of fit described in Section 16.2 were also based, in one way or another, on a comparison between these same two quantities.

The *Kolmogorov-Smirnov statistic D* is defined as

$$D = \max_x \left|F_n^o(x) - \hat{F}(x)\right|. \tag{16.6}$$

In words, the value of D is simply the single greatest difference in absolute value between the CDF of the sample distribution and that of the fitted model.

The determination of D is not completely straightforward and requires a bit of discussion. This discussion is aided by visual inspection of a graph comparing the two. In fact, we have already seen such a graph, namely Figure 16.5 in Section 16.2.1. Note that the graph of $F_n^o(x)$ is an upward stair step to the right. By contrast, the graph of $\hat{F}(x)$ is a continuously rising curve running upward to the right. However, both graphs start at zero and end at one, if the entire distribution is utilized.

It should be clear that the maximum difference between the two graphs must occur either just before (if $F_n^o(x)$ lies below $\hat{F}(x)$), or just after (if $F_n^o(x)$ lies above $\hat{F}(x)$) one of the "jumps" in the graph of $F_n^o(x)$. Therefore, it will be necessary to make twice as many calculations as there are jumps in order to determine D. If the sample is of size n and all the sample values are distinct, then there will be $2n$ calculations to make. If there are any duplicate values in the sample, then fewer calculations will be necessary.

There are some interesting contrasts that can be drawn between the K-S test of fit and the chi-square test of fit. The primary K-S test is designed to work with individual values from a continuous model, whereas the chi-square test requires grouping the data instead. The K-S test is not designed to work with discrete model distributions, whereas the chi-square test is ideally suited to be used with discrete distributions. Finally, the standard K-S test is two-tailed and the standard chi-square test is one-tailed.

The null hypothesis is the assumption of the distribution to be used as the fitted model. The issue then becomes one of accepting or rejecting the null hypothesis based on the value of D obtained. This requires reference to a *K-S table* and a comparison of D with the critical value.

Table 16.8 is an abbreviated K-S table for reference.

TABLE 16.8

Kolmogorov-Smirnov Table	
Significance Level α	**Critical Value**
$\alpha = .20$	$1.07/\sqrt{n}$
$\alpha = .15$	$1.14/\sqrt{n}$
$\alpha = .10$	$1.22/\sqrt{n}$
$\alpha = .05$	$1.36/\sqrt{n}$
$\alpha = .025$	$1.48/\sqrt{n}$
$\alpha = .01$	$1.63/\sqrt{n}$

The reader should note that the two-tailed nature of the K-S test is built directly into the K-S table. For example, the critical value of $1.22/\sqrt{n}$ places 5% probability into each tail to reach the 10% significance level.

Another consideration is the possibility of truncated or censored distributions. These modifications to the distributions do not present any significant difficulty in using the K-S test of fit. If the distribution is left truncated at some value $d > 0$, then no sample values will lie below d and both CDFs will begin at d and progress from there. If the distribution is right censored at some value $u > 0$, then the last comparison between the two CDFs should be at u. The value of D could not be to the right of u, if the data is right censored, since both CDFs are converging to one.

The primary purpose of introducing K-S in this text is to use it as a test of fit. Another common application for K-S, however, is to use it to construct confidence intervals for a model CDF based on the sample CDF. For example, consider a sample CDF which follows the familiar stair-step pattern. We can construct two more stair-step graphs, one above and one below the sample CDF by a distance of $1.22/\sqrt{n}$ on each side. In doing this, we have created a 90% confidence interval for the model CDF.

One final observation about the K-S test of fit is that it is *non-parametric* or *distribution-free*. In other words, the test can be used for any distribution chosen as the model.

EXAMPLE 16.8

Rework Example 16.1 using the KS test of fit with significance level 10%.

SOLUTION

The same data as used in Example 16.1 provides an excellent example with which to illustrate the K-S test of fit. The results of the K-S test are displayed in Table 16.9.

TABLE 16.9

Kolmogorov-Smirnov Test of Fit

x	$F_{10}^o(x)$	$\hat{F}(x)$	Difference
1_-	.000	.123	.123
1_+	.300	.123	.177
2_-	.300	.302	.002
2_+	.500	.302	.198
3_-	.500	.467	.033
3_+	.600	.467	.133
5_-	.600	.711	.111
5_+	.700	.711	.011
7_-	.700	.851	.151
7_+	.800	.851	.051
8_-	.800	.894	.094
8_+	.900	.894	.006
10_-	.900	.948	.048
10_+	1.000	.948	.052

Following are some observations about the construction of Table 16.9 and the resulting K-S test of fit:

(1) By inspection of the sample data, there are 7 distinct values among the 10 sample observations. Therefore, we know that the K-S table must have $2 \times 7 = 14$ lines.

(2) The values of x with a minus sign are those just before the jump in $F_n^o(x)$. The values of x with a plus sign are those just after the jump.

(3) The values of $\hat{F}(x)$ do not change before and after the jump, since $\hat{F}(x)$ is continuous.

(4) The largest difference occurs on line 4 of the table, so $D = .198$.

(5) The critical value for a 10% test is $\frac{1.22}{\sqrt{n}} = \frac{1.22}{\sqrt{10}} = .386$.

(6) Thus the result of the K-S test is $.198 < .386$, so that we accept as plausible the null hypothesis of a gamma distribution with the stated parameters in Example 16.1. ❐

EXAMPLE 16.9

A sample of 20 observations of a random variable X yields the following values:

0.5	1.0	1.5	2.0	2.5	3.0	3.5	4.0	4.5	5.0
6.0	7.0	8.0	9.0	10.0	11.0	12.0	13.0	14.0	15.0

The null hypothesis H_0 is that X has a uniform distribution on the interval [0, 20]. Perform a Kolmogorov-Smirnov test of fit at the 10%, 15%, and 20% significance levels.

SOLUTION

In this example there are 20 distinct sample values; if we construct a K-S table similar to that in Example 16.7, the table will have $2\times 20 = 40$ lines. This would be a lot of work, so we will look for a faster way to find a solution.

If we inspect the last sample value 15.0 and calculate the CDF values, we have $F_{20}^{o}(15)=1$ and $\hat{F}(15)=\frac{15}{20}=.75$. The absolute value of the difference at this point is equal to .25.

Can we find a bigger difference? By inspection of the sample data, we cannot. Interestingly, the difference is equal to .25 for all the sample values $5.0, 6.0, \ldots, 14.0, 15.0$, but it never becomes larger. Below 5.0 the difference clearly becomes smaller. Thus we have $D=.25$.

The critical values at the 20%, 15%, and 10% significance levels are

$$\frac{1.07}{\sqrt{20}} = .239,$$

$$\frac{1.14}{\sqrt{20}} = .255,$$

and

$$\frac{1.22}{\sqrt{20}} = .273,$$

respectively. We have a rejection at 20%, an acceptance as plausible (just barely) at 15%, and an acceptance as plausible at 10%. Interestingly, to two decimal places, the critical value for the 15% test is exactly equal to .25. ❐

EXAMPLE 16.10 (Simulation Illustration)

One application of simulation is to estimate the p-value (or critical region) for a hypothesis test. Consider the results of Example 16.9, shown above. Suppose we decide to estimate the p-value for this K-S test by running 100 simulations of 20 observations each, based on the null hypothesis H_0. The K-S statistic is then computed for each of these 100 simulations using the same procedure as in Example 16.9. The results are summarized in the following table:

K-S Statistic	Number of Simulations
.20 or less	25
.22	10
.24	20
.26	20
.28	15
.30 or greater	10

SOLUTION

The original hypothesis test in Example 16.9 produced a K-S statistic of .25. Of the 100 simulations used in redoing the test, a total of $25+10+20=55$ produced K-S values that were less than .25, and a total of $20+15+10=45$ produced K-S values that were greater. The estimate of the p-value for this hypothesis test, based on these 100 simulations, is equal to .45.

16.3.3 ANDERSON-DARLING TEST

Our third formal test of fit is the *Anderson-Darling test*,[3] often called the *A-D test* for short. This test can be thought of as a modification of the Kolmogorov-Smirnov test of fit. As the reader will recall, the K-S test statistic treats all CDF values equally. The intent of the A-D test is to place more weight in the tails and less in the middle of the distribution.

Whereas the K-S test statistic is simply the maximum absolute difference between $F_n^o(x)$ and $\hat{F}(x)$, the A-D test statistic represents the *weighted expected squared deviation* of $F_n^o(x)$ from $\hat{F}(x)$. The weight multiplying each squared deviation is the reciprocal of the variance of $F_n^o(x)$. Since $F_n^o(x)=1-S_n^o(x)$ is a binomial proportion random variable, then it follows from Equation (9.6b) that

$$Var[F_n^o(x)] = Var[S_n^o(x)] = \frac{S(x)\cdot F(x)}{n}, \tag{16.7}$$

where $S(x)$ and $F(x)$ denote the SDF and CDF, respectively, of the true, underlying distribution which we seek to estimate.

Consistent with the above description, the A-D test statistic is defined as

$$A^2 = \int_0^\infty \frac{n}{S(x)\cdot F(x)}\cdot\left[F_n^o(x)-\hat{F}(x)\right]^2\cdot f(x)\,dx, \tag{16.8a}$$

where $f(x)$, the PDF of the underlying distribution, is needed to create the expected value of the squared weighted deviation. The extra weighting for the tails is apparent by examining this denominator. At the median, the denominator would be $.50^2=.25$, and would become

[3] Proposed by Anderson and Darling [1].

progressively smaller when progressing into either the left tail or the right tail of the distribution.

Of course $f(x)$, $S(x)$, and $F(x)$ are not known; since $\hat{F}(x)$ is being hypothesized as representing $F(x)$, we evaluate the right side of Equation (16.8a) by using $\hat{f}(x)$, $\hat{S}(x)$, and $\hat{F}(x)$ in place of $f(x)$, $S(x)$, and $F(x)$, respectively. Then Equation (16.8a) becomes

$$A^2 = n\int_0^{\infty} \frac{\left[F_n^o(x) - \hat{F}(x)\right]^2}{\hat{S}(x)\cdot\hat{F}(x)} \cdot \hat{f}(x)\,dx. \tag{16.8b}$$

When working with complete individual data, Equation (16.8b) can be rewritten as

$$A^2 = -n - \frac{1}{n}\sum_{i=1}^{n}(2i-1)\left\{\ln\left[\hat{F}(x_i)\cdot\hat{S}(x_{n-i+1})\right]\right\}. \tag{16.8c}$$

The derivation of Equation (16.8c) from Equation (16.8b) is given in Appendix J.

As before, the null hypothesis is the assumption of the distribution to be used as the fitted model. The issue then becomes one of accepting or rejecting the null hypothesis based on the value of A^2 obtained. This requires reference to an *A-D table* and a comparison of A^2 with the critical value.

Table 16.10 is an abbreviated A-D table for reference.

TABLE 16.10

Anderson-Darling Table	
Significance Level α	**Critical Value**
$\alpha = .10$	1.933
$\alpha = .05$	2.492
$\alpha = .025$	3.070
$\alpha = .01$	3.857

Another consideration is the possibility of truncated or censored distributions. Left truncation does not present any significant difficulty in using the A-D test of fit. If the distribution is left truncated at some value $d > 0$, then the lower limit on the integral in Equation (16.8a) is equal to d and all the fitted values used in Equation (16.8c) are to the right of d.

Right censoring does present more of a problem. If the distribution is right censored at some value $u > 0$, then the upper limit on the integral in Equation (16.8a) is set equal to u, and only values to the left of u are used in Equation (16.8c). Since censoring automatically involves grouping of data, the A-D test should not be applied to that portion of the data.

EXAMPLE 16.11

Rework Example 16.1 using the Anderson-Darling test of fit with a significance level of 10%, by applying Equation (16.8c).

SOLUTION

The data of Example 16.1 provides an excellent example with which to illustrate the A-D test of fit. The results of the A-D test are displayed in Table 16.11 below.

TABLE 16.11

Anderson-Darling Test of Fit				
i	x_i	$\hat{F}(x_i)$	$\hat{S}(x_{11-i})$	$(2i-1)\left\{\ln\left[\hat{F}(x_i)\cdot\hat{S}(x_{11-i})\right]\right\}$
1	1	.12334	.05239	−5.04195
2	1	.12334	.10591	−13.01398
3	1	.12334	.14930	−19.97321
4	2	.30191	.28944	−17.06188
5	2	.30191	.53262	−16.44808
6	3	.46738	.69809	−12.32026
7	5	.71056	.69809	−9.11454
8	7	.85070	.87666	−4.39990
9	8	.89409	.87666	−4.14090
10	10	.94761	.87666	−3.52338
				−105.03809

Then applying Equation (16.8c), we have

$$A^2 = -10 - \frac{1}{10}(-105.03809) = .504.$$

The critical value for a 10% A-D test from Table 16.10 is 1.933, so the result of the A-D test is $.504 < 1.933$ and we accept as plausible the null hypothesis of a gamma distribution with the stated parameters in Example 16.1. ❐

16.4 SELECTING A MODEL

We have covered quite a bit of material on estimation of parametric models beginning in Chapter 13 and continuing into Chapter 16. The final issue we now face is actually making a decision on the model we intend to use for a particular purpose. Of course, this presumes that we have more than one distribution still under consideration!

The first step in this process is to identify a collection of potential distributions that might be plausible candidates. The second step is to estimate parameters for each of the potential distributions from the sample values obtained. The third step is to perform one or more tests of fit for each of the distributions under consideration. At this point some of the potential distributions might be eliminated if the tests of fit show that they are markedly inferior to other candidates.

Assuming that we still have more than one distribution under consideration, we now need to make a decision among the remaining candidates. There are two general categories of approaches that we consider in this section, namely (a) judgment-based approaches and (b) score-based approaches.

A separate subsection is devoted to each.

16.4.1 JUDGMENT-BASED APPROACHES

Judgment enters the selection process in a number of different ways. The entire selection process can be based on judgment. Even if a score-based approach is adopted as the primary decision criterion, judgment may still enter the process in some ways. Following is an illustrative list of ten possible ways in which judgment enters the process. The list is by no means exhaustive, but it should be helpful in illustrating the types of thought processes that a good modeler might go through prior to the final selection of a model.

(1) There is a fundamental decision as to whether to use a parametric model at all. Part III of this text contained a thorough discussion of tabular models which, in a sense, are an alternative to parametric models. This decision of model type is ultimately a judgment decision by the modeler.

(2) The experience of the modeler can be a valuable asset in the process. For example, perhaps the modeler has worked with similar situations before and that experience can be quite valuable. Also, consultation with colleagues who may have worked on similar problems in the past can be invaluable.

(3) The choice of models to be considered as candidates at the beginning requires a certain level of judgment. It clearly is not realistic to test every distribution we can find for every problem we might face. Good selection of potential candidates at the beginning involves a considerable element of judgment.

(4) The choice of models requires a decision as to whether to test discrete models, continuous models, or both. Often the choice between discrete and continuous distributions is relatively obvious, based on the problem at hand, but there may be exceptions.

(5) In some cases, the choice of distribution may be obvious. If we are dealing with repetitive trials of a process that has a binary outcome, is independent from trial to trial, and has constant probabilities from trial to trial, clearly the binomial distribution should be chosen without further analysis.

(6) The graphical comparison tests of fit discussed in Section 16.2 are totally judgmental. This again is where experience can be helpful. No graphical comparison is likely to look as good as we wish it would, but that does not mean that the fit is not acceptable. This is particularly true when the sample size is small.

(7) The level of symmetry or skewness in the sample data can be quite helpful in choosing appropriate candidates for consideration. The normal distribution will not work well for highly skewed data. Similarly, the Pareto distribution will not work well unless the sample data is highly skewed with a significant right tail.

(8) The modeler may wish to emphasize certain parts of the distribution more than others. For example, the modeler may be mostly concerned about a good fit where the large majority of outcomes occur in the middle of the distribution. Alternatively, the modeler may have a keen focus on extreme events far into one of the tails.

(9) No model selection is permanent. It has to be monitored and periodically updated or changed as additional experience is obtained. Thus, ease of updating in the future as conditions change may be an important matter. As the reader will recall from Chapter 15, this is one of the key advantages of using a Bayesian approach.

(10) Finally, assume that the modeler plans to use score-based approaches (to be discussed in the next section). However, suppose that the results from various score-based approaches do not produce a clear choice. At this point, the final decision as to the choice of model clearly involves an element of judgment.

EXAMPLE 16.12

Consider Example 16.1 in which the parameters of a gamma distribution were estimated using the method of moments. Analyze the choice of two possible alternative models, namely (a) the normal distribution, and (b) the Pareto distribution, using a judgment-based approach.

SOLUTION

(a) The normal distribution is symmetrical, but the sample data, by inspection, has positive skewness. The gamma distribution is quite versatile in fitting positively-skewed data and is almost certain to be a better model than the normal distribution, given the sample data.

(b) The Pareto distribution is highly skewed with a large right tail. Although the sample data does have positive skewness, there are not really any major outliers well into the right hand tail as might be expected with the Pareto. In fact, if we try to perform a method of moments parameter fit for the Pareto to this data, we will not even be able to get the technique to produce an answer that makes sense![4]

Therefore the gamma distribution should be superior to either the normal distribution or the Pareto distribution, given the sample data, purely on the basis of judgment without any extensive analysis being required. ❐

16.4.2 SCORE-BASED APPROACHES

We now examine more numerically-based decision criteria for the selection of a model. There are four approaches we will consider. The first three relate to the three formal tests of fit discussed in Section 16.3. The fourth one adapts the maximum likelihood technique for this pur-

---

[4] The parameter estimates $\hat{\alpha}$ and $\hat{\theta}$ both turn out to be negative numbers!

pose. The four score-based approaches to selecting the model distribution (together with its parameter estimates) can be summarized as the distribution that has (a) the smallest value of the chi-square test statistic, (b) the smallest value of the Kolmogorov-Smirnov test statistic, (c) the smallest value of the Anderson-Darling test statistic, or (d) the largest value of the likelihood function.

The logic behind all four of these approaches should be evident.

There is one attribute of the chi-square approach that distinguishes it from the other three. Consider the situation in which not all the potential candidates are distributions with the same number of parameters. Also assume the common situation in which all the parameters must be estimated from the sample data. The chi-square method will extract a "penalty" of sorts for the distributions with more parameters, since one degree of freedom is lost for each parameter being estimated. The other three methods do not have this attribute. The issue of simpler versus more complex distributions to use as the model distribution will be considered further in Section 16.5.

The preferred method for many modelers is the fourth one, which is based on the likelihood function. This is not surprising, given the popularity of maximum likelihood estimation and its many attractive characteristics. The reader should note that this method can be applied on a comparative basis among various competing distributions, even if one or more of the distributions being tested have parameters estimated by methods other than maximum likelihood.

The reader will recall that conceptually the likelihood function L is the probability (if discrete) or density (if continuous) of obtaining the sample outcome that was actually obtained. We want to choose the distribution, with its parameter estimates, that gives us the largest value of L. At this point we encounter an arithmetical problem.

Although the likelihood function is very useful as an analytical tool, numerically it can be an extremely small number. This is particularly true if the sample size is fairly large, since it is the product of a collection of numbers all lying between 0 and 1. Since many modelers find it inconvenient to work with numbers such as 3.72×10^{-18}, using the log likelihood function ℓ is a considerable improvement, although the ℓ's are all negative numbers.

A common convention is to work with the negative of the log of the likelihood functions, and then seek the smallest value among the competing distributions. This value is called NLL, negative log likelihood. Expressed as a formula we have

$$NLL = -\ln\prod_{i=i}^{n} f(x_i). \tag{16.9}$$

The distribution with the smallest NLL value is the leading candidate for selection based on this criterion.

EXAMPLE 16.13

Extending Example 16.1 even further, use the NLL criterion to choose among the three distributions of (a) gamma, (b) exponential, and (c) normal. Use the method of moments parameter estimates for all three distributions.

SOLUTION

In Example 13.2, the gamma distribution has parameter estimates $\hat{\alpha} = 1.63265$ and $\hat{\theta} = 2.45$.

The exponential distribution parameter estimate will be the sample mean, which is $\hat{\theta} = 4$.

From Example 7.1, the normal distribution has parameter estimates $\hat{\mu} = 4$ and $\hat{\sigma} = 3.13$.

The calculation of NLL values for the three distributions is given in Table 16.12 below.

We seek the distribution with the smallest NLL value, and the results are exactly what should be expected. In Example 16.11 we used a judgment-based argument to see that the gamma distribution should be superior to the normal distribution. A comparison of the NLL values for these two distributions confirms the judgment-based argument. The difference in NLL values is significant.

TABLE 16.12

NLL Comparison of Three Distributions			
	Gamma	Exponential	Normal
x	$f(x)$	$f(x)$	$f(x)$
1	0.17151	0.19470	0.08052
1	0.17151	0.19470	0.08052
1	0.17151	0.19470	0.08052
2	0.17679	0.15163	0.10392
2	0.17679	0.15163	0.10392
3	0.15192	0.11809	0.12112
5	0.09277	0.07163	0.12112
7	0.05074	0.04344	0.08052
8	0.03671	0.03383	0.05633
10	0.01869	0.02052	0.02030
NLL	23.2830	23.8630	25.6010

The gamma distribution also beats the exponential distribution, which should also be expected. The exponential distribution is a special case of the gamma distribution with one parameter. The regular gamma distribution with two parameters should be able to do everything that the exponential distribution can do, and more. A comparison of the NLL values for these two distributions confirms this argument. The two NLL values are rather close, however, reflecting the fact that this gamma distribution with these two particular parameter values is only slightly superior to an exponential distribution. ❐

16.5 PARSIMONY

In Section 16.4 we encountered situations in which two competing distributions had a different number of parameters. This is an issue needing further discussion, and Section 16.5 addresses this issue in more depth.

When using the NLL comparison test (or any other score-based approach, for that matter), it is likely that the winner of the competition will be one of the distributions with the largest number of parameters. Extra parameters give such distributions greater flexibility and ability to replicate underlying patterns in the sample data. In fact, this is certain to happen if the distribution with the fewer parameters is a special case of the distribution with the larger number of parameters. (See the comparison between the exponential and the gamma in Example 16.11 for an illustration of this phenomenon.)

Distributions with a greater number of parameters are more complex and harder to work with than distributions with fewer parameters. The principle of *parsimony* suggests that we should use a distribution with the fewest number of parameters that will give us a sufficiently close match to the sample data for the purpose at hand. Said in the contrapositive, we should not use a more complex distribution unless the use of that more complex distribution gives us enough greater accuracy to make it worth the trouble of using the more complex distribution.

The collection of distributions provided in Appendix A contains numerous continuous distributions, so the need for a systematic way to deal with the principle of parsimony is evident. There are two analytical approaches for applying the concept of parsimony that we consider in this section, namely, (a) the likelihood ratio test and (b) the Schwarz Bayesian criterion.

A separate subsection will be devoted to each.

16.5.1 LIKELIHOOD RATIO TEST

Our first test to implement the principle of parsimony is the *likelihood ratio test.* This test is constructed as the ratio of the likelihood functions for two proposed fitted distributions with differing numbers of parameters. The distribution with fewer parameters is typically a special case of the distribution with the greater number of parameters. A basic example would be an exponential distribution with one parameter as the simpler distribution and a gamma distribution with two parameters as the more complex distribution.

The distribution with the fewer parameters is assumed as the null hypothesis H_0. The likelihood function for the sample using this distribution is denoted by L_0. The distribution with the greater number of parameters then becomes the alternative hypothesis H_1. The likelihood function for the sample using this distribution is denoted by L_1.

The test statistic for the likelihood ratio test is denoted by K, and can be expressed in any of the following forms:

$$\begin{aligned} K &= \ln(L_1 / L_0)^2 \\ &= 2\ln(L_1 / L_0) \\ &= 2(\ln L_1 - \ln L_0) \\ &= 2(\ell_1 - \ell_0) \\ &= 2(NLL_0 - NLL_1) \end{aligned} \tag{16.10}$$

The test statistic K is approximately chi-square distributed, with a number of degrees of freedom equal to the number of parameters for the distribution in the alternative hypothesis minus the number of parameters for the distribution in the null hypothesis. The critical region for the hypothesis test is the right tail of the chi-square distribution.

EXAMPLE 16.14

Apply the likelihood ratio test to the gamma distribution and the exponential distribution analyzed in Example 16.12. Use a significance level of 10% for this test.

SOLUTION

The null hypothesis is the exponential distribution with one parameter. From Example 16.12 we have $NLL_0 = 23.863$ for the exponential distribution. The alternative hypothesis is the gamma distribution with two parameters. From Example 16.13 we have $NLL_1 = 23.283$ for the gamma distribution. The value of the test statistic from Equation (16.10) is then

$$K = 2(NLL_0 - NLL_1) = 2(23.863\text{–}23.283) = 1.160.$$

The number of degrees of freedom in the chi-square distribution is the difference between the number of parameters in the two distributions, which is $2-1=1$. The 90th percentile in the chi-square distribution with 1 degree of freedom is 2.706. Since $1.160 < 2.706$, we do not reject the null hypothesis H_0. ❐

Thus, based on the likelihood ratio test, we would be justified in using the simpler exponential distribution to model this data rather than the more complex gamma distribution. This does not mean that we should not use the gamma distribution, but it does indicate that the extra accuracy we obtain in doing so may not be sufficient to justify the extra effort involved.

16.5.2 SCHWARZ BAYESIAN CRITERION

Our second test to implement the principle of parsimony is the *Schwarz Bayesian criterion*, which we call SBC for convenience. The concept behind the SBC method of addressing the issue of parsimony is quite different than that used in the likelihood ratio test.

The SBC adjusts the NLL value of each distribution being tested by a *penalty* that increases as the number of parameters increases. An adjusted value of NLL, called NNL^S, is computed as

$$NLL^S = NLL + .50r \cdot \ln n, \tag{16.11}$$

where r is the number of parameters in the distribution and n is the sample size. The term $.50r \cdot \ln n$ is called the *penalty function*. Note that the penalty function is proportional to the number of parameters. Note also that the penalty function is added, not subtracted, because NLL is the negative of the log likelihood function from which the penalty is being subtracted.

EXAMPLE 16.15

Apply the Schwarz Bayesian criterion to the gamma distribution and the exponential distribution analyzed in Example 16.13.

SOLUTION

The unadjusted NLL values for the two distributions are $NLL_G = 23.283$ for the gamma and $NLL_E = 23.863$ for the exponential. On an unadjusted basis, we would choose the gamma distribution since its NLL value is smaller than that for the exponential distribution.

If we now apply the SBC, we compute adjusted NLL values as

$$NLL_G^S \; = \; NLL_G + .50r \cdot \ln n \; = \; 23.283 + 1 \cdot \ln 10 \; = \; 25.586$$

for the gamma, and

$$NLL_E^S \; = \; NLL_E + .50r \cdot \ln n \; = \; 23.863 + .50 \cdot \ln 10 \; = \; 25.014$$

for the exponential.

On the adjusted SBC basis, we would choose the exponential distribution since its adjusted NLL value is smaller than that for the gamma distribution. ❐

We reach the same conclusion with the Schwarz Bayesian criterion that we reached with the likelihood ratio test in Example 16.14. The two methods often reach the same conclusion, as in this case. The two methods may reach different conclusions in other cases, however. For example, note that the outcome of the likelihood ratio test may be affected by the size of the significance level chosen for the chi-square test. There is nothing comparable for the SBC, however, since its penalty function is determined strictly by the number of parameters and the sample size.

16.6 SUMMARY

In Chapter 16 we discussed testing various potential and competing models to be used in loss modeling and then developed criteria for selecting one. Three broad topics were discussed.

The first broad topic was to present a number of different tests of fit to assess how well each fitted model with estimated parameters fit the sample data. Several informal tests of fit were described. These tests all involved different types of graphical comparisons.

This was followed by the consideration of three formal tests of fit, all involving numbers-based decision criteria and formal hypothesis testing. These three were the chi-square test, the Kolmogorov-Smirnov test, and the Anderson-Darling test.

The second broad topic was the development of criteria for actually selecting a model from the group of contenders. Two categories of approaches were discussed. The first category involved a variety of judgment-based criteria. The second category involved score-based criteria. Four possibilities were considered, with primary focus devoted to the one based on maximizing the likelihood function. In practice, this technique is often implemented by minimizing the negative log likelihood function (NLL).

The third broad topic was consideration of parsimony. The goal of parsimony is to assess whether the better fit that typically accompanies selection of a model with more parameters is worth the extra complexity, or whether a simpler model with fewer parameters is "good enough" for the purpose at hand.

Two rather different techniques for assessing parsimony and reaching the decision as to which distribution to select were presented. The first was the likelihood ratio test, which is a technique widely used in mathematical statistics for a number of different purposes. The second was the Schwarz Bayesian criterion (SBC), which uses a penalty function proportional to the number of parameters that were estimated.

16.7 EXERCISES

16.1 Introduction
16.2 Graphical Comparisons

16-1 Consider the following ten sample outcomes:

Outcome	Number
1	5
2	1
3	3
4	1

We wish to fit an exponential distribution to this sample data using the method of moments, and then produce a graphical overlay of CDFs comparing the sample distribution and the fitted model. Find all points where the two graphs intersect.

16-2 Using the data of Exercise 16-1, calculate $D(2.50)$.

16-3 The graph shown in Figure 16.8 on the following page shows the *p-p* plot of a fitted distribution compared to the underlying sample distribution.

(a) Is the left tail of the fitted distribution too thick or too thin compared to the sample distribution?

(b) Does the fitted distribution have more or less probability around the median than does the sample distribution?

(c) Is the right tail of the fitted distribution too thick or too thin compared to the sample distribution?

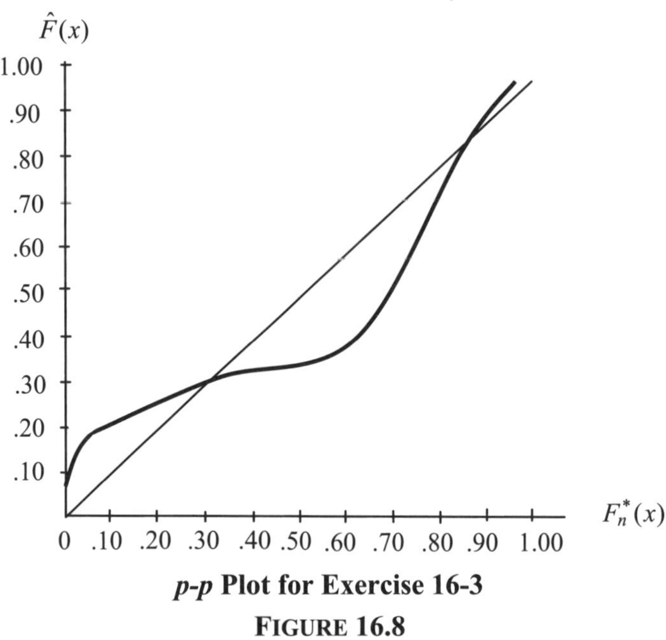

***p-p* Plot for Exercise 16-3**

FIGURE 16.8

16-4 Consider the *p-p* plot shown in Figure 16.9, which is based on the sample data

$$\{1, 2, 3, 15, 30, 50, 51, 99, 100\}.$$

Which of the following choices could be the fitted model underlying the *p-p* plot?

(i) $F(x) = 1 - x^{-.25}$, for $x \geq 1$

(ii) $F(x) = \frac{x}{1+x}$, for $x \geq 0$

(iii) Normal with mean 40 and standard deviation 40

(iv) Uniform on [1, 100]

(v) Exponential with mean 10

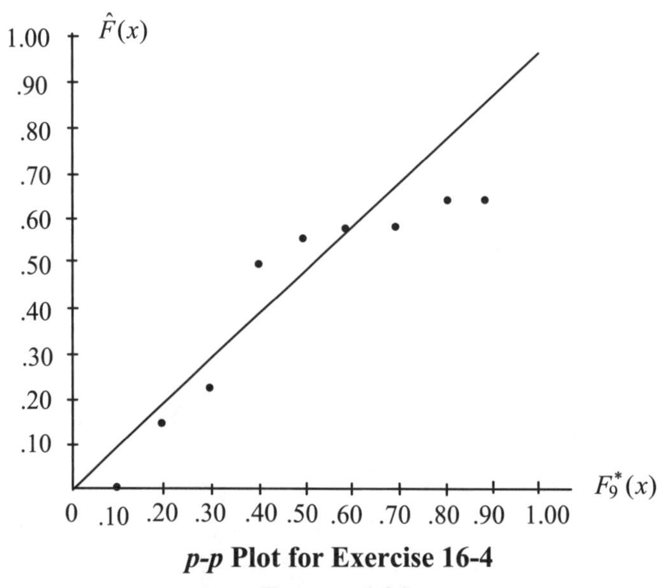

***p-p* Plot for Exercise 16-4**

FIGURE 16.9

16-5 The following data represent observed claim amounts:

$$\{400, 1000, 1600, 3000, 5000, 5400, 6200\}$$

An exponential distribution with $\theta = 3300$ is hypothesized for the data. The goodness of fit is to be assessed by both a *p-p* plot and a $D(x)$ plot. Let (s, t) be the coordinates of the *p-p* plot for a claim amount of 3000. Determine the value of $(s-t) - D(3000)$.

16-6 Consider the graph, shown in Figure 16.10, of the cumulative distribution functions of a fitted lognormal model and the empirical distribution. Determine, to the nearest integer, the difference between the mean of the lognormal model and the mean of the sample data.

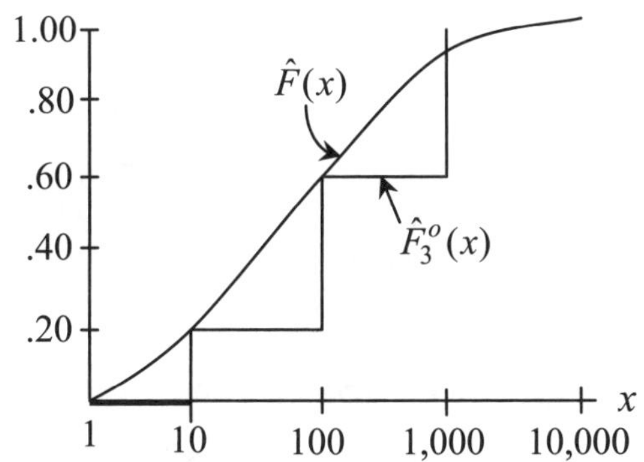

Graphic Overlay of CDFs for Exercise 16-6

FIGURE 16.10

16.3 Formal Tests of Fit

16-7 Consider the following observed claim frequency data collected over a period of 365 days:

Number of Claims Per Day	Observed Number of Days
0	50
1	122
2	101
3	92
4+	0

Fit a Poisson distribution to the above data using the maximum likelihood method. Group the data by number of claims per day into the four groups 0, 1, 2, and 3 or more. Apply the chi-square test of fit to test the null hypothesis that the claims follow a Poisson distribution.

(a) Calculate the value of the chi-square statistic.

(b) How many degrees of freedom should be used in this chi-square test?

(c) Find the smallest significance level that would result in a rejection of the null hypothesis, using the percentiles given in the chi-square table in Appendix C. (Do not interpolate in the table.)

16-8 We are given the following random sample of 30 automobile claims:

54	140	230	560	600	1,100
1,500	1,800	1,920	2,000	2,450	2,500
2,580	2,910	3,800	3,800	3,810	3,870
4,000	4,800	7,200	7,390	11,750	12,000
15,000	25,000	30,000	32,300	35,000	55,000

We wish to test the hypothesis that auto claims follow a continuous distribution function $F(x)$ with the following percentiles:

x	310	500	2,498	4,876	7,498	12,930
$F(x)$	.16	.27	.55	.81	.90	.95

Group the data using the largest number of groups such that the expected number of claims in each group is at least 5.

(a) Calculate the value of the chi-square statistic.

(b) How many degrees of freedom should be used in this chi-square test?

(c) Find the smallest significance level that would result in a rejection of the null hypothesis, using the percentiles given in the chi-square table in Appendix C. (Do not interpolate in the table.)

16-9 A total of 1000 workers insured under a workers compensation policy were observed for one year. The number of work days missed is as follows:

Number of Work Days Missed	Number of Workers
0	818
1	153
2	25
3 or more	4

The total number of work days missed was 230. The chi-square test of fit is used to test the hypothesis that the number of work days missed follows a Poisson distribution, where the Poisson parameter is estimated by the average number of work days missed. Any interval in which the expected number is less than one is combined with the previous interval.

(a) Calculate the value of the chi-square statistic.

(b) How many degrees of freedom should be used in this chi-square test?

(c) Find the smallest significance level that would result in a rejection of the null hypothesis, using the percentiles given in the chi-square table in Appendix C. (Do not interpolate in the table.)

16-10 The following is a sample of five claim payments:

$$\{29, 64, 90, 135, 182\}$$

Claims sizes are assumed to follow an exponential distribution, with parameter estimated by the method of moments. Calculate the value of the Kolmogorov-Smirnov test statistic.

16-11 The size of a claim for an individual insured follows an inverse exponential distribution with PDF

$$f(x\,|\,\theta) = \frac{\theta \cdot e^{-\theta/x}}{x^2},$$

for $x > 0$. The parameter θ, as a random variable, has a prior density function given by

$$\pi_\Theta(\theta) = \frac{e^{-\theta/4}}{4},$$

for $\theta > 0$. For a particular insured, the following five claims are observed:

$$\{1, 2, 3, 5, 13\}$$

Determine the value of the Kolmogorov-Smirnov statistic to test the goodness of fit of $f(x\,|\,\theta = 2)$.

16-12 The following is a random sample of five observations:

$$\{.20, .70, .90, 1.10, 1.30\}$$

We wish to use the Kolmogorov-Smirnov test for testing the null hypothesis that the PDF for the population is

$$f(x) = \frac{4}{(1+x)^5},$$

for $x > 0$.

(a) Calculate the value of the Kolmogorov-Smirnov test statistic.

(b) Find the smallest significance level that would result in a rejection of the null hypothesis, using the Kolmogorov-Smirnov values given in Table 16.8. (Do not interpolate in the table.)

16-13 Three sample values of .40, .70, and .90 are obtained from a population with CDF hypothesized to be

$$F(x) = x^2,$$

for $0 \le x \le 1$. Calculate the value of the Anderson-Darling test statistic A^2.

16-14 If the proposed model is appropriate, which, if any, of the following test statistics tends to zero as the sample size goes to infinity?

(a) Chi-square

(b) Kolmogorov-Smirnov

(c) Anderson-Darling

16.4 Selecting a Model

16-15 The distribution of accidents for 84 randomly selected policies is as follows:

Number of Accidents	Number of Policies
0	32
1	26
2	12
3	7
4	4
5	2
6	1
Total	**84**

Perform a comparison of the sample mean and sample variance to determine which of the following discrete distributions would be the best model to use for claim frequency:

(i) Poisson

(ii) Binomial

(iii) Negative binomial

16-16 We are given the following information from an unknown loss distribution for the random variable X:

Size k (000s)	**1**	**3**	**5**	**7**	**9**
Count of $X \ge k$	180	118	75	50	34
Sum of $X \ge k$	990	882	713	576	459

If we use the empirical mean excess loss (expected payment per payment) function to help select a distributional family for fitting the empirical data, which of the following would we expect to best fit the data:

(i) Pareto

(ii) Gamma $(\alpha > 1)$

(iii) Exponential

(iv) Normal

(v) Lognormal

16-17 We are given the following data displaying claim frequency on ten trials:

Number of Claims	Number of Outcomes
0	6
1	3
2	1

We fit both a Poisson distribution and a binomial distribution to this sample data using the method of moments.

(a) Calculate the NLL value for the Poisson fit.

(b) Calculate the NLL value for the binomial fit.

16-18 The distribution of the number of claims per policy during a one-year period for 10,000 insurance policies is as follows:

Number of Claims per Policy	Number of Policies
0	5000
1	5000
2 or more	0

If we fit a binomial model with parameters n and p using maximum likelihood, what is the NLL value when $n = 2$?

16.5 Parsimony

16-19 During a one-year period, the number of accidents per day was distributed as follows:

Number of Accidents	Days
0	209
1	111
2	33
3	7
4	3
5	2

Maximum likelihood is used to fit the data to a Poisson distribution and to a negative binomial distribution. The Poisson fit has an NLL value of 385.90, and the negative binomial fit has an NLL value of 382.40. Determine the likelihood ratio test statistic, treating the Poisson distribution as the null hypothesis.

16-20 We wish to fit a Pareto distribution to a sample of 200 claim amounts and use the likelihood ratio test to test the hypothesis that $\alpha = 1.50$ and $\theta = 7.80$. The maximum likelihood estimates are $\hat{\alpha} = 1.40$ and $\hat{\theta} = 7.60$. The value of the NLL function evaluated at the maximum likelihood estimates is 817.92. We are also given that $\sum \ln(x_i + 7.80) = 607.64$.

(a) Calculate the value of the likelihood ratio test statistic *K*.

(b) How many degrees of freedom should be used in this chi-square test?

(c) Find the smallest significance level that would result in a rejection of the null hypothesis, using the percentiles given in the chi-square table in Appendix C. (Do not interpolate in the table.)

16-21 The following is a random sample of five losses from a Weibull distribution:

$$\{595, 700, 789, 799, 1109\}$$

At the maximum likelihood estimates of θ and τ, we find that $\sum \ln f(x_i) = -33.05$. When $\tau = 2$, the maximum likelihood estimate of θ is 816.70. We wish to use the likelihood ratio test to test the hypothesis defined by $H_0: \tau = 2$ and $H_1: \tau \neq 2$.

(a) Calculate the value of the likelihood ratio test statistic.

(b) How many degrees of freedom should be used in this chi-square test?

(c) Find the smallest significance level that would result in a rejection of the null hypothesis, using the percentiles given in the chi-square table in Appendix C. (Do not interpolate in the table.)

16-22 For a sample of size $n = 100$, the NLL values associated with each of five different models are given in the following table:

Model	Parameters	NLL
Generalized Pareto	3	219.10
Burr	3	219.20
Pareto	2	221.20
Lognormal	2	221.40
Inverse Exponential	1	224.20

(a) Which of the five distributions should be chosen as the model based on the discussion in Section 16.4?

(b) Which of the five distributions should be chosen based on the Schwarz Bayesian criterion of Section 16.5.2?

16-23 Five different models are fitted to a sample of $n = 260$ observations with the following results:

Model	Parameters	Loglikelihood
I	1	-414
II	2	-412
III	3	-411
IV	4	-409
V	6	-409

Determine the model favored by the Schwarz Bayesian criterion.

APPENDIX A

SUMMARY OF CONTINUOUS DISTRIBUTIONS

This appendix includes primarily continuous distributions appearing or referenced in this text, plus several others that have appeared, or seem likely to appear, on the examinations of the Society of Actuaries and the Casualty Actuarial Society. For a more extensive survey of such distributions, see Appendix A of Klugman, et al. [21], from which some of the entries in this appendix have been taken.

A.1 UNIVARIATE CONTINUOUS DISTRIBUTIONS

This section summarizes distributions of a single variable, denoted by X in all cases.

A.1.1 ONE-PARAMETER DISTRIBUTIONS

The tables on the following two pages give basic functions for the continuous uniform, exponential, inverse exponential, shifted exponential, and single-parameter Pareto distributions. Note that we have omitted the survival distribution function $S(x)$, since, in all cases, $S(x)=1-F(x)$.

We have also omitted the generalized LEV function, $E[(X \wedge u)^k]$, for $k=2,3,\cdots$, except for distributions where it possesses a closed form expression. In those cases we show the function in a footnote.

Function	Single Parameter Uniform[1]	Exponential (Standard Parameterization)	Exponential (Alternate Parameterization)[2]
PDF $f(x)$	$\frac{1}{\omega}$, for $0 \le x \le \omega$; $\omega > 0$	$\beta \cdot e^{-\beta x}$, for $x > 0$; $\beta > 0$	$\frac{1}{\theta} \cdot e^{-x/\theta}$, for $x > 0$; $\theta > 0$
CDF $F(x)$	$\frac{x}{\omega}$	$1 - e^{-\beta x}$	$1 - e^{-x/\theta}$
HRF $\lambda(x)$	$\frac{1}{\omega - x}$	β	$\frac{1}{\theta}$
Mean $E[X]$	$\frac{\omega}{2}$	$\frac{1}{\beta}$	θ
k^{th} **Moment** $E[X^k]$	$\frac{\omega^{k+1}}{\omega(k+1)}$	$\frac{\Gamma(k+1)}{\beta^k}$ [3]	$\theta^k \cdot \Gamma(k+1)$ [4]
Mode $M(X)$	Equimodal at all x	0	0
Variance $Var(X)$	$\frac{\omega^2}{12}$	$\frac{1}{\beta^2}$	θ^2
MGF $M_X(t)$	$\frac{e^{\omega t} - 1}{\omega t}$	$\frac{\beta}{\beta - t}$	$\frac{1}{1 - \theta t}$
LEV $E[X \wedge u]$	$u - \frac{u^2}{2\omega}$	$\frac{1 - e^{-\beta u}}{\beta}$	$\theta(1 - e^{-u/\theta})$

[1] The more common two-parameter uniform distribution is presented in Section A.1.2 on page 488. The one-parameter version presented here relates primarily to survival models.

[2] In the alternative parameterization, with $\beta = \frac{1}{\theta}$, the exponential distribution constitutes a scale family of distributions where θ is a scale parameter.

[3] $E[X^k] = \frac{k!}{\beta^k}$ if k is a positive integer.

[4] $E[X^k] = \theta^k \cdot k!$ if k is a positive integer.

Function	Inverse Exponential (θ-form)	Shifted Exponential (θ-form)	Pareto (Single Parameter)[5]
PDF $f(x)$	$\frac{\theta \cdot e^{-\theta/x}}{x^2}$, for $x>0; \theta>0$	$\frac{1}{\theta} \cdot e^{-(x-\delta)/\theta}$, for $\delta<x<\infty; \theta>0$	$\frac{\alpha \cdot \theta^{\alpha}}{x^{\alpha+1}}$, for $x>\theta; \alpha>0$
CDF $F(x)$	$e^{-\theta/x}$	$1-e^{-(x-\delta)/\theta}$	$1-\left(\frac{\theta}{x}\right)^{\alpha}$
HRF $\lambda(x)$	$\frac{\theta \cdot e^{-\theta/x}}{x^2(1-e^{-\theta/x})}$	$\frac{1}{\theta}$	$\frac{\alpha}{x}$
Mean $E[X]$	Does Not Exist	$\delta+\theta$	$\frac{\alpha\theta}{\alpha-1}$, provided $\alpha>1$
k^{th} **Moment** $E[X^k]$	Does Not Exist for $k \geq 1$	$\theta^k \cdot e^{\delta/\theta} \cdot \Gamma(k+1) \cdot [1-\Gamma(k+1; \delta/\theta)]$	$\frac{\alpha\theta^k}{\alpha-k}$, provided $\alpha>k$
Mode $M(X)$	$\frac{\theta}{2}$	δ	θ
Variance $Var(X)$	Does Not Exist	θ^2	$\frac{\alpha\theta^2}{(\alpha-1)^2(\alpha-2)}$, provided $\alpha>2$
MGF $M_X(t)$	Does Not Exist	$\frac{e^{\delta t}}{1-\theta t}$	Does Not Exist
LEV $E[X \wedge u]$	$\theta \cdot \int_{\theta/u}^{\infty} t^{-1} e^{-t}\, dt + u(1-e^{-\theta/u})$	$\delta+\theta\left(1-e^{-(u-\delta)/\theta}\right)$, for $u>\delta$[6]	$\frac{\alpha\theta \cdot x^{\alpha-1}-\theta^{\alpha}}{(\alpha-1) \cdot x^{\alpha-1}}$, provided $\alpha>1$

[5] Example 14.6 on page 361 is an example of single-parameter Pareto with θ preestablished at $\theta=1$. Since θ can be preestablished at *any* positive value, it is retained in the general form of this distribution. For example,

$$f(x) = \frac{\alpha(1000)^{\alpha}}{x^{\alpha+1}},$$

for $x>1000$ and $\alpha>0$, is also a single-parameter Pareto density function.

[6] $E[X \wedge u]=u$, for $u \leq \delta$.

A.1.2 TWO-PARAMETER DISTRIBUTIONS

The tables on the following six pages give basic functions for the gamma, inverse gamma, general uniform, normal, lognormal, Pareto, inverse Pareto, Weibull, inverse Weibull, chi-square, and beta distributions. As in Section A.1.1, we have omitted the survival distribution function $S(x)$ and the generalized LEV function $E[(X \wedge u)^k]$, except for certain distributions where it appears in a footnote.

Note that some of the entries are expressed as a gamma function $\Gamma(r)$, which equals $(r-1)!$ if r is a positive integer, and others are expressed as an incomplete gamma function $\Gamma(r; y)$. (See Appendix K for more information on this function.)

Similarly, some entries for the beta distribution on page 492 make use of the incomplete beta function, which is defined as

$$\beta(a,b;x) = \frac{\Gamma(a+b)}{\Gamma(a)\cdot\Gamma(b)}\int_0^x t^{a-1}(1-t)^{b-1}\,dt,$$

where $a>0$, $b>0$, and $0<x<1$.

Function	Gamma (Standard Parameterization)	Gamma (Alternate Parameterization)[7]
PDF $f(x)$	$\frac{\beta^\alpha}{\Gamma(\alpha)} \cdot x^{\alpha-1} e^{-\beta x}$, for $x > 0$; $\alpha > 0$; $\beta > 0$	$\frac{(x/\theta)^\alpha \cdot e^{-x/\theta}}{x \cdot \Gamma(\alpha)}$, for $x > 0$; $\alpha > 0$; $\theta > 0$
CDF $F(x)$	$\frac{\beta^\alpha}{\Gamma(\alpha)} \cdot \int_0^x y^{\alpha-1} e^{-\beta y}\, dy = \Gamma(\alpha; \beta x)$	$\Gamma(\alpha; x/\theta)$
HRF $\lambda(x)$	$\lambda(x) = \frac{f(x)}{1-F(x)}$; there is no convenient closed-form expression	$\lambda(x) = \frac{f(x)}{1-F(x)}$; there is no convenient closed-form expression
Mean $E[X]$	$\frac{\alpha}{\beta}$	$\alpha\theta$
k^{th} **Moment** $E[X^k]$	$\frac{\Gamma(\alpha+k)}{\beta^k \cdot \Gamma(\alpha)}$ [8]	$\frac{\theta^k \cdot \Gamma(\alpha+k)}{\Gamma(\alpha)}$ [9]
Mode $M(X)$	$\frac{\alpha-1}{\beta}$, provided $\alpha > 1$	$\theta(\alpha-1)$, provided $\alpha > 1$
Variance $Var(X)$	$\frac{\alpha}{\beta^2}$	$\alpha\theta^2$
MGF $M_X(t)$	$\left(\frac{\beta}{\beta-t}\right)^\alpha$	$\left(\frac{1}{1-\theta t}\right)^\alpha$
LEV $E[X \wedge u]$	$\frac{\alpha}{\beta} \cdot \Gamma(\alpha+1; \beta u) + u[1-\Gamma(\alpha; \beta u)]$	$\alpha\theta \cdot \Gamma(\alpha+1; u/\theta) + u[1-\Gamma(\alpha; u/\theta)]$

[7] Like the exponential distribution, in the alternate parameterization the gamma distribution constitutes a scale family where θ is a scale parameter.

[8] $E[X^k] = \frac{(\alpha+k-1)!}{\beta^k \cdot (\alpha-1)!}$ if α and k are positive integers.

[9] $E[X^k] = \frac{\theta^k \cdot (\alpha+k-1)!}{(\alpha-1)!}$ if α and k are positive integers.

Function	**Inverse Gamma (θ-form)**	**Generalized Continuous Uniform**
PDF $f(x)$	$\frac{(\theta / x)^{\alpha} \cdot e^{-\theta / x}}{x \cdot \Gamma(\alpha)}$, for $x>0; \alpha>0; \theta>0$	$\frac{1}{b-a}$, for $a \leq x \leq b$
CDF $F(x)$	$1-\Gamma(\alpha; \theta / x)$	$\frac{x-a}{b-a}$
HRF $\lambda(x)$	No Closed Form Expression	$\frac{1}{b-x}$
Mean $E[X]$	$\frac{\theta}{\alpha-1}$, provided $\alpha>1$	$\frac{a+b}{2}$
k^{th} **Moment** $E[X^k]$	$\frac{\theta^k \cdot \Gamma(\alpha-k)}{\Gamma(\alpha)}$, provided $k<\alpha$	$\frac{b^{k+1}-a^{k+1}}{(k+1)(b-a)}$
Mode $M(X)$	$\frac{\theta}{\alpha+1}$	Equimodal at all x
Variance $Var(X)$	$\frac{\theta^2}{(\alpha-1)^2(\alpha-2)}$, provided $\alpha>2$	$\frac{(b-a)^2}{12}$
MGF $M_X(t)$	Does Not Exist	$\frac{e^{bt}-e^{at}}{t(b-a)}$
LEV $E[X \wedge u]$	$\frac{\theta}{\alpha-1}[1-\Gamma(\alpha-1; \theta / u)] + u \cdot \Gamma(\alpha; \theta / u)$	$\frac{bu-\frac{1}{2}u^2}{b-a}$

Function	Normal	Lognormal
PDF $f(x)$	$\frac{1}{\sigma\sqrt{2\pi}} \cdot e^{-\frac{1}{2}\left(\frac{x-\mu}{\sigma}\right)^2}$, for $-\infty < x < \infty;\ \sigma > 0$	$\frac{1}{x} \cdot \frac{1}{\sigma\sqrt{2\pi}} \cdot e^{-\frac{1}{2}\left(\frac{\ln x-\mu}{\sigma}\right)^2}$, for $x > 0;\ \sigma > 0$
CDF $F(x)$	$\Phi\left(\frac{x-\mu}{\sigma}\right)$ [10]	$\Phi\left(\frac{\ln x-\mu}{\sigma}\right)$
HRF $\lambda(x)$	No Closed Form Expression	No Closed Form Expression
Mean $E[X]$	μ	$e^{\mu+\sigma^2/2}$
k^{th} **Moment** $E[X^k]$	$\frac{d}{dt^k} M_X(t)\Big\|_{t=0}$; there is no convenient closed-form expression	$e^{k\mu+k^2\sigma^2/2}$
Mode $M(X)$	μ	$e^{\mu-\sigma^2}$
Variance $Var(X)$	σ^2	$e^{2\mu}(e^{2\sigma^2} - e^{\sigma^2})$
MGF $M_X(t)$	$e^{\mu t+\sigma^2 t^2/2}$	Does Not Exist for $t > 0$
LEV $E[X \wedge u]$	$u + (\mu-u) \cdot \Phi\left(\frac{u-\mu}{\sigma}\right) - \frac{\sigma}{\sqrt{2\pi}} \cdot e^{-\frac{1}{2}\left(\frac{u-\mu}{\sigma}\right)^2}$	$e^{\mu+\sigma^2/2} \cdot \Phi\left(\frac{\ln u-\mu-\sigma^2}{\sigma}\right) + u\left[1-\Phi\left(\frac{\ln u-\mu}{\sigma}\right)\right]$

[10] There is no closed form expression for the normal CDF. Values are obtained from a table of unit normal CDF values denoted by $\Phi(z)$, or by approximate integration.

Function	Pareto	Inverse Pareto
PDF $f(x)$	$\frac{\alpha \cdot \theta^{\alpha}}{(x+\theta)^{\alpha+1}}$, for $x>0; \alpha>0; \theta>0$	$\frac{\alpha\theta \cdot x^{\alpha-1}}{(x+\theta)^{\alpha+1}}$, for $x>0; \alpha>0; \theta>0$
CDF $F(x)$	$1-\left(\frac{\theta}{x+\theta}\right)^{\alpha}$	$\left(\frac{x}{x+\theta}\right)^{\alpha}$
HRF $\lambda(x)$	$\frac{\alpha}{x+\theta}$	$\frac{\alpha\theta \cdot x^{\alpha-1}}{(x+\theta)^{\alpha+1} - x^{\alpha}(x+\theta)}$
Mean $E[X]$	$\frac{\theta}{\alpha-1}$, provided $\alpha>1$	Does Not Exist
k^{th} **Moment** $E[X^k]$	$\frac{\theta^k \cdot \Gamma(k+1) \cdot \Gamma(\alpha-k)}{\Gamma(\alpha)}$	Does Not Exist for $k \geq 1$
Mode $M(X)$	0	$\frac{\theta(\alpha-1)}{2}$, provided $\alpha>1$
Variance $Var(X)$	$\frac{\alpha\theta^2}{(\alpha-1)^2(\alpha-2)}$, provided $\alpha>2$	Does Not Exist
MGF $M_X(t)$	Does Not Exist	Does Not Exist
LEV $E[X \wedge u]$	$\frac{\theta}{\alpha-1}\left[1-\left(\frac{\theta}{u+\theta}\right)^{\alpha-1}\right]$, provided $\alpha \neq 1$ [11]	$\alpha\theta \cdot \int_0^{u/(u+\theta)} y^{\alpha}(1-y)^{-1}\,dy + u\left[1-\left(\frac{u}{u+\theta}\right)^{\alpha}\right]$

[11] $E[X \wedge u] = \theta \cdot \ln\left(\frac{u+\theta}{\theta}\right)$ when $\alpha = 1$.

Function	Weibull [12]	Inverse Weibull [13]
PDF $f(x)$	$\frac{\tau \cdot (x/\theta)^\tau \cdot e^{-(x/\theta)^\tau}}{x}$, for $x>0; \tau>0; \theta>0$	$\frac{\tau \cdot (\theta/x)^\tau \cdot e^{-(\theta/x)^\tau}}{x}$, for $x>0; \tau>0; \theta>0$
CDF $F(x)$	$1-e^{-(x/\theta)^\tau}$	$e^{-(\theta/x)^\tau}$
HRF $\lambda(x)$	$\frac{\tau \cdot x^{\tau-1}}{\theta^\tau}$	$\frac{\tau \cdot \theta^\tau \cdot e^{-(\theta/x)^\tau}}{x^{\tau+1}\left(1-e^{-(\theta/x)^\tau}\right)}$
Mean $E[X]$	$\theta \cdot \Gamma\left(1+\frac{1}{\tau}\right)$	$\theta \cdot \Gamma\left(1-\frac{1}{\tau}\right)$, provided $\tau>1$
k^{th} **Moment** $E[X^k]$	$\theta^k \cdot \Gamma\left(1+\frac{k}{\tau}\right)$	$\theta^k \cdot \Gamma\left(1-\frac{k}{\tau}\right)$, provided $k<\tau$
Mode $M(X)$	$\theta\left(1-\frac{1}{\tau}\right)^{1/\tau}$	$\left(\frac{\tau \cdot \theta^\tau}{\tau+1}\right)^{1/\tau}$
Variance $Var(X)$	$\theta^2\left(\Gamma\left(1+\frac{2}{\tau}\right)-\left[\Gamma\left(1+\frac{1}{\tau}\right)\right]^2\right)$	$\theta^2\left(\Gamma\left(1-\frac{2}{\tau}\right)-\left[\Gamma\left(1-\frac{1}{\tau}\right)\right]^2\right)$
MGF $M_X(t)$	Does Not Exist	Does Not Exist
LEV $E[X \wedge u]$	$\theta \cdot \Gamma\left(1+\frac{1}{\tau}\right) \cdot \Gamma\left[1+\frac{1}{\tau};(x/\theta)^\tau\right]$ $+x \cdot e^{-(x/\theta)^\tau}$	$\theta \cdot \Gamma\left(1-\frac{1}{\tau}\right) \cdot \left[1-\Gamma\left[1-\frac{1}{\tau};(x/\theta)^\tau\right]\right]$ $+x\left[1-e^{-(x/\theta)^\tau}\right]$

[12] The exponential distribution, in scale parameter form, is the special case of the Weibull distribution with $\tau=1$.

[13] The inverse exponential distribution, in scale parameter form, is the special case of the inverse Weibull distribution with $\tau=1$.

Function	Chi-Square[14]	Beta
PDF $f(x)$	$\frac{x^{(n/2)-1}\cdot e^{-x/2}}{2^{n/2}\cdot\Gamma(n/2)}$, for $x>0; n>0$	$\frac{\Gamma(a+b)}{\Gamma(a)\cdot\Gamma(b)}\cdot x^{a-1}\cdot(1-x)^{b-1}$, for $0<x<1;\ a>0;\ b>0$
CDF $F(x)$	$\Gamma\left(\frac{n}{2};\frac{x}{2}\right)$	$\beta(a,b;x)$
HRF $\lambda(x)$	$\lambda(x) = \frac{f(x)}{1-F(x)}$; there is no convenient closed-form expression	$\lambda(x) = \frac{f(x)}{1-F(x)}$; there is no convenient closed-form expression
Mean $E[X]$	n	$\frac{a}{a+b}$
k^{th} **Moment** $E[X^k]$	$\frac{2^k\cdot\Gamma\left(\frac{n}{2}+k\right)}{\Gamma\left(\frac{n}{2}\right)}$ [15]	$\frac{\Gamma(a+b)\cdot\Gamma(a+k)}{\Gamma(a)\cdot\Gamma(a+b+k)}$ [16]
Mode $M(X)$	$n-2$, provided $n>2$	$\frac{a-1}{a+b-2}$
Variance $Var(X)$	$2n$	$\frac{ab}{(a+b)^2(a+b+1)}$
MGF $M_X(t)$	$\left(\frac{1}{1-2t}\right)^{n/2}$	$\sum_{k=0}^{\infty}\frac{t^k}{k!}\left(\frac{\Gamma(a+b)\cdot\Gamma(a+k)}{\Gamma(a)\cdot\Gamma(a+b+k)}\right)$
LEV $E[X\wedge u]$	$n\cdot\Gamma\left(\frac{n}{2}+1;\frac{u}{2}\right)+u\left[1-\Gamma\left(\frac{n}{2};\frac{u}{2}\right)\right]$	$\frac{a}{a+b}\cdot\beta(a+1,b;u)+u\left[1-\beta(a,b;u)\right]$

[14] The chi-square distribution is the special case of the gamma distribution with $\alpha=\frac{n}{2}$ and $\theta=2$. It is said to have n degrees of freedom.

[15] This reduces to $2^k\cdot\left(\frac{n}{2}+k-1\right)\cdot\left(\frac{n}{2}+k-2\right)\cdot\ \cdots\ \cdot\left(\frac{n}{2}\right)$ if k is a positive integer.

[16] This reduces to $\frac{(a+k-1)(a+k-2)\cdots(a)}{(a+b+k-1)(a+b+k-2)\cdots(a+b)}$ if k is a positive integer.

A.1.3 THREE-PARAMETER DISTRIBUTIONS

The tables on the following two pages give basic functions for the Burr, generalized Pareto, generalized gamma, and inverse generalized gamma distributions.

For each distribution, there is no convenient closed-form expression for the hazard rate function $\lambda(x)$, other than to express it as $\frac{f(x)}{1-F(x)}$, and there is no convenient closed-form expression for the variance $Var(x)$, other than to express it as $E[X^2]-(E[X])^2$.

As before, the survival distribution function is found as $S(x)=1-F(x)$. The moment generating function $M_X(t)$ is not shown, and, in most cases, does not even exist.

Some entries make use of the incomplete beta function, as defined on page 486.

Function	Burr	Generalized Pareto
PDF $f(x)$	$\dfrac{\alpha\tau(x/\theta)^{\tau}}{x[1+(x/\theta)^{\tau}]^{\alpha+1}}$	$\dfrac{\Gamma(\alpha+\tau)}{\Gamma(\alpha)\cdot\Gamma(\tau)}\cdot\dfrac{\theta^{\alpha}\cdot x^{\tau-1}}{(x+\theta)^{\alpha+\tau}}$
CDF $F(x)$	$1-[1+(x/\theta)^{\tau}]^{-\alpha}$	$\beta(\tau,\alpha;\,\frac{x}{x+\theta})$
Mean $E[X]$	$\dfrac{\theta\cdot\Gamma(1+\frac{1}{\tau})\cdot\Gamma(\alpha-\frac{1}{\tau})}{\Gamma(\alpha)}$	$\dfrac{\theta\tau}{\alpha-1}$
k^{th} **Moment** $E[X^k]$	$\dfrac{\theta^{k}\cdot\Gamma(1+\frac{k}{\tau})\cdot\Gamma(\alpha-\frac{k}{\tau})}{\Gamma(\alpha)}$	$\dfrac{\theta^{k}\cdot\Gamma(\tau+k)\cdot\Gamma(\alpha-k)}{\Gamma(\alpha)\cdot\Gamma(\tau)}$ [17]
Mode $M(X)$	$\theta\left(\dfrac{\tau-1}{\alpha\tau+1}\right)^{1/\tau}$, provided $\tau>1$	$\theta\left(\dfrac{\tau-1}{\alpha+1}\right)$, provided $\tau>1$
LEV $E[X\wedge u]$	$\dfrac{\theta\cdot\Gamma\left(1+\frac{1}{\tau}\right)\cdot\Gamma\left(\alpha-\frac{1}{\tau}\right)}{\Gamma(\alpha)}\cdot\beta\left(1+\frac{1}{\tau},\alpha-\frac{1}{\tau};1-\left[1+\left(\frac{x}{\theta}\right)^{\tau}\right]^{-1}\right)+x\left[1+\left(\frac{x}{\theta}\right)^{\tau}\right]^{-\alpha}$	$\dfrac{\theta\cdot\Gamma(\tau+1)\cdot\Gamma(\alpha-1)}{\Gamma(\alpha)\cdot\Gamma(\tau)}\cdot\beta\left(\tau+1,\alpha-1;\dfrac{x}{x+\theta}\right)$

[17] This reduces to $\frac{\theta^{k}\cdot(\tau+k-1)(\tau+k-2)\cdots(\tau)}{(\alpha-1)(\alpha-2\cdots(\alpha-k)}$ if k is a positive integer.

Function	**Generalized Gamma**	**Inverse Generalized Gamma**
PDF $f(x)$	$\dfrac{\tau\cdot(x/\theta)^{\tau}\cdot e^{-(x/\theta)^{\tau}}}{x\cdot\Gamma(\alpha)}$	$\dfrac{\tau\cdot(\theta/x)^{\alpha\tau}\cdot e^{-(\theta/x)^{\tau}}}{x\cdot\Gamma(\alpha)}$
CDF $F(x)$	$\Gamma\left(\alpha;(x/\theta)^{\tau}\right)$	$1-\Gamma\left(\alpha;(\theta/x)^{\tau}\right)$
Mean $E[X]$	$\dfrac{\theta\cdot\Gamma\left(\alpha+\frac{1}{\tau}\right)}{\Gamma(\alpha)}$	$\dfrac{\theta\cdot\Gamma\left(\alpha-\frac{1}{\tau}\right)}{\Gamma(\alpha)}$
k^{th} **Moment** $E[X^k]$	$\dfrac{\theta^{k}\cdot\Gamma\left(\alpha+\frac{k}{\tau}\right)}{\Gamma(\alpha)}$	$\dfrac{\theta^{k}\cdot\Gamma\left(\alpha-\frac{k}{\tau}\right)}{\Gamma(\alpha)}$
Mode $M(X)$	$\theta\left(\dfrac{\alpha\tau-1}{\tau}\right)^{1/\tau}$, provided $\alpha\tau>1$	$\theta\left(\dfrac{\tau}{\alpha\tau+1}\right)^{1/\tau}$
LEV $E[X\wedge u]$	$\dfrac{\theta\cdot\Gamma\left(\alpha+\frac{1}{\tau}\right)}{\Gamma(\alpha)}\cdot\Gamma\left(\alpha+\frac{1}{\tau};\left(\frac{x}{\theta}\right)^{\tau}\right)$ $+x\left[1-\Gamma\left(\alpha;\left(\frac{x}{\theta}\right)^{\tau}\right)\right]$	$\dfrac{\theta\cdot\Gamma\left(\alpha-\frac{1}{\tau}\right)}{\Gamma(\alpha)}$ $\cdot\left[1-\Gamma\left(\alpha-\frac{1}{\tau}\right);\left(\frac{\theta}{x}\right)^{\tau}\right]+x\cdot\Gamma\left(\alpha;\left(\frac{\theta}{x}\right)^{\tau}\right)$

A.2 MULTIVARIATE CONTINUOUS DISTRIBUTIONS

In this section we confine our attention to distributions of two variables only.

A.2.1 THE BIVARIATE NORMAL DISTRIBUTION

Two random variables X_1 and X_2 have a bivariate normal distribution if their joint density function is of the form

$$f(x_1, x_2) = \frac{1}{2\pi\sigma_1\sigma_2 \cdot \sqrt{1-\rho^2}} \cdot \exp\left\{\frac{-1}{2(1-\rho^2)}\left[\left(\frac{x_1-\mu_1}{\sigma_1}\right)^2 - 2\rho\left(\frac{x_1-\mu_1}{\sigma_1}\right)\left(\frac{x_2-\mu_2}{\sigma_2}\right) + \left(\frac{x_2-\mu_2}{\sigma_2}\right)^2\right]\right\},$$

where $-\infty < x_1 < \infty$, $-\infty < x_2 < \infty$, $\sigma_1 > 0$, and $\sigma_2 > 0$. The marginal distribution of X_i is normal with mean μ_i and standard deviation σ_i. The covariance of X_1 and X_2 is denoted by σ_{12}, and the correlation coefficient between X_1 and X_2 is

$$\rho = \frac{Cov(X_1, X_2)}{\sigma_1\sigma_2} = \frac{\sigma_{12}}{\sigma_1\sigma_2}.$$

A.2.2 THE BIVARIATE CONTINUOUS UNIFORM DISTRIBUTION

The random variables X and Y have a bivariate uniform distribution if their joint density function is the constant

$$f(x, y) = \frac{1}{A},$$

where $A > 0$ is the area of the joint domain in the (x, y) plane. The marginal distribution of X and Y are both continuous uniform, and X and Y are independent.

APPENDIX B

SUMMARY OF DISCRETE DISTRIBUTIONS

This appendix provides a condensed summary of the discrete distributions reviewed in Section 1.2. The alternative parameterization of the negative binomial is presented in Exercise 6-38.

B.1 UNIVARIATE DISCRETE DISTRIBUTIONS

Distribution	Probability Function $p(x)$	Expected Value $E[X]$	Variance $Var(X)$
Binomial[1]	$\binom{n}{x} \cdot p^x(1-p)^{n-x}$, for $x = 0, 1, \cdots, n$	np	$np(1-p)$
Bernoulli[2]	$p^x(1-p)^{1-x}$, for $x = 0,1$	p	$p(1-p)$
Poisson[3]	$\frac{e^{-\lambda}\lambda^x}{x!}$, for $x = 0, 1, 2, \cdots$	λ	λ
Negative Binomial[4]	$\binom{x+r-1}{r-1} \cdot p^r(1-p)^x$, for $x = 0, 1, 2, \cdots$	$\frac{rq}{p}$, where $q = 1-p$	$\frac{rq}{p^2}$, where $q = 1-p$
Geometric[5]	$p(1-p)^x$, for $x = 0, 1, 2, \cdots$	$\frac{q}{p}$, where $q = 1-p$	$\frac{q}{p^2}$, where $q = 1-p$
Negative Binomial (alternative parameterization)[6]	$\binom{x+r-1}{r-1} \cdot \frac{\beta^x}{(1+\beta)^{x+r}}$ for $x = 0, 1, 2, \cdots$	$r\beta$	$r\beta(1+\beta)$
Geometric (alternative parameterization)[7]	$\frac{\beta^x}{(1+\beta)^{x+1}}$, for $x = 0, 1, 2, \cdots$	β	$\beta(1+\beta)$

[1] In the binomial distribution, n is a positive integer and p must satisfy $0 < p < 1$.
[2] The Bernoulli distribution is the special case of the binomial distribution with $n = 1$.
[3] In the Poisson distribution, the parameter λ must satisfy $\lambda > 0$.
[4] In the negative binomial distribution, the parameter r must satisfy $r > 0$ but need not be an integer. Whether r is integral or not, the coefficient in the probability function can be evaluated using gamma functions as $\frac{\Gamma(x+r)}{\Gamma(r)\cdot\Gamma(x+1)}$.
[5] The geometric distribution is the special case of the negative binomial with $r = 1$.
[6] The relationship of the parameter p (in the standard parameterization) to the parameter β (in the alternate parameterization) is $p = (1/1+\beta)$, so that $1 - p = (\beta/1+\beta)$. The parameter r is the same in both versions.
[7] Again the geometric distribution is the special case of the negative binomial with $r = 1$.

Distribution	Moment Generating Function $M_X(t)$	Probability Generating Function $P_X(s)$
Binomial	$(q+pe^t)^n$, where $q=1-p$	$(q+ps)^n$, where $q=1-p$
Bernoulli	$q+pe^t$, where $q=1-p$	$q+ps$, where $q=1-p$
Poisson	$e^{\lambda(e^t-1)}$	$e^{\lambda(s-1)}$
Negative Binomial	$\left(\frac{p}{1-qe^t}\right)^r$, where $q=1-p$	$\left(\frac{p}{1-qs}\right)^r$, where $q=1-p$
Geometric	$\frac{p}{1-qe^t}$, where $q=1-p$	$\frac{p}{1-qs}$, where $q=1-p$
Negative Binomial (alternative parameterization)	$\left(\frac{1}{1+\beta-\beta e^t}\right)^r$	$\left(\frac{1}{1+\beta(1-s)}\right)^r$
Geometric (alternative parameterization)	$\frac{1}{1+\beta-\beta e^t}$	$\frac{1}{1+\beta(1-s)}$

B.2 MULTIVARIATE DISCRETE DISTRIBUTION

The multinomial distribution is a generalization of the binomial distribution. Its joint probability function, for the set of k random variables $X_1, X_2, \cdots, X_k$, is

$$p(x_1, x_2, \cdots, x_k) = \frac{n!}{x_1! x_2! \cdots x_k!} \cdot (p_1)^{x_1} (p_2)^{x_2} \cdots (p_k)^{x_k},$$

where n is a positive integer, $x_i = 0, 1, \cdots, n$ and $0 < p_i < 1$ for all $i = 1, 2, \cdots, k$, $\sum_{i=1}^{k} x_i = n$, and $\sum_{i=1}^{k} p_i = 1$. Its important properties are the following:

Expected Value $E[X_i]$	Variance $Var(X_i)$	Covariance $Cov(X_i, X_j)$
$n \cdot p_i$	$n \cdot p_i(1-p_i)$	$-n \cdot p_i \cdot p_j$

APPENDIX C

STATISTICAL TABLES

C.1 THE CHI-SQUARE DISTRIBUTION

Percentiles of the χ^2 random variable with r degrees of freedom:

r	.010	.025	.050	.100	.900	.950	.975	.990
1	0.000	0.001	0.004	0.016	2.706	3.841	5.024	6.635
2	0.020	0.051	0.103	0.211	4.605	5.991	7.378	9.210
3	0.115	0.216	0.352	0.584	6.251	7.815	9.348	11.34
4	0.297	0.484	0.711	1.064	7.779	9.488	11.14	13.28
5	0.554	0.831	1.145	1.610	9.236	11.07	12.83	15.09
6	0.872	1.237	1.635	2.204	10.64	12.59	14.45	16.81
7	1.239	1.690	2.167	2.833	12.02	14.07	16.01	18.48
8	1.646	2.180	2.733	3.490	13.36	15.51	17.54	20.09
9	2.088	2.700	3.325	4.168	14.68	16.92	19.02	21.67
10	2.558	3.247	3.940	4.865	15.99	18.31	20.48	23.21
11	3.053	3.816	4.575	5.578	17.28	19.68	21.92	24.72
12	3.571	4.404	5.226	6.304	18.55	21.03	23.34	26.22
13	4.107	5.009	5.892	7.042	19.81	22.36	24.74	27.69
14	4.660	5.629	6.571	7.790	21.06	23.68	26.12	29.14
15	5.229	6.262	7.261	8.547	22.31	25.00	27.49	30.58
16	5.812	6.908	7.962	9.312	23.54	26.30	28.84	32.00
17	6.408	7.564	8.672	10.08	24.77	27.59	30.19	33.41
18	7.015	8.231	9.390	10.86	25.99	28.87	31.53	34.80
19	7.633	8.907	10.12	11.65	27.20	30.14	32.85	36.19
20	8.260	9.591	10.85	12.44	28.41	31.41	34.17	37.57

C.2 THE STANDARD NORMAL DISTRIBUTION

Values of $\Phi(z) = \Pr(Z \le z)$, where Z is the standard normal random variable:

z	**0.00**	**0.01**	**0.02**	**0.03**	**0.04**	**0.05**	**0.06**	**0.07**	**0.08**	**0.09**
0.0	.5000	.5040	.5080	.5120	.5160	.5199	.5239	.5279	.5319	.5359
0.1	.5398	.5438	.5478	.5517	.5557	.5596	.5636	.5675	.5714	.5753
0.2	.5793	.5832	.5871	.5910	.5948	.5987	.6026	.6064	.6103	.6141
0.3	.6179	.6217	.6255	.6293	.6331	.6368	.6406	.6443	.6480	.6517
0.4	.6554	.6591	.6628	.6664	.6700	.6736	.6772	.6808	.6844	.6879
0.5	.6915	.6950	.6985	.7019	.7054	.7088	.7123	.7157	.7190	.7224
0.6	.7257	.7291	.7324	.7357	.7389	.7422	.7454	.7486	.7517	.7549
0.7	.7580	.7611	.7642	.7673	.7704	.7734	.7764	.7794	.7823	.7852
0.8	.7881	.7910	.7939	.7967	.7995	.8023	.8051	.8078	.8106	.8133
0.9	.8159	.8186	.8212	.8238	.8264	.8289	.8315	.8340	.8365	.8389
1.0	.8413	.8438	.8461	.8485	.8508	.8531	.8554	.8577	.8599	.8621
1.1	.8643	.8665	.8686	.8708	.8729	.8749	.8770	.8790	.8810	.8830
1.2	.8849	.8869	.8888	.8907	.8925	.8944	.8962	.8980	.8997	.9015
1.3	.9032	.9049	.9066	.9082	.9099	.9115	.9131	.9147	.9162	.9177
1.4	.9192	.9207	.9222	.9236	.9251	.9265	.9279	.9292	.9306	.9319
1.5	.9332	.9345	.9357	.9370	.9382	.9394	.9406	.9418	.9429	.9441
1.6	.9452	.9463	.9474	.9484	.9495	.9505	.9515	.9525	.9535	.9545
1.7	.9554	.9564	.9573	.9582	.9591	.9599	.9608	.9616	.9625	.9633
1.8	.9641	.9649	.9656	.9644	.9671	.9678	.9686	.9693	.9699	.9706
1.9	.9713	.9719	.9726	.9732	.9738	.9744	.9750	.9756	.9761	.9767
2.0	.9772	.9778	.9783	.9788	.9793	.9798	.9803	.9808	.9812	.9817
2.1	.9821	.9826	.9830	.9834	.9838	.9842	.9846	.9850	.9854	.9857
2.2	.9861	.9864	.9868	.9871	.9875	.9878	.9881	.9884	.9887	.9890
2.3	.9893	.9896	.9898	.9901	.9904	.9906	.9909	.9911	.9913	.9916
2.4	.9918	.9920	.9922	.9925	.9927	.9929	.9931	.9932	.9934	.9936
2.5	.9938	.9940	.9941	.9943	.9945	.9946	.9948	.9949	.9951	.9952
2.6	.9953	.9955	.9956	.9957	.9959	.9960	.9961	.9962	.9963	.9964
2.7	.9965	.9966	.9967	.9968	.9969	.9970	.9971	.9972	.9973	.9974
2.8	.9974	.9975	.9976	.9977	.9977	.9978	.9979	.9979	,9980	.9981
2.9	.9981	.9982	.9982	.9983	.9984	.9984	.9985	.9985	.9986	.9986

Values of z for selected values of $\Phi(z)$:

$\Phi(z)$	.80	.85	.90	.95	.975	.99	.995
z	0.842	1.037	1.282	1.645	1.960	2.327	2.575

APPENDIX D

THE FORWARD FINITE DIFFERENCE OPERATOR

The forward finite difference operator over the interval h, denoted by Δ_h, is defined by

$$\Delta_h f(x) = f(x+h) - f(x). \tag{D.1}$$

In words, the difference operator, when applied to a function at argument x in general, produces the difference $f(x+h) - f(x)$. In particular, at $h=1$ we have

$$\Delta f(x) = f(x+1) - f(x). \tag{D.2}$$

Note that when $h=1$, we use merely Δ rather than Δ_1. The remainder of this appendix will assume $h=1$ for simplicity.

The second order differencing operator, Δ^2, is defined by

$$\begin{aligned}
\Delta^2 f(x) &= \Delta\big[\Delta f(x)\big] \\
&= \Delta\big[f(x+1) - f(x)\big] \\
&= \Delta f(x+1) - \Delta f(x) \\
&= \big[f(x+2) - f(x+1)\big] - \big[f(x+1) - f(x)\big] \\
&= f(x+2) - 2f(x+1) + f(x).
\end{aligned} \tag{D.3}$$

Note that Δ^2 means a repetition of the differencing operation, and *not* Δ times Δ. (Since Δ is an operator, not an algebraic quantity, "multiplication" is not a meaningful concept.) Note also that the Δ operator is distributive and commutative with respect to a constant.

Higher order differences follow analogously. For example,

$$\begin{aligned}
\Delta^3 f(x) &= \Delta\big[\Delta^2 f(x)\big] \\
&= \Delta\big[f(x+2) - 2f(x+1) + f(x)\big] \\
&= \big[f(x+3) - f(x+2)\big] - 2\big[f(x+2) - f(x+1)\big] + \big[f(x+1) - f(x)\big] \\
&= f(x+3) - 3f(x+2) + 3f(x+1) - f(x).
\end{aligned} \tag{D.4}$$

By now the pattern should be clear. In general, $\Delta^n f(x)$ will involve $n+1$ terms, from $f(x+n)$ back through $f(x)$. We prefer to say it this way, rather than to say $f(x)$ up through $f(x+n)$, to aid in determining the signs of the coefficients. $f(x+n)$ is always positive, $f(x+n-1)$ will be negative, with signs alternating so that $f(x)$ will be positive or negative depending on whether n is even or odd. (Note the sign patterns in $\Delta^2 f(x)$ and $\Delta^3 f(x)$ above.) The coefficients of the $n+1$ terms in $\Delta^n f(x)$ are the binomial coefficients of order n.

An important property of finite differences is that the application of the Δ operator to a polynomial function reduces the degree of that polynomial by one. Thus, if $f(x)$ is a polynomial of degree n, $\Delta f(x)$ is a polynomial of degree $n-1$. In this respect, differencing is analogous to differentiation. It follows that if $f(x)$ is a polynomial of degree n, then $\Delta^n f(x)$ is a polynomial of degree 0, which is a constant. That is,

$$\Delta^n f(x) = c \tag{D.5}$$

if $f(x)$ is a polynomial of degree n, and, furthermore,

$$\Delta^{n+1} f(x) = 0. \tag{D.6}$$

It is for this reason that we say, for example, that requiring $\Delta^4 v_x$ to approach zero is to require the v_x sequence to approach a third degree polynomial (see Section 12.4.1).

APPENDIX E

DERIVATION OF THE WHITTAKER EQUATION (12.21) MINIMIZING VECTOR

We wish to show that the vector **v** which solves the matrix-vector equation represented by Equation (12.22) will minimize the composite measure M given by Equation (12.21). The demonstration depends on the result from matrix algebra which states that if a symmetric matrix **c** is positive definite, then it is non-singular (so that $\mathbf{c}^{-1}$ exists), and furthermore $\mathbf{c}^{-1}$ is also positive definite.

We observe that the matrix **c** is symmetric. Now **c** is positive definite if $\mathbf{y}^T\mathbf{c}\mathbf{y} \geq 0,$ and equals zero only when $\mathbf{y} = \mathbf{0}.$ For our **c**

$$\mathbf{y}^T\mathbf{c}\mathbf{y} \;=\; \mathbf{y}^T\mathbf{w}\mathbf{y} + h\mathbf{y}^T\mathbf{k_z}^T\mathbf{k_z}\mathbf{y} \;=\; \mathbf{y}^T\mathbf{w}\mathbf{y} + h(\mathbf{k_z}\mathbf{y})^T(\mathbf{k_z}\mathbf{y})\,.$$

Since h and w_x are positive, we see that $\mathbf{y}^T\mathbf{c}\mathbf{y}$ can be zero only if $\mathbf{y} = \mathbf{0}$. Thus **c** is positive definite.

Now we write Equation (12.21) as

$$(\mathbf{v}-\mathbf{u})^T\mathbf{w}(\mathbf{v}-\mathbf{u}) + h\mathbf{v}^T\mathbf{k}^T\mathbf{k}\mathbf{v},$$

dropping the subscript z from **k** for convenience. We expand the product $(\mathbf{v}-\mathbf{u})^T\mathbf{w}(\mathbf{v}-\mathbf{u})$ and combine the resulting $\mathbf{v}^T\mathbf{w}\mathbf{v}$ term with $h\mathbf{v}^T\mathbf{k}^T\mathbf{k}\mathbf{v}$ to introduce **c**. This produces

$$\mathbf{v}^T\mathbf{w}\mathbf{v} + h\mathbf{v}^T\mathbf{k}^T\mathbf{k}\mathbf{v} - \mathbf{u}^T\mathbf{w}\mathbf{v} - \mathbf{v}^T\mathbf{w}\mathbf{u} + \mathbf{u}^T\mathbf{w}\mathbf{u}$$

or

$$\mathbf{v}^T\mathbf{c}\mathbf{v} - \mathbf{u}^T\mathbf{w}\mathbf{v} - \mathbf{v}^T\mathbf{w}\mathbf{u} + \mathbf{u}^T\mathbf{w}\mathbf{u}.$$

Next we multiply each of the first three terms by the identity matrix $\mathbf{c}^{-1}\mathbf{c}$ (which is commutative, and, furthermore, $\mathbf{c}^T = \mathbf{c}$ due to symmetry). We also add and subtract $\mathbf{u}^T\mathbf{w}\mathbf{c}^{-1}\mathbf{w}\mathbf{u}$. We now have

$$\mathbf{v}^T\mathbf{c}\mathbf{c}^{-1}\mathbf{c}\mathbf{v} - \mathbf{u}^T\mathbf{w}\mathbf{c}^{-1}\mathbf{c}\mathbf{v} - \mathbf{v}^T\mathbf{c}\mathbf{c}^{-1}\mathbf{w}\mathbf{u} + \mathbf{u}^T\mathbf{w}\mathbf{c}^{-1}\mathbf{w}\mathbf{u} + \mathbf{u}^T\mathbf{w}\mathbf{u} - \mathbf{u}^T\mathbf{w}\mathbf{c}^{-1}\mathbf{w}\mathbf{u}.$$

Because the last two terms are constant (that is, they do not involve **v**), they can be ignored. The remaining four terms can be written as $(\mathbf{v}^T\mathbf{c}-\mathbf{u}^T\mathbf{w})\mathbf{c}^{-1}(\mathbf{cv}-\mathbf{wu})$, which is the same as $(\mathbf{cv}-\mathbf{wu})^T\mathbf{c}^{-1}(\mathbf{cv}-\mathbf{wu})$, due to the symmetry of **c** and **w**. Finally, since $\mathbf{c}^{-1}$ is positive definite, then $(\mathbf{cv}-\mathbf{wu})^T\mathbf{c}^{-1}(\mathbf{cv}-\mathbf{wu})$ can never be negative, and its minimum value is zero, which is obtained when $\mathbf{cv}=\mathbf{wu}$.

APPENDIX F

ITERATION METHODS

F.1 GENERAL BACKGROUND

A general formula for an equation to be solved using iteration is given by

$$f(x) = 0. \tag{F.1}$$

The roots of this equation are those values of r for which $f(r) = 0$. Many iteration methods express the formula for the equation to be solved in the alternative form

$$x = g(x). \tag{F.2a}$$

The iteration then proceeds by assuming a starting value x_0 and generating successive values $x_1, x_2, \ldots$ from

$$x_{n+1} = g(x_n). \tag{F.2b}$$

The iteration procedure described above will converge if

$$\left| g'(r) \right| < 1 \tag{F.3a}$$

and will diverge if

$$\left| g'(r) \right| \geq 1. \tag{F.3b}$$

The iteration stops when the desired level of accuracy is obtained for a converging iteration or when it is found that the iteration is diverging.

F.2 SUCCESSIVE BISECTION

This method requires two starting values, x_0 and x_1, which have functional values $f(x_0)$ and $f(x_1)$ of opposite sign. We bisect the interval, producing

$$x_2 = .50(x_0 + x_1), \tag{F.4}$$

and find its functional value. We then choose x_2 and *either* x_0 or x_1, such that $f(x_2)$ and the choice of $f(x_0)$ or $f(x_1)$ are of opposite sign. We continue the bisection process as many times as necessary to achieve the desired level of accuracy. This method is very simple to apply on a computer and convergence is guaranteed if $f(x)$ is continuous. The rate of convergence, however may be rather slow.

F.3 SUCCESSIVE INVERSE INTERPOLATION

This method also requires two starting values, x_0 and x_1, which have functional values $f(x_0)$ and $f(x_1)$ of opposite sign. The iteration formula is given by

$$x_{n+2} = \frac{x_n \cdot f(x_{n+1}) - x_{n+1} \cdot f(x_n)}{f(x_{n+1}) - f(x_n)}. \tag{F.5}$$

Two variations exist in applying this method after the first iteration. The first variation uses the two most recently computed values of x for which the associated values of $f(x)$ are of *opposite* sign. The second variation uses the two most recently computed values of x *regardless* of the signs of the associated $f(x)$.

F.4 NEWTON-RAPHSON METHOD

This iteration formula is given by

$$x_{n+1} = x_n - \frac{f(x_n)}{f'(x_n)}. \tag{F.6}$$

For this method, $g'(r) = 0$, which produces an extremely fast rate of convergence called *second-order convergence*. The method requires that $f'(x)$ can be computed and has a non-zero value.

APPENDIX G

ASYMPTOTIC PROPERTIES OF MAXIMUM LIKELIHOOD ESTIMATORS

As stated in Section 14.4.1, as the sample size $n \to \infty$ the maximum likelihood estimator of the parameter θ of a one-parameter underlying distribution possesses the properties of unbiasedness, consistency, and efficiency. Furthermore, if the density function of the underlying distribution satisfies certain conditions, then it is also true that the estimator random variable, $\hat{\theta}_n$, has a distribution that is approximately normal for large n and approaches a normal distribution as $n \to \infty$. The mean of this asymptotically normal distribution is

$$E[\hat{\theta}_n] = \theta,$$

confirming that $\hat{\theta}_n$ is asymptotically unbiased, and its variance is given by

$$Var(\hat{\theta}_n) = \left\{ n \cdot E\left[\left(\frac{d}{d\theta} \ln f(X;\theta) \right)^2 \right] \right\}^{-1}.$$

(The PDF of the underlying distribution is denoted $f(x;\theta)$, to remind us that it is a function of both x and θ. Whenever we consider the expected value of some function of the PDF, we replace x with X to remind us that the expectation is taken with respect to the underlying random variable X.)[1]

The conditions that $f(x;\theta)$ must satisfy in order that these results will ensue are the following:

(1) All three of the derivatives $\frac{d}{d\theta}\ln f(x;\theta)$, $\frac{d^2}{d\theta^2}\ln f(x;\theta)$, and $\frac{d^3}{d\theta^3}\ln f(x;\theta)$ exist.

(2) $\int_{-\infty}^{\infty} \frac{d}{d\theta} f(x;\theta)\,dx = 0$. Note that this also implies that $E\left[\frac{d}{d\theta}\ln f(X;\theta)\right] = 0$.

(3) $\int_{-\infty}^{\infty} \frac{d^2}{d\theta^2} f(x;\theta)\,dx = 0$

(4) The expected value $E\left[\frac{d^2}{d\theta^2}\ln f(X;\theta)\right]$ exists.

---

[1] The results are stated here without proof. For a proof of the theorem, see Rao [33] or Rohatgi [34].

Note that the theorem asserts Equation (14.14a) for the variance of the estimator random variable $\hat{\theta}_n$. We will therefore accept Equation (14.14a) as correct (which is verified by the proof of the theorem), and proceed to show that each of Equations (14.14b), (14.14c), and (14.14d) are equivalent to Equation (14.14a).

When we sample n times from an underlying distribution, we obtain a realized value, x_i, for the random variable X_i, for $i = 1, 2, \ldots, n$. Assuming that the X_i's are independent and identically distributed, with common density function $f(x;\theta)$, then the log likelihood function is

$$\ell(x;\theta) = \sum_{i=1}^{n} \ln f(x_i;\theta)$$

or

$$\ell(X;\theta) = \sum_{i=1}^{n} \ln f(X_i;\theta)$$

in terms of the random variables.[2] Then

$$\frac{d}{d\theta}\ell(X;\theta) = \sum_{i=1}^{n} \frac{d}{d\theta} \ln f(X_i;\theta),$$

$$\frac{d^2}{d\theta^2}\ell(X;\theta) = \sum_{i=1}^{n} \frac{d^2}{d\theta^2} \ln f(X_i;\theta),$$

and

$$E\left[\frac{d^2}{d\theta^2}\ell(X;\theta)\right] = \sum_{i=1}^{n} E\left[\frac{d^2}{d\theta^2} \ln f(X_i;\theta)\right].$$

Since the X_i's are identically distributed, it follows that the expectation $E\left[\frac{d^2}{d\theta^2} \ln f(X_i;\theta)\right]$ is the same for all i. Therefore the sum is equal to $n \cdot E\left[\frac{d^2}{d\theta^2} \ln f(X;\theta)\right]$, which establishes the equivalence of Equations (14.14b) and (14.14d).

Next we show the equivalence of Equations (14.14a) and (14.14c). Again we start with

$$\frac{d}{d\theta}\ell(X;\theta) = \sum_{i=1}^{n} \frac{d}{d\theta} \ln f(X_i;\theta)$$

so that

[2] Recall that we substitute data values for the x_i's when proceeding to estimate the parameter θ, but *not* when deriving expressions for the variance of $\hat{\theta}_n$.

$$\begin{aligned}\left(\frac{d}{d\theta}\ell(X;\theta)\right)^2 &= \left(\sum_{i=1}^{n}\frac{d}{d\theta}\ln f(X_i;\theta)\right)^2 \\ &= \sum_{i=1}^{n}\left(\frac{d}{d\theta}\ln f(X_i;\theta)\right)^2 + 2\cdot\sum_{i\neq j}\left(\frac{d}{d\theta}\ln f(X_i;\theta)\right)\left(\frac{d}{d\theta}\ln f(X_j;\theta)\right).\end{aligned}$$

Then

$$E\left[\left(\frac{d}{d\theta}\ell(X;\theta)\right)^2\right] = \sum_{i=1}^{n}E\left[\left(\frac{d}{d\theta}\ln f(X_i;\theta)\right)^2\right] + 2\cdot\sum_{i\neq j}E\left[\left(\frac{d}{d\theta}\ln f(X_i;\theta)\right)\left(\frac{d}{d\theta}\ln f(X_j;\theta)\right)\right].$$

Again, since the X_i's are identically distributed, the first term on the right side can be written as $n\cdot E\left[\left(\frac{d}{d\theta}\ln f(X;\theta)\right)^2\right]$. Since X_i and X_j are independent, then functions of them, such as $\frac{d}{d\theta}\ln f(X_i;\theta)$ and $\frac{d}{d\theta}\ln f(X_j;\theta)$, are independent as well and therefore the expected value of their product is the product of their expected values. Then the second term on the right side becomes

$$2\cdot\sum_{i\neq j}\left\{E\left[\frac{d}{d\theta}\ln f(X_i;\theta)\right]\cdot E\left[\frac{d}{d\theta}\ln f(X_j;\theta)\right]\right\},$$

which is zero by Condition (2) of the theorem. Therefore Equations (14.14a) and (14.14c) are equivalent.

Next we show the equivalence of Equations (14.14a) and (14.14d). We start with

$$\begin{aligned}\frac{d^2}{d\theta^2}\ell(X;\theta) &= \sum_{i=1}^{n}\frac{d^2}{d\theta^2}\ln f(X_i;\theta) \\ &= \sum_{i=1}^{n}\frac{d}{d\theta}\left[\frac{d}{d\theta}\ln f(X_i;\theta)\right] \\ &= \sum_{i=1}^{n}\frac{d}{d\theta}\left[\frac{\frac{d}{d\theta}f(X_i;\theta)}{f(X_i;\theta)}\right] \\ &= \sum_{i=1}^{n}\frac{f(X_i;\theta)\cdot\frac{d^2}{d\theta^2}f(X_i;\theta)-\left[\frac{d}{d\theta}f(X_i;\theta)\right]^2}{[f(X_i;\theta)]^2}.\end{aligned}$$

Then

$$E\left[\frac{d^2}{d\theta^2}\ell(X;\theta)\right] = \sum_{i=1}^{n}\left\{E\left[\frac{\frac{d^2}{d\theta^2}f(X_i;\theta)}{f(X_i;\theta)}\right] - E\left[\left(\frac{\frac{d}{d\theta}f(X_i;\theta)}{f(X_i;\theta)}\right)^2\right]\right\}$$

$$= -\sum_{i=1}^{n}E\left[\left(\frac{d}{d\theta}\ln f(X_i;\theta)\right)^2\right] + \sum_{i=1}^{n}\left[\frac{\frac{d^2}{d\theta^2}f(X_i;\theta)}{f(X_i;\theta)}\right],$$

by noting that $\dfrac{\frac{d}{d\theta}f(X_i;\theta)}{f(X_i;\theta)} = \dfrac{d}{d\theta}\ln f(X_i;\theta)$. But

$$E\left[\frac{\frac{d^2}{d\theta^2}f(X_i;\theta)}{f(X_i;\theta)}\right] = \int_{-\infty}^{\infty}\frac{\frac{d^2}{d\theta^2}f(x_i;\theta)}{f(x_i;\theta)}\cdot f(x_i;\theta)\,dx_i$$

$$= \int_{-\infty}^{\infty}\frac{d^2}{d\theta^2}f(x_i;\theta)\,dx_i = 0,$$

by Condition (3) of the theorem. Therefore we have

$$E\left[\frac{d^2}{d\theta^2}\ell(X;\theta)\right] = -n\cdot E\left[\left(\frac{d}{d\theta}\ln f(X;\theta)\right)^2\right],$$

which establishes the equivalence of Equations (14.14a) and (14.14d).

Finally, having already established the equivalence of Equations (14.14b) and (14.14d), we have now shown the equivalence of all four expressions for $Var(\hat{\theta}_n)$ in the asymptotic case.

APPENDIX H

INVERTING A 2 ×2 MATRIX

In linear algebra, a variety of methods are presented for inverting non-singular matrices. A simple and fast algorithm for inverting a 2×2 matrix is the following technique.

Let the matrix $\mathbf{A}$ be defined by

$$\mathbf{A} = \begin{vmatrix} a & b \\ c & d \end{vmatrix}.$$

The inverse of $\mathbf{A}$ is then given by

$$\mathbf{A}^{-1} = \frac{\begin{vmatrix} d & -b \\ -c & a \end{vmatrix}}{\det \begin{vmatrix} a & b \\ c & d \end{vmatrix}}, \tag{H.1}$$

where det denotes the determinant of the matrix that follows, which is $(ad - bc)$ in this case.

As a numerical example, let $\mathbf{A}$ be defined by

$$\mathbf{A} = \begin{vmatrix} 2 & 4 \\ 1 & 3 \end{vmatrix}.$$

Then the inverse of $\mathbf{A}$ is given by

$$\mathbf{A}^{-1} = \frac{\begin{vmatrix} 3 & -4 \\ -1 & 2 \end{vmatrix}}{\det \begin{vmatrix} 2 & 4 \\ 1 & 3 \end{vmatrix}} = \frac{\begin{vmatrix} 3 & -4 \\ -1 & 2 \end{vmatrix}}{2} = \begin{vmatrix} \frac{3}{2} & -2 \\ -\frac{1}{2} & 1 \end{vmatrix}.$$

Equation (H.1) can be derived by noting that if the inverse matrix is

$$\mathbf{A}^{-1} = \begin{vmatrix} w & x \\ y & z \end{vmatrix},$$

then it must be true that

$$\mathbf{A}\cdot\mathbf{A}^{-1} = \begin{vmatrix} a & b \\ c & d \end{vmatrix} \cdot \begin{vmatrix} w & x \\ y & z \end{vmatrix} = \begin{vmatrix} aw+by & ax+bz \\ cw+dy & cx+dz \end{vmatrix} = \begin{vmatrix} 1 & 0 \\ 0 & 1 \end{vmatrix}.$$

This leads to the linear equations

$$aw+by = 1,$$

$$cw+dy = 0,$$

$$ax+bz = 0,$$

and

$$cx+dz = 1,$$

where a,b,c,d are constants and we wish to solve for w,x,y,z. The first pair becomes

$$adw+bdy = d$$

and

$$cbw+bdy = 0,$$

which solves for $w=\frac{d}{ad-bc}$ and $y=\frac{-c}{ad-bc}$. Similarly, the second pair becomes

$$adx+bdz = 0$$

and

$$cbx+bdz = b,$$

which solves for $x=\frac{-b}{ad-bc}$ and $z=\frac{a}{ad-bc}$.

APPENDIX I

OTHER PARAMETER ESTIMATION TECHNIQUES

In Chapters 13-15 we discussed the four parameter estimation techniques of (1) method of moments, (2) percentile matching, (3) maximum likelihood, and (4) Bayesian estimation.

In this appendix we present two additional parameter estimation techniques, namely (1) minimum chi-square, and (2) minimum distance.

These two methods base the parameter estimates strictly on the sample values obtained, as is also the case with the first three methods listed above. These two additional methods have a close relationship with the tests of fit presented in Chapter 16, so they will produce parameter estimates that perform well when tests of fit are applied. This is an attractive feature of these methods.

I.1 MINIMUM CHI-SQUARE

The minimum chi-square method is ideally suited for use with grouped data. When applied in this situation, the parameter estimates obtained will automatically minimize the chi-square statistic in the chi-square test of fit. This is a highly desirable property of using this method.

Recall that the chi-square statistic used in the chi-square test of fit was defined in Section 16.3.1 by Equation (16.4) as

$$\chi^2 = \sum_{j=1}^{k} \frac{(E_j - O_j)^2}{E_j}. \tag{16.4}$$

We modify the notation in Equation (16.4) to use the standard notation for grouped data presented in Chapter 13, so the observed values in each of the k cells will be denoted by

$$O_j = n_j, \tag{I.1}$$

and the expected number in each cell will be denoted by the product of the probability mass in each cell multiplied by the total sample of size n, producing

$$E_j = n\left[F_n^o(c_j) - F_n^o(c_{j-1})\right]. \tag{I.2}$$

The unknown parameters will appear in the two CDF terms in each term of Equation (16.4), while everything else in Equation (16.4) will have known numerical values.

The minimization of χ^2 will be quite challenging, since the unknown parameters appear in both the numerator and denominator. This complication precludes a direct application of a standard least squares minimization approach. In order to obtain the parameter estimates, one technique would be to make an initial estimate of the parameters by one of the other methods (perhaps the method of moments), and then develop an iterative approach to refine the estimates.

A simpler approach that could be applied if less accuracy is required is to replace E_j in the denominator with O_j in each term in the summation. When this is done, the denominators all have known numerical values and a standard least squares minimization approach can be utilized.

I.2 MINIMUM DISTANCE

Recall that several of the tests of fit in Chapter 16 involve a comparison of the CDF in the empirical distribution with the CDF in the fitted model distribution. This generic approach was applied, in one fashion or another, for both the Kolmogorov-Smirnov and the Anderson-Darling tests of fit, as well as in several of the less formal graphical comparison methods.

The minimum distance statistic used in this appendix is not the same as the minimum distance statistic for any of the tests of fit in Chapter 16. Rather the minimum distance statistic used here is a variation of the *Cramer - von Mises statistic*, which appears in more advanced treatises on statistical inference. We present three variations of this test statistic, to provide greater flexibility to the practitioner when applying this method in practice.

The first variation can be applied with individual data. The test statistic Q for this case is defined as

$$Q = \frac{1}{n}\sum_{i=1}^{n}\left[F_n^o(x_i) - \hat{F}(x_i;\theta)\right]^2. \tag{I.3}$$

In words, this test statistic is a summation of squared differences between the two CDFs in which the summation occurs across each individual data point in the sample of size *n*. The goal, of course, is to find the parameter estimate that will minimize Q.

The second variation can be applied with grouped data. The test statistic Q for this case is defined as

$$Q = \sum_{j=0}^{k}\left[F_n^o(c_j) - \hat{F}(c_j;\theta)\right]^2. \tag{I.4}$$

In words, this statistic is a summation of squared differences between the two CDFs in which the summation occurs across the $k+1$ boundary points of the k cells into which the data has been grouped. Again the goal is to find the parameter estimate that will minimize Q.

The third variation is a generalization of the second, allowing the practitioner to place differential weights on the various cells. For example, more weight could be applied in the tails than in the middle of the distribution. Alternatively, perhaps the cells with more data should receive more weight. The test statistic Q for this case is defined as

$$Q = \sum_{j=0}^{k} w_j \left[F_n^o(c_j) - \hat{F}(c_j;\theta) \right]^2, \tag{I.5}$$

where w_j is the weighting function. Since the goal is to find the parameter estimate that minimizes Q, the actual values of the weights themselves are not significant. All that matters is the relative relationship of the weights to each other. For example, doubling each weight would not change the parameter estimate obtained by this technique.

The minimization of Q is relatively straightforward for any of these variations, using a standard least squares minimization approach from general statistics.

Although the test statistic used in this appendix is not the same as any of the test statistics used in Chapter 16, the results of this parameter estimation technique should nevertheless perform well when minimum distance tests of fit are performed.

APPENDIX J

DERIVATION OF EQUATION (16.8C) FOR THE ANDERSON-DARLING STATISTIC

In this appendix we show how the A^2 test statistic defined by Equation (16.8b) can be rewritten as Equation (16.8c), the formula from which A^2 would actually be calculated. We assume that the sample of size n has no duplicated values, and arrange the sample in ascending order so that $x_1 < x_2 < \cdots < x_n$.

We begin by noting that

$$F_n^o(x) = 1 - S_n^o(x)$$

and

$$\hat{F}(x) = 1 - \hat{S}(x),$$

so it follows that

$$[F_n^o(x) - \hat{F}(x)]^2 = [S_n^o(x) - \hat{S}(x)]^2.$$

Then Equation (16.8b) can be written as

$$A^2 = n \int_0^\infty \frac{[S_n^o(x) - \hat{S}(x)]^2}{\hat{S}(x) \cdot \hat{F}(x)} \cdot \hat{f}(x)\, dx. \tag{J.1}$$

We next note the definition of $S_n^o(x)$, as given by Equation (9.3) with t replaced by x. Substituting this expression for $S_n^o(x)$ in Equation (J.1) we have

$$\begin{aligned} A^2 &= \sum_{i=0}^{n-1} \int_{x_i}^{x_{i+1}} \frac{n}{\hat{S}(x) \cdot \hat{F}(x)} \cdot \left[\frac{n-i}{n} - \hat{S}(x)\right]^2 \cdot \hat{f}(x)\, dx \\ &\qquad + \int_{x_n}^\infty \frac{n}{\hat{S}(x) \cdot \hat{F}(x)} \cdot [0 - \hat{S}(x)]^2 \cdot \hat{f}(x)\, dx \end{aligned} \tag{J.2}$$

$$\begin{aligned} &= \sum_{i=0}^{n-1} \int_{x_i}^{x_{i+1}} \frac{n}{\hat{S}(x) \cdot \hat{F}(x)} \cdot \left[\left(\frac{n-i}{n}\right)^2 - 2\left(\frac{n-i}{n}\right) \cdot \hat{S}(x) + [\hat{S}(x)]^2\right] \cdot \hat{f}(x)\, dx \\ &\qquad + \int_{x_n}^\infty \frac{n}{\hat{S}(x) \cdot \hat{F}(x)} \cdot [\hat{S}(x)]^2 \cdot \hat{f}(x)\, dx \end{aligned}$$

$$\begin{aligned} &= \int_0^\infty \frac{n}{\hat{S}(x) \cdot \hat{F}(x)} \cdot [\hat{S}(x)]^2 \cdot \hat{f}(x)\, dx \\ &\qquad + \sum_{i=0}^{n-1} \int_{x_i}^{x_{i+1}} \frac{n}{\hat{S}(x) \cdot \hat{F}(x)} \cdot \left[\left(\frac{n-i}{n}\right)^2 - 2\left(\frac{n-i}{n}\right) \cdot \hat{S}(x)\right] \cdot \hat{f}(x)\, dx, \end{aligned} \tag{J.3}$$

by combining the two terms involving $[\hat{S}(x)]^2$ into one integral. Then (J.3) simplifies to

$$A^2 = n \cdot \int_0^{\infty} \frac{\hat{S}(x) \cdot \hat{f}(x)}{\hat{F}(x)} dx$$

$$- \sum_{i=0}^{n-1} 2(n-i) \cdot \int_{x_i}^{x_{i+1}} \frac{\hat{f}(x)}{\hat{F}(x)} dx + \sum_{i=0}^{n-1} \frac{(n-i)^2}{n} \cdot \int_{x_i}^{x_{i+1}} \frac{\hat{f}(x)}{\hat{S}(x) \cdot \hat{F}(x)} dx. \quad \text{(J.4)}$$

Consider the three integrals in (J.4). Let the indefinite integrals be represented by

$$I_1 = \int \frac{\hat{S}(x) \cdot \hat{f}(x)}{\hat{F}(x)} dx,$$

$$I_2 = \int \frac{\hat{f}(x)}{\hat{F}(x)} dx,$$

and

$$I_3 = \int \frac{\hat{f}(x)}{\hat{S}(x) \cdot \hat{F}(x)} dx.$$

Integration by parts is used to produce $I_1 = \ln \hat{F}(x) - \hat{F}(x)$. Straightforward integration produces $I_2 = \ln \hat{F}(x)$. Integration by partial fractions produces $I_3 = \ln \hat{F}(x) - \ln \hat{S}(x)$. Substituting these results into (J.4) produces

$$A^2 = n \cdot [\ln \hat{F}(x) - \hat{F}(x)]\Big|_0^{\infty}$$

$$- \sum_{i=0}^{n-1} 2(n-i) \cdot [\ln \hat{F}(x)]\Big|_{x_i}^{x_{i+1}} + \sum_{i=0}^{n-1} \frac{(n-i)^2}{n} \cdot [\ln \hat{F}(x) - \ln \hat{S}(x)]\Big|_{x_i}^{x_{i+1}}. \quad \text{(J.5)}$$

Next we simplify the three terms in (J.5). For convenience we call them A, B, and C, so that

$$A^2 = A - B + C.$$

A: This easily simplifies to

$$n \cdot [\ln \hat{F}(\infty) - \hat{F}(\infty) - \ln \hat{F}(0) + \hat{F}(0)].$$

Recall that $\hat{F}(\infty) = 1$, $\hat{F}(0) = 0$, and $\ln(1) = 0$. Thus we have

$$A = -n - n \cdot \ln \hat{F}(0). \quad \text{(J.6)}$$

We notice that $\hat{F}(0) = 0$ so we have the term $\ln(0)$, which is awkward to define. For now we will retain the notation $\ln \hat{F}(0)$.

B: This term simplifies to $2 \cdot \sum_{i=0}^{n-1} (n-i) \cdot [\ln \hat{F}(x_{i+1}) - \ln \hat{F}(x_i)]$, which is

$$2[n \cdot \ln \hat{F}(x_1) - n \cdot \ln \hat{F}(x_0) + (n-1) \cdot \ln \hat{F}(x_2) - (n-1) \cdot \ln \hat{F}(x_1) + \cdots + \ln \hat{F}(x_n) - \ln \hat{F}(x_{n-1})],$$

which simplifies to

$$2[\ln \hat{F}(x_1) + \ln \hat{F}(x_2) + \cdots + \ln \hat{F}(x_n) - n \cdot \ln \hat{F}(x_0)].$$

Thus we have

$$B = 2 \cdot \sum_{i=1}^{n} \ln \hat{F}(x_i) - 2n \cdot \ln \hat{F}(0), \tag{J.7}$$

since $x_0 = 0$.

C: This term can be written as

$$\frac{1}{n} \cdot \sum_{i=0}^{n-1} (n-i)^2 \cdot [\ln \hat{F}(x_{i+1}) - \ln \hat{F}(x_i) + \ln \hat{S}(x_i) - \ln \hat{S}(x_{i+1})].$$

Expanding the summation we have

$$\begin{aligned}\frac{1}{n}\Big\{ & n^2 \cdot [\ln \hat{F}(x_1) - \ln \hat{F}(0) + \ln \hat{S}(0) - \ln \hat{S}(x_1)] \\ & + (n-1)^2 \cdot [\ln \hat{F}(x_2) - \ln \hat{F}(x_1) + \ln \hat{S}(x_1) - \ln \hat{S}(x_2)] \\ & + \cdots + 1^2 \cdot [\ln \hat{F}(x_n) - \ln \hat{F}(x_{n-1}) + \ln \hat{S}(x_{n-1}) - \ln \hat{S}(x_n)] \\ & + 0^2 \cdot [\ln \hat{S}(x_n) - \ln \hat{F}(x_n)]\Big\},\end{aligned} \tag{J.8}$$

where the zero-value last line is added for symmetry. Now each of the terms $\ln \hat{F}(x_i)$ and $\ln \hat{S}(x_i)$, for $i = 1, \ldots, n$, appears twice in (J.8). Grouping these terms we find that (J.8) becomes

$$\begin{aligned}&\frac{1}{n}[\ln \hat{F}(x_1) \cdot \{n^2 - (n-1)^2\} + \ln \hat{F}(x_2) \cdot \{(n-1)^2 - (n-2)^2\} + \cdots + \ln \hat{F}(x_n) \cdot \{1^2 - 0^2\}] \\ &\quad - \frac{1}{n}[\ln \hat{S}(x_1) \cdot \{n^2 - (n-1)^2\} + \ln \hat{S}(x_2) \cdot \{(n-1)^2 - (n-2)^2\} + \cdots + \ln \hat{S}(x_n) \cdot \{1^2 - 0^2\}] \\ &\quad + n \cdot \ln \hat{S}(0) - n \cdot \ln \hat{F}(0).\end{aligned}$$

Since $\hat{S}(0) = 1$ and $\ln(1) = 0$, this expression can be written as

$$\frac{1}{n}\cdot\sum_{i=1}^{n}[(n-i+1)^2-(n-i)^2]\cdot\ln\hat{F}(x_i)$$

$$-\frac{1}{n}\cdot\sum_{i=1}^{n}[i^2-(i-1)^2]\cdot\ln\hat{S}(x_{n-i+1})-n\cdot\ln\hat{F}(0). \quad \text{(J.9)}$$

Next we make the simplifications

$$[(n-i+1)^2-(n-1)^2]=2(n-i)+1$$

and

$$[i^2-(i-1)^2]=2i-1.$$

Finally we can write term C as

$$C=-n\cdot\ln\hat{F}(0)+\frac{1}{n}\cdot\sum_{i=1}^{n}(2n-2i+1)\cdot\ln\hat{F}(x_i)$$

$$-\frac{1}{n}\cdot\sum_{i=1}^{n}(2i-1)\cdot\ln\hat{S}(x_{n-i+1}). \quad \text{(J.10)}$$

Combining $A^2=A-B+C$, we finally have

$$\begin{aligned}A^2 &= -n-n\cdot\ln\hat{F}(0)-2\cdot\sum_{i=1}^{n}\ln\hat{F}(x_i)+2n\cdot\ln\hat{F}(0)-n\cdot\ln\hat{F}(0)\\ &\quad+\frac{1}{n}\cdot\sum_{i=1}^{n}(2n-2i+1)\cdot\ln\hat{F}(x_i)-\frac{1}{n}\cdot\sum_{i=1}^{n}(2i-1)\cdot\ln\hat{S}(x_{n-i+1})\\ &= -n-\frac{1}{n}\cdot\sum_{i=1}^{n}(2i-1)\cdot\ln\hat{F}(x_i)-\frac{1}{n}\cdot\sum_{i=1}^{n}(2i-1)\cdot\ln\hat{S}(x_{n-i+1})\\ &= -n-\frac{1}{n}\cdot\sum_{i=1}^{n}(2i-1)\cdot\left\{\ln[\hat{F}(x_i)\cdot\hat{S}(x_{n-i+1})]\right\},\end{aligned} \quad \text{(J.11)}$$

which is Equation (16.8c).

APPENDIX K

REVIEW OF THE INCOMPLETE GAMMA FUNCTION

The incomplete gamma function is defined as

$$\Gamma(\alpha;x) = \frac{1}{\Gamma(\alpha)}\int_0^x t^{\alpha-1}e^{-t}\,dt, \tag{K.1}$$

where $\Gamma(\alpha)$ is the complete gamma function defined by

$$\Gamma(\alpha) = \int_0^\infty t^{\alpha-1}e^{-t}\,dt, \tag{K.2}$$

for $\alpha > 0$. In Section 1.3.4 we saw how this function arose in deriving the CDF of a gamma random variable. Values of both the complete and incomplete gamma functions are generally found from their definitions by numerical integration. Computer software that generates numerical values for these functions is readily available.

However, if α is a positive integer exact numerical values can be calculated. For example, if $\alpha = 1$ then Equation (K.1) gives

$$\begin{aligned}\Gamma(1;x) &= \frac{1}{\Gamma(1)}\int_0^x e^{-t}\,dt \\ &= \frac{1}{\Gamma(1)}\left(-e^{-t}\Big|_0^x\right) \\ &= \frac{1-e^{-x}}{\Gamma(1)} \\ &= 1-e^{-x},\end{aligned}$$

since $\Gamma(1)=1$. In general, the integral in Equation (K.1) evaluates using integration by parts as

$$\int_0^x t^{\alpha-1}e^{-t}\,dt = -t^{\alpha-1}e^{-t}\Big|_0^x + (\alpha-1)\int_0^x t^{\alpha-2}e^{-t}\,dt = -x^{\alpha-1}e^{-x} + (\alpha-1)\int_0^x t^{\alpha-2}e^{-t}\,dt.$$

The integral in the last expression is the same as that in Equation (K.1) with $\alpha-1$ replaced by $\alpha-2$, so a second integration by parts produces

$$-x^{\alpha-1}e^{-x}+(\alpha-1)\left[-x^{\alpha-2}e^{-x}+(\alpha-2)\int_0^x t^{\alpha-3}e^{-t}\,dt\right].$$

The integration by parts is repeated until the exponent of t becomes zero, and the residual integral at that point evaluates to $1-e^{-x}$, as shown above. Therefore we have

$$\begin{aligned}\Gamma(\alpha;x) = \frac{1}{\Gamma(\alpha)}\Big[&-x^{\alpha-1}e^{-x}+(\alpha-1)(-x^{\alpha-2}e^{-x})\\ &+(\alpha-1)(\alpha-2)(-x^{\alpha-3}e^{-x})+\cdots\\ &+(\alpha-1)(\alpha-2)\cdots(2)(-xe^{-x})\\ &+(\alpha-1)(\alpha-2)\cdots(1)(1-e^{-x})\Big].\end{aligned}$$

Recall that $\Gamma(\alpha)=(\alpha-1)!$, so we have

$$\Gamma(\alpha;x) = -\left[\frac{x^{\alpha-1}e^{-x}}{(\alpha-1)!}+\frac{x^{\alpha-2}e^{-x}}{(\alpha-2)!}+\frac{x^{\alpha-3}e^{-x}}{(\alpha-3)!}+\cdots+\frac{xe^{-x}}{1!}-1+e^{-x}\right] = 1-e^{-x}\sum_{r=0}^{\alpha-1}\frac{x^r}{r!}. \quad \text{(K.3)}$$

EXAMPLE K.1

Let X have a gamma distribution with parameters $\alpha=4$ and $\beta=.50$. Find the probability that X is between 10 and 14.

SOLUTION

First we note that $Pr(10<X<14)=F(14)-F(10)$. From Equation (1.58b) or from Table 6.1 we have $F(14)=\Gamma(4;7)$. Then we use Equation (K.3) to find

$$\begin{aligned}F(14) = \Gamma(4;7) &= 1-e^{-7}\left(1+\tfrac{7}{1!}+\tfrac{7^2}{2!}+\tfrac{7^3}{3!}\right)\\ &= 1-e^{-7}(1+7+24.5+57.1\dot{6})\\ &= .91823.\end{aligned}$$

Similarly,

$$\begin{aligned}F(10) = \Gamma(4;5) &= 1-e^{-5}\left(1+\tfrac{5}{1!}+\tfrac{5^2}{2!}+\tfrac{5^3}{3!}\right)\\ &= 1-e^{-5}(1+5+12.5+20.8\dot{3})\\ &= .73520.\end{aligned}$$

Then

$$Pr(10<X<14) = .91823-.73520 = .18303.$$

❐

The incomplete gamma function can also be evaluated by simulation. Because values of the complete gamma function defined by Equation (K.2) are readily available, we use simulation only to evaluate the integral part of Equation (K.1).[1] The approach is to evaluate the integrand $t^{\alpha-1}e^{-t}$ at n randomly selected values of t from the interval $[0,x)$, where n is very large, then sum them and divide by n to approximate the average value of the integrand. Multiplying this average value by x, the length of the interval, approximates the value of the integral.

EXAMPLE K.2

Estimate the value of the incomplete gamma function $\Gamma(3.5;5)$.

SOLUTION

We generate $n = 100,000$ random values from the uniform distribution over the interval $[0,5)$, evaluate the integrand $t^{2.5}e^{-t}$ at each value, sum them and divide by 100,000. Our result produced the average integrand value of .53977468. (Note that $f(t) = t^{2.5}e^{-t}$ is maximized at $t = 2.5$ with maximum value $f(2.5) = .81117362$.) From readily-available computer software we find $\Gamma(3.5) = 3.32335097$, so the incomplete gamma function is approximated as

$$\Gamma(3.5;5) = \frac{(5)(.53977468)}{3.32335097} = .81209401.$$

(Other software gives the actual value $\Gamma(3.5;5) = .817696$; our simulated value is within .7% of the actual value.) ❒

The incomplete gamma function arises in finding the limited expected value (LEV), given by $E[X \wedge x]$, for certain distributions. This is illustrated in the following two examples.

EXAMPLE K.3

Derive the expression for the LEV for the gamma distribution shown in Table 6.2.

SOLUTION

From Equation (6.34) we have

$$\begin{aligned} E[X \wedge x] &= \int_0^x [1-F_X(y)]\,dy \\ &= x - \int_0^x \Gamma(\alpha;\beta y)\,dy \\ &= x - \int_0^x \left(\frac{1}{\Gamma(\alpha)} \int_0^{\beta y} t^{\alpha-1}e^{-t}\,dt \right) dy \\ &= x - \frac{1}{\Gamma(\alpha)} \left[\int_0^{\beta x} \left(\int_{t/\beta}^x t^{\alpha-1}e^{-t}\,dy \right) dt \right], \end{aligned}$$

[1] The general idea of evaluating a definite integral by simulation is described in Herzog and Lord [16].

by reversing the order of integration. The inside integral evaluates to

$$(t^{\alpha-1}e^{-t})y\Big|_{t/\beta}^{x} = x(t^{\alpha-1}e^{-t}) - \frac{t^{\alpha}e^{-t}}{\beta},$$

so we have

$$\begin{aligned} E[X \wedge x] &= x - \frac{1}{\Gamma(\alpha)}\left[x\int_0^{\beta x} t^{\alpha-1}e^{-t}\,dt - \frac{1}{\beta}\int_0^{\beta x} t^{\alpha}e^{-t}\,dt\right] \\ &= x\left[1-\frac{1}{\Gamma(\alpha)}\int_0^{\beta x} t^{\alpha-1}e^{-t}\,dt\right] + \frac{1}{\beta}\left[\frac{\alpha}{\Gamma(\alpha+1)}\int_0^{\beta x} t^{\alpha}e^{-t}\,dt\right] \\ &= x[1-\Gamma(\alpha;\beta x)] + \frac{\alpha}{\beta}\cdot\Gamma(\alpha+1;\beta x). \end{aligned}$$

When written in the scale parameter form, by substituting θ for $\frac{1}{\beta}$, we have

$$E[X \wedge x] = x[1-\Gamma(\alpha;x/\theta)] + \alpha\theta\cdot\Gamma(\alpha+1;x/\theta),$$

as shown in Table 6.2. ❐

EXAMPLE K.4

Derive the expressions shown in Table 6.2 for the LEV for the (a) Weibull and (b) inverse Weibull distributions.

SOLUTION

(a) From Equation (6.34) we have

$$E[X \wedge x] = \int_0^x [1-F_X(y)]\,dy = \int_0^x e^{-(y/\theta)^{\tau}}\,dy.$$

We make the variable change $z=(y/\theta)^{\tau}$, so $y=\theta\cdot z^{1/\tau}$ and $dy=\frac{\theta}{\tau}\cdot z^{(1/\tau)-1}\,dz$. Then we have

$$\begin{aligned} E[X \wedge x] &= \int_0^{(x/\theta)^{\tau}} e^{-z}\cdot\frac{\theta}{\tau}\cdot z^{(1/\tau)-1}\,dz \\ &= \frac{\theta\cdot\Gamma(\frac{1}{\tau}+1)}{\tau\cdot\Gamma(\frac{1}{\tau}+1)}\int_0^{(x/\theta)^{\tau}} z^{(1/\tau)-1}e^{-z}\,dz \\ &= \frac{\theta\cdot\Gamma(\frac{1}{\tau}+1)}{\Gamma(\frac{1}{\tau})}\int_0^{(x/\theta)^{\tau}} z^{(1/\tau)-1}e^{-z}\,dz, \end{aligned}$$

since $\Gamma(\frac{1}{\tau}+1)=\frac{1}{\tau}\cdot\Gamma(\frac{1}{\tau})$. We recognize the integral, along with the denominator of $\Gamma(\frac{1}{\tau})$, to be $\Gamma\left(\frac{1}{\tau};(x/\theta)^{\tau}\right)$, so we have

$$E[X \wedge x] = \theta \cdot \Gamma(\tfrac{1}{\tau}+1) \cdot \Gamma\left(\tfrac{1}{\tau};(x/\theta)^\tau\right).$$

Alternatively, we can do one integration by parts on the original

$$E[X \wedge x] = \frac{\theta}{\tau}\int_0^{(x/\theta)^\tau} e^{-z} z^{(1/\tau)-1}\, dz$$

to reach

$$\begin{aligned} E[X \wedge x] &= \frac{\theta}{\tau}\left[\tau \cdot z^{1/\tau} e^{-z}\Big|_0^{(x/\theta)^\tau} + \tau\int_0^{(x/\theta)^\tau} z^{1/\tau} e^{-z}\, dz\right] \\ &= \frac{\theta}{\tau}\left[\tau(x/\theta)e^{-(x/\theta)^\tau} + \frac{\tau \cdot \Gamma(\frac{1}{\tau}+1)}{\Gamma(\frac{1}{\tau}+1)}\int_0^{(x/\theta)^\tau} z^{1/\tau} e^{-z}\, dz\right] \\ &= x \cdot e^{-(x/\theta)^\tau} + \theta \cdot \Gamma(\tfrac{1}{\tau}+1) \cdot \Gamma\left(\tfrac{1}{\tau}+1;(x/\theta)^\tau\right), \end{aligned}$$

which is the form given in Table 6.2.

(b) This time we have

$$E[X \wedge x] = \int_0^x [1 - e^{-(\theta/y)^\tau}]\, dy.$$

We make the variable change $z = (\theta/y)^\tau$, so $y = \theta \cdot z^{-(1/\tau)}$ and $dy = -\frac{\theta}{\tau} \cdot z^{-(1/\tau)-1}\, dz$. Then we have

$$E[X \wedge x] = -\int_{(\theta/x)^\tau}^{\infty} [1-e^{-z}] \cdot -\frac{\theta}{\tau} \cdot z^{-(1/\tau)-1}\, dz = \frac{\theta}{\tau}\left[\int_{(\theta/x)^\tau}^{\infty} [1-e^{-z}] \cdot z^{-(1/\tau)-1}\, dz\right].$$

We integrate by parts to obtain

$$\begin{aligned} E[X \wedge x] &= \frac{\theta}{\tau}\left[(1-e^{-z}) \cdot -\tau z^{-(1/\tau)}\Big|_{(\theta/x)^\tau}^{\infty} + \tau\int_{(\theta/x)^\tau}^{\infty} z^{-(1/\tau)} e^{-z}\, dz\right] \\ &= \frac{\theta}{\tau}\left[\tau(\theta/x)^{-1}\left(1-e^{-(\theta/x)^\tau}\right) + \tau\int_{(\theta/x)^\tau}^{\infty} z^{-(1/\tau)} e^{-z}\, dz\right] \\ &= x\left(1-e^{-(\theta/x)^\tau}\right) + \theta\int_0^{\infty} z^{-(1/\tau)} e^{-z}\, dz - \theta\int_0^{(\theta/x)^\tau} z^{-(1/\tau)} e^{-z}\, dz \\ &= x\left(1-e^{-(\theta/x)^\tau}\right) + \theta \cdot \Gamma(1-\tfrac{1}{\tau}) - \theta \cdot \Gamma(1-\tfrac{1}{\tau}) \cdot \Gamma\left(1-\tfrac{1}{\tau};(\theta/x)^\tau\right), \end{aligned}$$

as given in Table 6.2. ❐

In deriving the Table 6.2 expression for the inverse exponential distribution, a special situation arises. Using Equation (6.33), with $k=1$ and x in place of u, we have

$$E[X \wedge x] = \int_0^x z \cdot f_X(z)\,dz + \int_x^\infty x \cdot f_X(z)\,dz = \int_0^x z \cdot f_X(z)\,dz + x \cdot S_X(x).$$

For inverse exponential we have

$$E[X \wedge x] = x(1-e^{-\beta/x}) + \int_0^x z \cdot \frac{\beta \cdot e^{-\beta/z}}{z^2}\,dz = x(1-e^{-\beta/x}) + \beta \int_0^x \frac{1}{z} \cdot e^{-\beta/z}\,dz.$$

We let $t=\frac{\beta}{z}$, so $z=\frac{\beta}{t}$ and $dz=-\frac{\beta}{t^2}\,dt$. The integral then becomes

$$\int_\infty^{\beta/x} \frac{t}{\beta} \cdot e^{-t} \cdot -\frac{\beta}{t^2}\,dt = \int_{\beta/x}^\infty t^{-1} e^{-t}\,dt,$$

so we conclude that

$$E[X \wedge x] = x(1-e^{-\beta/x}) + \beta \int_{\beta/x}^\infty t^{-1} e^{-t}\,dt,$$

as shown in Table 6.2. (Note that the integral in the expression for $E[X \wedge x]$ cannot be expressed in terms of gamma functions. We could write

$$\int_{\beta/x}^\infty f(t)\,dt = \int_0^\infty f(t)\,dt - \int_0^{\beta/x} f(t)\,dt,$$

where here $f(t)=t^{-1}e^{-t}$. This is of the form $t^{\alpha-1}e^{-t}$, but for $\alpha=0$. Gamma functions, however, are defined only for $\alpha>0$.)

ANSWERS TO THE EXERCISES

CHAPTER 4

4-1 5.82200

4-2 .58559

4-3 1000

4-4 8

4-5 1

4-6 7.79

4-7 85

4-8 3478

4-9 2213

4-10 $\frac{44}{9}$

4-11 $\frac{19}{6}$

4-12 14,400

4-13 7

CHAPTER 5

5-2 .09022

5-3 .12500

5-4 .29289

5-5 .73497

5-7 (a) $[1+p(s-1)]^n$ (b) $\left(\frac{p}{1-(1-p)s}\right)^r$ (c) $\frac{p}{1-(1-p)s}$

5-8 $e^{\lambda_1[e^{\lambda_2(e^t-1)}-1]}$

5-9 $\frac{\lambda}{s}\cdot\sum_{k=1}^{s} k\cdot p_X(k)\cdot p_S(s-k)$

5-10 $e^{-\lambda[1-p_X(0)]}$

5-12 3.08885

5-13 (a) $\left(\frac{p}{1-q\cdot e^{\lambda(e^t-1)}}\right)^r$ (b) $\left(\frac{p}{1-q\cdot e^{(e^t-1)}}\right)^r$

5-14 .60944

5-15 .20

5-16 .3125

5-17 13.39954

5-18 (a) $\frac{\Gamma(a+b)\cdot\Gamma(n+1)\cdot\Gamma(a+x)\cdot\Gamma(b+n-x)}{\Gamma(a)\cdot\Gamma(b)\cdot\Gamma(x+1)\cdot\Gamma(n-x+1)\cdot\Gamma(a+b+n)}$

(b) $\frac{\Gamma(a+b)\cdot\Gamma(x+r)\cdot\Gamma(a+r)\cdot\Gamma(b+x)}{\Gamma(a)\cdot\Gamma(b)\cdot\Gamma(r)\cdot\Gamma(x+1)\cdot\Gamma(a+r+b+x)}$

5-20 .52378

5-21 (a) $\left(\frac{e^{-\lambda}}{1-e^{-\lambda}}\right)\left(\frac{\lambda^x}{x!}\right)$, for $x=1,2,\cdots$ (b) $\left(\frac{.65e^{-\lambda}}{1-e^{-\lambda}}\right)\left(\frac{\lambda^x}{x!}\right)$, for $x=1,2,\cdots$

5-22 3

5-23 163.75

5-24 .40601

5-25 (a) 5 (b) .01832

5-27 (a) 128 (b) 768 (c) .19657

5-28 $\frac{2}{9}$

5-29 .59546

5-31 .01556

5-32 93.55161

CHAPTER 6

6-5 (a) $\alpha\theta$ (b) $\alpha\theta^2$ (c) $\left(\frac{1}{1-\theta t}\right)^{\alpha}$ (d) $\Gamma(\alpha; x/\theta)$

6-10 $F_Y(y) = e^{-(\theta/y)^{\tau}}$; $f_Y(y) = \dfrac{\tau \cdot (\theta/y)^{\tau} \cdot e^{-(\theta/y)^{\tau}}}{y}$

6-11 (a) $\theta \cdot \Gamma(1+\frac{1}{\tau})$ (b) $\theta \cdot \Gamma(1-\frac{1}{\tau})$

6-12 $F_Y(y) = \left(\frac{y}{\theta+y}\right)^{\alpha}$; $f_Y(y) = \dfrac{\alpha \cdot \theta \cdot y^{\alpha-1}}{(\theta+y)^{\alpha+1}}$

6-15 .12049

6-17 (a) 64.50 (b) 3129.75 (c) .56247

6-18 .75662

6-19 (b) .92060

6-20 $\frac{3}{7}$

6-22 (a) 200.00 (b) 550.00 (c) 168.75

6-23 990,944.57

6-24 3.42857

6-25 1875

6-26 (b) $\theta \cdot \ln\left(\dfrac{d+\theta}{\theta}\right)$

6-27 175

6-28 166.42

6-29 (a) .20000 (b) .35524

6-30 .79917

6-31 38.91

6-32 .41631

6-33 1162.22

6-34 .43750

6-35 8%

6-36 Normal with mean 1050 and standard deviation 105

6-37 Negative binomial with $r^* = r$ and $p^* = \dfrac{p}{p + k(1-p)}$

6-40 .17156

6-42 (a) $\dfrac{1}{\beta}$ (b) $\dfrac{\frac{\theta}{\tau} \cdot \Gamma\left(\frac{1}{\tau}\right) \cdot \left[1 - \Gamma\left(\frac{1}{\tau}; (x/\theta)^{\tau}\right)\right]}{e^{-(x/\theta)^{\tau}}}$

6-43 $\dfrac{\omega + x}{2}$

6-44 $\dfrac{e^{\mu + \sigma^2/2} \cdot \left[1 - \Phi\left(\frac{\ln x - \mu - \sigma^2}{\sigma}\right)\right]}{1 - \Phi\left(\frac{\ln x - \mu}{\sigma}\right)}$

6-45 9.49122β

6-46 $g(t) = t$

6-48 $\dfrac{\omega k}{k+1}$

6-49 1000

6-50 4.74860

6-51 300.00

CHAPTER 7

7-2 2.35

7-3 (a) 1.50 (b) 2.175 (c) $\left[.90+.10(1-t)^{-1/2}\right]^{30}$

7-4 (a) 320; 760 (b) 320; 856

7-5 50; 25,000

7-6 9,710,400

7-7 209,030

7-8 15,361

7-9

x	$p^{*(0)}(x)$	$p^{*(1)}(x)$	$p^{*(2)}(x)$	$p^{*(3)}(x)$
0	1	.30	.09	.027
1	0	.30	.18	.081
2	0	.00	.09	.081
3	0	.40	.24	.135
4	0	.00	.24	.216
5	0	.00	.00	.108
6	0	.00	.16	.144
7	0	.00	.00	.144
8	0	.00	.00	.000
9	0	.00	.00	.064

7-10 165

7-11 .2826

7-12 .0760

7-13 .00083

7-14 .02902

7-15 5.225

7-16 .4375

7-17 65.28132

7-18 22.36

7-19 1940.89

7-20 67,500

7-21 (a)

x	$p_S(x)$	$F_S(x)$
0	.2097	.2097
1	.2421	.4518
2	.0351	.4869
3	.3255	.8124
4	.0936	.9060
5	.0108	.9168
6	.0624	.9792
7	.0144	.9936
8	.0000	.9936
9	.0064	1.0000

(b) .3984 (c) .5523 (d) 1.839

7-22 200,000

7-23 .10

7-24 2.25

7-25 $\frac{1}{\beta} \cdot e^{-\beta d}$

7-26 2895

7-27 120

7-28 2.064

7-29 .73653

CHAPTER 8

8-1 .50

8-2 $\frac{74}{11}$

8-3 .03090

8-4 110

8-5 .5625

8-6 7.20

8-7 75

8-8 2

8-9 I and II

8-10 1.60944

8-11 .018

8-12 800

8-13 I and II

8-14 20.79442

8-15 1.50

8-16 .60

8-17 4

8-18 10

8-19 $\dfrac{\theta r}{(1+\theta)r - e^r + 1}$

8-20 II and III

8-23 .90432

8-24 .19900

Chapter 9

9-1 7

9-2 3.75

9-3 7.50; 4.50

9-4 $\frac{11}{16}$

9-5 .21753

9-6 (a) p_j; $\frac{p_j q_j}{r_j}$

9-7 .43926

9-8 .95

9-9 .71454

9-11 (.18856, 1.36064)

9-12 $\frac{131}{192}$

9-13 120

9-14 (b) The density function at any point in the ith interval is estimated by the proportion of observations falling in that interval, divided by the length of the interval.

9-15

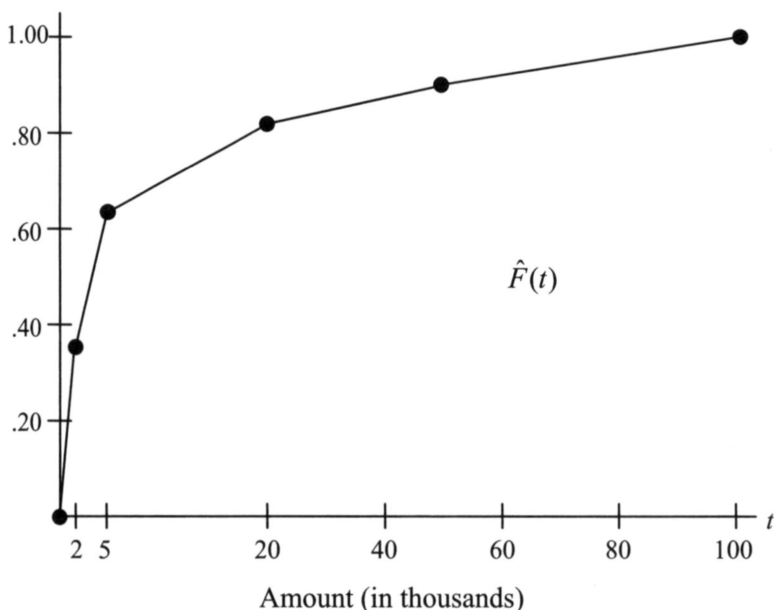

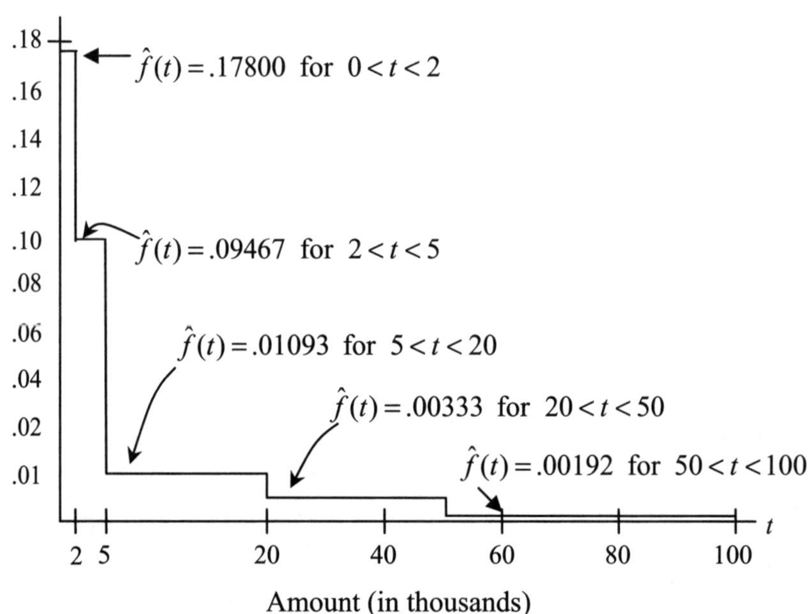

9-16 (a) .90 (b) .10 (c) 48,800

9-18 (a) $\frac{F(t_i)-F(t_{i-1})}{t_i-t_{i-1}}$ (b) $\frac{(F(t_i)-F(t_{i-1}))(1-F(t_i)+F(t_{i-1}))}{n(t_i-t_{i-1})^2}$

9-19 $\frac{n_i(n-n_i)}{n^3}$

9-20 $-\frac{({}_t|q_0)({}_r|q_0)}{n}$

9-21 $\frac{S(r)\cdot[1-S(t)]}{n}$

9-22 .90

9-23 .00009

9-25 .000084

9-26

Duration (t)	Observed Failures (d_t)	Observed Survivors (n_t)	Estimated Conditional Probability ($\hat{q}_t$)	Estimated Survival Function [$\hat{S}(t)$]
0	200	1000	.200	1.000
1	150	800	.188	.800
2	150	650	.231	.650
3	50	500	.100	.500
4	50	450	.111	.450
5	100	400	.250	.400
6	100	300	.333	.300
7	100	200	.500	.200
8	100	100	1.000	.100

Chapter 10

10-1 (a) incomplete (b) random censoring

10-2 Member 8 is now a planned (or scheduled) censored unit at time 30.

10-3 left truncation

10-4 (a) first, second, third, and fifth (b) second and third

10-5 3

10-6 2

10-8 .20

10-9 100

10-10 .58334

10-11 .90937

10-12 (.02160, 1.06412)

10-13 $r_1 = 7, r_2 = 6, r_3 = 5, r_4 = 3$

10-14 46.50

10-15 .52205

10-16 10

10-17 6

10-21 (a) .04227 (b) .00042963

10-22 .01722

Chapter 11

11-1

i	y_i	z_i	θ_i	ϕ_i
1	29.72	39.72	0	0
2	33.50	43.50	33.51	0
3	31.56	41.56	0	32.48
4	***	***	***	***
5	28.09	38.09	30.07	0
6	***	***	***	***
7	32.80	42.80	0	0
8	31.35	41.35	0	31.52
9	29.60	39.52	0	30.52
10	30.85	40.85	39.21	0
11	32.04	42.04	0	33.41
12	31.62	41.49	0	41.10
13	29.82	39.56	0	0
14	31.28	40.86	37.14	0
15	30.11	39.21	0	37.57
16	29.83	38.72	0	0
17	32.36	41.39	39.17	0
18	29.75	38.23	0	34.49
19	31.58	40.18	0	0
20	31.86	39.90	0	34.55
21	30.00	38.05	35.23	0
22	31.39	39.06	0	0
23	29.73	37.42	0	0
24	31.62	38.93	0	32.62
25	29.53	36.45	0	36.33
26	30.04	37.25	32.12	0
27	31.97	39.32	0	36.74
28	31.65	38.78	36.70	0
29	29.90	36.73	0	0
30	30.60	37.60	0	33.07
31	30.80	37.40	0	0
32	29.56	36.11	0	0
33	31.32	38.06	36.19	0
34	30.08	36.41	0	31.04
35	30.47	36.31	0	0
36	31.34	37.50	0	35.69
37	31.38	36.84	34.38	0
38	30.52	35.92	0	0
39	32.16	37.32	0	33.92
40	31.22	36.16	0	0
41	29.67	34.46	0	0
42	31.04	35.70	31.75	0
43	30.14	34.43	0	32.94
44	30.35	34.08	0	0
45	31.97	35.99	0	0
46	31.34	35.15	0	31.62
47	30.15	33.62	0	31.15
48	29.89	33.38	0	32.89
49	31.62	34.99	0	0
50	30.29	33.81	32.54	0
51	30.37	33.27	0	32.24
52	30.41	33.13	0	0
53	32.26	35.32	33.74	0
54	29.69	32.30	0	30.02
55	31.76	34.11	0	0
56	30.08	32.37	0	0
57	30.59	32.98	0	0
58	30.66	32.74	31.37	0
59	32.22	34.41	0	32.31
60	31.84	33.91	0	0
61	29.69	31.68	0	30.10
62	31.20	32.84	0	0
63	29.94	31.38	31.06	0
64	32.20	33.49	0	33.37
65	29.70	30.61	0	0
66	32.24	33.29	0	33.24
67	31.47	32.15	0	0
68	30.04	30.45	0	0
69	31.67	31.87	0	0
70	***	***	***	***

***Member is not involved in the study

11-2

x	k_x
30	1
31	3
32	2
33	2
34	1
35	1
36	2
37	1
39	2

11-3

Interval	(EE_x)
(28,29]	.91
(29,30]	4.98
(30,31]	24.22
(31,32]	35.33
(32,33]	44.20
(33,34]	35.80
(34,35]	28.06
(35,36]	23.83

Interval	(EE_x)
(36,37]	16.27
(37,38]	10.53
(38,39]	8.72
(39,40]	4.72
(40,41]	2.18
(41,42]	1.10
(42,43]	.80
Total	**241.65**

11-4

x	$\hat{q}_x$
30	.04045
31	.08141
32	.04424
33	.05433
34	.03501
35	.04110
36	.11567
37	.09060
39	.34540

11-6 .25641

11-7 .14876

11-8

i	y_i	z_i	θ_i	ϕ_i
1	30	39	0	0
2	*	*	*	*
3	32	41	0	32
4	*	*	*	*
5	28	37	29.95	0
6	*	*	*	*
7	34	43	0	0
8	*	*	*	*
9	30	39	0	31
10	32	41	39.62	0
11	33	42	0	34
12	32	41	0	0
13	30	39	0	0
14	31	40	36.86	0
15	30	39	0	37
16	30	38	0	0
17	32	41	38.81	0
18	30	38	0	35
19	32	40	0	0
20	32	40	0	35
21	30	38	35.23	0
22	31	38	0	0
23	30	37	0	0
24	32	39	0	33
25	30	36	0	0
26	30	37	32.08	0
27	32	39	0	37
28	32	39	37.05	0
29	30	36	0	0
30	31	38	0	33
31	31	37	0	0
32	30	36	0	0
33	31	37	35.87	0
34	30	36	0	31
35	30	35	0	0

*Policyholder is not involved in the study

i	y_i	z_i	θ_i	ϕ_i
36	31	37	0	35
37	31	36	34.01	0
38	31	36	0	0
39	32	37	0	34
40	31	35	0	0
41	30	34	0	0
42	31	35	31.71	0
43	30	34	0	33
44	30	33	0	0
45	32	36	0	0
46	31	34	0	31
47	30	33	0	31
48	30	33	0	33
49	32	35	0	0
50	30	33	32.25	0
51	30	32	0	32
52	30	32	0	0
53	32	35	33.48	0
54	30	32	0	30
55	32	34	0	0
56	30	32	0	0
57	31	33	0	0
58	31	33	31.71	0
59	32	34	0	32
60	32	34	0	0
61	30	31	0	30
62	31	32	0	0
63	30	31	0	0
64	32	33	0	33
65	*	*	*	*
66	32	33	0	33
67	*	*	*	*
68	*	*	*	*
69	*	*	*	*
70	*	*	*	*

11-9

x	k_x	n_x
28	0	1
29	1	1
30	0	24
31	2	33
32	2	43
33	1	34
34	1	29
35	2	22
36	1	15
37	1	10
38	1	7
39	1	4
40	0	2
41	0	1
42	0	1
Total	**13**	**227**

11-10

	$x = 30$		$x = 31$		$x = 32$	
t	$k_{[x]+t}$	$n_{[x]+t}$	$k_{[x]+t}$	$n_{[x]+t}$	$k_{[x]+t}$	$n_{[x]+t}$
0	0	23	2	13	0	15
1	0	19	0	11	1	13
2	2	16	0	9	0	9
3	0	11	1	9	0	7
4	0	10	1	6	0	6
5	1	8	1	4	1	5
6	0	4	0	2	1	4
7	0	2	0	1	0	3
8	0	1	1	1	0	2
9					0	1
10					0	1
Total	**3**	**94**	**6**	**56**	**3**	**66**

11-11

i	y_i	z_i	θ_i	ϕ_i
1	32	40	0	0
2	*	*	*	*
3	*	*	*	*
4	*	*	*	*
5	*	*	*	*
6	*	*	*	*
7	35	43	0	0
8	*	*	*	*
9	*	*	*	*
10	33	41	38.86	0
11	*	*	*	*
12	34	42	0	41.11
13	32	40	0	0
14	33	41	36.78	0
15	32	40	0	37.86
16	31	39	0	0
17	34	42	39.28	0
18	31	39	0	34.76
19	33	41	0	0
20	32	40	0	34.15
21	31	39	35.68	0
22	32	40	0	0
23	30	38	0	0
24	31.19	39	0	32.19
25	29.58	37	0	36.38
26	30.29	38	32.37	0
27	32.15	40	0	36.92
28	31.37	39	36.42	0
29	29.67	37	0	0
30	30.50	38	0	32.97
31	30.90	38	0	0
32	29.95	37	0	0
33	31.76	39	36.63	0
34	30.17	37	0	31.13
35	30.66	37	0	0

*Member is not involved in the study

i	y_i	z_i	θ_i	ϕ_i
36	31.34	38	0	35.69
37	31.04	37	34.04	0
38	30.10	36	0	0
39	32.34	38	0	34.10
40	31.56	37	0	0
41	29.71	35	0	0
42	30.84	36	31.55	0
43	30.21	35	0	33.01
44	30.77	35	0	0
45	31.48	36	0	0
46	31.69	36	0	31.97
47	30.03	34	0	31.03
48	30.01	34	0	33.01
49	31.13	35	0	0
50	29.98	34	32.23	0
51	30.60	34	0	32.47
52	30.78	34	0	0
53	32.44	36	33.92	0
54	29.89	33	0	30.22
55	32.15	35	0	0
56	30.21	33	0	0
57	30.11	33	0	0
58	30.42	33	31.13	0
59	32.31	35	0	32.40
60	31.43	34	0	0
61	29.51	32	0	29.92
62	30.86	33	0	0
63	30.06	32	31.18	0
64	32.21	34	0	33.38
65	29.59	31	0	0
66	32.44	34	0	33.45
67	31.82	33	0	0
68	30.09	31	0	30.53
69	31.30	32	0	0
70	33.54	34	0	0

11-12

x	$(EE)_x$	k_x	$\hat{q}_x$
31	29.88	3	.09553
32	39.05	2	.04993
33	33.77	1	.02918
34	29.05	1	.03384
35	24.37	1	.04020
36	19.13	3	.14514
38	8.86	1	.10673
39	6.28	1	.14720

11-13

x	n_x	k_x	$\hat{q}_x$
31	33	3	.09091
32	41	2	.04878
33	33	1	.03030
34	30	1	.03333
35	25	1	.04000
36	20	3	.15000
38	9	1	.11111
39	7	1	.14286

11-14

x	$q_x'^{(w)}$
30	.11650
31	.10704
32	.12694
33	.13035
34	.06880
35	.04110
36	.11567
37	.09060
41	.59711

11-15

x	$k_x^{(w)}$	n_x
28	0	1
29	0	1
30	5	26
31	2	34
32	6	45
33	4	36
34	2	29
35	1	23
36	1	15
37	1	11
38	0	7
39	0	4
40	0	2
41	0	1
42	0	1

11-16

x	$q_x^{(f)}$	$q_x^{(w)}$
29	1.00000	---
30	---	.19231
31	.05882	.05882
32	.04444	.13333
33	.02778	.11111
34	.03448	.06897
35	.08696	.04348
36	.06667	.06667
37	.09091	.09091
38	.14286	---
39	.25000	---

Chapter 12

12-2 .48500

12-3 .53125

12-5 $$\hat{f}(x) = \begin{cases} .075x - .225 & \text{for} \quad 3 \le x < 5 \\ .050x - .100 & \text{for} \quad 5 \le x < 7 \\ 1.125 - .125x & \text{for} \quad 7 \le x < 8 \\ .725 - .075x & \text{for} \quad 8 \le x < 9 \\ .050x - .400 & \text{for} \quad 9 \le x < 10 \\ .600 - .050x & \text{for} \quad 10 \le x \le 12 \end{cases}$$

12-7 (a) .05, .15, .65, 1.00
(b) .05, .15, .60, 1.00

12-8 .42668

12-9 .11353

12-11 .22036

12-12 (a) $\sum_t p_n^o(t)\cdot\left(1-e^{-x/t}\right)$ (b) $\sum_t p_n^o(t)\cdot\left(\frac{t(\alpha-1)}{x+t(\alpha-1)}\right)^{\alpha}$

12-16 (a)

$$\begin{vmatrix} 1 & a & a^2 & a^3 & 0 & 0 \\ \vdots & \vdots & \vdots & \vdots & \vdots & \vdots \\ 1 & h_1 & h_1^2 & h_1^3 & 0 & 0 \\ 1 & h_1+1 & (h_1+1)^2 & (h_1+1)^3 & (h_1+1-k_1)^3 & 0 \\ \vdots & \vdots & \vdots & \vdots & \vdots & \vdots \\ 1 & h_2 & h_2^2 & h_2^3 & (h_2-k_1)^3 & 0 \\ 1 & h_2+1 & (h_2+1)^2 & (h_2+1)^3 & (h_2+1-k_1)^3 & (h_2+1-k_2)^3 \\ \vdots & \vdots & \vdots & \vdots & \vdots & \vdots \\ 1 & b & b^2 & b^3 & (b-k_1)^3 & (b-k_2)^3 \end{vmatrix}$$

12-17 6285

12-18 450

12-19

$$\begin{vmatrix} 1 & -2 & 1 & 0 & 0 & 0 \\ 0 & 1 & -2 & 1 & 0 & 0 \\ 0 & 0 & 1 & -2 & 1 & 0 \\ 0 & 0 & 0 & 1 & -2 & 1 \end{vmatrix}$$

12-20

$$\begin{vmatrix} -1 & 3 & -3 & 1 & 0 & 0 & 0 \\ 0 & -1 & 3 & -3 & 1 & 0 & 0 \\ 0 & 0 & -1 & 3 & -3 & 1 & 0 \\ 0 & 0 & 0 & -1 & 3 & -3 & 1 \end{vmatrix}$$

12-22 63

12-23 8.50

12-24 .96552

12-25 6

Chapter 13

13-1 $\hat{\mu}=1.14740$ and $\hat{\sigma}=.69122$

13-2 The sample variance is greater than the sample mean.

13-3 369.36641

13-4 $\hat{n}=8$ and $\hat{p}=.15$

13-5 20

13-6 $-.24$

13-7 1.87287

13-8 $12{,}129.3\dot{3}$

13-9 4,859

13-10 $\hat{a}=2.77976$ and $\hat{\theta}=11{,}884$

13-11 $3{,}958.3\dot{3}$

13-12 3,587.96

13-13 $208.3\dot{3}$

13-14 160

13-15 384

13-16 .63497

13-17 .3446

13-18 118.31914

13-19 248.53365

13-20 6

13-21 4.00267

13-22 $\hat{k} = .30$ and $\hat{\theta} = 20$

13-23 104.46472

13-24 $\frac{n+1}{n} \cdot \theta^2$

Chapter 14

14-1 2.45339

14-2 16.74257

14-3 2391

14-4 $\hat{\beta} = \frac{\overline{x}}{r}$

14-5 2

14-6 4.32746

14-7 $\theta^{-3} \cdot e^{-1100/\theta}$

14-8 1997

14-9 3326

14-10 471.35349

14-11 5.65685

14-12 3.08865

14-14 $\frac{n}{\alpha} + n \cdot \ln\theta - \sum_{i=1}^{n} \ln(x_i + \theta) = 0$ $\frac{n\alpha}{\theta} - (\alpha+1) \cdot \sum_{i=1}^{n} \frac{1}{x_i + \theta} = 0$

14-15 .16013

14-16 $\frac{3\theta^2}{n}$

14-17 $21\theta^4$

14-18 .07856

14-20 .7951

14-21 .01867

14-22 (.23407, .68733)

14-23 1

14-24 282.51935

14-25 $\left[\frac{p\cdot e^{-1}}{100}+\frac{(1-p)\cdot e^{-.01}}{10{,}000}\right]\left[\frac{p\cdot e^{-20}}{100}+\frac{(1-p)\cdot e^{-.20}}{10{,}000}\right]$

14-26 10.12237

14-27 7.60

Chapter 15

15-1 .70918

15-2 .14844

15-3 10,322

15-4 10/19

15-5 1.25

15-6 .68088

15-7 $\frac{4\theta^2\cdot e^{-2\theta}}{1-13e^{-4}}$

15-8 3.25

15-9 .07143

15-10 .29375

15-11 .62247

15-12 .64

15-13 .72115

15-14 $.2777\dot{7}$

15-15 9

15-16 3

15-17 (a) 6 (b) 3

15-18 (a) 1 (b) 2.25

15-19 1.10

15-20 .50

15-21 $\lambda_R^2 - \lambda_L^2 = 100 \ln\left(\frac{\lambda_R}{\lambda_L}\right)$

$e^{-(\lambda_L/10)^2} - e^{-(\lambda_R/10)^2} = .90$

15-22 (a) (1.02598, 4.47214) (b) (1, 3.16228) (c) .627

15-23 .21752

15-25 $\mathbf{v} = [.0295, .0479, .1323, .2819]^T$; decrease

15-26 $\mathbf{v} = \left[\frac{13}{9}, \frac{34}{7}, \frac{120}{7}\right]^T$

15-27 $\mathbf{A} = \begin{vmatrix} .0022 & .0024 & .0013 & .0004 & 0 & 0 \\ .0024 & .0032 & .0034 & .0020 & .0006 & 0 \\ .0013 & .0034 & .0045 & .0053 & .0029 & .0010 \\ .0004 & .0020 & .0053 & .0077 & .0085 & .0054 \\ 0 & .0006 & .0029 & .0085 & .0117 & .0150 \\ 0 & 0 & .0010 & .0054 & .0150 & .0238 \end{vmatrix}$

15-28 $\frac{7}{20}$

15-29 21

15-30 $108\lambda^2 \cdot e^{-6\lambda}$

Chapter 16

16-1 (0, 0) (1, .393) (1.386, .5) (3, .777)

16-2 −.113

16-3 (a) Too thick (b) Less probability (c) Too thin

16-4 Choice (i)

16-5 −.071

16-6 94

16-7 (a) 7.55 (b) 2 (c) 025 level

16-8 (a) 6.65 (b) 3 (c) .10 level

16-9 (a) 9.35 (b) 2 (c) .01 level

16-10 .273

16-11 .168

16-12 (a) .680 (b) .025 level

16-13 .193

16-14 (a) No (b) Yes (c) No

16-15 Negative binomial

16-16 Exponential

16-17 (a) 9.158 (b) 9.123

16-18 7781

16-19 7

16-20 (a) 7.7 (b) 2 (c) .025 level

16-21 (a) 4.46 (b) 1 (c) .05 level

16-22 (a) Generalized Pareto (b) Pareto

16-23 I

BIBLIOGRAPHY

1. Anderson, T.W. and D.A. Darling, "A Test of Goodness of Fit," *JASA*, 49 (1954), 765.

2. Asimow, L.A. and M.M. Maxwell, *Probability and Statistics with Applications: A Problem-Solving Text*. Winsted: ACTEX Publications, Inc., 2010.

3. Batten, R.W., *Mortality Table Construction*. Englewood Cliffs: Prentiss-Hall, Inc., 1978.

4. Bowers, N.R., et al., *Actuarial Mathematics* (Second Edition). Schaumburg: Society of Actuaries, 1997.

5. Box, G.E.P and M.E. Muller, "A Note on the Generation of Random Normal Deviates," *Annals of Mathematical Statistics*, Vol. 29, No. 2 (1958), 610.

6. Camp, K., "New Possibilities in Graduation," *TSA*, VII (1955), 6.

7. Cunningham, R.J., T.N. Herzog, and R.L. London, *Models for Quantifying Risk* (Fourth Edition). Winsted: ACTEX Publications, 2011.

8. DeBoor, C., *A Practical Guide to Splines*. New York: Springer-Verlag, 1978.

9. Gompertz, B., "On the Nature of the Function Expressive of the Law of Human Mortality," *Phil. Trans.*, Royal Society of London, 1825.

10. Greenwood, M., "A Report on the Natural Duration of Cancer," Reports on Public Health and Medical Subjects, H. M. Stationery Office, 33 (1926), 1.

11. Greville, T.N.E. (Editor), *Theory and Application of Spline Functions*. New York: Academic Press, 1969.

12. Hassett, M.J. and D.G. Stewart, *Probability for Risk Management* (Second Edition). Winsted: ACTEX Publications, Inc., 2006.

13. Henderson, R., "A New Method of Graduation," *TASA*, XXV (1924), 29.

14. Henderson, R., "Further Remarks on Graduation," *TASA*, XXVI (1925), 52.

15. Herzog, T.N., *Introduction to Credibility Theory* (Fourth Edition). Winsted: ACTEX Publications, Inc., 2010.

16. Herzog, T.N. and G. Lord, *Applications of Monte Carlo Methods to Finance and Insurance.* Winsted: ACTEX Publications, Inc., 2002.

17. Hogg, R.V., J.W. McKean, and A.T. Craig, *Introduction to Mathematical Statistics* (Sixth Edition). Upper Saddle River: Pearson Prentiss Hall, 2005.

18. Hogg, R.V. and E.A. Tanis, *Probability and Statistical Inference* (Eighth Edition). Upper Saddle River: Pearson Prentiss Hall, 2010.

19. Kaplan, E.L. and P. Meier, "Nonparametric Estimation from Incomplete Observations," *JASA*, 53 (1958), 457.

20. Kimeldorf, G.S. and D.A. Jones, "Bayesian Graduation," *TSA*, XIX (1967), 66.

21. Klugman, S.A., H.H. Panjer, and G.E. Willmot, *Loss Models: From Data to Decisions* (Third Edition). Hoboken: John Wiley and Sons, 2008.

22. Knuth, D.E., *The Art of Computer Programming*, Vol. 2 (Third Edition). Reading: Addison-Wesley, 1997.

23. Lehmer, D.H., "Mathematical Models in Large-Scale Computing Units," *Annals of the Computation Laboratory of Harvard Universit*, 26: *Proceedings of the Second Symposium on Large-Scale Digital Calculating Machinery* (September 13-16, 1949). Cambridge: Harvard University Press, 1951.

24. Lewis, P.A.W., A.S. Goodman, and J.M. Miller, "A Pseudorandom Number Generator for the System/360," *IBM Systems Journal*, Vol.8 (1969), 136.

25. London, D., *Graduation: The Revision of Estimates*. Winsted: ACTEX Publications, Inc., 1985.

26. London, D., *Survival Models and Their Estimation* (Third Edition). Winsted: ACTEX Publications, Inc. 1997.

27. Lowrie, W.B., "An Extension of the Whittaker-Henderson Methopd of Graduation," *TSA*, XXXIV (1982), 329.

28. Makeham, W.M., "On the Law of Mortality, and the Construction of Annuity Tables," *JIA*, VIII (1860).

29. McCutcheon, J.J., "Recently Published U.K. Mortality Tables: Methods of Construction and Possible Developments Therefrom," *ARCH*, 1980.2, 61.

30. McCutcheon, J.J., "Some Remarks on Splines," *TFA*, XXXVII (1981), 421.

31. Miller, M.D., *Elements of Graduation*. New York: Actuarial Society of America and American Institute of Actuaries, 1946.

32. Nelson, W.A., "Theory and Applications of Hazard Plotting for Censored Failure Data," *Technometrics*, 14 (1972), 945.

33. Rao, C.R., *Linear Statistical Inference*. New York: John Wiley and Sons, 1965.

34. Rohatgi, V.K., *An Introduction to Probability Theory and Mathematical Statistics*. New York: John Wiley and Sons, 1976.

35. Ross, S.M., *A First Course in Probability* (Sixth Edition). Old Tappen: Prentiss-Hall, 2001.

36. Ross, S.M., *Introduction to Probability Models* (Eighth Edition). San Diego: Academic Press, 2003.

37. Ross, S.M., *Simulation* (Fourth Edition). San Diego: Academic Press, 2006.

38. Schuette, D.R., "A Linear Programming Approach to Graduation," TSA, XXX (1978), 73.

39. Spoerl, C.A., "The Whittaker-Henderson Graduation Formula A, the Mixed Difference Case," TASA, XLII (1941), 292.

40. Whittaker, E.T., "On a New Method of Graduation," *Proc. Edin. Math. Soc.*, XLI (1923), 63.

INDEX